# HANDBOOK OF SECURITY AND NETWORKS

# HANDBOOK OF SECURITY AND NETWORKS

editors

**Yang Xiao**
*The University of Alabama, USA*

**Frank H Li**
*The University of South Carolina Upstate, USA*

**Hui Chen**
*Virginia State University, USA*



World Scientific

NEW JERSEY • LONDON • SINGAPORE • BEIJING • SHANGHAI • HONG KONG • TAIPEI • CHENNAI

*Published by*

World Scientific Publishing Co. Pte. Ltd.
5 Toh Tuck Link, Singapore 596224
*USA office:* 27 Warren Street, Suite 401-402, Hackensack, NJ 07601
*UK office:* 57 Shelton Street, Covent Garden, London WC2H 9HE

**British Library Cataloguing-in-Publication Data**
A catalogue record for this book is available from the British Library.

**HANDBOOK OF SECURITY AND NETWORKS**


ISBN-13 978-981-4273-03-9
ISBN-10 981-4273-03-1

Typeset by Stallion Press
Email: enquiries@stallionpress.com

Printed by FuIsland Offset Printing (S) Pte Ltd. Singapore

# CONTENTS

## PREFACE

As computing and networking technologies are gradually integrated with every aspect of human lives and activities, computer and network security has become a critical issue. The Handbook of Security and Networks presents a collection of recent advances in computer networking and security areas. These include applied cryptography, access control, authentication, anonymity, network attacks, malware, key management, anomaly detection, network security applications, and other security issues in computer networks.

More than fifty internationally recognized authorities in the field of security and networks contribute articles in their areas of expertise. These international researchers and practitioner are from highly-respected universities, renowned research institutions and IT companies from all over the world. This handbook is an essential source of reference for professionals and researchers in the areas of security in computer and networks, and as a text for graduate students in these fields.

This book is made possible by the great efforts of our contributors and publishers. We are indebted to our contributors, who have sacrificed days and nights to put together these chapters for our readers. We would like to thank our publishers. Without their encouragement and quality work, we could not have this book. Finally, we are grateful that our families have continuously supported us.

*Yang Xiao*
*Department of Computer Science*
*The University of Alabama*
*101 Houser Hall, Box 870290*
*Tuscaloosa, AL 35487-0290 USA*
*E-mail: yangxiao@ieee.org*

*Frank Haizhon Li*
*Division of Mathematics and Computer Science*
*University of South Carolina Upstate*
*Spartanburg, SC 29303, USA*
*E-mail: fli@uscupdate.edu*

*Hui Chen*
*Department of Mathematics and Computer Science*
*Virginia State University*
*P.O.Box 9068, Petersburg, VA 23806 USA*
*E-mail: huichen@ieee.org*

## ABOUT EDITORS

**Dr. Yang Xiao** worked in industry as a MAC (Medium Access Control) architect involving the IEEE 802.11 standard enhancement work before he joined Department of Computer Science at The University of Memphis in 2002. Dr. Xiao is currently with Department of Computer Science (with tenure) at The University of Alabama. He was a voting member of IEEE 802.11 Working Group from 2001 to 2004. He is an IEEE Senior Member. He is a member of American Telemedicine Association. He currently serves as Editor-in-Chief for International Journal of Security and Networks (IJSN), International Journal of Sensor Networks (IJSNet), and International Journal of Telemedicine and Applications (IJTA). He serves as a panelist for the US National Science Foundation (NSF), Canada Foundation for Innovation (CFI)'s Telecommunications expert committee, and the American Institute of Biological Sciences (AIBS), as well as a referee/reviewer for many national and international funding agencies. He serves on TPC for more than 100 conferences such as INFOCOM, ICDCS, MOBIHOC, ICC, GLOBECOM, WCNC, etc. He serves as an associate editor for several journals, e.g., IEEE Transactions on Vehicular Technology. His research areas are security, telemedicine, robot, sensor networks, and wireless networks. He has published more than 300 papers in major journals, refereed conference proceedings, book chapters related to these research areas. Dr. Xiao's research has been supported by the US National Science Foundation (NSF), U.S. Army Research, Fleet & Industrial Supply Center San Diego (FISCSD), and The University of Alabama's Research Grants Committee. Dr. Xiao is a Guest Professor of Jilin University (2007–2012), and was an Adjunct Professor of Zhejiang University (2007–2009).

Frank Haizhon Li is an assistant professor of Computer Science at the University of South Carolina Upstate. He received his Ph.D. degree from the University of Memphis. Prior to pursuing his career in Computer Science, he has worked as a chemical engineer for four years. His research interests include modeling and analysis of mobile, wireless, ad hoc and sensor networks, Quality of Service and MAC enhancement for IEEE 802.11 wireless LANs, adaptive network services, multimedia services and protocols over wireless networks, and Computer Security. Frank has served as technical program committee member for many conferences such as IEEE ICC and IEEE WCNC. Email: fli@uscupstate.edu

Hui Chen is a geophysicist turned computer programmer and computer science researcher. From 1996 to 2001, he spent most of his time in research on computational aspects of geophysics. He late worked as a software developer in industry. Out of his interest in research and teaching, and his desire to learn, he joined the faculty of the Department of Mathematics and Computer Science at Virginia State University in 2007. While retaining interest in computational problems in Earth sciences, he primarily works on computer systems, networking, and security areas such as design and analysis wireless networks, sensor networks, caching for wireless systems, operating system and network security as well as applied computing. He served and is serving as technical program committee member for many conferences such as IEEE Globecom and IEEE ICC. He was and is a guest editor of a few journals, such as special issues of "Wireless Telemedicine and Applications" and "Wireless Network Security" of the EURASIP Journal on Wireless Communications and Networking. He is member of IEEE and ACM. Email: huichen@ieee.org

# CONTRIBUTORS

Sheila B. Banks
Calculated Insight
Orlando, Fl 32828, U.S.A.

Haifeng Chen
NEC Laboratories America
Princeton, NJ 08540, U.S.A.

Thomas M. Chen
Institute of Advanced Telecommunications
Swansea University
Singleton Park, Swansea SA28PP, UK

Whai-En Chen
Institute of Computer Science and Information Engineering
National I-Lan University
Taiwan

Xiaotie Deng
Department of Computer Science
City University of Hong Kong
83 Tat Chee Avenue, Kowloon, Hong Kong

Qi Dong
Department of Computer Science and Engineering
The University of Texas at Arlington
416 Yates Street, Arlington, TX 76001, U.S.A.

Shawn Embleton
School of Electrical Engineering and Computer Science
University of Central Florida
Orlando, FL 32816, U.S.A.

Xinxin Fan
Department of Electrical and Computer Engineering
University of Waterloo
Waterloo, Ontario, N2L3G1, Canada

Xiaofeng Gao
Department of Computer Science
University of Texas at Dallas
800 W. Campbell Road, Richardson, TX 75080, U.S.A.

Guang Gong
Department of Electrical and Computer Engineering
University of Waterloo
Waterloo, Ontario, N2L3G1, Canada

Ahsan Habib
Siemens Technology-To-Business Center
Berkeley, CA, U.S.A.

Mohamed Hefeeda
School of Computing Science
Simon Fraser University
250-13450 102nd Ave, Surrey, BC V3T0A3, Canada

Ahmed Helmy
Computer and Information Science and Engineering Department
University of Florida
Gainesville, Florida, U.S.A

Fei Hu
Department of Computer Engineering,
College of Engineering,
RIT, Rochester, New York

Hung-Chung Huang
Department of Sys. Bio. and Trans. Med.
Texas A&M Health Science Center,
Temple, TX 76504, U.S.A.

Ting-Kai Huang
Department of computer Science
National Chiao Tung University
1001, Ta Hsueh Road, Hsinchu, Taiwan

Raj Jain
Computer Science and Engineering Department
Washington University in St. Louis
1 Brookings Drive, Saint Louis MO, 63108, U.S.A.

Nasir Jamily
Dept. of Electrical Engineering
Southern Methodist University
Dallas, Texas 75275, U.S.A.

Guofei Jiang
NEC Laboratories America
Princeton, NJ 08540, U.S.A

Yixin Jiang
Department of Electrical and Computer Engineering
University of Waterloo
200 University Ave. W., Waterloo,
Ontario, Canada

Muhi Ahmed Ibne Khair
University of Manitoba
Winnipeg, Manitoba, Canada

Donghyun Kim
Department of Computer Science
University of Texas at Dallas
800 W. Campbell Road, Richardson, TX 75080, U.S.A.

Yongjin Kim
Qualcomm
5775 Morehouse Drive, San Diego,
California, U.S.A.

Donggang Liu
Department of Computer Science and Engineering
The University of Texas at Arlington
416 Yates Street, Arlington, TX 76001, U.S.A.

Wenyuan Li
Department of Molec. and Compu. Bio.
University of Southern California
U.S.A.

Jon W. Mark
Department of Electrical and Computer Engineering
University of Waterloo
200 University Ave. W., Waterloo, Ontario, Canada

Prabhaker Mateti
Department of Computer Science and Engineering
Wright State University
Dayton, Ohio 45435, U.S.A.

Xiaoqiao Meng
NEC Laboratories America
Princeton, NJ 08540, U.S.A.

Jelena Misic
University of Manitoba
Winnipeg, Manitoba, Canada

Vojislav B. Misic
University of Manitoba
Winnipeg, Manitoba, Canada

Kianoosh Mokhtarian
School of Computing Science
Simon Fraser University
250-13450 102nd Ave, Surrey, BC V3T0A3, Canada

Benjamin Murray
Department of Computer Science and Engineering
Wright State University
Dayton, Ohio 45435, U.S.A.

Venkat Pothamsetty
Department of Computer Science and Engineering
Wright State University
Dayton, Ohio 45435, U.S.A

Meikang Qiu
Department of Electrical Engineering
University of New Orleans
New Orleans, LA 70148, U.S.A.

Humphrey Rutagenwa
Radio Communications Technologies
Communications Research Centre
Ottawa, Canada

Abhishek Sharma
NEC Laboratories America
Princeton, NJ 08540, U.S.A.

Xuemin Shen
Department of Electrical and Computer Engineering
University of Waterloo
200 University Ave. W., Waterloo, Ontario, Canada

Minghui Shi
Department of Electrical and Computer Engineering
University of Waterloo
200 University Ave. W., Waterloo, Ontario, Canada

Sherri Sparks
School of Electrical Engineering and Computer Science
University of Central Florida
Orlando, FL 32816, U.S.A.

Martin R. Stytz
The Institute for Defense Analyses
Calculated Insight
Washington, DC, U.S.A.

Abdel Karim Al Tamimi
Computer Science and Engineering Department
Washington University in St. Louis
1 Brookings Drive, Saint Louis MO, 63108, U.S.A.

Sapon Tanachaiwiwat
Innovative Scheduling, Inc.

Nidhi Verma
Department of Computer Engineering
College of Engineering,
RIT, Rochester, New York

Chun-Chieh Wang
Information and Communications Research Laboratories
Industrial Technology Research Institute
195 Chung Hsing Rd., Sec.4 Chu Tung, Hsin Chu, Taiwan

Duncan S. Wong
Department of Computer Science
City University of Hong Kong
83 Tat Chee Avenue, Kowloon, Hong Kong

Jiande Wu
Department of Electrical Engineering
University of New Orleans
New Orleans, LA 70148, U.S.A.

Weili Wu
Department of Computer Science
University of Texas at Dallas
800 W. Campbell Road, Richardson, TX 75080, U.S.A.

Guomin Yang
Department of Computer Science
City University of Hong Kong
83 Tat Chee Avenue, Kowloon, Hong Kong

Kenji Yoshihira
NEC Laboratories America
Princeton, NJ 08540, U.S.A.

Hui Zhang
NEC Laboratories America
Princeton, NJ 08540, U.S.A.

Dongmei Zhao
Department of Electrical and Computer Engineering
McMaster University
Hamilton, Canada

Cliff C. Zou
School of Electrical Engineering and Computer Science
University of Central Florida
Orlando, FL 32816, U.S.A.

Feng Zou
Department of Computer Science
University of Texas at Dallas
800 W. Campbell Road, Richardson, TX 75080, U.S.A.

**ACKNOWLEDGEMENT**

This work is supported in part by the US National Science Foundation (NSF) under the grant numbers CCF-0829827, CNS-0716211, and CNS-0737325.

# Part I: Overview of Network Security

# Chapter 1

## SECURITY IN WIRELESS DATA NETWORKS

Abdel-Karim Al Tamimi* and Raj Jain†
*Department of Computer Engineering,*
*Yarmouk University, Irbid, 21163, Jordan*

*Science and Engineering Dept.,*
*Washington University in St. Louis*
*1 Brookings Drive, Saint Louis MO,*
*63108, USA*
*abdelkarim.tamimi@gmail.com
†jain@cse.wustl.edu

This chapter illustrates the key concepts of security, wireless networks, and security over wireless networks. Wireless security is demonstrated by explaining the main specifications of the common security standards like 802.11 WEP, 802.11 WPA, WPA2 (802.11i) and Bluetooth security standards. Moreover, it explains the concept of WMAN (Wireless Metropolitan Access Network) and its security specifications. Finally, it sums up with thoughts and suggestions about wireless security, along with chosen examples of the current proposals in wireless security.

### 1.1. Introduction

Security in computer world determines the ability of the system to manage, protect and distribute sensitive information. Data Security issues have been researched for many years before the advent of wireless communication due to the mankind's need to send information (in war or in peace time) without exposing its content to others. The first and most known machine (Enigma) was used in WWII by the German military to encrypt their messages. The machine was something similar to a simple typing machine with a scrambler unit to obfuscate the content of the messages [25], [26].

From that time till now, many solutions to security threats have been introduced, and most of them were abandoned or replaced by better security standards. These ongoing changes have promoted the security field to be a permanent hot topic. In the wireless world security threats were not known to public people till prices of wireless equipment went down around the beginning of this century. Before that date, the military was the number one client for wireless security products especially during the cold war [4], [6].

This chapter aims to give a better understanding of security measures and protocols available in the market, along with a brief analysis of each security scheme's weaknesses and points of strength. The chapter starts with an introduction to security and wireless worlds to give the right background for understanding the evolution of security standards. Section 3 gives a brief description about security standards in wireless LANs. Section 4 describes WMAN 802.16 protocol and the current security schemes used with it. Section 5, Thoughts on wireless security, explores some of the practical suggestions to increase the level of network security. Since security in wireless networks is still a work in progress. Section 6 discusses some of the recent proposals to enhance current security standards like PANA (Protocol for carrying Authentication for Network Access). Finally, Section 7 concludes this chapter.

## 1.2. Security and Wireless Overview

An overview of security and wireless communications is presented in this section. Although this introduction does not cover all the aspects of both topics, it gives a descent amount of information that allows the reader to go through the chapter without the necessity of referring to other books or papers. Section 2.1 gives a crash course in security for both wired and wireless networks. Section 2.2 describes the current wireless systems and infrastructures. Finally, a list of the common security threats and attacks are discussed in Section 2.3.

### 1.2.1. *Introduction to Security*

This section outlines some of the basic concepts in security. It starts by defining the goals behind implementing security in computer networks (Section 2.1.1). Then it discusses encryption and decryption concepts (Section 2.1.2), the implementation of both block and stream ciphers (Section 2.1.3), and finally a brief description of the most common encryption standards.

#### 1.2.1.1. *Security goals*

Every security system must provide a bundle of security functions that can assure the secrecy of the system. These functions are usually referred to as the goals of the security system. These goals can be listed under the following five main categories [2], [5]:

*Authentication*: This means that before sending and receiving data using the system, the receiver and sender identity should be verified.

*Secrecy or Confidentiality*: Usually this function (feature) is how most people identify a secure system. It means that only the authenticated people are able to interpret the message (data) content and no one else.

*Integrity*: Integrity means that the content of the communicated data is assured to be free from any type of modification between the end points (sender and receiver). The basic form of integrity is packet check-sum in IPv4 packets.

*Non-Repudiation*: This function implies that neither the sender nor the receiver can falsely deny that they have sent a certain message.

*Service Reliability and Availability*: Since secure systems usually get attacked by intruders, which may affect their availability and quality of service they offer to their users. Such systems should provide a way to grant their users the quality of service they expect.

1.2.1.2. *Data encryption: Symmetric and asymmetric encryption*

To send data securely between two nodes, the system must encrypt the data or "systematically scramble information so that it cannot be read without knowing the coding key" [27]. This operation determines to a certain level the strength of the security system; the harder it is to decode the encrypted message the better security levels provided by the system. Figure 1.1 shows the common use of encryption/decryption techniques, where unsecured messages (plain text) are encrypted using an encryption technique, sent over the network, and then decrypted at the destination to be viewed back as unencrypted messages.

Data encryption procedures are mainly categorized into two categories depending on the type of the security keys used to encrypt/decrypt the secured data. These two categories are: asymmetric and symmetric encryption techniques.

*Symmetric Encryption*

In this type of encryption, the sender and the receiver agree on a secret (shared) key. Then they use this secret key to encrypt and decrypt their messages. Figure 1.2 shows the process of symmetric cryptography. Node A and B first agree on the encryption technique to be used in encryption and decryption of communicated data. Then they agree on the secret key that both of them will use in this connection. After the encryption setup finishes, node A starts sending its data encrypted with the shared key, on the other side node B uses the same key to decrypt the encrypted messages.

The main concern behind symmetric encryption is how to share the secret key securely between the two peers. If the key gets exposed for any reason, the whole system security collapses. The key management for this type of encryption is troublesome, especially if a unique secret key is used for each peer-to-peer

Fig. 1.1. Data encryption and decryption.

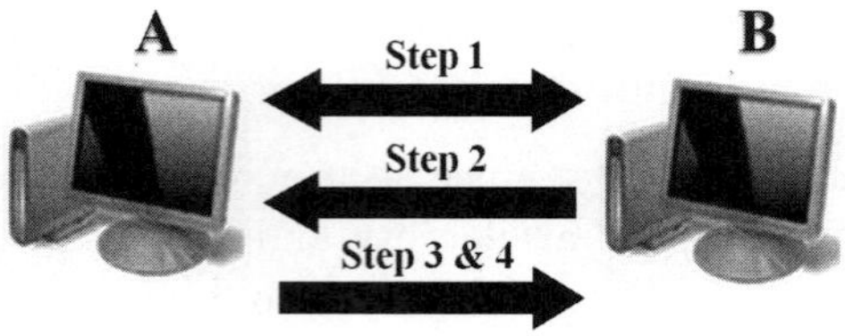


1- A and B agree on a cryptosystem

2- A and B agree on the key to be used

3- A encrypts the messages using the shared key

4- B decrypts the ciphered messages using the shared key

Fig. 1.2. Symmetric encryption.

connection, then the total number of secret keys to be saved and managed for n-nodes will be $n(n-1)/2$ keys [4].

*Asymmetric Encryption*

Asymmetric encryption is the type of encryption where two keys are used. What Key1 can encrypt only Key2 can decrypt, and vice versa. It is also known as Public Key Cryptography (PKC), because users need two keys: public key, which is known to the public and private key which is only known to the user. Figure 1.3 below illustrates the use of the two keys between node A and node B. After agreeing on the type of encryption to be used in the connection, node B sends its public key to node A. Node A uses the received public key to encrypt its messages. Then when the encrypted messages arrive, node B uses its private key to decrypt them.

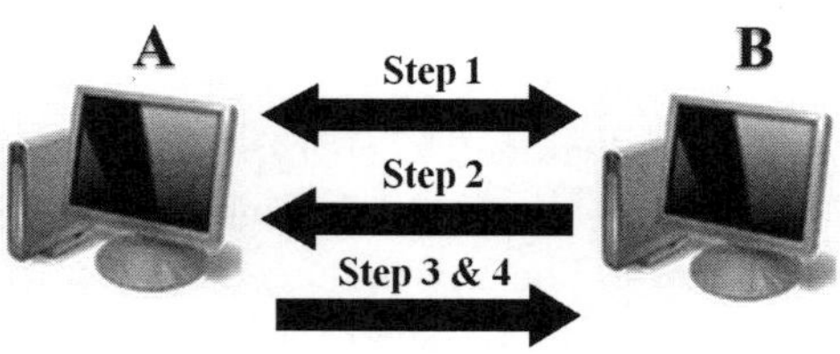


1- A and B agree on a cryptosystem

2- B sendsits public key to A

3- A encrypts the messages using the negotiated cipher and B's public key received in Step 2.

4- B decryptsthe ciphered messages using its private key and the negotiated cipher

Fig. 1.3. Asymmetric encryption.

Asymmetric encryption overcomes the symmetric encryption problem of managing secret keys. But, on the other hand, this unique feature of public key encryption makes it mathematically more prone to attacks. Moreover, asymmetric encryption techniques are almost 1,000 times slower than symmetric techniques, because they require more computational processing power [4], [6].

To get the benefits of both methods, a hybrid technique is usually used. In this technique, asymmetric encryption is used to exchange the secret (shared) key, symmetric encryption is then used to transfer data between sender and receiver.

#### 1.2.1.3. *Block and stream ciphers*

Another commonly used categorization method to differentiate encryption techniques is based on the form of input data they operate on. The two types are: Block Cipher and Stream Cipher. This section discusses the main features offered by the two types, operation modes, and compares them in terms of security and performance.

##### *Block Cipher*

In this method data is encrypted and decrypted in the form of blocks. In its simplest mode, the plain text is divided into blocks which are then fed into the cipher system to produce blocks of cipher text.

There are many variations of block cipher, where different techniques are used to strengthen the security of the system. The most common methods are: ECB (Electronic Codebook Mode), CBC (Chain Block Chaining Mode), and OFB (Output Feedback Mode). ECB is the basic form of block cipher where data blocks are encrypted directly to generate its correspondent ciphered blocks (shown in Figure 1.4). CBC mode uses the cipher block from the previous step of encryption in the current one, which forms a chain-like encryption process. OFB operates on plain text in a way similar to stream cipher that will be described next, where the encryption key used in every step depends on the encryption key from the previous step [1], [4].

##### *Stream Cipher*

Stream cipher works on a stream of data by operating on it bit by bit. Stream cipher consists of two major components: a key stream generator, and a mixing function. Mixing function is usually just an XOR function, while key stream generator is the main unit in the stream cipher encryption technique. For example, if the key stream generator produces a series of zeros, the outputted ciphered stream will be identical to the original plain text.

To start the series of a key stream, an Initialization Vector (IV) is sent to set the initial value. A common IV between the sender and the receiver is usually imposed

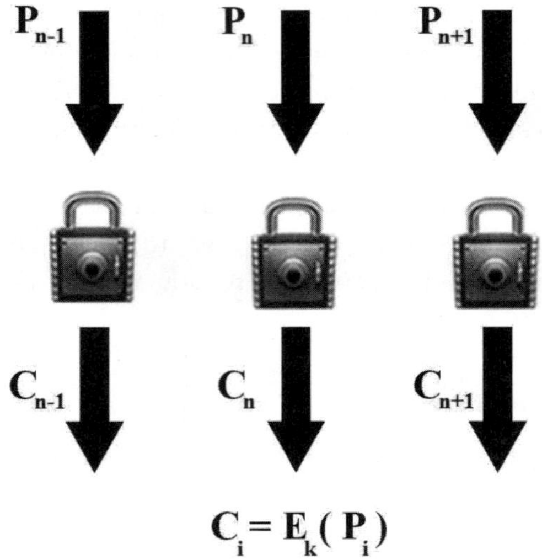


Fig. 1.4. Block cipher — ECB mode.

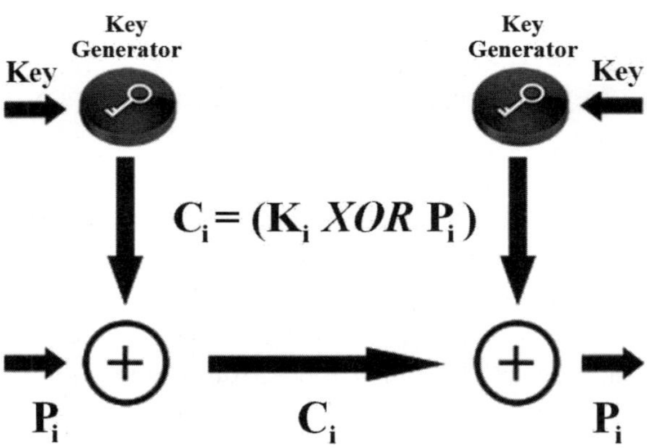


Fig. 1.5. Stream cipher — Simple mode.

to keep both of them synchronized. The IV can be auto-generated or incremented on each packet, which depends on the capabilities of the system.

The stream cipher techniques can be categorized into two modes: synchronous stream cipher, and self-synchronizing stream cipher. In synchronous stream cipher, the key stream generator depends only on the base key used for encryption. Figure 1.5 shows how synchronous stream mode (the "simple" mode) operates on the both sender and receiver sides. The sender uses only the base (shared) key to encrypt the outgoing stream; on the other side the receiver decrypts the stream using the same key. The main disadvantage of this method is that if the base key gets known the whole system is compromised.

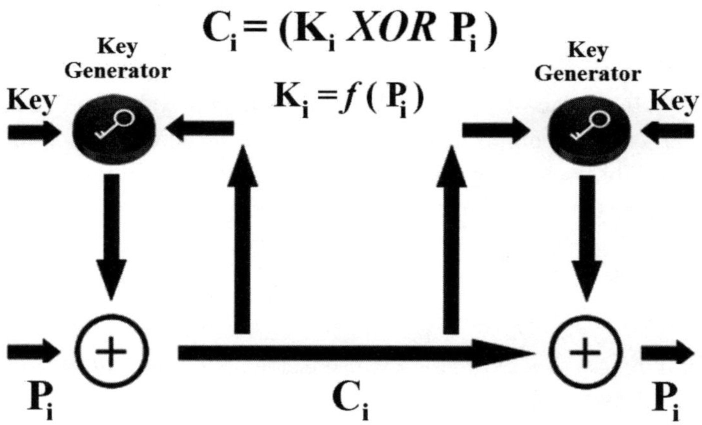


Fig. 1.6. Stream cipher — self synchronizing mode.

The other mode is called self-synchronizing stream cipher. In this mode, the state of key stream generator (the key used at that instant of time) depends on the previous states of cipher text bits. The previous states number is fixed and defined by the algorithm. Self-synchronizing method is more secure than the previous mode, but it is slower. Figure 1.6 shows the process undertaken by self-synchronizing stream cipher to encrypt/decrypt data.

Stream cipher has a well known advantage over block cipher because of its speed and simplicity of operation. But at the same time it is a known fact that stream ciphers are less secure than block ciphers. Today's standards recommend using block cipher techniques [1].

### 1.2.1.4. *Data encryption standards: DES, AES and RC4*

After taking a quick look at the major classification of data ciphers (both stream and block ciphers), in this section we describe briefly some of the well known and used encryption standards. Moreover, we mention the key features and merits of each standard.

#### *DES*

DES (Data Encryption Standard), was the first encryption standard to be recommended by NIST (National Institute of Standards and Technology). It is based on the IBM proposed algorithm called Lucifer. DES became a standard in 1974 [28]. Since then, many attacks and methods have been published that exploit the weaknesses of DES, which proved it as an insecure block cipher. As an enhancement to DES, the 3DES (Triple DES) encryption standard was proposed. The 3DES encryption method is similar to DES but it is applied 3 times to increase the encryption strength. 3DES is known to be slower than most of other block cipher methods.

*AES*

AES (Advanced Encryption Standard), is another encryption standard recommended by NIST to replace DES. Rijndael (pronounced Rain Doll) algorithm was selected in 1997 after a competition to select the best encryption standard. Brute force attack is the only effective attack known against it, in which the attacker tries to test all character combinations to unlock the encryption. Both AES and DES are block ciphers.

*RC4*

RC4 or ARC-Four is the most widely used stream cipher. It is used with SSL (Secure Socket Layer), which is used to secure identification information and money transfer transactions over the Internet. Moreover, it is used in WEP (Wired Equivalent Privacy) which is responsible for securing wireless data. RC4 is secure enough for certain systems, but it lacks the required level of security for wireless communications, making it fall short for many security standards [1].

### 1.2.2. *Introduction to the Wireless Networking*

Wireless data networks have spread among home users and companies alike in an increasing fashion. The main reason behind this fast adaptation is due to the nature of wireless networks, since they provides the flexibility and freedom that wired networks lack. The increasing bandwidth capabilities have inspired people to think seriously about replacing wired networks with wireless networks especially in places where it is hard or expensive to have wired networks. One of the main places that can benefit from these ideas is rural areas, where wired networks infrastructure is either difficult or impossible to create due to physical obstacles.

The main standards in wireless networking are: 802.11 standard which describes the Wireless LAN architecture, and 802.16 standard which describes the Wireless MAN architecture. These two wireless standards are usually known by two acronyms: WiFi (Wireless Fidelity) for WLAN, and WiMAX (Worldwide Interoperability for Microwave Access) for WMAN.

#### 1.2.2.1. *Wireless LAN (WLAN)*

Wireless LANs are designed to imitate the structure of the wired LANs, using another medium to transfer data rather than cables. This medium is electromagnetic waves which are mainly either radio frequency (RF) or infrared frequency (IR).

Wireless LANs consist mainly of two entities: clients or end-user devices and Access Points (APs). Clients are equipped with devices that allow them to use the RF medium to communicate with other wireless devices. AP functions like a regular switch or a router in wired networks for the wireless devices. Moreover, it represents a gateway between the wireless devices and wired networks.

Fig. 1.7. Wireless LAN.

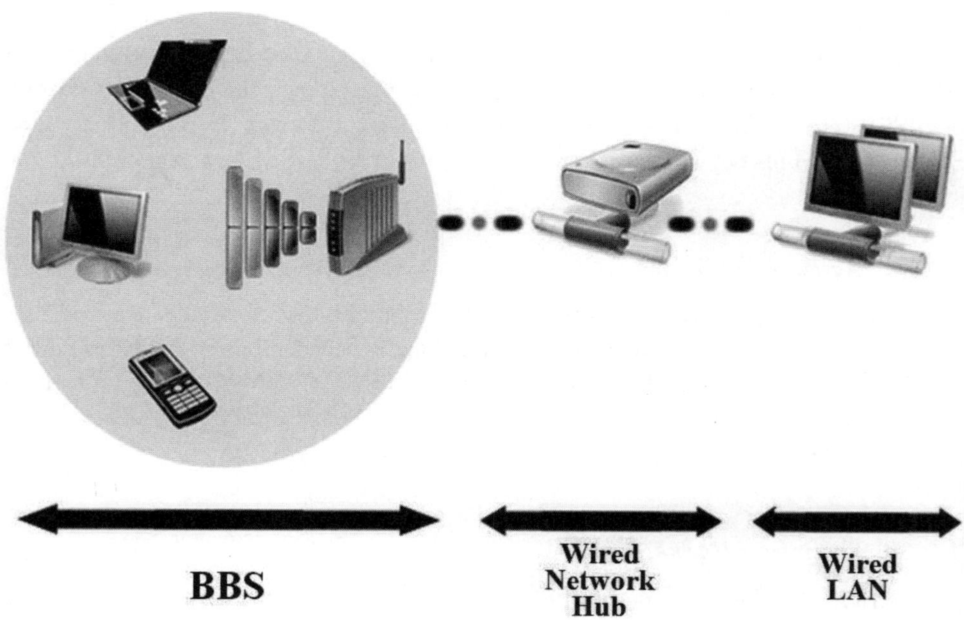


Fig. 1.8. WLAN — BSS structure.

The basic structure of a Wireless LAN is called BSS (Basic Service Set) shown in Figure 1.8, in which the network consists of an AP and several wireless devices. When these devices try to communicate among themselves they propagate their data through the AP device. In order to form the network, AP keeps broadcasting its SSID (Service Set Identifier) to allow others to join the network.

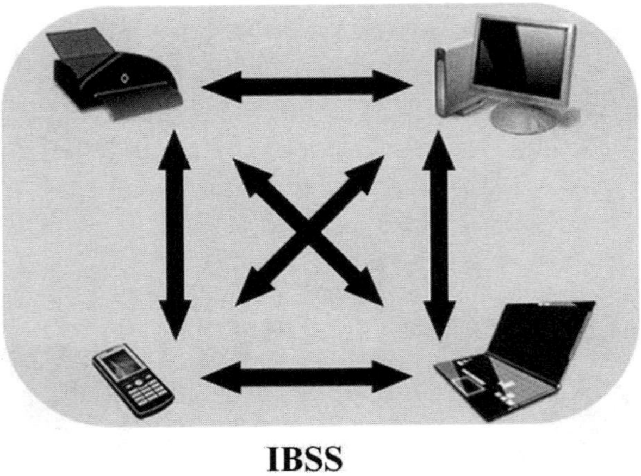


Fig. 1.9. WLAN — IBSS structure.

If the BSS did not have an AP device, and the wireless devices were communicating with each other directly, this BSS is called an Independent BSS (IBSS) and works in a mode called "ad hoc mode" (shown in Figure 1.9). Group of BSSs (either BSS or IBSS) can be combined to form an ESS (Extended Service Set). This set is created by chaining groups of BSSs to a single backbone system.

#### 1.2.2.2. *Wireless MAN (WMAN)*

The idea behind using WMAN is to offer a broadband internet service using wireless infrastructure over a metropolitan area. The idea is very similar to a TV broadcast network (shown in Figure 1.10). The theoretical speed of WMAN could be as high as 75 Mbps with a range extends to several miles, which will offer a replacement to cable and DSL connections [6].

### 1.2.3. *Security Attacks*

As mentioned before, the main difference between wired and wireless networks is the medium they transfer their data through. This difference makes the burden of securing the network heavier. The broadcast nature of wireless networks makes it easy for everyone to attack the network if not secured, due to the absence of physical barriers, where the range of wireless transmission ranges from 300 ft to several miles [10].

The exponential growth of wireless networks adds another obstacle on enhancing the network security. People tend to keep things the way they are instead of doing what is right. Also such enhancement of security is expensive in terms of time, money and effort that many users do not have or do not wish to spend.

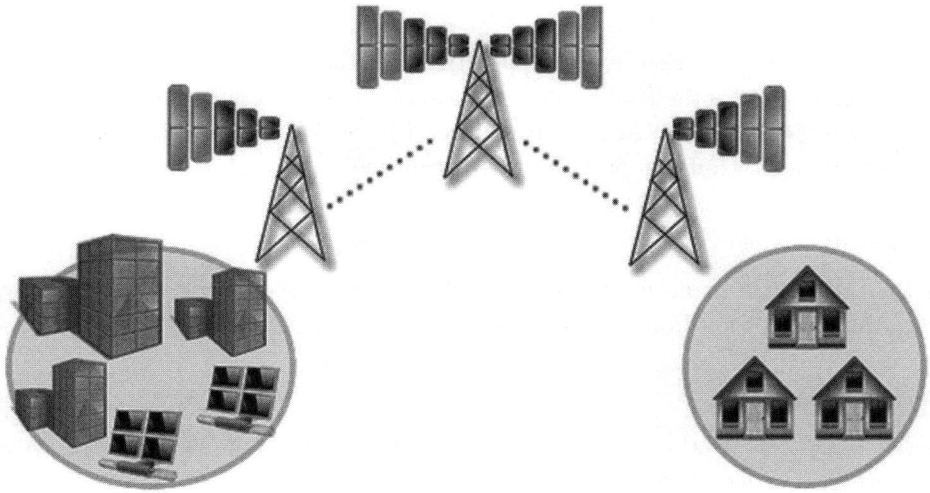

Fig. 1.10. Wireless MAN.

Below is a list of the most common attack types known in both wired and wireless networks. Most of the security attacks and threats are listed under the following categories:

*Traffic Analysis*

In this type of attacks the attacker uses the statistics of network connectivity and activity to find information about the attacked network. Information includes: AP location, AP SSID and the type of protocol used by the analysis of size and types of packets [3].

*Passive Eavesdropping*

Attackers of this type set themselves in sniffing mode, where they listen to all the network traffic hoping to extract information from it. This type of attack is only useful with unencrypted networks and stream cipher encrypted ones.

*Active Eavesdropping*

Similar to passive eavesdropping but the attacker tries to change the data on the packet, or to inject a complete packet in the stream of data.

*Unauthorized Access*

This type of attack is also known by many other names, such as war-driving, war-walking, or war-flying [5]. This is the most common attack type, where the attacker tries to get access to a network that she is not authorized to access. The main reason behind such attacks is just to get Internet access for free [11].

*Man-in-the-middle Attacks*

In this attack, the attacker gets the packets before the intended receiver does. This allows her to change the content of the message. One of the most known subset of this attack is called ARP (Address Resolution Protocol) attacks, where the attacker redirects network traffic to pass through her device [3].

*Session Hijacking*

In this Attack the attacker attacks the integrity of the session by trying to hijack an authorized session from an authorized user.

*Replay Attacks*

In this type of attack the attacker uses the information from previous authenticated sessions to gain access to the network.

*Rouge AP*

Some of the devices allow themselves to appear as an AP. This will make people confused and sometimes they may connect to this false AP exposing their information to it. This can be solved by imposing mutual authentication between AP and network devices.

*DoS Attacks*

DoS (Denial of Service) attacks are the most difficult type of attacks to protect against. Attackers use radio devices to send continuous noise on a specific channel to ruin network connectivity. It is known in the wireless world as RF Jamming [3].

There are many other threats that can be placed under one of the categories above. These different types of attacks make it harder for the standard regulators to find the best way to come up with the best solutions to the security hazards without sacrificing network usability or speed.

## 1.3. Security in WLAN 802.11

In this section, we will go through the steps wireless LAN security community took to achieve its current status of implementing 802.11i security protocol. First we will discuss the difficulties faced in creating the standard, and then describe the 802.11 standard itself. After that we will take a journey through the different security modules that have been proposed to solve the security issues related to wireless networks starting from WEP and ending with WPA2.

Wireless media are known to be more difficult to secure than wired media because of its broadcast nature [10]. This property makes creating a well secured protocol that is comparable to the used wired security modules a hard task. In addition to that, mobile units that use wireless security protocols differ from regular PCs in many aspects. There are constraints related to processing power, battery capacity, and flexibility to facilitate inter-operability. In addition to that, there is a need for tamper proofing techniques in case mobile units fall into the hands of malicious entities [14].

### 1.3.1. *IEEE 802.11 Standard*

The IEEE 802.11 standard was first standardized in 1997. It consists of three layers: Physical layer, MAC (Medium Access Control) layer, and LLC (Logical Link Control) layer (Figure 1.11). The first version of the standard supported only 2 Mbps data rate, which motivated the developing teams to come up with standards to support higher speeds.

Protocol designers took into consideration the necessity of making the physical layer supports more than one signaling technique and interface, as shown in Figure 1.11. The physical layer is responsible for providing an interface to exchange frames with the MAC layer, transmitting and signaling packets, and works as a media activity sensor for the MAC layer.

The MAC layer supports the functionality needed to allow reliable transfer to the upper layers in a manner similar to the data link layer in the OSI (Open System Interconnection) model. It provides the functionality to control media access, and it is a connectionless layer. The LLC provides addressing and data link control, and it is independent from the lower layers (MAC and PHY). LLC provides connection oriented service to the upper layers.

*802.11 Authentication*

To allow clients to access the network they must go through two steps: getting authenticated by the AP, then getting associated. There are two types of authentications used: Shared Key Authentication and Open Key Authentication [5].

In the WEP (Wired Equivalent Privacy) standard (the first security module used with 802.11) both of the authentication modes were supported. In the new

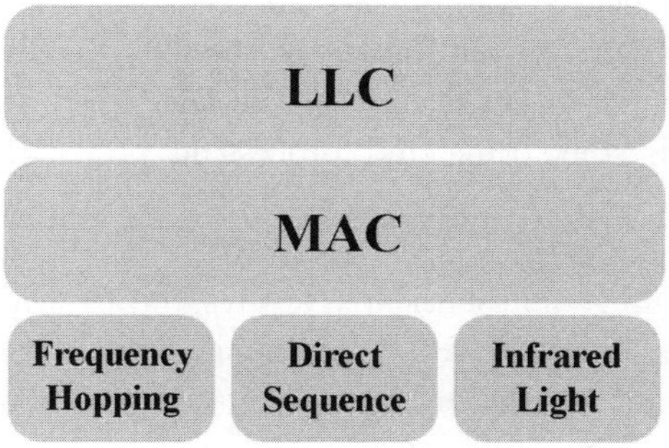


Fig. 1.11. 802.11 layers.

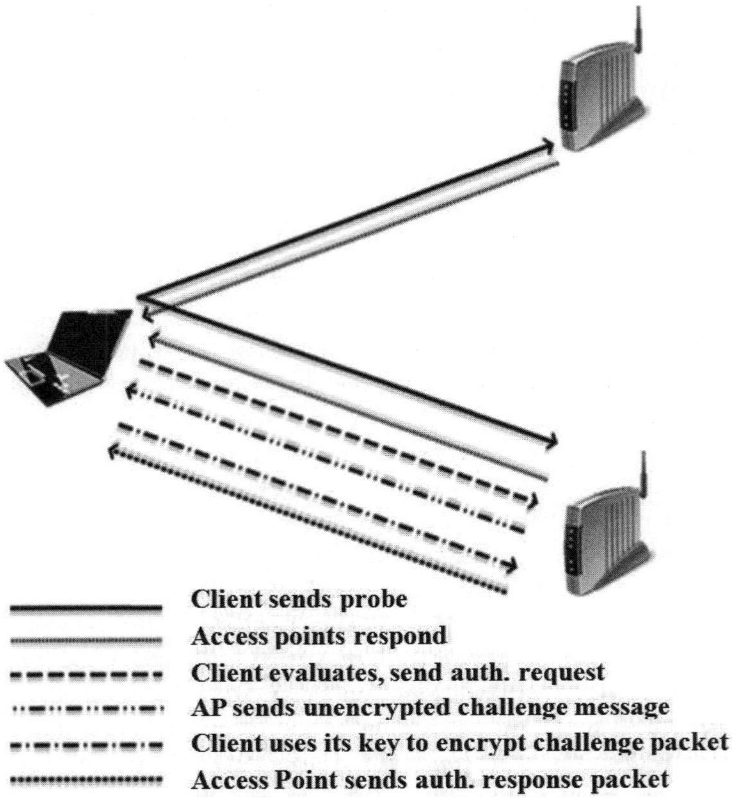


Fig. 1.12. Shared key authentication.

security standards the use of use of shared key authentication is not recommended. Figure 1.12 shows how Shared Key Authentication works. When the client wants to connect to the AP, it sends a request. Upon that request the AP sends a challenge packet in clear text (unencrypted). The client then encrypts it with its WEP key and sends it back. The AP tries to decrypt the message using its WEP key. If the decryption process succeeds that means the client is an authenticated user, otherwise the access is denied. In this case if someone is sniffing the traffic, they will get a copy of the encrypted and clear text versions of the message. With some time and processing power the WEP key can be obtained.

Open Key Authentication does not involve challenge/response messages exchange. The client will get authenticated always, but to send and receive messages she needs to have the correct WEP key. Although Open Key Authentication does not offer any kind of authentication, it is more secure. The reason behind the last statement is that Open Key Authentication does not expose the WEP key to traffic sniffers [33].

### 1.3.2. *WEP (Wired Equivalent Privacy)*

WEP had three goals to achieve for wireless LAN: confidentiality, availability and integrity [5]. WEP is now considered insecure for many reasons; nonetheless it still one of the most used security modules in the wireless world.

WEP uses encryption to provide confidentiality. The encryption process is only between the client and the AP, meaning that the transmitted packets after the AP (on wired LAN) point are unencrypted. WEP uses RC4 (discussed earlier) for encryption. Since RC4 is a stream cipher it needs a seed value to start its key stream generator. This seed is called IV (Initialization Vector). The IV and the shared WEP key are used to encrypt/decrypt the transferred packets (Figure 1.13). In the encryption process, the Integrity check (IC) value is computed and then attached to the payload, after that the payload is XORed with the key stream generated using encryption key that consists of two sections (IV and WEP Key). The packet is then forwarded with the IV value sent in plain text (Figure 1.14).

WEP uses CRC (Cyclical Redundancy Checking) to verify message integrity. On the other side (receiver: AP) the decryption process is the same but reversed. The AP uses the IV value sent in plain text to decrypt the message by joining it with the shared WEP key. To get a better understanding of the operation, Figure 1.14 shows both encryption and decryption process between the client and AP.

In this section we have described the way the WEP security protocol operates and the main features or properties it possesses. In the following section we will go through WEP weaknesses and flaws.

### 1.3.3. *WEP Weaknesses*

Many people still think that WEP is secure. They argue that because no big accident has occurred, that is related to wireless security yet, means “no news is good news”.

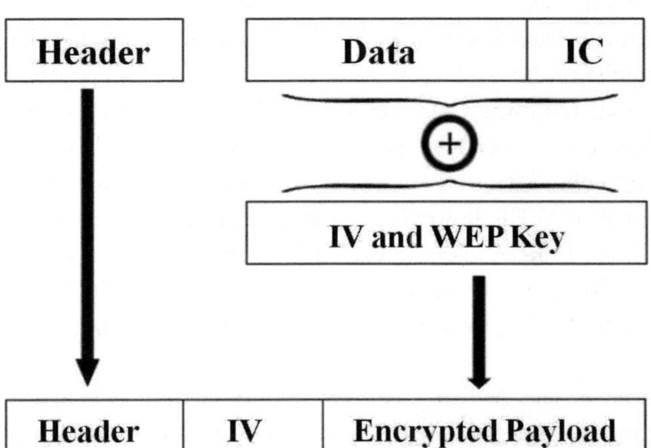


Fig. 1.13. WEP packet encryption.

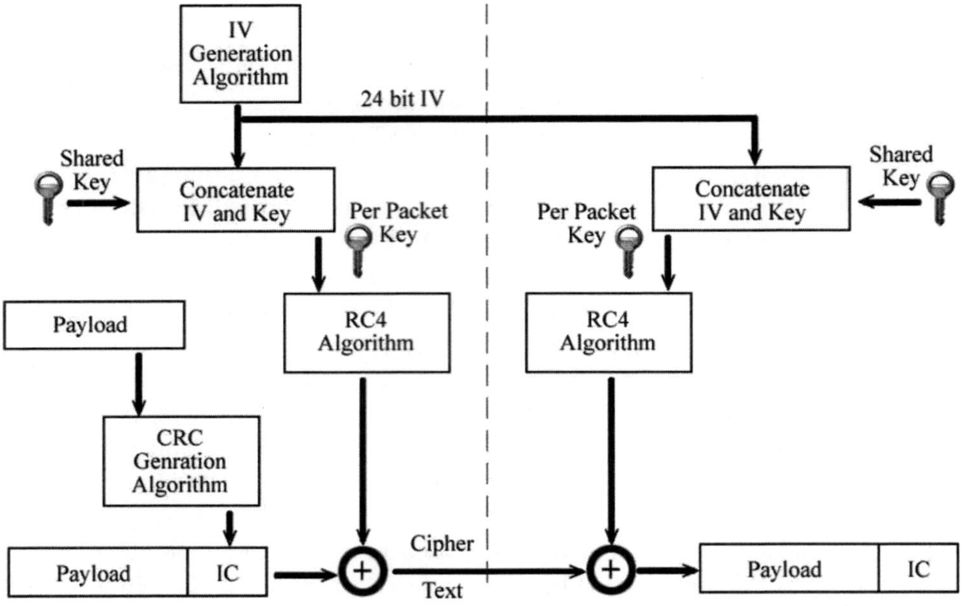


Fig. 1.14. WEP encryption and decryption processes.

The argument completely contradicts with the meaning of security, where you have to predict the risk and work to secure yourself from it before it happens.

Other people believe that attacking a wireless network is an expensive and a complex process; it requires high processing power and complex techniques to break into the network. Today's computers have high processing power and they are continuously becoming cheaper. A wireless attacker does not need to know much about cryptography or security modules; there are many online tools that can ease the process for them [30].

One of the major reasons behind WEP weaknesses is its key length. WEP has a 40-bit key, which can be broken in less than five hours using parallel attacks with the help of normal computer machines [17]. This issue urged vendors to update WEP from using 40-bit to 104-bit key; the new release is called WEP2.

This update helped to resolve some of the security issues with WEP. The main disadvantage of WEP however, is the lack of key management. Some SOHO (Small Office/Home Office) users never change their WEP key, which once known puts the whole system in jeopardy. In addition to that, WEP does not support mutual authentication. It only authenticates the client, making it open to rouge AP attacks.

Another issue is the use of CRC to ensure integrity. While CRC is a good integrity provision standard, it lacks the cryptography feature. CRC is known to be linear. By using a form of induction, knowing enough data (encrypted packets) and acquiring specific plaintext the WEP key can be resolved [17].

RC4 suffers from a deadly symptom. It tends to repeat IV values (even if it is auto generated), making the exposing of the traffic easier. Mathematically, if the same IV is used to encrypt two packets (with the same WEP key) and you have a pair of encrypted/plaintext message, then by applying the following simple rule:

$$C_1 \otimes C_2 = P_1 \otimes P_2 \tag{1.1}$$

(where P1(plain text message #1), C1 (ciphered message #1) and C2 are already known), this makes it very easy to know the content of the new encrypted packet P2 [3].

These weaknesses forced the architects of WLAN security modules to be more cautious in their designs. They also demonstrate the result of not designing the security module from the ground up taking into consideration all applicable risks. In the next section, we will go through some of the new standards that came after WEP to overcome these vulnerabilities.

### 1.3.4. *IEEE 802.1x: EAP over LAN (EAPOL)*

The IEEE 802.1x standard was designed for port-based authentication for IEEE 802 networks. 802.1x does not care what encryption techniques is used, it is only used to authenticate users. EAP (Extensible authentication Protocol) was designed to support multiple authentication methods over point to point connections [34]. EAP allows any of the encryption schemes to be implemented on top of it, adding flexibility to the security design module. EAPOL (EAP over LAN) is EAP's implementation for LANs [35].

The 802.1x framework defines three ports or entities: Supplicant (client wants to be authenticated), Authenticator (AP that connects the supplicant to the wired network), and Authentication Server (AS) which performs the authentication process on the supplicant based on their credentials [5], [6], [35].

The authentication server in the 802.1x framework uses Remote Authentication Dial-In User Service (RADIUS) protocol to provide Authentication, Authorization and Accounting (AAA) services for network clients [2], [36]. The protocol creates an encrypted tunnel between the Authentication Server (AS) and the Authenticator (AP). Authentication messages are exchanged inside the tunnel to determine if the client has access to the network or not. Figure 1.15 below shows the network layout.

### 1.3.5. *IEEE 802.11i Standard*

The IEEE 802.11i (released June 2004) security standard is the IEEE 802.11i committee's solution to wireless security issues. It improves authentication, integrity and data transfer. Due to the market need for a better substitute to WEP, vendors (WiFi Alliance) took a subset of it and marketed the new product before the final release under the name WPA (WiFi Protected Access), which was released

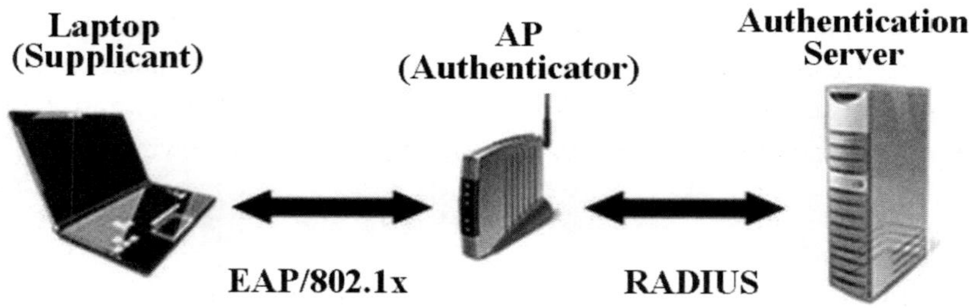


Fig. 1.15. 802.1x authentication.

in April 2003. After the final release of 802.11i the vendors implemented the full specifications under the name WPA2. This section will explore the details of 802.11i and its features [37].

802.11i supports two methods of authentication. The first method is the one described before by using 802.1x and EAP to authenticate users. For users who cannot or do not want to implement the first method, another method was proposed to use per-session key per-device. This method is implemented by having a shared key (like the one in WEP) called GMK (Group Master Key), which represents the base key to derive the other used keys. GMK is used to derive PTK (Pair Transient Key) and PSK (Pair Session Key) to do the authentication and data encryption.

To solve the integrity problem with WEP, a new algorithm named Michael is used to calculate an 8-byte integrity check called MIC (Message Integrity Code). Michael differs from the old CRC method by protecting both data and header. Michael implements a frame counter which helps to protect against replay attacks [39], [40].

To improve data transfer, 802.11i specifies three protocols: TKIP, CCMP and WRAP. TKIP (Temporal Key Integrity Management) was introduced as a "band-aid" solution to WEP problems [17]. One of the major advantages of implementing TKIP is that you do not need to update the hardware of the devices to run it. A simple firmware/software upgrade is enough. Unlike WEP, TKIP provides per-packet key mixing, a message integrity check and a re-keying mechanism [38]. TKIP ensures that every data packet is encrypted with its own unique encryption key. TKIP is included in 802.11i mainly for backward compatibility.

WRAP (Wireless Robust Authenticated Protocol) is the LAN implementation of the AES encryption standard introduced earlier. It was ported to wireless to get the benefits of AES encryption. WRAP has intellectual property issues, where three parties have filed for its patent. This problem caused IEEE to replace it with CCMP [17], [41].

CCMP (Counter with Cipher Block Chaining Message Authentication Code) Protocol is considered the optimal solution for securing data transfer under 802.11i. CCMP uses AES for encryption. The use of AES will require a hardware upgrade to support the new encryption algorithm.

### 1.3.6. *RSN*

RSN (Robust Secure/Security Network) is a part of 802.11i for providing a method to exchange the clients and the AP capabilities of implementing security methods. RSN uses RSN IE (Information Element) frames to exchange this type of information. RSN increases the flexibility of wireless security network standards and provides options to define the security policies implemented in organizations [5].

### 1.3.7. *WAP*

WAP stands for Wireless Application Protocol. WAP came as a result of an initiative lead by Unwired Planet, Motorola, Nokia and Ericson. WAP is not considered to be a formal standard yet [45].

WAP was designed to provide web browser capabilities to wireless devices, especially handhelds and mobile phones. The connection between the client mobile device and the Internet goes through a WAP gateway (shown in Figure 1.16). WAP gateway is usually a server that resides inside the carrier network [46]. WAP gateway has four main functions:

1. Convert WAP devices requests to HTTP requests.
2. Convert WML (Wireless Markup Language) Internet websites responses to the binary format comprehendible by mobile devices.
3. Convert between SSL (Secure Socket Layer) capabilities used in the Internet and WTLS (Wireless Transport Layer Security) protocol used in WAP.
4. Bridges the communication between Internet TCP and WAP WDP (Wireless Datagram Protocol) [48].

WAP Forum [46] (which has consolidated into the Open Mobile Alliance OMA) proposed a protocol suite to allow competing standards to work on top of it. WAP defines also the wireless application environment (WAE) to enable 3rd parties to develop WAP services and applications [49].

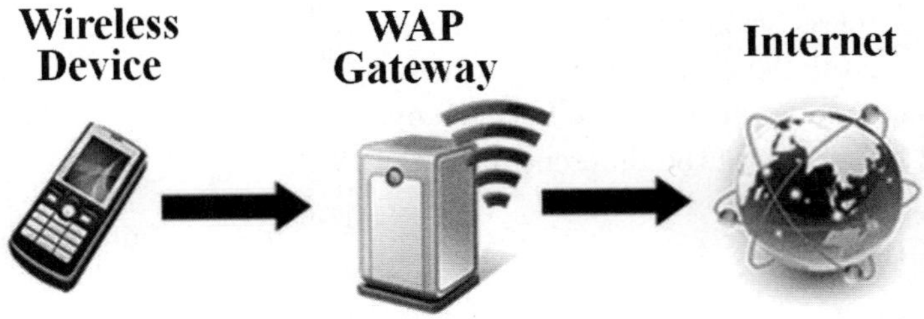


Fig. 1.16. WAP connection through WAP gateway.

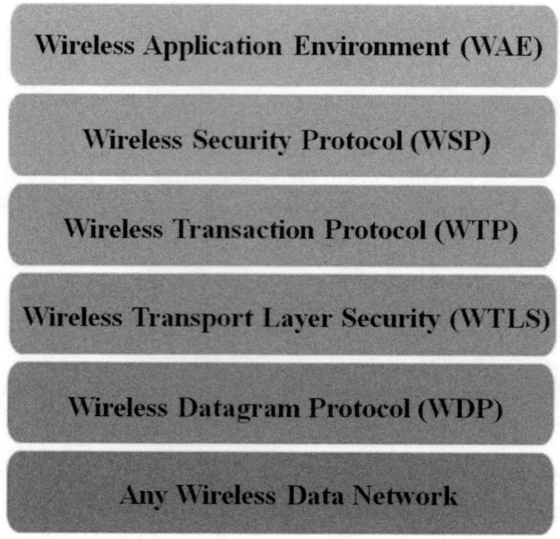


Fig. 1.17. WAP protocol suite.

*WAP Protocol Suite*

As shown in Figure 1.17, WAP provides a suite of protocols that allows the interoperability of WAP equipment and software with many different network technologies.

WDP (Wireless Datagram Protocol) is considered to be the wireless version of UDP where it provides unreliable but a uniform transport layer to the upper layers. By providing this layer, the upper layers can work independently of the types of technology used in the carrier network.

WTLS (Wireless Transport Layer Protocol) provides public key encryption functionality. It provides integrity, privacy and authentication. WTLS is based on the TLS (Transport Layer Security) protocol [50]. The use of WTLS is optional.

Packet loss is considered to be a common problem in wireless networks. This problem makes wired network TCP protocol to behave in undesired way. A modified version of TCP is introduced to overcome this setback. This version is called WTP (Wireless Transaction Protocol).

WSP (Wireless Session Protocol) provides two connectivity modes: connection-oriented mode (also called CO-WSP) which operates on top of the WTP layer. Connectionless mode (also called CL-WSP) operates on top of WTLS or WDP [51]. Figure 1.18 below shows the different modes of WSP.

*Security in WAP*

When the security option is used in WAP, all communication requests between the WAP device and the WAP gateway are encrypted with the help of WTLS, the

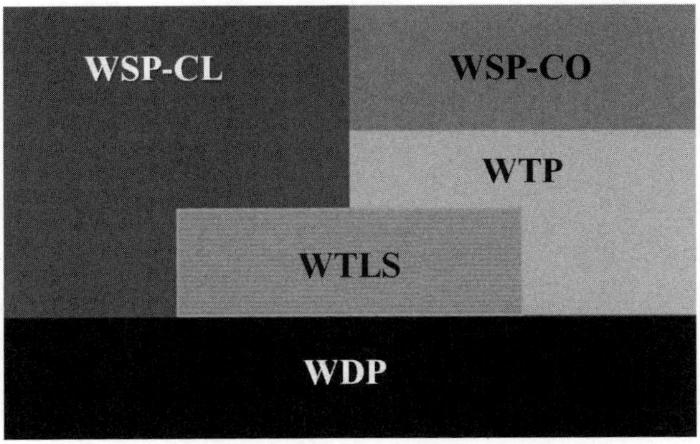


Fig. 1.18. WSP modes of operations.

gateway then decrypts these requests and re-encrypt them using SSL. This method has two main obvious drawbacks: using WTLS is entirely optional, and WTLS itself allows for weak encryption algorithms [52].

A further investigation into the common threats in the WTLS model yields the following threat points. First is the use of linear IV computation; which leads to predictable IVs which ease plain-text attacks. WTLS uses DES with a 35-bit key, which result in weak encryption capabilities. Unauthenticated error messages used in WTLS, which are sent in clear text, are also considered a possible hole in the security system. These kinds of messages although may not result in ending the session, they use a sequence number that can be used by the attacker to send unauthenticated alert messages instead of actual data packets without being detected. This is usually called truncation attack. It has also been found that brute force attack can be easily mounted on block ciphers in WTLS [53].

## 1.4. Security in Bluetooth Networks

Bluetooth is a wireless protocol to facilitate communication among low power, fixed and mobile devices in a short range and what is called Personal Area Networks (PANs). While WLAN targets to replace wired LANs, Bluetooth technology focuses on small wireless networks like PANs, which is supposed to cover only the gadgets around the person's body. As a result of these different goals, different security architecture approaches have been considered.

To facilitate the usage of Bluetooth networks and to allow their operations on low-cost and low-power devices, many security sacrifices or tradeoffs have been taken. For instance Bluetooth devices broadcast all the services they provide to ease the communication and setup procedures between it and other nearby devices. For these reasons Bluetooth is better suited as an ad-hoc network.

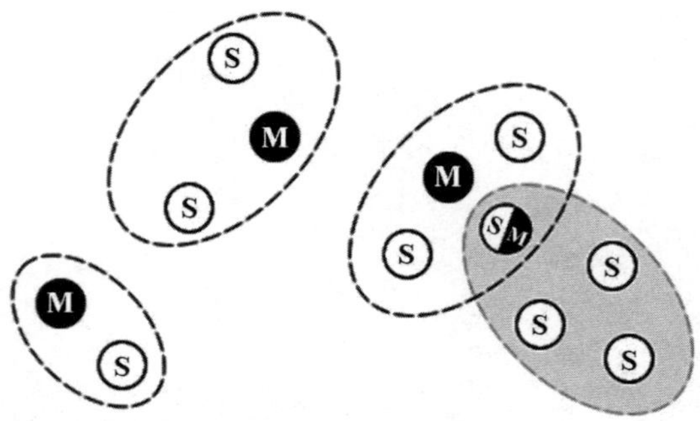


Fig. 1.19. Piconets structure and interaction.

Bluetooth networks are formed using piconets. Each piconet allows up to eight devices to connect to it. Communications among nodes inside a piconet is determined in master-slave manner. There is one master and one to seven other active slaves at most [56].

This structure does not limit the scalability of Bluetooth networks, since Bluetooth devices are allowed to connect to more than one piconet by dividing time between the connected piconets, and allowing the nodes to behave as a slave and a master node at the same time for different piconets. Figure 1.19 shows some of the possible configurations of Bluetooth networks.

Security in Bluetooth networks is affected by the fact that most of Bluetooth devices are within a close range of each other. Also most Bluetooth are not expected to have sophisticated security capabilities if at all. These variations of Bluetooth devices urged the designers to consider the functionality of a security manager where the devices capabilities and services are taken into consideration before establishing the secure connection.

Bluetooth General Access Profile (GAP) defines three modes of connection, aided by the decision of the security manager:

1. Mode 1: {None}. Communication is not restricted in any way.
2. Mode 2: {Application Layer Security}: Which guarantees the connection's security past connection establishment and it operates using application layer functionalities.
3. Mode 3: {Link Layer Security}: Security is enforced prior to connection establishing phase, using level 2 (link layer) functionalities.

Other security levels are used in Bluetooth to identify physical layers as: reliable or unreliable, and devices as: trusted or untrusted [57].

Though Bluetooth security is considered to be mature and offers a lot of sophisticated methods to secure exchanged data including methods similar to the previously discussed WLAN security methods, it is still prone to many of the same security threats.

Bluetooth is no exception in its vulnerability to DoS attacks. And because of its limited power the consequences of this attack are even more severe. DoS attack drains the battery power and leaves the device unusable. Bluetooth also suffers from possible attacks to expose devices confidentiality or steal their identity due to the weaknesses in the key generation process and its handshaking mechanism, mainly because of the use of PIN code in these processes.

In this section we gave a simple introduction to both Bluetooth network concept and its security modules, and explained some of the security threats that it can be exposed to.

## 1.5. Security in WMAN IEEE 802.16

As mentioned before, the WMAN or WiMAX was proposed to solve the "last mile" problem. The IEEE 802.16 standard was released in Dec 2001. That gave the designers time to learn from the mistakes made in designing the 802.11 WEP security protocol. In the following sections the architecture of 802.16 will be discussed along with its security volunaribilitis.

### 1.5.1. *The 802.16 Protocol Layers*

802.16 protocol consists of four layers (shown in Figure 1.20):

*Physical Layer*

802.16 protocol operates in three major frequency bands:

1. 10 to 66 GHz (licensed bands)
2. 2 to 11 GHz (licensed bands)
3. 2 to 11 GHz (unlicensed bands)

To support these three bands, the protocol specifies multiple physical layers.

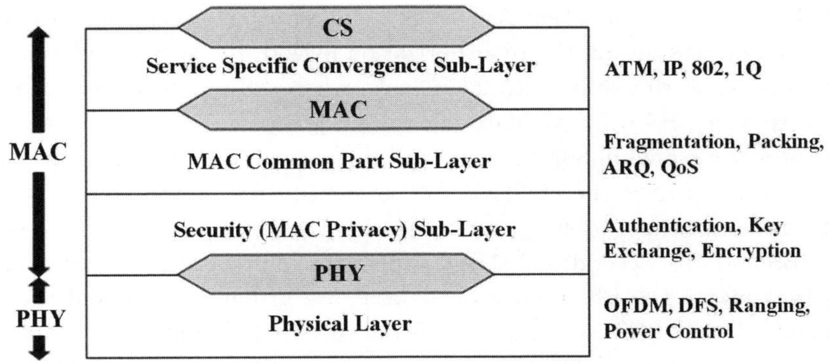


Fig. 1.20. IEEE 802.16 layers.

*Security Sub-layer or MAC Sub-layer*

This layer focuses on the security functions in the MAC layer. It consists of two component protocols:

- Encapsulation protocol: This component describes how the authentication is processed and the types of algorithms to be used in encrypting packets between the Base Station (BS) and the Subscriber Station (SS).
- Key Management protocol: This component describes how to distribute and manage connection keys. The default protocol used here is Privacy Key Management (PKM). Each connection between the BS and SS or Mobile Station (MS) has a unique Connection ID (CID).

*MAC Common Part Sub-layer*

It is a connection oriented sub-layer, and it includes the mechanisms to request bandwidth. Authentication and registration is also a part of this layer's function.

*MAC Convergence Sub-layer (Service Specific Convergence Sub-layer)*

Dividing the MAC layer into two sub-layers aims to solve the problem of having different protocols, where the common part sub-layer provides common functionality units to the upper layer (MAC convergence sub-layer). The MAC convergence sub-layer implements different services on top of the common part sub-layer. It is also responsible for bandwidth allocation and QoS [29].

As mentioned before the key management protocol used in 802.16 is PKM. PKM is used by SS to obtain the authorization to use the media. PKM uses 3DES as its encryption algorithm. PKM protocol operates in two phases: Authorization Key (AK) phase, and Traffic Encryption Keys (TEK). AK represents the secret key used to obtain TEK in the exchanges between SS and BS in subsequent phases.

In each connection session between SS and BS, both of them keep track of the two AK keys. The reason is that AK needs to be refreshed periodically. In order to keep all the packets during the reauthorization period, the two AK lifetimes must overlap. The same rule applies to TEK keys, where SS has to estimate the time period after which BS will invalidate the old TEK key [6].

The security model in 802.16 ensures that specific requirements are supported. The first requirement is the ability of BS to identify the MS to allow it to access the network. Once this is done, a master session key (MSK) is transferred securely between BS and MS. Secondly, WiMAX supports a multicast and broadcast service (MBS) that allows the BS to distribute data to a group of registered users. The system must be able to control access to the distributed content by using a per-group secret key. Finally, WMAN security system provides per-MPDU (MAC Packet Data Unit) integrity protection and reply protection.

Now that we have briefed about WiMAX (WMAN) architecture, and explained the main functionalities of each layer and summarized the security techniques used to keep the traffic secure, in the next section we summarize the security threats for IEEE 802.16 security systems.

### 1.5.2. *WMAN Security Concerns*

Although the designers of 802.16 security module have benefited from the loop holes found in 802.11 WEP design, they still had some shortcomings in their security design. The possible reason behind these unexpected outcomes is the fact that they incorporated the use of the pre-existing standard DOCSIS (Data over Cable Service Interface Specifications) that was used to solve the "last mile" problem for cable communication. Since wired networks differ from wireless networks, 802.16 security modules failed to protect the 802.16 link as was hoped [13]. This section will briefly highlight some of these threats.

*Physical Layer Attacks*

Since the security layer of 802.16 operates completely in the MAC layer, there is no protection for the PHY layer. Attacks like water torture where the attacker sends a series of packets to drain the receiver battery resources are possible [13]. Not to forget that the radio jamming attack is also applicable to 802.16 networks.

*No Specific Definition for SA*

Security Association (SA) holds a security state relevant to a certain connection. 802.16 designers did not specify the authorization SA, which led to making the system vulnerable to replay attacks.

*No Mutual Authentication*

One of the major flaws in the 802.16 security module is the lack of BS authentication, allowing attacks of rouge AP type.

*PKM Authorization Vulnerabilities*

- Insufficient key length and wrong choices in choosing the correct cipher modes: WiMAX uses DES-CBC cipher with 56-bit key length. This cipher requires a guarantee of unpredictable IV to initialize CBC mode. TEK uses 3DES encryption, but operates it in ECB mode which is not secure enough.
- Lack of Integrity Protection of MPDUs: PKM initially lacked the message integrity protection. This has been fixed in 802.16-2004 specification.
- Small Key ID for AK and TEK: AK ID is only 4-bit long, where TEK ID is only 2-bit long. This opens the possibility of reusing keys without detection.

These obvious vulnerabilities motivated people to propose PKMv2. PKMv2 introduced a solution to mutual authentication and promoted a key hierarchy structure to reduce the cost of key exchanges in PKM. PKMv2 uses X.509 certificates to authenticate both SS and BS [6].

In this section we discussed the common and known threats in 802.16 security module. Moreover, we highlighted the motivation behind proposing a new key management system for 802.16, which is PKMv2.

## 1.6. Thoughts on Wireless Security

This section will briefly discuss the best practices for installing wireless security in your home or company taking into consideration all the security threats mentioned earlier. Moreover, we will discuss the main reasons behind the lack of security even with the existence of good security systems.

### 1.6.1. *Best Practices*

WEP has many flaws in its security system, but this is not the main reason why most of the wireless networks are attacked. Less than half of wireless networks are well configured and are running correctly. In addition to that most APs default settings do not implement any type of encryption or authentication [9].

One of the best practices in home networks is to change the WEP key on a regular basis; this will weaken the chances of getting attacked. One of the most common techniques to bulletproof your network security is by using attacker tools that might be used to hack your network. There are many tools online that you can use, and they are available for different operating systems [30].

### 1.6.2. *Security Policy*

The same security techniques are not sufficient for companies where many computers are attached to the network. In this situation a security policy must be described and written down to allow managers as well as technicians to react correctly to undesired circumstances [9]. It is not surprising that the main reason for security breaches is the human error factor or what is also known as social engineering, where the network security is shared or revealed intentionally or unintentionally to unwanted parties. APs can also be configured to stop broadcasting its SSID which will make it harder for the attacker to forge a rouge AP.

There are three levels of security policies: Organization specific, Issue specific (for certain type of technologies), and Systems-specific for individual PCs that hold important information [9]. The availability of the wireless network and the downtime for the network must be taken into consideration while writing these specifications.

Switching to WPA and WPA2 technologies will solve many of the problems on both user and company levels. The users have to be cautious about implementing the new network, since WPA supports backward compatibility, devices that still implement WEP will jeopardize the entire network security. It is due to the fact that security system's strength is determined by the strength of the weakest chain.

### 1.6.3. *Is the Security Problem Solved?*

With all these proposed new technologies and security standards over the last few years to solve the wireless security problems, we still cannot say that our wireless networks are secure. The human factor is the major drawback. Despite the fact that people want security, they tend to prefer less secure system in favor of ease of use. Moreover, adding security features to wireless components makes it more expensive than other less secure systems, and many people prefer cheap equipments over good equipments [19].

This section described what the user or the administrator of the wireless network can do to prevent most of the known security threats.

## 1.7. Recent Proposals

This section discusses some of the recent proposals to enhance wireless security mechanisms. The first topic is about PANA (Protocol for Carrying Authentication for Network Access). PANA's target is to improve the authentication and authorization process between WLAN clients and AAA servers. LWAPP (Light Weight Access Point Protocol) is the subject for the second topic. Finally we will discuss a new proposal called DRKH (Dynamic Re-keying with Key Hopping) to provide 802.11i security level for mobile power-limited devices.

### 1.7.1. *PANA*

PANA is a new method to authenticate WLAN users over IP based networks. The goal of this proposal is to identify a link-layer protocol to allow hosts and networks to authenticate each other for network access. The protocol runs between PANA Client (PaC) and PANA Authentication Agent (PAA). The purpose of this protocol is to provide the carrier for the existing security protocols.

The protocol design is limited only to defining a messaging protocol that will allow authentication payload to be carried between the host/client (PaC) and an agent/server (PAA) in the access network for authentication and authorization purposes regardless of the AAA infrastructure that may (or may not) reside on the network[42]. As a network-layer protocol, it will be independent of the underlying access technologies and applicable to any network topology.

PANA is intended to be used in situations where no prior trust between PAA and PaC exists. As shown in Figure 1.21, PANA defines four integral parts: PaC, Enforcement Point (EP) the physical point where inbound and outbound traffic filters are applied, and PAA which represent the access authority on the network.

In this proposal, if a client wishes to gain access to a network it has to go through a specific scenario. PaC must first discover the IP address of PAA, after

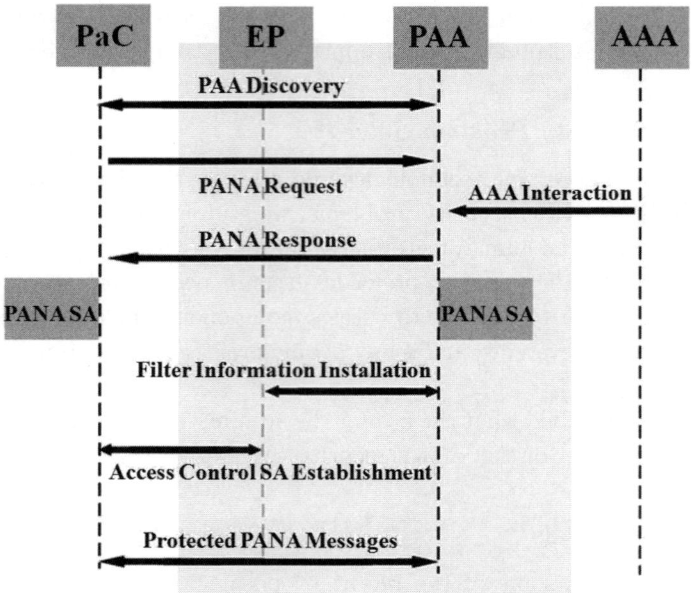


Fig. 1.21. PANA framework.

that it starts sending messages to authenticate itself on the network. Authentication can be granted from AAA server or from the local PAA depending on the network authentication infrastructure. Once the client is authenticated, PANA SA is created on both PAA and PaC. Furthermore, information filters are installed on the EP. Even after the client is authenticated, there might be other authentication messages exchanged between PaC and PAA during the connection session.

PANA also provides a mechanism to prevent DoS attacks by using ISN (Initial Sequence Number), and cookie based authentication between PAA and PaC. It also works as a carrier for EAP packets [42]–[44].

PANA is still being developed and there are many discussions about its strength and flexibility. These ongoing discussions are aiming to provide a very reliable substitute to the 802.1x/EAP authentication scheme.

### 1.7.2. *LWAPP*

LWAPP (Light Weight Access Point Protocol) represents the current trend of favoring the centralized authentication and authorization access points over localized points. LWAPP specifies the protocol used between the centralized access point and other Wireless Termination Points (or Light Weight Access Points). The main benefit of using such a protocol is that it provides a uniform layer 2 protocol to ease the development and deployment of WTPs.

LWAPP views the wireless network as a collection of mobile nodes connected to the wired network via WTPs. These WTPs provide the functionalities needed to

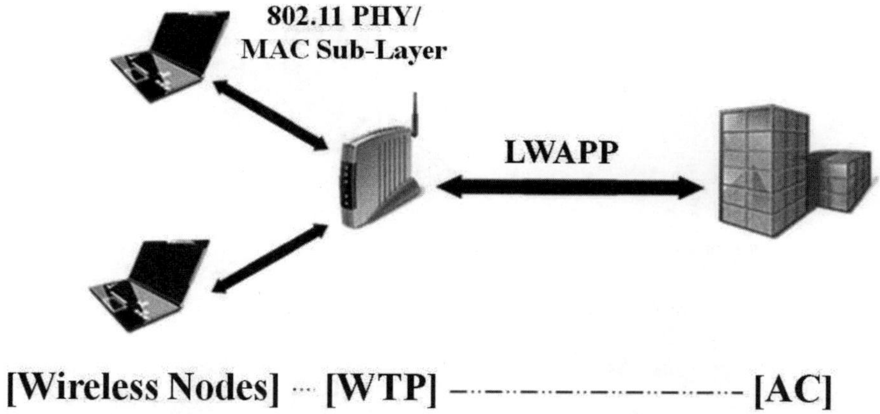


Fig. 1.22. LWAPP architecture.

connect to the wired network. WTPs are controlled by a centralized Access Control (AC) point. LWAPP is the bridge protocol between the AC and the WTPs as shown in Figure 1.22.

LWAPP designers have set three main goals for this protocol. First, reduced cost and higher efficiency in constructing wireless LANs are achieved by providing a central point for authentication, authorization and forwarding yields. Secondly, shifting the responsibility from WTP to a centralized point will mainly reduce the cost of manufacturing WTPs. In addition to that it will permit WTPs to efficiently use their computing power to provide a higher level of access control service. Third, providing a generic encapsulation and transport protocol leads to the possibility of applying the protocol to different access points in the future.

LWAPP defines two types of messages to be exchanged between the WTPs and the central AC. The two types are: LWAPP Data messages which contain data wireless frames, and LWAPP control messages. LWAPP transport header uses a specific bit called "C-bit" to distinguish between control and data messages. If LWAPP is used over IP, control and data messages are sent using different ports.

The AC discovery mechanism executed on WTPs starts with discovery request messages sent by WTPs that causes all ACs receiving that request to respond with a discovery response. Depending on the responses the WTP chooses the best AC to connect to, this operation is done by sending a join request. Figure 1.23 shows the steps of LWAPP discovery and join mechanisms.

Once the join-operation is completed, the configuration and link settings are exchanged. For example, if the packets arriving at the WTP are larger than the frame size agreed on, WTP fragments the frames. Another type of information exchanged between WTP and AC is the statistical information about the 802.11 devices connected to a specific WTP. Finally, if the AC appears to be dead for

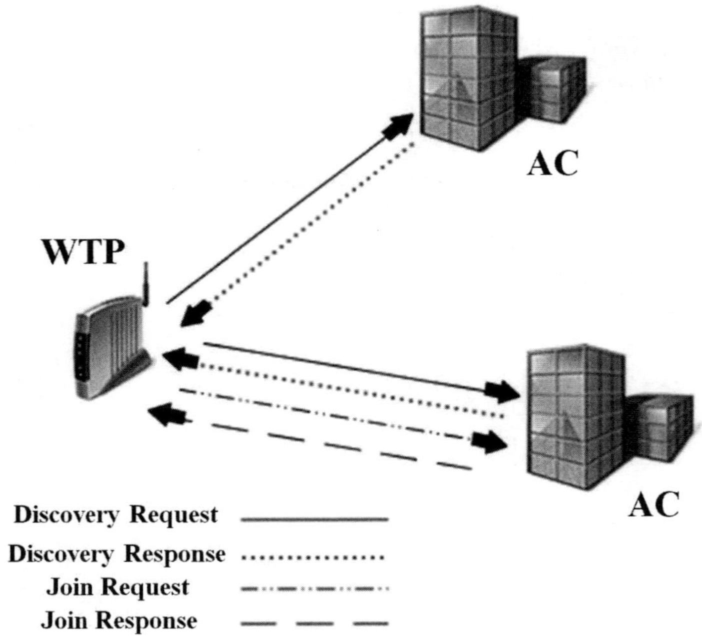


Fig. 1.23. LWAPP AC discovery mechanism.

a certain amount of time, WTP does the discovery mechanism again to specify another AC to communicate through.

*LWAPP Security*

In order to deliver better service for network users, LWAPP designers tolerated some security risks. There are four main assumptions behind LWAPP security architecture. The first assumption states that LWAPP may be accessible to sophisticated attackers. IPSec can be used to provide end-to-end encryption mechanism. Some of the control messages exchanged between WTP and AC should be secured especially if they carry important information about user's session keys. Finally, AC is trusted to generate strong keys.

Since data traffic can be secured using IPSec as stated earlier, LWAPP protocol specifies only the mechanism of securing control messages. LWAPP uses AES-Counter with CBC-MAC (CCM) to encrypt control messages. Control packets, used in both discovery and join operations, are not encrypted since they do not carry security association information. After a successful join operation the network enters the configuration phase where the base key will be exchanged to derive other required session keys. LWAPP requires that control frames be encrypted during the configuration phase using AES-CCM block cipher.

Initial key generation can be achieved either using a pre-shared key or certificate based security. LWAPP requires that WTP and AC to have separate IV keys for transmitting and receiving. Since WTP-AC connection is considered to have a long connection period "re-keying" or refreshing the keys is necessary to tighten the security. Key life-time is a parameter agreed on during the configuration phase between WTP and AC, when the key reaches 95% of its life-time, the refreshing process is initiated.

As stated before certificate based security can be used in the initial key generation phase. LWAPP uses x.509v3 certificates to ensure that the functionalities of WTP or AC are carried out only by these entities. A special name extension is added to these certificates to differentiate WTP certificates from AC ones [54].

### 1.7.3. *DRKH*

This section describes one of the suggestions to improve power consumption efficiency while maintaining the same level of security. Dynamic Re-keying with Key Hopping (DRKH) [55] provides a low complexity computational security architecture that is suitable for solar powered hand-held devices. Designers of DRKH aim to resolve the extensive power consumption in the recent security proposals to overcome WEP security inefficiency. Such solutions favor using complex cryptographic methods that consume a lot of power and are not suitable for low power wireless devices.

DRKH replaces the flawed key scheduling algorithm used in WEP with a strong one-way hash function. In DRKH the AP and the wireless node exchange five different keys; the fifth key is used to encrypt/decrypt authentication messages. The AP is responsible for determining the session counter value, period, start time and end time. It is also responsible for making the connected nodes aware of the session parameters.

DRKH security algorithm uses four static pre-shared keys with the session counter as inputs to the one-way hash function to produce a set of four session keys. The use of the generated session keys to encrypt and decrypt packet data protects the original four static keys. WEP and WPA reinitialize RC4 state on every packet using KSA; DRKH uses a nonlinear look-up table to mix the session with its corresponding IV value to reinitialize RC4 state.

The use of the correct session key (among the four keys) to encrypt and decrypt data packets depends on a pre-agreed key hopping sequence. Although the number of session keys is only four, the key sequence hopping can specify their usage in infinitely different ways. The two communicating nodes keep using the same four session keys till the end of the session when they have to rehash the four static keys to regenerate another set of session keys to be used in the new session. Figure 1.24 below shows the schematic diagram of DRKH protocol.

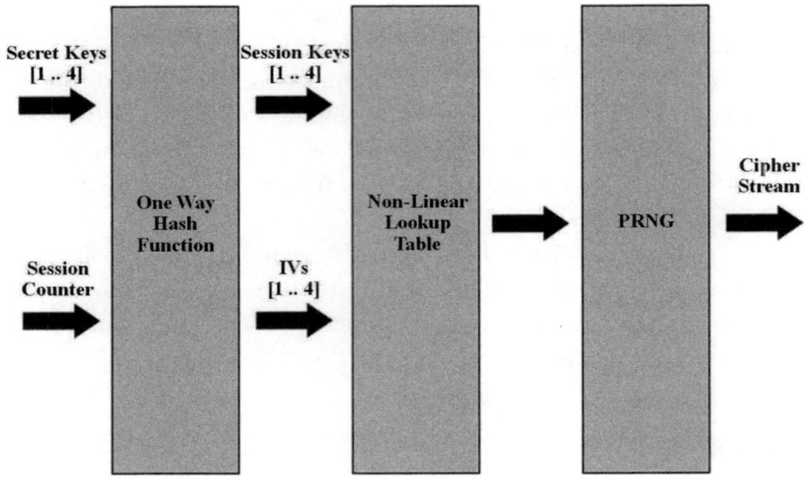


Fig. 1.24. Schematic diagram of DRKH protocol.

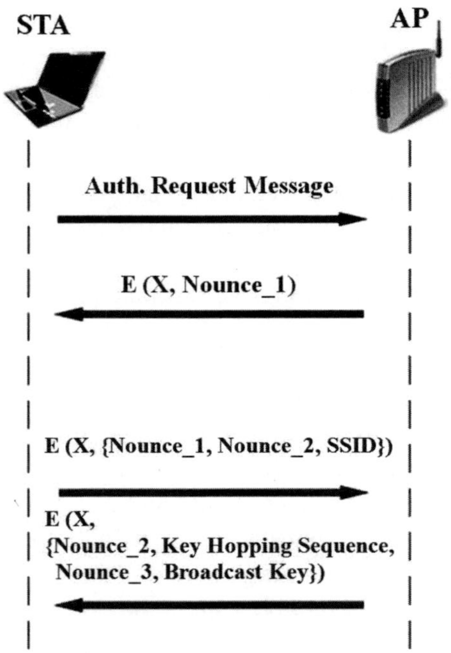


Fig. 1.25. DRKH authentication process.

*DRKH Authentication Process*

A four way authentication scheme is used to mutually authenticate the two communicating nodes as shown in Figure 1.25. Using one of the key management schemes AP and the other wireless devices share a long secret key (the fifth key)

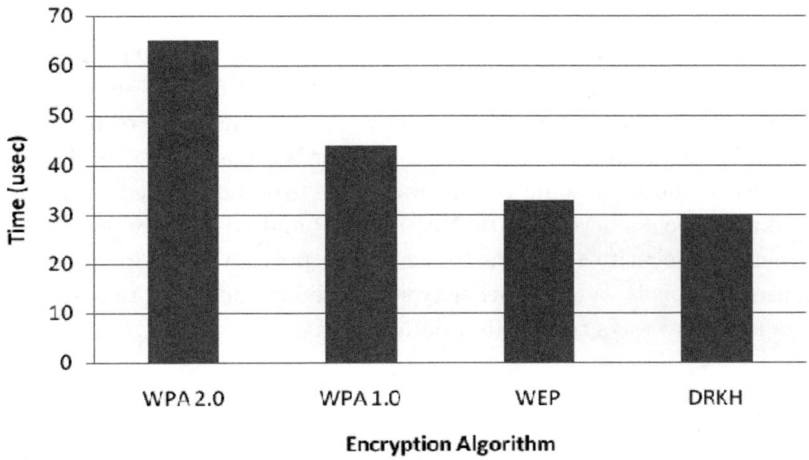


Fig. 1.26. Processing cost comparison.

to encrypt/decrypt authentication messages. The wireless device starts by sending Authentication. Request Message to the AP, the AP responds with a challenge message E (X, Nonce_1). The challenge message contains a nonce that is encrypted using the fifth secret key (X). Using nonce is effective against replay attacks.

In step 3, the wireless node sends an encrypted message that contains the first nonce, another generated nonce and the SSID (Service Set ID). The AP checks for the validity of the information and sends back another encrypted message containing: Nonce_2, the key hopping sequence, Nonce_3, and broadcast key. Broadcast key is used to encrypt the session counter. After these four steps both sides are mutually authenticated and this method is immune to man in the middle type of attacks.

DRKH protocol supports a power saving mode, where the wireless device can go to sleep mode when there is no transmission activity without losing the connection with the AP. This can be achieved using a session period as a multiple of Target Beacon Transmission Time (TBTT) and the wireless device has to wake up every TBTT to listen to possible new notifications from the AP.

The main aim of this new proposal is to achieve a high level of security for low power devices. Experiments have shown that this approach saves a lot of energy by minimizing the execution time needed for each packet. Figure 1.26 shows the results of executing a packet with the size of 1,500 bytes using WPA 2.0, WPA 1.0, WEP and DRKH.

## 1.8. Summary

In this chapter, we reviewed how security in wireless data networks has evolved over the last few years. We have discussed also how the difference in the data transfer medium between wired and wireless networks plays a key role in exposing the system to more possible attacks. Security hazards will always be around; they can only be avoided if the correct policies and standards are used. The 802.11i protocol promises to fix most of the security holes found in its predecessor WEP, but since the standard is relatively new, it did not have the proper period of time to be tested thoroughly. Only the future can tell us if the current standards are as secure as they promise. Moreover, we mentioned some of the ways that can be utilized to improve the security of the wireless networks. PANA, LWAPP and DRKH are new proposals in wireless network security that aim to achieve to provide better performance than existing used protocols. Wireless security still evolving and it will remain a hot topic as long as there are ways to threaten data security.

## References


[1] P. Chandra, Bulletproof Wireless Security: GSM, UMTS, 802.11, and Ad Hoc Security (Communications Engineering), Newnes, 2005.

[2] H. Imai, Wireless Communications Security, Artech House Publishers, 2006.

[3] D. Welch and S. Lathrop, Wireless security threat taxonomy. Information Assurance Workshop, *IEEE Systems, Man and Cybernetics Society*, **18**(20), pp. 76–83, 18–20 June 2003.

[4] J. Edney and W.A. Arbaugh, Real 802.11 Security: Wi-Fi Protected Access and 802.11i, Addison Wesley, 2003.

[5] A.E. Earle, Wireless Security Handbook, Auerbach Publications, 2005.

[6] T. Hardjono and L.R. Dondeti, Security in Wireless LANS and MANS, Artech House Publishers, 2005.

[7] J. Rittinghouse and J.F. Ransom, Wireless Operational Security, Digital Press, 2004.

[8] N. Prasad and A. Prasad, 802.11 WLANs and IP Networking: Security, QoS, and Mobility, Artech House Publishers, 2005.

[9] M.E. Manley, C.A. McEntee, A.M. Molet, and J.S. Park, Wireless security policy development for sensitive organizations. Systems, Man and Cybernetics (SMC) Information Assurance Workshop, *Proceedings from the Sixth Annual IEEE*, pp. 150–157, 15–17 June 2005.

[10] W.A. Arbaugh, Wireless security is different, *Computer*, **36**(8), Aug. 2003, pp. 99–101.

[11] B. Potter, Wireless security's future, Security & Privacy Magazine, *IEEE*, **1**(4), pp. 68–72, July–Aug. 2003.

[12] F.C.C. Osorio, E. Agu, and K. McKay, Measuring energy-security tradeoffs in wireless networks, Performance, Computing, and Communications Conference, 2005. IPCCC 2005. 24th IEEE International, pp. 293–302, 7–9 April 2005.

[13] D. Johnston and J. Walker, Overview of IEEE 802.16 security, Security & Privacy Magazine, *IEEE*, **2**(3), pp. 40–48, May–June 2004.

[14] S. Ravi, A. Raghunathan, and N. Potlapally, Securing Wireless Data: System Architecture Challenges, In *Proc. Intl. Symp. System Synthesis*, pp. 195–200, October 2002.

[15] K.J. Hole, E. Dyrnes, and P. Thorsheim, Securing Wi-Fi networks, *Computer*, **38**(7), pp. 28–34, July 2005.

[16] J.-C. Chen, M.-C. Jiang, and Y.-W. Liu, Wireless LAN security and IEEE 802.11i. Wireless Communications, *IEEE*, **12**(1), pp. 27–36, Feb. 2005.

[17] B. Brown, 802.11: the security differences between b and i. Potentials, *IEEE*, **22**(4), pp. 23–27, Oct–Nov 2003.

[18] M. Barbeau, WiMAX/802.16 threat analysis, International Workshop on Modeling Analysis and Simulation of Wireless and Mobile Systems.
[19] J. Viega, Security—problem solved? Queue, Security: a war without end, **3**(5), June 2005.
[20] Wireless LANs, http://cnscenter.future.co.kr/hot-topic/wlan.html [This page sums up all the organizations, papers, resources, ... etc related to WLAN]; cited on May 30, 2008.
[21] The Unofficial 802.11 Security Web Page. http://www.drizzle.com/~aboba/IEEE/ [This page tries to gather relevant papers and standards to 802.11 Security in a single place.]; cited on May 30, 2008.
[22] CTIA: Wireless Internet Caucus: Standards & Tech. http://www.wirelessenterpriseinfo.org/wic/standardsandtech.htm. [Links to all groups that have been involved in the identification and development of standards and requirements for mobile data solutions]; cited on May 30, 2008.
[23] Wi-Fi Planet, http://www.wi-fiplanet.com/ [The Source for Wi-Fi Business and Technology]; cited on May 30, 2008.
[24] ITtoolbox Security Knowledge Base, http://security.ittoolbox.com/ [ITtoolbox Security Knowledge Base provides the latest community-generated content from the IT market. Share knowledge with your peers and work together to form experience-based decisions.]; cited on May 30, 2008.
[25] Enigma Machine, http://homepages.tesco.net/~andycarlson/enigma/about_enigma.html [Description about Enigma Machine and how it works]; cited on May 30, 2008.
[26] Security History, http://csrc.nist.gov/publications/history/ [Group of papers that explain security history in computer world]; cited on May 30, 2008.
[27] Glossary Terms, http://www.sabc.co.za/manual/ibm/9agloss.htm [Definition of security]; cited on May 30, 2008.
[28] DES Overview, http://www.tropsoft.com/strongenc/des.htm [Explains how DES works in details, features and weaknesses]; cited on May 30, 2008.
[29] B. Cohen and D. Deutsch, 802.16 Tutorial, WiFi Planet, August 26, 2003.
[30] War Driving Tools, http://www.wardrive.net/wardriving/tools/ [War driving tools to hack/test wireless networks for different OSes]; citen on May 30, 2008.
[31] WPA2 Routers List, http://www.bbwexchange.com/publications/newswires/page546-1160883.asp [contains a list of the WPA2 routers from different companies]; cited on May 30, 2008.
[32] CompNetworking: 802.11 standards, http://compnetworking.about.com/cs/wireless80211/a/aa80211standard.htm [Describe briefly 802.11 standards and their specifications]; cited on May 30, 2008.
[33] Shared vs Open authentication method, http://www.startawisp.com/index2.php?option=com_content&do_pdf=1&id=147 [Explains why shared Authentication is considered less secure than open authentication] cited on May 30, 2008.
[34] B. Aboba, L. Blunk, J. Vollbrecht, J. Carlson, and H. Levkowetz, Ed. RFC3748: Extensible Authentication Protocol (EAP).
[35] IEEE 802.1X: EAP over LAN (EAPOL) for LAN/WLAN Authentication & Key Management, http://www.javvin.com/protocol8021X.html [Explanation of 802.1x, EAPOL]; cited on May 30, 2008.
[36] RADIUS-Wikipedia, the free encyclopedia., http://en.wikipedia.org/wiki/RADIUS [Wikipedia definition and related resources about RADIUS]; cited on May 30, 2008.
[37] Wi-Fi Protected Access — Wikipedia, http://en.wikipedia.org/wiki/Wi-Fi_Protected_Access, [Wikipedia definition and related resources about WPA]; cited on May 30, 2008.

[38] TKIP — Wikipedia, http://en.wikipedia.org/wiki/TKIP. [Wikipedia definition and related resources about TKIP]; cited on May 30, 2008.

[39] Overview of the WPA wireless security update in Windows XP, http://support.microsoft.com/?kbid=815485 [Explains the security features in WPA]; cited on May 30, 2008.

[40] Tech-FAQ: What is MIC?. http://www.tech-faq.com/mic-message-integrity-check.shtml [Short definition for MIC and how it works]; cited on May 30, 2008.

[41] Tech-FAQ: What is WRAP?. http://www.tech-faq.com/wrap-wireless-robust-authenticated-protocol.shtml , [Explaining why WRAP is not the recommended data transfer encryption standard for 802.11i]; cited on May 30, 2008.

[42] A. Yegin, Ed., Y. Ohba, R. Penno, G. Tsirtsis, and C. Wang, RFC4058: Protocol for Carrying Authentication for Network Access (PANA) Requirements.

[43] M. Parthasarathy, RFC4016: PANA Threat Analysis and Security Requirments.

[44] Dan Forsberg, Yoshihiro Ohba, Basavaraj Patil, H. Tschofenig, and A. Yegin, PANA Solution, http://people.nokia.net/~patil/IETF56/PANA/PANA_Solution_Slides_7.pdf; cited on May 30, 2008.

[45] Webopedia: What is WAP?. http://www.webopedia.com/TERM/W/WAP.html; cited on May 30, 2008.

[46] WAP Forum website, http://www.wapforum.org/; cited on May 30, 2008.

[47] Ssi service strategies, WAP gateway products. http://www.ssimail.com/WAP_gateway.htm; cited on May 30, 2008.

[48] The Wireless FAQ, http://www.thewirelessfaq.com; cited on May 30, 2008.

[49] IEC: Online Education: WebPro Forum, http://www.iec.org/online/tutorials/wap/index.html; cited on May 30, 2008.

[50] WTLS definition. WiFi Planet, http://wi-fiplanet.webopedia.com/TERM/w/WTLS. html; cited on May 30, 2008.

[51] Wireless Session Protocol. Wiki WireShark. http://wiki.wireshark.org/Wireless_Session_Protocol; cited on May 30, 2008.

[52] Philip Mikal, WTSL: The good and Bad of WAP Security. http://www.advisor.com/Articles.nsf/aid/MIKAP001; cited on May 30, 2008.

[53] Markku-Jujani Saarinen, Attacks against the WAP WTLS protocol. http://www.freeprotocols.org/harmOfWap/wtls.pdf; cited on May 30, 2008.

[54] P. Calhoun, B. O'Hara, R. Suri, N. Cam Winget, S. Kelly, M. Williams, and S. Hares, Light Weight Access Point protocol. http://www.watersprings.org/pub/id/draft-ohara-capwap-lwapp-03.txt

[55] A.M. Kholaif, M.B. Fayek, H.S. Eissa, and H.A. Baraka, DRKH: A Power Efficient Encryption Protocol for Wireless Devices, lcn, pp. 822–829, The IEEE Conference on Local Computer Networks 30th Anniversary (LCN'05)l, 2005.

[56] C. Gehrmann, J. Persson, and B. Smeets, Bluetooth Security, Artech House Publishers 2004.

[57] H. Labiod, H. Afifi, and C. De Santis, Wi-Fi, Bluetooth, Zigbee and WiMAX. Springer 2007.

# Chapter 2

# ENABLING INFORMATION CONFIDENTIALITY IN PUBLISH/SUBSCRIBE OVERLAY NETWORKS

Hui Zhang*, Guofei Jiang†, Haifeng Chen‡, Xiaoqiao Meng§, Kenji Yoshihira¶ and Abhishek Sharma‖
*NEC Laboratories America*
*Princeton, NJ 08540*
* *huizhang@nec-labs.com*
† *gfj@nec-labs.com*
‡ *haifeng@nec-labs.com*
§ *xqmeng@nec-labs.com*
¶ *kenji@nec-labs.com*
‖ *absharma@nec-labs.com*

"*Alice has a piece of valuable information which she is willing to sell to anyone interested in; she is too busy and wants to ask Bob, a professional broker, to sell that information for her; but Alice is in a dilemma where she cannot trust Bob with that information but Bob cannot help her find her customers without knowing that information*".

In this chapter, we propose a security mechanism called *information foiling* to address the above and other new confidentiality problems arising in pub/sub overlay services. Information foiling extends Rivest's "Chaffing and Winnowing" work, and its basic idea is carefully generating a set of fake messages to hide an authentic message. Information foiling requires no modification inside the broker network so that the routing/filtering capabilities of broker nodes remain intact.

We formally present the information foiling mechanism in the context of publish/subscribe overlay services, and discuss its applicability in other Internet applications. For publish/subscribe applications, we propose a suite of *optimal* schemes for fake message generation in different scenarios. Real data traces are used in our evaluation to demonstrate the effectiveness of the proposed schemes.

## 2.1. Introduction

Content-based publish/subscribe (pub/sub) [12] enables a dynamic many-to-many communication paradigm for information dissemination: information providers (publishers) and consumers (subscribers) are decoupled through a broker (overlay) network which stores the registered interests of subscribers (subscriptions), and does content-based routing on the messages from publishers (events) to subscribers based on the latter's interests. There are many services suitable for pub/sub-style interactions, such as stock quotes [3], online auctions [4], located based services [5], enterprise activity monitoring and consumer event notification systems [6,7], and mobile alerting systems [8,9].

For the benefits such as scalability and performance, a third-party broker overlay network is usually designed for a wide-area pub/sub service with a large and dynamic population of publishers and subscribers. However, data security and privacy concerns over the pub/sub information (e.g., commercial real-time stock price information, the highest price a bidder can consider, current physical location of a customer) may cause publishers/subscribers to place no trust in those third-party broker nodes; a publisher and a subscriber may not know each other in advance and thus have no default trust between each other. In such an environment, a set of new confidentiality problems arise in pub/sub overlay services, as identified in [10]:

- *Information confidentiality*: can the broker network perform content-based routing without the publishers trusting the broker network with the event content?
- *Subscription confidentiality*: can subscribers obtain dynamic, content-based data without revealing their subscription functions (content) to the publishers or broker network?
- *Publication confidentiality*: can publishers control which subscribers may receive particular events?

Existing approaches address the above problems with various cryptographic techniques. For example, Wang *et al.* [10] suggest the application of *computing with encrypted data* technique [11] for the information confidentiality problem. Raiciu and Rosenblum [12] design a secure pub/sub protocol by extending the secure multiparty computation model PSM [13]. EventGuard [14] relies on a pre-trusted server for the distribution of symmetric keys among publishers and subscribers; all messages communicated between a publisher and its subscribers are encrypted by a symmetric key before entering the broker network and the broker network is utilized only for overlay channel-based multicasting. Those approaches share one or more of the following drawbacks:

- some secrets (cryptographical keys) have to be distributed in advance among the publishers and subscribers, either through direct connections or a pre-trusted proxy, which is not scalable and conflicts with the dynamic many-to-many communication model.
- many secure computing protocols are often computationally intensive and require a large amount of communication overhead, which could be prohibitively expensive to carry out.
- the filtering/routing capabilities of the broker nodes are weakened by the poor expressivity of subscription functions with the input of encrypted data.

We observe that in many pub/sub services, it is not difficult to make a rough estimation on the contained information in a routed message used for content-based routing. For example, in stock quote dissemination where the current stock price is the protected information, a rough range of the stock price for a stock symbol can be given based on its recent performance; in location-aware mobile services where the current location of a user is privacy-sensitive, an approximate area can be guessed based on the assigned IP address; in an online auction session where the current bidding price is the protected information, a rough upper bound can be put on it based on the item's intrinsic worth. However, the rough estimation is useless (or even possibly harmful when in usage, e.g., in stock trading decisions) in the context of those applications as being valuable is *the accurate information delivered in real time.*

Following the observation, we propose a new security mechanism called *information foiling* to enable data confidentiality in pub/sub overlay services. The basic idea in information foiling originates from Rivest's "Chaffing and Winnowing" [15]: for a message to be protected, a set of *fake* messages are carefully generated and sent along with the authentic message, all in plain text; the information contained in all the messages as a whole is sufficiently confusing to be useless to an attacker sitting inside the broker network; the attacker still has some chance to catch the authentic message (by guessing which is the authentic one), but the catching probability is a controllable parameter in the mechanism. Notice that information foiling requires no modification inside the broker network so that the routing/filtering capabilities of broker nodes are preserved maximally.

Information foiling extends Rivest's "chaffing and winnowing" by

- providing a protocol design for enabling confidentiality without encryption in a new application, pub/sub overlay services;
- formalizing the fake message generation problem, and defining the metrics on measuring the performance of potential solutions;
- presenting the preliminary results on the design and evaluation of specific fake message generation schemes in pub/sub services.

The core component of information foiling is fake message generation (FMG), a challenging problem in general. We define two metrics to measure the performance of a FMG scheme: *indistinguishability* and *truth deviation.* For publish/subscribe overlay services, we propose a suite of *optimal* FMG schemes based on various assumptions about the knowledge available to the attacker and and the information foiler on the routed messages. In the context of stock quote dissemination, real stock price data are used in our simulation study to demonstrate the effectiveness of the proposed schemes.

While we focus on pub/sub overlay services in the exposition, we believe that information foiling is also applicable to other Internet applications. For example, many other applications built on content-based routing, such as Internet file sharing [16], have the same confidentiality requirements as those from pub/sub applications. When we look ahead into the future Internet with the expected popularity of *asymmetric communications* [17], where one end of the communication is a high-end server but the other end is a low-end device which has constrained computing resources and cannot support a strong security protocol, information foiling can be an attractive confidentiality scheme that offers both simplicity and effectiveness to many new applications. We briefly discuss the generalization of information foiling in Section 2.6.

The remainder of the chapter is organized as follows. Section 2.2 gives the problem definition, and Section 2.3 presents the information foiling mechanism. In Section 2.4, we propose three FMG schemes for publish/subscribe overlay services. The experiment results are shown in Section 2.5, and a generalization of information foiling in the new asymmetric communication paradigm is presented in Section 2.6. Section 2.7 describes the related work, and Section 2.8 concludes the chapter.

## 2.2. Problem Definition

### 2.2.1. *Pub/Sub Confidentiality*

We formulate pub/sub confidentiality as a communication problem. As shown in Figure 2.1, there are three entities: a publisher, a subscriber, and a broker. Both the publisher and the subscriber have private information sources ($R_p$ and $R_s$). Based on the inputs, the publisher generates a potentially unlimited sequence number of event messages $E$, and the subscriber has a potentially unlimited number of subscriptions $S$. At the broker, a subset of the subscriber's subscriptions are stored, which is called the active subscription set. The publisher sends the sequence of events to the broker independently of the subscriber, and the broker sends a sequence of notifications $N$ to the subscriber based on both $E$ and $S$. Upon an event $e$, the broker must be able to determine if each subscription $s$ in the active subscription set matches the event based on a function $f(e, s)$, but without learning the information contained in $e$ and $s$. Contained in the events are essentially data tuples and those in subscriptions are usually selection criteria, such as number comparisons or regular expressions, and the related parameters. The problem definition generalizes naturally to the multi-party case where the number of publishers and subscribers is arbitrarily large.

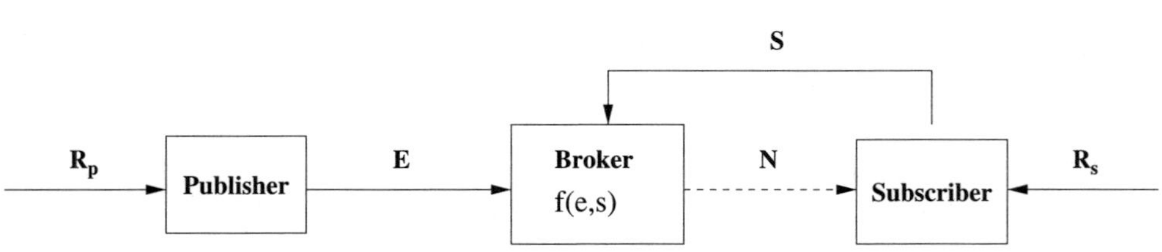


Fig. 2.1. Formulation of pub/sub confidentiality as a communication problem.

### 2.2.2. *Threat Model*

Our threat model is the same as in [12]. A pub/sub broker is assumed to be computationally bounded and exhibits a semi-honest behavior. That is, the broker follows the protocol as prescribed but may record messages to subsequently deduce information not obtainable solely from protocol output (i.e., the outcome of the matching). In the rest of the chapter, we use the words "broker" and "attacker" interchangeably when referring to entities in the broker network that try to obtain the authentic information contained in pub/sub messages.

We assume that publishers are honest and publish only valid events. We also assume that subscribers are honest, and a subscriber does not reveal events he/she receives to other subscribers. Otherwise, this would be equivalent to solving the digital copyright problem.

Other security concerns, such as authorization, authentication, integrity, and reliability against DoS attacks, are not the focus of this paper, and existing cryptographical techniques can address those issues as presented in [14].

## 2.3. Information Foiling

### 2.3.1. *Information Foiling Mechanism*

We observe that in many pub/sub services, it is not difficult to make rough estimation on the contained information of a routed message used for content-based routing. For example, in stock quotes dissemination where the current stock price is the protected information, a rough range of the stock price for a stock symbol can be given based on its recent performance; in location-aware mobile services where the current location of a user is privacy-sensitive, an approximate area can be guessed based on the assigned IP address; in an online auction session where the current bidding price is the protected information, a rough up bound can be put on it based on the item's intrinsic worth. However, the rough estimation is often useless (or even possibly harmful when in usage, e.g., in stock trading or auction bidding decisions) in the context of those applications as being valuable is *the accurate information delivered in real time.*

We propose a mechanism called *information foiling* which achieves data confidentiality by fooling the attacker with fake information. As shown in Figure 2.2,

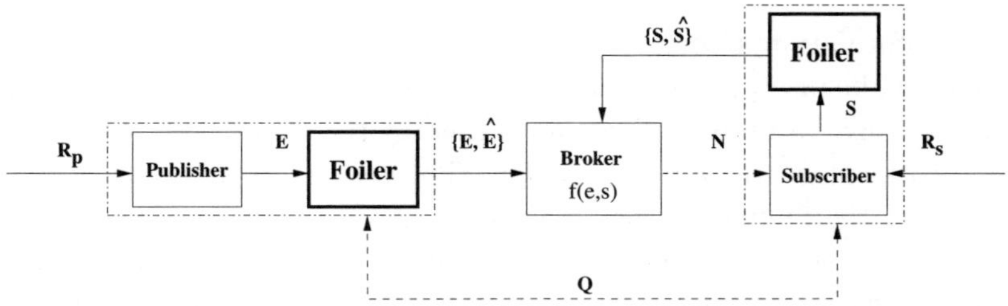


Fig. 2.2. The information foiling mechanism.

information foiling introduces a new component, *foiler*, on both publisher and subscriber sides. The functionality of a foiler is to generate a set of $k$ fake messages (called foiling messages in the rest of the chapter) $\hat{m}^k = \{\hat{m}_1, \hat{m}_2, \ldots, \hat{m}_k\}$ with an input message $m$, and we call the message set $\{m, \hat{m}^k\}$ a composite set. The number $k$ is a parameter decided by the confidentiality requirement, and can be personalized for each publisher or subscriber. Both an authentic message and its foiling messages are in plain text when arriving the broker, and they all are valid input for the function $f(e, s)$.

The information foiling mechanism works as following:

(1) Subscriber: for each active subscription, generates $k_s$ foiling subscriptions, and send them in a random order to the broker which store them all as active subscriptions.
(2) Publisher: for each event, generates $k_p$ foiling events, and send them in a random order to the broker.
(3) Broker: upon each arriving event $e$, decides the subset of the active subscription set and send one notification for each matched subscription.
(4) (optional) Subscriber: upon a notification associated with one authentic subscription, sends a confirmation request to the publisher.
(5) (optional) Publisher: upon a confirmation request, sends a reply to the subscriber upon the authenticity of the related event.

Step 4 is optional as we can optimize the confirmation overhead with a shared secret $Q$ between the publisher and subscriber. For example, the publisher can use a hash chain to decide the random position of an authentic message in the composite message set and the chain length is 100 authentic events; if a subscriber sends a confirmation request for the 50th authentic event in a round, the publisher can include the seed of that hash chain in its reply, and the subscriber does not need to ask a confirmation for any notification due to the next 50 authentic events.

Step 5 is optional as besides the same reason for Step 4, there can be access control policy applied by the publisher to decide if a reply is necessary at all.

Last, we note that information foiling requires no modification inside the broker network so that the routing/filtering capabilities of broker nodes remains intact.

### 2.3.2. *Performance Metrics*

Intuitively, information foiling should satisfy two basic requirements. The first requirement can be interpreted as robustness: most (if not all) of the foiling messages should survive any data filtering technique used by the attacker so that the attacker is not able to identify the correct message. The second requirement is referred to as effectiveness: the foiling messages can serve as a deterrent against attacks if the cost of incorrect guess is significant for the attacker. For example, in the case of stock prices, if the stock prices contained in fake messages differ significantly from the true stock price, the profit obtained by the attacker from guessing the correct stock price in a small number of instances can be offset by heavy losses incurred when the attacker believes the stock price contained in one of the fake messages as the true stock price.

Assume the attacker has a function $F : \{e, \hat{E}_e\} \rightarrow G$, that takes the composite message set $\{e, \hat{E}_e\}$ as input and outputs a message set $G \subseteq \{e, \hat{E}_e\}$ consisting of messages that the attacker perceives as useful. Then, we can measure the information foiling performance based on the following metrics:

- *indistinguishability*: defined as $\frac{I(e,G)}{|G|}$, where $I(e, G) = 1$ if $e \in G, 0$ otherwise. We assume $|G| \neq 0$, i.e., the attacker will pick at least one message. This metric captures the robustness of the information foiling mechanism. A value of 0 for this metric implies that the attacker failed to identify the correct message whereas a value of 1 implies that the attacker was able to do so. However, if the *indistinguishability* is $1/r$ $(r > 1)$, then the attacker is not able to distinguish the correct message from $(r - 1)$ foiling messages. The best case is when *indistinguishability* equals to $1/(k + 1)$ (where $k$ is the number of fake messages). *Indistinguishability* can also be interpreted as the probability of identification of the true message by the attacker.
- *truth deviation*: defined as $\sum_{g \in G} \frac{D(e,g)}{|G|}$ where $D(e, g)$ is the difference between the values of messages $e$ and $g$. This metric captures the effectiveness of the information foiling mechanism.

A third metric, *communication overhead*, is also important in measuring information foiling performance. Since it depends not only on the information foiling mechanism but also on the actual data distributions of the authentic events and subscriptions, we investigate it separately from the other two metrics in the next section.

### 2.3.3. *Communication Overhead*

In terms of content matching, a cryptography-based solution essentially replaces the attribute values in an event with wild-card characters generated using the encryption scheme. Our foiling method associates $K$ additional values with the attributes in an event in addition to the original value. The cryptography-based solution will incur a much higher communication overhead as any event (publication) containing attribute $A$ must be delivered to all the subscribers interested in content containing attribute $A$, regardless of the value for the attribute $A$ specified by the subscriber. A subscriber then needs to decrypt the value associated with attribute $A$ in the event to determine if the event is of its interest. To fix ideas, consider a pub/sub system with 1 million subscriptions per topic and an average subscription hit ratio (defined as the fraction of subscriptions for a topic that a event on that topic is relevant to) of 0.01. On any new event, the original pub/sub system without any security mechanisms delivers $10^6 \times 0.01 = 10K$ messages in total to the subscribers, the cryptography-based solution delivers 1 million messages in total (one to each subscriber), and our foiling scheme with $K = 2$ incurs a communication overhead of $10^6 \times 3 \times 3 \times 0.01 = 90K$ total messages (assuming both the events and subscriptions are protected via information foiling) delivered to the subscribers and $10^6 \times 3 \times 0.01 + 10^6 \times 0.01 = 40K$ total messages due to the confirmation procedure. Hence, the total communication overhead of our foiling scheme is $130K$ which is significantly less compared to the 1 million messages in the case of the cryptography-based scheme.

Of course, as the subscription hit ratio increases, our foiling scheme would incur more communication overhead. For $X_{total}$ subscriptions for a topic with subscription hit ratio $p$ and a fixed $K$, the communication overhead (for a new event) in our foiling scheme is $pX_{total}(K^2 + K + 1)$. The communication overhead of the cryptography-based system is independent of $p$ and is always $X_{total}$. Hence, for $p \leq 1/(K^2+K+1)$, our foiling scheme will incur a lower communication overhead compared to the cryptography-based scheme. For $p = 0.01$, generating up to $K = 8$ fake messages to protect each event and subscription would still incur a lower communication overhead than any cryptography-based scheme. As the communication overhead is directly proportional to $K$, in practice, one can decide on the security and communication overhead trade-off according the nature of the data being protected.

### 2.3.4. *Discussions*

#### 2.3.4.1. *Pub/Sub confidentiality revisited*

In pub/sub setting, information foiling offers valuable flexibility for publishers and subscribers to decide independently on exerting confidentiality control or not. Therefore, anyone that does not care about its confidentiality does not have to pay the cost in associated with activating the security mechanism.

In pub/sub services, another security issue related to publication confidentiality is *auditability* [10]: *Can publishers audit the accounting to verify that they are being paid fairly for the subscriptions they deliver?* Clearly, information foiling naturally addresses this problem as the confirmation procedures in information foiling offer the opportunity for publishers to audit the delivery of their services.

## 2.4. Fake Message Generation in Content-based Pub/Sub

### 2.4.1. *A Simple Probabilistic Model*

In content-based pub/sub model, information used in content-based routing is attribute based. For events, it is a set of attribute and its value, $(A_i, V_i)$, pairs. We assume that subscriptions are expressed as a conjunction of predicates, with predicate $i$ containing information about the range of values for attribute $A_i$ that the subscriber is interested in. The aim of the information foiling scheme is to prevent the attacker from determining the value $V_i$ for any event or the range of values for any attribute that a subscription specifies. In this chapter, we describe and evaluate the various components of our information foiling scheme in the context of events; the details of information foiling for subscriptions are similar and not presented for the sake of brevity.

To fix ideas, consider a event message $m$ with $L$ attributes. Let the value $V_i$ for attribute $A_i$ in $m$ be a random variable taking values in $V$ according to a probability mass function (pmf) $p_{V_i}$. Let $V_m = (V_1, V_2, \ldots, V_L)$, i.e., $V_m$ is a vector of random variables associated with message $m$ taking values in $V^L$. If the attribute value random variables are independent of each other, then the pmf for $V_m$ is

$$p_{V_m} = \prod_{i=1}^{L} p_{V_i}$$

Each of the $K$ foiling messages generated by the information foiling scheme for $m$ can be thought of as a random variable taking values in $V^L$. In this scenario if the attacker does not know the pmf $p_{V_m}$, the aim of the information foiling scheme can be to maximize the entropy $H(M)$ [18] of the composite message set $M = \{m, \hat{m}^K\}$ (defined in Section 2.3.1). We discuss other fake message generation schemes for different scenarios next.

### 2.4.2. *Fake Message Generation Schemes*

In order to achieve good *indistinguishability* results, the fake message generation scheme must adapt to the available information at the attacker. Different scenarios can be defined based on the various assumptions about the knowledge available to the attacker and to the foiler at the subscriber. In this chapter, it is not our intent to provide an analysis of every possible scenario that may be encountered in practice, but we do investigate a few scenarios that provide further insight into the challenging problem of *optimal* fake message generation.

*Scenario I*: The attribute values in the event messages are generated according to a random model known both to the foiler at the publisher as well as the attacker. For example [19], presents such a model for stock prices. But the accurate pmf is known only to the foiler. In this scenario, fake messages can be generated by corrupting the true message with noise. The aim of the information foiling scheme would be to maximize *truth deviation* without comprising on *indistinguishability* with minimum communication overhead. The attacker may use techniques from signal processing to filter out the noise from the fake messages to help her determine the correct message. We investigate this scenario in detail in Section 2.5. The technique of generating fake messages by adding noise to the true message can also be applied even to the situations where neither the foiler nor the attacker do not know much about how the true messages are generated (for example. the pmf for attribute values is unknown).

*Scenario II*: The foiler knows the pmf for attribute values $V_i$ but the attacker does not, and the attacker does not even know the random model of how $V_i$ is generated. This scenario was described in detail earlier and to achieve the best *indistinguishability* performance, the aim of fake message generation scheme should be to maximize the entropy of the composite message (true and fake messages taken together). This can be done by generating the fake messages in such a way that the composite message is uniformly distributed over its support set.

*Scenario III*: Both the foiler and the attacker know the pmf for attribute values $V_i$. In this scenario, we think a conservative FMG approach is appropriate which takes maximizing *indistinguishability* as the highest priority and then maximizing true deviation. According, we propose the following bucketing FMG algorithm:

- A FIFO (First In, First Out) queue is maintained in the foiler to cache $m(V_i, \hat{V_i}^1, \ldots, \hat{V_i}^k)$ vectors generated in the past. Initially it is empty;
- If the current value of $V_i$ can be found in some vector at the FIFO queue, the same values of $(V_i, \hat{V_i}^1, \ldots, \hat{V_i}^k)$ from that vector is used for this run, and the FIFO queue is updated accordingly;
- Otherwise: the foiler divides the range into $(k+1)$ sub-ranges (buckets) with equal cumulative probability. The foiler picks one value proportionally to its PDF from each bucket except the bucket where the real value falls into, and the resulting $(V_i, \hat{V_i}^1, \ldots, \hat{V_i}^k)$ vector is used as the composite data set to be delivered and also put into the FIFO queue for caching.

When multiple attribute values are to be protected in a message and they are independent from each other, the above bucketing algorithm is applied to each attribute individually. When multiple attribute values are to be protected in a message and they are dependent from each other, a master attribute is specified by the foiler and the bucketing algorithm is applied to this attribute; the fake values of the rest attributes are then decided based on the correlation with the master attribute.

Intuitively, the fake values generated by the bucketing algorithm look probabilistically the same to any attacker, which leads to the maximal *indistinguishability* of $\frac{1}{k+1}$; the range bucketing is for keeping the distance of the authentic value to any of the fake values, and we speculate that the bucketing algorithm achieves the maximal true deviation when $D(e, g) = |e - g|^2$, given the condition of reaching the best *indistinguishability* performance.

### 2.5. Evaluation

We evaluate *information foiling* in pub/sub stock quotes dissemination service where the current stock price is the content (event) to be protected. Stock prices were collected from [20] with one minute frequency. We use the two metrics — *indistinguishability* and *truth deviation* — introduced in Section 2.3.2 to assess the efficacy of our scheme.

### 2.5.1. *Experimental Setup*

**Fake Message Generation**: For each day's closing price for some stock, we generate $K$ fake messages containing false closing prices for that stock [19]. presents the following discrete-time model describing the how the stock prices change:

$$\frac{\triangle S}{S} = \mu \triangle t + \sigma \epsilon \sqrt{\triangle t} \tag{2.1}$$

$$\Rightarrow \triangle S = \mu S \triangle t + \sigma S \epsilon \sqrt{\triangle t} \tag{2.2}$$

where $\triangle S$ is the change in the stock price, $S$ in a small interval of time, $\triangle t$, and the random variable $\epsilon$ has the standard normal distribution. $\mu$ is the expected rate of return per unit time from the stock and $\sigma$ captures the stock price volatility. Both $\mu$ and $\sigma$ are assumed constant and as in [19], we set $\mu = 0.12$ and $\sigma = 0.15$. From Eqn. (2.2), it is evident that for a fixed stock price $S$, $\triangle S$ is normally distributed with mean $\mu S \triangle t$ and standard deviation $\sigma S \sqrt{\triangle t}$.

For the stock price at time $t$, $S_t$, we generate the $K$ fake messages as follows:

$$\tilde{S}_t^i = S_t + \eta_i, \quad i = 1 \ldots K \tag{2.3}$$

where $\tilde{S}_t^i$ is the $i_{th}$ fake message for $S_t$ and $\eta_i$ is white Gaussian noise. Keeping the variance of $\eta_i$ the small creates fake messages whose values are close to the correct stock price and is desired as per the *indistinguishability* criterion. However, the *average deviation* is directly proportional to the variance of $\eta_i$ and to achieve higher *average deviation*, we need the variance of $\eta_i$ to be larger than $\triangle S_{t-1}$. We explore this trade-off in more detail later.

**Attacker's Strategy**: In our experiments, the attacker eavesdropping on the data through the pub/sub broker network uses the following two strategies to guess the correct message out of $K + 1$ messages for each event (closing stock price).

- *Uniform Sampling*: The attacker picks each of the $K + 1$ messages as the correct message with the same probability. Hence, on an average, the attacker guesses the correct message with probability $1/(K+1)$ and the *indistinguishability* constraint is satisfied.
- *Extended Kalman Filter* [21]: Assuming that the attacker knows Eqn. (2.1), she can use an extended Kalman filter to filter out the noise and generate estimates, $\hat{S}_t^i$ of the true stock price from the fake message, $\tilde{S}_t^i$ she observes. She then picks the observed message $j$ as the correct one where

$$j = \arg\min |\tilde{S}_t^i - \hat{S}_t^i| \quad i = 1, ..., K + 1$$

The motivation for looking at the difference between the observations and their corresponding Kalman filter stock price estimates is the following. One of the $K + 1$ messages observed by the attacker contains the true stock price and hence for at least one of the observed messages the difference between the message and the Kalman filter estimate corresponding to that observation is going to be small (proportional to the estimation error of the filter). If the publisher adds noise $\eta_i$ of high variance (to achieve greater *average deviation*), then all the $K$ fake messages will differ significantly from their estimates obtained using the Kalman filter enabling the attacker to identify the message containing the correct information.

### 2.5.2. *Results: Indistinguishability*

For the results presented in this section, the variance of white, Gaussian noise added to the correct stock price to generate the fake messages was of the same order as the variance of $\triangle S$ (i.e., equal to the volatility of the change in stock price at a given price $S$). Figure 2.3 shows the probability of identification of the correct stock price by the adversary. The curves labeled "Uniform" and "EKF" refer to the uniform sampling and the Kalman filter strategies used by the attacker, respectively. We explain the curve labeled "Sig. Events" later. We also generated the results for many other companies including IBM, Amazon, and Microsoft, and skipped them in this chapter due to the similarity.

For $K = 1$ (only one foiling message), the Kalman filter approach leads to slightly higher correct identifications than uniform sampling. However, as $K$ is increased the adversary can guess correctly more often by doing uniform sampling. Hence, information foiling can achieve *message indistinguishability* even when the attacker resorts to sophisticated signal processing techniques to filter out the noise.

As seen in Figure 2.3, a small number for fake messages ($K = 2$) are enough to severely reduce the adversary's ability to identify the correct message. It is important to fool the adversary with only a small number of fake messages per

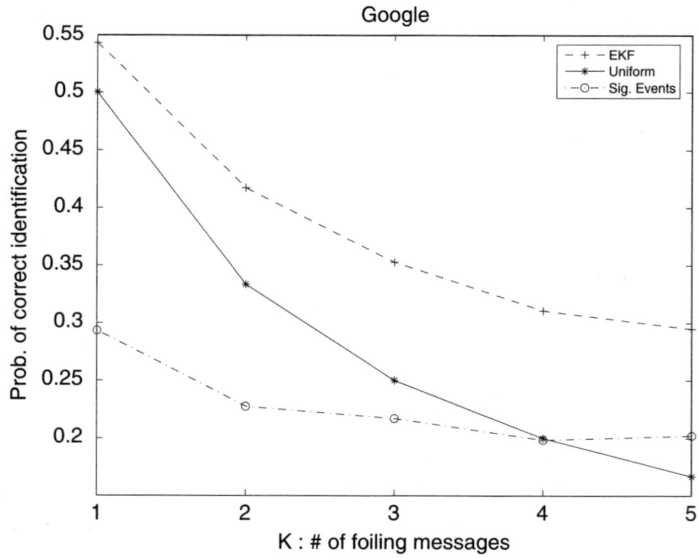


Fig. 2.3. Indistinguishability results: Google data set.

correct message because the communication overhead for the pub/sub broker network is directly proportional to $K$. Also, increasing $K$ beyond a point does not reduce the probability of correct identification significantly. Hence, depending on the data to be protected, a small number of fake messages would be enough to drastically reduce the probability of correct identification.

**Significant Events**: We refer to a comparatively large change in the current stock price as a significant event. The curve labeled "Sig. Events" shows the probability of correct guess by the adversary for significant events.

Because of the time (iterations) needed by the Kalman filter estimates to adapt to the sudden change in the stock price, the Kalman filter approach does much worse compared to uniform sampling when the stock price changes by a large amount. As shown in Figure 2.3, the performance of the Kalman filter approach degrades by more than 20% compared to its overall performance in the case of significant events (for $K \geq 3$).

In the case of stock prices, (winning) bids, location informations etc., the events were their value changes by a large amount are arguably more important than when their value remains constant (or changes by a small amount). From this perspective, it is an important result that the information fake approach severely reduces the adversaries ability to identify the correct message.

***Truth deviation* vs *indistinguishability***: We now explore the trade-off between having a higher *truth deviation* (to hurt the attacker more on an incorrect guess) and the ability of the attacker to identify the correct message. In our evaluation, the function $D(e, g)$ in truth deviation is materialized as $D(e, g) = |e - g|$. Table (2.1) lists the *avg. truth deviation* (over 500 rounds) achieved for data on Google's stock prices by adding noise with different variances. A value of 10 for "Factor" means the variance of the noise was 10 times the variance of $\triangle S$. As expected, higher variance for the added noise achieves a higher *truth deviation.*

Figure (2.4) shows the performance of the Kalman filter based approach for the different scenarios listed in Table (2.1). For higher noise variance, the Kalman filter based approach does quite well and the adversary sees a more than two-fold improvement in its ability to identify the correct message and performs better than uniform sampling. The reason for it is as follows. One of the $K + 1$ messages

Table 2.1. Google dataset: Truth Deviation (avg. price change per minute = 0.167)

| Factor | Avg. Truth Deviation |
|---|---|
| 1 | 0.0131 |
| 10 | 0.414 |
| 25 | 0.0509 |
| 50 | 0.093 |
| 100 | 0.1314 |

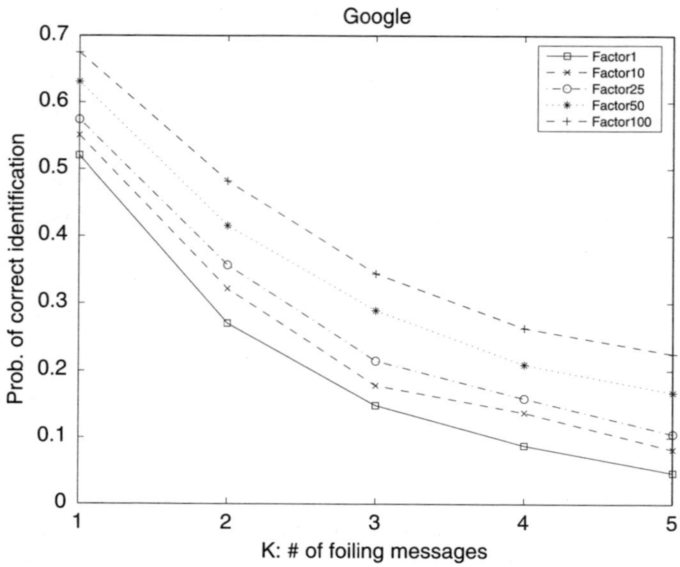


Fig. 2.4. Google data set: Indistinguishability

observed by the attacker contains the true stock price and hence, for at least one of the observed messages, the difference between the message and the Kalman filter estimate corresponding to that observation is going to be small (proportional to the estimation error of the Kalman filter). If the publisher adds noise of high variance (to achieve greater *truth deviation*), then all the $K$ fake messages will differ significantly from their estimates obtained using the Kalman filter enabling the attacker to identify the message containing the correct information. It is worth noting that even in high variance noise scenario, the efficacy of the Kalman filter based approach continues to decrease with increasing $K$.

## 2.6. Asymmetric Communications: Generalization of Information Foiling

The idea of information foiling is applicable to many other Internet applications for security and privacy. In this section, we present a family of such applications in the context of *asymmetric communications*.

### 2.6.1. *Asymmetric Communications*

Traditionally, network security addresses symmetric communications on the Internet, where two computers can learn about each other out of band or through some hand-shaking protocol, and then start secure communications with a strong cryptographical protocol.

However, new communication paradigms and network devices lead to the proliferation of *asymmetric communications*: the two end nodes, not necessarily regular computers, in a communication have asymmetric information or computing resources between each other so that existing cryptography-based mechanisms are not applicable to new security requirements from such communications. Examples of asymmetric communications and their new security requirements include:

- **Content-based routing**. In a content-based routing process, the communication relationship between a message initiator and a responder is decided dynamically based on the content the sender is looking for and the data the receiver owns. For the issues like scalability and performance, a third-party (overlay) router node sits in the middle of the routing path to help the sender find the receiver. However, the content used for the routing decision can be sensitive so that confidentiality problems like the following naturally arise [10]: can the router node perform content-based routing without the sender trusting it with the routing content?
- **Sensor Network Data Communications**. The predominant communication models in sensor networks are — *query dissemination* and *data collection.* They both require communication between computation, memory and power constrained sensors and base-stations/sinks (with orders of magnitude higher resources). How to design an efficient mechanism to ensure the secrecy of sensed data from eavesdroppers is one of the various security challenges [22].
- **RFID tracking**. In radio-frequency identification (RFID), a tiny microchip, called *tag*, communicates its identifier in response to a query from a nearby reader. Low-cost RFID tags are computationally weak and in the case of passive tags, even the power for operation is transmitted by the reader. Privacy concerns lead to security challenges like the following [23]: with the tags not being able to distinguish between authorized and unauthorized reader, could only an authorized application be able to identify them?
- **Ubiquitous computing with embedded networked devices**. In the future Internet, when ubiquitous computing comes to reality with sensor nodes and other embedded devices integrated into our home and work environment and hooked directly to the Internet, security and privacy issues arise on those low-end networked devices like the following [24]: without sufficient computing resources to support a strong security protocol, can the embedded devices be trusted to securely sense, aggregate, and carry sensitive information (such as the location, activity, or health of a monitored patient)?
- **Denial of Service and worm attacks**. Arguably, DoS and worm attacks are asymmetric communications where one end node has no information about the other end node. The current solutions to DoS and worm attacks can be categorized into two directions: 1. restore the communications to be symmetric, i.e., recovering the sender ID (e.g., IP traceback [25]); 2.prevent the asymmetric communications by hiding the receiver's ID (e.g., secure overlay services [26]).

### 2.6.2. *Asymmetric Communication Confidentiality*

In the asymmetric communication confidentiality problem, there are three entities: a sender, a receiver, and an adversary. The sender sends a message $e$ to the receiver and $e$ has to be in plain text due to the inapplicability of encryption/decryption schemes. An adversary is sitting between the sender and the receiver, and participates in the communication protocol as a message forwarder. It is assumed to be semi-honest. That is, the adversary correctly follows the communication protocol, but yet attempts to learn additional information by analyzing the transcript of the message received during the execution.

### 2.6.3. *Application of Information Foiling*

Information foiling is applicable to many network applications with asymmetric communications. For example, in Internet file sharing applications with anonymity requirements, information foiling could be a plausible approach with node ID and file ID foiling in the routing. In ubiquitous computing, to allow a low-end embedded device with constrained computing resources to protect its data privacy, information foiling can be applied as following: an embedded device shares with its legitimate data receiver some secret information (e.g., a seed for a random generator) out of band; the data sender protects the delivered messages by applying some fake message generation scheme and permuting the composite data set based on a series of random numbers generated with the seed; the receiver knows how to identify the authentic message given the same random seed. In sensor networks, data perturbation on sensor readings with the techniques proposed in [27] can be combined with aggregation tree based routing schemes to deliver a confidential data collection solution where an application server can accurately estimate the distribution of original readings with a complete set of (perturbed) reading data, and an adversary needs to eavesdrop on the transmissions from a significant fraction of the total sensors to make a good estimation of the statistics of the original readings.

## 2.7. Related Work

Rivest's "chaffing and winnowing" mechanism [15] motivated our work on information foiling. In his original work, information confidentiality is enabled using only authentication primitives. A message to be delivered is split into many equal sized parts and a valid MAC is appended to each part as a separate packet. For each authentic packet, called "winnowing", some packets, called "chaffing", are generated with random values for the message part and appended with the same MAC. The two types of packets are mixed and then sent to the receiver. Anyone with the authentication key for the MAC values can distinguish the authentic packets from fake ones. However, no details on fake message generation were presented in the original paper.

Wang *et al.* [10] identified the new security issues arising in pub/sub overlay services, including the confidentiality problems studied in this chapter. Wang *et al.* [10] also suggested several cryptographic protocols as potential solutions to the confidentiality problems, including computing with encrypted data [11] for information confidentiality, private information retrieval [28] and secure multi-party computation [29] for subscription confidentiality. Both [10] and [12] discussed the insufficiency of the above existing techniques in solving the confidentiality problems.

EventGuard [14] offers a dependable framework for pub/sub overlay services and addresses many security issues including authenticity, confidentiality, integrity, and availability. On confidentiality, it relies on a pre-trusted server for the distribution of symmetric keys among publishers and subscribers. All messages communicated between a publisher and its subscribers are encrypted by some symmetric key before entering the broker network, and the broker network is utilized only for overlay channel-based multicasting.

Raiciu and Rosenblum [12] propose a secure pub/sub protocol by extending the secure multi-party computation model Private Simultaneous Messages [13], and designs two new algorithms that implement a form of approximate matching in the context of secure routing for complex regular expressions. The protocol requires that publishers and subscribers share a common secret key in advance, and it has the communication complexity that is quadratic in the size of the input [12] also shows that in pub/sub setting information-theoretic security is impossible.

Information hiding [30,31] is an active research area with the applications including watermarking, fingerprinting, and copyright protection for digital media. A generic information hiding problem can be described as finding an embedding approach to hide a message in a hosted data set against an attacker who attempts to remove the message from the hosted data set. While the formal description of information foiling in Section 2.3.1 bears similarity to the information hiding problem model in [31], there are three critical distinctions:

- Information foiling has the constraint of computation compatibility due to intermediate processing (i.e., content-based matching in pub/sub services), which is not a concern in information hiding.
- The hosted data set in information hiding is an input from outside the system, while the fake message set in formation foiling is generated by the information foiler itself.
- The hider in information hiding can corrupt the composite data set (the protected message and its hosted data set) for information protection, e.g., through encryption, while the foiler in information foiling may not be able to or allowed to corrupt the protected message.

Privacy preserving data mining (PPDM) [32–34] addresses the problem of getting valid data mining results without disclosing the underlying data values. While some of the PPDM techniques like data obscuring [32,33] look similar to the information foiling mechanism in that both generate fake messages by perturbing the original data value, three key points distinguish our work from them:

- Data obscuring does not disclose the authentic data and only exposes the altered data value, while information foiling has to disclose the authentic data for the correctness of content-based routing.
- In PPDM the attacker has no knowledge about the authentic data distribution, while in information foiling we take the attacker knowing the authentic data distribution as one application scenario.
- The noise data distribution in data obscuring is constrained by the goal of maintaining the statistics property of the whole authentic data set unchanged, while information foiling chooses the fake data distribution with the optimization goal on indistingushability and truth deviation.

## 2.8. Conclusions

In this chapter, we introduced a new security mechanism called *information foiling* that addresses the confidentiality issues involved in content-based routing via a pub/sub broker network. Our scheme is complementary to the traditional cryptography-based security schemes and offers probabilistic guarantees on information confidentiality. The efficacy of our mechanism depends upon the quality of *fake messages* generated. We analyzed the performance of the new mechanism and explored the security and communication overhead trade-off in fake message generation schemes using real data traces on US stock price.

We highlight several open problems following our initial work. The need for a stronger guiding theory to better understand the fundamental limits of any information foiling system is quite evident. An analytic study on the fundamental trade-off between the fake message number, indistinguishability, and truth deviation is important. Investigating the interaction between a foiler and an attacker in game theory is interesting. Last but not the least, the designs of optimal FMG schemes for other interesting and important application scenarios are needed.

## References

[1] P. Eugster, P. Felber, R. Guerraoui, and A. Kermarrec, The many faces of publish/subscribe. In *ACM Computing Surveys*, **35**(2), 114–131, (2003).

[2] F. Fabret, H.A. Jacobsen, F. Llirbat, J. Pereira, K.A. Ross, and D. Shasha, Filtering algorithms and implementation for very fast publish/subscribe systems. In *ACM SIGMOD*, (2001).

[3] Y. Wang, L. Qiu, D. Achlioptas, G. Das, P. Larson, and H. Wang., Subscription partitioning and routing in content-based publish/subscribe networks. In *Proc. International Symposium on Distributed Computing*, (2002).

[4] D.X. Song and J.K. Millen, Secure auctions in a publish/subscribe system. In Available at http://www.csl.sri.com/users/millen/, (2000).

[5] X. Chen, Y. Chen, and F. Rao, An efficient spatial publish/subscribe system for intelligent location-based services. In *Proceedings of the 2nd international workshop on Distributed event-based systems*, (2003).
[6] L. Cabrera, M. Jones, and M. Theimer, Herald: Achieving a global event notification service. In *Proc. of HotOS-VIII*, (2001).
[7] A. Carzaniga, D. Rosenblum, and A. Wolf, Design of a scalable event notification service: Interface and architecture, (1998).
[8] http://mobile.yahoo.com/wireless/alert.
[9] Y. Huang and H. Garcia-Molina, Publish/subscribe in a mobile environment. In *Proceedings of the 2nd ACM international workshop on Data engineering for wireless and mobile access*, (2001).
[10] C. Wang, A. Carzaniga, D. Evans, and A.L. Wolf, Security issues and requirements for internet-scale publish-subscribe systems. In *Proc. of the HICSS-35, Big Island, Hawaii*, (2002).
[11] M. Abadi, J. Feigenbaum, and J. Kilian, On hiding information from an oracle. In *Proc. of the 19th Annual ACM Conference on Theory of Computing*, (1987).
[12] C. Raiciu and D.S. Rosenblum. A secure protocol for content-based publish/subscribe systems. (http://www.cs.ucl.ac.uk/staff/C.Raiciu/files/secure_pubsub.pdf).
[13] Y. Ishai and E. Kushilevitz, Private simultaneous messages protocols with applications. In *Israel Symposium on Theory of Computing Systems*, pp. 174–184, (1997).
[14] M. Srivatsa and L. Liu, Securing publish-subscribe overlay services with eventguard. In *the Proceedings 12th ACM Conference on Computer and Communication Security*, (2005).
[15] R.L. Rivest, Chaffing and winnowing: Confidentiality without encryption. In *RSA Laboratories CryptoBytes*, **4**(1), (1998).
[16] I. Clarke, O. Sandberg, B. Wiley, and T. Hong, Freenet: A distributed anonymous information storage and retrieval system. (Freenet White Paper, http://freenetproject.org/freenet.pdf, (1999).
[17] Report of nsf workshop on new architectures and disruptive technologies for the future internet: The wireless, mobile and sensor network perspective. Dipankar Raychaudhuri, Mario Gerla, Editors. August (2005).
[18] T.M. Cover and J.A. Thomas, Elements of information theory. In *WileyInterscience*, (1991).
[19] R.R. Gallati. Securities, random walk on wall street. (http://ocw.mit.edu/NR/rdonlyres/Sloan-School-of-Management/15-433InvestmentsSpring2003/040F67B1-EF93-4C0D-B902-4C5241D6E609/0/154332random_walk.pdf).
[20] http://finance.yahoo.com.
[21] D. Simon, *Optimal State Estimation*, chapter 13. John Wiley and Sons, New York, (2006).
[22] E. Shi and A. Perrig, Designing Secure Sensor Networks. In *IEEE Wireless Communications* (Dec., 2004).
[23] S.E. Sarma, S.A. Weis, and D.W. Engels, RFID Systems and Security and Privacy Implications. In *Proc. of Workshop on Cryptographic Hardware and Embedded Systems*, (2002).
[24] D. Kotz, Digital living 2010: Sensors, privacy, and trust. In *NSF Workshop on grand chanllenges in distributed systems*, (2005).
[25] A.C. Snoeren, C. Partridge, L.A. Sanchez, C.E. Jones, F. Tchakountio, S.T. Kent, and W.T. Strayer, Hash-based ip traceback. In *ACM SIGCOMM*, (2001).

[26] A. Keromytis, V. Misra, and D. Rubenstein, Sos: Secure overlay services. In *ACM SIGCOMM*, (2002).
[27] R. Agrawal and R. Srikant, Privacy-Preserving Data Mining. In *Proc. of ACM SIGMOD Conference on Management of Data*, (2000).
[28] B. Chor, E. Kushilevitz, O. Goldreich, and M. Sudan, Private information retrieval, *J. ACM.* **45**(6), 965–981, (1998).
[29] A. Yao, How to generate and exchange secrets. In *Proc. of the 27th IEEE Symposium on Foundations of Computer Science (FOCS)*, (1986).
[30] M.D. Swanson, M. Kobayashi, and A.H. Tewfik, Multimedia data–embedding and watermarking strategies. In *Proc. IEEE*, **86**(6), pp. 1064–1087, (June 1998).
[31] P. Moulin and J.A. O'Sullivan. Information-theoretic analysis of information hiding. In *IEEE Transactions on Information Theory*, **49**(3), 563–593, (March 2003).
[32] D. Agrawal and C.C. Aggarwal. On the design and quantification of privacy preserving data mining algorithms. In *Symposium on Principles of Database Systems*, (2001).
[33] R. Agrawal and R. Srikant, Privacy-preserving data mining. In *Proc. of the ACM SIGMOD Conference on Management of Data*, pp. 439–450, (2000).
[34] S. Rizvi and J. Haritsa, Maintaining data privacy in association rule mining, (2002).

# Chapter 3

## SECURITY ENHANCEMENT OF NETWORK PROTOCOL RFCs

Prabhaker Mateti
*Department of Computer Science and Engineering*
*Wright State University, Dayton, Ohio 45435*
*pmateti@wright.edu*

Venkat Pothamsetty
*Cisco Systems, Austin, TX 78727*
*vpothams@cisco.com*

Benjamin Murray
*Barracuda Networks, Ann Arbor, MI 48104*
*bmurray@barracuda.com*

The description methods of network protocol RFCs have not changed in decades. As a specification, a typical RFC leaves much to be desired. Using specific examples, we point out how ambiguities in protocol RFCs have lead to security vulnerabilities.

First, we suggest fixing the RFC so that there is no ambiguity for the implementer in those areas where past exploit techniques exist and future exploits can be predicted. Secondly, we classify the "bad" packets in the state-space through formal methods based on discrete mathematics and logic. Third, at certain locations in the source code implementation of the protocol, we suggest insertion of assertions based on this classification.

We offer advice to RFC writers, implementers and RFC approval bodies. The most effective solution to reducing network security incidents is to fix the RFCs in such a way that the implementers are forced to write an exploit-robust implementation.

### 3.1. Introduction

Sending cleverly crafted packets to a protocol engine so that it is impaired has become a common attack technique. Cleverly crafted, but obeying the RFC of the protocol. The TCP/IP suite has many security issues [1]. A network device rebooting is not an uncommon sight when a packet with large sized data or a zero length data is sent to it. It is also not uncommon to observe memory leaks on a device because the corresponding protocol stack did not implement timeouts for various connection stages. Of course, RFCs are not responsible for all these, but some vulnerabilities of the past could have been avoided had the RFCs been better.

### 3.1.1. *Security Robustness*

Security robustness is generally well-understood, but has not been well articulated. It encompasses the following.

(1) No matter what the packets are, a protocol engine must not crash or hang.
(2) Serve only legitimate packets.
(3) Do not send an invalid response to a valid request from a legitimate client and user combination.
(4) Do not send a valid response to a bogus request.
(5) Do not delay sending a response, beyond computing power and network traffic limitations, unless it is never to be sent.

### 3.1.2. *Blame the Protocol Design?*

A protocol design itself may be exploitable. TCP sniper attacks, ARP poisoning, DNS attacks are examples of these. During the early design of new protocols, security considerations ought to play an important role. From a purely theoretical point of view, it may be deducible that certain states cannot occur. In practice, they do because certain assumptions made are not satisfied at some other level of design and implementation.

### 3.1.3. *Blame the Implementation?*

Typical software engineering principles suggest that an implementer should faithfully follow the given specification and produce the desired output only when the input satisfies specified input conditions. He is not expected to assume or deal with conditions and inputs which do not conform to the given specification. Should that become necessary, one should go back to the requirements analysis phase and update the protocol design.

Many vulnerabilities, e.g., buffer overflows, are due to implementers not following secure programming recommendations. But, a large number of vulnerabilities occur because the corresponding implementation failed to anticipate packets that do not correspond to the protocol specification.

Implementers must, and by and large do, faithfully implement an RFC. However, implementers usually take any silence in a specification as "design freedom". Even though the protocol implementers are network specialists, they often are not knowledgeable about network security and cryptography issues. Past exploits and common attack techniques can impact the security of a protocol module, and consequently, the whole system.

### 3.1.4. *Blame the RFC?*

An RFC should include advice on all topics of RFC 3552 [2] and considerably more. Past RFCs have been unsatisfactory and a number of vulnerabilities can be traced to their failings [3] [4]. The next section is devoted to several such examples.

We suggest the RFC be revised as an Enhanced RFC for security robustness. In the ERFC, there is no ambiguity for the implementer in those areas where past exploit techniques exist and future exploits can be predicted. The enhancement is written with an awareness of the "seven sins" (Section 3.2.1). As a part of bringing security robustness, we classify the "bad" packets in the state-space through formal description techniques.

### 3.1.5. *Better RFCs*

In this paper, we consider the following problem. We assume that a protocol is designed (perhaps) without security considerations first, and it is written up as an RFC. We may also be given the design and/or source code of an implementation that is "based on" the RFC. We are also given reports of (past or possible future) exploits of the protocol and of the implementation. We are asked to reduce the security risk posed by the protocol and its implementation. We assume that rejection of either the protocol or its present implementation is not an option. The space of acceptable solutions includes enhancing the protocol with minimal incompatibilities resulting in an ERFC. We expect making the code more robust by careful revision of code in the light of the ERFC. We assume that it is permissible to have a range of solutions that depend on issues such as the computing power of the platform.

This is a paper on security of general network protocols, not on cryptography-based security protocols. We are also not focused on the editorial process of how RFCs come to be published (see `http://www.rfc-editor.org/howtopub.html` and dissenting opinions such as `http://www.ietf.org/mail-archive/web/ietf/current/msg30229.html`).

## 3.2. Inadequacies in Protocol RFCs

RFCs are written up as technical reports in English. This is prone to ambiguities and misinterpretation. It is a well-known but perhaps unacknowledged fact that different network protocol stacks would not be inter-operable had it not been for the wide accessibility of source code that implemented the early and "infrastructure" protocols such as TCP. Even today, one can safely predict that, if an implementation team is given only the RFCs and denied all access to source code of any implementations, the result would not be inter-operable. Protocol problems continue to be discussed; see, e.g., "ICMP attacks against TCP" `http://tools.ietf.org/html/draft-ietf-tcpm-icmp-attacks-00` of 2006.

The structure of the RFCs has not changed in over two decades. RFCs can be significantly improved. There are obvious needs to modernize, for example to include better diagrams than ASCII and at least use pseudo-code rather than prose descriptions of algorithms.

### 3.2.1. *Missing Specification Qualities*

An RFC is a specification. Yet a typical RFC does not posses the technical qualities described in [5]. A typical RFC commits all the "seven sins" [6]:

*Noise* The presence in the text of an element that does not carry information relevant to any feature of the problem. Variants: redundancy; remorse.

*Silence* The existence of a feature of the problem that is not covered by any element of the text.

*Over-specification* The presence in the text of an element that corresponds not to a feature of the problem but to features of a possible solution.

*Contradiction* The presence in the text of two or more elements that define a feature of the system in an incompatible way.

*Ambiguity* The presence in the text of an element that makes it possible to interpret a feature of the problem in at least two different ways.

*Forward reference* The presence in the text of an element that uses features of the problem not defined until later in the text.

*Wishful thinking* The presence in the text of an element that defines a feature of the problem in such a way that a candidate solution cannot realistically be validated with respect to this feature.

#### 3.2.1.1. *Inappropriate silence*

Presently, most of the protocol RFCs try to define the "right" packets relevant to the protocol and they specify what the response should be for such packets. They remain silent on what a protocol implementation should do for malformed packets, particularly in the middle of a long conversation between a server-client pair. They often remain silent on time-outs; if there is no time-out in certain states the RFC should explicitly say so.

An implementer takes the "silence" in the specification as design freedom, but usually they have not factored in the security issues.

The protocol implementer also usually does not have knowledge of security issues, past exploits, common attack techniques that impact his module and hence the overall network stack and device.

#### 3.2.1.2. *Ambiguity of technical prose*

RFCs have used many ambiguous terms (e.g., "silently discard", "tightly packed", "is-caused-by", "not required to honor"), but a few such as "universally unique numbers" and "unpredictable random numbers" deserve special attention (see Section 3.5.1).

A part of the ambiguity arises because of the words the RFCs chose as building blocks of the RFC — "Must", "Should" and "May" (see RFC 2119). Historically, the design intent of the RFCs has been to interpret the packets leniently, and words like "may" are deliberately intended to allow protocol implementations to be lenient in the interpretation.

However, for a protocol implementation to be secure, it must be strict in interpretation. Many a vulnerability (e.g., buffer overflows) today are due to sloppy implementations which do not *validate* the packets before parsing them. The problem however is that the implementers do not have a rigorous specification against which they can *validate* their implementation.

### 3.2.2. *Poor Definition of Valid Packets*

Quite a few RFCs are ambiguous or silent about the range, type and size of valid header values, permitting illegal combinations of flags and lengths. Though some of these validity conditions are derivable, the not-so-direct specification of header values result in an implementation not checking for the type and values inside the packet headers before parsing. Should an RFC recommend about order of parsing headers? For example, length should be checked first before parsing the whole packet etc. Only a few RFCs, e.g., RFC 2408: Internet Security Association and Key Management Protocol (ISAKMP), have general packet processing recommendations.

#### 3.2.2.1. *Not specifying valid types*

In cases where the value of a header or data must have only specific types of values (strings in the case of email address, e.g.), RFCs should explicitly specify the type and bind the implementer to check the validity of the type of values before parsing.

*Example 1 (MIME Protocol Interpretation of Characters)*: Many vulnerabilities exist in the MIME protocol (RFCs 2045–2049) because different vendors interpreted RFCs comments on interpreting characters in different ways. (see `www.niscc.gov.uk/niscc/docs/al-20040913-00537.html`) The corresponding vulnerabilities become more dangerous when the characters have special meanings, such as the back-slash and null characters in web applications. (see `www.webappsec.org/projects/threat/classes/path_traversal.shtml`)

#### 3.2.2.2. *Unexpected flexibility in fields*

*Example 2 (RADIUS)*: Each RADIUS packet (RFC 2865) can be up to 4096 bytes. It implicitly allows packing > 2000 attributes into a single packet. Some RADIUS servers' implementations allocate maximum attribute length for each attributes, it means for each attributes > 256 bytes of memory will be allocated. It is possible to lock about 512 K of memory and waste CPU time with a single 4 K packet resulting in an easy denial of service attack. (see `http://www.securiteam.com/exploits/6K00J2035U.html`)

*Example 3 (Ping of Death)*: This classic exploit happened because the ICMP RFC did not put a limit on the data portion of the ICMP packet (see `http://www.insecure.org/sploits/ping-o-death.html`).

*Example 4 (Telnet Options)*: Within every BSD derived `telnet` daemon under UNIX, the telnet options are processed by the `telrcv` function. This function parses the options according to the telnet protocol and its internal state. During this parsing the results which should be sent back to the client are stored within the `netobuf` buffer. This is done without any bounds checking, since it is assumed that the reply data is smaller than the buffer size (which is `BUFSIZ` bytes, usually).(see `www.monkey.org/openbsd/archive/misc/0107/msg01332.html`) The corresponding buffer overflow has lead to multiple vulnerabilities.(see `www.cert.org/advisories/CA-2001-21.html`) Had the Telnet RFC 854 specified explicit limits on the size of the options (see `http://www.iana.org/assignments/telnet-options`), this vulnerability could have been avoided.

*Example 5 (SSL)*: There are a few vulnerabilities in SSL because SSL did not put a limit on the data portion client certificates(see `archives.neohapsis.com/archives/bugtraq/2002-02/0313.html`).

#### 3.2.2.3. *Malformed packets*

*Example 6 (ISAKMP Malformed Payloads)*: "An ISAKMP packet with a malformed payload having a self-reported payload length of zero will cause isakmpd to enter an infinite loop, parsing the same payload over and over again."

"An ISAKMP packet with a malformed IPSEC SA payload will cause isakmpd to read out of bounds and crash."

"An ISAKMP packet with a malformed Cert Request payload will cause an integer underflow, resulting in a failed `malloc()` of a huge amount of memory." (see `http://www.securityfocus.com/archive/1/358386`)

"An ISAKMP packet with a malformed delete payload having a large number of SPIs will cause isakmpd to read out of bounds and crash." (see `CVEID: CAN-2004-0221`)

*Example 7 (Malformed H.225.0 messages)*: Malformed H.225.0 messages were insufficiently checked and caused various parsing and processing functions to fail, which resulted in system crashes and reboots. (see `http://www.cisco.com/warp/public/707/cisco-sa-20040113-h323.shtml`)

*Example 8 (TCP)*: RFC 793 and others in defining the functional specification for TCP do define how systems should respond to legitimate packets, but they don't explain how systems should handle illegal combinations of flags. Consequently, different operating systems respond differently to illegal flag combinations. Attackers now exploit this to finger print the operating system. (see `www.securityfocus.com/infocus/1200/`)

*Example 9 (SNMP Headers)*: Many of the vulnerabilities indicated by the test cases released by `www.ee.oulu.fi/research/ouspg/` for the SNMP protocol are because the corresponding implementation did not have code to handle header values that are inconsistent with the protocol specification. (see `www.cert.org/advisories/CA-2002-03.html`).

*Example 10 (Teardrop)*: Overlapping IP fragments crashed the servers upon re-assembly. (see `http://www.cert.org/advisories/CA-1997-28.html`)

*Example 11 (Land)*: Source address and port are spoofed to be the same as the destination in an IP packet crashed the servers. (see `http://www.cert.org/advisories/CA-1997-28.html`) (see `http://www.cisco.com/warp/public/770/land-pub.shtml`)

*Example 12 (Devious IP options)*: Devious IP options caused denial of service (see `http://www.securiteam.com/unixfocus/IP_options_processing_Denial_of_Service_in_BSD.html`).

*Example 13 (Valid Values of Fields)*: A classic example is how RFCs specify the *length* field of a header. E.g., ISAKMP RFC2408 has this on page 24: "Length (4 octets) — Length of total message (header + payloads) in octets". However, it leaves many questions unanswered: Can the payload be of zero bytes? What is the minimum size of payload? What is the maximum possible length of the payload? In the absence of such specification, the implementer will try to take the value as-is and try to interpret the rest of the packet as per the supplied value, leading to a multitude of vulnerabilities. E.g., implementation of ISAKMP daemon in OpenBSD had vulnerabilities because the length of the received packet is not validated against valid and possible data values(see `xforce.iss.net/xforce/xfdb/15518`).

Had the specification been written (e.g., by specifying the min and max values of length) so that the implementer is forced to ascertain the value before parsing, many vulnerabilities (see `CAN-2005-0340,CAN-2005-0482, CAN-2004-1002,CAN-2004-0899.`) could have been avoided.

### 3.2.3. *Weak Handling of Security Issues*

Most RFCs do not (thoroughly) follow RFC 3552 Guidelines for Writing RFC Text on Security Considerations (2003). Consider the following selected examples.

(1) *RFC 3928 Lightweight Directory Access Protocol (LDAP)* does not methodically consider all attack scenarios. It considers flooding attacks and ignores the rest.
(2) *RFC 3937 A Uniform Resource Name (URN) Namespace* claims, without justifying, that the RFC brings no additional threats.

(3) *RFC 3952 Real-time Transport Protocol (RTP) Payload Format for internet Low Bit Rate Codec (iLBC) Speech, Dec 2004, Experimental* identifies a potential denial of service (DoS) but does not analyze how the protocol counters that threat.

### 3.2.4. *Prone to Denials of Service*

#### 3.2.4.1. *Flooding*

*Example 14 (SYN Floods)*: The vulnerabilities related to SYN floods and ARP floods are because the RFC and the implementations failed to anticipate such packets. Irrespective of these classic attack patterns, we have seen RFCs continuing to be silent on this aspect. E.g.,

*Example 15 (Floods in IKE)*: IKE RFC2409 failed to anticipate a flood of initial (Main Mode) packets, and the implementations continue to be vulnerable (see `www.securiteam.com/windowsntfocus/6N00G0A3F0.html`).

#### 3.2.4.2. *Memory exhaustion*

*Example 16 (TCP Reassembly)*: RFC 793 TCP did not specify re-assembly time-outs of out-of-sequence numbers, and RFC 791 IP did not specify fragmented datagrams, which lead the implementers follow different waiting schema for packet re-assembly. (see `attrition.org/security/advisory/idefense/idefense-04-03-02.freebsd`)

*Example 17 (ISAKMP Order of Packets)*: ISAKMP RFC 2408 did not specify the sequence of payloads and BSD ISAKMPD suffered.(see `http://www.openbsd.org/errata31.html`)

*Example 18 (Cisco Catalyst)*: Numerous "memory leak exploits" are due to the protocol engine not reclaiming the memory resources before exiting a state (see `http://www.cisco.com/warp/public/707/catalyst-memleak-pub.shtml`),

*Example 19 (NNTP service in Windows)*: The implementation does not release the memory used by a previous state. (see `www.securiteam.com/windowsntfocus/5EP0B1F550.html`)

*Example 20 (RDP)*: When an RDP (Remote Data Protocol) packet contains a specific type of malformation, a memory leak "depletes overall server memory by a small amount." (see `http://support.microsoft.com/?kbid=292435&sd=RMVP`)

#### 3.2.4.3. *Time-outs*

Many RFCs either ignore time-outs or specify too long a time-out. IKE RFC 2409, for example, does not specify time-outs for connections in various modes, including "Main Mode" and "Quick Mode".

*Example 21 (Windows Telnet DoS)*: If a client does not reset a session (e.g., the client connects to a session and idles), it might effectively cause denial of service on other legitimate users. Windows Telnet daemon had such vulnerability.(see `www.securityfocus.com/bid/2018`)

*Example 22 (Resource Exhaustion)*: Since a protocol state is essentially a collection of all variables, overlong time-outs can cause memory consumption on routing/ fire-walling devices. As a result, several fire-walling devices were vulnerable. (see `www.kb.cert.org/vuls/id/539363`)

### 3.2.5. *Prone to Unauthorized Use*

3.2.5.1. *Spoofing*

*Example 23 (TCP Connection Termination)*: See RFC 4953 Defending TCP Against Spoofing Attacks.

*Example 24 (IP Spoofing Attacks and Hijacked Terminal Connections)*: (see `http://www.cert.org/advisories/CA-1995-01.html`)

3.2.5.2. *Packet Replay and Header Reuse*

*Example 25 (Session-Based Authentication)*: Earlier specifications of SSH (as opposed to RFC4251-6) (see `http://www.kb.cert.org/vuls/id/565052`), Kerberos (see `http://www.hut.fi/~autikkan/kerberos/docs/phase1/pdf/LATEST_replay_attack.pdf`), and TACACS (see `http://www-arc.com/sara/cve/tacacs_server.html`) have all been exploited with replay.

*Example 26 (SNMP)*: Most of the vulnerabilities arising from the test cases released by OUSPG for SNMP protocol are because the corresponding implementation did not have code to handle header values inconsistent with the protocol specification. (see `http://www.cert.org/advisories/CA-2002-03.html`)

3.2.5.3. *Entering and exiting a state*

*Example 27 (POP3 Webmail Unauthorized Access)*: If the implementation does not reset all the variables of a session, it is possible for the next user to gain unauthorized access to the prior user's variables. (see `www.securityfocus.com/bid/9807/discuss`)

3.2.5.4. *Dictionary attacks*

*Example 28 (Kerberos)*: See `www.securiteam.com/tools/6V0070A6AS.html`.

*Example 29 (WEP)*: See `www.airscanner.com/pubs/wep.pdf` and [7].

3.2.5.5. *Authentication*

*Example 30 (RIP v1)*: RFC 1058 RIP v1 was vulnerable to spoofing. (see `CVE-1999-0111`) RIP v2 (RFC 1723 and RFC 2082) includes plain text and MD5 authentication mechanisms.

*Example 31 (OSPF and BGP)*: These had to do go through the same phases, they needed to be extended to include authentication mechanisms. Later OSPF (RFC 2328) and BGP (RFC 2385) RFCs have authentication mechanisms, but it is not known how many installations actually use these authentication mechanisms as the protocol does not mandate the use of those authentication mechanisms.

*Example 32 (Original SIP)*: RFC 3261 employed HTTP's authentication mechanism for request messages but not for registration messages. Therefore, the registration message is spoofable.

3.2.5.6. *Authorization*

RFCs do not typically analyze the authorization issues that will crop up when a protocol is deployed in large scale.

*Example 33 (H323 Random Ports)*: H323 protocol suite and SIP recommend opening up random ports for transferring media, and it has become hard for firewalls to employ fix-ups (so that only authorized persons have access to that traffic) and secure the corresponding traffic.

3.2.5.7. *Confidentiality and integrity*

The non-cryptographic RFCs (as opposed to cryptography-based RFCs like IPSec) typically do not specify any mechanisms for protecting protocol communication.

*Example 34 (H323 and SIP)*: The H323 protocol suite and SIP (RFC 3261 Session Initiation Protocol) protocols did not think deeply about cryptographic issues in encrypting the signal and media traffic when the RFCs were written. As a result, it took quite a while for the industry to figure out what the right encryption mechanisms are for Voice-Over-IP traffic.

## 3.3. Specifications v. Designs v. Implementations

In this paper, we are considering the RFCs and their implementations, not the design of the protocol and how it came to be published as an RFC. If PI stands for the source code of a protocol implementation, we consider the corresponding RFC its specification, and discuss the design and implementation of a PI.

### 3.3.1. *Explicit Description of Design Freedoms*

A specification document should not be taken as an outline of a suggested design, but this happens. This can be prevented by making clarity the goal of the specification, and deliberatingly relegating performance to a separate section. Thus, the ERFCs we are suggesting would be ingloriously inefficient if viewed as design outlines.

A specification document ought to permit as much design freedom as possible. When a specification is silent on an item, the interpretation in the past has been that the particular item is irrelevant to the specification and that the implementer may freely choose it to help his design, usually without factoring in the security issues. We believe this should change. Design freedoms must be explicitly identified. Silent items that become important during the design phase must be brought back to the attention of the specifiers and resolved early in the development life-cycle.

### 3.3.2. *Formal Methods Brief*

We recommend a moderate amount of formal methods usage in RFCs. Below we give a whirlwind summary of definitions and examples of some of the terms and ideas of formal methods used in this article. The books [8], [9], and [10] are three classics that can together give an excellent background on formal methods to a practical programmer.

#### 3.3.2.1. *Assertions*

An assertion is a logical expression on the variables of a program. E.g.,

$$x - \delta_1 \leq (sqrt(x))^2 \leq x + \delta_2,$$

for some small values $\delta_1$ and $\delta_2$, is an assertion about a square-root algorithm named *sqrt*.

The logical expression may use well-known mathematical and programmer-defined functions. In this expression, we may not only use the Boolean and, or, not, ..., but also the $\forall$ (for all) and $\exists$ (there exists) quantifiers. E.g., at the end of an algorithm sorting an array $a[1:n]$ of numbers, we expect to have

$$\forall i : 1 \leq i < n \rightarrow a[i] \leq a[i+1] \wedge bag(a) = bag(a.old).$$

It is possible to convert some (not all) assertions into executable watch-dog code.

#### 3.3.2.2. *Pre- and post-conditions*

A pre-condition is an assertion that is expected to be true immediately upon entering a procedure/ function/ method. The body of the method assumes this and proceeds to accomplish its task. A post-condition is an assertion that describes what the procedure will accomplish. A pre-condition involves parameters to the procedure and globals. It must never involve variables local to the procedure. A post-condition involves the current values of the parameters, globals, and local variables, and relates them to the values the globals had upon entry.

#### 3.3.2.3. *Invariants*

An invariant is an assertion whose value remains true every time control reaches it. A loop invariant is inserted at a location inside a loop. A class invariant must be true as both pre- and post-condition of every public method of a class.

#### 3.3.2.4. *Abstraction function*

An abstraction function maps the concrete state to a more mathematically amenable abstract model. The concrete state vector is likely to use various data structures whose details are irrelevant to the issues at hand. For example, that something is a linearly linked list is irrelevant. Considering it as a sequence of certain values is more useful. An abstraction function drops irrelevant detail from concrete data structures of a program.

E.g., a program may be implementing a set using an array `int a[100]`, whose abstraction function maps the array into the set it represents:

$$abstract(a) = \{a[i] : 0 \leq i < 100\}$$

The abstract models uses sets, sequences, tuples, graphs, etc. but not pointers. The abstraction function is necessary in the analyses. It is a function mathematically well-defined. It is not necessarily programmed into an executable method.

### 3.3.3. *Specification Language ÖM*

We use ÖM [11] as the defining language where an RFC uses only English prose. ÖM is designed to have a familiar programming feel. Its syntax can be further revised to cater to protocol implementations. Even so, formal languages such as ÖM are not expected to be self-explanatory; like programs, they also need careful commentary. In this paper, a typical ÖM fragment is followed by a brief explanatory note or two regarding the syntax and semantics.

## 3.4. Protocol Engine

This section is an overview of an architecture for client-server protocol specifications. All protocols are defined using a collection of finite state machines that is often called a protocol engine. This engine has never been a pure finite state machine; e.g., it always had time related transitions. In this section, we will be introducing security inspired extensions. We present these as if we are starting from a given protocol RFC, and revising it into an ERFC.

### 3.4.1. *States and State Vectors*

A *state* is an abstract identifier that captures an important situation in a protocol in following a specific server-client conversation. In typical diagrams, states are shown as circles or boxes with an alphanumeric identifier written inside them. Transitions are shown as arrows often with labels of the form $a/b$, with $a$ indicating the "inputs", and $b$ indicating the "outputs".

The ERFC identifies all variables essential to the protocol specification. By a "state vector", we mean the collection of all such variable-value pairs at any moment. This includes packets received, global variables, contents of certain files, the content of the run-time stack, etc. A quick, if imprecise, description is that the state vector is the "core dump". As the protocol engine executes it makes changes to the state. In the engine, certain control points correspond to the states shown in the state machine.

The state vector is the input to the state that will lead a transition into another state. It is unlikely that all of the state vector is relevant to a given state. The output of a state is the state vector resulting as the engine ends the current state and begins the transition to the next state. It is likely that much of the output state vector is identical to the input state. In many RFCs the time it takes to go through the transition is implicitly assumed to be zero.

#### 3.4.1.1. *Auxiliary variables*

With the entire state machine and/or with some chosen states, we introduce certain auxiliary variables. Some of these variables are abstractions of concrete variables needed for the normal functioning of the protocol; the remaining variables are introduced solely to enhance security. The auxiliary variables can capture timing issues, such as when the packet arrived, real time elapsed in that state, or time spent by the CPU in that state. They can also deal with resource consumption issues, such as number of bytes allocated to various data structures, and even number of system calls. An ERFC should use formulas to estimate average and worst case scenarios. These are similar to the big-Oh statistics from analysis of algorithms, but must not ignore constant factors; e.g., $100 * n^2$ is considered better than $120 * n^2$.

We will occasionally use the term the essential state vector for a given state as one that excludes the auxiliary variables.

#### 3.4.1.2. *Partitioning the state space*

The state space is the collection of all possible state vectors. A large subset of these state vectors will not occur simply because of the control flow in the protocol engine. Current RFCs describe only the reachable state vectors, but, in an ERFC, it is very helpful to describe the unreachable states. The reachable-and-legal and reachable-but-illegal and the unreachable-and-hence-illegal state spaces are defined using techniques of discrete mathematics and logic. This is a task for the security specialist with the help of a formal methods person.

States are legal or illegal ("should not occur" but do happen) from the perspective of the protocol. The definition of legality is based on whether a valid transition is defined for that state vector in a given state.

#### 3.4.1.3. *Introduction of new states and transitions*

The ERFC introduces certain states for the sole purpose of dealing with illegal state vectors and defines transitions to them. The transition from a good state $X$ to a bad state $Y$ occurs when a state vector is illegal in $X$. When an engine is in these "bad-or-tentative" states, all further processing should be done with greater care if we are to be exploit-robust. The ERFC should also describe if, when, and how it is possible to join a good state from one of these bad states.

#### 3.4.1.4. *Quiescent state*

In all protocols, there is (conceptually) a *quiescent* state where the server process is awaiting a request having finished all outstanding requests. Reusable resource (e.g., memory) consumption should remain the same in these states.

### 3.4.2. *Time Stamps and Time Outs*

We limit ourselves to the situation where the protocol engine is running on one host machine, perhaps using multiple processes. Thus, the notion of a clock is clear, unambiguous, and computationally tractable. We assume that this clock is fine-grained enough that at any instant at most one event occurs.

A number of RFCs view the arrival of an entire packet as a single event. But this may not realistically model security situations, whereas associating a time-stamp with the arrival each byte or field may be too demanding. Realistically, packets should be given two time stamps: the arrival beginning and ending. A typical RFC does not describe what an implementation may do as soon as a packet begins to arrive; this is an explicit design freedom.

The sending of an entire packet can also be viewed as a single time-stamped event. As above, we propose that packet sending be given two time stamps: the begin and end of the sending.

### 3.4.3. *Histories and Logs*

A *snapshot* is a time-stamped record of the state vector, including the auxiliary variables. Snapshots are used in the analyses of a protocol engine. *History* is a sequence of snapshots. Obviously, history is immutable. We use history as an abstraction in clearly stating certain vulnerabilities or attacks in progress. Another commonly used term for snapshot is "checkpoint".

Note that in an actual implementation, not only the size of the snapshot can be very large, it may also mean that the protocol engine cannot run in real-time. However, in order to prevent various exploits, such as flooding, from occurring, an implementation has to record portions of history and re-examine upon suspicion of attacks. We discuss in Section 3.5.6.1, as a protocol implementation task, an efficient design for recording history.

A log is a concrete record of history. Because of size reasons, the ERFC must carefully select what gets recorded.

### 3.4.4. *Servers*

A server is a process that responds to requests from the client process. These may or may not be "processes" as the host OS defines the term, but these are processes from the perspective of the ERFC. In many protocols, a server becomes a client and vice-versa for brief durations. A server may have one or more clients. Many protocols deal with other services, such as authentication and proxy.

When a server process starts it generally must identify itself and register its service. This can be a "broadcast" that a servers of servers listens to, and later helps clients in their discovery of appropriate servers. Similarly, when a server is about to terminate, it de-registers its service.

#### 3.4.4.1. *Conversation with a client*

A typical client engages in a conversation that involves several requests to the server, and several responses to the client.

A server is set up to start listening to requests from clients. On receiving a request, a server should (i) authenticate the client, (ii) validate the request, and (iii) provide the service in that order. Between a server and a client there may be an exchange of several request-responses, not necessarily strictly alternating. Often a request can be identified as the beginning of a conversation, and a response to the client as the end. Such a sequence of request-responses is often called a *session.*

A client may request a server process and its host machine to authenticate themselves. Thus, a server process must submit its credentials.

Typical servers are expected to provide service to clients that they may not already know. This necessitates the authentication of the client.

#### 3.4.4.2. *Request validation*

Servers are expected to serve clients with certain service parameters (rights, privileges, resource limits, etc.) associated with a given client. Validation of a request also depends on the history of the client.

When a request is invalid, the essential state vector must remain unchanged. The ERFC describes the details of the server response: a client may be informed of the request being invalid, or the server may choose to be quiet and silently discard the request.

### 3.4.5. *Clients*

A client is a process that generates requests to a server process. The protocol describes how a client discovers servers, how it chooses a server, and the time outs.

## 3.5. Security Enhanced RFCs

This section gathers security-sensitive issues in protocol RFCs. We admit into the RFC such things as history logs that were previously considered implementation artifacts.

An RFC must (now) have a security considerations section as in RFC 3552 for it to be accepted. The security considerations section is a good start; however, it is not mandatory that RFC writers propose an exhaustive set of security mechanisms for a newly proposed protocol.

A single security considerations section does not effectively address attacks that could happen at various stages during the protocol. For example, attacks (such as message insertion, and flooding), security techniques (such as authentication) and security measures (such as error recovery) depend on the state that the protocol is in. We believe that the threats could be effectively addressed in relevant sections all through the RFC, and not just at the end.

We expect the RFCs to describe the handling of common attack techniques. The present RFCs are silent on what the implementation should do with respect to common attacks related to packets, for example flooding, sniffing, spoofing, replay, and not responding with an appropriate "reply", or deliberately delaying the reply.

### 3.5.1. *RFC Terms*

This section reviews and refines a few terms that RFCs frequently use.

#### 3.5.1.1. *Reserved*

A packet field when labeled as "reserved" informs that the content of this field is expected to be ignored at the time of the writing of an RFC, but may acquire a significant role later. Such fields have become useful in covert channels [12].

Experimental is a word used to mean that a value, field, or action has been suggested, but that it may change "soon".

#### 3.5.1.2. *Is-caused-by*

This is a relation between two events or actions to be understood with its normal English meaning. If event $e_2$ is caused by event $e_1$, it must have been the case that the time stamp of $e_1$ is earlier than that of $e_2$. If action $a_2$ is caused by action $a_1$, it must have been the case that the time stamp of $a_1$ is earlier than that of $a_2$. A similar statement holds between events and actions.

3.5.1.3. *Simple Network Data Types*

```
model byte is 0 .. 2^8 - 1;
model short is 0 .. 2^16 - 1;
model long is 0 .. 2^32 - 1;
```

The models above are subsets of ***unsigned integer***. ÖM's ***integer*** is the mathematical view of an integer; the sum of two positive integers, no matter how large, will never overflow anything.

3.5.1.4. *Octets v. bytes*

An octet is a sequence of 8 bits. Unless otherwise stated, it is viewed as an unsigned integer in the range of 0 .. 255. A byte is the smallest unit of addressable memory in modern computers. It is equivalent to an octet. There have been computers where the smallest unit of addressable memory was called a "word". Depending on the system, the size of the word varied from 16 bits to 60. On such a system, talking about a byte is inappropriate, and an octet alignment on a bit-index within the word needs to be specified. Networking literature continues to use the term octet, but in our opinion, this term should now be retired.

3.5.1.5. *Tightly packed*

This means that there are no gaps in the byte sequence in the representation of a value composed from values of differing data types.

3.5.1.6. *Left to right*

This phrase is used as in "The fields are transmitted from left to right." We take it for granted that (i) a `long` occupies 4 consecutive bytes, (ii) a `short` occupies 2 consecutive bytes, and (iii) all integers (including short, and long) are in network byte order. Composite values are transmitted with lowest indexed byte first.

3.5.1.7. *Undistinguished octets*

This means that the bytes are uninterpreted 8-bit values – not to be treated as characters, integers, text, string, or whatever. There are several other phrases with the same meaning: "opaque data", "opaque octets".

3.5.1.8. *Time-outs*

Time-outs are the maximum time durations that a server or client may have to wait (usually for an event such as packet arrival) in a particular protocol state. Time-outs play a significant role in the security of a protocol.

In general, network protocols require the specification of various time-outs. Some protocols have specified these as constants. Even when these are carefully chosen, evolving technologies etc. make them too long. It is better to give a time-out's initial value as a formula based on the computing platform and the network delays being experienced at the moment of computing this value.

To specify something using a "short span" (RFC 2865, line 778) of time is inherently ambiguous. In ERFC 2865, we used ***time-to-process*** to specify the time taken by a RADIUS server to process a request and a corresponding ***time-out-server-response*** in the clients.

### 3.5.1.9. *Silently discard*

The phrase "silently discard" occurs 9 times in RFC 2865. "This means the implementation discards the packet without further processing" (line 257) explains a bit, but does not define it. It also omits the general understanding that the networking community has: the server will not indicate to the client it is dropping the request.

It can be, in principle, resolved as follows. It is (i) as if the silently discarded packet never arrived (hence "unreplied"), and (ii) the future behavior of the entity that received this packet is unaltered. The first aspect, even though it is very easy to understand, is not mathematically specifiable, unless we exclude resource consumption issues. Note that determining if a packet is to be discarded silently does take CPU time and memory resources. Hence, packets that will be silently discarded can be used as part of a DoS attack. While it is wise to log all discarded packets, this in itself can become a DoS by filling up file systems. Further, once we log something we violate (i) even more.

The second aspect of "silently discard" can be formulated in a functional programming framework. Suppose we have a sequence $s = a + b + c$, where the $+$ sign denotes catenation. We specify that a computation $C$ silently discard $b$ by demanding $C(a+b+c) = C(a+c)$ for all $a, c$. Obviously, we assumed that $b$ is not a sub-sequence of either $a$ or $c$.

### 3.5.1.10. *Unpredictable*

This and the next two subsections consider certain difficult to define properties often mentioned in RFCs even though a satisfactory rigorous definition is still elusive.

Consider the following example where an RFC requires that the *request* authenticator value should "be unpredictable and unique over the lifetime of the shared secret"(RFC 2865, line 812).

"Unpredictable" is arguably a mathematically undefinable concept. Note that to be able to speak of values in a probabilistic manner makes it predictable. We presume that the intended meaning is that *for a third party, having observed a sequence of certain values of a field being exchanged between two parties, it is computationally infeasible to compute what the future values of exchange will be.*

"The phrase 'computationally infeasible' is used frequently in cryptography but is rarely defined. The general consensus on its meaning is as follows. If the time complexity of an algorithm $A$ is a function that grows faster than any polynomial, we consider $A$ to be computationally infeasible. A similar meaning with respect to memory (and other) resources required is included in the meaning of the phrase. On a practical level, we should understand the phrase to stand for any computation that requires either extremely long time or extremely high resource requirements even on the fastest (parallel, cluster, etc.) computer systems. Extremely long here is in the class of several (zillion?) years." [13].

"Unique over the lifetime of the shared secret" can certainly be specified, but would be near-infeasible to implement unless the shared secret does get changed frequently, in the range of once every few seconds.

Note that the "unpredictable" property regarding a certain number in a field usually has further dependencies on other field values that are known, e.g., in the RADIUS protocol, the shared secret, the server id, and the client id that share this secret.

### 3.5.1.11. *Universally unique numbers*

RFCs require many GUIDs (Globally Unique Identifier), which are ill-defined. Globally here implies both world-wide and for-all-time. Often, an RFC overstates its needs: The RFC 2865 requires that the request authenticator value should "exhibit global uniqueness"(RFC 2865, line 819). Clearly, global is used in the sense of "word-wide." There is no IANA dealing with request authenticators. Is this not wishful thinking?

Consider as an example the following paragraph as a definition or as a description. GUID is "a unique 128-bit number that is produced by the Windows OS or by some Windows applications to identify a particular component, application, file, database entry, and/or user. For instance, a Web site may generate a GUID and assign it to a user's browser to record and track the session. A GUID is also used in a Windows registry to identify COM DLLs. Knowing where to look in the registry and having the correct GUID yields a lot information about a COM object (i.e., information in the type library, its physical location, etc.). Windows also identifies user accounts by a user-name (computer/domain and user-name) and assigns it a GUID. Some database administrators even will use GUIDs as primary key values in databases. GUIDs can be created in a number of ways, but usually they are a combination of a few unique settings based on specific point in time (e.g., an IP address, network MAC address, clock date/time, etc.)." (see `http://webopedia.internet.com/TERM/G/GUID.html`)

### 3.5.1.12. *Temporal uniqueness*

RFC 2865 requires that the *request authenticator* value should (1) "be ... unique over the lifetime of the shared secret"(RFC 2865, line 812) and (2) "exhibit ... temporal uniqueness"(RFC 2865, line 819).

We suspect what was intended was that it be *unique over a period of time*, from the beginning of establishing a shared secret till it is changed to another. This is unambiguous but makes it computationally infeasible because of the enormous storage needs of maintaining the history and CPU time needed in generating such a unique number.

A number of protocols require that certain numbers (e.g., request authenticators in RADIUS RFC2865, MAC addresses in Ethernet, IP addresses in IP) they use should be (i) *universally unique numbers* and/or (ii) *temporally unique*. The terms are generally described loosely, and often imply that the two terms are equivalent. But, they are not. It turns out that it is not too difficult to rigorously define the terms [14] using discrete mathematics and logic. The essence of the difference is that (ii) refers to uniqueness in the context of what has transpired so far, whereas (i) is time independent, i.e., unique from "big bang" of the distant past to "apocalypse" of the unknown future.

The difficulty with respect to (i) and (ii) is in arriving at a practical implementation that hopes to do justice to the two obligations: (a) the "sender" should generate such a number, and (b) the "receiver" should be algorithmically able to verify that the received number is one such. Depending on whether we chose interpretation (i) or (ii), the difficulties are different.

Traditionally, the problems of (i) are "solved" by using number granting authorities and associated query/answer protocols. Because these solutions are inadequate, various spoofing attacks became possible.

Regarding (ii), note that this kind of uniqueness is obviously in the context of a group of "connected" senders and receivers. Hosts A and B are "connected" not in the sense of TCP-connected, but in the sense that they exchanged a message of the protocol, or transitively there was a third party C with which they did. The problems of (ii) are solvable (if we put aside the resource requirements) as follows. Every sender and receiver has access to a global historical record of what has transpired. Using such records, (a) and (b) can be implemented. But, the resource requirements — in particular, space to store the history, and the distributed computing mechanisms to keep it up-to-date across all hosts — are immense even when the group of connected hosts is small.

### 3.5.1.13. *New this implies new that*

The phrase "new X" appears only in the context of values for a field or attribute named X. It is defined as true iff the current value of X, say $x$, has never been a value for this field. Requiring this property in an RFC is to commit the sin of wishful thinking unless the life time of X is so short that an implementation can maintain complete history of values used.

### 3.5.2. *Validity of Packet Structure*

Defining valid packets needs to be done at multiple levels: (i) simple data types, (ii) individual packets, (iii) as an item in a sequence of packets, and (iv) finally in the context of a client-server conversation. It is helpful to design a packet format so that full syntax validity (i.e., (i)–(iii)) is checkable fast without requiring deep interpretations of fields (their types and values).

Many protocols have a provision for sending varying number of headers (typically to advertise the protocol's capabilities, so that the other end of the protocol can choose the appropriate one). RFCs typically do not specify the valid size of the accompanying payload, or the limitations on the number of such inner headers an implementation should entertain. Because of this silence, the implementation often continues to parse headers leading to vulnerabilities.

As can be seen from the examples of Section 3.2.2.3, many implementations trusted the packets to be valid without verification. There should be a global statement in RFCs that "The validity of a packet must be ascertained before any state transitions are allowed. Any server/client should function as described in the RFC if valid packets are received. Any server/client must ignore all invalid packets."

In addition to such protocol field anomalies, there are protocol data anomalies that depend on the semantics of the payload of the packets.

#### 3.5.2.1. *Individual packet structure*

RFCs have long used ASCII diagrams and programming language notations to describe the layout of packets, leaving to prose the description of constraints. Many invalid packets also satisfy such ambiguous specifications. But, in languages like ÖM, it is possible to fully specify packets. We illustrate this with a fragment from [14].

```
model RADIUS-packet is composite (
  code, identifier: byte,
  length: short,
  authenticator: Authenticator,
  attribute-bytes: seq byte,
) such that
  for all r: RADIUS-packet (
    r.code: {1 .. 5, 11, 12, 13, 255},
    r.length == 20 + # r.attribute-bytes <= 4096,
    r.length <= r.sizeof,
    valid-attribute-bytes(r)
  )
```

#### 3.5.2.2. *Sequences of packets*

The validity of a packet often depends on packets received earlier. SEQ/ACK numbers in packets are a simple example of this. In more complex case, the maintenance of recent history of packets may be needed, and upon the discovery of an illegal packet the proper thing to do is to go back to a previously good state restoring the snapshot at that state.

### 3.5.3. *Actions for Illegal Packets*

The RFCs are typically ambiguous/silent/non-exhaustive about the conditions that need to be fulfilled before entering a protocol state and after leaving a protocol state. Here are the recommendations of a vulnerability taxonomy [15].

(1) For secure state transitions, specify all the pre-conditions for every state: Trust pre-conditions, such as authentication and authorization conditions, resource pre-conditions, such as amount of memory that must be available. Do not initiate any transitions until the pre-conditions are verified.
(2) At state hand-over, all resources allocated to the connection should be reclaimed, and all changes that are made to the system should be reset/undone.
(3) The connections at later stages should not be affected by the connections at preliminary stages. The connections should have time-outs and a secure exit strategy, including either handing over the connection to the previous state or terminating the connection.

RFCs also do not exhaustively specify the actions that the implementation needs to take in case of illegal packets. The actions may be (a) drop the packet, (b) close the connection, (c) send an error packet, (d) do a transition fork (see Section 3.5.3.1), or (e) any combinations of these actions. In the absence of such conditions, the implementer will be free to accept and interpret such packets. In many cases the implementer will continue to interpret, store the information, and pass on the packet to other modules causing vulnerabilities.

The simple corrective action for wrong header values is to simply drop the offending packet and remain in the current state, but it is possible to take more sophisticated actions such as alerting an IDS, or begin gathering more packets that may arrive from the same source address.

#### 3.5.3.1. *Impact rollover*

This vulnerability refers to the impact on a state rolling over and impacting the previous states as well. A well-known example of this type of exploit is the SYN floods on a port affecting the already ESTABLISHED connection [4].

An ERFC should be alert to the possibility of state transition path fork that may have to be undone. A snapshot S at the current state C is taken and transitions are tentatively allowed as needed by the sequence of packets, but if we then end up in a bad state, we roll back to state C with S as its state vector. The idea is simple, but a feasible implementation requires considerable work because of active use of history. This idea is essentially the converse of non-deterministic transitions in finite state machine theory.

Reaching a previously saved safe state is also the recommended action for header reuse or when we get a copy of an earlier session.

### 3.5.4. *Denial of Service*

While DoS can happen legitimately, more often than not it is the result of an attack. A rigorous definition of what constitutes DoS that is useful/implementable in all contexts is difficult. But in specific protocols, such as RADIUS, one can give highly implementable definitions. An ERFC should contain suggestions to implementers on how to detect and prevent DoS. The typical DoS prevention strategy is to drop packets that appear to be suspicious based on a fast (and usually superficial) analysis of the packet in question.

#### 3.5.4.1. *Resource exhaustion*

A DoS occurs because of resource exhaustion. The typical resources that an ERFC is concerned about are: memory, CPU time, disk space, number of sys-calls, number of time-outs, number of packets, etc. An ERFC must not remain silent; it should discuss these. It should use formulas to estimate average and worst case scenarios. These are similar to the big-Oh statistics from analysis of algorithms, but must not ignore constant factors; e.g., $100 * n^2$ is considered better than $120 * n^2$.

As an example, in a RADIUS server implementation there is a quiescent state (Section 3.4.1.4) where the server process is awaiting a request having finished all outstanding requests. Memory consumption should remain the same in these states. This is easier to track if each request is handled by a separate thread.

#### 3.5.4.2. *Flooding*

RFCs typically do not have the machinery needed to even define "flooding." Flooding refers to an abnormally high arrival rate of packets. It is inherent in all client-server protocols. We should of course define flooding carefully so that we do not identify legitimate traffic as a flooding attack. Flooding vulnerabilities arise when an implementation can not handle large volume of packets in a secure way.

Since this is a common attack technique, the ERFC should address it. The maximum rate of Access-Request messages that a RADIUS server is expected to handle should be defined in terms of the computing power of the platform, but here as a sketch of an example, we specify that a server silently drop packets from a client if more than 10 Access-Request messages are received in the last one-second interval.

In the ÖM code below, the `servers-past` is a packet history including the `Time-Stamp` of arrival/sending a packet. Without further ado, we assume that this is the

32-bit Unix time stamp (the number of seconds elapsed since January 1st, 1970). Let *sq* be the sub-sequence of *servers-past* of packets that arrived in the last one second; the expression *[ a: servers-past such that a.2 >= ct - 1 ]* makes a sequence by selecting all entries of *servers-past* that have a time-stamp of *ct - 1* or more recent. The expression *sq // source-address* makes a sequence of only the source IP addresses from *sq*.

```
var servers-past: seq (IP-UDP-packet, Time-Stamp);

function noccurs(ip: IP-address) returns ni (
  let ct be current-time(),
  let sq be [ a: servers-past such that a.2 >= ct - 1 ],
  let iq be sq // source-address,
  let ni be ip #: iq
)

function is-flooding(ip: IP-address) returns boolean (
  noccurs(ip) > 10
)
```

This example illustrates *the* essential technique in detecting a flooding attack. That we are being flooded cannot be discovered unless we are aware of the history of packets with timestamps. On the other hand, reckless use of history will make an implementation infeasible.

#### 3.5.4.3. *Time-out*

Associated with every state, unless explicitly exempted, there should be time outs specified as a function of the computing platform and network conditions. This prevents resource exhaustion caused by withholding response packets.

### 3.5.5. *Unauthorized Use*

#### 3.5.5.1. *Sniffing and spoofing*

It is no longer reasonable to think that packet contents are not sniffed. When the packets are unencrypted, the attacker can make immediate productive use of the connection beyond just DoS. Encrypted packets add computational burden of decyphering not only to the receiving hosts but also to the sniffer (who may not possess the relevant keys and hence must resort to brute-force). Note that there is enormous pressure on making receiving hosts (especially on embedded devices such as IP phones and wireless access points) inexpensive, implying that their computational powers are meager. Depending on the nature of the protocol, the trade-off between leaving the packet unencrypted (fast processing of unencrypted packet contents together with loss of confidentiality) versus encrypted packets must be evaluated.

Nearly all of the protocols designed in the past (say, prior to 1990) lacked a cryptographic means of authenticating packets or verifying their integrity. A third party can therefore replace selected fields of a sniffed packet without being detected.

So that dictionary attacks become time consuming, the ERFCs need to specify a reasonable length for passwords as well. Note that encryption simply postpones this into a replay; after a successful dictionary attack, previously sniffed and stored history is available to the attacker.

### 3.5.6. *Implementation Issues*

All implementers need an attitude adjustment: Distrust the received packets. At certain locations in the source code implementation of the protocol, validity assertions should be inserted. If the platform on which the protocol implementation is running is powerful enough, we can enable the assertions as run-time checks. An ERFC should recommend such ideas specialized to the protocol being described.

#### 3.5.6.1. *Recording history efficiently*

Exploit prevention depends heavily on being able to access the history of the protocol engine. On the other hand, straightforward implementations would make the engines useless in practice. However, there is now a large body of literature on control flow transition forks using `setjmp` and `longjmp` undo/redo techniques, taking checkpoints that has not become a standard technique in protocol implementations.

## 3.6. Discussion

In this section, we present answers to some questions we imagined or heard in the context this article.

### 3.6.1. *Formal Methods*

#### 3.6.1.1. *Formal methods and languages for protocol analysis*

Are Formal Languages the Best Solution? From our perspective, the answer is "Yes." Recall that C, C++, and Intel Assembler language are all formal languages. Using suitable formal languages in protocol design and implementation makes it possible to "compile" a high-level description into feasible code. Today we do not debate whether a skilled assembly programmer can produce better code for an algorithm described in C. We only debate the productivity of such an endeavor.

Several languages and methods have been proposed over the years for the precise and unambiguous descriptions of protocols. The paper [16] is a good introduction to how formal methods are applied to the analysis of secure protocols. [17] is an introduction to formal languages developed for protocol descriptions. This article gives a bird's eye view of SDL, Promela and Lotos. There is considerable literature on formal analysis and design verification of crypto protocols (see e.g., [18]). Interestingly enough, we could not find any past work, related to removing the ambiguity of protocol specifications through formal methods or improving the robustness of specifications against common attack techniques. The reasons for their non-adoption by protocol designers and implementers have not been analyzed, but perhaps the methods were too "foreign", too deeply rooted in mathematics and logic to appeal to them. Perhaps many formal languages are gratuitously difficult. Using a notation and semantics already familiar to implementers has not been a concern of the designers of languages like Lotos. This is not to say that by merely making the notation C-like all problems of comprehension and training are solved.

#### 3.6.1.2. *What "protocol problems" did formal languages solve?*

Let us defuse the question by answering "None." The answer of course really depends on what is meant by "solve." E.g., did formal languages/methods help (i) find flaws in protocols after the protocol is some how designed and formulated? (ii) find bugs and vulnerabilities? (iii) help generate acceptable implementations from formal descriptions? (iv) Did formal methods help security-harden existing implementations of protocols? We do not know of such work. Can formal methods help generate differing implementations intended to run on platforms with varying degrees of computing power? Yes. Can we address device specific issues like CPU inside the specification? Yes. Some protocols (especially public protocols like web and mail) require accepting a packet from any client. In that case, in order to implement the "Flood Heuristic" function above, we need to take the device's CPU level and memory consumption into consideration. It is another question whether our ERFC should talk about what constitutes such heuristics. We would argue that we should, because we are trying to solve the problem of "non security-savvy" implementer.

#### 3.6.1.3. *Can formal methods replace testing?*

Testing and formal methods should be seen as being orthogonal. To repeat a famous quote, "Testing reveals the presence of bugs not their absence." Formal methods typically focus on guaranteeing the absence of bugs.

### 3.6.2. *Code Analysis and Generation*

#### 3.6.2.1. *Code generation*

We expect to be able to generate C-like code, from the functional programming constructs used in the FDT, that is realistic in terms of resources through the interactive use of a software tool to be developed.

There is a sizable body of literature (e.g., [19], [20] [21], [22]) on this topic.

#### 3.6.2.2. *Code analysis tools*

Splint [23] is a compile-time tool that analyzes C source code based on formal annotations given by the programmer, and can pin point many errors. [24] is an example of how the Splint tool helped locate buffer-overflow problems in `wu-ftpd`. Several RADIUS implementations were audited using Splint and other tools [25].

A technique called meta-compilation has been successful in identifying bugs in software systems (see e.g., [26]). The NRL protocol analyzer [27] has been used by many. There is considerable activity on CAPSL [28].

#### 3.6.2.3. *Attack techniques against implementations*

There is considerable progress in the last few years in testing of protocol implementations. Automated tools based on testing techniques known as "fuzzing", "fault injection" and "boundary testing" are becoming more common. [29] [30] [31]. There are sophisticated techniques for generating test cases as well [32] [33].

There are even a few attack tools available on this technique. Spike API, a fuzzer creation kit (see `http://www.immunitysec.com/resources-freesoftware.shtml`), is one such tool concentrating on HTTP protocol. Fuzzing tools are both commercially available, like Codenomicon (see `http://www.codenomicon.com`), and being privately developed, like the one used in BGP Vulnerability Testing (see `http://www.nanog.org/mtg-0306/pdf/franz.pdf`). We believe that sophisticated open source protocol fuzzing tools are around the corner.

### 3.6.3. *Specifiers'/Implementers' Problem?*

Industry has few options to counter the problem of non-robust implementations. Static analysis tools cannot effectively catch vulnerabilities arising due to inherent protocol design problems, nor do they point out vulnerabilities arising due to common attack techniques. Security education of network software engineers is an effective solution, but the solution is only as good as the implementer is.

The most effective solution is to fix the RFCs. The specifications should be written in such a way that if the implementer follows the specification (he will by contract), the resulting implementation will automatically be robust, withstand common attack techniques and will have incorporated security measures.

Furthermore, it is much easier to educate relatively few specifiers than an uncountable and scattered implementers. We acknowledge that some of the attacks are dependent on platform specific resource limitations, which the specifier has no control over. However, in such cases, we recommend that the specifier explicitly acknowledge the issue, and recommend implementation considerations to the implementer.

#### 3.6.3.1. *Will RFC writers use ERFC to write all RFCs in the immediate future?*

Almost nil. We consider our effort a success even if we were only able to get IETF accept ERFC as an "informational RFC".

Whether or not RFC writers will be persuaded to use ERFC like languages will depend on the need to do so. We guess that sophisticated open source fuzzing tools would expand such a need.

Since there are no other solutions now, we want to put our solution out there. We hope that it will be refined and developed as per the community needs and will be ready when such a time comes.

#### 3.6.3.2. *Should the RFC writers be aware of attack techniques?*

Yes. One of the goals of our effort is to make the specification aware of the attack techniques so that the implementers do not have to worry about them.

Furthermore, the "attack techniques" do not change from protocol to protocol and it would not be hard to acquire such knowledge through the example ERFC that we would be writing. Note that even though the attack techniques don't change, the replies (drop, reject, error, or safe state) would change as per the requirements of various protocols.

## 3.7. Conclusion

A large number of protocol implementations can be impaired by sending them cleverly crafted sequence of packets. Such vulnerabilities occur because the corresponding implementation failed to anticipate packets that do not correspond to the protocol specification.

In this document, we proposed a solution to this problem consisting of the following steps. (i) We fix the specification as given in the original RFC in such a way that there is no ambiguity for the implementer in those areas where past exploit techniques exist and future exploits can be predicted. We call the resulting document an Enhanced RFC. (ii) We classify the "bad" packets in the state-space through formal description techniques. (iii) At certain locations in the source code implementation of the protocol, we insert assertions based on this classification. If the platform on which the protocol implementation is running is powerful enough, we can enable the assertions as run-time checks.

Our approach depends on a careful use of the history of the concrete state vector of the protocol engine, and progressively refining into a feasible implementation. Our approach makes use of advances in the design of very-high level programming languages, compilation techniques, formal methods, and security improvement techniques.

### 3.7.1. *Advice to RFC Writers*

Knowing how an implementer should/would understand an RFC is important to the authors of RFCs. We argue that RFCs should provide "advice" to implementers as well.

**Be Aware of Silence** A protocol RFC deals with three main elements: (i) the structure of a packet, (ii) the sequences of packets, and (iii) the states of the protocol engine. The "standard" interpretation of silence is not the same for all three elements. In (i) and (ii), silence implies invalidity: That is, any packet that does not satisfy the described requirements must be considered invalid. In (iii), silence implies design freedom. Where you wish to give design freedom, do so explicitly. Make an explicit statement to the effect that any situation not covered by the RFC is an illegal one, and an RFC-compliant implementation must detect these situations and be robust. If you wish to be silent on a certain item, say so explicitly.

**Be Aware of Ambiguity** If non-determinism is desired, say so explicitly. By "non-determinism" we mean the following. That there are multiple, but unambiguously described, actions that are acceptable. A single choice must be made among the alternatives. Any choice so made among these need not be consistent either.

**Be Aware of Infinite Sequences** Protocol sequences can be infinitely long, but every implementation can only store a finite amount of it. Do not describe properties based on infinite sequences. "Unpredictable", "unique" are some examples of this.

**Timeouts** Specify minimum and maximum time delays between certain bookmarks of the packet sequence if not between consecutive packets. Obviously, as the technology changes, so will these timeouts.

### 3.7.2. *Advice to RFC Approval Bodies*

The RFC approval process is rigorous. But, this process still does not give enough importance to security issues.

**Independent Implementations** Do not approve RFCs unless at least two independent implementations that "agree" exist. Consider, e.g., the standards of publication of results in biological sciences where an experiment can take years or decades and blind studies are required.

**Completeness of Packets** An approved RFC must rigorously define *valid* packets. All packets that do not satisfy this definition must be considered *invalid* packets. An approved RFC must separately state what the actions are in response to (i) valid and (ii) invalid packets.

A "good" RFC will further divide the invalid packets into (a) invalid but harmless packets, (b) invalid and resource-exhausting packets, (c) invalid and causes-hangs packets, and (d) invalid and causes-halts packets.

**Completeness of States** An approved RFC must rigorously define (i) what constitutes a *state* of the protocol engine, (ii) the *valid states*, and (iii) all the rest of the states as *invalid* states. An engine must never reach a valid state consuming invalid packets. An engine must never reach an invalid state consuming valid packets. Once an invalid state is entered, the engine remains in the invalid state, transitioning into a valid state only via explicitly described packets in the RFC.

**Timeouts** An approved RFC must define timeouts for every state (both valid and invalid). A timeout causes a state transition. Such transitions must be explicitly described.

### 3.7.3. *Advice to Implementers*

Even if an RFC is not written following the advice above, implementers should follow the best practices as suggested below.

**Ascertain Packet Validity** Packet validity must be ascertained *before* any action is taken. Any gain in computational efficiency obtained by ignoring this advice is doomed.

**Design Freedom and Silence** Do not interpret silence as design freedom. Caution on the side of packet validity (item above) and interpret silence as invalid packets (item below).

**Invalid Packet Processing** Unless the protocol explicitly describes how invalid packets should be dealt with, an implementer must "silently drop" such packets. This means that the protocol engine remains in the state that it was in prior to receiving the invalid packet. Other than a small amount of computational time, no resources are consumed. Any allocated resources are released. Logging of invalid packets is advised, but one must consider the requirements and security risks posed by logging.

**Timeouts** Implement a timeout for practically every state of the protocol engine, except for a tiny few states explicitly identified as quiescent states.

**Think About Worst-Case Scenarios** The implementer should consider the worst case scenarios before taking any action based on the contents of a packet. Some examples: (i) Make sure all resources needed will be/are available (ii) Analyze possible deadlock and live-lock scenarios and consider the corresponding prevention techniques.

### 3.7.4. *Future Work*

We are actively working on solutions to make the RFCs more secure. Our work includes (i) Developing a specification language for writing RFCs, with the following design goals: (i.a) The language would give enough flexibility to the specification writer to write unambiguous RFCs. (i.b) The language should force the implementers to validate the packets and do all the right things for security. (i.c) The language would be easily understandable by the implementers. (ii) Supplying methods for incorporating security techniques into RFCs. (iii) Supplying methods for incorporating attack technique knowledge into RFCs. (iv) Publish an example eRFC work (see, e.g., [14]) of an existing RFC, enhancing it to include all the above mentioned functionalities.

### 3.7.5. *Conclusions*

RFCs should be written in a way that none of the sections are ambiguous. Invariants on header values and sizes should be specified in the RFC so that the implementer would not have freedom for sloppy interpretation of packets.

It should be mandatory that the RFC writers take the protocol specification through a reasonable threat model and consider possible attack scenarios.

It should be mandatory that the RFCs propose ways to handle common attack techniques such as spoofing, flooding, replay, and reuse at all stages of the protocol.

It should be mandatory that the RFCs propose security mechanisms for providing confidentiality, integrity, authentication, authorization and non-repudiation at all stages of the protocol.

## References

[1] P. Mateti. Security issues in the TCP/IP suite. In eds. Y. Xiao and Y. Pan, *Security in Distributed and Networking Systems*, chapter 1, pp. 3–30. World Scientific Publishing (Aug, 2007). ISBN 978-981-270-807-6.

[2] E. Rescorla and B. Korver. Guidelines for writing RFC text on security considerations. Technical Report RFC 3552, ftp.rfc-editor.org (July, 2003). `ftp://ftp.rfc-editor.org/in-notes/rfc3552.txt`.

[3] R. Stewart, M. Tuexen, and G. Camarillo. Security attacks found against the stream control transmission protocol (SCTP) and current countermeasures. Technical Report RFC 5062, ftp.rfc-editor.org (September, 2007).

[4] W. Eddy. TCP SYN flooding attacks and common mitigations. RFC 4987 (Informational) (Aug., 2007). URL `http://www.ietf.org/rfc/rfc4987.txt`.

[5] C. A. R. Hoare, The quality of software, *Software: Practice & Experience*, **2**(2), 103–105, (1972).

[6] B. Meyer, On formalism in specifications, *IEEE Software*, **2**(1), 6–26 (Jan., 1985). ISSN 0740-7459.

[7] A. Bittau, M. Handley, and J. Lackey, The final nail in WEP's coffin, *IEEE Symposium on Security and Privacy*, **0**, 386–400, (2006). ISSN 1081-6011.

[8] E. W. Dijkstra, *A Discipline of Programming*. (Prentice-Hall, 1976).

[9] D. Gries, *The Science of Programming*. (Springer, New York, 1981).

[10] D. Björner and C. B. Jones, *Formal Specification & Software Development*. (Prentice-Hall, 1982). ISBN 0-13-329003-4.

[11] P. Mateti. ôM: A design specification language. Technical Report WSU-CS-90-07, Wright State U (Jan, 1990).

[12] S. Zander, G. Armitage, and P. Branch, A survey of covert channels and countermeasures in computer network protocols, *IEEE Communications Surveys & Tutorials*, **9**(3), 44–57, (October, 2007).

[13] P. Mateti. Cryptography in Internet Security. In *Lectures on Internet Security*. Wright State University (April, 2002). `http://www.cs.wright.edu/~pmateti/InternetSecurity/Lectures/Cryptography/index.html`.

[14] P. Mateti. RADIUS Protocol Annotated in OM. Technical report, Wright State U (May, 2005).

[15] V. Pothamsetty and B. Akyol. A vulnerability taxonomy for network protocols: Corresponding engineering best practice countermeasures. In *Communications, Internet and Information Technology 2004*, Virgin Islands (November, 2004). `http://www.iasted.org/`.

[16] S. Older and S.-K. Chin, Formal methods for assuring security of protocols, *The Computer Journal*, **45**(1), 46–54, (2002). ISSN 0010-4620.

[17] F. Babich and L. Deotto, Formal methods for specification and analysis of communication protocols, *IEEE Communications Surveys and Tutorials*, **4**(1), 2–20, (2002).

[18] S. Schneider and R. Delicata, Verifying security protocols: An application of CSP, *Lecture Notes in Computer Science*, **3525**, 243–263, (2005).

[19] C. Castelluccia, W. Dabbous, and S. O'Malley, Generating efficient protocol code from an abstract specification, *IEEE/ACM Trans. Networking*, **5**(4), 514–524, (1997). ISSN 1063-6692. doi: http://doi.acm.org/10.1145/262028.262034.

[20] I. S. Abdullah and D. A. Menasc. Protocol specification and automatic implementation using XML and CBSE. In *Proc. of Int. Conf. on Communications, Internet and Information Tech. (CIIT2003)*, p. 6pp, Scottsdale, AZ, (2003).

[21] T. M. McGuire. *The Austin Protocol Compiler Reference Manual* (May, 2004). `www.cs.utexas.edu/users/mcguire/software/ apc/reference/reference.html`.

[22] T. M. McGuire. *Correct Implementation of Network Protocols*. PhD thesis, The University of Texas at Austin (May, 2004). Adviser: Mohamed G. Gouda.

[23] D. Evans. Splint — Secure Programming Lint. Technical report, University of Virginia, (2002). `http://www.splint.org`.

[24] D. Evans and D. Larochelle, Improving security using extensible lightweight static analysis, *IEEE Software*, **19**(1), 42–51 (Jan/Feb, 2002). ISSN 0740-7459.

[25] P. Mateti, B. Murray, and J. Uphaus. Source code audit of FreeRADIUS, OpenRADIUS and GNU RADIUS Implementations of RFC 2865. Technical report, Wright State University, (2006).

[26] M. Musuvathi and D. R. Engler. Model checking large network protocol implementations. In *USENIX Symposium on Networked Systems Design and Implementation NSDI 2004*, San Francisco, CA 94108, (2004). USENIX.

[27] C. Meadows, Formal methods for cryptographic protocol analysis: Emerging issues and trends, *IEEE Journal on Selected Areas in Communication*, **21**(1), 44–54, (Jan, 2003).

[28] J. Millen. CAPSL Common Authentication Protocol Specification Language Web site. `http://www.csl.sri.com/users/millen/capsl`, (2004).

[29] S. Dawson, F. Jahanian, and T. Mitton, Experiments on six commercial TCP implementations using a software fault injection tool, *Software: Practice and Experience*, **1**(1), 1–26 (Jan 01, 1997).

[30] PROTOS. Security testing of protocol implementations, (2004). `http://www.ee.oulu.fi/research/ouspg/protos/index.html`.

[31] A. Vasan and A. M. Memon. ASPIRE: Automated systematic protocol implementation robustness evaluation. In *Australian Software Engineering Conference (ASWEC 2004)*, Melbourne, Australia, (2004).

[32] P. Sinha and N. Suri. Identification of test cases using a formal approach. In *Symposium on Fault-Tolerant Computing*, pp. 314–321, (1999).

[33] R. Kaksonen, M. Laakso, and A. Takanen. Software security assessment through specification mutations and fault injection. In *IFIP TC6/TC11 Fifth Joint Working Conference on Communications and Multimedia Security (CMS'01)*, (2001).

# Chapter 4

## AUTHENTICATION OF SCALABLE MULTIMEDIA STREAMS

Mohamed Hefeeda and Kianoosh Mokhtarian
*School of Computing Science, Simon Fraser University*
*250-13450 102nd Ave, Surrey, BC V3T 0A3, Canada*

Multimedia services such as Internet streaming and video conferencing are increasingly getting very popular among all sectors of society and all ages. Many users rely on these services for activities related to their work, education, and entertainment. Users typically receive multimedia content over open network channels, where malicious attackers could potentially intercept and manipulate such content for political, financial or other reasons. Therefore, ensuring the authenticity of received multimedia streams is clearly an important problem. This chapter first proposes a set of requirements that an authentication scheme designed for multimedia streams should meet. It then surveys the most important schemes in the literature for authenticating non-scalable as well as scalable multimedia streams. Unlike non-scalable streams, scalable streams provide flexible adaptation to accommodate the dynamic network conditions and the diversity of receiving devices. Moreover, the chapter presents a qualitative comparison among the presented schemes using the proposed set of requirements, and it outlines potential directions for future research on authentication of multimedia streams.

### 4.1. Introduction

The demand for multimedia services has been rapidly increasing over the past few years, and this demand is expected to even accelerate in the future. This is confirmed by numerous market studies for different multimedia services, such as video conferencing, Internet streaming, and Internet Protocol Television (IPTV). For example, the US Internet streaming media market (network and content services) is expected to grow from about $900 million in 2005 to more than $6 billion in 2011 [1]. In addition, it is estimated that the revenue of the video conferencing market (services and equipment) will reach $11.9 billion by 2010, up from $6.7 billion in 2007 [2]. Furthermore, the worldwide revenue of IPTV is forecasted to reach $38 billion in 2009 with almost 53 million subscribers [3].

As more users rely on multimedia services for many aspects of their daily lives, including work, education, and entertainment, the security of such services will be of great importance. This chapter focuses on an important aspect of securing multimedia services: authentication of multimedia streams. Other security issues such as access control and confidentiality are outside the scope of this chapter. Authentication of multimedia streams means ensuring that streams played out by receivers are original and have not been tampered with by malicious attackers. In general, the communication channel between senders and receivers cannot be perfectly secure. Thus, an attacker could potentially capture and modify multimedia streams on their way to receivers. The motivations for attackers to tamper with multimedia streams can range from just curiosity and showing off attackers' skills to political and commercial gains. For example, an attacker may modify parts of an important documentary video to hide or change some facts to support certain political views or to spread some rumors. An attacker may also insert a few video frames containing unauthorized commercial adds in an Internet broadcast of a popular program for financial reasons.

Authentication of multimedia streams is done in two steps. First, the sender or the creator of a multimedia stream generates some authentication information and sends it to the receiver along with the multimedia content itself. Second, the receiver verifies the authenticity of the received multimedia stream using the authentication information. The generation and verification of the authentication information for multimedia streams should consider the special characteristics of those streams. These characteristics include, the possibility that multimedia streams are *adapted* to meet various constraints imposed by the receiver or the network. Adaptation of multimedia streams implies removing parts of the data to reduce their bit rate, frame rate, or resolution. Thus, an authentication scheme for multimedia streams should be able to verify the authenticity of adapted streams. This is unlike authentication schemes for other types of data such as documents and software packages where all bits of the data are always used. There are several other important characteristics of multimedia streams that should be considered as well. In Section 4.2, we elaborate more on these characteristics and propose a set of requirements that an authentication scheme designed for multimedia streams should meet. We will use these requirements to guide our discussion and comparison between different schemes proposed in the literature. These requirements can also be useful for other researchers designing new schemes for authenticating multimedia streams.

The adaptation of multimedia streams depends on the method used to encode and compress them. In general, there are two categories of encoding multimedia streams: scalable and non-scalable. We present a brief background on these categories in Section 4.2, defining several terminologies and concepts that will be used in the rest of the chapter. Streams encoded in non-scalable manner should be obtained in full in order for the receiver to be able to decode and play them out. Thus, limited adaptation options are provided by such streams, and they usually require transcoding the original streams into different ones. Scalable streams, in contrast, provide easier adaptation because they allow decoding of partial streams. Currently, non-scalable streams are widely used, while in the future it is expected that scalable streams gain more adoption, because of the increased diversity of the devices used for viewing multimedia content — these devices can range from high-end workstations with fast network access to limited-capacity cell phones and PDAs with low bit rate and noisy wireless channels. We present authentication schemes for non-scalable streams in Section 4.3, and for scalable streams in Section 4.4. In our presentation, we focus on the main ideas of the different schemes, as well as how they meet the requirements that we define in Section 4.2 and at what cost. We summarize all presented schemes and compare them against each other in Section 4.5. We conclude the chapter in Section 4.6 by outlining potential directions for future research on authentication of multimedia streams.

## 4.2. Background

In this section, we first propose a set of requirements that captures all dimensions of the multimedia stream authentication problem. Then, we present background materials and definitions that will be used throughout the chapter. A list of acronyms used in this chapter is given in the Appendix for a quick reference.

### 4.2.1. *Requirements for Multimedia Authentication Solutions*

Authentication of multimedia streams poses different challenges than authentication of regular data such as documents and software packages. We define six main requirements to study the multimedia stream authentication problem. We use these requirements in the rest of this chapter to evaluate and compare current solutions for the authentication problem. These requirements can also be used to guide the design of future multimedia stream authentication solutions.

- *R1: Authenticity.* The first and foremost requirement is ensuring that a received multimedia stream is authentic. That is, any malicious tampering with the media must be detected. Tampering can occur within frames (intra-frame) or across frames (inter-frame). Intra-frame tampering involves changing the visual content of individual images of the video. On the other hand, frame removal, insertion, or reordering are possible forms of inter-frame tampering.
- *R2: Robustness to Adaptations and Losses.* Multimedia streams are usually served to heterogeneous clients. Heterogeneity comes from many sources, including processing capacity, network bandwidth, network delay, and screen resolution. In addition, most multimedia streams are transported over the Internet, which is a dynamic environment with changing packet loss rates, delays, and available bandwidth. Therefore, multimedia systems need to dynamically *adapt* to network conditions and clients' available resources. This adaptation requires alterations of the multimedia streams (intra- and/or inter-frame). Thus, an important metric for any authentication scheme is whether it can verify the authenticity of an adapted, i.e., genuinely modified, multimedia stream. We call this metric robustness to adaptations.

As explained in the following subsection, adaptation of multimedia streams depends on the way they are encoded. Multimedia streams can be encoded in nonscalable or scalable manner; see [4] for a good overview of video coding. A nonscalable stream cannot be decoded unless its data is being fully received by the decoder. To adapt such streams, either the frame rate is reduced by dropping some frames, or a transcoding process is performed. Transcoding [5] means transforming the encoded steam into another stream with different bit rate and/or spatial resolution. A scalable stream, on the other hand, provides flexible and efficient adaptation by removing parts of the stream, while the remaining parts can be decoded. Note that when the media is scalably coded, its scalable structure should be preserved by the authentication scheme. This means that the authentication scheme should not dictate or limit possible truncation ways/points; all regular truncations should be acceptable and the truncated substream should be verifiable as authentic.

In addition to adaptation, it is desirable for the authentication scheme to be able to tolerate some data losses that may occur during the transportation of multimedia streams over lossy channels, which is the common case in real systems. Two types of losses should be considered: loss of the video data, and loss of the authentication information.

- *R3: Overheads and Client Buffer.* At least three types of overheads are imposed by an authentication scheme: computation, communication, and buffering. Computation overhead is the additional CPU cycles needed to create and verify the authentication information. The communication overhead is the number of bytes that the authentication information needs. In addition, some authentication schemes may require a client to receive (and buffer) a certain amount of data before it can start the verification process. Accounting for the overheads is important especially for supporting limited-capacity clients such as PDAs and cell phones, and for scaling the streaming servers.
- *R4: Online Production and Verification.* An important class of multimedia services is live streaming, in which multimedia streams need to be encoded and streamed in real-time. For such applications, the creation (or production) of the authentication information must be created in real time as well, and therefore cannot depend on or use future video data. In contrast, for pre-encoded multimedia streams in video on-demand systems, the production of the authentication information can be done offline. This means that the authentication scheme may have the freedom to choose any part of the stream in the authentication information. However, the verification of the stream authenticity need to be done in real time for both live and pre-encoded streams.
- *R5: Supported Transportation Modes.* There are several possible methods for transporting multimedia streams from their sources to destinations. These include unicast (one sender, one receiver) and multicast (one sender, multiple receivers). In addition, the presence of multimedia proxies as intermediaries between senders and receivers should be considered. Finally, a recent trend in

multimedia streaming is the use of multi-senders to one receiver, as in the case of distributed streaming for path diversity and better quality [6], and peer-to-peer streaming [7–10] because of the limited capacity of the senders. Therefore, it is important to assess the ability of the authentication scheme to function with different transportation methods.

- *R6: Number of Trusted Entities.* The final important metric for evaluating authentication schemes is the entities in the system that need to be trusted. Clearly, the fewer the number of the assumed-trusted entities is, the better the authentication scheme will be. The best case is to trust only the producer of the multimedia stream. Other third parties, e.g., proxies or peers, should not be trusted.

### 4.2.2. Background and Common Techniques

We provide below basic definitions, abbreviations, and functions that will be used in the rest of the chapter. These are divided into three classes: basic cryptographic functions, erasure codes to tolerate losses, and non-scalable and scalable video coding.

*Basic Cryptographic Functions.* Several cryptographic functions and techniques are usually used in authentication schemes. For more details see [11]. For example, Message Authentication Code (MAC) is used for assuring authenticity of a message using a secret key $K$. A MAC is a short digest calculated over an arbitrary-length message $x$ using the secret key $K$ as input, $y = MAC(x, K)$. Since they are based on symmetric cryptography, MAC codes are very inexpensive to compute. However, because of being based on a shared secret key, they cannot make a commitment between a message and one particular signer. That is, if one is able to verify a MAC, i.e., he or she has the key, then he or she is able to alter the message and compute a new forged MAC.

Another cryptographic primitive is the one-way hash function, which is very useful for providing authentication with low overhead. One-way hash functions take as input a message $x$ of any length and produce a fixed-length output, $y = h(x)$, to which we interchangeably refer as the hash value or the message digest. Given $x$, computation of $h(x)$ is easy, whereas if $y$ is given, finding $x$ is infeasible. Moreover, finding two messages $x_1$ and $x_2$ such that $h(x_1) = h(x_2)$ is infeasible. Therefore, if $h(\cdot)$ is a secure hash function, authenticity of $h(x)$ implies authenticity of the message $x$. SHA-1 [12] and MD5 [13] are two commonly-used such functions.

Digital signatures provide authentication as well as non-repudiation, i.e., the signer cannot repudiate or refuse the validity of his or her signature. Conventional digital signatures, such as RSA (by Rivest, Shamir, and Adleman) [14] and DSS (Digital Signature Standard) [15], are based on asymmetric cryptography, and are thus computationally expensive. Another type of digital signatures are one-time signatures, which use symmetric cryptographic functions to sing/verify a single message using a key pair, i.e., they cannot use the same key pair for authenticating multiple messages. However, they are much faster than conventional digital signatures such as RSA [14] and DSS [15].

*Erasure Codes to Tolerate Losses.* Authentication information as well as video data can be lost or damaged during transmission from sender to receivers. Forward Error Correction (FEC) is a class of methods that provides controllable robustness to data loss or damage. The idea is to intelligently introduce some redundancy to the data $D$ to be used in case of losses. The redundancy-added data is then split into $n$ pieces to be transmitted, where any subset of $k \leq n$ pieces can reconstruct the original message. That is, the loss of up to $n-k$ pieces can be tolerated. Information Dispersal Algorithm (IDA) [16] does that in a space-optimal way, that is, the length of each piece is equal to $|D|/k$. However, it has a quadratic decoding time. Tornado Codes [17] have linear coding and decoding time, but have a slight overhead; they are sub-optimal in terms of space overhead.

*Non-scalable and Scalable Video Coding.* A video consists of a sequence of images that have a strong temporal correlation. Taking advantage of such correlation, a video frame can be encoded predictively, i.e., encoded as the difference of its contents with a close previous or next one. However, not the entire video can be predictively coded; some frames need to be coded independently to act as synchronization points in the video for supporting VCR-like functionalities and for avoiding propagation of errors and losses. Therefore, besides inter-coded frames, some frames are intra-coded. Intra-coded video frames, which are called I-frames, are directly coded using transform coding, i.e., the way JPEG images are compressed. Inter-coded frames carry prediction information needed to re-construct the frame based on other frames. The prediction can be done using a single reference or by averaging the estimation obtained from two references; one earlier frame and a later one. Frames coded in the former way are called Predicted frames (P-frames) and those coded in the latter way are called Bidirectionally predicted frames (B-frames). I, P, and B frames in a sample video sequence are illustrated in Figure 4.1.

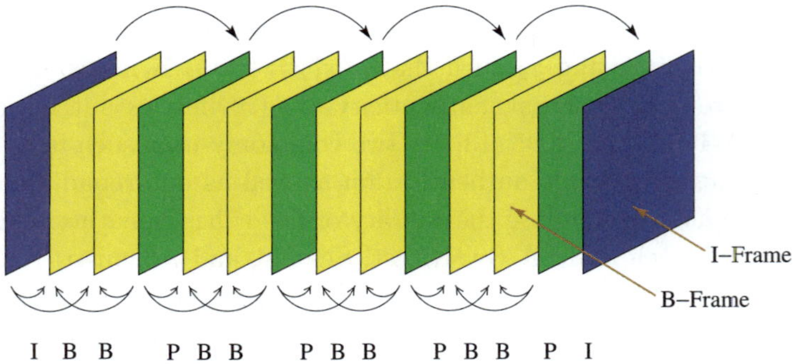


Fig. 4.1. I, P, and B frames in a video sequence.

The prediction basically consists of motion estimation. First, each image is segmented into macroblocks of $16 \times 16$ pixels. A macroblock, if inter-coded, is predictively coded as its displacement relative to the best matching macroblock in a reference frame. After motion estimation, prediction error blocks are DCT transformed, quantized, and finally run-length encoded. For more details on video coding please refer to ch. 9 of [18].

The above technique for video coding results in an efficiently encoded video with a single layer or quality level. That is, the stream needs to be decoded, and no partial substream can be decoded. Since devices participating in such sessions have different capabilities, multiple quality levels are needed. The traditional way for supporting this diversity is to encode the video into multiple separate streams with different qualities and bitrates. This requires storing and managing multiple files for each stream, and typically supports only a few levels of quality. Another technique is to encode the media into multiple streams that are partially disjoint, referring to each sub-stream as a description. In this technique, which is called Multiple Description Coding (MDC) [19], any subset of descriptions suffices to decode the original stream. The more the number of descriptions received, the higher the quality the receiver obtains. However, MDC has not been widely used, mainly due to its complexity and overhead. The more recent way of supporting receiver diversity is using scalable video coding.

The idea of scalable video coding is to create a single stream that can be partially received and decoded, based on capabilities of the receiver. Traditionally, a scalable video consists of a base layer and a number of enhancement layers that progressively improve the quality. Receiver devices ask for a proper number of layers or subscribe to multicast streams up to the layer they can receive and decode. This leads to less load on the transmitting server and higher efficiency for receivers to adapt to dynamic changes in network conditions. This traditional form of layered scalability is called Coarse-Grained Scalability (CGS). The base layer is the minimum receivable information that serves a low-quality video. Each enhancement layer needs and progressively enhances the video obtained from the base layer and previous enhancement layers. There are three common scalability techniques: temporal, spatial, and signal-to-noise ratio (SNR). In temporal scalability, the frame rate is decreased to lessen the bitrate of the video. Thus, videos re-constructed by each layer have same spatial resolution, but different frame rates. On the other hand, in spatial scalability, the spatial resolution of the image is customized. Hence, the frame rate of different-layer videos is the same but with different spatial resolutions. SNR scalability, which is also called quality or fidelity scalability [20], preserves the frame rate and the spatial resolution in different layer videos, but with different qualities, which is typically achieved by designating different quantization accuracies for the layers.

In CGS, each enhancement layer either should be received completely or has no enhancing effect. In order to overcome this defect, Fine-grained Scalability (FGS) is introduced [21,22] to make the scalability levels contiguous (with fine-granularity of 1 bit). That is, every received bit can be used for enhancing the quality. In FGS, the base layer can be coded using any motion-compensated prediction video coding method. The enhancement layer, which is the difference between the original image and the reconstructed image from the base layer, is coded based on a fine-granular coding method, such as bit-plane coding (used in MPEG-4 FGS [21]). Bit-plane coding consists of storing the zigzag-traversed quantized coefficients of each DCT block in the following manner. First, the most significant bit (MSB) of all coefficients is placed, which forms the first bit-plane. Then comes the second MSB of them, and so on. The resulting bit-planes are coded by (RUN, EOP) symbols. RUN is number of consecutive zeros before a 1, and EOP (end-of-plane) tells whether any 1 is left in the bit-plane or not. For example, the bit-plane $001000100\cdots00$ is represented as $[(2,0),(3,1)]$. Finally, this coded string is Variable-Length Coded (VLC) for more compactness to form the output bitstream.

FGS offers an excellent granularity, but the coding efficiency it provides is considerably less than CGS. One reason is that in MPEG-4 FGS, motion compensation is done only in the base layer. This results in elimination of any drift, i.e., the loss of an enhancement packet does not cause propagation of an error in other frames. However, lower coding efficiency is unavoidable, since the higher quality picture of an enhancement layer is not used for motion prediction. In addition, decoding FGS streams is more complicated that decoding CGS streams.

To strike a balance between CGS and FGS, Medium-Grained Scalability (MGS) is introduced as a part of the Scalable Video Coding (SVC) extension of the H.264/AVC Standard [20]. MGS comes with a hybrid of temporal and SNR/spatial scalability. Images of the coarsest temporal level are transmitted as *key pictures*, and only for these images the corresponding base layer is used in motion compensation. These key-pictures can be thought of as synchronization points for controlling drift propagation among video frames. For all other temporal refinement frames, the highest available quality image is used as reference for motion compensation. This is to improve coding efficiency. Furthermore, for offering finer granularity than CGS, MGS prioritizes packets of enhancement layers. Hence, packets with lower priorities are dropped if needed, and packet level granularity is provided. MGS follows a similar structure to CGS, but provides the feature that if part of an enhancement layer is lost, the received part is still usable.

## 4.3. Authentication of Data Streams and Nonscalable Video Streams

As mentioned in Section 4.2, while scalable streams are expected to be used in the future, most current streaming systems employ nonscalable video streams. It is therefore important to study the main authentication schemes for nonscalable streams. These schemes are summarized in this section. We start, in Section 4.3.1, by presenting authentication schemes for *data* streams, which address the authenticity of continuously generated data. The data can, for example, be stock quotes transmitted by a server, or measurements collected by monitoring sensors. Data stream authentication methods do not assume or use any characteristics of video streams such as temporal dependency and redundancy among successive video frames. Yet, they can be applied on packets belonging to video streams. In Section 4.3.2, we present authentication schemes explicitly designed for nonscalable *video* streams.

### 4.3.1. *Authentication of Data Streams*

Gennaro *et al.* in [23] introduced two techniques to authenticate offline and online (possibly infinite) data streams. For the former case, all packets of the stream are available for the authentication scheme, while in the latter, packets are authenticated as they are being generated. For offline streams, the technique puts the hash of each packet in its previous packet, then the first packet of the stream is signed. Therefore, the entire stream can be authenticated. Figure 4.2 illustrates this technique. For authenticating online streams, the authors use one-time signatures [24]. one-time signatures are much faster than conventional digital signatures that use asymmetric cryptography. The key pair for one-time signature, however, can be used to sign only one message. The authentication scheme is illustrated in Figure 4.3 and works as follows. With each packet $p_i$, a pair of public and private keys are generated for signing/verifying packet $p_{i+1}$. The public key to verify packet $p_{i+1}$ is inserted in packet $p_i$. Then the data of packet $p_i$ and the public key to verify packet $p_{i+1}$ are signed with the private key corresponding to packet $p_i$. The signature of a packet is attached to it before it is transmitted. Here, production of the signed stream can be done online, while it could not be in the former technique (hash chaining). Verification in both techniques can be done online; a packet is verified once it is received. The techniques require

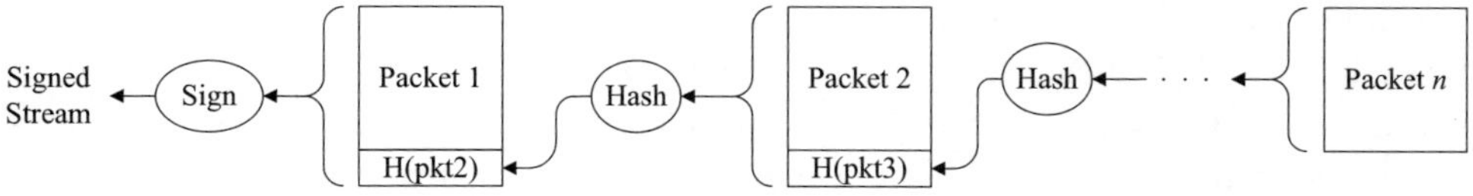


Fig. 4.2. Stream authentication using hash chaining.

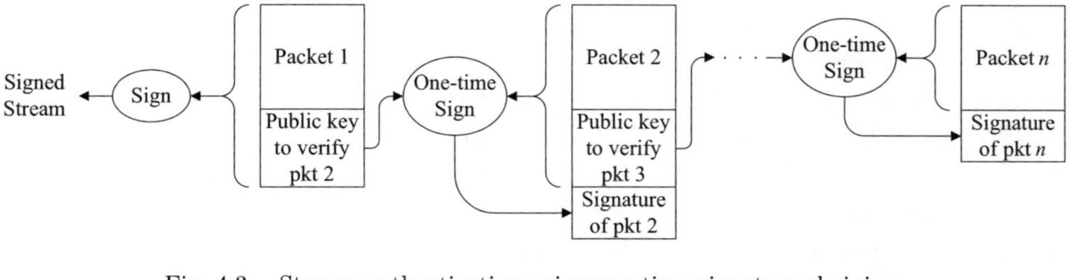


Fig. 4.3. Stream authentication using one-time signature chaining.

no expensive computation. However, the second one incurs high communication overhead inherited from one-time signatures. In both techniques, no buffering is needed for authentication purposes at the receiver side except for a hash value or public key of a one-time signature. Both techniques tolerate no packet loss, that is, they require reliable and in-order delivery of packets.

Wong and Lam [25] presented two techniques for stream authentication: star chaining and tree chaining. The authors also presented extensions to the Feig-Fiat-Shamir (FFS) [26] digital signature scheme to speed up the signing rate while keeping the verification rate as high as that of RSA [14]. In the two schemes presented, packets are divided into groups, and one signature is designated for each group. In star chaining, the digest and the signature of a group of $n$ packets $p_1, p_2, \ldots, p_n$ would simply be $H = h(h(p_1)||h(p_2)|| \ldots ||h(p_n))$ and $Sign(H)$ respectively, where $h(\cdot)$ is a one-way hash function and $||$ denotes concatenation. In order for each packet to be individually verifiable, each packet needs to carry the signature of the group it belongs to, its location in the group, and the hash of other packets. Thus, the communication overhead is linearly proportional to the group size.

In the tree chaining technique, a balanced binary Merkle hash tree is built over packets of each group. In a Merkle hash tree, each node represents the digest of its children. The root of this tree is then signed. Due to the collision-free property of the hash function, the whole set of leaf packets is authenticated if the root of the tree is successfully verified. In order to verify a packet without having the entire group, we need to traverse the tree from the node corresponding to the given packet to the root by reconstructing each node on the path, and to verify the root digest using the given signature. Note that for this procedure, only siblings of the nodes on the path are needed. Therefore, each packet carries the signature of the group, its location in the group, and the set of siblings on the path from it to the root. Hence, the communication overhead is logarithmically proportional to the group size. For example, if SHA-1 [12] is used as the message digest algorithm and 1024-bit RSA [14] is used as the digital signature scheme, each packet in a group of 64 packets would carry $20 \times 6 + 128 = 248$ bytes, which is considered low for packets of a few kilobytes and high for packets of broadcast scenarios with smaller sizes. The computational cost of these two schemes is in tradeoff with the delay and buffering overheads, and both depend on the group size and packet rate. For having low computational cost, the delay and buffer would be longer. Since each packet is individually verifiable, packet loss has no impact on this scheme, assuming that a packet together with its authentication information either arrives or gets lost. This scheme functions in any transportation scenario, with only the producer needed to be trusted.

Perrig *et al.* proposed TESLA (Timed Efficient Stream Loss-tolerant Authentication) and EMSS (Efficient Multi-chained Stream Signature) in [27] to authenticate online streams in presence of packet losses. The core idea is to take advantage of the online nature of the stream. That is, after a packet is received, any forgery on the content of that packet is of no danger. The authentication procedure is similar to hash chaining somehow. The Message Authentication Code (MAC) digest is calculated for packet $p_i$ using a key $k_i$, and the digest is appended to the packet itself. The key $k_i$ needed to verify the authenticity of packet $p_i$ is embedded in a later packet $p_{i+d}$, where $d$ is a delay parameter. Therefore, when calculating the MAC of packet $p_i$, the key that $p_i$ carries ($k_{i-d}$), should be taken into account as well. For assuring security, the receiver must make sure that $p_i$ is arrived before the sender sends out $p_{i+d}$. Otherwise, if $p_{i+d}$ is already sent out, the MAC key $k_i$ that is carried by $p_{i+d}$ is revealed and $p_i$ is exposed to forgery. Therefore, the value $d$ plays a key role. It depends on parameters such as packet rate, network conditions, and maximum tolerable verification delay. Because the packet rate may be variable, the delay parameter is determined based on a time interval basis, not on a packet index basis. Accordingly, there is a need for time synchronization between the sender and receivers, though loose, but with an uncertainty below a threshold. This synchronization lets receivers check the security condition for a packet, i.e., whether or not the packet is received before its key is revealed, without knowing the exact sending schedule of each packet.

For working with time-based indices, the sender groups the packets into time intervals, and uses the same MAC key for all packets within each interval. Note that the number of packets in each interval may vary, while the time it takes to transmit the packets of an interval is fixed. In addition to the payload and its MAC, each packet in the "$i + d$"th interval carries its interval index and the MAC key for packets of the "$i$"th interval. For the value $d$, there is a tradeoff between the packet rate and the tolerable delay, which determines the packet buffer size. If packets are expected to be verified almost immediately, packets of the "$i + 1$"st interval must not be sent out before packets of the "$i$"th interval are received by all receivers. On the other hand, if packet rate is to be arbitrarily high, the value $d$ needs to be large enough. Therefore, for supporting heterogeneous receivers with various buffering capabilities and different delays relative to the origin, multiple MAC key chains are designated with different $d$ values. However, besides the communication overhead it brings, the buffering needed at a receiver far from the origin is a problem, especially for devices with limited capabilities. Packet loss is tolerated in TESLA by correlating the MAC keys. Each key $K_i$ can be calculated using any later key $K_j (j > i)$, since the keys $K_1, \ldots, K_{n-1}$ are the result of consecutively applying a pseudorandom function $F(\cdot)$ on a random number $K_n$ (the last key), i.e., $K_i = F(K_{i+1})$. Therefore, if a key $K_j$ was not received due to packet loss, it is retrievable from subsequent keys. Note that knowledge of $K_i$ does not reveal any information about $K_{i+1}$ or other later keys.

As an improvement on TESLA, EMSS provides the non-repudiation feature, and it does not require any time synchronization. On the other hand, it loses some error robustness and has more computational cost. For a group of packets, the hash of each packet is put in some later packets of the group. Then, a signature is put in the last packet of the group. The signature suffices for certifying authenticity of the entire group of packets. While the sender does not have to buffer any packet, the need for keeping a buffer of packets exists at the receiver side, and immediate verification of packets is not possible, because the receiver must wait till the last packet of the group. In order to deal with packet losses, the authors proposed to use Information Dispersal Algorithm (IDA [16]) with EMSS to split a hash value over multiple later packets.

Computations needed for TESLA are inexpensive, since they only consists of MAC calculations. Computational cost of EMSS depends on the size of packet groups, i.e., on the rate of signature packets in the packet stream. If they are not so frequent, computational overhead is lower, but the receiver delay and buffer size are higher. Communication overhead of TELSA depends on the number of MAC key chains (designated for different $d$ values), which is low in case of using very few chains. Communication overhead of EMSS depends on its packet group size, and the parameters of the IDA algorithm, which is in tradeoff with tolerability of packet loss.

The above authors extended their TESLA in [28] to provide immediate authentication. That is to avoid requiring buffering of packets at the receiver side. Like TESLA, in packet $p_i$ a MAC of packet $p_i$ is inserted whose key will come in packet $p_{i+vd}$, as well as the hash of that later packet $p_{i+vd}$. $d$ is the delay parameter as in TESLA, and $v$ is the number of packets in each time interval. Intuitively, this is sort of shifting the buffering requirement from receiver side to sender side, and also increasing the delay, in order to avoid receiver costs. $p_{i+vd}$ will be immediately authenticated given that the authenticity of packet $p_i$ is already verified, since the certified hash of $p_{i+vd}$ has come with $p_i$ before. In case of losing $p_i$, $p_{i+vd}$ can still be authenticated. This time, it is done by its MAC, whose key will come in packet $p_{i+2vd}$. Therefore, The receiver needs to buffer only those packets whose authenticity is not immediately verified, because earlier packets containing their hashes have been lost. Note that in applications were the data packets have to be consumed in-order, the need for buffering a packet and waiting for its MAC key also indicates waiting for all of its subsequent packets, unless we drop the waiting packet instead of buffering it; this is not a rational choice. Therefore, a packer loss causes a short pause in consumption of data at the receiver side. Note that the need to afford the buffer still exists, even though it is not always full. Like TESLA, computation and communication overheads of this scheme are low. Particularly, MAC key chains are designated appropriately in a way that multiple MAC key chains, which let receivers with lower network delays experience shorter key disclosure delays, are utilized with only one key per packet.

Park *et al.* [29] presented SAIDA (Signature Amortization using Information Dispersal Algorithm) for stream authentication. SAIDA divides the stream into groups of $m$ packets. Then, it hashes each packet and concatenates the hash values. Let us denote that by $F = h(p_1)||h(p_2)||\cdots||h(p_m)$. $F$ along with a signature

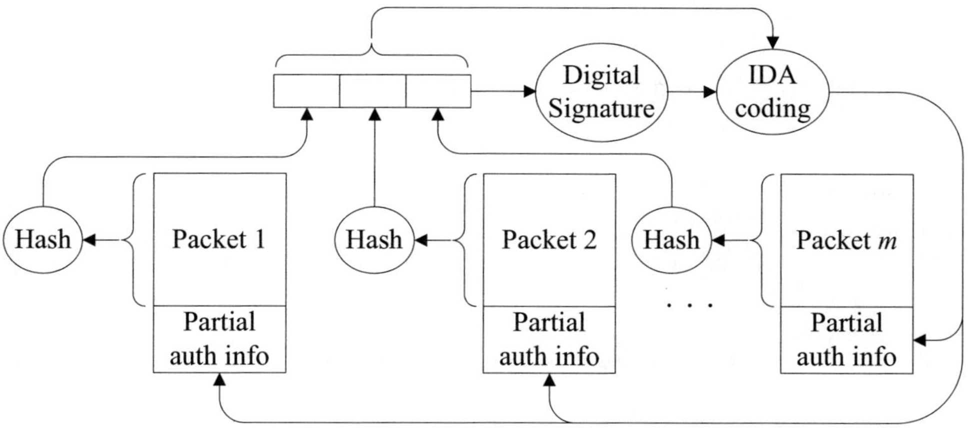


Fig. 4.4. Stream authentication using SAIDA.

on $h(F)$ is IDA coded into $m$ chunks and split over all packets of the group. Any $k(\leq m)$ chunks suffice to re-construct the hashes and the signature to verify authenticity of the entire group. The SAIDA authentication scheme is illustrated in Figure 4.4. In SAIDA, the tradeoff between verification delay, loss resilience, and communication/computation overhead is controllable by changing the parameters $m$ and $k$. Typically, as always, if low computations are desired, the delay and the buffer would be longer. Both the sender and the receivers have to wait and buffer packets of a group till almost the end of the group. Pannetrat *et al.* [30] developed an improvement of SAIDA, which follows a similar procedure to SAIDA, but uses a more systematic way of employing FEC coding to reduce the overhead. Like SAIDA, it requires arrival of a group of packets (or a possibly large portion of it) to verify authenticity of any of the packets in the group.

Habib *et al.* [31] presented TFDP (Tree-based Forward Digest Protocol) for the many-to-one media streaming scenario, where that "many" are not necessarily trusted. As in SAIDA [29], the data is partitioned into blocks, each of which consists of a number of packets. However, only one signature is generated for the whole stream, not one for each block. Similar to tree chaining [25], hash values of packets are placed as leaves of a Merkle hash tree [32]. Packets belonging to the same block will be children of one node corresponding to that block. Thus, the second deepest depth of the tree consists of nodes associated with packet blocks. Then, the Merkle hash tree is completed over these nodes. Figure 4.5 depicts a sample of such structure over 12 blocks (packets of each block are not shown). In this figure, the leaves of the tree are hash values corresponding to data blocks $B_1, B_2, \ldots, B_{12}$. Each higher level node consists of hash of its children. At the beginning of the streaming session, the client authenticates himself to the server and receives the root of the hash tree along with a list of senders. The client asks one of the senders for digests needed to verify a number ($n$) of blocks. Having received the digests, the client

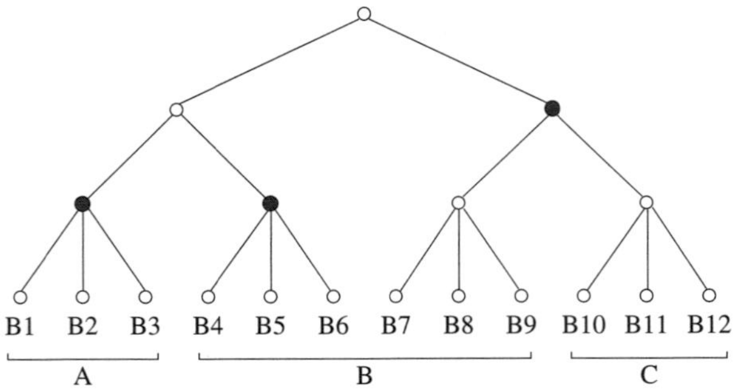


Fig. 4.5. Stream authentication using TFDP [31].

checks their genuineness by re-calculating the root hash. Once verified, they can be used for verifying authenticity of the $n$ data blocks, one by one once they arrive. In the example of Figure 4.5, the client asks node $A$ for digests needed to verify the first three data blocks. These digests are highlighted in the figure with dark circles. As can be seen, the root hash is computable using these digests. The client repeats the same procedure for the next sets of blocks; it asks $B$ and $C$ for digests needed to verify data blocks $B_4, \ldots, B_9$ and $B_{10}, \ldots, B_{12}$ respectively. Using this method, the overhead is amortized over a number of blocks. Robustness against packet loss is achieved by FEC-coding the digests. The client only has to buffer packets of one block. However, because the whole tree is constructed and the root hash is signed before beginning to stream any packet, this scheme is not suitable for live streaming.

In addition to various techniques we reviewed above, a number of works have focused on the loss resilience aspect of the stream authentication schemes. The basic idea is to attach the hash of a packet to multiple packets. In general, they divide the stream of packets into groups, and designate a signature for each group. The group can be modeled by a Directed Acyclic Graph (DAG), whose nodes represent data packets and each directed edge from node $A$ to node $B$ indicates that the hash of packet $A$ is attached to packet $B$, i.e., if packet $B$ is verified then packet $A$ is verified. The hash chaining technique [23] we saw at the beginning of this section is thus modeled by a graph of $n$ nodes ($n$ is the number of packets), which has $n - 1$ directed edges each of which is from a node $i\,(2 \leq i \leq n)$ to node $i - 1$, and the first packet is signed. Generally, a packet is verifiable if there is a path from its corresponding node to the signature node. When loss occurs in the group of packets, some nodes of the graph and their associated edges are removed, which threatens the verifiability of some received packets. Golle and Modadugu [33] build such DAG, initially by attaching the hash of each packet $p_i$ to packets $p_{i+1}$ and $p_{i+a}$, where $a$ is an integer parameter that affects resistance against bursty losses as well as receiver delay/buffer. Then, in order to shift some buffering load from receiver to sender side, a number of additional packets as well as their relevant edges are inserted in the chain to make it an *augmented chain*. Song *et al.* [34]

proposed the use of expander graphs, which have the property that every subset of the nodes has many neighbors. Zhang *et al.*[35] proposed to use butterfly graphs, where the nodes are divided into a number of stages, and each node of a stage is linked to two nodes of its previous stage, while there is no link between two nodes of the same stage. Zhu *et al.* [36] also proposed to put the nodes into a number of layers and link the nodes between two adjacent layers. Butterfly graphs impose a number of limitations: they have fixed overhead, they do not work for any arbitrary number of packets, and the signature packet size grows in proportion to packet group size. Thus, the authors later extended their work to utilize a more generalized butterfly graph [37]. These works differ mainly in their packet loss resilience capability. Their overheads, delay, and buffering requirements are roughly the same as the other works [25,29] summarized above, which divide packets into groups and designate one signature for each group. However, the graph-based approaches have typically a higher communication overhead, since multiple hash values (at least 2) are designated for each packet, while for example SAIDA [29] with about 1.5 hash values per packet (using FEC) achieves a high robustness of over 95% against bursty losses at rate 20%.

### 4.3.2. *Non-scalable Media Stream Authentication*

Now, we present authentication schemes that use some characteristics of the video stream. Liang *et al.* [38] proposed a method for extracting a content-based feature vector from video. The goal is to inexpensively extract the feature vector such that it is robust against transcoding operations. The feature vector is then embedded back into the video as a watermark. The authentication scheme works as follows. The video sequence is divided into shots using the algorithm proposed in [39]. A feature vector is computed for each shot. For each shot, the DCT coefficient blocks of all I-frames (intra-coded frames) are averaged to form a distribution matrix $M$ for the shot. I-frames are chosen because the authors assume that they are not changed in many video transcoding operations such as frame dropping. The matrix $M$ is divided into $m$ sub-regions where $m$ is the length of the desired binary feature vector. If the total number of macroblocks of a frame is $n$, each sub-region would contain $n/m$ macroblocks. Denote the energy of each sub-region by $E_i (1 \leq i \leq m)$, which is the sum of coefficient values of all blocks inside the sub-region. Also, let $E_c$ denote the median value of "$E_i$"s. Each bit $b_i$ of the feature vector of the shot is obtained by comparing $E_i$ to $E_c$. That is, $b_i = 0$ if $E_i < E_c$, and $b_i = 1$ otherwise. The feature vector, which is roughly to reflect the energy distribution of frames in the shot, is coded using a secret key and embedded back into the luminance blocks of video frames. The scheme depends on a shared key between the two parties of the communication, which is not desirable. Besides, I-frames are not always invariant. The video cannot be generated in an online manner, neither can its verification be. More importantly, the result of shot determination at the sender side (on the original video) and at the receiver side (on the transcoded/tampered vide) are assumed the same, while they may not be so. In this scheme, the energy distribution used as the feature vector does not have strong security; it may be possible for an attacker to change the video in a "meaningful" way while preserving the energy distribution used as the feature vector. Moreover, P- and B-frames are left totally unprotected.

Sun *et al.* [40] extended an earlier work of theirs on image authentication [41] for video authentication with robustness against transcoding. In [41], some content-based invariant features of an image are extracted, and the feature vector is FEC-coded. The resulting codeword can be partitioned into two parts: the feature vector itself and parity check bits. Only the parity check bits are taken as a Message Authentication Code (MAC) for the image and are then embedded back into the image as a watermark. Furthermore, the whole FEC codeword (extracted feature vector and its parity check bits) is hashed and then signed to form the signature of the image. The signature can either be attached to the image or again be embedded back into the image as another watermark. At the receiver side, to verify the authenticity, the feature vector is extracted from the content, which together with the watermark (parity check bits) can re-construct the FEC codeword whose signed hash is received and ready for verification. Feature extraction and watermark embedding are done in the transform domain, since transcoding operations are usually performed in that domain. Three inputs must be given to this scheme: the producer's key pair (for signing and verification), the authentication strength (a degree for distinguishing between benign and malicious manipulations), and possible transcoding ways. Possible transcodings considered in this paper are re-quantization, frame dropping, and frame resizing. Robustness against re-quantization is achieved by following the approach taken in an earlier work [42]. Basically, it considers the invariance of the relationship between two coefficients in a block pair before and after JPEG compression. Frame-dropping is tolerated by FEC coding the watermark bitstream of a frame over multiple frames instead of in the frame itself alone. For surviving against frame-resizing transcodings, such as conversion from Common Intermediate Format (CIF) to Quarter CIF (QCIF) (from $352 \times 288$ to $176 \times 144$ resolution), the invariant features can be extracted in either QCIF or CIF, while the watermark is embedded in CIF in such a way that it is still extractable from the corresponding QCIF video [43]. In this scheme, high computational cost of digital signatures can be relaxed by dividing the frames into groups and performing the above operations on the group. Thus, sender and receiver delay as well as receiver buffering are necessary. This scheme requires only the producer of the video to be trusted, is applicable to multiple-senders scenario, and has low communication overhead.

As an example of a watermark embedding technique for authentication, Zhang *et al.* [44] targeted watermarking of the popular video format H.264/AVC [45]. In H.264/AVC standard, a $16 \times 16$ macroblock can be partitioned into sub-macroblocks of smaller sizes for better quality and higher coding efficiency. The best mode for a macroblock is selected among all possible modes using the Lagrangian optimization technique of H.264/AVC. It can be observed that for stationary areas of the picture that have no motion, a partition mode of $16 \times 16$ is the best. On the other hand, for the areas having a lot of detailed motions, smaller sub-macroblock sizes are desired. Watermark bits are embedded in these small partition modes, since in such areas of the picture it is more difficult for the human eye to detect the little distortion imposed by the watermark. In motion error blocks of smaller partitioning modes, all non-zero DCT coefficients starting from the 10th one are replaced with the watermark symbols. This process is integrated with the Lagrangian optimization technique done for H.264/AVC encoding to have minimal rate-distortion performance penalty.

Another instance of content-based approaches is the scheme presented by Pradeep *et al.* [46] for video authentication based on Shamir's secret sharing [47]. They divide a video into shots, and then extract a number of key frames from each shot. The goal is to calculate three levels of authentication frames in the raw image domain that are robust against lossy compressions while sensitive to malicious manipulations. The three authentication levels create one authentication frame for (i) each sequence of frames between two successive key frames, (ii) each shot, and (iii) the whole video. First, shots are determined using an arbitrary shot boundary detection algorithm. Then, for each video frame of a given shot, the luminance values of pixels are quantized, which maps similar pixels into the same value. After quantization, assuming the first and last frames of a shot are key frames, the rest of key frames are extracted. For each frame, a differential energy value between the frame and the last key frame is computed and compared to a threshold to determine whether the frame is the next key frame or not. After determining key frames, assuming $F_i$ and $F_j$ $(j > i)$ are two consecutive key frames within the given shot, an authentication frame $F_{auth}$ for the sequence of frames $F_{i+1}, F_{i+2}, \ldots, F_{j-1}$ located between $F_i$ and $F_j$ is obtained as the following. In $F_{auth}$, each pixel $P_{auth}(x, y)$ is obtained based on the (quantized) luminance value of pixels located at $(x, y)$ in $F_{i+1}, F_{i+2}, \ldots, F_{j-1}$, say $P_{i+1}(x, y), P_{i+2}(x, y), \ldots, P_{j-1}(x, y)$. From this sequence of quantized luminance values, only unique values are chosen, and the rest are ignored. Then, using polynomial interpolations, similar to that of an $(r, r)$ secret sharing threshold scheme [47], and a shared secret key, the value of $P_{auth}(x, y)$ is calculated. Some weights can be given as input to make some regions of the picture more important in the authentication process, such as face, after a face recognition algorithm determines the position of face in a set of frames. The authentication frames described above are called key-secrets, i.e., authenticators at key-frame level. The next level of authenticators, shot-secrets, are calculated in a similar fashion for each shot using key-secrets and key-frames of the shot. Lastly, a master-secret is similarly computed to form the authenticator of the whole video. These three levels of signatures can be used for different scenarios: where real-time verification of authenticity is more important, where robustness against frame dropping is more important, and where authentication can be done offline, for the three aforementioned levels, respectively. For verification, a real number is calculated between 0 and 1 as a measure of how significantly the video has been changed. That is done by comparing the authentication frame received and the one calculated over the received video. The comparison is done block by block (blocks of $8 \times 8$ pixels) with respect to the weight of each block, which is in turn calculated from the input weights.

In this scheme, the quantization factor can control the boundary between benign and malicious manipulations, but there is no clear such boundary, i.e., there is no totally-clear choice for this and other threshold parameters. Computations needed include expensive interpolations and extrapolations. They might be unaffordable by some users. If high security and low robustness is desired, the quantization factor should be small. Consequently, computation and communication cost would be significantly higher due to the increase in the degree of polynomial being interpolated and extrapolated. The authenticated video cannot be produced online. Also, verification is delayed at least until the reception of the next key frame. Verification delay can be shortened by changing the parameter governing the key frame extraction process so as to extract more key frames, i.e., decreasing the differential energy threshold parameter. However, a larger number of key frames in turn increases computation and communication overhead. In this scheme, there must be some secrets shared between the sender and the receiver. In addition to problems related to agreeing upon a secret, the video is exposed to malicious operations by legitimate users of the system. More importantly, the techniques used for calculating a signature over a sequence of frames (after quantization and removal of similar values) could have been simply replaced by MAC codes, which would have had equal security at much lower computational cost.

For detecting forgery of offline (recorded) videos, Wang *et al.* [48] approached authentication of MPEG-coded video by detecting the effects of double MPEG compression. Recall the video coding process where each Group of Pictures (GoP) consists of an I-frame followed by a number of P- and B-frames. When a sequence of frames is removed from (or inserted to) a video and the video is encoded again, the type (I, P, or B) of some frames could change. Accordingly, two frames belonging to a GoP in the new video might belong to two different GoPs in the old one. Since the retrieved content of P- and B-frames is mainly based on the motion vectors, there is a strong correlation between frames belonging to the same GoP. However, when some frames are in different GoPs in the old video and in the same GoP in the new one, this correlation becomes weaker, and the motion error is increased; this increased motion error is observed periodically in the video sequence. In addition to migration between GoPs, there is another effect when a video is compressed twice. For the I-frames that still remain I-frame in the new coded video, the quantization factor would be different if the old and new videos are encoded at different bitrates. Such double quantization results in a detectable statistical pattern that occurs periodically in the histogram of DCT coefficients. Taking advantage of these two behaviors, a forgery can be detected. However, there is a possibility to do removal or insertion in the video without letting the above techniques notice, e.g., removing/inserting one or more entire GoPs, and re-encoding with same quantization factors. Thus, the security of this scheme is questionable.

## 4.4. Scalable Media Authentication

Authentication of scalable multimedia streams has received less attention in the literature than authentication of nonscalable streams. Zhu *et al.* [49] surveyed a number of earlier works on scalable media security. In regards to authentication, a few scalable authentication schemes for JPEG 2000 images are surveyed in [50–52], but no work about authentication of scalable video (streaming or offline) is presented. This section provides a survey on different methods of authenticating scalable multimedia streams.

An authentication scheme for a scalable media bitstream must be able to authenticate all valid substreams that can be extracted from it. In order to achieve that, most previous works for authentication of scalable media are based on two techniques: hash chaining and Merkle hash trees. These works are surveyed in Sections 4.4.1 and 4.4.2, respectively.

### 4.4.1. *Approaches Based on Hash Chaining*

In an early work on scalable media authentication, Skraparlis [53] proposed to extend stream authentication techniques, e.g., hash chaining or tree chaining (see Section 4.3.1 for these methods), to two dimensions. One dimension is time (the temporal axis) and the other one is the video layers. Thus, a single media stream is stored on the server and different sub-streams can be extracted and successfully verified.

A similar framework is presented in [54]. Basically, video frames can be chained by attaching the hash of each frame to its previous one, and signing the first frame. For supporting scalable media, the chain is extended to two dimensions. The hash of each enhancement layer is attached to the previous layer, and hash of the base layer of a frame is attached to the base layer of its previous frame. The hash of the very first base layer is then signed. This authentication scheme is illustrated in Figure 4.6.

Computation and communication overheads of this method are low. Besides, it requires only a small buffer at the receiver side to keep some hash values; video frames/layers need not to be buffered for authentication purposes. Security is high since the content is deterministically verified based on a collision-free hash. Although verification of the received stream can be done online, the authenticated stream cannot be produced online. In other words, the framework is not applicable for live streaming. Proxies conducting adaptations are not involved in the authentication, so the only entity needed to be trusted is the producer of the video. The scheme is designed for coarse-grained scalability and is not applicable to medium- and fine-grained scalable videos. Lastly, when used for streaming, this framework is very

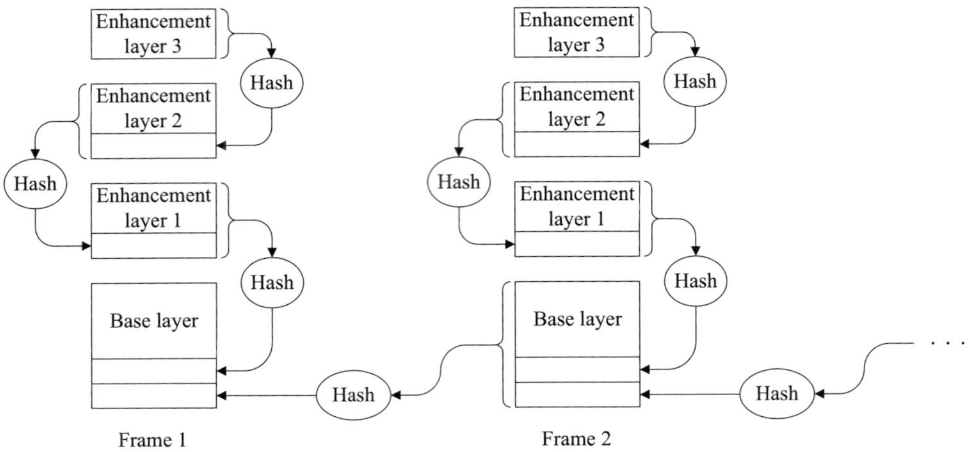


Fig. 4.6. Two-dimensional hash chaining for scalable media.

sensitive to packet loss. An improvement on this framework is presented in [55] to achieve loss resilience by using Multiple Description Coding (MDC) [19], which increases the overhead considerably.

### 4.4.2. *Approaches Based on Hash Trees*

Li *et al.* [56] proposed an authentication framework for multi-source streaming of MPEG-4 media. The proxies, at which adaptations are done, and the sources are assumed to be trusted. The MPEG-4 hierarchical structure is utilized to form the authentication data. An MPEG-4 Video Sequence (VS) consists of a number of Video Objects (VOs) [57]. Each VO is encoded as multiple Video Object Layers (VOLs), which enables scalable transmission. A VOL includes a sequence of two-dimensional shapes at different time intervals called Video Object Planes (VOPs). VOPs are partitioned into $16 \times 16$ macroblocks, which are in turn divided into $8 \times 8$ blocks. This is illustrated in Figure 4.7. According to this tree-like structure of MPEG-4, each source builds a hash tree over the group of packets it is providing, and sings the root. These signatures form the authentication data. For truncation adaptations, the hash of the truncated part of this tree is signed and appended to the authentication data by the proxy. In case of adaptations consisting of truncation and insertion from multiple stream sources, the proxy removes authentication information of removed sub-trees and adds those of the inserted sub-trees along with its signature on them. The authentication information of a group of packets is distributed over the packets using FEC coding to tolerate packet loss. For reducing the size of signatures, aggregate signature schemes are used. Such signature can aggregate $n$ signatures made on $n$ distinct messages from $n$ signers into a single signature (see [58] for the details of such a scheme). Despite the reduction in size of signatures, the cost of verification at the receiver side grows in proportion to

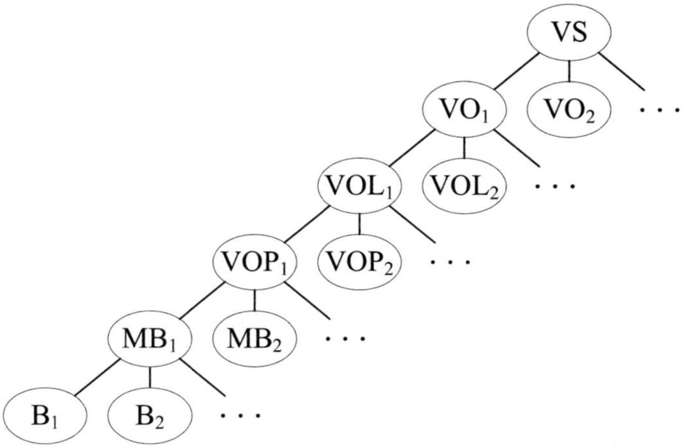


Fig. 4.7. Hierarchical structure of an MPEG-4 video sequence.

the number of proxies that have done adaptations, which might be several. The adaptation cost is even higher, because it requires generation of a digital signature, which is much more expensive than signature verification. Therefore, the high load on proxies limits the scalability of the framework. In this scheme, the authenticated video cannot be produced online. Moreover, verification is not possible in real-time; it is delayed because the receiver has to wait for the reception of many packets before being able to verify them. In the meanwhile, the receiver has to buffer received packets. Lastly, the method does not support fine-grained scalability of the media.

The use of Merkle tree for multimedia authentication is also suggested by Kaced *et al.* [59]. They divide the content into media objects, and place them as leaves of a balanced binary tree to be hashed as a Merkle hash tree. The producer side signs the root of the tree. This signature forms the initial authentication data. Having removed some media objects or inserted some adapted ones, proxies perform necessary updates to the tree and modify the authentication data. For removal, the extra verification data needed to successfully re-build the tree is supplied. For insertion of new content, such as a new format of some media objects, proxies need to sign the inserted content. The verification key (or the location to retrieve it) for signatures of proxies is already signed by the original producer. Similar to the method in [56], there is a heavy load on proxies doing adaptations, and also on receivers especially if the media is passed through multiple proxies. Moreover, the approach is not applicable for online streaming, since neither production of the video nor its verification can be done in an online manner. Accordingly, media objects need to be buffered until they are verified. However, unlike [56], random packet loss is not handled. The authors presented the implementation of their work in [60].

Suzuki *et al.* [61] proposed a similar approach. However, for insertion they make an enhancement by using a trapdoor hash function. Being denoted by $H_Y(m, r)$, it is similar to a typical hash function $H(m)$, but has a pair of public and private keys $Y$ and $X$. $Y$ is needed for verification. On the other hand, knowing $X$ lets an entity obtain a separate pair of messages $(m', r')$ whose hash is the same as a given hash value: $H_Y(m', r') = H_Y(m, r)$. A proxy generates random values $m, r$, calculates $T = H_Y(m, r)$, and sends it to the original producer to be signed. Now the proxy has a placeholder $T$. Later, when the proxy needs to insert some media data $m'$, it computes $r'$ such that $H_Y(m', r') = T$, which is already certified by the server. Space overhead of placeholders can be reduced by structuring them as Merkle trees and using a simple modification to use a single placeholder for multiple times. However, computation of such hash values is very expensive, because it involves modular exponentiation and multiplication. The space overhead of this scheme is proportional to the number of proxies that have done adaptations, but can be reduced using aggregate signatures. Again, online production of the media and online verification of it are not possible; same as the above similar method. Accordingly, the client has to buffer stream packets until they are verified.

Gentry *et al.* [62] approach authentication of scalable streams by hash chains and Merkle trees. They also consider the case when the producer produces multiple versions of the streams such that a proxy may dynamically switch between these versions. Denote the $m$ streams by $M^{(1)}, \ldots, M^{(m)}$ and the $n$ frames of stream $j$ by $M_1^{(j)}, \ldots, M_n^{(j)}$. In their first scheme, called LISSA, each frame of each stream is first hashed. Then, the hash values of the first frame of all streams, i.e., $M_1^{(1)}, M_1^{(2)}, \ldots, M_1^{(j)}$, are combined to generate the hash of the overall first frame. The hashes of the rest of the frames are computed in a similar fashion. Then, these hash values are combined to be signed for forming the signature of all streams. Therefore, for each frame, proxies send $m - 1$ extra hash values. Although the communication overhead may be reduced by modifications such as grouping before hashing, it is still considerable. In this scheme, production of the authenticated media cannot be done in an online manner, but its verification can be. The authors of LISSA propose a second scheme, called TRESSA, in which they compute a Merkle hash tree for each stream and sign the combination of the roots. The combination of roots may be tree-like or chain-like. Again, upon modification the proxy sends necessary additional information. In this scheme, verification cannot be done online. In both schemes in [62], computations are not expensive since they only consist of hash computations. Furthermore, random loss is tolerated using FEC. Lastly, although proxies conducting adaptations are involved in authentication mechanism, they need not to be trusted.

Wu *et al.* [63] presented three authentication schemes for MPEG-4 streams. In the first scheme, called flat authentication, data units (e.g., groups of bytes) of a packet are hashed and then XORed to form the hash of the packet. These packet hashes are then concatenated (along with their indices) and hashed to form the hash value of the packet group, which is then signed. When a proxy removes a number of data units of a packet, it adds the XOR of their hashes to the packet. Thus, a receiver can still verify the authenticity of the packet group, given that the proxies are trusted. In their second scheme, packet hashes are computed as follows. Denoting data units of packet $p_i$ by $p_{i_1}, p_{i_2}, \ldots, p_{i_n}$, where priority of each unit $p_{i_j}$ is higher than the next one $p_{i_{j+1}}$, the progressive hash of packet $p_i$ would be $h(H_1||i)$ where $H_i = h(p_i||H_{i+1})$. Hence, unlike in the flat authentication scheme, in this scheme a malicious proxies cannot insert content. Because hashes are chained together and alteration becomes impractical due to the one-way property of the hash function. In the third scheme, hierarchical authentication, a Merkle tree is built with the hierarchical structure of MPEG-4, similar to [56]. The leaves of the tree are the smallest units: blocks of $8 \times 8$ pixels. As we get far from the bottom of the tree, less-deep levels in the tree correspond to macroblocks, VOPs, VOLs, and VOs. They are arranged with respect to their priorities. For example, in a VO, $VOL_1$ has more priority than $VOL_2$, because $VOL_2$ is prior than $VOL_1$ for dropping. Thus, $VOL_2$ would be a child of $VOL_1$ in the tree, and $VOL_1$ a child of the VO itself. On the other hand, this relationship does not exist between the VOP and macroblock level: all macroblocks of a VOP are direct children of it; no macroblock would be a child of another macroblock. This structure is illustrated in Figure 4.8. After completely building this tree, the hash of the root is signed. For bitrate reduction, when dropping a sub-tree, the proxy replaces it by the corresponding hash value. Based on the erasure correction coding, verification is done when a certain number of packets of a group are received to recover the signature and packet hash values.

In the last two schemes above, only the producers need to be trusted. The security is high since authenticity of the content can be deterministically verified assuming a collision-free hash and a secure digital signature. The number of hash

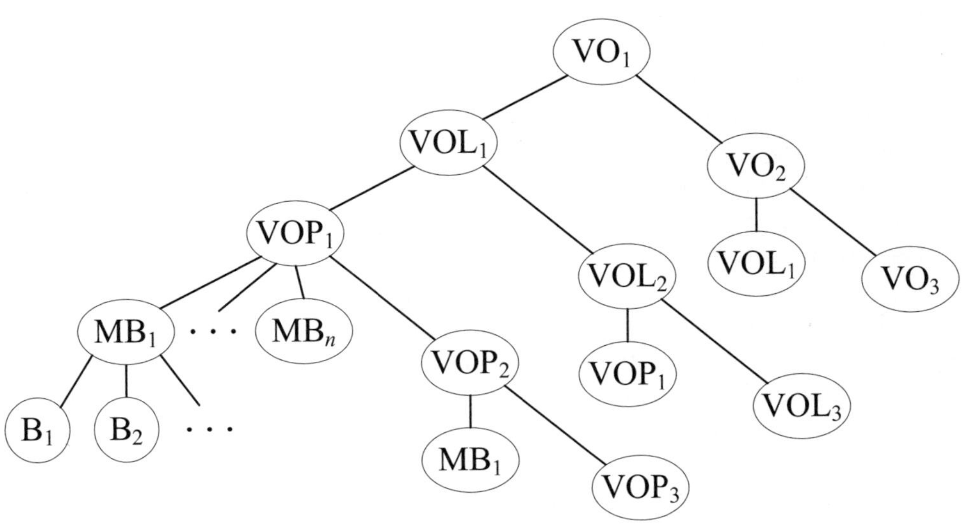


Fig. 4.8. Tree structure for the layers based on priorities.

computations is controllable by choosing what entities to put as the leaves of the tree, which in turn impacts the granularity of the authenticated video. For example, for having an authentication as fine-grained as a macroblock, a large number of hashes must be calculated. Random packet loss is tolerated by FEC coding the signatures and packet hashes. Neither producing the authenticated video nor verifying that can be done online. For verification, the receiver must wait until reception of all the packets of a group that is signed, e.g., the entire video. If groups are made small, the number of signature verifications will grow. Communication overhead depends on the number of signatures, which is typically low if there is only one signature for the entire video or for each VO. Lastly, in these schemes proxies must be involved in the authentication mechanism, but they do not need to be trusted.

### 4.5. Comparison

In this section, we present a qualitative comparison among the different schemes discussed in the previous sections. Tables 4.1 and 4.2 summarize how each of the works surveyed meets requirements discussed in Section 4.2.1. Each row corresponds to one of the requirements. We briefly highlight a number of points worthwhile to mention about some of the them.

Schemes that are based on cryptographic hash functions inherit the high security of these functions, as listed in the first row. On the other hand, content-based approaches may have acceptable security but not a hundred percent assured; from a criticizing perspective, there is no clear boundary for differentiating benign and malicious operations, which can leave a possibility for an attacker to take advantage of this weakness by spending enough time and effort. Computational cost of the receiver, shown in the second row of the tables, typically excludes hash computations if the number of them is reasonable, while it is mainly affected by digital signatures. Given that the frequency of digital signature verifications is low, computational cost would be low too. Besides, content-based techniques involve other expensive operations than hash and digital signature, as discussed in Section 4.3.2, and thus typically have high computational cost. Communication overhead, the third row, is normally low in the works summarized, except where space-consuming techniques are utilized, such as one-time signatures in [23] or MDC [54].

A buffer for keeping stream data until their authentication information arrives is assumed negligible if it stores a small number (typically 1–10) of packets. We assume a buffer of over 20–30 packets as considerable. Many of the works involve a tradeoff between computational cost and buffer/delay. In these cases, we assume the computational cost must be low so as to be affordable by most of the receivers, and then judged the buffering/delay overheads. Loss tolerance is usually achieved by Forward Error Correction (FEC). Content-based techniques in the table achieve loss tolerance based on a content-based manner, and thus their loss tolerance cannot

Table 4.1. Comparison among general stream authentication methods.

| | [23] (hash chaining) | [23] (one-time signature chaining) | [25] (tree chaining) | [27,28] (TESLA) | [27] (EMSS) | [29] (SAIDA) and [30] | [31] (TFDP) |
|---|---|---|---|---|---|---|---|
| Security | High | High | High | High | High | High | High |
| Computation overhead | Low | Low | Low (given enough buff/delay) | Low | Low (given enough buff/delay) | Low (given enough buff/delay) | Low |
| Communication overhead | Low | High | Medium | Low | Low | Low | low |
| Buffer needed | Negligible | Negligible | Considerable (for low comp' cost) | Considerable (for low comp' cost) | Considerable (for low comp' cost) | Considerable (for low comp' cost) | Can be small |
| Loss tolerance | No | No | No | Yes | Yes | Yes | yes |
| Supported scenarios | Any, only offline streams | Any | Any | One to many, only online streams | Any | Any | Any, only offline Streams |
| Who needs to be trusted | Only producer | Only producer | Only producer | Only producer | Only producer | Only producer | Only producer |
| Online production | No | Yes | Delayed | Yes in [27], delayed in [28] | Yes | Delayed | No |
| Online verification | Yes | Yes | Delayed | Delayed | Delayed; no delay if network is loss-free in [28] | Delayed | Delayed (can be less than [25,27,29]) |

Table 4.2. Comparison among media stream authentication methods.

| | [38,40,46] (content-based) | [53–55] (2D hash chaining) | [56,59,61–63] (Merkle trees) |
|---|---|---|---|
| Security | Acceptable, questionable in [38] | High | High |
| Computation overhead | Typically high | Low | Typically low |
| Communication overhead | Low-medium | Low in [53,54] , higher in [55] | Typically low |
| Buffer needed | Typically considerable | Small | Can be considerable |
| Robustness against adaptations | To some extent | Yes | Yes |
| loss tolerance | To some extent | No in [53,54] , yes in [55] | Yes in [56,62,63] , no in [59,61] |
| Scalability preservation | No | Yes | Yes |
| Supported scenarios | Any, single sender multiple trusted receivers in [46] | Any | Any |
| Proxies involvement | Not involved | Not involved | Involved |
| Who needs to be trusted | Only producer, producer and receivers in [46] | Only producer | Producer and proxies in [56,59,61], only producer in [62,63] |
| Online production | No or delayed | No or delayed | No or delayed |
| Online verification | No or delayed | Yes | No or delayed |

be clearly determined. How to employ FEC for achieving best resilience against network losses is an important matter, as pointed in Section 4.3.1, though we did not take those details into account in the tables. Regarding the supported transmission scenarios, if digital signatures are the basis of a scheme, then the scheme is easily functioning in any scenario, i.e., single-sender single-receiver, one-to-many and man-to-many. But if the scheme is dependent on shared secrets or on a limit on the delay between transmission and reception of a packet, it cannot be applied to cases such as P2P, systems where any peer is potentially untrusted and delay management is of high difficulty.

It should be mentioned that in the last column of Table 4.2 which represents [56,59,61–63], the linear (chain-based) schemes presented in [62] and [63] are not considered and the comparison only involves their tree-based schemes; their chain-based schemes are more or less similar to other chain-based ones, which are listed in the second last column of that table.

## 4.6. Conclusion and Research Directions

In this chapter, we surveyed the most important techniques proposed in the literature to authenticate multimedia streams. We classified multimedia streams based on the encoding method they use into two classes: nonscalable and scalable. The first class provides limited flexibility for adapting the multimedia streams, while the second does provide such adaptability at the expense of some complexity and inefficiency in compression. To authenticate nonscalable multimedia streams, we may consider them as data packets without paying attention to their special characteristics such as temporal correlation among video frames. In this case, schemes developed for authenticating general data streams can be used — we presented and analyzed several schemes in this category.

We also presented authentication schemes that analyze the video content of nonscalable multimedia streams. These schemes usually extract key features of the multimedia content to create some authentication information based on these features. The security of content-based authentication schemes assumes that it is infeasible for an attacker to tamper with a multimedia content without changing its key features. Thus, any such tampering will be detected.

Authentication of scalable multimedia streams is more challenging, especially the recent streams that provide different types of scalability. These streams are usually encoded into multiple layers. We presented two categories of authentication schemes for scalable streams. The first one uses hash chaining, where two dimensional chaining (over layers of the same frame, and across frames) is performed. The second category is based on hash trees, where a tree of hashes on different parts of the stream is created.

We proposed a set of requirements that can be used to evaluate different authentication schemes. These requirements capture the most important aspects of the stream authentication problem, such as overheads involved in the authentication, robustness to stream adaptation, entities that need to be trusted, and the ability to authenticate and verify in real time. We used these requirements to conduct a qualitative comparison among all presented authentication techniques. The comparison puts all schemes side-by-side and exposes the strengths and weaknesses of each. In summary, each of the earlier works attempts to provide a suitable balance between multiple metrics to address the requirements of a given class of applications. For example, when an authentication scheme provides online production of authenticated videos and online verification of them are as in live streaming applications scheme usually, the computational cost incurs high. Or when an authentication scheme does not trust mid-path proxies responsible for adaptation, the size of the authentication information grows.

Based on our analysis, we conclude that there are rooms for improving current solutions and/or developing new ones. We discuss below a few possible directions for further research. First, new authentication schemes need to be developed for recent scalable streams, because they are not well supported by current schemes. For example, authentication of FGS-coded streams with current techniques results in incomplete authentication of the content. Given a receiver who ignores any non-verified portion of the stream, the fine-granularity of the stream will be useless. In an attempt for authentication of FGS, the authors of [64] embed a watermark bit in every $8 \times 8$ bit-plane of the FGS-coded video by adjusting the even-odd parity of "1" bits in the bit-plane. However, an attacker can forge the video while preserving the watermark, because the attacker needs only to preserve the even-odd parity of blocks. In addition to FGS, the recent and well-favored Scalable Video Coding (SVC) extension of H.264/AVC standard proposes the concept of MGS (see Section 4.2.2). An MGS video is basically coded like CGS but with some modifications to allow finer granularity in scalability while preserving coding efficiency. Authentication at a layer basis will result in high overhead, because there could be many MGS layers within a frame.

A second potential research direction is to develop more efficient cryptographic tools. Conventional cryptographic primitives used in media authentication methods are devised for general data security; they protect all portions of the data equally. However, considering the special characteristics of multimedia streams, computation and communication overhead of the cryptographic techniques may significantly be reduced. For example, there is a strong correlation between consecutive video frames or between partially-enhanced images within a frame, while a conventional hash function treats each of them as an isolated chunk of data. In addition, a multimedia stream needs to be authentic only during the playback time of a streaming session. Thus, the cryptographic techniques used can be less secure and more efficient than conventional ones for general data. Another way of reducing communication and/or computation overhead is to precisely identify the importance of different portions of the content and unequally protect them. Furthermore, allowing receivers to choose security proportional to their capabilities is an interesting feature, which future authentication schemes can support.

A final research direction could be developing new authentication schemes for distributed and peer-to-peer (P2P) media streaming, which has recently seen wide deployment in practice. These schemes may capitalize on the unique features of the P2P environment, such as the large number of potential senders. Given many senders, a receiver can, for example, verify the stream by downloading parts of the data and the authentication information from multiple intelligently-chosen senders and compare them.

### A.1. Acronyms

| Acronym | Description |
|---|---|
| B-frame | Bidirectionally predicted frame |
| CGS | Coarse-Grained Scalability |
| CIF | Common Intermediate Format |
| DCT | Discrete Cosine Transform |

| Acronym | Description |
|---|---|
| DSS | Digital Signature Standard |
| EMSS | Efficient Multi-chained Stream Signature |
| FEC | Forward Error Correction |
| FFS | Feige-Fiat-Shamir |
| FGS | Fine-Grained Scalability |
| GoP | Group of Pictures |
| I-frame | Intra-coded frame |
| IDA | Information Dispersal Algorithm |
| MAC | Message Authentication Code |
| MB | MacroBlock |
| MDC | Multiple Description Coding |
| MGS | Medium-Grained Scalability |
| MSB | Most Significant Bit |
| P-frame | Predicted frame |
| QCIF | Quarter Common Intermediate Format |
| RSA | Rivest-Shamir-Adleman |
| SAIDA | Signature Amortization using Information Dispersal Algorithm |
| SNR | Signal-to-Noise Ratio |
| SVC | Scalable Video Coding |
| TESLA | Timed Efficient Stream Loss-tolerant Authentication |
| TFDP | Tree-based Forward Digest Protocol |
| VCR | Video Cassette Recorder |
| VLC | Variable-Length Coding |
| VO | Video Object |
| VOL | Video Object Layer |
| VOP | Video Object Plane |
| VS | Video Sequence |

## References


[1] Streaming media, IPTV, and broadband transport: Telecommunications carriers and entertainment services 2006–2011. Technical report, The Insight Research Corporation, 718 Main Street, Boonton, NJ (April, 2006). `http://www.insight-corp.com/execsummaries/iptv06execsum.pdf`.

[2] Video conferencing — a global strategic business report. Technical report, Global Industry Analysts Inc., 5645 Silver Creek Valley Road, San Jose, CA (July, 2007). `http://www.strategyr.com/MCP-1062.asp`.

[3] Global IPTV market analysis (2006–2010). Technical report, RNCOS (August, 2006). `http://www.rncos.com/Report/IM063.htm`.

[4] G. Sullivan and T. Wiegand, "Video compression — from concepts to the H.264/AVC standard", *Proceedings of the IEEE*, **93**(1), 18–31, (January, 2005).

[5] J. Xin, C. Lin, and M. Sun, Digital video transcoding, *Proceedings of the IEEE*, **93** (1), 84–97 (January, 2005).

[6] T. Nguyen and A. Zakhor, Distributed video streaming over Internet. In *Proc. of Multimedia Computing and Networking (MMCN'02)*, San Jose, CA (January, 2002).

[7] J. Liu, S. Rao, B. Li, and H. Zhang, Opportunities and challenges of peer-to-peer internet video broadcast, *Proceedings of the IEEE*, **96**(1), 11–24 (January, 2008).

[8] M. Hefeeda, A. Habib, D. Xu, B. Bhargava, and B. Botev, CollectCast: A peer-to-peer service for media streaming, *ACM/Springer Multimedia Systems Journal*, **11**(1), 68–81 (November, 2005).

[9] M. Hefeeda, A. Habib, B. Botev, D. Xu, and B. Bhargava. PROMISE: Peer-to-peer media streaming using CollectCast. In *Proc. of ACM Multimedia 2003*, pp. 45–54, Berkeley, CA (November, 2003).

[10] Y. Cui and K. Nahrstedt. Layered peer-to-peer streaming. In *Proc. of ACM International Workshop on Network and Operating Systems Support for Digital Audio and Video (NOSSDAV'03)*, Monterey, CA (June, 2003).

[11] A. Menezes, S. Vanston, and P. Van Oorschot, *Handbook of Applied Cryptography.* (CRC Press, Boca Raton, FL, 1996), 1st edition.

[12] Federal information processing standards (FIPS) publication 180: Secure hash standard. Technical report, National Institute of Standards and Technology (NIST) (May, 1993).

[13] R. Rivest. RFC1321; the MD5 message-digest algorithm. IETF (April, 1992).

[14] R. Rivest, A. Shamir, and L. Adleman, A method for obtaining digital signatures and public-key cryptosystems, *Communications of the ACM*, **21**(2), 120–126 (Februrary, 1978).

[15] Federal information processing standards (FIPS) publication 186: Digital signature standard (DSS). Technical report, National Institute of Standards and Technology (NIST) (May, 1994).

[16] M. Rabin, Efficient dispersal of information for security, load balancing, and fault tolerance, *Journal of the ACM*, **36**(2), 335–348 (April, 1989).

[17] M. Luby, M. Mitzenmacher, M. Shokrollahi, D. Spielman, and V. Stemann. Practical loss-resilient codes. In *Proc. of ACM Symposium on Theory of Computing (STOC'97)*, pp. 150–159, El Paso, TX (May, 1997).

[18] Y. Wang, J. Ostermann, and Y. Zhang, *Video Processing and Communications.* (Prentice Hall, 2002).

[19] V. Goyal, Multiple description coding: Compression meets the network, *IEEE Signal Processing Magazine*, **18**(5), 74–93 (September, 2001).

[20] H. Schwarz, D. Marpe, and T. Wiegand, Overview of the scalable video coding extension of the H.264/AVC standard, *IEEE Transactions on Circuits and Systems for Video Technology*, **17**(9), 1103–1120 (September, 2007).

[21] W. Li, Overview of fine granularity scalability in MPEG-4 video standard, *IEEE Transactions on Circuits and Systems for Video Technology*, **11**(3), 301–317 (March, 2001).

[22] H. Radha, M. van der Schaar, and Y. Chen, The MPEG-4 fine-grained scalable video coding method for multimedia streaming over IP, *IEEE Transactions on Multimedia*, **3**(1), 53–68 (March, 2001).

[23] R. Gennaro and P. Rohatgi, How to sign digital streams. In *Proc. of Advances in Cryptology (CRYPTO'97)*, vol. 1294, *LNCS*, pp. 180–197, Santa Barbara, CA (August, 1997). Springer-Verlag.

[24] R. Merkle. A digital signature based on a conventional encryption function. In *Proc. of Advances in Cryptology (CRYPTO'87)*, vol. 293, *LNCS*, pp. 369–378, Santa Barbara, CA (August, 1987). Springer-Verlag.

[25] C. Wong and S. Lam, Digital signatures for flows and multicasts, *IEEE/ACM Transactions on Networking*, **7**(4), 502–513 (August, 1999).

[26] U. Feige, A. Fiat, and A. Shamir. Zero knowledge proofs of identity. In *Proc. of ACM Symposium on Theory of Computing (STOC'87)*, pp. 210–217, New York, NY (mAY, 1987).

[27] A. Perrig, R. Canetti, J. Tygar, and D. Song. Efficient authentication and signing of multicast streams over lossy channels. In *Proc. of IEEE Symposium on Security and Privacy (S&P'00)*, pp. 56–73, Berkeley, CA (May, 2000).

[28] A. Perrig, R. Canetti, D. Song, and J. Tygar, Efficient and secure source authentication for multicast. In *Proc. of Network and Distributed Systems Security Symposium (NDSS'01)*, pp. 35–46, San Diego, CA (February, 2001).

[29] J. Park, E. Chong, and H. Siegel, Efficient multicast stream authentication using erasure codes, *ACM Transactions on Information and System Security*, **6**(2), 258–285 (May, 2003).

[30] A. Pannetrat and R. Molva. Efficient multicast packet authentication. In *Proc. of Network and Distributed System Security Symposium (NDSS'03)*, San Diego, CA (February, 2003).

[31] A. Habib, D. Xu, M. Atallah, B. Bhargava, and J. Chuang, A tree-based forward digest protocol to verify data integrity in distributed media streaming, *IEEE Transactions on Knowledge and Data Engineering*, **17**(7), 1010–1014 (July, 2005).

[32] R. Merkle. A certified digital signature. In *Proc. of Advances in Cryptology (CRYPTO'89)*, vol. 435, *LNCS*, pp. 218–238, Santa Barbara, CA (August, 1989). Springer-Verlag.

[33] P. Golle and N. Modadugu. Authenticating streamed data in the presence of random packet loss. In *Proc. of Network and Distributed System Security Symposium (NDSS'01)*, pp. 13–22, San Diego, CA (February, 2001).

[34] D. Song, J. Tygar, and D. Zuckerman. Expander graphs for digital stream authentication and robust overlay networks. In *Proc. of IEEE Symposium on Security and Privacy*, pp. 258–270, Berkeley, CA (May, 2002).

[35] Z. Zhang, Q. Sun, and W. Wong, A proposal of butterfly-graph based stream authentication over lossy networks. In *Proc. of IEEE International Conference on Multimedia and Expo (ICME'05)*, pp. 784–787, Amsterdam, The Netherlands (July, 2005).

[36] X. Zhu, Z. Zhang, Z. Li, and Q. Sun. Flexible layered authentication graph for multimedia streaming. In *Proc. of IEEE Workshop on Multimedia Signal Processing (MMSP'07)*, pp. 349–352, Chania, Crete, Greece (October, 2007).

[37] Z. Zhishou, Q. Apostolopoulos, J. Sun, S. Wee, and W. Wong, Stream authentication based on generalized butterfly graph. In *Proc. of IEEE International Conference on Image Processing (ICIP'07)*, vol. 6, pp. 121–124, San Antonio, TX (September, 2007).

[38] C. Liang, A. Li, and X. Niu, Video authentication and tamper detection based on cloud model. In *Proc. of Conference on Intelligent Information Hiding and Multimedia Signal Processing (IIHMSP'07)*, vol. 1, pp. 225–228, Splendor Kaohsiung, Taiwan (November, 2007).

[39] C. Roover, C. Vleeschouwer, F. Lefbvre, and B. Macq, Robust video hashing based on radial projections of key frames, *IEEE Transactions on Signal Processing*, **53**(10), 4020–4037 (October, 2005).

[40] A. Sun, D. He, Z. Zhang, and Q. Tian, A secure and robust approach to scalable video authentication. In *Proc. of IEEE International Conference on Multimedia and Expo (ICME'03)*, vol. 2, pp. 209–212, Baltimore, MD (July, 2003).

[41] Q. Sun, S. Chang, M. Kurato, and M. Suto, A new semi-fragile image authentication framework combining ECC and PKI infrastructure. In *Proc. of IEEE International Symposium on Circuits and Systems (ISCAS'02)*, vol. 2, pp. 440–443, Phoenix-Scottsdale, AZ (May, 2002).

[42] C. Lin and S. Chang, Semi-fragile watermarking for authenticating JPEG visual content. In *Proc. of SPIE Security and Watermarking of Multimedia Content II*, vol. 3971, pp. 140–151, SanJose, CA (January, 2000).

[43] D. He, T. Ng, Z. Zhang, and Q. Sun, A practical watermarking scheme aligned with compressed-domain CIF-to-QCIF video transcoding. In *Proc. of the Joint Conference of the 4th International Conference on Information, Communications and Signal Processing, and the 4th Pacific Rim Conference on Multimedia (ICICS-PCM'03)*, vol. 2, pp. 1168–1172, Meritus Mandarin Singapore Hotel, Singapore (December, 2003).

[44] J. Zhang and A. Ho, Efficient video authentication for H.264/AVC. In *Proc. of International Conference on Innovative Computing, Information and Control (ICICIC'06)*, vol. 3, pp. 46–49, Beijing, China (August, 2006).

[45] T. Wiegand, G. Sullivan, G. Bjontegaard, and A. Luthra, Overview of the H.264/AVC video coding standard, *IEEE Transactions on Circuits and Systems for Video Technology*, **13**(7), 560–576 (July, 2003).

[46] P. Atrey, W. Yan, and M. Kankanhalli, A scalable signature scheme for video authentication, *Multimedia Tools and Applications*, **34**, 107–135 (July, 2007).

[47] A. Shamir, How to share a secret, *Communications of the ACM*, **22**, 612–613 (November, 1979).

[48] W. Wang and H. Farid. Exposing digital forgeries in video by detecting double MPEG compression. In *Proc. of ACM Multimedia and Security Workshop*, pp. 37–47, Geneva, Switzerland (September, 2006).

[49] B. Zhu, M. Swanson, and S. Li, Encryption and authentication for scalable multimedia: Current state of the art and challenges. In *Proc. of SPIE Internet Multimedia Management Systems V*, vol. 5601, pp. 157–170, Philadelphia, PA (October, 2004).

[50] R. Deng, D. Ma, W. Shao, and Y. Wu, Scalable trusted online dissemination of JPEG2000 images, *Multimedia Systems*, **11**(1), 60–67 (November, 2005).

[51] R. Grosbois, P. Gerbelot, and T. Ebrahimi, Authentication and access control in the JPEG2000 compressed domain. In *Proc. of SPIE Applications of Digital Image Processing XXIV*, vol. 4472, pp. 95–104, San Dieog, CA (December, 2001).

[52] C. Peng, R. Deng, Y. Wu, and W. Shao, A flexible and scalable authentication scheme for JPEG2000 image codestreams. In *Proc. of ACM Multimedia Conference*, pp. 433–441, Berkeley, CA (November, 2003).

[53] D. Skraparlis, Design of an efficient authentication method for modern image and video, *IEEE Transactions on Consumer Electronics*, **49**(2), 417–426 (May, 2003).

[54] H. Yu, Scalable streaming media authentication. In *Proc. of IEEE International Conference on Communications (ICC'04)*, vol. 4, pp. 1912–1916, Paris, France (June, 2004).

[55] H. Yu. A loss resilient and scalable streaming media authentication scheme. In *Proc. of IEEE Consumer Communications and Networking Conference (CCNC'05)*, pp. 60–64, Las Vegas, NV (January, 2005).

[56] T. Li, H. Zhu, and Y. Wu. Multi-source stream authentication framework in case of composite MPEG-4 stream. In *Proc. of International Conference on Information and Communications Security (ICICS'05)*, vol. 3783, *LNCS*, pp. 389–401, Beijing, China (December, 2005). Springer.

[57] F. Pereira and T. Ebrahimi, *The MPEG-4 Book.* (Prentice Hall, July 2002).

[58] A. Lysyanskaya, S. Micali, L. Reyzin, and H. Shacham. Sequential aggregate signatures from trapdoor permutations. In *Proc. of Advances in Cryptology — EUROCRYPT 2004*, vol. 3027, *LNCS*, pp. 74–90, Interlaken, Switzerland (May, 2004). Springer.

[59] R. Kaced and J. Moissinac. Multimedia content authentication for proxy-side adaptation. In *Proc. of International Conference on Digital Telecommunications (ICDT'06)*, Cap Esterel, Cote d'Azur, France (August-September, 2006).

[60] R. Kaced and J. Moissinac. SEMAFOR: A framework for authentication of adaptive multimedia content and delivery for heterogeneous networks. In *Proc. of International Conference on Internet Surveillance and Protection (ICISP'06)*, p. 28, Cap Esterel, Cote d'Azur, France (August, 2006).

[61] T. Suzuki, Z. Ramzan, H. Fujimoto, C. Gentry, T. Nakayama, and R. Jain. A system for end-to-end authentication of adaptive multimedia content. In *Proc. of IFIP Conference on Communications and Multimedia Security (IFIP CMS'04)*, vol. 175, *LNCS*, pp. 237–249, Windermere, The Lake District, United Kingdom (September, 2004). Springer.

[62] C. Gentry, A. Hevia, R. Jain, T. Kawahara, and Z. Ramzan, End-to-end security in the presence of intelligent data adapting proxies: The case of authenticating transcoded streaming media, *IEEE Journal on Selected Areas in Communications*, **23**(2), 464–473 (February, 2005).

[63] Y. Wu and R. Deng, Scalable authentication of MPEG-4 streams, *IEEE Transactions on Multimedia*, **8**, 152–161 (February, 2006).

[64] C. Wang, Y. Lin, S. Yi, and P. Chen. Digital authentication and verification in MPEG-4 fine-granular scalability video using bit-plane watermarking. In *Proc. of Conference on Image Processing, Computer Vision, and Pattern Recognition (IPCV'06)*, pp. 16–21, Las Vegas, NV (June, 2006).

# Chapter 5

## EXPLAINING SYSTEM SECURITY ISSUES TO COMPUTER PROFESSIONALS

Prabhaker Mateti*
*Department of Computer Science and Engineering*
*Wright State University*
*Dayton, Ohio 45435*

We consider the security of a system running a Linux distribution. This starts with (i) choosing a distribution, (ii) installing it, and (iii) configuring it so that the system is secure. Then onwards, the system is (iv) booted and run. The administrator (v) watches, (vi) modifies the configuration, and (vii) controls the running system. As needed, the system is (viii) rebooted. We describe how in each of the steps, except in watching the system run (v), new security violations can happen, and for item (v), we describe what information may be hidden. These explanations range from describing the classic buffer overflow exploits to TCP/IP weaknesses to kernel hardening ideas. We also discuss the technical reasons behind what permits these attacks to succeed, and how they can be prevented.

### 5.1. Introduction

Computer systems have become the targets of attack both from users who have console access as well as those arriving via networks. Every computer user is aware of the exploits at the newspaper headline levels. Surprisingly many computer professionals are not better informed. This paper attempts to explain security issues assuming that the reader is familiar with operating system internals.

Our goal here is not to list and explain every exploit that has happened, but to select a few important ones and explain them well-enough, and where possible suggest prevention and detection techniques. We also discuss the technical reasons behind what permits these attacks to succeed, and how they can be prevented, which requires the background material of Sections 5.3 and 5.2. In this paper, we do not consider the motivations of the attackers.

This paper focuses on describing Linux-specific details. Here are two stats, perhaps unreliable, to judge how important Linux OS and Linux security have

---

*`http://www.cs.wright.edu/~pmateti/`

become. A `www.Amazon.com` search for books on "Linux security" produced 21 total matches in October 2001, and 1371 in October 2008. A search on `www.Google.com` with the search phrase "Linux security" produced ten pages of results (about ten results per page) in 2001 compared with 2,240,000 in 2008.

We consider the security of a system running a Linux distribution. This starts with (i) choosing a distribution (Section 5.9), (ii) installing it and (iii) configuring it so that the system is secure (Section 5.8). Then onwards, the system is (iv) booted (Section 5.5) and run. The administrator (v) watches, (vi) modifies the configuration, and (vii) controls the running system (Section 5.10). As needed, the system is (viii) rebooted. We describe how in each of the steps, except in watching the system run (v), new security violations can happen, and for item (v), we describe what information may be hidden. These explanations range from describing the classic buffer overflow exploits (Section 5.6) to TCP/IP network exploits (Section 5.7) to kernel hardening ideas (Section 5.10).

## 5.2. Attack Techniques

Attack techniques are composed of reconnaissance and deception to either cause denial of service or gain unauthorized access to a system.

### 5.2.1. *Reconnaissance*

#### 5.2.1.1. *Sniffing*

Attackers sniff the data necessary in the exploits they are planning to execute. In the so called promiscuous mode, an NIC captures all frames that pass by it, and the sniffer running on the local machine saves them. The volume of such frames makes it a real challenge for an attacker to either immediately process all such frames fast or clandestinely store them for later processing. An attacker at large on the Internet has other techniques that make it possible to install remotely a sniffer on the victim machine.

#### 5.2.1.2. *Finger printing a system*

An attacker wants to remotely scan entire LANs and identify what services run where, etc. and to identify the exact version of an OS running on a targeted victim because operating system exploits will usually only work against a specific operating system or software running. Nuances in the TCP/IP stacks implemented in the various OS, and versions of the same OS, make it possible to remotely probe the victim host and identify the OS. Such probing deliberately constructs illegal packets, and attempts to connect to each port and observes the responses it gets. The tool called nmap (`http://insecure.org/nmap/`) is comprehensive in this regard. To make such finger printing difficult, a scrubber should be deployed.

### 5.2.2. *Deception*

#### 5.2.2.1. *Spoofing*

Spoofing refers to altering portions of a packet so that the overall packet remains structurally legitimate (e.g., check-sums are valid) but the "info" it contains is fake. Spoofing often accompanies sniffing, but may newly manufacture packets with fake values.

#### 5.2.2.2. *Poisoning*

Many network services are essentially mappings implemented as table look-ups. The mappings are dynamic, and update methods are well-defined. Unfortunately, who is qualified to provide the updates, and how messages that provide update information are to be authenticated are ill-defined. An attacker takes advantage of this, and provides fake updates causing the table to be "poisoned".

#### 5.2.2.3. *Root-kits*

A root-kit is a set of programs and modules that an attacker installs on a compromised system so that the next visit is easier. Root-kit programs replace several observer programs such as `ls, ps, md5sum, lsmod` with Trojaned versions to hide their activity, install hooks inside the kernel to redirect various system calls to their custom implementations, and install such programs as a password protected backdoor, a log wiper program, a network sniffer, and a command line sniffer.

### 5.2.3. *Denial of Service*

The goal of a denial of service (DoS) attack is to prevent legitimate clients from receiving service(s). Since the service being performed is almost always a constant time operation, it is easy for an external observer process to detect a DoS attack. These attacks are generally transient.

Of course such things as `/.xsession-errors` making a file volume full, or NFS problems or broken device causing a system hang should not be considered DoS.

#### 5.2.3.1. *Buffer overflow*

TBD: prev section; A large number of TCP/IP server programs suffer from a class of programming errors known as buffer overflows. Many of these server programs run with the privileges of a super user. Among the many servers that suffer from such bugs are several implementations of FTP servers, the ubiquitous DNS server program called bind, the popular mail server called sendmail, and the Web server IIS, to name a few. An attacker supplies cleverly constructed inputs to such programs causing them to transfer control to executable code she has supplied. A typical code produces a shell that she can interact with from a remote machine with all the privileges of the super user.

#### 5.2.3.2. *Illegal packets*

Packets containing "unexpected" values in some of the fields are illegal in the sense that a legitimate sender would not have constructed them. Software in the receiver ought to check for such illegal packets, but RFCs were ambiguous and/or legacy software was not cautious. Attackers have written special programs that construct illegal packets and cause the receiving network hosts to crash or hang. The so-called Ping of Death attack of 1996 sent an ICMP echo request (ping) packet that was larger than the maximum permissible length (216 1). TCP segments have a number of flags that have, collectively, a strong influence on how the segment is processed. However, not all the flags can be independently set or reset. For example, syn + fin, syn + fin + psh, syn + fin + rst, and syn + fin + rst + psh are all illegal combinations. Past implementations have accounted only for valid combinations, ignoring the invalid combinations as "will not happen." An IP packet should not have source address and port equaling the destination address and port. The 1997 attack tool called land exploited this vulnerability.

#### 5.2.3.3. *Storms*

A storm is the flow of a certain kind packets that is abnormally high. For example, if 50 ARP requests per second is normal, we would consider, say, 500 per second abnormally high. Storms are often created by a few packets generated on a compromised host. The attackers send the packets to intermediary machines (amplifiers or reflectors). The packets are often source spoofed also. There have been several attacks that generate enormous numbers of packets rendering (portions of) a network ineffective. These amplify the numbers of packets into a "storm." Section 1.8.8 describes an ACK storm. Clever use of broadcast or multi-cast addresses helps the storms.

#### 5.2.3.4. *Distributed denial of service*

An attack whose main gaol is DoS, and the attack is conducted by a coordinated set of hosts, it is termed a distributed denial of service (DDoS) attack. The hosts (often called zombies) that participate in overflow. The attacker prepares the zombies ahead of the DDoS attack, and issues a start up command remotely through an installed backdoor.

A DDoS attacker covertly distributes (portions of) his attack tools over many machines spread across the Internet, and later triggers these intermediary machines into beginning the attack and remotely coordinates the attack.

## 5.3. Kernel Architecture

OS designs and implementations have been performance-centric and security-naive. In the next few subsections, we summarize security ideas that are (being) incorporated in current kernels in varying degrees.

### 5.3.1. *Loadable Kernel Modules*

A loadable kernel module (LKM) is a specially linked executable. On a typical Linux system, most of the device drivers (e.g., ethernet cards), and several file systems (e.g., NTFS) are built as modules that are dynamically loaded on demand, keeping the core kernel small. The modules reside as files in the `/lib/modules` directory.

### 5.3.2. *Network Filter Modules*

Linux has a collection of LKMs known as `netfilter`. After these are loaded, a root user can insert rules that examine the contents of network packets and filter them. The rules are inserted, modified, and saved with the `iptables` utility that shares its name with the kernel internal data structures also called `iptables`. Each rule within an `iptable` consists of a number of classifiers that describe (i) a packet template to match and (ii) when the match succeeds the action to take, such as drop the packet, replace a field of then packet. Sophisticated firewalls can be built with the `netfilter`.

### 5.3.3. *Fine-Grained Privileges*

On a standard Linux system, security is based on privileges assigned to user and group IDs, and permissions on files. There is one user ID, called the `root` or *super user*, that can bypass all permissions on files, etc. A number of services (daemons) and programs run with super user privileges. Binding to a privileged port, loading kernel modules, and managing file systems are examples of things that typically can only be done by root. The `ping` command, that many ordinary users invoke, runs with the privileges of the root in order to open a raw socket to create the necessary ICMP packet for the echo request. There are bugs in many of these programs that can be exploited by an attacker to gain root access.

The granularity of permissions is also coarse. E.g., the owner of a file cannot grant permission to append to a file without permitting rewriting.

Common operations often pose interesting dilemmas. In order to backup a system, should the backup operator be permitted read-access to all files? Could we limit privileges of the backup program to read all files from certain devices only if they are about to be copied over to certain other devices? Should the super user be able to reboot a system via a remote login?

The inability to grant or deny such rights on a finer granularity is a weakness. The rest of this subsection explores how this coarse granularity can be broken down so that it is no longer necessary to run certain programs `setuid` root.

### 5.3.3.1. *Subjects, objects, access control, etc*

An *object* is an operand, the subject an "operator" (usually, a process). The access matrix has objects as rows, subjects as columns, and each cell describes the access rights the subject has on that object. The request for an operation is intercepted by a *reference monitor* that consults the matrix and grants or denies. A column of the matrix is referred to as an access control list (ACL).

Clearly, access control lists support fine-grained permissions. There are several Linux kernel access control projects. Common penetration techniques that involve tricking the system into running the intruder's own program in privileged mode are blocked by this approach.

A *role* can be thought of as a subset of permissions that a group of users collectively have. Thus, the role of backup-operator may involve multiple users, and when they are acting in this role can be permitted to read the files of all users.

*Authorization* is an attribute of a user account that enables the user to execute a subset of the available programs. *Privileges* are attributes assigned to programs that give them different grades of access to system resources. Together, these two sets of attributes enable programs to behave differently toward different users. Applications can be extended to define and check new authorizations, providing a standardized protocol by which applications and the operating platform can communicate to grant permissions to users. Authorizations can be used to divide administrative duties into separate roles, which can then be assigned to different users.

*Security attributes* are arbitrary name-value pairs that are associated with system resources such as files, processes, network ports, interfaces, and host addresses. Port 21, for example, can have an attribute that grants access to it only to the `ftp` subsystem. Even a program running with root privileges would not then be able to use port 21. Incoming packets from a network interface can be assigned attributes based on the source IP address or the network interface. Outgoing packets can be assigned attributes based on the process or daemon that created them. An incoming or outgoing packet will be dropped if the attribute of the packet is not valid for both the interface and the remote host.

### 5.3.3.2. *Capabilities*

A capability is a "token" used by a process to prove that it is allowed to do an operation on an object. The capability identifies both the object and the operations allowed on that object. Operations on capabilities themselves include copying, transferring to other processes, modifying, and revoking a capability. A capability often has a notion of an "owner" who is able to invalidate all copies and derived versions of a capability.

POSIX capabilities partition the privileges of the super user into 30+ finer grained, non-overlapping privileges, such as the ability to alter the priority of a process, boot the system, or open a privileged port. Linux kernels 2.4 and later implement several of the POSIX capabilities and an additional number that are specific to Linux. These capabilities include the ability to change file ownership, kill processes, kernel module management, reboot or shutdown the machine, manipulate the system clock. See `include/linux/capability.h` in the Linux kernel source for the full list.

#### 5.3.3.3. *Access control*

Role based access control (RBAC) is discussed thoroughly in [1]. Medusa[2] is an implementation of RBAC. Objects (files) and subjects (processes) are separated into domains, named virtual spaces. An object can be member of any number of virtual spaces simultaneously. Each subject is assigned a set of abilities, one for each access type. Ability is a set of virtual spaces. Access is granted when the object and the subject share at least one common virtual space for the given access type.

Mandatory access control (MAC) enforces access controls on the basis of security attributes attached to subjects and objects. Users have no choice regarding their attributes. Discretionary access control (DAC) denies or grants access to an object based on permissions set by, typically, the owner. What is discretionary is the control exercised by a user, not the access decision made by the system. The standard Linux system provides the DAC model.

## 5.4. Boot Exploits

The boot-up sequence can be divided into events that occur (i) prior to the beginning of an OS boot loader, (ii) prior to the invocation of an OS kernel (iii) prior to the spawning of the first process, `init`, and (iv) following the spawning of `init` until the system enters a normal "run level". In this paper, we are also concerned with the shutdown.

### 5.4.1. *BIOS*

Events that occur prior to the beginning of an OS boot loader are the result of the ROM-resident BIOS being executed. This boot-strapping stage starts a computer system from a powered-on-but-halted or just-powered-on state ending with the invocation of a loader of operating system kernels.

BIOS discovers boot-able devices. The user has the option to change the order of these devices. BIOS reads the boot-sector of the first device and begins execution of instructions present there.

BIOS changes require giving a password. There are also backdoor BIOS passwords published on websites for many brands of motherboards. The user-set passwords are both resettable via jumpers on the mother board and easy to crack.

On many motherboards, BIOS is "re-flashable" through an OS. After a root compromise, it is a simple matter to install a rogue BIOS.

Two open source BIOS projects are CoreBoot `http://www.coreboot.org/` and OpenBIOS `http://www.openfirmware.info/`. Trusted BIOS is discussed in [3] and [4].

### 5.4.2. *OS Boot Loaders*

The operating system boot loader is responsible for loading an OS kernel. Linux Loader (LILO), and GRand Unified Boot loader (GRUB) are the Linux-native boot loaders. LoadLin and Syslinux are for booting Linux from MS-DOS. Pxelinux is a syslinux derivative that can boot Linux off of a network server, using a network ROM conforming to the Intel PXE (Pre-Execution Environment) specification. Isolinux is a syslinux derivative that is used to boot Linux off of CDs or DVDs.

All these can pass parameters and flags to the invoked Linux kernel. The collection of the parameters is either interactively or through configuration files. The authentication of both the interactive and the config files is rudimentary. A Trojaned kernel can be invoked, exploitable parameters can be passed, etc.

### 5.4.3. *OS Kernel Initialization*

The initialization behavior of the kernel is controlled by the parameters the kernel has built-in or received from the OS boot loader. The boot sector of the kernel contains pre-built configuration parameters. The kernel parses the command line from the boot loader. A command-line argument which has the character "=" in it is classified as an environment variable. The other parameters are passed to the `check setup()` function which checks if the parameter is meant for the kernel. The parameters which are neither environment variables nor kernel parameters are considered as arguments to the `init` program. The kernel then invokes the `init` thread. The `init` thread discovers the location of the first program `init`, and invokes it. Control enters the kernel from now on only when an interrupt occurs, when a fault (such as page fault, divide by zero) occurs, or when a system call is made.

There are problems when the users have access to the OS loader. There are three kernel parameters, given to it by the OS loader, that affect the `init`.

- `root=` This specifies the root file volume to be used by the kernel. The attacker can boot an entirely different system ("parallel universe") by specifying an alternate root.
- `init=` This specifies the path name of the `init` program to be executed by the kernel as `init`. A Trojan `init` can be specified. Note that the typical kernel does not authenticate `init` nor are there any file integrity checkers in place yet.
- `S` When present, this parameter is passed by the kernel to to the `init` program that `init` should enter a so-called "single" user mode. In the single user mode, a typical `init` configuration spawns a root shell and does not perform any authentication procedures.

## 5.5. Init Process Exploits

The idea of having a first process that does a lot of leg work is universal. It is present not only in Unix-like systems, but also in other OS that claim a disjoint ancestry from Unix. In this section, we focus on init as it appears in Linux/Unix systems.

### 5.5.1. *Expectations of an Init*

Init is, by definition, the first program to be invoked as a process. But, any arbitrary program without regard to its functionality can be given as the init to the kernel. There are many `init` programs [5] widely differing in size and in their degree of support for features described here. The kernel does not evaluate the script or ELF binary program it is about to invoke if it qualifies in some way to be *the* init process. The following functionality is expected of any program if it were to serve as a "full service" `init`.

(i) Ancestor of All Processes: The `init` process is assigned the process ID of 1. Older Unix kernels did indeed create this as the very first process. Newer Unix kernels, including current Linux kernels, actually construct several internal processes. For legacy reasons, `init` continues to be the process numbered 1. The internal processes are kernel *threads* expected to be alive while the system is up sharing not only the kernel address space but all the kernel resources. Compared to other threads, these kernel-threads have process control block data structures describing them.

The `init` is the only user-space process explicitly created by the kernel. All other processes are created by system calls made by `init` or its descendants.

(ii) Discovered by the Kernel: The `init` program that the kernel invokes can be an ELF binary or a script. The full path name of the `init` is discovered through two methods. (i) The boot-loaders can pass the path name of the file to be executed as `init` using the `init=` directive when invoking the kernel. (ii) If not, the kernel executes the first file that turns out to be an executable file in the ordered list of four hard-coded full path names: `/sbin/init`, `/etc/init`, `/bin/init` and finally `/bin/sh`. If neither succeeds, the kernel panics with the `init not found` message.

The above did not eliminate any arbitrary program from being considered an `init`, even though such arbitrary selection may make the system useless or even dangerous. On the basis of utility alone, we cannot but accept a shell, e.g., `/bin/bash`, as an `init` program.

This is too loose for our purpose here, and we use the following as tighter criteria. The `init` program is often coupled with the `shutdown`, `halt` and `reboot` programs and `init` takes an active part in shutting down the system. A program must have the functionalities listed below before we can include it in the `init` class of programs.

(iii) Customizable Behavior: A classic `init` program is generic, and the needed customizations at a specific installation are specified in a file, usually at path

`/etc/inittab`. The location of this file, and the the syntax and semantics of this file vary with different `inits`, but overall the behavior of `init` must be governed by this file. So, an init will read the `/etc/inittab` file as soon as possible. There are typically no checks on its authenticity.

As a further mechanism contributing to customization of a specific installation, `init` programs execute script files during the three different states described below.

(iv) Life Span: The life span of an `init` is the lifespan of the system.

A computer system can be considered to be in one of three states. It is in a (i) transient state, called *system initialization*, as it continues to boot from `init` being just invoked to a (ii) *normal stable state*. A computer system is in a (iii) transient state, called *system shutdown*, as it is making the transition from the normal stable state to state of reboot or halt.

The life of `init` begins with the beginning of (i) and ends with the ending of (iii).

(v) System Initialization: An `init` should be capable of recognizing the special needs of this phase and orchestrating it as specified in `/etc/inittab`. The event marking the beginning of system initialization is essentially the same as the invocation of `init`(). The end of this state is specified in `/etc/inittab`.

(vi) Normal Stable State: This state if often subdivided with popular names such as *single user mode*, *multi user mode*, or *GUI/X11 mode*. A multi-user system will expect multiple login processes allowing multiple users to work on the system simultaneously. An embedded system's `init` will expect closer monitoring of processes. The expected functionality in this state depends on the kind of system that this `init` is a part. But, the technical need is to spawn and re-spawn processes.

An `init` program is capable of spawning (i.e., `fork()` followed by `execve()`) children processes. It is able to monitor its children, and respawn them should they terminate as specified in `/etc/inittab`.

(vii) System Shutdown: An `init` program is able to orchestrate proper shutting down as specified in `/etc/inittab` of the system. This involves informing all processes (except itself) to terminate, waiting for them to actually die, and should some processes not terminate within a timeout period forcing termination using kernel facilities.

(viii) Robustness: An `init` must be robust. It must not crash or hang. In practice, this amounts to handling (i) all *signals* that can be raised, and (ii) syntactic and other errors in `/etc/inittab`.

Traditionally, signals are used to indicate state transitions.

(ix) Collect Dead Processes: An `init` program should collect its child processes when they terminate. E.g., the Linux kernel makes the first process the parent for all zombie processes. More abstractly, a kernel is designed to maintain an invariant regarding the resources it controls, and the init process plays a crucial role.

(x) Re-Execute Self: An `init` is able to re-execute itself (i.e., do an `execve("/sbin/init", ...)` without a `fork()`). Using techniques such as setting a global variable, it is possible for an `init` to determine if it is being executed for the first time or if it is being re-executed. Typically, an `init` will re-read the `/etc/inittab` so that recent changes made are in effect.

(xi) Logging: An `init` program should have the capability to log its activity.

### 5.5.2. *A Tour of Past Exploits*

We present a few past exploits that involve `init`.

#### 5.5.2.1. *Replace* `/etc/inittab`

All the existing `init` programs use an external configuration file (typically at `/etc/inittab`) which they read at run-time for their configuration commands.

Replacing the `/etc/inittab` file is one of the easy exploits to implement and is applicable to more than one `init` program. (i) The original `/etc/inittab` file is moved to a temporary location. (ii) The attacker copies his Trojan `/etc/inittab` file as `/etc/inittab`. (iii) Attacker sends a SIGHUP signal[a] to the `init` program which instructs the `init` program to re-read the `/etc/inittab` file. (iv) The Trojan `/etc/inittab` file is read and the new instructions are executed. (v) The original content of `/etc/inittab` is restored.

As the `/etc/inittab` file was moved/ renamed by the `/bin/mv` command the `i-node` of the file is not modified, hence file integrity checkers do not detect any change.

#### 5.5.2.2. *Replacing boot-up scripts*

This is also an easy exploit that is applicable to all the existing `inits`. The attacker replaces one or more of the boot-up scripts with custom versions where along with the intended service some Trojans are also started.

The limitation for this exploit is that it can be detected by a file integrity checker easily. If the program is supposed to be running always on the system, without appropriate Trojan programs installed, the program can be noticed by an administrator.

#### 5.5.2.3. **BSD* `procfs` *secure level exploit*

This exploit [6] was developed for the BSD variants FreeBSD, OpenBSD and NetBSD operating systems.

The BSD kernel security model is based on a variable called `securelevel` that has has four different values or "levels" that have the following meaning.

---

[a] `kill -1 1`

(i) [Permanently Insecure mode, −1]: This is the default `securelevel` value. (ii) [Insecure mode, 0]: Immutable and append-only flags maybe turned off and the devices can be read or written subject to their permissions. (iii) [Secure mode, 1]: Immutable and append-only flags may not be turned off; disks for mounted file systems, `/dev/mem` and `/dev/kmem` cannot be opened for writing; kernel modules cannot be loaded or unloaded. (iv) [Highly Secure mode, 2]: This level is the same as secure mode with the added protection to disks whose file systems are not mounted; (v) [Network Secure mode, 3]: This level is the same as 2, with the addition that IP packet filter rules cannot be modified.

The `securelevel` can be incremented, but never decremented except by `init`. The increment can only be done by a super-user process.

The `init` process during boot-up checks the value of the `securelevel` variable and if the value is 0, it raises the security level to 1. The `init` program needs to be able to bring the system down into the single-user mode from a multi-user mode, and so `init` is granted exclusive privileges for decreasing the value of the `securelevel` variable.

The `proc` file system implementation of the BSD variants contains a link to the memory region of a process under the `/proc/processid` as a normal writable file. A super-user process can write to this file, thus modifying the process image.

The exploit modifies the process image of the `init` program so that it decreased the security level of the system during a state transition. The code required to accomplish this is trivial. In the `multi_user()` routine, the machine code bytes of `if (getsecuritylevel() == 0) setsecuritylevel(1);` were modified to the equivalent of `if (getsecuritylevel() != 0) setsecuritylevel(0);`

#### 5.5.2.4. *umask 0000 vulnerability*

Older Linux kernels set the `umask` of all the kernel threads to "0000", which also included the `init` program. This umask was also applicable to the files that were created by the `init` program as the child processes inherit the parent process's permissions.

#### 5.5.2.5. *Open file descriptor exploit*

In Linux, file descriptors that are open in the parent process are visible to its children unless the files are explicitly closed or the flag `close-on-exec` is set for the files.

The exploit of [7] was specifically designed for `Simpleinit` and `Simpleinit-MSB`. Both the programs had a flaw which left the file descriptor of the control FIFO open in its children processes. A local user process which inherits this open file descriptor from `Simpleinit` can execute arbitrary commands with super-user privileges. The descriptor in question is used by `Simpleinit` to read messages from (`/dev/initctl`) FIFO. Programs named `initctl`, `need` and `provide` pass instructions to `Simpleinit` which opens this FIFO in the read/write mode, hence any process which inherits this FIFO can also insert instructions to `Simpleinit`. The processes started through the `bootprog=`, `finalprog=` and `ctrlaltdel=` actions of the `/etc/inittab` file will inherit this file descriptor. If a program that accepts input from an untrusted source is started using one of these three `/etc/inittab` fields, then the system is vulnerable to even remote exploits.

5.5.2.6. *Init replacing root kits*

Several root kits play switcharoo with `init`. Superkit [8], `suckIT` [9], `poiuy` [10] and `kist` (kernel intrusion system Trojan) [11] root kits replace the `init` program with their own.

### 5.5.3. *Trojaned* `inits`

The Trojan space for the `init` program is unlimited. It can modify any file on any file volume, currently mounted or not. It can control logging, and alter configuration files, libraries, scripts and program binaries including those of file system checkers, intrusion detection systems, or whatever other security enhancements are present. It can spawn processes that are unobservable.

It is a root-owned process limited to the user address space, and cannot directly access kernel space, but can load Trojan kernel module that can.

A compromise of the `init` process is hard to detect. There are no security mechanisms embedded in standard Unix/Linux kernels to detect a Trojan `init`. File integrity check on `init` can be performed only after it is "in charge".

The pristine `init` can be replaced so that during the next boot the Trojan-ed `init` program file is executed. The file replacement can be accomplished by an LKM. when the system is being shutdown. Replacing a file while it is "busy" is possible on UNIX-like systems. During the shutdown procedure, file integrity checkers are stopped and will not be available until the system is completely booted up during the subsequent boot. Toward the end of the shutdown all file volumes are remounted read-only. This period of time between the IDS shutdown and read-only remount is vulnerable.

Once the Trojan `init` program replaces the pristine `init` program it needs to hide itself from the administrator. The `inits` cannot be detected as easily as the other Trojan programs due to the fact that it can cover its tracks before the system is able to invoke other programs.

The standard Linux kernel does not verify the file that it executes as `init` during the subsequent boot-up. This Trojan `init` can restore the pristine copy so that, once the system boots up, file integrity checkers will not be able to detect any change in the `/sbin/init` binary files attributes such as i-node number, time stamps, or its content. Whenever a request is made with respect to the `init` binary the system call diversion hooks redirect them to the pristine copy of the `init` binary stored on the disk. The loaded module is unlinked from the list of all modules that the kernel maintains so that an `lsmod` list will not show it.

### 5.5.4. *Checking the Integrity of* `init`

The modifications designed by [5] enable the kernel [12] to verify the integrity of `init` both before invocation and during its life time. An MD5 check-sum of `init` is computed just before being invoked and is compared with one inserted into the kernel during its compilation. The check is performed on the binary discovered to become the `init` (usually `/sbin/init`). There is a mutual authentication protocol used by `init` and the kernel to authenticate each other. There is a secret key that is shared between the kernel and `init` and an HMAC hash is computed and exchanged through system calls for verification. This ensures that the system is not booted using an alternate `init` program or kernel.

MD5 check-summing of `init`'s text pages and the text pages of shared libraries used by `init` on the system memory detects any system call redirection or replacing `init`'s program image on-the-fly.

## 5.6. Buffer Overflow Exploits

Exceeding array bounds is a common programming error known as a "buffer overflow". There is not a single OS that is free from this error. Buffer overflows have been causing serious security problems for decades. In the most famous example, the Internet worm of 1988 used a buffer overflow in `fingerd`. What is surprising is that a number of security oriented software such as SSH and Kerberos also have had these errors.

In the buffer overflow attack, code is injected into the run-time stack or heap or bss address locations of a running process using essentially assignment statements or data-move operations, and control is cleverly pointed to the location of these deposited instructions so that they are executed.

### 5.6.1. *The Buffer Overflow Error*

A buffer overflow occurs when an object of size `m + d` is placed into a container of size `m`. This can happen in many situations where the programmer does not take proper care to bounds check what their functions do and what they are placing into variables inside their programs. The essence of this problem can be explained by the following. Using `strcpy(p, q)` to copy a string q to p is a common piece of code in most systems programs. An example of this is: `char env[32]; strcpy(env, getenv("TERM"));` The `strcpy(p, q)` is proper only when (i) $p$ is pointing to a char array of size $m$, (ii) $q$ is pointing to a char array of size $n$, (iii) $m \geq n$, and (iv) $q[i] =$ '\0' for some $i$ where $0 \leq i \leq n-1$. Unfortunately, only a few programs verify or can assert that all the above hold prior to invoking `strcpy(p, q)`. If $m < n$ in the `strcpy(p, q)` of above an area of memory beyond `&p[m]` gets overwritten.

### 5.6.2. *Stack Smashing*

Stack-smashing attacks target programs that use variables allocated on the program's run-time stack such as local variables and function arguments as the destination in a `strcpy()` or the like. The idea is straightforward: Inject attack code (for example, code that invokes a shell) somewhere and overwrite the stack in such a way that the return address is replaced with that of the attack code. If the program being exploited runs with root privilege, the attacker gets that privilege in the interactive session.

Buffer overflow exploit code intimately depends on (i) the CPU, (ii) the OS and (iii) the compiler of the language that the code is in. "Smashing The Stack For Fun And Profit" [13] describes the technique in great detail, and is required reading. It is written in 1990s, and the examples are based on a Linux version running on an x86 32-bit machine. Further more, it has a few inaccuracies [14].

Heap overflows are harder to exploit than stack overflows [15].

### 5.6.3. *Techniques of Avoiding Buffer Overflow*

There are many techniques that can detect and prevent buffer overflow attacks [16]. Most modern programming languages are immune to this problem, either because they automatically resize arrays (e.g., Perl, and Java), or because they normally detect and prevent buffer overflows (e.g., Ada95 and Java). However, the C language provides no protection against such problems, and C++ can be easily used in ways to cause this problem too.

#### 5.6.3.1. *C/C++ library functions*

C/C++ users must avoid using functions that do not check bounds unless it can be asserted that the bounds will never get exceeded. Functions to avoid include: `strcpy()`, `strcat()`, `sprintf()`, and `gets()`. These should be replaced with functions such as `strncpy()`, `strncat()`, `snprintf()`, and `fgets()` respectively. Other functions that may permit buffer overruns include `fscanf()`, `scanf()`, `vsprintf()`, `realpath()`, `getopt()`, `getpass()`, `streadd()`, `strecpy()`, and `strtrns()`.

Note that `strncpy()` and `strncat()` have somewhat surprising semantics. E.g., the function `strncpy (p, q, m)` does not NUL-terminate the destination string $p$ if the source string $q$ is longer than $m - 1$. There is also a performance penalty with `strncpy()` because of NUL-filling the remainder of the destination and because we should do both bounds checking and NUL character checking at every character being copied.

Newer libraries for C include

```
size_t strlcpy (char *dst, const char *src, size_t size);
size_t strlcat (char *dst, const char *src, size_t size);
```

Both `strlcpy` and `strlcat` take the full size of the destination buffer as a parameter (not the maximum number of characters to be copied) and guarantee to NUL-terminate the result (as long as size is larger than 0). The `strlcpy` function copies up to `size-1` characters from the NUL-terminated string `src` to `dst`, NUL-terminating the result. The `strlcat` function appends the NUL-terminated string `src` to the end of `dst`. It will append at most `size - strlen(dst) - 1` bytes, NUL-terminating the result.

One nuisance is that these two functions are not, by default, installed in most Unix-like systems.

### 5.6.3.2. *Compilation enhancements*

Modern compilers are mechanizing stack protection techniques. StackGuard [17] is a modification of the GNU C compiler. It inserts a "canary" value in front of the return address. If a buffer overflow overwrites the return address, the canary's value changes and the system detects this before using it. There are also tools that can statically check, at compile time, based on additional annotations that the programmer provides [18].

### 5.6.3.3. *Non-executable stack*

Linux 32-bit kernels do not use the protection features offered by the segmentation unit and prefers the paging unit. Linux kernel implements the basic flat segmentation model in which all the segments are mapped to the same range of the linear address space. Any page, which is readable, is executable. Because of this in the IA-32 based Linux kernel there is no protection against execution of a page that contains only data.

The page tables of Linux kernel's text are set with read and write permissions enabled. As a result a malicious process in kernel mode can modify the kernel's text. A malicious kernel module, once inserted into the kernel, can access and modify any part of the kernel's memory and can even hide itself from the system administrator's monitoring tools.

It is possible to modify the Linux kernel so that the stack segment is not executable [19], or make certain pages non-executable. However, this is not built into the standard Linux kernels. In Linux 2.6.x kernels, you must chose grsecurity configuration options. Part of the rationale is that this is less protection than it appears; attackers can simply force the system to call other "interesting" locations already in the program (e.g., in its library, the heap, or static data segments). Also, sometimes Linux does require executable code in the stack, e.g., to implement signals and to implement GCC "trampolines".

Even in the presence of non-executable stack, exploits are still possible. "It is really easy. You do something like this: 1) overflow the buffer on the stack, so that the return value is overwritten by a pointer to the `system()` library function. 2) the next four bytes are crap (a "return pointer" for the system call, which you don't care about) 3) the next four bytes are a pointer to some random place in the shared library again that contains the string `"/bin/sh"` (and yes, just do a `strings` on the thing and you'll find it). Voila. You didn't have to write any code, the only thing you needed to know was where the library is loaded by default. And yes, it is library-specific, but hey, you just select one specific commonly used version to crash. Suddenly you have a root shell on the system. So it is not only doable, it is fairly trivial to do. In short, anybody who thinks that the non-executable stack gives them any real security is very very much living in a dream world. It may catch a few attacks for old binaries that have security problems, but the basic problem is that the binaries allow you to overwrite their stacks. And if they allow that, then they allow the above exploit. It probably takes all of five lines of changes to some existing exploit, and some random program to find out where in the address space the shared libraries tend to be loaded" (from a public email of Linus Torvalds).

#### 5.6.3.4. *No set-user-Id programs*

An attacker targets set-user-id (suid) root programs so that after the exploit he is the root, and can do arbitrary things. Thus, it is helpful to reduce the number of suid programs on a system. But, many network services run as root (and generally for no good reason other than to make use of a privileged low port), and some not-so-good sysadmins, in order to get something to work properly, have set entire directories of programs to setuid root.

## 5.7. Network Exploits

The TCP/IP suite has many design weaknesses [20] so far as security and privacy are concerned, all perhaps because in the era (1970s) when the development took place network attacks were unknown. The flaws present in many implementations exacerbate the problem. A number of these are due to the infamous buffer overflow. However, considerable blame belongs to the many ambiguous RFCs [21].

This section is an overview of security attacks on the core protocols (IP, UDP, and TCP) and infrastructure protocols (ARP, ICMP, DNS) to the extent that they affect a single computer system. We do not address the exploits in various application protocols, but do focus on additional issues such as covert channels.

### 5.7.1. *IPv4 Exploits*

#### 5.7.1.1. *IP address spoofing*

The IP layer of the typical OS simply trusts that the source address, as it appears in an IP packet, is valid. Replacing the true IP address of the sender (or, in rare cases, the destination) with a different address is known as IP spoofing. Because the IP layer of the OS normally adds these IP addresses to a data packet, a spoofer must circumvent the IP layer and talk directly to the raw network device. IP spoofing is used as a technique aiding an exploit on the target machine. For example, an attacker can silence a host A from sending further packets to B by sending a spoofed packet announcing a window size of zero to A as though it originated from B. Note that the attackers machine cannot simply be assigned the IP address of another host T, using `ifconfig` or a similar configuration tool. Other hosts, as well as T, will discover (through ARP, for example) that there are two machines with the same IP address.

We can monitor packets using network-monitoring software. A packet on an external interface that has both its source and destination IP addresses in the local domain is an indication of IP spoofing. Another way to detect IP spoofing is to compare the process accounting logs between systems on your internal network. If the IP spoofing attack has succeeded on one of your systems, a log entry on the victim machine shows a remote access; on the apparent source machine, there will be no corresponding entry for initiating that remote access. There are more advanced methods for detecting spoofed packets [22].

All routers must employ proper IP filtering rules. They should only route packets from sources that could legitimately come from the interface the packet arrives on.

#### 5.7.1.2. *IP fragment attacks*

A well-behaving set of IP fragments is non-overlapping. Unfortunately, in the IP layer implementations of nearly all OS, there are bugs and naive assumptions in the reassembly code. A pair of carefully crafted but malformed IP packets that have illegal fragment offsets causes a server to crash during reassembly. The 1997 attack tool called `teardrop` exploited this vulnerability.

### 5.7.2. *UDP Exploits*

A UDP flood attack sends a large number of UDP packets to random ports. Such ports may be open or closed. If open, an application listening at that port needs to respond. If closed, the network layer of the OS, replies with an ICMP Destination Unreachable packet. Thus, the victim host will be forced into sending many ICMP packets and wasting computing cycles. If the flooding is large enough, the host will eventually be unreachable by other clients. The attacker will also IP-spoof the UDP packets, both to hide and to ensure that the ICMP return packets do not reach him.

An attack called `fraggle` used packets of UDP echo service in the same fashion as the ICMP echo packets. To defend, most hosts disable many UDP services such as the `chargen` and `echo`.

### 5.7.3. *TCP Exploits*

#### 5.7.3.1. *TCP sequence number prediction*

TCP exploits are typically based on IP spoofing and sequence number prediction. In establishing a TCP connection, both the server and the client generate an initial sequence number (ISN) from which they will start counting the segments transmitted. Host Y accepts the segments from X only when correct SEQ/ACK numbers are used. The ISN is (should be) generated at random and should be hard to predict. However, some implementations of the TCP/IP protocol make it rather easy to predict this sequence number. The attacker either sniffs the current SEQ+ACK numbers of the connection or can algorithmically predict them.

Current OSs use "SYN cookies" [23] that help make better choices of initial TCP sequence numbers.

#### 5.7.3.2. *Closing connections*

An established TCP connection is expected to be close by the 4-way handshake that involves sending FIN segments. An attacker can enact this easily. The attacker constructs a spoofed FIN segment and injects it fast. It will have the correct SEQ number, that is computed from segments sniffed from the immediate past, so that it is accepted by the targeted host. This host would believe the (spoofed) sender had no data left. Any segments that may follow from the legitimate sender would be ignored as bogus. The rest of the four-way handshake is also supplied by the attacker. A similar connection killing attack using RST is also well known.

#### 5.7.3.3. *Connection hijacking*

If an attacker on machine Z can sniff the segments between X and Y that have a TCP connection, Z can hijack the connection. Z can send segments to Y spoofing the source address as X, at a time when X was silent. (Z can increase the chances of this by launching a denial of service attack against X.) Y would accept these data and update ACK numbers. X may subsequently continue to send its segments using old SEQ numbers, as it is unaware of the intervention of Z. As a result, subsequent segments from X are discarded by Y. The attacker Z is now effectively impersonating X, using "correct" SEQ/ACK numbers from the perspective of Y. This results in Z hijacking the connection: host X is confused, whereas Y thinks nothing is wrong as Z sends "correctly synchronized" segments to Y. If the hijacked connection was running an interactive shell, Z can execute any arbitrary command that X could. Having accomplished his deed, a clever hijacker would bow out gracefully by monitoring the true X. He would cause the SEQ numbers of X to match the ACK numbers of Y by sending to the true X a segment that it generates of appropriate length, spoofing the sender as Y, using the ACK numbers that X would accept. Such connection forgery is also possible to do "blind", i.e., without being able to sniff. The attacker guesses that a connection exists, and guesses a valid port and sequence numbers. Note that well-known routers use well-known ports and stay connected for fairly long periods. ACK storms are generated in the hijack technique described above. A host Y, when it receives packets from X after a hijack has ended, will find the packets of X to be out of order. TCP requires that Y must send an immediate reply with an ACK number that it expects. The same behavior is expected of X. So, X and Y send each other ACK messages that may never end.

#### 5.7.3.4. *Connection flooding*

TCP RFC has no limit set on the time to wait after receiving the SYN in the three-way handshake. An attacker initiates many connection requests with spoofed source addresses to the victim machine. The victim machine maintains data related to the connection being attempted in its memory. The SYN+ACK segments that the victim host sends are not replied to. Once the implementation imposed limit of such half-open connections is reached, the victim host will refuse further connection establishment attempts from any host until a partially opened connection in the queue is completed or times out. This effectively removes a host from the network for several seconds, making it useful at least as a stepping tool to other attacks, such as IP spoofing. Chen describes defenses against TCP SYN flooding attacks under different types of IP spoofing.30 A server that uses SYN cookies sends back a SYN+ACK, when its SYN queue fills up. It also must reject TCP options such as large windows, and it must use one of the eight MSS values that it can encode. When the server receives an ACK, it checks that the secret function works for a recent value of a 32-bit time counter, and then rebuilds the SYN queue entry from the encoded MSS.

#### 5.7.3.5. *TCP reset attack*

The recent (2004) TCP reset attack lead to severe concerns in the routing protocol BGP used in large routers. This is attack does not involve sniffing, but does depend on having done enough reconnaissance regarding the BGP partners and the source port numbers they use. TCP protocol requires that a receiver close a connection when it receives an RST segment, even if it has a sequence number that is not an exact match of what is expected, as long as the number is within the window size. Thus, the larger the window size the easier it is to guess a sequence number to be placed in a spoofed TCP RST segment. [24] gives a detailed account of this attack.

#### 5.7.3.6. *Low-rate/shrew TCP attacks*

The low-rate TCP attack, also known as the shrew attack [25], exploits the congestion control mechanism, forces other well-behaving TCP flows to back off, and enter the retransmission timeout state. This sort of attack is difficult to identify due to a large family of attack patterns. Detection and defense mechanisms capable of mitigating the attack are being developed by several groups [26].

#### 5.7.3.7. *Illegal segments: SYN+FIN*

The TCP specification does not specify clearly certain transitions. As an example, suppose an attacker sends a TCP segment with both the SYN and the FIN bit set. Depending on the TCP implementation, victim host processes the SYN flag first, generates a reply segment with the corresponding ACK flag set, and perform a state-transition to the state SYN-RCVD. Victim host then processes the FIN flag, performs a transition to the state CLOSE-WAIT, and sends the ACK segment back to attacker. The attacking host does not send any other segment to victim. TCP state machine in the victim for this connection is in CLOSE-WAIT state. The victim connection gets stuck in this state until the expiry of the keep-alive timer.

### 5.7.4. *DNS Exploits*

Domain name service (DNS) is about associating names such as `osis110.cs.wright.edu` with their IP addresses and vice-versa. There have been serious attacks of large scale DNS servers (see e.g., (`http://news.zdnet.com/2100-1009_22-151146.html`)). A domain is hijacked when an attacker is able to redirect queries to servers that are under the control of the attacker. This can happen because of (i) cache poisoning, (ii) forgery, or (iii) a domain server has been compromised.

DNS cache poisoning can happen on large DNS servers as well as on an ordinary system. Cache poisoning happens when the OS updates ("poisons") its local table of DNS information, known as cache, based on misinformation supplied by DNS server in the control of an attacker. This may be about just one domain name or an entire DNS zone.

The DNS answers that a host receives may have come from an attacker who sniffs a query between the victim resolver and the legitimate name servers and responds to it with misleading data faster than the legitimate name server does. The attacked host may in fact be a DNS server.

The server programs that provided DNS service were, over the years, almost without exception, prone to buffer overflow exploits.

An effective counter measure against DNS poisoning is to populate the local `etc/hosts` file with DNS entries of important servers. Note that DNS forgeries can be detected by noticing multiple DNS replies. While this cannot prevent a hijack, it can certainly be used in cleaning the cache.

### 5.7.5. *ICMP Exploits*

The attack tool of 1997, called `smurf` sends ICMP ping messages. It made possible several other attacks such as route redirection, reconnaissance and scanning. Arkin [27] describes an OS finger printing method based on ICMP. Covert channels are enabled by ICMP (see Section 5.7.7).

### 5.7.6. *ARP Poisoning*

ARP discovers the (Ethernet) MAC address of a device whose IP address is known. The translation is performed with a table look-up. Local operating systems maintain this table known as the ARP cache. When an entry is not found in the cache, the OS uses ARP to broadcast a query.

ARP poisoning is an attack technique that corrupts the ARP cache with wrong Ethernet addresses for some IP addresses. An attacker accomplishes this by sending an ARP response packet that is deliberately constructed with a "wrong" MAC address. ARP poisoning enables the so-called man-in-the-middle attack that can defeat cryptographic communications such as SSH, SSL and IPSec.

ARP packets are not routed, and this makes it very rewarding to the attacker if a router can be ARP poisoned. To defend, we must monitor changes in the ARP cache using tools such as `arpwatch`. Unfortunately, it is not possible to block the poisoning other than after-the-fact "immediate" cleanup. Setting static mapping of IP to MAC addresses eliminates the problem but this does not scale to large networks. Note that ARP does not use an IP header and tracking the attackers is difficult. It is often suggested that one should periodically broadcast MAC address of important servers and gateway, which cleans up poisoning of corresponding entries.

There are proposals for new secure ARP: [28], and [29]. There are several ideas to detect ARP spoofing; see, e.g., [30].

### 5.7.7. *Covert Channels*

A covert channel is "any communication channel that can be exploited by a process to transfer information in a manner that violates the systems security policy". Covert channels do not modify the TCP/IP stack. The make legitimate use of the protocols. Obviously, covert channels need either specialized client and/or servers to inject and retrieve covert data.

Covert channels are the principle enablers in a distributed denial of service (DDoS) attack that causes a denial of service to legitimate machines. Covert channels are possible in nearly all the protocols of the TCP/IP suite.

### 5.7.8. *Traffic Scrubbing*

Scrubbing refers to forcing the TCP/IP traffic to obey all the rules of the RFCs [31]. Reserved fields can be set to a random value; illegal combinations of flags are checked, and so on. Scrubbing is expected to be done not only at the originating hosts but also on the routers and especially in firewalls.

Scrubbing adds to the computational burden of the hosts. Because of hidden assumptions made by programs beyond the specifications of the RFCs, scrubbing may disrupt interoperability.

## 5.8. Secure Installation

The life of a secured system begins with the choice of an appropriately secured distribution that includes a secured kernel and only secured programs. These should have been properly installed and properly configured. Any installation be made "secure" if we permit ourselves the freedom to (i) not only configure the installed components, but also (ii) replace entire *sub*systems. Securing a system is a continuing effort. As exploits become known, detection, prevention, and repair procedures need to be adjusted.

Let us further assume that the system has been running well, and connected to the Internet for a few days without incident. Have We Booted Securely? While the system is running, is everything secure? How can we be sure that buffer overflow bugs, set-user-id scripts, bugs in kernel code have not been exploited? This section is about answering such questions.

### 5.8.1. *Terminology*

We should distinguish proper configuration, "fortification", and hardening of an installation.

*Proper Configuration* of the system as given is a prerequisite to either fortifying or hardening. Systems as distributed are often loosely configured. Occasionally this is due to sloppiness of the distributor. More commonly it is because the distributor has tried to configure a generic appeal-to-all setup. So, it is important that we examine the configuration at length and determine what if any changes must be made.

*Fortification* is about adding a layer of protection beyond proper configuration of the OS and applications. This layer of protection consists of tools that help detect changes in the system and monitor (suspicious) system activity. Fortification is the addition (and in some cases *deletion*) of packages to improve security. It should be done after a system has been properly configured with the supplied components. Fortification frequently will discard a supplied component in preference to a carefully chosen added component.

*Hardening* refers to the redesign of the OS and its components and/or source code modifications that tighten security prior to the compilation rather than after their deployment.

### 5.8.2. *Proper Configuration*

Many so-called hardening guides are actually about proper configuration. For example, the Bastille Hardening Program (`http://bastille-linux.sourceforge.net/`) is a script that is expected to be run soon after a fresh installation. It draws from the advice of a number of reputable sources on Linux security. As it runs, Bastille Linux educates the installing administrator about the security issues involved in each of the script's tasks.

The `cert.org` has many guides on proper configuration.

### 5.8.3. *Fortification*

#### 5.8.3.1. *Security violation detection tools*

Detection of malware must be an important function included in the requirements of a secure distribution. This includes detection of viruses, worms, and Trojans, and intrusion detection subsystems.

An attacker often installs root-kits to hide their presence on the system. These are Trojaned command replacements for system binaries and libraries. Tools to detect the presence of root-kits must be included.

File integrity checking via cryptographic signatures of all system files is necessary.

The current Linux kernels include IP filtering abilities. The distribution should make use of `iptables`. It should include tools such as `snort`.

#### 5.8.3.2. *Watching an OS*

A user/ sysadmin should know what processes are expected to be present and be able to tell when unusual processes appear.

Services (or daemons) are processes that are expected to be alive until an explicit termination signal is sent. The daemons are alive while the OS is alive and fully functional. A death of a daemon is a sign of something gone wrong with the system.

`Init` is the first daemon created by the kernel. This process has to continuously run in order to keep the OS completely functional and if we happen to terminate this process, the system is surely going to crash.

The `syslogd` daemon logs all system events into a text file, typically `/var/log/messages`. The system administrator determines which events are worth keeping track of. This is a very important process in terms of security since the attacker takes care to see that he eludes this process from monitoring his events. Only an incompetent attacker tries to kill this process, which makes it too obvious to the system administrator that something is wrong with the system.

The `klogd` process is similar to the syslogd process but it monitors the events of the kernel. This process records the return values of the functions that are run, and creates a log file so that it is available for fault detection at a later time.

`inetd` is the "server of servers" through which all network serving connections are established. For example, if some other machine requests a `ssh` connection the, inetd process grants the connection. In this action, two configuration files `/etc/inetd.conf` and `/etc/services` are consulted.

`portmap` contains the map of all the active ports of the system. This process allocates the port for a request by a local server, and can answer a remote client regarding where a certain service is listening.

`getty` processes run on different virtual terminals on the Linux system. The getty process is in charge of a user's attempt to login.

## 5.9. Secure Distributions of Linux

On various Linux portal sites, many distributions are described as secured. We use the phrase "secured Linux" in a more restrictive manner coupled with a number of expectations.

> "The open-source movement is not inherently guaranteed to come up with secure software unless there is significant discipline in the development, distribution, operation and administration of the resulting systems. So it's important to realize that we have a lot of weak links, all of which have to be addressed. The idea that hiding the source code is going to solve the problem is utterly ridiculous". – Peter G. Neumann.

### 5.9.1. *Definition of a Distribution*

A collection of system tools, applications and of course the kernel are packaged together with an install script as a so-called "distribution". Securing a distribution therefore includes securing the kernel itself (see Section 5.10). By securing a distribution, we mean the proper selection of various tools and applications and how well they are configured with respect to security in their default installation. We would like to distinguish the "security of a distribution" from that of an installed system after it has been properly configured. Without this distinction, all distributions can be considered to be equally secure.

A typical distribution of Linux today (2008) uses up more than 5 GB of hard disk. In this section, we exclude the X11, KDE, GNOME and other desktop GUI components, all games, compilers, interpreters and other development tools for various languages. These components do contribute to insecurity, but to keep this section from becoming too long we exclude them.

It is possible to specifically list system tools by their names. But different distributions make different choices. So, we describe them here by their "group names": Standard C libraries, shells, services (daemons), management tools for user accounts, network, and in general system, printing subsystem, mail subsystem.

### 5.9.2. *What Makes a Distribution Secure?*

(i) Size Versus Functionality: It should be obvious that the more limited the collected functionality of a distribution is the more secure it is going to be.

It is an unfortunate fact of the programming world that the larger a program is the higher the number of bugs it contains. We expect the distributions to prefer smaller programs of similar functionality, and also to contain as few programs as possible also.

For a given functionality, having multiple tools is a similar situation. The typical distribution tries to cater to different "tastes" of users, and may include a dozen different text editors, three different desktop environments, four different browsers, and so on. A secure distribution should not do so unless the choices provided are among equally secure packages.

(ii) Functionality that can be Sacrificed: It is often acknowledged that a secure system is less "convenient" than a loose one. If the super user wishes to edit configuration files remotely, even if it is via `ssh`, the system will be less secure than that of a system where such functionality is sacrificed. A system that includes LIDS [32], for example, requires a reboot with LIDS disabled in order to modify its configuration. It is also obvious that a completely closed is the most secure but useless. So, what can be sacrificed is a balancing act.

(iii) Security of Included Components: Consider an example component that is infamous for containing exploitable bugs: sendmail. A distribution should either use a different mail agent that is known to be more secure, or at least include a version of sendmail that incorporates patches to all known vulnerabilities.

(iv) Free from Buffer Overflows: All buffer overflow exploits (see Section 5.6) and format string exploits are due to bugs. There are now tools such as [33] that can spot these errors at compile-time. There are also kernel modifications, that make the run time stack non-executable. Hence, if a component of a secure distribution yield to these exploits, we should downgrade the security ranking of the distribution.

(v) Audited Source Code: Every component should be audited by at least one person other than the author. Unfortunately, even though Linux is a product of the open source movement, it has not followed the path of systematic audits. We believe source code audit of every component of a distribution is a minimum requirement for it be considered secure. However, we are afraid, on this basis no distribution is secure.

(vi) Security Patches: Many distributors have been diligent in generating fixes within days or weeks after being notified of an exploit. That there should be no exploitable bugs appears to be an unachievable goal. That the distributor must supply patches within, say, two weeks is quite a realistic requirement.

(vii) Services: Most distributions enable a service when the corresponding package is installed. Such services either get started during boot time or are invoked via the inetd. The installed presence of an unneeded service is questionable, but just because it is installed to enable it is even more questionable.

All the services should have been revised so that they run in chroot-jails [34].

Most services should be run without the privileges of the root.

(viii) Safe Defaults: Every subsystem gets installed with certain default values so that it is functional. Instead of easy-to-use and "all features available", the default settings must be secure. Many of the options available in complex software are never used at the vast majority of sites, but still pose security risks if left enabled. This applies to services (daemons).

(ix) Correct Permissions on Files and Directories: Many logs and configuration files should be unreadable, unwriteable etc to nearly all users except perhaps the root. Directories such as `/bin`, `/sbin`, `/usr/bin`, and `/usr/bin` should not be writable when the system is running in the normal mode. Both these requirements are frequently violated.

(x) Discarding Insecure Tools: A secure distribution should opt to discard an insecure tool when secure alternatives are not available and incur the inconvenience. For example, it is no longer acceptable to include plain `telnet` and `rlogin` class of tools.

(xi) Authentication: User authentication should be based on better schemes than having `/etc/passwd` and `/etc/shadow`. The password database should be accessible to only a few programs such as `login`. All passwords should be at least 8 characters and checked for their guess-ability extensively. Host authentication also must be included.

(xii) Careful Logging: Logs are an aid in discovering intrusion. Unfortunately, several distributions leave them readable to everyone, and on occasion even writable. A secure distribution should provide for append-only logs, and have a way out when the file system becomes full.

A typical Linux distribution does not log all TCP connections, but rather only connections to "well-known" ports, or those ports listed in the `/etc/services` file. There are tools, such as `tcplogd`, and `icmpinfo`, that can be added to log any TCP connection to any port.

## 5.10. Kernel Hardening

*Kernel Hardening* refers to the redesign of the kernel and/or source code modifications that tighten security prior to the compilation of OS kernels rather than after their deployment. A security hardened kernel should be untamperable. It should make it impossible for applications to bypass access controls.

The word "kernel" is used variously in the OS literature. In this article, we need a working a definition. Rather than enter into a long debate trying to settle this definition, we consider the following to be the Linux kernel.

By *kernel source* we mean all the source code that compiles and links into (i) the file `bzImage`, that is typically installed as `/boot/vmlinuz` (ii) the files collectively known as *loadable kernel modules* that are typically installed into the directory `/lib/modules`. (iii) the following system utilities: `insmod, rmmod, modprobe` that operate on kernel modules, and a few others such as `ifconfig, route, iptables, ld.so` that are typically located in the `/sbin` directory.

### 5.10.1. *Kernel Exploits*

Kernel exploits exist for every OS. Below we highlight a few in the context of Linux.

#### 5.10.1.1. *Chroot jails*

`chroot` system call changes the directory that is considered the root ("the slash") of a process. All subsequent absolute path names of a file are resolved with respect to the new root. The process cannot access files that are outside of the tree rooted at the new root directory, even in the presence of hard or symbolic links. Such a process is said to be in a "jail" or "chroot jail". Server daemons, such as anonymous FTP server, and web server, where the processes need access to a limited sub tree only, are run inside a `chroot` jail for security reasons.

Unfortunately, weaknesses exist, and a jailed superuser process can break out of it. Linux `chroot` restricts only the "real" (e.g., persistent storage media) file system access of the processes in the jail. Using inter process communication mechanisms such as domain sockets, shared memory segments, pipes, and signals, a jailed process can damage the rest of the system.

#### 5.10.1.2. *LKM root-kits*

Loadable kernel modules (LKM) bring run-time modularity. On the negative side, LKM root-kits are the easiest and most "elegant" way to modify the running kernel. Linux kernel does not have a proper authentication system for inserting the kernel modules. It also does not restrict a loaded module from accessing any part of the kernel's memory. As a result LKM has become the best place for installing kernel root-kits. In a modularized kernel the attacker can insert root-kits into kernel once he gains root privileges. Through LKM root-kit the attacker can modify any part of the kernel. Typically LKM root-kits would redirect the system calls to the attacker's own implementation.

The Linux kernel has a `sys_call_table[]`, an array of 7-byte elements consisting of a 3-byte jump instruction and a 4-byte address of a function. The attacker diverts selected system calls such as `open, read, write` to Trojan versions by resetting corresponding jump table entries to point to the Trojans.

The binaries of the Trojan system calls is often contained in an LKM, and the table resetting is done in the `init-module`. The code of Trojan system call functions is often a wrapper. It can be as simple as checking their arguments, handling the cases of interest to them, and invoking the original system calls for all non-interesting cases. More elaborate Trojan system call functions modify the output of the original system call and/or modify the inputs before submitting them to the original system call.

The location of the jump table and the header node of the module list are kernel version specific. These are found in `/boot/System.map`, if available. Otherwise, the attacker fingerprints the OS and has more work to do to discover them.

A variation of this technique [35] goes one step deeper in the kernel internals in order to evade detection. The attacker replaces the `do_execve()` kernel internal function called by the `sys_execve()` system call function. This gives the Trojan the actual arguments as dissected by the system call `sys_execve()` and passed to the `do_execve()` function eliminating the need to extract the arguments from the "registers" for manipulating them.

#### 5.10.1.3. `/dev/kmem` *root-kits*

`/dev/kmem` is a "character device" that is an image of the kernel's virtual memory. Through this device, an attacker can modify the kernel's text or data, and can drastically change the behavior of kernel. Other memory devices which can similarly be exploited are `/dev/mem` and `/dev/port` which give direct access to physical memory of the system.

Superkit [8] does not depend upon LKM support in the kernel. Instead, it uses `/dev/kmem` to install itself. The `execve()` system call is redirected to a custom version that executes pristine init every time `/sbin/init` is the argument to `execve()`. The files and programs that need to be hidden are all suffixed by `sk`. The Superkit program executes a file named `.rc` present in the home directory of the root kit which is configured during compilation. This file is used to start programs fancied by the attacker during every boot. The contents of `/etc/inittab` are also copied into this file so that during every boot the compromised system starts all the programs and services as usual.

The fundamental weakness that gives away root kits is that they must reside in a persistent storage device. The not-so clever root kits install themselves as normal files with with tricky names. The clever root kits make use of free blocks of a storage device.

Root kits are discoverable through well-known root kit detectors as well as file integrity checkers because the typical root kits have not gone far enough in replacing standard libraries, and analyzing the system to see what root kit detectors are in place. The kernel module root-kit detectors, such as StMichael_LKM [36], have built-in signatures for the standard system call functions and check the existing system call functions of the kernels and can detect if they have been replaced with custom functions of a root-kit. These kernel root-kit detectors examine the first 7 bytes of the system call functions and compare them with their database of the function signatures.

#### 5.10.1.4. *Race conditions*

Often, a privileged process first probes the state of a file and then takes subsequent action based on the results of that probe. If these two actions are not together atomic, an attacker can race between the actions (after the probe but before the resultant action), and exploit them. For example, a server process may require a file in `/tmp` directory be created, and so it would check the existence of a file with a certain name. Once it is confirmed that file does not exist it creates the file. An attacker would learn of the name from prior observations. Between checking and creation, the attacker would race and create a soft link to a security sensitive file, with same name. The server process which is not aware of this would access the link file and writes into it.

RaceGuard [37] can detect attempts to exploit temporary file race vulnerabilities. It works fast enough that the attack can be halted before it takes effect.

5.10.1.5. *ptrace exploit*

For debugging purposes, Linux provides `ptrace` system call that one process can use to completely control another process. This system call is often exploited to take control of the privileged processes and let them damage the system.

5.10.1.6. *Close files on execve*

When a process invokes the `execve` system call, the file descriptors are not closed unless close-on-exec flag is set on individual files. The process has to explicitly close them before the system call or it should set close-on-exec flag on the file descriptor. Sloppy developers forget to close files before calling `execve`. Attackers often take control of such vulnerable process and can access or modify the contents of the file which is left open.

### 5.10.2. *Kernel Patches*

This section summarizes various contributions of concrete code that can be merged into the Linux kernel source. Kernel patches for Linux are released at the source code level. These replace section(s) of code in a specific version of the kernel. Often a patch is in response to a newly discovered security hole. But, there are proactive modifications also in the open source OS.

5.10.2.1. *Janus*

A "sand box" is a virtual machine (VM) that is capable of restricting the activities of a process. This is called the "sand box" approach because the process is kept within a safe environment where it can do no damage to itself or "others".

Janus [38] is a security tool for sandboxing untrusted applications within a restricted execution environment. This can be used to limit the harm that can be caused by any successful compromise of the application. We have successfully used Janus to jail Apache, bind, and other programs within a limited sandbox without disturbing application behavior, and we continue to seek experience with using this approach in production environments.

5.10.2.2. *Domain and type enforcement*

DTE is a simplified form of capabilities. Domains and types are attributes respectively of processes and files. Hallyn [39] implements DTE as a Linux Security Module, and provides tools for the composition and analysis of policies.

#### 5.10.2.3. *LSM, linux security modules*

The Linux Security Module (LSM) [40] project has developed a light-weight access control framework that permits many different access control models to be implemented as loadable kernel modules. Linux capabilities, Security Enhanced Linux, Domain, and Type enforcement have been adapted to use LSM framework.

#### 5.10.2.4. *SE-Linux*

SE-Linux Security Enhanced Linux [41] supports a combination of type enforcement (TE) and role-based access controls (RBAC). The type enforcement component defines an extensible set of domains and types. Each process has an associated domain, and each object has an associated type. The configuration files specify how domains are allowed to access types and to interact with other domains. They specify what types (when applied to programs) can be used to enter each domain and the allowable transitions between domains. They also specify automatic transitions between domains when programs of certain types are executed. Such transitions ensure that system processes and certain programs are placed into their own separate domains automatically when executed.

The RBAC component defines an extensible set of roles. Each process has an associated role. This ensures that system processes and those used for system administration can be separated from those of ordinary users. The configuration files specify the set of domains that may be entered by each role. Each user role has an initial domain that is associated with the user's login shell. As users execute programs, transitions to other domains may, according to the policy configuration, automatically occur to support changes in privilege.

Processes and other subjects perform operations on objects based on certain conditions. Conditions are formulas involving operations, objects, time, events, history, processes, files, semaphores, shared memory segments, signals, and many kernel-internal data structures.

#### 5.10.2.5. *OpenWall*

Typical stack smashing overwrites a function's return address via a buffer overflow. Another way is to point the return address to a function in `libc`, usually `system()`. OpenWall makes the stack non-executable, and also changes the default address that shared libraries are `mmap()`-ed at.

Directories that include a `+t` are for the creation and use of temporary files. Establishing symbolic links and hard links in such directories is a source for race conditions. Openwall does not allow users to create hard links to files they do not own, unless they could read and write the file (due to group permissions).

Openwall also restricts writes into untrusted FIFOs (named pipes), to make data spoofing attacks harder.

Openwall also restricts the permissions on /proc so that non-root users can see their own processes only, and nothing about active network connections, unless they're in a special group.

File descriptors 0, 1, and 2 are expected to be corresponding to stdin, stdout and stderr. An attacker can close these, and open other files, and then execute a SUID/SGID binary. Depending on the order in which the open() is invoked it can yield the same numbers. Openwall ensures that if any of the 0, 1, or 2 is closed, the device `/dev/null` will be opened for it.

A denial of service situation develops if too many processes are created. Openwall strengthens the checks that the standard kernel makes in this regard.

Shared memory segments are not counted in the resource usage of a process. Frequently, unattached segments continue to live. Openwall destroys shared memory segments when their attach count becomes zero after a detach or a process termination. It will also destroy segments that were created, but never attached to.

Openwall ensures that only root can bind sockets to addresses of privileged aliased interfaces.

#### 5.10.2.6. *Linux trustees*

Linux "trustees" is a permission management system (`http://sourceforge.net/projects/trustees/`) based on special objects, called *trustees*, that are bound to every file and directory. A trustee describes the permissions granted (or denied) to certain user or group (or all except user or group), with the default being deny.

#### 5.10.2.7. *REMUS*

One must protect the contents of memory (and hence processes, and various kernel data structures), the contents of persistent media (configuration files, MD5 sums, files, executables, and boot sectors), and the contents of firmware (BIOS, CMOS tables). This is most effectively done by system call interception, and verification. Having intercepted a system call, it is often necessary maintain state information regarding the specific objects these calls are manipulating.

"Reference Monitors" check the parameters, and either permit the operation to go through as if the system call had never been monitored, or deny it altogether when the called returned an error value.

REMUS (REference Monitor for Unix Systems) (`http://remus.sourceforge.net`) [42] is implemented both as a loadable kernel module and as a kernel patch. It intercepts system calls without requiring changes to syntax and semantics of existing system calls, and can detect illegal invocations of system calls. It isolates a subset of system calls and tasks critical to system security and hence allow reduction of monitoring overhead. It can also prevent loading of certain kernel modules. It also integrates the Access Control Database (ACD) with the Unix standard virtual file system `/proc`.

5.10.2.8. *GR security*

"Grsecurity" is a set of security patches for Linux (`http://www.grsecurity.net/`) that provides non-executable stack, an ACL system, `/proc` restrictions, `chroot` restrictions, linking and FIFO restrictions, `exec` and `set*id` logging, secure file descriptors, trusted path execution, randomized PIDs, randomized TCP source ports, altered ping ids, randomized TTL, better IP stack randomness, socket restrictions, sysctl support on nearly all options, secure keymap loading, stealth networking enhancements, signal logging, failed fork logging, time change logging, and others.

5.10.2.9. *LIDS*

Linux Intrusion Detection System (LIDS) [32] (`http://www.lids.org/`) is a kernel patch whose main focus is on access control lists. Other enhancements include Linux capabilities, protecting important processes, and port scan detection, stack smashing protection, disabling the loading of modules, locking routing tables, protecting daemons from signals, read-only and append-only flags to protect programs or log files from a root intruder.

LIDS also provides read-only file system protection at a finer granularity of protection on individual files. With LIDS, a file or directory can be made read-only, or append-only. LIDS implements it own ACLs in the kernel and they are integrated into VFS so that it would not depend on the file system type. LIDS ACLs are enforced during boot-up scripts as soon as mounting is done and it cannot be turned off till administrator decides to turn off entire LIDS.

### 5.10.3. *Synthesis of a New Kernel*

Standard Linux kernels installed by many distributions are not as secure as they can be. Only a few of the patches made available by security groups are applied to the standard source code tree of Linux. We can only speculate the causes for this non-acceptance. The main reason is fear of performance loss when some of the security patches are applied. The secondary reason is that the patches are not thoroughly audited. The tertiary reason is that the supplied patches are considerably behind the latest kernel development.

New hardened kernels should guarantee that the following old exploit techniques do not succeed any more. In the new kernels, a few poorly written but legitimate programs may crash, and we believe this price is worth the enhancement in security.

5.10.3.1. *Better software engineering*

> "How should I know if it works? That's what beta testers are for. I only coded it." – Linus Torvalds.

The development of the Linux kernel, and the rest of its system is such an amazing phenomenon of world-wide collaboration that there are excellent studies written up about it [43]. Even with thousands of eyes examining its source code, and millions recompiling it with different configurations, the kernel contains critical bugs [44].

Secure kernels should undergo evaluation of their overall design, verification of the integrity and reliability of their source code, and systematic, independent penetration evaluation. Testing is necessary to reveal the vulnerability of old attack techniques, but is not sufficient to detect new exposures. Code audit should not to be confused with a security audit of a system. The source code of kernel needs to be reviewed by people who are knowledgeable in kernel internals and current literature.

Kernels included in the major distributions are compiled by specific versions of GNU gcc. Often, other compilers would produce a kernel that crashes. It is then a difficult question of figuring out whether the kernel source is using ambiguous C constructs, or the compiler is generating incorrect code.

#### 5.10.3.2. *Stealth*

There is a need to be as invisible as possible to an attacker and to even engage in counter espionage. An attacker often tries to first identify the system he wishes to attack because he can then use more specific techniques. In days past, an attempt to remotely login would bring on the screen a prompt screen from the remote system identifying its CPU and OS version. Today, most systems are silent.

Modern UNIX systems mount a pseudo file system called the `proc` file system at `/proc`, which acts as an interface to the data structures of the kernel. The `proc` file system is a virtual file system which is not associated with a block device, but exists only in the kernel memory. It can be used to obtain information about the processes, and also to modify certain kernel data structures dynamically. Initially when `proc` file system was introduced, it was an optional feature. Today's Linux `proc` is so extensive that many utilities depend on the `/proc` files for reading and writing kernel data structures instead of using system calls. With the information provided by the `proc` file system, the system can be attacked more easily.

#### 5.10.3.3. *Random numbers*

The standard kernel generates numbers in several contexts whose specific value is irrelevant. For example, the id of the next process forked need not be one-higher than the last. Apart from the tradition that the init process is numbered 1, there are no expectations regarding process IDs. In TCP/IP, sequence numbers when initiating connections can be random. Several old exploits have used the predictable nature of these numbers.

The general recommendation is to use random numbers for all kernel-internal purposes where specific values do not matter. It is also not considered safe to use a pseudo random number generator. Instead, there are now "character" devices, `/dev/random` and `/dev/urandom`, which provide random data at any time for any application such as generating random passwords, seeding TCP sequence numbers, generating PGP keys, and SSH challenges. `/dev/random` is high quality entropy, generated from measuring the system interrupt times and other events which are non-deterministic. Unfortunately, `/dev/random` can run out of random bytes and can block the call for a long time waiting for new user-generated entries. `/dev/urandom` is similar, but when the store of entropy is running low, it will return a cryptographically strong hash of available bits.

#### 5.10.3.4. *Packet drops*

A secure kernel should drop incoming packets not aimed at it (received while an interface is in promiscuous mode) as soon as possible, even before they are processed by such modules as `iptables`. This fixes the characteristic reply to packets 'with my IP address but bogus MAC' while in promiscuous mode that allows easy sniffer detection. Bad flag packets should also be silently dropped, but other bogus packets to unserved ports should be replied with a TCP RST or an ICMP port unreachable.

#### 5.10.3.5. *Defeating TCP/IP stack fingerprinting*

An attacker often tries to first identify the system he wishes to attack because he can then use more specific techniques. In days past, an attempt to remotely login would bring on the screen a prompt screen from the remote system identifying its CPU and OS version.

The TCP/IP stack fingerprint scrubber works at both the network and transport layers to convert ambiguous traffic from a heterogeneous group of hosts into sanitized packets that do not reveal clues about the hosts' operating systems.

#### 5.10.3.6. *New additions*

There are a number of standard items that are easily watchable because the OS gives built-in support. However, their granularity is too large. E.g., we cannot see the actual physical page frame numbers of a process.

For forensic purposes, it is essential to log all important events. In any system worthy of being protected, logging is necessary when system calls that require superuser privileges are invoked, when a general protection error occurs, when kernel denies a resource allocation to a process, and during module loading. All the kernel messages are written to a buffer which is read by a user process called `klogd`, through a system call, and are written to a file on the local system. Logging is insecure in standard Linux kernel.

#### 5.10.3.7. *Deletions*

Often, unneeded services are exploited by the intruders. A well-secured server system would have pruned the services that are run, and would have carefully configured the services that do run. The construction process of secure kernels should provide pruning control at the level of system calls, capabilities, memory devices, network interface configuration, routing table configuration, and `ext` file system attributes. Many of these items should be eliminated at compile-time whereas the remainder should be frozen at run-time soon after the initial boot.

#### 5.10.3.8. *Performance sacrifice*

Making a kernel as described in this paper will also make it slower and bulkier than a standard kernel. We may make a kernel very secure, but there is little point if such a kernel is not widely adopted. It appears that users of Linux systems can bear the increase in bulk but not the loss of performance.

#### 5.10.3.9. *Kernels for servers*

Kernels are designed with considerable generality so that processes of extreme variety of functionality can be run. But in the case of server systems, where the processes are dedicated to a particular service, not all the functionality offered by an operating system is required. Standard Linux kernel construction does not control pruning the unneeded features from the kernel both at compile-time and/or at run-time. By cutting down the kernel to exactly fit the requirement of server, we mitigate the powers of a superuser, and intrusion becomes harder.

As a feasibility study of the above requirements, Gadi [12] describes and constructs security hardened Linux kernels intended for anonymous FTP servers, web servers, mail servers, and file servers. These kernels have several interesting features. First, they prevent or mitigate buffer overflow attacks, `chroot` breaking, temporary file race conditions, file descriptor leakage, LKM based root-kits, and `/dev/kmem` root-kits. Second, based on kernel threads, there is a new *kernel logger* for secure logging in addition to `syslogd`, and a new *kernel integrity checker* that can detect on-the-fly kernel modifications as well as yet-to-be discovered attacks. Third, *trusted path mapping* is added to the kernel for preventing the execution of binaries from arbitrary path names. Finally, in these kernels a file system can be treated as read-only that works more robustly and more securely than merely mounting it as read-only.

## 5.11. Conclusion

We explained security issues assuming that the reader is familiar with operating system internals. Our goal here was not to list and explain every exploit that has happened, but to select a few important ones and explain them, and where possible suggest prevention and detection techniques. We also discussed the technical reasons behind what permits these attacks to succeed, and how they can be prevented. We summarized several ideas that enhance the support that a kernel provides for security focusing on Linux-specific details.

We discussed proper configuration, and fortification of a Linux installation.

We set standards for a distribution to claim that it is a secure distribution, but shied away from specifically naming the ones labeled as "secured" on various Linux portal sites but are not.

We described the issues involved in securing a Linux kernel. We described areas of tightening security prior to the compilation of OS kernels rather than after their deployment.

We described how a secure kernel can be put together incorporating all compatible security enhancements from the standard components as distributed by the Linux kernel group.

### *Acknowledgments*

Portions of Sections 5.5 and 5.10 are from the work of my graduate students Karthik Mohanasundaram [5] and Sunil Gadi [12].

### References

[1] R. Sandhu, E. Coyne, H. Feinstein, and C. Youman, Role-based access control models, *IEEE Computer*, **29**(2), 38–47, (1996).

[2] M. Zelem, M. Pikula, M. Ockajak, J. Varga, R. Varga, and R. Dobozy, *Medusa DS9*, (2004). http://medusa.terminus.sk.

[3] W.A. Arbaugh, D.J. Farber, and J.M. Smith, A secure and reliable bootstrap architecture. In *IEEE Symposium on Security and Privacy*, pp. 65–71, Oakland, CA, USA (May, 1997). IEEE.

[4] Z. Zhou and R. Xu, *BIOS Security Analysis and a Kind of Trusted BIOS.* (Springer, 2007).

[5] K. Mohanasundaram, Security hardening of the process init of Linux. Master's thesis, Wright State University (September, 2004). Adviser: Prabhaker Mateti.

[6] A. Nash and T. Newsham, Vulnerability in 4.4BSD procfs. http://www.insecure.org/sploits/BSD.procfs.securelevel.subversion.html (June, 1997).

[7] P. Smith and R. Gooch, Simpleinit open file descriptor vulnerability. http://www.securityfocus.com/bid/5001/info/ (June, 2002).

[8] Mostarac. Superkit. http://packetstormsecurity.org.pk/UNIX/penetration/rootkits/index6.html (November, 2003).

[9] SD and Devik, Linux on-the-fly kernel patching without LKM, *Phrack*, **11**(58), 7 (December, 2001). http://phrack.org/phrack/58/p58-0x07.

[10] G. Harrison, The poiuy rootkit, and my struggles with it. http://www.mandrake.net/features/03/05/14/152221.shtml (May, 2003).

[11] Optyx. Kernel intrusion system (KIS) Trojan. http://www.linuxathome.net/articles/kis_trojan.php (July, 2001).

[12] S. S. Gadi, Security hardened kernels for Linux servers. Master's thesis, Wright State University (April, 2004). Adviser: Prabhaker Mateti.

[13] Aleph One, Smashing the stack for fun and profit, *Phrack*, **7**(49), (1996). http://phrack.org/phrack/49/P49-14.

[14] P. Mateti, Buffer overflow. Technical report, Wright State University, (2002). http://www.cs.wright.edu/~pmateti/InternetSecurity/Lectures/BufferOverflow/.

[15] M. Conover and w00w00 Security Team. w00w00 on heap overflows. Technical report, www.w00w00.org, (1999). www.w00w00.org/files/article/heaptut.txt.

[16] B.A. Kuperman, C.E. Brodley, H. Ozdoganoglu, T.N. Vijaykumar, and A. Jalote, Detection and prevention of stack buffer overflow attacks, *Commun. ACM*, **48**(11), 50–56, (2005). ISSN 0001-0782.

[17] C. Cowan and C. Pu. StackGuard: Automatic Adaptive Detection and Prevention of Buffer-Overflow Attacks. In *Proceedings of 7th USENIX Security Symposium*, San Antonio, TX, (1998). USENIX.

[18] D. Evans and D. Larochelle, Improving security using extensible lightweight static analysis, *IEEE Software*, **19**(1), 42–51 (Jan/Feb, 2002). ISSN 0740-7459. http://www.cs.virginia.edu/~evans/pubs/ieeesoftware.pdf.

[19] B. Spengler, Grsecurity. www.grsecurity.net (November, 2003).

[20] P. Mateti, Security issues in the TCP/IP suite. In eds. Y. Xiao and Y. Pan, *Security in Distributed and Networking Systems*, chapter 1, pp. 3–30. World Scientific Publishing (Aug, 2007). ISBN 978-981-270-807-6.

[21] P. Mateti, V. Pothamsetty, and B. Murray, Security enhancement of network protocol RFCs. In eds. Y. Xiao, F. Li, and H. Chen, *Handbook on Security and Networks*, chapter 18. World Scientific Publishing, (2009).

[22] S.J. Templeton and K.E. Levitt, Detecting spoofed packets. In *DISCEX (1)*, p. 12pp. IEEE Computer Society, (2003). ISBN 0-7695-1897-4. URL http://doi.ieeecomputersociety.org/10.1109/DISCEX.2003.1194882.

[23] D.J. Bernstein, SYN cookies. http://cr.yp.to/syncookies.html.

[24] P. Watson, Slipping in the window: TCP reset attacks. In *CanSecWest Security Conference.* (October, 2003).

[25] A. Kuzmanovic and E.W. Knightly, Low-rate TCP-targeted denial of service attacks (the shrew vs. the mice and elephants), *Submitted to IEEE/ACM Transactions on Networking, March 2004.* (July 30. 2003). URL http://citeseer.ist.psu.edu/689629.html;http://www-ece.rice.edu/networks/papers/dos.ps.gz.

[26] H. Farhat, Protecting TCP services from denial of service attacks. In *LSAD '06: Proceedings of the 2006 SIGCOMM workshop on Large-scale attack defense*, pp. 155–160, New York, NY, USA, (2006). ACM Press. ISBN 1-59593-571-1. doi: http://doi.acm.org/10.1145/1162666.1162674.

[27] O. Arkin, A remote active OS fingerprinting tool using ICMP, *;login: the USENIX Association newsletter*, **27**(2), 14–19 (Apr., 2002). ISSN 1044-6397. URL http://www.usenix.org/publications/login/2002-04/pdfs/arkin.pdf.

[28] M.G. Gouda and C.-T. Huang, A secure address resolution protocol, *Computer Networks*, **41**(1), 57–71, (2003). URL http://dx.doi.org/10.1016/S1389-1286(02)00326-2.

[29] D. Bruschi, A. Ornaghi, and E. Rosti, S-ARP: a secure address resolution protocol. In *19th Annual Computer Security Applications Conference*, pp. 66–75. IEEE Computer Society, (2003). ISBN 0-7695-2041-3. URL http://csdl.computer.org/comp/proceedings/acsac/2003/2041/00/20410066abs.htm.

[30] V. Ramachandran and S. Nandi, Detecting ARP spoofing: An active technique. In eds. S. Jajodia and C. Mazumdar, *Information Systems Security, First International Conference, ICISS*, vol. 3803, *Lecture Notes in Computer Science*, pp. 239–250, Kolkata, India (December, 2005). Springer. ISBN 3-540-30706-0. URL http://dx.doi.org/10.1007/11593980_18.

[31] D. Watson, M. Smart, G.R. Malan, and F. Jahanian, Protocol scrubbing: network security through transparent flow modification, *IEEE/ ACM Transactions on Networking*, **12**(2), 261–273 (Apr., 2004). ISSN 1063-6692.

[32] H. XIE and P. Biondi, LIDS Linux intrusion detection system. www.lids.org (October, 2003).

[33] D. Evans, Splint — Secure Programming Lint. Technical report, University of Virginia, (2007). http://www.splint.org.

[34] Simes. How to break out of a chroot jail. Technical report, www.bpfh.net, (2002). www.bpfh.net/simes/computing/chroot-break.html.

[35] Palmers, Five short stories about execve (Advances in kernel hacking II), *Phrack*, **11**(59), 5, (2002). http://phrack.org/phrack/59/p59-0x05.txt.

[36] T. Lawless, The Saint Jude project. http://sourceforge.net/projects/stjude (October, 2002).

[37] C. Cowan, S. Beattie, C. Wright, and G. KroahHartman, RaceGuard: Kernel Protection From Temporary File Race Vulnerabilities. In *Proceedings of 10th USENIX Security Symposium*, Washington D.C (August, 2001). USENIX.

[38] I. Goldberg, D. Wagner, R. Thomas, and E.A. Brewer, A secure environment for untrusted helper applications: Confining the wily hacker. In *1996 USENIX Security Symposium*. USENIX, (1996). http://www.cs.berkeley.edu/~daw/janus/, 2000.

[39] S.E. Hallyn, *Domain and Type Enforcement in Linux*. PhD thesis, The College of William & Mary in Virginia (September, 2003). Adviser: J. Phil Kearns.

[40] C. Wright, C. Cowan, S. Smalley, J. Morris, and G. Kroah-Hartman, Linux Security Modules: General Security Support for the Linux Kernel. In *Proceedings of USENIX Security '02*, SanFransico, CA, (2002). USENIX.

[41] B. McCarty, *SELinux: NSA's Open Source Security Enhanced Linux*. (O'Reilly Media, Inc., 2004). ISBN 0596007167.

[42] M. Bernaschi, E. Gabrielli, and L.V. Mancini, Remus: a security-enhanced operating system, *ACM Trans. Inf. Syst. Secur.*, **5**(1), 36–61, (2002). ISSN 1094-9224. doi: http://doi.acm.org/10.1145/504909.504911.

[43] J.Y. Moon and L.S. Sproull, Essence of distributed work: The case of the Linux kernel, *First Monday*, **5**(11), (2000). URL http://www.firstmonday.org/issues/issue5_11/moon/index.html.

[44] A.C. Chou, *Static analysis for bug finding in systems software*. PhD thesis, Stanford University, Stanford, CA, USA, (2003). Adviser: Dawson Engler.

# Part II: Attacks on Networks

# Chapter 6

## ATTACKER TRACEBACK IN MOBILE MULTI-HOP NETWORKS

Yongjin Kim
*Qualcomm, 5775 Morehouse Drive*
*San Diego, California, U.S.A*
*yongjink@qualcomm.com*

Ahmed Helmy
*Computer and Information Science and Engineering*
*(CISE) Department, University of Florida*
*Gainesville, Florida, U.S.A*
*helmy@cise.ufl.edu*

Flooding-type Denial-of-Service (*DoS*) and Distributed DoS (*DDoS*) attacks can cause serious problems in mobile multi-hop networks due to its limited network/host resources. *Attacker traceback* is a promising solution to take a proper countermeasure near attack origins, for forensics and to discourage attackers from launching the attacks. However, attacker traceback in mobile multi-hop networks is a challenging problem. Existing IP traceback schemes developed for the fixed networks cannot be directly applied to mobile multi-hop networks due to the peculiar characteristics of the mobile multi-hop networks (e.g., dynamic/autonomous network topology, limited network/host resources such as memory, bandwidth and battery life). We perform systematic risk analysis on mobile multi-hop networks. Mobile attackers can intentionally exploit mobility to avoid traceback and launch sophisticated attack. In addition, legitimate mobility of intermediate and victim's mobility can largely affect traceback performance. Based on our observations, we propose attacker traceback scheme in mobile multi-hop networks. We take traffic monitoring-based approach and utilize MAC and network layer information. We show that the proposed scheme successfully tracks down attacker under diverse mobile multi-hop network environment (e.g., high background traffic, DDoS attack, partial node compromise, and node mobility) with low communication, computation, and memory overhead.

### 6.1. Introduction

Mobile multi-hop networks include Mobile Ad-hoc NETworks (MANET), wireless mesh networks, and wireless sensor networks, among others. Various types of mobile multi-hop networks have been under active research recently due to its numerous promising applications and practical deployment is near. However, in general, security issues are not properly addressed in the design of such networks.

DoS/DDoS attack can cause serious problems in mobile multi-hop networks since (1) it is easy to perform attack using existing tools without technical expertise, and (2) in general, mobile multi-hop networks are severely limited in network resources (e.g., bandwidth) and host resources (e.g., battery, memory, etc).

Different types of DoS/DDoS attacks can be broadly classified into two classes: software exploiting attack and flooding-type attacks. In software exploits (e.g., Land attack, teardrop attack, [1], [18]), attacker sends a few packets or even single packet to exercise specific software bugs within the target's OS or application disabling or harming the victim. On the other hand, in flooding-type attacks, one or more attackers send incessant streams of packets aimed at overwhelming link bandwidth or computing resources at the victim. We focus on flooding-type DoS/DDoS attack since it cannot be fixed with software debugging.

In flooding-type DoS/DDoS attack, an attacker transmits a large number of packets towards a victim with spoofed source address. For instance, in SYN Flood [2], at least 200–500 pps (packet per second) of SYN packets are transmitted to a single victim. UDP Echo-Chargen [4] and Smurf [3] also attacks victim using a large amount of packets with spoofed address. It is reported that DoS attack occurs more than 4,000 times per week and more than 600,000 pps of attack packets are used for attack in some cases [9] in the Internet.

In general, we can say that the following are some characteristics of flooding-type DoS/DDoS attacks: (I) Traffic volume is abnormally increased during attack period. (II) Attackers routinely disguise their location using incorrect/spoofed addresses. (III) Such attacks may persist for tens of minutes and in some case for several days [1].

We define our goal of attacker traceback as the ability to identify the machines that directly generate attack traffic and the network path this traffic subsequently follows [6], or at least identify their neighborhood (e.g., location, neighboring nodes) if not identity. Attacker traceback is a useful technique not only for forensics, but also to take a proper countermeasure near attack origin and discourage attackers from launching attacks. There are several attacker traceback schemes proposed for the Internet such as packet marking [17], logging [16], and ICMP traceback [7]. Such traceback schemes were developed for the fixed networks and are not directly applicable to mobile multi-hop networks due to the following particular characteristics of mobile multi-hop networks. (1) In mobile multi-hop networks, there is no fixed infrastructure, gateways or firewalls. Each node works as an autonomous terminal, acting as both host and a router. (2) Each node can move in and out of the network, frequently changing network topology. (3) In general, network bandwidth and battery power are severely limited. (4) It may be difficult to physically secure a mobile node that could be captured, compromised to later rejoin the networks as a Byzantine node.

In addition to the peculiar characteristics of mobile multi-hop networks, "mobility" poses significant challenge in attacker traceback. Node mobility can be classified into two classes; intentional/malicious attacker's mobility and legitimate mobility of intermediate/victim nodes. Intentional/malicious attacker's mobility can cause numerous problems and illusions in traceback. To identify various risks caused by attacker's mobility, we propose *multi-dimensional set-based risk analysis* method. In addition, we analyze how various innocent mobility of intermediate and victim can affect traceback performance.

We provide a protocol framework for attacker traceback in mobile multi-hop networks. For efficient traceback, we focus on statistical abnormality in attack traffic. The protocol framework consists of abnormality detection, abnormality characterization, abnormality searching, and abnormality matching. We use cross-layer (i.e., network and MAC layer) information to increase traceback efficiency with decreased operational overhead. We also effectively utilize overhearing capability of the wireless MAC layer, to drastically increase robustness against node compromise and mobility and to reduce false positive and negative rates. We also propose traceback-assisted countermeasure, which provides an effective defense strategy. Finally, we propose mobile attacker traceback scheme.

## 6.2. Related Work

In general, attacker traceback scheme is a method to assist in revealing the true identity of an attacker even under address spoofing. It can help restore normal network functionality by blocking attacks near the origin of the generator of the attack packets, and prevent reoccurrences. In addition, it holds attackers accountable for their crime. Current attacker traceback schemes [6] can be classified as follows from several different standpoints:

- Preventative vs. Reactive:
  Ingress filtering is an example of preventative scheme, in which incoming packets addresses are checked at the router and packets are blocked if the address does not belong to proper subnet address space. On the other hand, in the reactive scheme, traceback is performed after the attack is detected by intrusion detection systems. Link testing [8], logging [16], iTrace [7], and packet marking [17] are classified as reactive schemes.
- On-going vs. Post-mortem:
  In on-going traceback schemes, traceback must be completed while the attack is in progress. It is useless once the attack is over. It could be effective for small controlled networks. An example is link testing [8]. In post-mortem capable schemes, traceback can be performed after the attack is complete. It basically records tracing information as packets are routed through the network. Then the information is pieced together to form the attack path resulting in attacker identification. Examples of such a scheme include logging [16], iTrace [7], and packet marking [17].
- End-host storage vs. infrastructure storage:
  In end host storage scheme, some information to trace back attacker is delivered to the end host. End-host takes responsibility of reconstructing the attack path from the attacker to the victim. Examples of end-host storage scheme are packet

marking [17] and iTrace [7]. On the other hand, in infrastructure-storage scheme, information for traceback is stored in the network and a victim requests the information to reconstruct the attack path. An example of the traceback scheme is logging-based traceback [16].

## 6.3. Design Requirements

To analyze and identify design requirements for traceback protocol in mobile multi-hop networks, we classify the main building blocks of the attacker traceback protocol as follows: (I) information searching and gathering, (II) information storage,and (III) information analysis. Information searching and gathering are the processes to put together or seek clues on the attack traffic. Information storage is the process to store the gathered clue in some storage for analysis. Information analysis is the process to reconstruct the attack path based on the clue obtained through information storing process or real-time data provided by information searching and gathering processes. Based on the classified building blocks, we identify the design requirements (Table 6.1) for our traceback protocol in mobile multi-hop networks.

- Information searching and gathering
  For robust and efficient information searching and gathering in mobile multi-hop networks, we need to satisfy the following protocol requirements: First, the traceback scheme should be robust against route instability due to node mobility and topology change. Second, it may be difficult to physically secure nodes that could be captured, compromised and later rejoin the networks as Byzantine node. Hence, we need robustness against node compromise. Third, in general, mobile multi-hop networks are severely limited in networks resource (i.e., bandwidth). In addition, energy conservation is one of major concern. Hence, we need to reduce communication overhead and energy consumption through an energy efficient searching scheme.

  Existing attacker traceback schemes (e.g., PPM [17], iTrace [7]) rely on hop-by-hop traceback. Hence, when one intermediate node moves out or powered down, the traceback process fails. In addition, when several nodes are compromised, the traceback process stops at the compromised nodes.

Table 6.1. Design requirements for attacker traceback in mobile multi-hop networks.

| Protocol building block | Design requirement |
|---|---|
| Information searching and gathering | Robustness against topology change and mobility |
| | Robustness against node collusion |
| | Low communication overhead and energy consumption |
| Information storage | Low storage consumption |
| Information analysis | Low computational overhead |
| | Low delay |

Consequently, a majority-based scheme is required in mobile multi-hop networks, which is robust against multiple node compromise and failure.

- Information storage

  Clue information, obtained through information searching and gathering processes, needs to be stored for traceback. Information can be stored at the end-host or inside the network. However, in general, nodes in mobile multi-hop network have limited storage space. Hence, it is important to reduce storage.

  iTrace [7] or PPM [17] is end-host storage scheme. ICMP or marked packets are stored at the end-host and used for path reconstruction. The logging scheme in [16] is a network-storage scheme, where clue information is stored in inside networks. An obvious drawback of these schemes is that large amount of data needs to be stored at either the end-host or inside the network since per-packet information is required. On the other hand, controlled flooding [8] does not require information storage. However, it consumes network bandwidth, which is highly undesirable in resource constrained mobile multi-hop networks.

- Information analysis

  Information analysis in existing schemes (e.g., iTrace [7], PPM [17], logging [16]) incurs high processing overhead and delay since it takes per-packet analysis approach. For instance, in iTrace, end host first searches the database, which stores packet information. Then, based on the packet information, end-host should reconstruct the attack path.

## 6.4. Risk Analysis

Mobility poses several challenges for attacker traceback. First, the attacker(s) can maliciously exploit mobility to avoid traceback, and increase attack efficiency. Second, mobility of intermediate and victim nodes can degrade traceback performance even without malicious intention. To systematically analyze how mobility can affect traceback performance, we take a *multi-dimensional approach.* In this approach, mobile multi-hop network domains are classified into multiple dimensions: (1) temporal transition domain, (2) spatial transition domain, (3) address domain, (4) area domain, and (5) the node coordination domain. These domains were selected after a careful process. We show that the combination of each domain attributes can identify a class of attack scenarios with a unique risk in mobile multi-hop networks.

### 6.4.1. *Mobile Multi-hop Network Domains*

- Temporal Transition Domain ($T$-domain)

  The $T$ domain defines the temporal relation among attack traffic observed at different location. T domain consists of three attributes: temporal continuity ($T_c$), temporal discontinuity ($T_d$), and temporal randomness ($T_r$) as described in Table 6.2. $T0$, $T1$, and $T2$ are the time slots during which the attack is observed.

In Figure 6.1(a), attack signatures $\xi1$, $\xi2$, and $\xi3$ are observed at $T0, T1$, and $T2$ time slots continuously (Temporal continuity). On the other hand, temporal discontinuity is observed in Figure 6.1(b). The attack signatures ($\xi1$ and $\xi2$) are observed at discontinuous time slots at $T0$ and $T2$.

- Spatial Transition Domain (S-domain)
  S-domain defines spatial relation among attack occurrence. S-domain has three attributes: (1) spatial continuity ($S_c$) (2) spatial discontinuity ($S_d$) (3) spatial randomness ($S_r$). For instance, in mobile DoS attack, the attack signature is observed in a spatially continuous manner (Figure 6.2(a)). In general, spatial discontinuity is observed in DDoS attack as in Figure 6.2(b). Note that DDoS attack can also show spatial continuity. In that case, we can distinguish between DDoS attack and mobile DoS attack using temporal relation (i.e., T-domain).

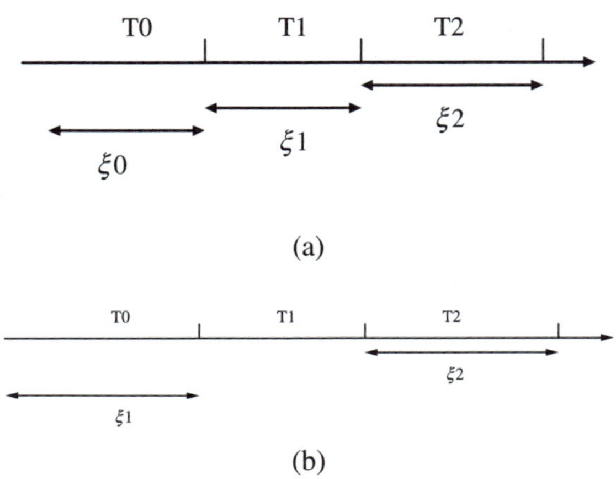


Fig. 6.1. Three attributes of the temporal $T$-Domain. (a) Temporal continuity (Attribute $T_c$) (b) Temporal discontinuity (Attribute $T_d$).

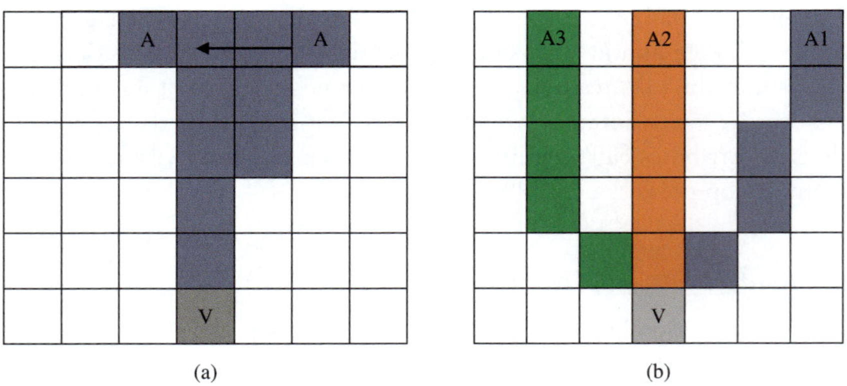


Fig. 6.2. (a) Spatial continuity of mobile DoS attack. Attacker, $A$, is moving from right to left attacking victim $V$. (b) Spatial discontinuity of DDoS attack. Attackers, $A1$, $A2$, and $A3$ are launching attacks towards victim $V$. Each cell logically corresponds to contact vicinity.

- Address domain (AD-domain)
  An attacker can perform malicious attack by spoofing, sometimes using multiple addresses. Some possible attack scenarios include (1) single random address ($AD_{sr}$) (2) multiple random addresses ($AD_{mr}$) (3) targeted single address ($AD_{st}$), and (4) targeted multiple addresses ($AD_{mt}$). Unlike fixed networks, the address is not fixed in mobile multi-hop networks. An attacker can easily use false, changing addresses.
- Area domain (A-domain)
  In mobile multi-hop networks, an attacker can choose its location freely, where an attacker can choose: (1) single random area ($A_{sr}$) (2) multiple random areas ($A_{mr}$) (3) targeted single area ($A_{st}$) (4) targeted multiple areas ($A_{mt}$).
- Node coordination domain (N-domain)
  Coordination of multiple nodes can lead to serious confusion to a victim. Coordination maybe: (1) temporal coordination of compromised nodes ($N_t$), or (2) spatial coordination of compromised nodes ($N_s$).

### 6.4.2. *Mobile Attack Identification*

Using various combinations of domain assignments we can identify numerous attack scenarios and assess their risks. We define the combinational set as the *set* of *minimal necessary entities* in mobile network domains/attributes to perform certain attack. We identify some of the attack scenarios in this section. Note that these are five example attacks to show the usefulness of the combinational-set based approach and not exhaustive set of all attack scenarios.

- Mobility Misuse (MM) Attack
  MM is the simplest form of attack exploiting mobility. In the MM attack, attacker sends attack traffic continuously to a victim. To avoid traceback, the attacker constantly changes its location. The MM attack has the following domain setting:

  $$MM\ Domain\ Setting = \{T_c, S_c, A_{mr}\}$$

  As a result of the MM attack, a victim can be confused between DDoS attack and mobile attack. Without considering attacker's mobility, existing traceback schemes will infer that attack traffic is coming from distributed locations, which leads to false positive in distributed nodes.
- Mobility and Address Misuse (MAM) Attack
  In MAM attack, an attacker sends attack traffic continuously to a victim. To avoid traceback, attacker changes not only its location but also it address.

  $$MAM\ Domain\ Setting = \{T_c, S_c, AD_{mr}, A_{mr}\}$$

  Similar to MM attack, a victim will be confused between DDoS attack and mobile attack. In addition, since the attacker changes its address, some preventive techniques such as firewalls or filtering become useless.

- False Mobility Generation (FMG) Attack
  In FMG attack, the attackers intentionally generate false mobility. That is, the attack is performed from multiple nodes with spatial and temporal continuity.

  $$FMG\ Domain\ Setting = \{T_d, S_c, N_s, N_t\}$$

  A traceback mechanism capable of detecting mobile attack (e.g., MM attack) may be misled by FMG attack. That is, even if the attack is launched from distributed nodes, a victim might conclude that attacker is moving and performing MM attack.
- Distributed Blinking (DB) Attack
  The drawback of FMG attack is that the continuity of the attack is detectable. To overcome this, DB attack can be performed by an attacker. In DB attack, the attacker compromises multiple nodes and performs the attack from distributed random nodes at random times. Attack is launched with spatial/temporal transition randomness.

  $$DB\ Domain\ Setting = \{T_r, S_r, N_s, N_t\}$$

  From victim's point of view, attack traffic comes from random location for short period of time. However, bulk attack traffic comes continuously to a victim since multiple nodes are compromised.
- Disabling Targeted Area (DTA) Attack
  In DTA attack, the attacker is aware of the countermeasure after traceback process. The attacker intentionally generates attack traffic near targeted area where attacker wants to disable or harm networking through expected countermeasure (e.g., packet filtering, or rate limiting). Attacker launches attack at targeted area.

  $$DTA\ Domain\ Setting = \{T_c, A_{st}\}$$

  Once the traceback mechanism identifies the attack origin(s), countermeasures are taken near those origin(s). However, since the attacker may intentionally choose the attack origin, legitimate traffic may also be dropped by the countermeasure.

### 6.4.3. *Impact of Legitimate Mobility on Traceback*

Legitimate mobility of nodes can affect traceback performance. The negative impact of legitimate node mobility occurs due to the following factors:

- Reduction of witness nodes
  Intermediate nodes that observe abnormality (i.e., witness nodes) can move away from the attack route(s). The problem can become worse when we rely only on intermediate nodes that relayed the attack traffic. Once the relay nodes move away from the attack route, the traceback cannot proceed after that point.

- Abnormality mismatching
  For traceback, we need to find intermediate nodes that observe similar attack signature as victim. However, during attack period, new nodes can move into the attack route, which can reduce signature matching level due to insufficient abnormality monitoring.

In the following sections, we define mobility metrics to systematically analyze how mobility affects traceback performance. Some of metrics are borrowed from earlier work [5].

6.4.3.1. *Mobility metrics*

- Directional Correlation (DC):
  DC is defined as follows:

$$DC(i,j,t) = \frac{\vec{v}_i(t) \bullet \vec{v}_j(t)}{|\vec{v}_i| * |\vec{v}_j|}, \tag{6.2}$$

  where, $\vec{v}_i(t)$ and $\vec{v}_j(t)$ are the velocity vectors of nodes $i$ and $j$ at time $t$. High DC implies, two nodes $i$ and $j$ are moving in the same direction. One the contrary, low DC implies two nodes $i$ and $j$ are moving in opposite directions.
- Speed Correlation (SC):
  SC is defined as follows.

$$SC(i,j,t) = \frac{\min(|\vec{v}_i(t)|, |\vec{v}_j(t)|)}{\max(|\vec{v}_i(t)|, |\vec{v}_j(t)|)}. \tag{6.3}$$

  High SC implies that two nodes $i$ and $j$ are moving with similar speed. One the contrary, low DC implies two nodes $i$ and $j$ are moving at different speed.
- Geographic Restriction (GR):
  Geographic restriction represents the degree of freedom of node movement on a map. More specifically, the degree of freedom represents the number of directions a node can go.
- Reference Restriction (RR):
  Reference restriction represents the degree of freedom of reference point nodes. When all the nodes are going to the same reference point, high RR is observed.

6.4.3.2. *Mobility dependency*

By using the mobility metrics defined above, we can further define mobility dependency among nodes or among groups of nodes as follows.

- Mobility Dependency between attacker and victim
  We define mobility dependency between attacker and victim as follows.

$$MD(a,v,t) = DC(a,v,t) * SC(a,v,t) \tag{6.4}$$

  When attacker ($a$) and victim ($v$) have high directional correlation and speed correlation, mobility dependency becomes high.

- Mobility Dependency among intermediate nodes
  Mobility dependency between intermediate nodes is defined as follows.

$$MD(i, i', t) = DC(i, i', t) * SC(i, i', t) \tag{6.5}$$

When intermediate nodes ($i$ and $i'$) move in a similar direction with similar speed, the mobility dependency becomes high. Mean mobility dependency among nodes $N$ during time duration $T$ is also defined as follows:

$$\overline{MD}(i) = \frac{\sum_{i=1}^{N} \sum_{t=1}^{T} \sum_{t'=1}^{T} MD(i, i', t)}{P} \tag{6.6}$$

- Mobility Dependency among attacker, intermediate, and victim

$$MD(a, v, i, t) = MD(a, v, t) * \overline{MD}(i) \tag{6.7}$$

When attacker, victim and intermediate nodes are moving in a similar direction with similar speed, the dependency becomes high.

We note that mobility can affect traceback performance. Different mobility models have different characteristics (i.e., high/low DC, SC, GR, RR, and mobility dependency). Depending on mobility model and its characteristics, attacker traceback performance can largely vary.

### 6.5. Traffic Monitoring-based Traceback

We propose traffic-monitoring-based attacker traceback protocol for mobile multi-hop networks. Our protocol consists of the following five components: (1) abnormality detection, (2) abnormality characterization, (3) abnormality searching, (4) abnormality matching, and (5) countermeasures.

Abnormality is monitored by all nodes in the network. Each node monitors network and MAC layer activity (e.g., number of packet, busy time in MAC layer). Once abnormality is detected, the information is captured and logged. We introduce several classes of detection technique to accurately detect attack with low overhead. We classify abnormality into two classes: coarse-grained abnormality and fine-grained abnormality. Basically, with coarse-grained abnormality, we trace-back attackers using only packet counters, without using payload-level details. Coarse-grained abnormality monitoring is further divided into the following two classes: Coarse-grained Network Layer Monitoring (C-NLM) and Coarse-grained MAC Layer Monitoring (C-MLM). On the other hand, with fine-grained traceback, we trace-back attackers by analyzing payload-level details. Fine-grained abnormality monitoring is further divided into the following three classes: Fine-grained Network Layer Monitoring (F-NLM), Fine-grained MAC Layer Monitoring (F-MLM) and Fine-grained Cross-layer Monitoring (F-CM) that includes both network layer and MAC layer monitoring. There exists a clear tradeoff between the two above mechanisms. In coarse-grained abnormality-based traceback, computational/storage overhead is minimized by sacrificing payload level analysis for traceback. It is an effective way of traceback in many cases when attack traffic shows obvious abnormality and background traffic is low or moderate, as we shall show. In fine-grained abnormality-based traceback, payload-level information is considered and analyzed to trace back attackers. It requires more computation/storage overhead because we need to store and analyze more detailed information, but it can more accurately trace back attackers. Fine-grained abnormality-based traceback becomes essential in the following cases: (1) in DDoS attacks only reduced abnormality is observed near the edges of the attack route. Hence, we need to differentiate between attack traffic and background traffic accurately, and (2) high background traffic makes the abnormality less obvious. We show that we can increase traceback accuracy even under low abnormality and high background traffic by using fine-grained abnormality monitoring by filtering much of the noise traffic (i.e., background traffic). The fine-grained cross-layer information can further filter out background traffic. With the various classes of abnormalities defined above, we perform the following traceback process.

- Abnormality detection:
  Each node monitors protocol layer activity. Once abnormality is detected, the node logs the abnormality information as candidate attack signature. Later, during the search phase the candidate attack signature is compared with the attack signature which is characterized by a victim. To detect abnormality, we need to define a threshold. If the observed value exceeds the threshold, it is defined as abnormality. Threshold can be set either as fixed value or adaptive value. For fixed threshold, we use the Fractional Deviation from the Mean (FDM), and we use the Pivot method for the adaptive threshold.
- Abnormality characterization and matching:
  Once abnormality is detected, the abnormality needs to be characterized for traceback. Characterized abnormality at the victim is called the 'attack signature' and abnormality characterized at an intermediate node is called 'candidate attack signature'. Then, abnormality matching is performed between the attack and candidate attack signatures. If it shows high match level, we can infer that the attack traffic has passed through the corresponding intermediate nodes (those that observed the candidate attack signature). Once abnormality is detected, the abnormality needs to be characterized. We characterize the abnormality as time series data. That is, attack signature is defined by the sequence of *number of frames* in $n$ time slots, $(a_1, a_2, \ldots, a_n)$, where $a_i$ $(1 \leq i \leq n)$ is the number of frames at time slot $i$. Sampling window, $D$, is expressed as:

  $$D = n \bullet d, \tag{6.6}$$

  Where $d$ is the time slot length. For fine-grained characterization, destination address, and previous hop MAC address are used (Table 6.2). There is obvious tradeoff between coarse-grained and fine-grained characterization. When coarse-grained characterization is used, space complexity for abnormality logging

Table 6.2. Abnormality table using cross-layer information.

| Destination_addr | Source_MAC_addr | Abnormality |
|---|---|---|
| 1 | 2 | $\xi(1,2)$ |
| 1 | 3 | $\xi(1,3)$ |
| . | . | . |
| . | . | . |
| . | . | . |
| . | . | . |

becomes $O(1)$. However, abnormality matching and subsequent traceback result becomes less accurate. On the other hand, when fine-grained characterization is used, space complexity becomes $O(N * M)$, where $N$ is the number of destination network addresses and $M$ is the number of previous hop source MAC addresses. $N$ can grow to the number of nodes in the network, and $M$ is the average node degree (number of direct neighbors). However, traceback accuracy is improved since we can reduce noise traffic, as we shall show later in this section.

Once abnormality is characterized, abnormality matching is done between candidate attack signature and attack signature. If the two signatures are closely matching, we can infer the attack route. We use KS-fitness test for signature matching test.

- Abnormality searching:
  To perform the abnormality matching process, we need to find nodes that observe candidate attack signature. To provide energy efficiency and robustness against false reports, we use majority voting. Majority voting is performed by multiple nodes that observe or overhear abnormality in a certain region. We also utilize the small world model to increase the search efficiency. Helmy[10][11] show that path length in wireless networks can be drastically reduced by adding a few random links (resembling a small world). These random links need not be totally random, but in fact may be confined to small fraction of the network diameter, thus reducing the overhead of creating such network. The random links can be established using contacts [11].
- Countermeasure:
  After we identify the attack origin(s), we carry out countermeasures to ameliorate the intensity of (or stop) the attack. Existing countermeasures (e.g., packet filtering, rate-limiting) suffer from several drawbacks. A packet filtering scheme drops a large volume of legitimate packets. While in a rate-limiting scheme it is hard to find the optimal limiting rate. We take a hybrid approach of packet filtering and rate limiting. We use matching level — that we call 'confidence index' — to find a reasonable limiting rate.

We also propose mobile attacker traceback scheme. To track down mobile attackers effectively, we utilize spatio-temporal relation of attack signature. Our mobile attacker traceback scheme is built on top of the basic traceback components

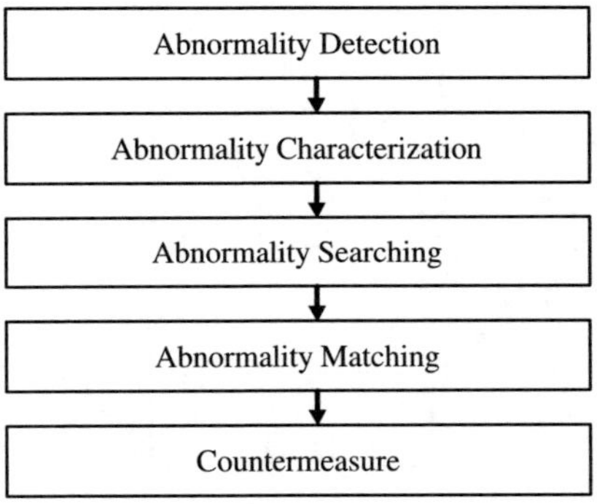


Fig. 6.3. Attacker Traceback Protocol Framework.

described above. The overall traceback architecture is built on a contact-based hierarchy using vicinities, and supports attack detection, abnormality matching, directional search and countermeasures for DoS and DDoS attacks.

### 6.5.1. *DoS Attacker Traceback*

We describe overall DoS attacker traceback scheme as follows: (1) when a victim node, $V$, detects attack such as SYN flooding, it first extracts attack signature. It, then, sends queries to nodes within its vicinity and level-1 contacts specifying the depth of search ($D$), indicating the number of contact levels to search. The queries contains Sequence Number (*SN*) and attack signature. (2) As the query is forwarded, each node traversed records the *SN*, and $V$. If a node receives a request with the same *SN* and $V$, it drops the query. This provides for loop prevention and avoidance of re-visits to the covered parts of the network.

(3) In the case high local attack signature energy is observed by vicinity nodes and contacts the first step of traceback is completed. For instance, victim ($V$) sends queries to its vicinity nodes and 2 level-1 contacts ($CL\_1a$ and $CL\_1b$) around the victim in Figure 6.4 (transmission arrows to vicinity nodes by each contact are omitted in the figure). Then, one level-1 ($CL\_1b$) contact reports to the victim that it observed high local attack signature energy. To reduce the risk of false matching report from vicinity nodes, we use 'majority voting' where a contact node requests candidate attack signatures observed by the vicinity nodes at given time slots instead of distributing attack signature to all its vicinity nodes and waiting for individual attack signature energy response. A matching test is done at each contact node. Although this does not completely remove the risk of false matching report, it reduces such risk dramatically as we shall show.

(4) Next, only the contact, $CL\_1b$ in our example, that observes high local attack signature energy in its vicinity, sends a report back to $V$ and (based on $V$'s request) further sends queries to level-2 contacts ($CL\_2c$, and $CL\_2d$) with the partial attack path appended to the queries. It also reduces $D$ by 1. This processing by the contact nodes is called *in-network* processing. Other contacts that do not

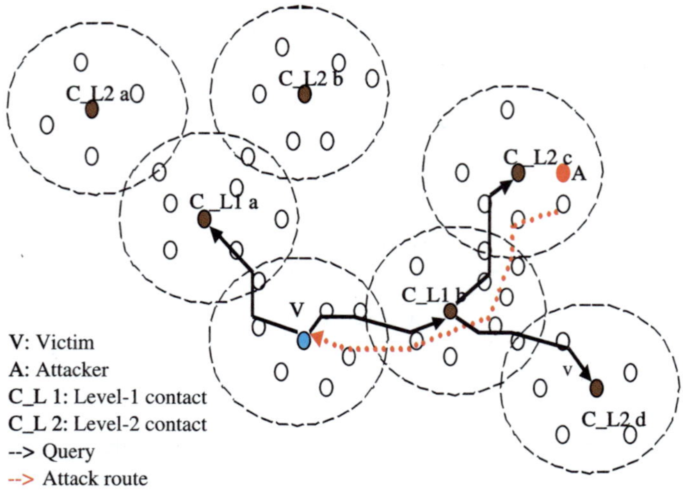


Fig. 6.4. Victim ($V$) sends queries with attack signature to the first level contacts, ($CL\_1a$, $CL\_1b$). Only $CL\_1b$ that observed matching attack signature within its vicinity sends next level queries to level-2 contacts ($CL\_2c$, $CL\_2d$). $CL\_1a$ suppresses further queries. $CL\_2c$ sends final attack route to the victim.

observe high local attack signature energy in their vicinities, suppress forwarding further queries. This results in directional search towards the attacker. (5) When there are no more contact reports or there are no more nodes outside the vicinity, the last contact ($CL\_2c$) reports the complete attack route to the victim.

Our scheme is based on majority node reporting. That is, even if some nodes move out of the attack route or are compromised, we can still find the attack route using information available from neighboring nodes around attack route. This will become clearer later during mobility analysis.

### 6.5.2. *DDoS Attacker Traceback*

DDoS attacks involve a number of compromised nodes to send useless packets toward a victim at the same time. The sum of that traffic constitutes the attack traffic. The magnitude of the combined traffic is usually significant enough to jam, or even crash, the victim or connection links.

Similar to the DoS attack case, a victim node sends queries to its vicinity nodes and level-1 contacts with its characterized attack signature. In DDoS attacker traceback, multiple candidate attack signatures are observed and returned from multiple contacts. For instance, in Figure 6.5, three sets of responses are returned from level-1 contacts ($CL\_1a$, $CL\_1b$, and $CL\_1c$) and the victim first identifies branch attack signatures from all combinations of candidate attack signatures. Then, local attack signature energy is calculated with each branch attack signatures. In this example, local attack signature energy shows the highest values in regions of $CL\_1a$, and $CL\_1b$. As a result, a victim concludes that the attack traffic comes

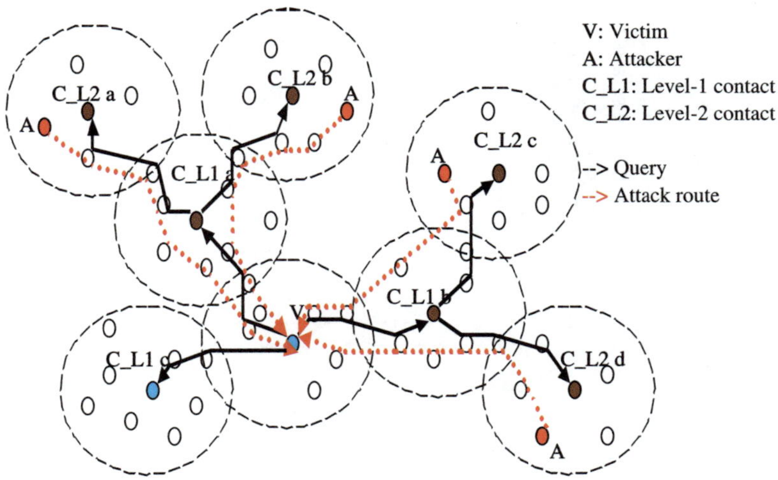


Fig. 6.5. Victim ($V$) sends queries with attack signature to level-1 contacts (i.e., $CL\_1a$, $CL\_1b$, $CL\_1c$). Two level-1 contacts (i.e., $CL\_1a$, $CL\_1b$) that observe matching attack signature within their vicinities sends next level queries to level-2 contacts (i.e., $CL\_2a$, $CL\_2b$, $CL\_2c$, $CL\_2d$). Final level-2 contacts send distributed attack routes to the victim.

through $CL\_1a$ and $CL\_1b$ regions. Contacts that are determined to be on the attack routes by the victim node perform next level query in a recursive manner. Each level-1 contact finds two other branches of attack route in two level-2 ($CL\_2a$, $CL\_2b$, $CL\_2c$, and $CL\_2d$) contacts. The final attack route is reported to $V$ by the last contact nodes. The searching process leads to multi-directional searching. Note that the search initiated by the victim follows the same protocol for both DoS and DDoS attacks since the victim cannot differentiate a-priori between these types of attacks.

### 6.5.3. *Performance Analysis*

We compare traceback success rate for DoS and DDoS attacker traceback. Traceback success is defined as the event of identifying all the attack origins that generated the attack traffic. We set up a simulation network size of 2,750 m × 2,750 m with transmission range of each node set to 150 m and about 20 hops network diameter. We repeat each simulation 10 times in random topology with 1,000–3,000 static nodes and calculate the average value. We also set $NoC$ (Number of Contacts) = 6, $R$ (vicinity radius) = 3, $r$ (contact distance) = 3, $d$ (search depth) = 5 for contact selection. DSDV is used as underlying routing protocol. DoS attacker is 17 hops away from a victim, and DDoS attackers are 10 hops away from a victim.

Figure 6.6 shows success rate for DoS attacker traceback with C-MLM and F-MLM. F-MLM shows higher success rate (Avg. 20% higher than C-MLM). The improvement becomes significant as background traffic is increased. It is because F-MLM uses fine-grained information (i.e., previous-hop MAC address). Figure 6.7 shows further improvement (100% success rate) when we use F-CM

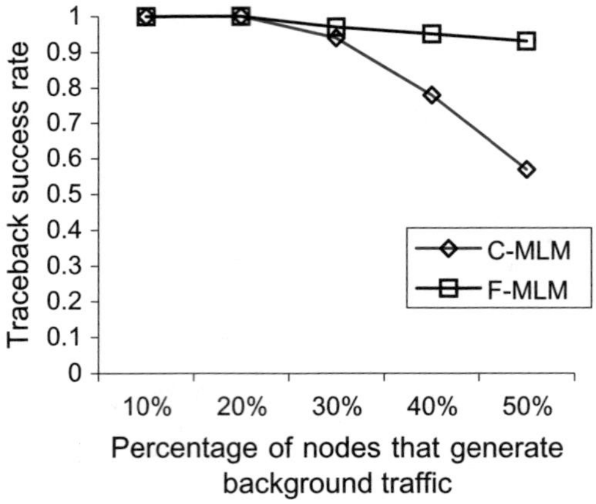


Fig. 6.6. DoS attacker traceback success rate comparison between C-MLM and F-MLM.

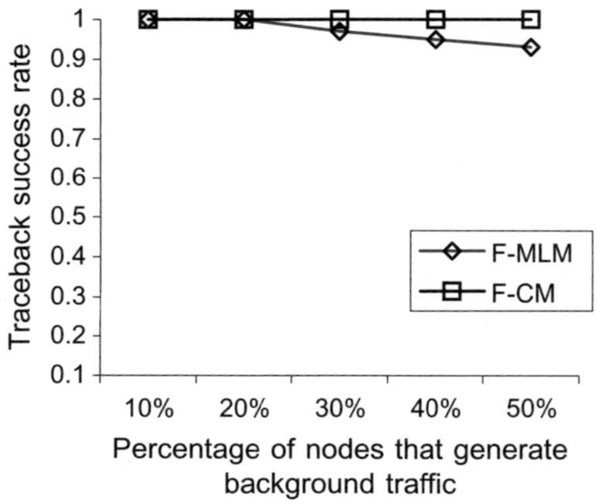


Fig. 6.7. DoS attacker traceback success rate comparison between F-MLM and F-CM.

since we use network layer information to filter out more background noise traffic. Figures 6.8 and 6.9 show success rate for DDoS attacker traceback with 25% of background traffic. C-MLM shows low performance since branch attack traffic has low abnormality. F-MLM shows high success rate when average number of one-hop neighbor is large. However, when average number of one-hop neighbor is small (<4), traceback success goes down in even F-MLM. It is because more noise (i.e., background traffic) is carried over the link where the attack traffic passes.

In Figure 6.9, the success rate drastically increases (Avg. 51%) by using fine-grained network-layer information (i.e., destination address) in addition to fine-grained MAC-layer information. It is because network layer information can filter out most of the noise traffic.

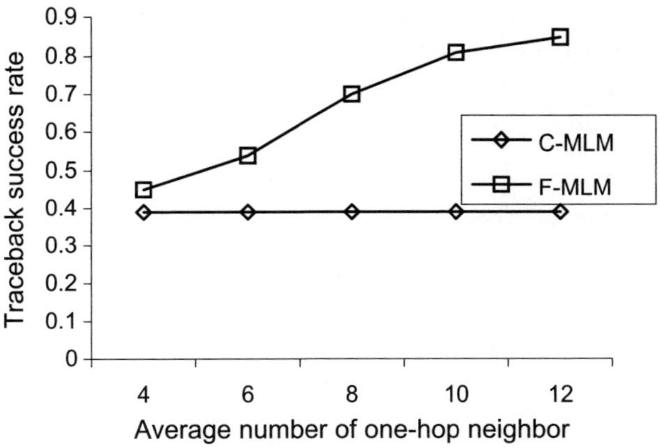


Fig. 6.8. DDoS Attacker traceback success rate comparison between C-MLM and F-MLM.

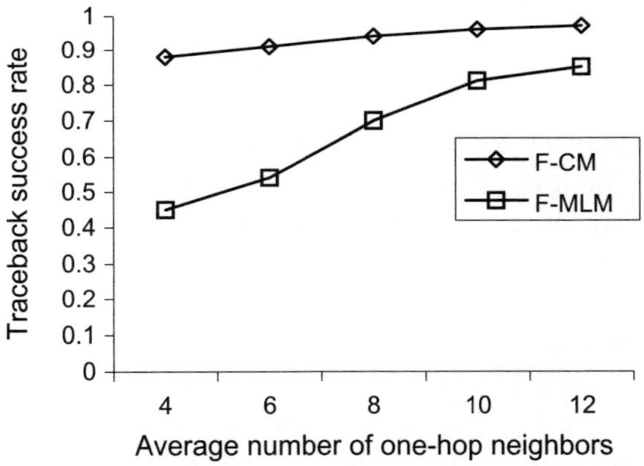


Fig. 6.9. DDoS attacker traceback success rate comparison between F-MLM and F-CM.

## 6.6. Mobile Attacker Traceback

In this section, we propose a mobile attacker traceback scheme. Our scheme consists of: (1) information gathering, and (2) information fusion processes.

### 6.6.1. *Information Gathering*

Information gathering in mobile attacker traceback has the following features: (1) In addition to traceback information used in static attacker traceback, age information is gathered by contact nodes. More specifically, spatio-temporal attack signatures $(\xi, t_S, t_L, S)$ are gathered. $\xi$ is candidate attack signature, $S$ is the relative position of attacker (e.g., 2 hops away from level-1 contact $i$), $t_S$ is the start time of (or time since) abnormality and $t_L$ is the last (or most recent) time when abnormality is observed. This spatio-temporal attack signature is effectively used to classify attack type (e.g., DDoS attack, mobile attack, etc). (2) All the attack signature information (i.e., spatio-temporal attack signature) from every level of contact needs to be returned to the victim for network-wide analysis.

### 6.6.2. *Information Fusion*

Information fusion is the process to correlate and analyze the spatio-temporal signature information obtained through the information gathering process.

To quantitatively represent spatial relation among candidate attack signatures, we define Spatial Relation Factor (SRF) as follows:

$$SRF = \frac{\alpha \bullet P}{\sum_{\eta_{C\_1}=1}^{N_{C\_1}} \sum_{\eta_{C\_2}=1}^{N_{C\_2}} D_S(\eta_{C\_1}, \eta_{C\_2}, \xi_{C\_1}, \xi_{C\_2})} \tag{6.8}$$

Where,

$$\alpha = \frac{n_S}{N_{C\_1} + N_{C\_2}} \tag{6.9}$$

$N_{c-1}$ is the total number of vicinity nodes of contact $c\_1$ and $N_{c-2}$ is the total number of vicinity nodes of contact $c\_2$. $n_S$ is the number of nodes that observe attack signature, $\xi_{c-1}$ and $\xi_{c-2}$ in the vicinity of contacts $c\_1$ and $c\_2I$, respectively. $\eta_{c-1}$ is a vicinity node of contact $c\_1$ and $\eta_{c-2}$ is a vicinity node of contact $c\_2$. $D_S$ $(\eta_{c-1}, \eta_{c-2}, \xi_{c-1}, \xi_{c-2})$ is the hop count between node $\eta_{c-1}$ and $\eta_{c-2}$ that observe the attack signature $\xi_{c-1}$, and $\xi_{c-2}$ respectively. The hop count information can be obtained using underlying routing table or through explicit query. $D_S$ $(\eta_{c-1}, \eta_{c-2}, \xi_{c-1}, \xi_{c-2}) = 0$ if node $\eta_{c-1}$ and $\eta_{c-2}$ do not observe any candidate attack signature. $P$ is the total number of pairs of $(\eta_{c-1}, \eta_{c-2})$, where $D_S$ $(\eta_{c-1}, \eta_{c-2}, \xi_{c-1}, \xi_{c-2}) > 0$. $\alpha$ is majority voting factor. For a high value of $\alpha$, we can infer that attack is occurring near the central region of $c\_1$'s vicinity and $c\_2$'s vicinity. It is because more vicinity nodes can overhear the abnormality when attack traffic passes through the central region of the contact's vicinity. When $\alpha$ is small, we can infer that the attack traffic is not passing through the central region of the contact's vicinity or the candidate attack signature report is not reliable (false reporting). When attacker moves from vicinity of $c\_1$ to vicinity of $c\_2$, we can observe small $D_S$ $(\eta_{c-1}, \eta_{c-2}, \xi_{c-1}, \xi_{c-2})$ and high SRF. When $c\_1$ and $c\_2$ is not adjacent contacts and $\eta_{c-1}$ and $\eta_{c-2}$ are far away, large $D_S$ $(\eta_{c-1}, \eta_{c-2}, \xi)$ is obtained, which leads to low SRF.

We also quantitatively formulate temporal relation of candidate attack signatures as Temporal Relation Factor (TRF).

$$TRF = \frac{\alpha \bullet P}{\sum_{\eta_{C\_1}=1}^{N_{C\_1}} \sum_{\eta_{C\_2}=1}^{N_{C\_2}} D_T(t_L(\eta_{C\_1}), t_S(\eta_{C\_2}), \xi_{C\_1}, \xi_{C\_2})} \tag{6.10}$$

Where, $D_T(t_L(\eta_{c-1}), t_S(\eta_{c-2}), \xi_{c-1}, \xi_{c-2})$ is the time difference between the start time (i.e., $t_S(\eta_{c-2})$) when attack signatures $\xi_{c-2}$ is observed by node $\eta_{c-2}$ and the last (or most recent) time (i.e., $t_L$ $(\eta_{c-1})$) when the attack signature $\xi_{c-1}$ is observed by $\eta_{c-1}$ where $t_S$ $(\eta_{c-2}) \geq t_S$ $(\eta_{c-1})$. Under mobile attack, temporal continuity is observed and TRF becomes large since $D_T(t_L(\eta_{c-1}), t_S(\eta_{c-2}), \xi_{c-1}, \xi_{c-2})$ becomes small.

We use SRF and TRF metrics to infer attack type as follows: (I) When high SRF and high TRF is observed, we can infer that mobile attack has occurred. (II) When high SRF and low TRF are observed, we can infer that attack traffic has been intermittently generated from geographically clustered attackers. (III) When high SRF and negative TRF are observed, we can infer that DDoS attack has occurred from clustered attackers (clustered DDoS attack) (IV) When low SRF and high TRF are observed, we can infer that attack has occurred from geographically spread attackers with temporal continuity. (V) When low SRF and low TRF are observed, we can infer that attack traffic has been generated from geographically spread attackers. (VI) When low SRF and negative TRF are observed, we can infer that DDoS attack from geographically spread attackers has been generated (spread DDoS attack). These results have been validated via extensive simulations.

### 6.6.3. *Examples for Mobile Attacker Traceback*

- Mobile DoS attacker Traceback
  Figure 6.10(a) shows the example of mobile DoS attacker traceback using the TRF and SRF metrics. In the figure, attacker moved from region 10 → 9 → 8 → 7. Attack paths from each attack origin are as follows: (10 → 6 → 4 → 2 → 1 → $v$), (9 → 6 → 3 → 2 → 1 → $v$), (8 → 5 → 3 → 2 → 1 → $v$), (7 → 5 → 3 → 2 → 1 → $v$). A victim will find the first level temporal/spatial relation in regions 3 and 4. In region 3 and region 4, high TRF and high SRF are observed. At this point, we can infer that mobile attack is occurring. Similarly, in region 5 and 6,

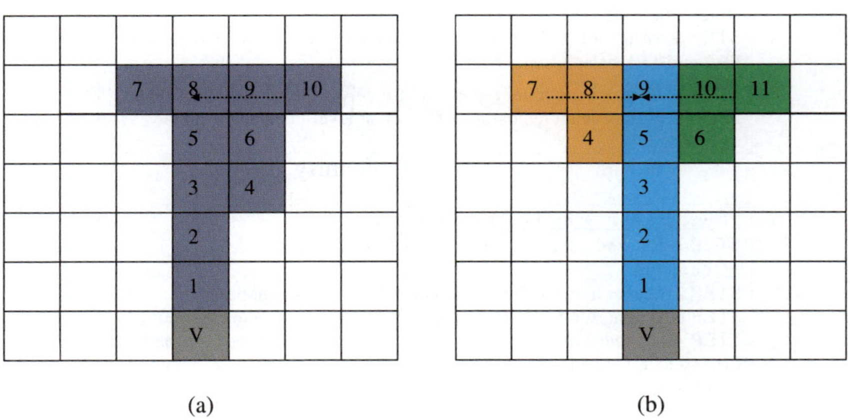


Fig. 6.10. Illustration of mobile attacks. (a) Mobile DoS attack (b) Crossing mobile DDoS attack.

high TRF and high SRF are observed. Lastly, in region 7, 8, 9, 10, high TRF and SRF are observed, which leads us to conclude that attacker is moving and currently located in the region 7. Vertical or diagonal movement of attacker can be detected similarly.

- Mobile DDoS attacker Traceback
  Basically, mobile DDoS attacker can be detected and tracked down using the same mechanism mentioned above with separate threads for each branch attack route. A difficult problem in mobile DDoS attack occurs when multiple attackers are crossing each other as in Figure 6.10(b). The crossing mobile DDoS attack can be detected by using TRF and SRF metrics plus attack signature surge detection. For instance, in Fig. 36(b), the first attacker is moving $7 \rightarrow 8 \rightarrow 9$ and the second attacker is moving $11 \rightarrow 10 \rightarrow 9$. Attack traffic is merged on the path $9 \rightarrow 6 \rightarrow 3 \rightarrow 2 \rightarrow 1$. Region 4, and 5 observe high SRF and high TRF. In addition, region 5, and 6 also observe high SRF and high TRF. The relations enable us to infer mobile attack has occurred in (4,5) regions and (5, 6) regions. In addition, region 5 observes attack traffic surge, which allows us to infer the crossing of mobile attack traffic. Similarly, region 7, 8 and 9 observe high SRF and high TRF. In addition, region 11, 10, and 9 observe high SRF and high TRF. Region 9 will also observe attack signature surge. Consequently, relative location of an attacker can be inferred from gathered information at contact region 9. The overall algorithm to detect and trace mobile DDoS attack is outlined in Figure 6.11.

**Procedure at victim *v***
STEP 1: Detect flooding-type DoS/DDoS attack.
STEP 2: Send attack signature query to level-*1* contacts.
STEP 3: If there are multiple signature reports from contacts, calculate SRF and TRF.
STEP 4: If SRF > SRF_thresh and TRF > TRF_thresh between contact $c_{1a}$ and $c_{1b}$, infer that attacker is moving from region $c_{1a}$ to region $c_{1a}$.
STEP 5: Check signature surging. If the surging exists, infer that multiple attackers are crossing.
STEP 6: Wait for matching report from higher level contact and perform SRF and TRF calculation.
STEP 7: If there is no more reports after receiving level-*N* contact report, infer the current relative position of attack at level-*i* contact, with the largest age.

**Procedure at intermediate contact $c_i$**
STEP 1: Receive attack signature query from contact $c_{i-1}$ or victim.
STEP 2: Gather abnormality information from vicinity nodes.
STEP 3: If abnormality exists, report the attack signature to the victim.
STEP 4: If abnormality is observed and level depth is not reached yet then select contact ($c_{i+1}$) and send next-level query $c_{i+1}$. Otherwise suppress query.

Fig. 6.11. Algorithm for mobile DDoS attack trace-back.

Table 6.3. Attack classification using SRF and TRF metrics.

| | SRF ($m^{-1}$) | TRF ($s^{-1}$) |
|---|---|---|
| Mobile DoS | 0.17 | 28.1 |
| Clustered DDoS | 0.18 | $5.12 \times 10^{-3}$ |
| Spread DDoS | 0.032 | $5.38 \times 10^{-3}$ |

### 6.6.4. *Performance Analysis for Mobile Attacker Traceback*

To evaluate and show the effectiveness of our mobile attacker traceback scheme, we compare the SRF and TRF values in DDoS attacks and mobile DoS attacks. DDoS attacks are performed from six randomly selected nodes. In mobile DoS attacks, the attacker and 5% of intermediate nodes move with random waypoint mobility model ($V_{\max} = 2\,\text{m/s}$, pause time $= 2.5\,\text{s}$). Average SRF and TRF values are calculated where mobility is detected. We exclude the regions where $\alpha$ (Eq. 6.9) is small (<0.1) since it implies that the nodes that report the attack signature moved out from original attack path. As shown in Table 6.3, SRF is high (>0.1) in both in mobile attack and clustered DDoS the attack since attack is observed in a close region. SRF shows low value (<0.1) when DDoS attacks are performed from geographically spread locations. TRF can differentiate between mobile attacks and clustered DDoS attacks since DDoS attacks are launched at around the same time regardless of the observation region. Consequently, we can effectively differentiate between DDoS attacks and mobile attacks using combination SRF and TRF metrics.

## References

[1] CERT Advisory CA-97.28, IP Denial-of-Service Attacks, May 26, 1996.
[2] CERT Advisory CA-96.21, TCP SYN Flooding and IP Spoofing Attacks, Sept. 24, 1996.
[3] CERT Advisory CA-98.01, Smurf IP Denial-of-Service Attacks, Jan. 5, 1998.
[4] CERT Advisory CA-96.01, UDP Port Denial-of-Service Attack, Reb. 8, 1996.
[5] F. Bai, N. Sadagopan, A. Helmy, "The IMPORTANT Framework for Analyzing the Impact of Mobility on Performance of Routing for Ad Hoc Networks," AdHoc Networks Journal — Elsevier, Vol. 1, Issue 4, 2003.
[6] A. Belenky and Nirwan Ansari, "On IP Traceback", IEEE Communication Magazine, July 2003.
[7] S.M. Bellovin, "ICMP Traceback Messages," IETF draft 2000; http://www.research.att.com/smb/papers/draft-bellovin-itrace-00.txt.
[8] H. Burch, *et al.*, "Tracing Anonymous Packets to Their Approximate Source", Proc. 2000 USENIX LISA Conf., pp. 319–327, Dec. 2000.
[9] R.K.C. Chang, "Defending against Flooding-Based Distributed Denial-of-Service Attacks: A Tutorial," IEEE Communication Magazine, Oct. 2002.
[10] A. Helmy, "Small World in Wireless Networks", IEEE communication letters, 2001.
[11] A. Helmy, *et al.*, "A Contact-based Architecture for Resource Discovery in Ad Hoc Networks", ACM Baltzer MONET Journal, 2004.
[12] X. Hong, M. Gerla, G. Pei, and C.-C. Chiang, "A group mobility model for ad hoc wireless networks", ACM/IEEE MSWiM, Aug. 1999.

[13] G. Mansfield, *et al.*, "Towards trapping wily intruders in the large", Computer Networks, Vol. 34, pp. 650–670, 2000.
[14] S. Milgram, "The small world problem", Psychology Today 1, 61 (1967).
[15] C.E. Perkins and P. Bhagwat, "Highly dynamic destination sequenced distance vector routing (DSDV) for mobile computers", ACM SIGCOMM, 1994, pp. 234–244.
[16] Alex C. Snoeren, *et al.*, "Hash-Based IP Traceback", ACM SIGCOMM, 2001.
[17] Stefan Savage, *et al.*, "Practical Network Support for IP Traceback", ACM SIGCOMM, 2000.
[18] Microsoft Corporation, "Stop 0A in tcpip.sys when receiving out of band (OOB) data", support.microsoft.com/support/kb/articles/Q143/4/78.asp.
[19] Hogg and Tanis, Probability and Statistical Inference, Prentice Hall, 2001.
[20] F. Bai, N. Sadagopan, B. Krishnamachari, and A. Helmy, "Modeling Path Duration Distributions in MANETs and their impact on Routing Peformance", IEEE Journal on Selected Areas of Communications (JSAC), Vol. 22, No. 7, pp. 1357–1373, September 2004.

# Chapter 7

## DETECTING DOS ATTACKS AND SERVICE VIOLATIONS IN QOS-ENABLED NETWORKS

Mohamed Hefeeda and Ahsan Habib*
*School of Computing Science, Simon Fraser University*
*250-13450 102nd Ave, Surrey, BC V3T 0A3, Canada*

The Internet currently plays a critical role in society, and it thus requires careful protection from malicious activities such as dental of service (DoS) attacks. DoS attacks can consume memory, CPU, and network bandwidth of a victim site, and they could hinder its operation or temporarily shut it down. The first part of this chapter is devoted to studying different types of DoS attacks and the of mechanisms proposed in the literature to defend against them. The second part of the chapter focuses on attacks on quality of service (QoS) enabled networks, which offer different levels of service. Attacks on QoS-enabled networks include stealing network resources, e.g., bandwidth, and degrading the service perceived by other users. We present network monitoring techniques to detect service violations and to infer DoS attacks in early stages. The last part of the chapter provides a quantitative comparison among all defense schemes for DoS and QoS attacks. The comparison highlights the merits of each scheme and estimates the overhead (both processing and communication) introduced by it. The comparison also provides guidelines for selecting the appropriate defense scheme, or a combination of schemes, based on the requirements and how much overhead can be tolerated.

### 7.1. Introduction

The Internet has become a critical infrastructure for businesses, industries, entertainment activities, banking, and almost all aspects of our every day lives. The role of the Internet in society is even growing as more and new services are continually offered electronically, and the speed and quality of communication networks improve. Because of its prevalence and importance, the Internet has also become a target for malicious activities. A prime example of such malicious activities is the denial of service attacks (DoS), which is the subject of this chapter.

The aim of a DoS attack is to consume the resources of a victim or the resources on the way to communicate with a victim. By wasting the victim's resources, the attacker disallows it from serving legitimate customers. A victim can be a

*Ahsan Habib is with the Siemens Technology-To-Business Center, Berkeley, CA

host, server, router, or any computing entity connected to the network. Inevitable human errors during software development, configuration, and installation open several unseen doors for these type of attacks [1]. In addition, the original design of the Internet focused primarily on interconnectivity among diverse networks and reliability against failures [2]. This design has led to a stateless Internet core — internal routers do not keep any information about packets passing through them. The stateless nature of the Internet does not provide enough deterrents for attackers, because they cannot easily be tracked down.

Wide spectrum of motivation behind these DoS attacks exists. They range from political conflicts and economical benefits for competitors to just curiosity of some computer geeks. Furthermore, cyber terrorism may not be excluded in the future. Several DoS attacks are known and documented in the literature [3–7]. Flooding a victim with an overwhelming amount of traffic is the most common. This unusual traffic clogs the communication links and thwarts all connections among the legitimate users, which may result in shutting down an entire site or a branch of the network. This happened in February of 2000 for the popular web sites Yahoo, E*trade, Ebay, and CNN for several hours [4].

Numerous DoS attacks are occurring every day over the Internet [1]. For example, the San Diego Supercomputer Center reported 12,805 DoS attacks over a three-week period in February of 2001 [5]. The DoS attacks can be severe if they last for a prolonged period of time preventing legitimate users from accessing some or all of computing resources. Imagine an executive of a financial institution deprived of access to the stock market updates for several hours or even several minutes. In [5], the authors showed that whereas 50% of the attacks lasted less than ten minutes, unfortunately, 2% of them lasted greater than five hours and 1% lasted more than ten hours. There were dozens of attacks that spanned multiple days.

The first part of this chapter (Section 7.2) is focused on studying DoS attacks in the Internet. It defines various types of DoS attacks (in Section 7.2.1), and it provides a classification of mechanisms proposed in the literature to defend against them. These mechanisms are divided into two categories: (i) Detection and Reaction (presented in Section 7.2.2), and (ii) Prevention and Suppression (presented in Section 7.2.3). Approaches in the first category focus on detection of DoS attacks, and then identifying and punishing the attackers. Whereas approaches in the second category try to prevent DoS attacks from happening by filtering their traffic.

In addition to DoS attacks, the quality of service (QoS) enabled networks are vulnerable to another type of attacks, namely, the QoS attacks. A QoS-enabled network, such as a differentiated services network [8], offers different classes of service for different costs. Differences in the charging rates may entice some users to steal bandwidth or other network resources. We define an attacker in this environment as a user who tries to get more resources, i.e., a better service class, than what he has signed (paid) for. QoS attacks are classified into two kinds: attacking the *network provisioning process* and attacking the *data forwarding process*. Network provisioning involves configuration of routers in a QoS network.

This process can be attacked by injecting bogus configuration messages, modifying the content of real configuration messages, or delaying such messages. Networks can be secured against such attacks by encrypting the configuration messages of the signaling protocols.

Attacks on the data forwarding process are of a more serious nature. These attacks inject traffic into the network with the intent to steal bandwidth or to cause QoS degradation for other flows — a traffic flow refers to the sequence of packets flowing from a source to a destination. Since the differentiated services framework is based on aggregation of flows into service classes, legitimate customer traffic may experience degraded QoS as a result of the illegally injected traffic. Taken to an extreme, that excess traffic may result in a denial of service attack. This creates a need for developing an effective defense mechanism that automates the detection and reaction to attacks on the QoS-enabled networks.

In the second part of this chapter (Section 7.3), we study the QoS-enabled networks and possible attacks on them. In particular we present network monitoring techniques to detect service violations and to infer DoS attacks. Network monitoring has the potential to detect attacks in early stages before they severely harm the victim. The basic idea is that a DoS attack injects a huge amount of traffic into the network, which may alter the internal characteristics (e.g., delay and loss ratio) of the network. The monitoring scheme watches for these changes and identifies the congested links, which helps in locating the attacker and alerting the victim. We analyze the performance and overheads of various monitoring techniques.

In the final part of this chapter (Section 7.4), we conduct a comparative evaluation study among the approaches presented for defending against DoS and QoS attacks. The aim of the study is to compare the behavior of the approaches under different situations of the underlying network. We draw insightful comments from the comparison that guide the selection of one or more defending approaches suitable for a given environment. We conclude the chapter in Section 7.5.

## 7.2. Denial of Service Attacks

In the literature, there are several approaches to deal with denial of service (DoS) attacks [3,9,10]. In this section, we provide an updated taxonomy of these approaches, and we describe the main features of each approach. We start in Section 7.2.1 by defining different types of DoS attacks. Then, we present various approaches to detect and thwart DoS attacks. We divide the approaches for dealing with DoS attacks into two main categories: (i) *Detection and Reaction*, and (ii) *Prevention or Suppression*. The first category, presented in Section 7.2.2, capitalizes on the fact that appropriately punishing wrong doers (attackers) will deter them from re-attacking again, and will scare others to do similar acts. The second category, presented in Section 7.2.3, tries to thwart attacks before they harm the victim.

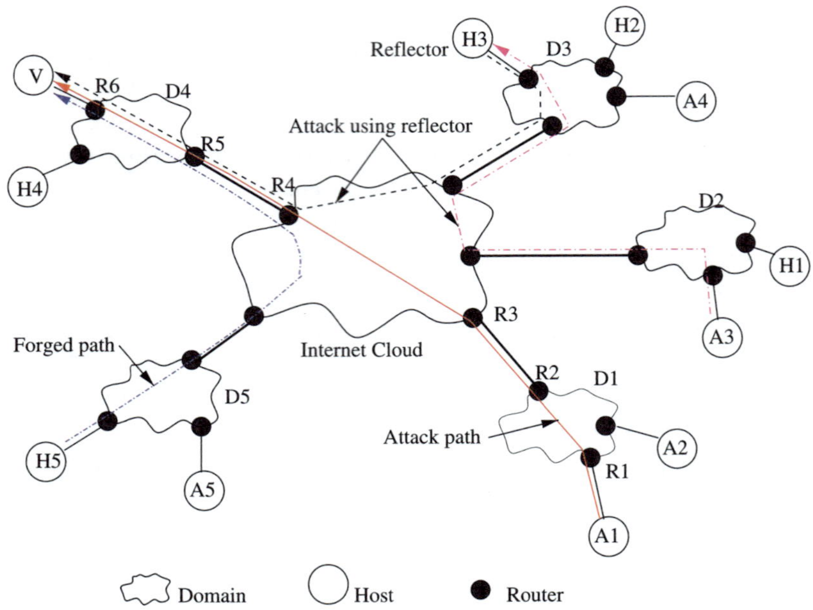


Fig. 7.1. Different scenarios for DoS attacks. Attacker $A1$ launches an attack on the victim $V$. $A1$ spoofs IP address of host $H5$ from domain $D5$. Another attacker $A3$ uses host $H3$ as a reflector to attack $V$.

To clarify the presentation, we use the hypothetical network topology shown in Figure 7.1 to demonstrate several scenarios for DoS attacks and how the different approaches react to them. The figure shows several hosts (denoted by $Hs$) connected to four domains. Throughout the chapter, we use "domain" to refer to an Autonomous Systems (AS) domain, which is a network administered by a single entity. $D1, D2, D3$, and $D4$ are four domains interconnected through the Internet cloud. In the figure, $A_i$ represents an attacker $i$ while $V$ represents a victim.

### 7.2.1. *Types of Denial of Service Attacks*

The goal of a DoS attack is to deprive legitimate users access to services offered by the target of the attack (the victim). Attackers employ different schemes to launch DoS attacks. These attacking schemes can roughly lead to three categories of attacks: Application attacks, Vulnerability attacks, and Flooding (also known as network or bandwidth) attacks. We describe these attacks below. Notice that these categories are not strict in the sense that some attacks can fall in multiple categories at the same time, or attacks can be transformed from one category to another by changing the environment and/or the behavior of the attackers.

**Application Attacks.** In this type of attacks, the attacker submits a valid request to the victim, but the request is expensive to fulfill. For example, the attacker may submit a lengthy database query that requires extensive disk operations, or a request that consumes too many CPU cycles and/or memory space. The attacker sends many such expensive requests to the victim to consume its resources, which results in degradation or even denial of service for legitimate users. Since requests are usually small-size messages, submitting many of them is easily doable even by limited-capacity attackers. A few approaches can be used to defend against applications attacks. For example, the victim server can stop automatically generated requests by using CAPTCHA-based techniques [11], which can differentiate requests issued by humans from those issued by machines. Another approach is that the server requires the machine submitting a request to pay some CPU or memory cycles (by solving a computational challenge) [12], or pay actual or virtual currency [13]. In this case, the attacker cannot submit too many requests. An interesting recent approach [14] for defending against application attacks is to encourage legitimate users to actually increase their sending rates such that they can take a larger share of the server's resources than the attacker, assuming that the attacker is already sending at its maximum rate and the sever can handle the increased traffic volume.

**Vulnerability Attacks.** In vulnerability attacks, the attacker exploits some software bugs or configuration errors of the software systems running on the victim server. Currently there is a numerous number of such vulnerabilities, and this number has even been increasing over the past few years [1,3]. An example of such attacks is the Ping of Death attack, which exploited a vulnerability in the network stack. This attack caused buffer overflow and crash of many systems by sending a ping packet with size larger than 65,535 bytes, which is the maximum allowed size for an IP packet. This vulnerability has been fixed in the late 1990s. The only method to mitigate the effects of vulnerability attacks is by following best practices in regularly patching and properly configuring servers connected to the Internet. Several web sites such as [1] periodically publish recently discovered vulnerabilities and possible remedies for them.

**Flooding or Bandwidth Attacks.** This kind of attacks is the main focus of this chapter. Attackers flood a victim with an overwhelming amount of network traffic. This unusual traffic clogs the communication links and thwarts all connections among the legitimate users, which may result in shutting down an entire site or a branch of the network. Several flooding attacks are known and documented in the literature [3–7]. TCP SYN flooding is an instance of the flooding attacks [15]. Under this attack, the victim is a host and usually runs a Web server. A regular client opens a connection with the server by sending a TCP SYN segment. The server allocates buffer for the expected connection and replies with a TCP ACK segment. The connection remains half-open (backlogged) till the client acknowledges the ACK of the server and moves the connection to the established state. If the client does not send the ACK, the buffer will be deallocated after an expiration of a timer. The server can only have a specific number of half-open connections after which all requests will be refused. The attacker sends a TCP SYN segment pretending a desire to establish a connection and making the server reserves buffer for it. The attacker does not complete the connection. Instead, it issues more TCP SYNs, which lead the server to waste its memory and reach its limit for the backlogged connections. Sending such SYN requests with a high rate keeps the server unable to satisfy connection requests from legitimate users.

Schuba *et al.* [15] developed a tool to alleviate the SYN flooding attack. The tool watches for SYN segments coming from spoofed IP addresses and sends TCP RST segments to the server. The RST segments terminate the half-open connections and free their associated buffers. Other types of flooding attacks include TCP ACK and RST flooding, ICMP and UDP echo-request flooding, and DNS request flooding [5,7]. This list is by no means exhaustive.

A DoS attack can be more severe when an attacker uses multiple hosts over the Internet to storm a victim. In this case, the attack is called a Distributed DoS (DDoS) attack. To achieve this, the attacker compromises many hosts and deploys attacking agents on them. The attacker signals all agents to simultaneously launch an attack on a victim. Barros [16] shows that DDoS attack can reach a high level of sophistication by using *reflectors*. A reflector is like a mirror that reflects light. In the Internet, many hosts such as Web servers, DNS servers, and routers can be used as reflectors because they always reply to (or reflect) specific type of packets. Web servers reply to SYN requests, DNS servers reply to queries, and routers send ICMP packets (time exceeded or host unreachable) in response to particular IP packets. The attackers can abuse these reflectors to launch DDoS attacks. For example, in Figure 7.1, an attacking agent ($A1$) sends a SYN request to a reflector ($H3$) specifying the IP address of the victim ($V$) as the source address of the agent. The reflector will send a SYN ACK to the victim. There are millions of reflectors in the Internet and the attacker can use these reflectors to flood the victim's network by sending a large amount of packets. Paxson [17] analyzes several Internet protocols and applications and concludes that DNS servers, Gnutella servers, and TCP-based servers are potential reflectors.

### 7.2.2. *Detection and Reaction Approaches*

The detection and reaction approaches rely on finding the malicious party who launched a DoS attack and consequently punish or hold him liable for the damage he has caused. Thus, there are two steps in these approaches. The first is to detect the existence of an attack, and the second is to react to the attack. To react for an attack, the real attacker needs to be identified. We present below the main methods for detecting DoS attacks and identifying the attackers.

#### 7.2.2.1. *Attack detection*

The goal of the detection process is to differentiate between packets belonging to legitimate traffic and malicious traffic. A number of approaches have been proposed in the literature to detect denial of service attacks, e.g., [10,18–20]. Many of these methods detect an attack by observing the deviation of some statistics of the traffic from the normal behavior of the traffic. We classify the detection methods into three categories, based on the detection location: (i) near the victim, (ii) near the attack source, and (iii) in the network.

Carl *et al.* present a recent survey on DoS detection methods that can be used near the victim, which are usually the preferred methods for administrators as they aim at protecting their own networks. These methods inspect packet headers to collect statistics on connection patterns, distribution of source and destination IP addresses, and average packet rate. These statistics can be compared against normal levels to detect anomalous behavior, using for example a chi-square test. More sophisticated methods such as analyzing the time series representing samples periodically taken from the traffic using wavelet analysis can also be used [20].

Detecting DoS attacks near their sources is also possible, although might be less effective because the traffic volume near the source is usually low — the DoS traffic aggregates from various sources toward the victim. Nonetheless, some characteristics of the DoS traffic can be used to detect it. For example, the DoS traffic usually does not obey the TCP congestion control algorithm, and it may have asymmetric packet rates between local and remote hosts. Asymmetric packet rates appear because the attacking machine typically sends much more packets than it receives. Using this idea, Mirkovic *et al.* [20] proposed the D-WARD defense system. D-WARD is to be deployed at edge routers to monitor the asymmetry in the two-way packet rates.

Several works advocate detecting the attack traffic inside the network itself [18,19,21]. For example Yuan and Mills [18] monitor the spatial-temporal correlation among various characteristics of aggregate traffic flows, that is, they observe the macroscopic behavior of many traffic connections. The idea is that congestion at routers happens as a result of interaction among many flows crossing the network from different directions. Therefore, congestion near victim servers that are destinations for DoS attacks would reveal correlation among their aggregate traffic flows. The authors propose collecting information about packet flows from a limited number of monitoring points in the network. Then, they conduct a cross-correlation analysis of the traffic matrix constructed on the packet flows. They compute the eigenvalues and eigenvectors of the matrix. Correlation among traffic flows is typically exposed by the components of the eigenvector corresponding to the largest eigenvalue. The authors then define a weight vector by grouping the components of the eigenvector that belong to the same destination. Thus, using these weights, the influence of each destination on the whole network can be studied, and a network-wide view of the shifting traffic patterns and where the congested destinations are can be created.

Finally, Sekar *et al.* [19] propose an automated system for detecting DoS attacks, which is called LADS. LADS uses a multistage detection approach, where each stage is triggered by its predecessor and operates on data of finer granularity. More specifically, LADS first uses a light-weight stage to detect possible anomalies in the traffic patterns close to the victim. This stage uses coarse-grained traffic statistics provided by SNMP (Simple Network Management Protocol) agents running on routers. Although coarse-grained, anomalies in these statistics are usually indicative because links close to the victim (Internet access links) typically have limited capacity. Coarse-grained statistics include, for example, traffic volume (packets or bytes per second), packet drop rate, and router CPU utilization. The collected statistics are compared against expected ones, and thresholds are used to detect anomalies and possible attacks. If a potential attack is detected, a second stage of more elaborate traffic analysis is triggered. The second stage collects detailed traffic statistics from routers running monitoring software such as NetFlow. The detailed statistics include per-flow information, which can be used to cluster and aggregate traffic flows based on their source-destination prefixes — a prefix is a network address specified by the leftmost bits in the IP address. This aggregation helps in identifying the heavy hitters and potential attackers.

#### 7.2.2.2. *Attacker identification*

The reaction to an attack includes identifying the attacker and blocking or filtering the attacking traffic. Pinning the real attacker down, however, is not a straightforward task, because the attacker usually spoofs the source IP address of the attacking packets. In addition, the Internet is *stateless*, which means whenever a packet passes through a router, the router does not store any information (or traces) about that packet. Therefore, mechanisms such as ICMP traceback and packet marking are devised to figure out the real attacker. In this subsection, we describe the traceback and packet marking techniques used to identify attackers.

**ICMP Traceback.** Bellovin *et al.* [22] propose the idea of using ICMP Traceback messages, where every router samples the forwarded packets with a very low probability, e.g., 1 out of 20,000, and sends an ICMP Traceback message to the destination. An ICMP Traceback message contains the previous and next hop addresses of the router, timestamp, portion of the traced packet, and authentication information. In Figure 7.1, while packets are traversing the network path from the attacker $A1$ to the victim $V$, the intermediate routers ($R1, R2, R3, R4, R5$, and $R6$) sample some of these packets and send ICMP Traceback messages to the destination $V$. With enough messages, the victim can trace the network path $A1 \rightarrow V$. The pitfall of this approach is that the attacker can send many false ICMP Traceback messages to confuse the victim.

To address Distributed DoS (DDoS) attacks by reflectors, Barros [16] proposes a modification to the ICMP Traceback messages. In his refinement, routers sometimes send ICMP Traceback messages to the *source*. In Figure 7.1, $A3$ launches a DDoS attack by sending TCP SYN segments to the reflector $H3$ specifying $V$ as the source address. $H3$, in turn, sends SYN ACK segments to the victim $V$. According to the modification, routers on the path $A3 \rightarrow H3$ will send ICMP Traceback messages to the source, i.e., to $V$. This *reverse trace* enables the victim to identify the attacking agent from these trace packets. The *reverse trace* mechanism depends only on the number of attacking agents, and not on the number of reflectors [17]. This achieves scalability because the number of available reflectors is much higher than the number of attacking agents on the Internet.

Snoeren *et al.* [23] propose an attractive hashed-based system that can trace the origin of a single IP packet delivered by a network in the recent past. The system is called Source Path Isolation Engine (SPIE). SPIE uses an efficient method to store information about packets traversing through a particular router. The method uses $n$ bits of the hashed value of the packet to set an index of a $2^n$-bit *digest table.* When a victim detects an attack, a query is sent to SPIE, which queries routers for packet digests of the relevant time periods. Topology information is then used to construct the attack graph from which the source of the attack can be determined.

**Packet Marking.** Instead of having routers send separate messages for the sampled packets, Burch and Cheswick [24] propose to inscribe some path information into the header of the packets themselves. This marking can be deterministic or probabilistic. In the deterministic marking, every router marks all packets. The obvious drawback of the deterministic packet marking is that the packet header grows as the number of routers increases on the path. Moreover, significant overhead will be imposed on routers to mark every packet.

The probabilistic packet marking (PPM) method encodes the path information into a small fraction of the packets. The assumption is that during a flooding attack, a huge amount of traffic travels towards the victim. Therefore, there is a great chance that many of these packets will be marked at routers throughout their journey from the source to the victim. It is likely that the marked packets will give enough information to trace the network path from the victim to the source of the attack.

Savage *et al.* [6] describe efficient mechanisms to encode the path information into packets. This information contains the XOR (exclusive OR) of two IP addresses and a distance metric. The two IP addresses are for the start and the end routers of the link. The distance metric represents the number of hops between the attacker and the victim. To illustrate the idea, consider the attacker $A1$ and the victim $V$ in Figure 7.1. Assume there is only one hop between routers $R3$ and $R4$. If Router $R1$ marks a packet, it will encode the XOR of $R1$ and $R2$ addresses into the packet and sets the distance metric to zero, that is, it will encode the tuple $\langle R1 \oplus R2, 0\rangle$. Other routers on the path just increase the distance metric of this packet, if they don't decide to mark it again. When this packet reaches the victim, it provides the tuple $\langle R1 \oplus R2, 5\rangle$. Similarly, some packets may get marked at routers $R2, R3, R4, R5$, and $R6$ and they will provide the tuples $\langle R2 \oplus R3, 4\rangle$, $\langle R3 \oplus R4, 3\rangle$, $\langle R4 \oplus R5, 2\rangle$, $\langle R5 \oplus R6, 1\rangle$, $\langle R6, 0\rangle$, respectively, when they reach the victim. The victim can retrieve all routers on the path by XORing the collected messages sorted by the distance. (Recall that $Rx \oplus Ry \oplus Rx = Ry$.) This approach can reconstruct most network paths with 95% certainty if there are about 2,000 marked packets available, and even the longest path can be resolved with 4,000 packets [6]. For DoS attacks, this amount of packets is clearly obtainable because the attacker needs to flood the network to cause a DoS attack. (Moore *et al.* [5] report that some severe DoS attacks had a rate of thousands of packets per second.) The authors describe ways to reduce the required space and suggest to use the identification field (currently used for IP fragmentation) of IP header to store the encoding of the path information. They also propose solutions to handle the co-existence of marking and fragmentation of IP packets [6]. The recent work in [25] improves the efficiency and accuracy of probabilistic packet marking.

The main limitation of the PPM approaches stems from the fact that, nothing prevents the attacker from marking packets. If a packet marked by the attacker does not get re-marked by any intermediate router, it will confuse the victim and make it harder to trace the real attacker. Park and Lee [26] show that for single-source DoS attacks, PPM can identify a small set of sources as potential candidates for a DoS attack. For DDoS attacks, however, the attacker can increase the uncertainty in localizing the attacker. Therefore, PPM is vulnerable to distributed DoS attacks [26].

### 7.2.3. *Prevention and Suppression Approaches*

Prevention approaches try to stop a DoS attack by identifying the attack packets and discarding them before reaching the victim. We summarize several packet filtering techniques that achieve this goal.

#### 7.2.3.1. *Ingress filtering*

Incoming packets to a network domain can be filtered by ingress routers. These filters verify the identity of packets entering into the domain, like an immigration security system at the airport. Ingress filtering, proposed by Farguson and Senie [27], is a restrictive mechanism that drops traffic with IP address that does not match a domain prefix connected to the ingress router. As an example, in Figure 7.1, the attacker $A1$ resides in domain $D1$ with the network prefix a.b.c.0/24. The attacker wants to launch a DoS attack to the victim $V$ that is connected to domain $D4$. If the attacker spoofs the IP address of host $H5$ in domain $D5$, which has the network prefix x.y.z.0/24, an input traffic filter on the ingress link of $R1$ will thwart this spoofing. $R1$ only allows traffic originating from source addresses within the a.b.c.0/24 prefix. Thus, the filter prohibits an attacker from using *spoofed* source addresses from outside of the prefix range. Similarly, filtering foils DDoS attacks that employ reflectors. In Figure 7.1, ingress filter of $D2$ will discard packets destined to the reflector $H3$ and specifying $V's$ address in the source address field. Thus, these packets will not be able to reach the reflector.

Ingress filtering can drastically reduce the DoS attack by IP spoofing if *all* domains use it. It is hard, though, to deploy ingress filters in *all* Internet domains. If there are some unchecked points, it is possible to launch DoS attacks from that points. Another concern is that some legitimate traffic can be discarded by an ingress filtering when Mobile IP is used to attach a mobile node to a foreign network [27]. Packets from the mobile node will have source addresses that do not match with the network prefix where the mobile node is currently attached.

Unlike ingress filters, egress filters reside at the exit points of a network domain and checks whether the source address of exiting packets belong to this domain. Aside from the placement issue, both ingress and egress filters have similar behavior.

#### 7.2.3.2. *Route-based filtering*

Park and Lee [28] propose route-based distributed packet filtering, which rely on route information to filter out spoofed IP packets. For instance, suppose that $A1$ belongs to domain $D1$ and is attempting a DoS attack on $V$ that belongs to domain $D4$. If $A1$ uses the spoofed address $H5$ that belongs to domain $D5$, the filter at domain $D1$ would recognize that a packet originated from domain $D5$ and destined to $V$ should not travel through domain $D1$. Then, the filter at $D1$ will discard the packet. Route-based filters do not use/store individual host addresses for filtering, rather, they use the topology information of Autonomous Systems (ASes). The authors of [28] show that with partial deployment of route-based filters, about 20% in the Internet AS topologies, it is possible to achieve a good filtering effect that prevents spoofed IP flows reaching other ASes. These filters need to build route information by consulting BGP routers of different ASes. Since routes on the Internet change with time [29], it is a challenge for route-based filters to be updated in real time.

Finally, all filters proposed in the literature so far fall short to detect IP address spoofing from the domain in which the attacker resides. For example, in Figure 7.1, if $A1$ uses some unused IP addresses of domain $D1$, the filters will not be able to stop such forged packets to reach the victim $V$.

## 7.3. Monitoring to Detect Service Violations and DoS Attacks

In this section, we show how network monitoring techniques can be used to detect service violations and to infer DoS attacks. Network monitoring is also used in security and quality monitoring [30] as well as detection of traffic anomalies in multimedia transmission [31].

We believe that network monitoring has the potential to detect DoS attacks in early stages before they severely harm the victim. Our conjecture is that a DoS attack injects a huge amount of traffic into the network, which may alter the internal characteristics (e.g., delay and loss ratio) of the network. Monitoring watches for these changes and our proposed techniques can identify the congested links and the points that are feeding them. We describe the monitoring schemes in the context of a QoS-enabled network, which provides different classes of service for different costs. The schemes are also applicable to best effort (BE) networks to infer DoS attacks, but not to detect service violations because there is no notion of service differentiation in BE networks.

To monitor a domain, we measure three parameters: delay, packet loss ratio, and throughput. We refer to these parameters collectively as the service level agreement (SLA) parameters, since they indicate whether a user is achieving the QoS requirements contracted with the network provider. In our discussion, delay is the end-to-end latency; packet loss ratio is defined as the ratio of number of dropped packets from a flow[a] to the total number of packets of the same flow entered the domain; and throughput is the total bandwidth consumed by a flow inside the domain. Delay and loss ratio are good indicators for the current status of the domain. This is because, if the domain is properly provisioned and no user is misbehaving, the flows traversing through the domain should not experience high delay or loss ratio inside that domain. It is worth mentioning that delay jitter, i.e., delay variation, is another important SLA parameter. However, it is flow-specific and therefore, is not suitable to use in network monitoring.

The SLA parameters can be estimated with the involvement of internal (core) routers in a network domain or can be inferred without their help. We describe both *core-assisted* monitoring and *edge-based* (without involvement of core routers) monitoring in the following subsections. Then, in Section 7.3.3, we describe how these monitoring schemes can be used to detect service violations and DoS attacks. Finally, in Section 7.3.3.1, we present a brief survey on other monitoring approaches in the literature.

### 7.3.1. *Core-based Monitoring*

The core-assisted monitoring estimates the SLA parameters with the involvement of the core routers in a network domain. These measurements are similar to the literature [32,33] on measuring delay, loss, and throughput in the Internet. However, we follow different strategies to measure each parameter to make it more suitable for the monitoring process. Other monitoring schemes that involve both core and edge routers are proposed in the literature, see for example [34–36]. Now we briefly discuss the measurement of SLA parameters and how these measurements are used to monitor a network domain.

**Monitoring Algorithm:**

Let $E$ be the set of all edge routers, both egress and ingress. One of these routers can act as an SLA Monitor (SLAM), or a separate entity can be used to act as SLAM. The algorithm proceeds as follows:

(1) Each ingress router copies the header of user packets with probability $p_{probe}$ to probe the network for delay measurement.
(2) When an egress router receives these probes, the egress stamps its identity on the packet and resends them back to the source (ingress). The egress replies

[a]A flow can be a micro flow with five tuples (addresses, ports, and protocol) or an aggregate one that is a combination of several micro flows.

the delay probe to the ingress because by this way the monitor determines the receiver egress routers for the probing.

(3) The monitor computes the average edge-to-edge delay and updates the average delay of the user.

(4) During congestion, the SLAM receives packet drop information from different core routers. Then, it polls the egress routers to obtain the packet count, which is required to calculate the loss ratio.

(5) The SLAM probes the network for throughput approximation when the loss is higher than the pre-configured threshold.

(6) For users with higher delay, loss, and bandwidth consumption, the monitor decides about possible SLA violation. The monitor knows the existing traffic classes and the acceptable SLA parameters per class. If there is any loss at the core for the EF traffic class and if the AF loss ratio exceeds a certain level, an SLA violation is flagged. DoS attack is checked by comparing the total bandwidth achieved of a user with it $SLA_{bw}$. For each violation, it takes proper action, such as throttling the particular user traffic using flow control mechanism.

### 7.3.2. *Edge-based Monitoring*

We describe two edge-based monitoring schemes: *stripe-based* and *distributed*. Both schemes measure delay and throughput using the same techniques as the previous core-based scheme. They differ, however, in measuring the packet loss ratio.

**Stripe-based Monitoring.** This scheme uses the same mechanism to measure delay and throughput as it is described in the core-assisted monitoring scheme. The main difference between the two lies in measuring loss. The stripe-based monitoring scheme probes a network domain to infer loss characteristics of each individual links. The loss inference makes the stripe-based monitoring scalable.

The real challenge of this work is to determine an algorithm that monitors the network in real time nature. We need to determine how often the stripes should be sent and to which receivers to monitor all links. As this mechanism involves only edge routers, the monitoring scheme will be scalable. We show how to infer loss ratios for unicast traffic as explained in [37] and refer the reader to [38] for the multicast traffic case. The scheme sends a series of probe packets, called a stripe, with no delay between them. Usually, a stripe consists of three packets. To simplify the discussion, consider a two-leaf binary tree spanning nodes 0, $k$, $R_1$, $R_2$, as shown in Figure 7.2. The loss ratio of the link $k \rightarrow R_1$, for instance, can be estimated by sending stripes from the root 0 to the leaves $R_1$ and $R_2$. The first packet of a 3-packet stripe is sent to $R_1$, while the last two are sent to $R_2$. If a packet reaches to any receiver, we can infer that the packet must have reached the branching point $k$. Further, if $R_2$ gets the last two packets of a stripe, it is likely that $R_1$ receives the first packet of that stripe. The packet loss probability is calculated based on whether all packets sent

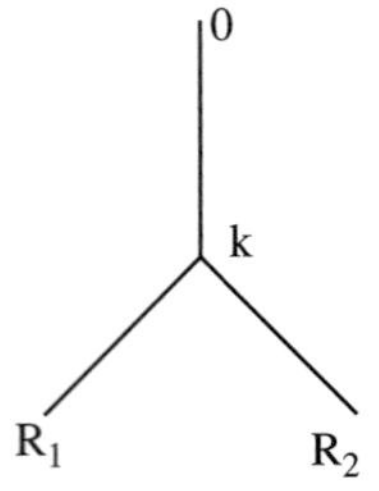


Fig. 7.2. Inferring loss ratio from the source 0 to receivers $R_1$ and $R_2$.

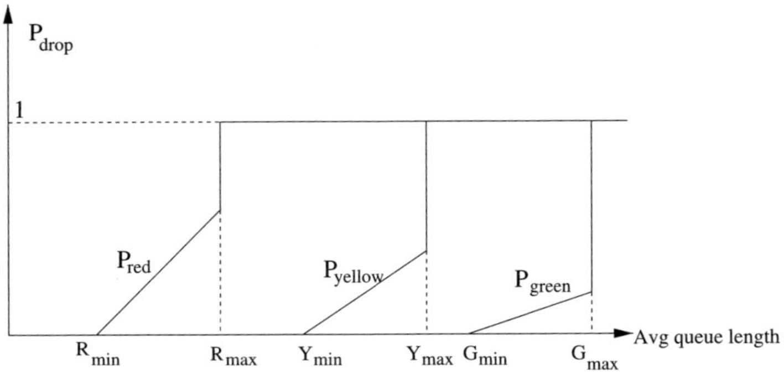


Fig. 7.3. RED Parameters for an active queue with three drop precedences.

to $R_1$ and $R_2$ reach their destination. Similarly, the loss ratio of the link $k \to R_2$ is inferred using a complementary stripe, in which the first packet is sent to $R_2$ and the last two are sent to $R_1$. The loss ratio of the common path from $0 \to k$ can be estimated by combining the results of the previous two steps. For general trees, this inference technique sends stripes from the root to all ordered pairs of the leaves of the tree.

The unicast probing scheme is extended in [39] for routers with active queue management, e.g., 3-color RED [40]. This queue has different drop precedences. We have to adjust the loss inference to cope with the drop precedences. The new scheme will be used to monitor loss inside a QoS network domain.

Figure 7.3 shows the drop probabilities of a three drop precedence active queues. The red traffic has higher probability to drop than yellow and green traffic. The packets are dropped with these probabilities when the queue length falls in between minimum and maximum threshold. Below minimum threshold there is no drop, and after maximum threshold there is absolute drop. The Assured Forwarding (AF) mechanism is realized using four queues where each queue has three drop precedences referred to as green, yellow, and red. The red traffic is dropped with a probability $P_{red}$ when the average queue size lies between two thresholds $R_{min}$ and $R_{max}$. All incoming red packets are dropped when the average queue length is $\geq R_{max}$. Let $\mathcal{P}_{red}$ be the percentage of packet drops due to the behavior of active queue management for red packets, and let $\mathcal{P}_{yellow}$ and $\mathcal{P}_{green}$ be defined similarly. These percentages can be computed as:

$$\mathcal{P}_{red} = \frac{R_{max} - R_{min}}{R_{max}} \times P_{red} + \frac{G_{max} - R_{max}}{B} \times 100, \tag{7.1}$$

$$\mathcal{P}_{yellow} = \frac{Y_{max} - Y_{min}}{Y_{max}} \times P_{yellow} + \frac{G_{max} - Y_{max}}{B} \times 100, \tag{7.2}$$

$$\mathcal{P}_{green} = \frac{G_{max} - G_{min}}{G_{max}} \times P_{green}, \tag{7.3}$$

where $B$ is the buffer (queue) size in the router.

Let, $\mathcal{P}'_{red} = 1 - \mathcal{P}_{red}$, be the percentage of *red* packets accepted by the active queue. We can define percentages for yellow and green traffic similarly using equations (7.2) and (7.3). Link loss can be inferred by subtracting of transmission probability. Therefore, if $L_g$, $L_y$, and $L_r$ are the inferred losses of green, yellow and red traffic, respectively, the overall loss of a class is expressed as shown in equation (7.4), where $n_i$ is number of samples taken from $i$ types of traffic. To put equal weight to all traffic, we can use $n = n_i, \forall i$. However, when loss of green traffic is zero, we average yellow and red losses. When the loss of yellow traffic is zero, we report only loss of red probes.

$$L_{class} = \frac{n_g \mathcal{P}'_{green} L_g + n_y \mathcal{P}'_{yellow} L_y + n_r \mathcal{P}'_{red} L_r}{n_g + n_y + n_r}. \tag{7.4}$$

Our goal is to detect SLA violations with minimal communication and implementation overhead. To achieve that, we propose to eliminate unnecessary probing when there is no traffic or when there are no misbehaving flows.

The essence of the proposed approach is to detect which egress and ingress routers are active at a certain time. This can be done using delay probes, which are anyway periodically transmitted. If many edge routers are idle or many links are under-utilized, the SLAM does not probe the whole network for loss information. This reduces the set of edge routers used as receivers in the stripe-based probing.

**Distributed Monitoring.** The distributed monitoring approach is proposed in [39] to further reduce the monitoring overhead. In this mechanism, the edge routers of a domain form an overlay network on top of the physical network. Figure 7.4(a) shows the spanning tree of the domain's topology. The edge routers form an overlay network among themselves, as shown in Figure 7.4(b). This overlay is used to build tunnel for probe packets on specified paths. The internal links for each end-to-end path in the overlay network are shown in Figure 7.4(c). In the distributed monitoring approach, an SLA monitor sits at any edge router. The monitor probes the network regularly for unusual delay patterns. The delay and throughput measurements are the same as described in *stripe-based* scheme. The two schemes differ in measuring loss. Since service violation can be detected without exact loss values, we need only to determine whether a link has higher loss than the specified threshold or not.

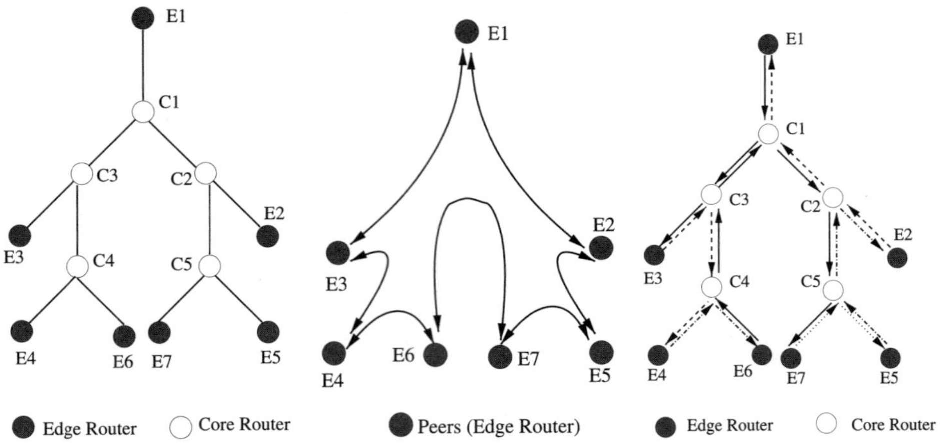


(a) The spanning tree of the domain's topology.

(b) An overlay constructed over all edge routers.

(c) Direction of probing the internal links

Fig. 7.4. Network monitoring using the distributed mechanism.

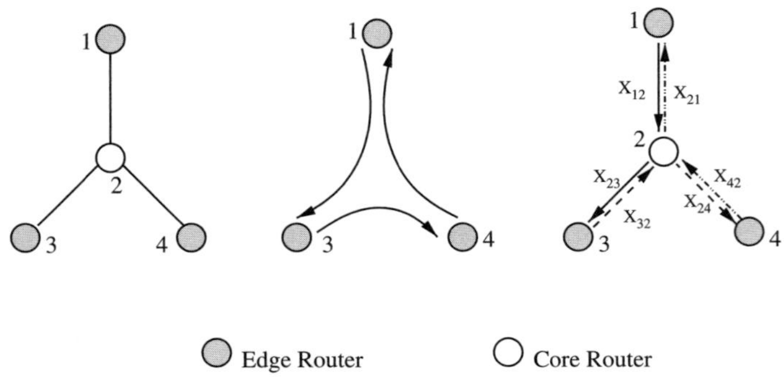


Fig. 7.5. (a) Spanning tree of a simple network topology. (b) Each edge router probes its neighbor edge router in counter-clockwise direction (c) Direction of internal links for each probing.

The link with high loss is referred to as a congested link. The goal of the distributed monitoring is to detect all congested links.

Our solution contains two rounds of probing in the Simple method. One in the counter-clockwise direction, and in the clock-wise direction starting from any edge router. The former one is referred to as *first round* of probing, and the latter one is referred to as *second round* of probing. In each round, probing is done in parallel.

We describe the loss monitoring scheme with a simple network topology. In this example, Figure 7.5(b), edge router 1 probes the path $1 \to 3$, router 3 probes the path $3 \to 4$, and 4 probes the path $4 \to 1$. Let $P_{i,j}$ be a boolean variable that represents the outcome of a probe between edge routers $i$ to $j$. $P_{i,j}$ takes on value 1 if the measured loss exceeds the threshold in any link within the probe path, and 0 otherwise. Notice that $P_{i,j} = 0, \forall_{ij}, i = j$. We express the outcome of a probe in terms of combination of all link status. Let $X_{i,j}$ be a boolean variable to represent the congestion status of an internal link $i \rightarrow j$. We refer $X$ to a *congestion variable.* From Figure 7.5(c), we can write equations as follows:

$$X_{1,2} + X_{2,3} = P_{1,3} \quad X_{3,2} + X_{2,4} = P_{3,4} \quad X_{4,2} + X_{2,1} = P_{4,1}, \qquad (7.5)$$

where (+) represents a boolean "OR" operation. We express status of internal links of any probe path of a network topology in terms of probe outcomes.

Note that loss in path $1 \rightarrow 3$ might not be same as loss in path $3 \rightarrow 1$. This path asymmetry phenomenon is shown in [41]. In general, $X_{i,j}$ is independent of $X_{j,i}, \forall_{ij}, i \neq j$.

The second round of probing, Figure 7.5(a), is done from $1 \rightarrow 4$, $4 \rightarrow 3$, and $3 \rightarrow 1$. We express the outcome of this round of probing in terms of internal links as follows:

$$X_{1,2} + X_{2,4} = P_{1,4} \quad X_{4,2} + X_{2,3} = P_{4,3} \quad X_{3,2} + X_{2,1} = P_{3,1}. \qquad (7.6)$$

For an arbitrary topology,

$$X_{i,k} + \sum_{n=k}^{n=l-1} X_{n,n+1} + X_{l,j} = P_{i,j}. \qquad (7.7)$$

The sets of equations (7.5 and 7.6) are used to detect congested link in the network. For example, if the outcome of the probing shows $P_{1,3} = 1$, $P_{1,4} = 1$, and rest are 0, we get the following:

$$X_{1,2} + X_{2,3} = 1 \qquad X_{1,2} + X_{2,4} = 1. \qquad (7.8)$$

All other probes do not see congestion on its path, i.e., $X_{3,2} = X_{2,4} = X_{4,2} = X_{2,1} = X_{2,3} = 0$. Thus, the equation set (7.8) reduces to $X_{1,2} = 1$. Similarly, if any of the single link is congested, we can isolate the congested link. Suppose, two of the links, $X_{1,2}$ and $X_{2,3}$, are congested. The outcome of probing will be $P_{1,3} = 1$, $P_{1,4} = 1$, and $P_{4,3} = 1$, which makes $X_{3,2} = X_{2,4} = X_{4,2} = X_{2,1} = 0$. This leaves the solution as shown in equation (7.9). Thus, the distributed monitoring scheme can isolate links with high loss in this topology.

$$X_{1,2} + X_{2,3} = 1 \qquad X_{1,2} = 1 \qquad X_{2,3} = 1. \qquad (7.9)$$

The strength of this method comes from the fact that congestion variables in one equation of any round of probing is distributed over several equations in the other round of probing. If $n$ variables appear in one equation in the first round of probing, no two (out of the $n$) variables appear in the same equation in the second round of probing or vice versa. This property helps to solve the equation sets efficiently. If any single probe path is congested with arbitrary number of links, the simple method can identify all the congested links. It determines the status of a link with very high probability when the congestion is low.

We refine the solution by conducting a few more probing with the probes that can resolve to the unknowns so far. Let the set of equations with undecided variables so far be $\mathbb{E}$. For each variable in equation set $\mathbb{E}$, we need to find two nodes that can be used to probe the network. Each probe requires one start node and one end node. For an undecided link $v_i \to v_j$, we look for leaves descended from node $v_i$ and $v_j$. First, the algorithm searches for a node in the direction on a subtree descended from $v_i$ and then in the direction on a subtree descended from $v_j$. For any node $v$, we explore all siblings of $v$ to choose a path in a specified direction. The function avoids previously visited path and known congested path. It marks already visited path so that the same path will not be repeated in exploration of an alternate path.

If the network is congested in a way that no solution is possible, the refinement can not add anything to the simple method. If there is a solution, the refinement can obtain probes because this is an exhaustive search on the topology tree to find edge-to-edge paths that are not already congested. More can be found at [39].

The distributed monitoring scheme requires less number of total probes, $O(n)$, compared to the stripe-based scheme, which requires $O(n^2)$, where $n$ is the number of edge routers in the domain. The distributed scheme is able to detect violation in both directions of any link in the domain, whereas the stripe-based can detect a violation only if the flow direction of the misbehaving traffic is the same as the probing direction from the root. To achieve same ability like distributed one, the stripe-based needs to probe the whole tree from several points, which increases the monitoring overhead substantially. Narasimha *et al.* provide theoretical bounds on the growth rate of the number of measurements by relating the congestion localization in networks to the problem of decoding linear error correcting codes (ECC) over a binary symmetric channel in coding theory [42].

### 7.3.3. *Violation and DoS Detection*

In both the *stripe-based* and *distributed-based* monitoring schemes, when delay, loss, and bandwidth consumption exceed the pre-defined thresholds, the monitor decides on possible SLA violation. The monitor knows the existing traffic classes and the acceptable SLA parameters per class. High delay is an indication of abnormal behavior inside the domain. If there is any loss for the guaranteed traffic class and if the loss ratios of other traffic classes exceed certain levels, an SLA violation is flagged. This loss can be caused by some flows consuming bandwidth beyond their SLA. Bandwidth theft is checked by comparing the total bandwidth achieved by a user against the user's SLA for bandwidth. The misbehaving flows are controlled at the ingress routers.

To detect DoS attacks, set of links $L$ with high loss are identified. For each congested link, $l(v_i, v_j) \in L$, the tree is divided into two subtrees: one formed by leaves descendant from $v_i$ and the other from the leaves descendant from $v_j$. The first subtree has egress routers as leaves through which high aggregate bandwidth flows are leaving. If many exiting flows have the same destination IP prefix, we can infer that either this is a DoS attack or the traffic is a going to a popular site [43]. Decision can be taken with consulting the destination entity. If it is an attack, we can stop it by triggering filters at the ingress routers that are leaves of the *other* subtree.

We illustrate a scenario of detecting and controlling DoS attack using Figure 7.4. Suppose, the victim's domain $\mathcal{D}$ is connected to the edge router $E6$. The monitor observes that links $C3 \rightarrow C4$ and link $C4 \rightarrow E6$ are congested for a time duration $\Delta t$ sec. From both congested links, we obtain the egress router $E6$ through which most of these flows are leaving. The destination IP prefix matching at $E6$ reveals that an excess amount of traffic is heading towards the domain $\mathcal{D}$ connected to $E6$. To control the attack, the monitor needs to figure out through which ingress routers the suspected flows are entering into the domain. The algorithm to identify these ingress routers is discussed in [39]. The monitor activates filters at these ingress routers to regulate the flows that are destined to $\mathcal{D}$.

The advantage of the monitoring-based attack detection is that the neighbor domains of the victim can detect the attack early by observing the violation of SLA parameters. By consulting with the potential victim, these domains can regulate the intensity of the attack and even an early detection can thwart the attack. For each violation, the monitor takes actions such as throttling a particular user's traffic using a flow control mechanism.

#### 7.3.3.1. *Other monitoring approaches*

An Internet service provider needs to monitor its network domain to ensure the network is operating well. One obvious way of monitoring is to log packets at various points throughout the network and then extract information to discover the path of any packet. This scheme is useful to trace an attack long after the attack has been accomplished. The effectiveness of logging is limited by the huge storage requirements especially for high speed networks. Stone [44] suggested to create a virtual overlay network connecting all edge routers of a provider to reroute *interesting* flows through tunnels to central tracking routers. After examination, suspicious packets are dropped. This approach also requires a great amount of logging capacity.

Many proposals for network monitoring [34,36] give designs to manage the network and ensure that the system is operating within desirable parameters. In efficient reactive monitoring [36], the authors discuss ways to monitor communication overhead in IP networks. Their idea is to combine global polling with local event driven reporting. In contrast, the core-assisted monitoring scheme, presented in Section 7.3.1, depends on local event driven reporting to detect SLA violation and performs global polling only when it is absolutely necessary. Breitbart *et al.* [34] identify effective techniques to monitor bandwidth and latency in IP networks. The authors present *probing-based* techniques, where path latencies are measured by transmitting probes from a single point of control. The paper describes algorithms to compute an optimal set of probes to measure latency of paths in a network.

A large variety of network monitoring tools can be found at [45]. Many tools use SNMP [46], RMON [47], or NetFlow [48], which are built-in functionality for most routers. Using these mechanisms, a centralized or decentralized model can be built to monitor a network. The centralized approach to monitor network latency, jitter, loss, throughput, or other QoS parameters suffers from scalability. One way to achieve scalability is to use a hierarchical architecture [49,50]. Subramanyan *et al.* [50] design an SNMP-based distributed network monitoring system that organizes monitoring agents and managers in a hierarchical fashion. Both centralized or decentralized models obtain monitoring data by polling each router of a network domain, which limits the ability of a system to scale for a large number of flows. The alternative way of polling is to use an event reporting mechanism that sends useful information typically in a summarized format only when the status of a monitored element changes. A more flexible way of network monitoring is by using mobile agents [51] or programmable architecture [52]. However, periodic polling or deploying agents in high speed core routers put non-trivial overhead on them.

In [35], a histogram-based aggregation algorithm is used to detect SLA violations. The algorithm measures network characteristics on a hop-by-hop basis and uses them to compute end-to-end measurements and validate end-to-end SLA requirements. In large networks, efficient collection of management data is a challenge. While exhaustive data collection yields a complete picture, there is an added overhead. The authors propose an *aggregation* and *refinement* based monitoring approach. The approach assumes that the routes used by SLA flows are known, citing VPN and MPLS [53] provisioning. Though routes are known for double ended SLAs that specify both ingress and egress points in the network, they are unknown in cases where the scope of the service is not limited to a fixed egress point.

## 7.4. Quantitative Comparison

In this section, we conduct a quantitative analysis of the overhead imposed by different schemes to detect and prevent DoS attacks. The objective of this comparison is to show the characteristics of each scheme and how they behave when different configuration parameters of a domain are changed. We do not emphasize on numeric overhead values of any specific scheme, rather, we draw a relative comparison among them. The comparison provides guidelines for selecting the appropriate scheme, or a combination of schemes, based on the requirements and how much overhead can be tolerated. The schemes we compare here are: Ingress Filtering (*Ingf*), route-based packet filtering (*Route*), traceback with probabilistic packet marking (*PPM*), core-based network monitoring (*Core*), stripe-based monitoring (*Stripe*), and distributed monitoring (*Distributed*).

### 7.4.1. *Setup*

For each scheme, we calculate two different overheads: processing and communication. The processing overhead is due to extra processing required at all routers of a domain per unit time. The communication overhead is due to extra packets injected into a domain. The communication overhead is computed as the number of extra *bytes* (not packets) injected per unit time. For processing overhead, the extra processing at routers may contain: more address lookups, changing some header fields, checksum re-computation, and any CPU processing needed by the scheme. For example, filters need to check the source IP address to verify whether a packet is coming from a valid source. This requires one extra address lookup (to check the source IP address) for each packet. The monitoring schemes inject probe packets into the network. Each router inside a domain requires processing such as address lookup, TTL field decrement, checksum computation for each probe packet. For simplicity, we charge the filtering scheme $\alpha_1$ processing units, the marking scheme $\alpha_2$ processing units, and the monitoring schemes $\alpha_3$ processing units for each packet processed. We express the processing overhead in terms of $\alpha_1, \alpha_2$, and $\alpha_3$ (processing units), and the communication overhead in terms of the total kilobytes (KB) injected in the domain.

We consider a domain $\mathcal{D}$ with $M$ edge routers and $N$ core routers. We assume there are $F$ flows traversing through each edge router and each flow has $P$ packets on average. We define $\theta$ as the percentage of misbehaving flows that may cause DoS attacks. We denote $\mathcal{C}_{sch}$ as the communication overhead and $\mathcal{P}_{sch}$ as the processing overhead respectively for scheme *sch*. Table 7.1 lists the variables used in the comparison and their values.

### 7.4.2. *Overhead Calculation*

Filtering and marking techniques do not incur any communication overhead. The monitoring schemes have both processing and communication overhead.

**Ingress filtering.** The processing overhead of ingress filtering depends on the number of packets entering a domain. It requires one processing unit to check

Table 7.1. Symbols used in the comparison and their values.

| Symbol | Description | Values |
|---|---|---|
| $\mathcal{P}_{sch}$ | Processing overhead for scheme *sch* | — |
| $\mathcal{C}_{sch}$ | Communication overhead for scheme *sch* | — |
| $M$ | Number of edge routers | [10–20] |
| $N$ | Number of core routers | 12 |
| $F$ | Number of flows entering through each edge router | 100,000 |
| $P$ | Number of packets per flow | 10 |
| $p$ | Probability to mark a packet | [0–0.20] |
| $\theta$ | Percentage of misbehaving flows | [0–20%] |
| $h$ | Path length inside a domain or hop count | 4, 6 |
| $s$ | Length of a stripe | 3 |
| $f_s$ | Frequency of stripes in stripe-based monitoring | 20 |
| $f_d$ | Frequency of probes in distributed monitoring | 30 |
| $\alpha_1$ | Processing overhead for filtering | — |
| $\alpha_2$ | Processing overhead for marking | — |
| $\alpha_3$ | Processing overhead for monitoring | — |

the source IP address of every packet. For our domain $\mathcal{D}$, the total entering packets is $M \times F \times P$. Thus, the total processing overhead of ingress filtering is given by:

$$\mathcal{P}_{Ingf} = M \times F \times P \times \alpha_1. \tag{7.10}$$

**Route-based filtering.** We need to deploy ingress filters in every domain in the Internet to effectively stop all possible attacks. The route-based filtering scheme, on the other hand, does not require every single domain to have a filter. Park *et al.* show that placing this filter at approximately 20% of all autonomous systems can prevent DoS to a great extent [28]. For a domain that deploys a router-based filter, the overhead is the same as the ingress filter. Globally speaking, the overhead of route-based filtering is one fifth of the overhead of ingress filtering on the average. In our comparison, we use

$$\mathcal{P}_{Route} = 0.2 \times \mathcal{P}_{Ingf}. \tag{7.11}$$

**Probabilistic packet marking (PPM).** *PPM* does not incur any communication overhead but adds extra $\alpha_2$ processing units for every packet that gets marked at an intermediary router. *PPM* might need sophisticated operation such as taking hash of certain IP fields. The traceback with *PPM* marks packets with a probability $p$ at each router on the path to the victim. If a packet passes through $h$ hops, on the average, in the network domain $\mathcal{D}$, the processing overhead is computed as:

$$\mathcal{P}_{PPM} = M \times F \times P \times p \times h \times \alpha_2 \tag{7.12}$$

**Core-based monitoring.** The monitoring schemes inject probe traffic into the network and add processing overheads as well. The total number of injected probes and the size of each probe packet are used to calculate the communication overheads in terms of bytes. The *Core* scheme depends on the number of packets that core routers send to the monitor to report drop history. The drop history at each core router depends on the flows traversing the network domain and the percentage of these flows that are violating their SLAs at a particular time. For the domain $\mathcal{D}$, if $d$ bytes are required to record the drop information of each flow, then each core needs to send $C = max(1, \frac{F \times \theta \times d}{packet\_size})$ control packets to the monitor. The *packet_size* is the size of a control packet, which depends on the MTU of the network. To obtain *loss ratio*, the monitor queries all edges for packet count information of the misbehaving flows. Every edge replies to this query. The total number of packets exchanged among all edge routers and the monitor is $(2M + N) \times C$ packets. Therefore, the communication overhead is given by:

$$\mathcal{C}_{Core} = (2M + N) \times max\left(1, \frac{F \times \theta \times d}{packet\_size}\right) \times packet\_size, \tag{7.13}$$

and the processing overhead is given by:

$$\mathcal{P}_{Core} = (2M + N) \times max\left(1, \frac{F \times \theta \times d}{packet\_size}\right) \times h \times \alpha_3, \tag{7.14}$$

where $packet\_size$ is a configurable parameter.

**Stripe-based monitoring.** In the stripe-based monitoring scheme, a stripe of $s$ packets is sent from the monitor to every egress router pairs. For the network domain $\mathcal{D}$, the total number of probing packets is $s \times (M-1) \times (M-2) \times f_s$, where $f_s$ is the frequency by which we need to send stripes per unit time. The communication overhead and the processing overhead are shown in equation (7.15) and equation (7.16) respectively.

$$\mathcal{C}_{Stripe} = s \times (M-1) \times (M-2) \times f_s \times packet\_size, \tag{7.15}$$

$$\mathcal{P}_{Stripe} = s \times (M-1) \times (M-2) \times f_s \times h \times \alpha_3. \tag{7.16}$$

**Distributed monitoring.** For the distributed monitoring, each edge router probes its left and right neighbors. If it requires $f_d$ probes per unit time, the communication overhead is:

$$\mathcal{C}_{Distributed} = 2 \times M \times f_d \times packet\_size. \tag{7.17}$$

On the average, each probe packet traverses $h$ hops and thus the processing overhead can be calculated as:

$$\mathcal{P}_{Distributed} = 2 \times M \times f_d \times h \times \alpha_2 \tag{7.18}$$

### 7.4.3. *Results and Analysis*

To visualize the differences among all schemes, we plot the processing and communication overhead for one of the domain shown in Figure 7.1. Usually, DoS attacks are directed towards a particular host or a set of hosts connected to a relatively small size domain. In the example, Figure 7.1, the DoS attack is directed towards domain $D4$ and the attack traffic is coming from various other domains. For our comparison, we use the parameters' values shown in Table 7.1 for domain $D$. We use *sec* as unit time in all comparisons.

Figure 7.6(a) shows the processing overhead in terms of $\alpha_1$ for ingress filtering, route-based filtering, and PPM when packet marking probability is varied along the X-axis. The route-based filtering requires less processing than marking scheme for $p \geq 0.07$ because this filtering scheme does not need to be deployed at all routers of all domains. Savage *et al.* use marking probability $p = 0.04$ in their traceback analysis [6]. Using this probability, the marking mechanism has less overhead than others. We use two different path lengths in the plot; one is $h = 4$ and another is $h = 6$. The path length does not increase the overhead substantially because the path length does not go up very high for a small-size domain. Figure 7.6(b) shows

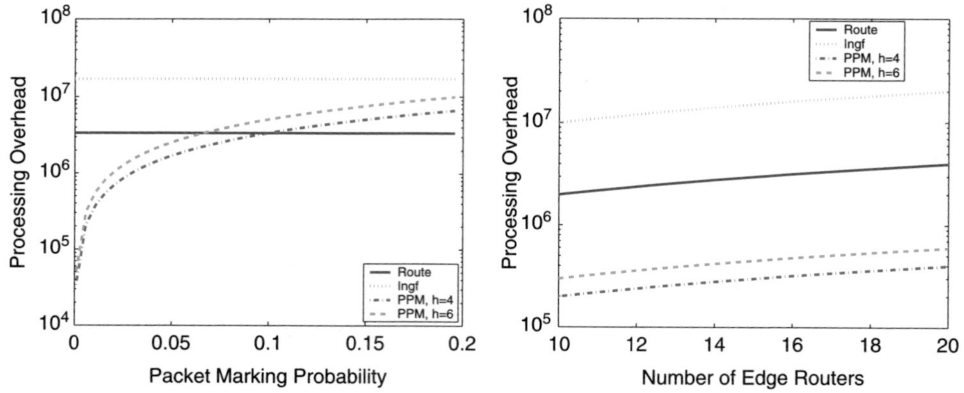


(a) Effect of varying the marking probablility on the processing overhead.

(b) Effect of varying the number of edge routers on the processing overhead.

Fig. 7.6. The processing overhead per unit time for filters and probabilistic packet marking (PPM) schemes. Marking scheme has less processing overhead than filtering scheme if the marking probability is not too high (e.g., $p \leq 0.07$).

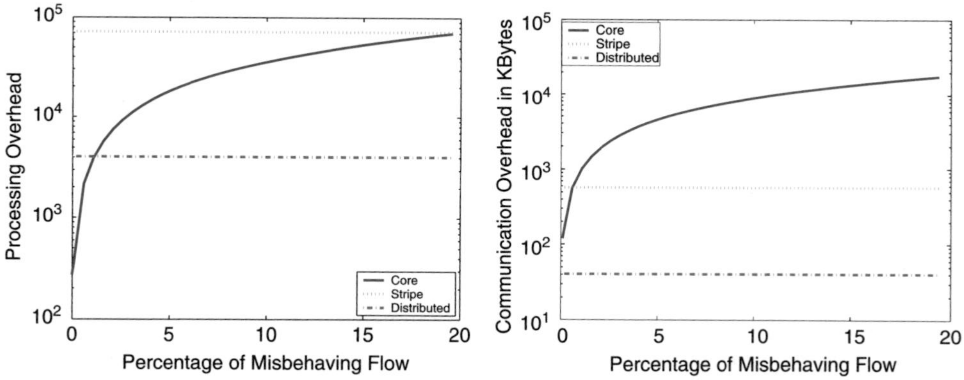


(a) Processing overhead.

(b) Communication overhead.

Fig. 7.7. The processing and communication overhead for the monitoring schemes when the percentage of misbehaving flows is increased. The *Core* scheme has less communication overhead than *Stripe* scheme for $\theta < 20\%$. Both *Stripe* and *Distributed* schemes have less communication overhead than *Core* unless $\theta$ is very low.

that when number of edge routers are increased in a domain the processing over is increased for all schemes.

Figure 7.7 shows both processing and communication overhead for different monitoring schemes. The processing overhead is low for *Core* scheme than the *Stripe* scheme for $\theta \leq 20\%$. This is because the control packet size of *Core* can be set equal to the maximum transmission unit of the network to minimize total number of packets sent, whereas the probe packet size of the *Stripe* is 20 bytes with 20 bytes of IP header. However, if the attack intensity is high, i.e., the value of $\theta$ is high, the

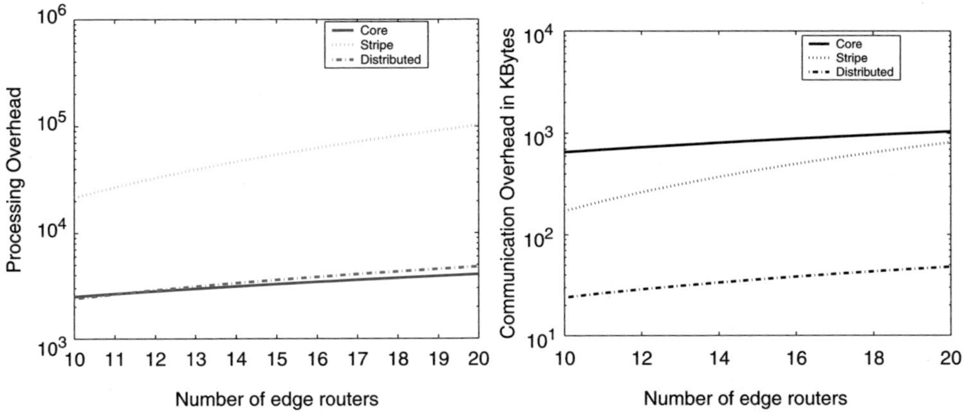


(a) Processing overhead. (b) Communication overhead.

Fig. 7.8. The processing and communication overhead for the monitoring schemes when the number of edge routers in a domain is increased. The *Core* scheme has less processing overhead than both edge-based schemes when the number of edge routers in the domain is increased. Edge-based schemes always impose less communication overhead than the *Core* scheme. The *Core* might perform better than *Stripe* for a large domain (e.g., $M > 20$) depending on the value of $\theta$.

overhead of *Core* exceeds the overhead of both edge-based schemes. In this example, probes injected by *Stripe* scheme consumes 600 K bytes of bandwidth per sec, which is distributed over all links of the domain. If all links are OC3 type, on average each link experiences probe traffic less than 0.015% of the link capacity. The *Distributed* scheme consumes ten times less than the *Stripe* one in this setup.

In Figure 7.8, we vary the domain size changing the number of edge routers while keeping the number of core routers fixed to $N = 12$. The percentage of misbehaving traffic $\theta$ is fixed and equals 1%. Figure 7.8(a) shows that *Core* can result in less computation overhead than edge-based schemes when the number of edge routers increases. Even though the overhead of *Core* scheme depends on both core and edge routers, this scheme reduces processing overhead by aggregating flows when it reports to the monitor. When number of edge routers increases, overhead for both *Core* and *Distributed* schemes increase linearly. The overhead for *Stripe* increases substantially with the increase of edge routers. Depending on $\theta$, Figure 7.8(b) shows that the communication overhead for *Stripe* may exceed the communication overhead of *Core* when $M > 20$.

### 7.4.4. *Summary*

We summarize the important features of all schemes in Table 7.2. Ingress filtering and core-assisted monitoring schemes have high implementation overhead because the former needs to deploy filters at all ingress routers in the Internet and the latter needs support from all edge and core routers in a domain. But filtering and monitoring can provide better safety compared to the traceback approach

Table 7.2. Comparison among different schemes to detect/prevent service violations and DoS attacks.

| Property | PPM | Ingress filtering | Route-based filtering | Core-assisted monitoring | Stripe-based monitoring | Distributed monitoring |
|---|---|---|---|---|---|---|
| Overhead depends on | attack volume | number of incoming packets | number of incoming packets | number of flows violating SLAs | routers, topology, attack traffic | routers, topology, attack traffic |
| Implementation overhead | all routers | all ingress edge routers | all routers of selective domains | all edge and core routers | all edge routers | all edge routers |
| Clock synchronization | — | — | — | at edge and core routers | at edge routers | at edge routers |
| Response | reactive | proactive | proactive | reactive | reactive | reactive |
| SLA violation detection | no | no | no | yes | yes | yes |
| Detect attacks initiated using | any IP | spoofed IP from other domains | spoofed IP from other domains | any IP | any IP | any IP |

which only can identify an attacker after the attack has occurred. All monitoring schemes need clock synchronization to measure SLA parameters, which is an extra overhead. But, they can detect service violations and DoS attacks as well. Filters are proactive in nature while all other schemes are reactive. Filters can detect attacks by spoofed packets whereas the rest of the schemes can detect an attack even if the attacker does not use spoofed IP addresses from other domains.

## 7.5. Conclusions

In this chapter, we investigated several methods to detect service level agreement violations and DoS attacks. We showed that there is no single method that fits all possible scenarios. Specifically, in ICMP traceback and probabilistic packet marking mechanisms, the attacker may be able to confuse the victim by sending false ICMP traceback packets and by randomly marking attacking packets. Ingress filters need global deployment to be effective, whereas route-based filters strive against the dynamic change of the routing information.

We showed that network monitoring techniques can be used to detect service violations by measuring the SLA parameters and comparing them against the contracted values between the user and the network provider. We also argued that monitoring techniques have the potential to detect DoS attacks in early stages before they severely harm the victim. Our argument is based on the fact that a DoS attack injects a huge amount of traffic into the network, which may alter the internal characteristics (e.g., delay and loss ratio) of the network. The monitoring techniques watch for these changes and identify the congested links, which helps in locating the attacker and alerting the victim.

The presented comparative study showed several issues. First, it showed that while marking imposes less overhead than filtering, it is only a forensic method. Filtering, on the other hand, is a preventive method, which tries to stop attacks before they harm the system. Second, the core-based monitoring scheme has a high deployment cost because it needs to update all edge as well as core routers. However, the core-based scheme has less processing overhead than the stripe-based scheme because it aggregates flow information when it reports to the monitor. Third, The stripe-based monitoring scheme has lower communication overhead than the core-based scheme for relatively small size domains. For large domains, however, core-based may impose less communication overhead depending on the attack intensity. Fourth, The distributed scheme outperforms the other monitoring schemes in terms of deployment cost and overhead in many of the cases.

## References

[1] CERT. CERT web site. http://www.cert.org/.

[2] D. Clark. The design philosophy of the DARPA Internet protocols. In *Proc. of ACM SIGCOMM'88*, pp. 106–114, Stanford, CA (August, 1988).

[3] T. Peng, C. Leckie, and K. Ramamohanarao, Survey of network-based defense mechanisms countering the DoS and DDoS problems, *ACM Computing Surveys*, **39**(1) (April, 2007).

[4] L. Garber, Denial of Service attacks rip the Internet, *IEEE Computer*, **33**(4), 12–17 (April, 2000).

[5] D. Moore, G. Voelker, and S. Savage, Inferring Internet denial-of-service activity. In *Proc. of USENIX Security Symposium*, Washington, DC (August, 2001).

[6] S. Savage, D. Wetherall, A. Karlin, and T. Anderson, Network support for IP traceback, *IEEE/ACM Transactions on Networking*, **9**(3), 226–237, (June, 2001).

[7] G. Spafford and S. Garfinkel, *Practical Unix and Internet Security.* (O'Reilly & Associates, Inc, 1996), second edition.

[8] S. Blake, D. Black, M. Carlson, E. Davies, Z. Wang, and W. Weiss, An architecture for Differentiated Services. IETF RFC 2475, (December 1998).

[9] J. Mirkovic and P. Reiher, A taxonomy of DDoS attack and DDoS defense mechanisms, *ACM Computer Communications Review*, **34**(2), 39–53 (April, 2004).

[10] G. Carl, G. Kesidis, R. Brooks, and S. Rai, Denial-of-service attack detection techniques, *IEEE Internet Computing.* pp. 82–89 (January-February, 2006).

[11] L. Ahn, M. Blum, and J. Langford, Telling humans and computers apart automatically, *Communications of the ACM*, **47**(2), 56–60 (February, 2004).

[12] X. Wang and M. Reiter. Defending against denial-of-service attacks with puzzle auctions. In *Proc. of IEEE Symposium on Security and Privacy (SP'03)*, pp. 78–92, Oakland, CA (May, 2003).

[13] D. Mankins, R. Krishnan, C. Boyd, J. Zao, and M. Frentz, Mitigating distributed denial of service attacks with dynamic resource pricing. In *Proc. of IEEE Computer Security Applications Conference (ACSAC'01)*, pp. 411–421, New Orleans, LA (December, 2001).

[14] M. Walfish, M. Vutukuru, H. Balakrishnan, D. Karger, and S. Shenker, DDoS Defense by Offense. In *Proc. of ACM SIGCOMM'06*, pp. 303–314, Pisa, Italy (September, 2006).

[15] C. L. Schuba, I. V. Krsul, M. G. Kuhn, E. H. Spafford, A. Sundaram, and D. Zamboni, Analysis of a denial of service attack on TCP, *IEEE Symposium on Security and Privacy, Oakland, CA.* (May 1997).

[16] C. Barros. A proposal for ICMP traceback messages. Internet Draft (September, 2000). http://www.research.att.com/lists/ietf-itrace/2000/09/msg00044.html.

[17] V. Paxson, An analysis of using reflectors for distributed denial-of-service attacks, *ACM Computer Communications Review*, **31**(3), (July 2001).

[18] J. Yuan and K. Mills, Monitoring the macroscopic effect of DDoS flooding attacks, *IEEE Transactions on Dependable and Secure Computing*, **2**(4), 324–335 (October–December, 2005).

[19] V. Sekar, N. Duffield, O. Spatscheck, J. Merwe, and H. Zhang. LADS: large-scale automated DDoS detection system. In *Proc. of USENIX Annual Technical Conference*, pp. 171–184, Boston, MA (May, 2006).

[20] J. Mirkovic, G. Prier, and P. Reiher, Attacking DDoS at the source. In *Proc. of IEEE International Conference on Network Protocols (ICNP'02)*, pp. 312–321, Paris, France (November, 2002).

[21] J. Ioannidis and S. Bellovin, Implementing pushback: Router-based defense against DDoS attacks. In *Proc. of Network and Distributed Systems Security Symposium (NDSS'02)*, San Diego, CA (February, 2002).

[22] S. Bellovin, M. Leech, and T. Taylor, ICMP traceback messages. Internet draft (February, 2003).

[23] A. Snoeren, C. Partridge, L. Sanchez, W. Strayer, C. Jones, and F. Tchakountio, Hashed-based IP traceback. In *Proc. of ACM SIGCOMM'01*, pp. 3–14, San Diego, CA (August, 2001).

[24] H. Burch and H. Cheswick, Tracing anonymous packets to their approximate source. In *Proc. of USENIX Conference on System Administration*, pp. 319–327, New Orleans, LA (December, 2000).

[25] M. Goodrich, Probabilistic packet marking for large-scale IP traceback, *IEEE/ACM Transactions on Networking*, **16**(1), 15–24 (February, 2008).

[26] K. Park and H. Lee. On the effectiveness of probabilistic packet marking for IP traceback under Denial of Service attack. In *Proc. of IEEE INFOCOM'01*, pp. 338–347, Anchorage, AK (April, 2001).

[27] P. Ferguson and D. Senie, Network ingress filtering: Defeating denial of service attacks which employ ip source address spoofing. IETF RFC 2827 (May, 2000).

[28] K. Park and H. Lee, On the effectiveness of route-based packet filtering for distributed dos attack prevention in power-law internets. In *Proc. of ACM SIGCOMM'01*, pp. 15–26, San Diego, CA (August, 2001).

[29] V. Paxson, End-to-end Internet packet dynamics, *IEEE/ACM Transactions on Networking*, **7**(3), 277–292 (June, 1999).

[30] P. Sakarindr, N. Ansari, R. Rojas-Cessa, and S. Papavassiliou, Security-enhanced quality of service SQoS design and architecture. In *Proc. of Advances in Wired and Wireless Communication* (April, 2005).

[31] H. Luo and M.-L. Shyu, Differentiated service protection of multimedia transmission via detection of traffic anomalies. In *Proc. of IEEE Multimedia and Expo (ICME'07)* (July, 2007).

[32] V. Paxson. *Measurement and Analysis of End-to-End Internet Dynamics.* PhD thesis, University of California, Berkeley, Computer Science Division, (1997).

[33] V. Paxson, G. Almes, J. Mahdavi, and M. Mathis, Framework for IP performance metrics. IETF RFC 2330 (May, 1998).

[34] Y. Breitbart, C. Chan, M. Garofalakis, R. Rastogi, and A. Silberschatz, Efficiently monitoring bandwidth and latency in IP networks. In *Proc. of IEEE INFOCOM'01*, pp. 933–942, Anchorage, AK (April, 2001).

[35] M. C. Chan, Y.-J. Lin, and X. Wang, A scalable monitoring approach for service level agreements validation. In *Proc. of IEEE International Conference on Network Protocols (ICNP'00)*, pp. 37–48, Osaka, Japan (November, 2000).

[36] M. Dilman and D. Raz, Efficient reactive monitoring. In *Proc. of IEEE INFOCOM'01*, pp. 1012–1019, Anchorage, AK (April, 2001).

[37] N. Duffield, F. L. Presti, V. Paxson, and D. Towsley, Inferring link loss using striped unicast probes, *Proc. of IEEE INFOCOM'01*. pp. 915–923 (April, 2001).

[38] R. Cáceres, N. Duffield, J. Horowitz, and D. Towsley, Multicast-based inference of network-internal loss characteristics, *IEEE Transactions on Information Theory*, **45**(7), 2462–2480 (November, 1999).

[39] A. Habib, *Monitoring and Controlling QoS Network Domains: An Edge-to-Edge Approach.* PhD thesis, Purdue University, Department of Computer Science, West Lafayette, (2003).

[40] S. Floyd and V. Jacobson, Random early detection gateways for congestion avoidance, *IEEE/ACM Transactions on Networking*, **1**(4), 397–413 (August, 1993).

[41] S. Savage, Sting: a TCP-based network measurement tool. In *Proc. of USENIX Symposium on Internet Technologies and Systems (USITS'99)*, Boulder, CO (October, 1999).

[42] R. Narasimha, S. Dihidar, C. Ji, and W. McLaughlin, A scalable probing-based approach for congestion detection using message passing. In *Proc. of IEEE International Conference on Communications (ICC'06)*, pp. 640–645, Istanbul, Turkey (June, 2006).

[43] R. Mahajan, S. Bellovin, S. Floyd, J. Ioannidis, V. Paxson, and S. Shenker, Controlling high bandwidth aggregates in the network, *ACM SIGCOMM Computer Communication Review*, **32**(3), 62–73, (2002).

[44] R. Stone, Centertrack: An IP overlay network for tracking DoS floods. In *Proc. of USENIX Security Symposium*, Denver, CO (August, 2000).

[45] IEPM. Web Page of Internet End-to-end Performance Monitoring. http://www-iepm.slac.stanford.edu/.

[46] J. Case, M. Fedor, M. Schoffstall, and J. Davin, A Simple Network Management Protocol (SNMP). IETF RFC 1157 (May, 1990).

[47] S. Waldbusser, Remote network monitoring management information base. IETF RFC 2819, (May 2000).

[48] Cisco, Cisco Netflow services and applications. http://www.cisco.com/.

[49] E. Al-Shaer, H. Abdel-Wahab, and K. Maly, HiFi: a new monitoring architecture for distributed systems management. In *Proc. of IEEE International Conference on Distributed Computing Systems (ICDCS'99)*, pp. 171–178, Austin, TX, (May 1999).

[50] R. Subramanyan, J. Miguel-Alonso, and J. A. B. Fortes, A scalable SNMP-based distributed monitoring system for heterogeneous network computing. In *Proc. of High Performance Networking and Computing Conference (SC'00)*, Dallas, TX (November, 2000).

[51] A. Liotta, G. Pavlou, and G. Knight, Exploiting agent mobility for large-scale network monitoring, *IEEE Network* (May/June. 2002).

[52] K. G. Anagnostakis, S. Ioannidis, S. Miltchev, J. Ioannidis, M. Greenwald, and J. M. Smith, Efficient packet monitoring for network management. In *Proc. of IEEE Network Operations and Management Symposium (NOMS'02)*, Florence, Italy (April, 2002).

[53] R. Callon, P. Doolan, N. Feldman, A. Fredette, G. Swallow, and A. Viswanathan, A framework for multiprotocol label switching. Internet Draft, (2000).

# Part III: Key and Key management

# Chapter 8

## KEY ESTABLISHMENT — SECRECY, AUTHENTICATION AND ANONYMITY

Guomin Yang*, Duncan S. Wong† and Xiaotie Deng‡
*Department of Computer Science*
*City University of Hong Kong*
*83 Tat Chee Avenue, Kowloon, Hong Kong*
* *csyanggm@cs.cityu.edu.hk*
† *duncan@cs.cityu.edu.hk*
‡ *deng@cs.cityu.edu.hk*

Authenticated Key Establishment (AKE) is a method for two or more parties communicating over an insecure network to establish a shared symmetric key in a secure and authenticated manner. This shared key, generally called session key, will then be used for establishing a secure communication channel among the parties. In this chapter, we will discuss some advanced topics regarding AKE for interconnected wired and wireless networks. Those topics include two-factor AKE, AKE in roaming networks, and user privacy protection in AKE protocols.

### 8.1. Introduction

Confidentiality and authenticity are two of the most prominent requirements in network security. Confidentiality is about ensuring data secrecy when messages are transferred over an insecure channel. This insecure channel is considered to have adversaries such as eavesdroppers who are trying to obtain the transferring messages by monitoring the channel. Authenticity is about ensuring the integrity of the transferring messages against adversaries who are *active* in the sense that they can alter messages in transfer. In order to facilitate confidentiality and authenticity for the communication among the communicating parties over an insecure network which may have both passive (i.e., eavesdroppers) and active adversaries, the parties should first establish a shared symmetric key securely. This key will then be used to create secure channels among the parties by using techniques such as symmetric-key encryption and message authentication codes. This key is generally called a *session key*.

The establishment of a session key is necessary for providing efficient encryption and message authentication. It is also important for providing some additional security properties. By using a session key to protect one session of communication rather than using static and long-term cryptographic keys such as communicating parties' public keys or pre-shared long-term symmetric keys, we target to ensure confidentiality and authenticity for each of the sessions efficiently. Desirably, we usually require that all established and previous sessions should remain secure even after all the long-term keys have been compromised. This requirement is called perfect forward secrecy. Diffie-Hellman key exchange [1] is the building block of realizing perfect forward secrecy.

Besides key establishment for setting up efficient secure channel and supporting higher security properties, *entity authentication* should also be provided. This is because the insecure network used by the communicating parties for establishing the session key could have active adversaries which may launch various impersonation attacks with the purpose of compromising the session key. Man-in-the-middle attack against the Diffie-Hellman key exchange is a well-known type of active attacks which illustrate the importance of mutual entity authentication.

**Authenticated Key Establishment** (AKE, for short) is a method for two or more parties to communicate over an insecure network (e.g., the Internet) in a secure and authenticated manner. Due to the variety of applications and security requirements, there are many types of AKE protocols. In this chapter, we focus on AKE protocols for interconnected wired and wireless networks and introduce three advanced topics. They are two-factor AKE using smart cards and passwords, AKE in roaming networks, and user privacy protection in AKE protocols. We first give a brief introduction to these topics.

(1) (*Two-Factor AKE*) When doing remote access, user authentication is the fundamental requirement. Besides that, due to the presence of passive and active adversaries in the insecure networks, server authentication and key establishment are also important. The current practice of doing user authentication is password based. As the applications of remote access become ubiquitous, for example, online banking, online shopping, etc., password-based user authentication mechanism becomes one of the most vulnerable aspects in the corresponding systems as more users are using the systems, it is more likely that one of the users' password could be compromised. Weak password becomes the major issue of many existing user authentication systems and alternative solutions have been proposed lately and adopted. One of the widely deployed solutions is the use of two secrets for user authentication. For example, using both password and hardware token, say a smart card, is a common method to do secure remote access. In the next section, we provide more details on how this technology is defined, how the security requirements are formalized and how to build an efficient protocol of this type.
(2) (*AKE for Secure Roaming*) As computer networks are booming, there are many heterogenous networks operated by different service providers that are now interconnected. A customer (so-called subscriber) of one service provider may want to access the network provided by another service provider for various

reasons, for example, for increasing the geographical coverage of service that the customer can enjoy, or for increasing the reliability of the service by being able to access multiple networks at the same time. When a customer of one service provider is accessing a network provided by another service provider, this communication scenario is called *roaming.* In this chapter, we discuss the security issues of secure roaming and propose some efficient solutions for them.

(3) (*Anonymous AKE for Secure Roaming*) In a typical AKE protocol, the identities of the communicating parties are usually publicly known. However, it may become undesirable in some applications. For example, in a roaming network, a customer of one service provider may not want the foreign service provider to trace the roaming information or his/her whereabouts when the customer is roaming and hopping from one foreign network to another. For preventing tracing, the customer has to hide his/her identity from all the foreign service providers. However, the home service provider should still be able to identify the customer and find out where the customer is. This is required in practice because of the billing purpose and the support of incoming calls. In this chapter, we give more details on the problem and propose methods for solving it.

In Sec. 8.2, we discuss the security requirements for two-factor authentication and key establishment protocols, review some attacking techniques against this type of protocols, and describe an efficient protocol. In Sec. 8.3, we first discuss the secure roaming setting. This is followed by the description of an attack which is specific to the roaming setting. A secure and efficient AKE for secure roaming is also described. In Sec. 8.4, we review some protocols for anonymous roaming and identify some security issues related to user anonymity. We then describe an anonymous AKE for secure roaming. The protocol is an extension of the one described in Sec. 8.3. We conclude this chapter in Sec. 8.5.

## 8.2. Two-Factor AKE Using Smart Cards and Passwords

As explained above, mutual entity authentication is important in AKE for defending against active attacks. If we consider two parties where one party is a user (or a client) and the other party is a server, then mutual entity authentication is about client authentication and server authentication. This is a typical remote access application, for example, when a user is trying to logon to a web-based email server or access a company system when the user is on the road. User authentication is usually carried out by asking the user to show his/her knowledge on a human-memorizable password. However, it is found in many real applications that password-based user authentication may not be secure enough. This is because the passwords chosen by users are sometimes easy to guess. In some of the existing systems, adversaries may be able to find out a user's password by launching an *offline dictionary attack*. This attack requires an adversary to eavesdrop or impersonate a communicating party for a short period of time so that the adversary can obtain some information which will be useful for the adversary to try different passwords offline and verify the trial passwords using the information obtained. For systems which require high security protection, for example, online banking, higher security measures are emerged for enhancing the current password-only user authentication practice.

Two-factor authentication uses a combination of two different factors to authenticate a user. These two factors could be any two of something you *know*, something you *have*, and something you *are*. One of the most commonly used two-factor user authentication mechanisms nowadays is based on smart card and password. This technology has been widely deployed in various kinds of authentication applications which include remote host login, online banking, access control of restricted vaults, activation of security devices, and many more. Schemes of this type usually have session keys established for securing subsequent communication. In this following, we discuss the security requirements and some constructions of this type of two-factor AKE protocols.

A two-factor *smart-card-based password AKE* protocol involves two parties: a client $A$ (with identity $ID_A$) and a server $S$. The protocol consists of two phases: *registration phase* and *login-and-authentication phase*. During the registration phase, $S$ securely issues a smart card to $A$. The smart card is personalized with $ID_A$ and an initial password. This phase is carried out only once for each client. It is also commonly referred to as the smart-card issuing stage. In the real world, this stage may require the client who is requesting for registration to show up in person at the server's office and then have a smart-card initialized and personalized using a secure and isolated machine after successful identification and authentication of the client. The smart-card is finally issued securely to the client at the end of the stage. There is no specific security requirement related to the communication channel between the registration server and the client as it is usually assumed and ensured that the (physical) security protection of the entire process is adequate. However, we should emphasize that a comprehensive and well practiced set of security systems, policies and management procedures should be established and executed effectively in the entire system. For the second phase, login-and-authentication phase, the client $A$ can access $S$ for as many times as needed. In this phase, there could have various kinds of passive and active network adversaries in the communication channel between $A$ and $S$. We have to consider such a hostile environment because in the real world, the honest parties $A$ and $S$ usually do not have much control on the security of the communication channel between them. For example, when $A$ and $S$ are communicating over the Internet, we cannot assume that all the routers and nodes on the forwarding path between them are all benign. Instead, we should consider the worst case scenario where there could have various kinds of passive and active adversaries. The adversaries may eavesdrop and even modify, remove or insert messages into the communication channel between $A$ and $S$. The security goal of the protocol in this phase is to ensure mutual entity authentication and session key establishment and secrecy between $A$ and $S$. In particular, with respect to the two-factor property, it is required that $A$ should both *have* the smart card and *know* the password in order to carry out the protocol, that is, to successfully convince $S$ that the counter-party is indeed the client who claims to be.

There are some other requirements for the two-factor smart-card-based password AKE protocol that are desirable in practice. For example, $A$ may want to *change password* from time to time without interacting with or notifying $S$. Conventionally, changing password requires $A$ to communicate with $S$ and have $S$ update its password database accordingly. Here we promote the idea of letting $A$ change the password at will without interacting with or notifying $S$, and also eliminating any password database at the server side. This helps improve the efficiency and reduce the operational cost and complexity of the system.

Regarding the adversarial capabilities and attacks against two-factor smart-card-based password AKE protocols, one of the most important attacks that the protocol designer has to consider is *offline guessing attack* (also known as *offline dictionary attack*). The purpose of offline guessing attack is to compromise a client's password through exhaustive search of all possible password values after obtaining some information about the password under attack where the information only needs to be adequate for verifying whether a trial password is correct or not. In a password-based setting, passwords are considered to be short and human memorizable, and the corresponding password space is so small that an adversary is able to enumerate all possible values in the space within a reasonable amount of time. For example, in many web-based email implementations, the email server authenticates a client by sending a random challenge in clear and having the client send back a response which is the hashed value of the password and the challenge. Although the password is not transmitted in clear, an adversary can readily launch offline guessing attack for finding out the password after eavesdropping the challenge and the response. This is because the adversary is able to check the hashed value of a trial password and the challenge against the response. If they are equal, then generally with overwhelming probability that the trial password is the correct password. For a secure two-factor smart-card-based password AKE protocol, we require that the client's password should remain secure against offline guessing attack even after the client's smart card is compromised.

### 8.2.1. *Security Requirements and Adversarial Capabilities*

We now give a list of security goals and desirable properties for a secure two-factor smart-card-based password AKE protocol.

(1) (*Client Authentication*) The server is sure that the communicating party is indeed the registered client that claims to be at the end of the protocol.
(2) (*Server Authentication*) The client is sure that the communicating party is indeed the server $S$ at the end of the protocol.

(3) (*Key Establishment*) The client and the server establish a fresh session key which is known only to them at the end of a successful protocol execution.
(4) (*Server Knows No Password*) $S$ should not get any information of the password of a registered client or anything derived from the password.
(5) (*Freedom of Password Change*) A client's password can freely be changed by the client without any interaction with server $S$. $S$ can be totally unaware of the change of the client's password.
(6) (*Short Password*) All passwords in the password space are human-memorizable.

We consider a network adversary $\mathcal{A}$ who has the full control of the communication channel between the server $S$ and any of the *registered* clients. $\mathcal{A}$ can obtain all the messages transmitted between the server $S$ and a registered client; $\mathcal{A}$ can also modify or block transmitting messages; and even make up then send fake messages to any entity in the system while claiming that the messages are from another entity (i.e., impersonation). To simulate *insider attack*, that is, the adversary *is* a malicious but real client, we also allow $\mathcal{A}$ to know the passwords and the information stored in the smart cards of all the clients except those of a client who is under attack from $\mathcal{A}$. In addition, we also allow $\mathcal{A}$ to compromise *either* the password *or* the smart card of the client under attack, but not both. However, $\mathcal{A}$ is not allowed to compromise $S$.

As described above, $\mathcal{A}$ can interact with registered clients only rather than unregistered ones. This explicitly prevent $\mathcal{A}$ from intervening the registration process of the clients, as we assume that the communication channel between the clients and $S$ in the registration phase is always secure and authenticated, and operations in this phase are all carried out according to the protocol specification.

In the list of desirable properties above, the first two constitute the primary security requirement of a secure two-factor smart-card-based password AKE protocol, that is, mutual authentication between the server $S$ and a registered client $A$. The fourth property helps solve the scalability problem at the server side. In addition, since there is no information about clients' passwords stored at the server side, the property also alleviate damage entailed to the clients if the server is compromised. The fifth property will help improve the user friendliness of the system as there is no additional communication overhead when a client changes its password.

Also notice that Property 4 does not imply Property 5. It is possible to construct a scheme such that the server does not have any information of a client's password while the client cannot change the password either once after registration. For example, the smart-card of the client contains a signature of $S$ on the commitment of the client's password. When carrying out authentication, the client needs to send the signature of $S$ on the commitment to the server and do a zero-knowledge proof on the knowledge of the password with respect to the commitment. If the client wants to change the password, the client needs to request for a new signature from $S$.

Property 6 means that we always consider that if an adversary launches an attack which needs to search through the password space (for example, an offline guessing attack), the adversary can always evaluate all the possible values in the space within the running time of the adversary. To prevent an adversary from launching offline guessing attack successfully, we therefore need to make sure that the protocol does not leak any information useful about the client's password so that the adversary can use the information for checking if a trial password is the correct one.

Another attack which is related to offline guessing attack is *online* guessing attack. In this attack, the adversary impersonates one of the communicating parties and sends messages based on a trial password chosen by the adversary. If the connection is rejected, the adversary tries another trial password and repeats until a successful connection is granted. An adversary can always launch the *online* guessing attack. However, a secure protocol should make sure that the adversary can only test at most one trial password in each impersonation and the failure of impersonation should be detectable. If the adversary tries another trial password and repeats the impersonation, the communicating party can record the number of consecutive failure of authentication and block further runs of the protocol if a certain number of unsuccessful runs of the protocol is reached with respect to the same identity under investigation. Online guessing attack is usually easy to defend against if each unsuccessful attack is detectable by the server. For example, a system can set up a policy mandating that if the password of a client is entered incorrectly for five times in a row, then the client will be blocked and refused to connect any further. This policy works well in practice and can effectively defend against online guessing attack if the attack only allows the adversary to try one password in each impersonation attack. However, we should also note that a secure protocol should not allow the adversary to test two passwords or more in each of this impersonation attack.

Another remark is that, we do not make assumption on the existence of any special security features supported by the smart cards. Instead, we simply consider a smart card to be a memory card with an embedded micro-processor for performing required operations specified in a two-factor smart-card-based password AKE protocol. Therefore, we assume that once a smart card is stolen by an adversary, all the information stored in it would be known to the adversary. In addition, after a smart card is compromised, the card holder may not be aware of it. For example, the adversary simply *steals* all the information stored in the card using a fraudulent card reader without being noticed by the card-holder rather than stealing the card itself. Hence in our model, we still let the card-holder to use the card and for a secure two-factor smart-card-based password AKE protocol, we require that the adversary cannot compromise mutual authentication or key establishment even when this case happens, that is, when the smart-card of the client under attack is compromised but not the password.

### 8.2.2. *Offline Dictionary Attack*

Since Lamport [2] introduced remote user authentication in 1981, there have been many two-factor smart-card-based password AKE (or purely authentication) protocols proposed. However, many of these protocols were later broken. The design and security analysis of two-factor smart-card-based password AKE protocols is not a trivial task, and new attacks are continually being discovered. Therefore, it is utmost important to define a strong security model which can capture the strongest while reasonable adversarial capabilities, and construct provably secure protocols accordingly. In this chapter, we do not discuss the formalization of the adversarial capabilities [3]. Instead, we first illustrate the meaning of two-factor authentication by going through the cryptanalysis of an actual two-factor smart-card-based password AKE protocol, then describe a protocol which has been proven secure under the strongest security model currently available for two-factor smart-card-based password AKE protocols. The attack below shows that a protocol fails to achieve two-factor authentication if the authentication is failed after any one of the factors has been compromised.

Let $p$ be a large prime, for example, 1024 bits long, $g$ a random generator of $\mathbb{Z}_p^*$, so that the discrete logarithm problem in $\mathbb{Z}_p^*$ is intractable. Let $h$ be a cryptographic hash function (e.g., SHA-256). At the very beginning, the server $S$ chooses a secret key $x$, for example, a random 160-bit string. In the following, we review a protocol that appears in [4].

**Registration phase**: Server $S$ issues a smart card to a client $A$ as follows.

(1) $A$ arbitrarily chooses a unique identity $ID_A$ and password $PW_A$. $A$ then calculates $h(PW_A)$ and sends $(ID_A, h(PW_A))$ to $S$.
(2) $S$ calculates $B = g^{h(x\|ID_A)+h(PW_A)} \bmod p$ and issues $A$ a smart card which has $(ID_A, B, p, g)$ in it.

**Login-and-authentication phase**: $A$ attaches the smart card to an smart-card reader and types in $ID_A$ and $PW_A$. Afterwards, $S$ and $A$ (the smart-card) carry out the following steps.

(1) $A$ sends a login request to $S$.
(2) On receiving the login request, $S$ calculates $B'' = g^{h(x\|ID_A)R} \bmod p$ where $R \in \mathbb{Z}_p^*$ is a random number, and sends $h(B'')$ and $R$ to $A$.
(3) Upon receiving the message from $S$, $A$ calculates $B' = (Bg^{-h(PW_A)})^R \bmod p$ and checks if $h(B'') = h(B')$. If they are not equal, $S$ is rejected. Otherwise, $A$ calculates $C = h(T\|B')$ where $T$ is a timestamp, and sends $(ID_A, C, T)$ to $S$.
(4) Let $T'$ be the time when $S$ receives $(ID_A, C, T)$. $S$ validates $A$ using the following steps.

(a) $S$ checks if $ID_A$ is in the correct format[a]. If it is incorrect, $S$ rejects.
(b) Otherwise, $S$ compares $T$ with $T'$. If $T' - T \geq \Delta T$, $S$ rejects, where $\Delta T$ is the legal time interval for transmission delay.
(c) $S$ then computes $C' = h(T\|B'')$ and checks if $C = C'$. If they are not equal, $S$ rejects. Otherwise, $S$ accepts.

This completes the description of the protocol. The steps in the registration phase are carried out once only for each smart card while the steps in the login-and-authentication phase are then carried out as many times as needed. In the following, we describe an attack which compromises user authentication once after the smart card is compromised. This means that the protocol cannot provide two-factor authentication.

Suppose client $A$'s smart card is compromised by an adversary $\mathcal{A}$. $\mathcal{A}$ can carry out the offline guessing attack as follows.

(1) $\mathcal{A}$ impersonates $A$ and sends a login request to $S$.
(2) $S$ calculates $B'' = g^{h(x\|ID_A)R} \bmod p$ and sends back $(h(B''), R)$.
(3) $\mathcal{A}$ then carries out offline guessing attack by checking if

$$h(B'') = h((Bg^{-h(PW_A^*)})^R \bmod p)$$

for each trial password $PW_A^*$ (i.e., $\mathcal{A}$'s guess of $PW_A$).

Note that after $\mathcal{A}$ receives the message from $S$ in step (2), $\mathcal{A}$ does not need to provide any response to $S$ and therefore $S$ does not know whether the communicating party is launching an attack or simply the message sent by $S$ is lost during transmission. This makes the guessing attack described above difficult to detect. In addition, if $\mathcal{A}$ possesses a past communication transcript between $A$ and $S$, $\mathcal{A}$ can perform the offline guessing attack directly without interacting with $S$.

### 8.2.3. *A Secure Two-Factor Smart-Card-Based Password AKE*

In [3], Yang *et al.* proposed a novel approach for constructing smart-card-based password AKE protocols. Their idea is to "upgrade" a conventional password AKE to a two-factor version. They proved the security of their protocol in a strong security model due to Canetti and Krawczyk [5], and further extended their protocol to a generic construction framework.

Let $G, g, q$ be the group parameters defined in Sec. 8.2.2, and $k$ a security parameter such that $k \geq 160$. The server maintains a key pair $(\mathrm{PK}_S, \mathrm{SK}_S)$ for public key encryption, a key pair $(\mathrm{PK}'_S, \mathrm{SK}'_S)$ for digital signature, and a long-term secret $x$ which is a random binary string of length $k$. Let $H : \{0,1\}^* \to \{0,1\}^k$ denote a target collision resistant hash function and $PRF_K : \{0,1\}^k \to \{0,1\}^k$ a

[a]In [4], the format of identity $ID_A$ was not given. We hereby assume that there is some pre-defined format for all the identities used in their system.

pseudorandom function keyed by $K$. Also let $H' : \{0,1\}^* \rightarrow \{0,1\}^k$ denote a hash function which preserves the entropy of its input.

**Registration phase**: Server $S$ issues a smart card to client $A$ as follows.

(1) $A$ arbitrarily chooses a unique identity $ID_A$ and sends it to $S$.
(2) $S$ calculates $B = PRF_x(H(ID_A)) \oplus H'(PW_0)$ where $PW_0$ is the initial password (e.g., a default password such as a string of all '0').
(3) $S$ issues $A$ a smart card which contains $\mathrm{PK}_S, \mathrm{PK}'_S, ID_A, B, p, g, q$. In practice, all these parameters except $B$ can be "burned" in the read-only memory of the smart card when the smart card is manufactured.
(4) Upon receiving the smart-card, $A$ changes the password immediately by performing the password-changing activity (described below).

**Login-and-authentication phase**: $A$ attaches the smart card to an input device, and then keys in $PW_A$. The smart card retrieves the value $LPW_A = B \oplus H'(PW_A)$. $A$ (performed by the client's smart-card) and $S$ then uses $LPW_A$ as the password to perform a password AKE protocol illustrated in Figure 8.1. Here "sid" denotes the session ID of one communication session.

**Password-changing activity**: If $A$ wants to change the password, $A$ performs the following steps.

(1) Select a new password $PW'_A$.
(2) Compute $Z = B \oplus H'(PW_A) \oplus H'(PW'_A)$, where $PW_A$ is the old password.
(3) Replace $B$ with $Z$ in the smart-card.

In [3], the authors showed that server authentication security and session key secrecy of the above protocol are both maintained as in the original password AKE protocol, and there are only two disjoint cases that need to be considered for client authentication:

(1) The client's password is leaked while the smart card remains secure; and
(2) the client's smart card is compromised but the password remains secure.

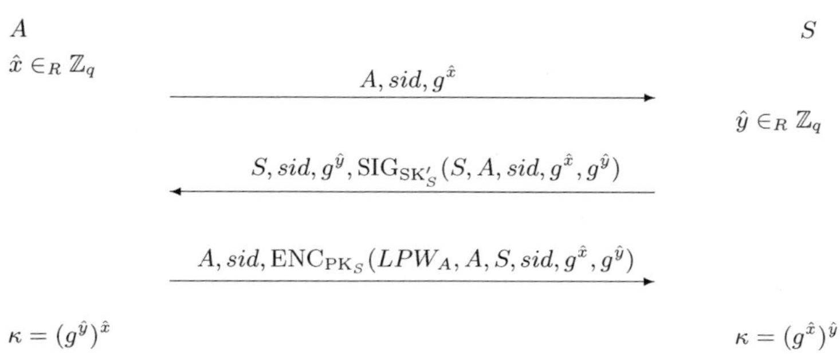


Fig. 8.1. A password AKE protocol.

They proved that, in the first case, their protocol can provide a cryptographic key level security for client authentication, in other words, the security of the password AKE is "upgraded" by making use of smart cards. In the second case, they showed that the protocol can also provide the same security level as the password AKE.

From the protocol above, we can see that a two-factor smart-card-based password AKE protocol may be built directly from any secure password AKE protocol. By taking a secure password AKE protocol, we only need to change the password to the secret value stored (in some encrypted form) in the smart card (i.e., $LPW_A$) for constructing a secure two-factor smart-card-based password AKE protocol. This "upgrading" technique is quite efficient. During the login-and-authentication phase, the smart-card only needs to carry out one hash function and one exclusive-or operation in addition to the operations incurred by the underlying password AKE protocol. The generic construction framework allows us to choose a password AKE protocol which is efficient enough when implemented on smart-cards.

In the next section, we move to another advanced topic in AKE, that is, the AKE for secure roaming.

## 8.3. Authenticated Key Establishment in Roaming Networks

With the advancement of mobile technology, wireless networks have been becoming widely available and more importantly have been interconnecting with each other and also the wired networks closely. People may travel around with their mobile devices persistently getting connected. Service providers are now able to provide services to their customers without being much limited by the geographical area or the coverage provided solely by their own networks. Instead, the services may actually be provided by some partnering service providers.

One commonly available and important service that is needed for enabling the wide availability of service coverage is *roaming*. A typical roaming scenario involves three parties: *a roaming user* $A$, *a home server* $H$, and *a foreign server* $V$. During roaming, $A$ subscribed to $H$ is in a foreign network and wants to get services from $V$. Typical examples include the roaming service in cellular networks, hopping across meshed WLANs (Wireless Local Area Networks) administered by different individuals, joining and leaving various wireless ad hoc networks operated by different foreign operators, etc.

In the roaming scenario, $V$ may first authenticate $A$ before providing the requested services. However, the authentication performed here is different from the conventional user authentication. In the roaming scenario, what $V$ wants to make sure is that $A$ is indeed a legitimate subscriber of some server $H$ whose subscribers are allowed to get the requested services. Usually $H$ will be called in as a guarantor for giving a promise to $V$ that $A$ is indeed a legitimate subscriber of it. So in the roaming scenario, we call this process *Subscription Validation* instead of *User Authentication*. In each successful execution of a secure roaming protocol, the following three requirements should be satisfied simultaneously.

(1) (*Foreign Server Authentication*) The roaming user is sure about the identity of the foreign server.
(2) (*Subscription Validation*) The foreign server is sure about the legitimation of the roaming user under a valid home server.
(3) (*Key Establishment*) The roaming user and the foreign server establish a fresh session key which is known only to them.

Regarding the third item above, some roaming protocols allow the home server to obtain or even generate the session key (e.g., the GSM [6] and 3GPP [7] AKE protocols). Here we promote the requirement that the home server should not obtain the session key. The reason is that services are provided by the foreign server to the roaming user but not to the home server. For the privacy of both user and foreign server, it is their interest of not letting the home server from accessing their secure channel. This also does not prevent the home server from making correct billing.

Among these three security requirements, subscription validation is specific for the roaming scenario and is different from the conventional user authentication. The security goal seems straightforward, but achieving such a goal is not as trivial as it might first appear. Below is an interesting attack discovered by Yang, Wong and Deng [8].

### 8.3.1. *Deposit-case Attack Against Secure Roaming*

Subscription validation is intuitively related to the financial interests of the foreign server. However, in [8], the authors showed that subscription validation is also related to the financial interest of the roaming user. They presented an attack named *Deposit-case Attack* which incurs the following two results simultaneously.

(1) The attack allows a malicious server to persuade the visiting foreign server of a roaming user that the malicious server is the user's home server without being noticed by the roaming user nor the real home server.
(2) The roaming user, however, believes that the foreign server has obtained the correct identity of its home server.

An attack of this kind is called deposit-case attack as such an attack is profitable to the malicious server when the user is accessing the foreign server to 'deposit' some information of value to its home server. In [8], the authors showed the insecurity of several roaming protocols against deposit-case attack, in the following, we review one of them.

The attack is against an anonymous roaming protocol described in [9]. Let $A$, $V$, $H$ denote a roaming user, a foreign server and the home server of the roaming user, respectively. $\mathcal{H}_1$ and $\mathcal{H}_2$ are cryptographic hash functions. Let $(\hat{S}_H, P_H) \in \mathbb{Z}_q \times G$ denote $H$'s private/public key pair such that $P_H = g^{\hat{S}_H}$, and $(\hat{S}_V, P_V) \in \mathbb{Z}_q \times G$

| | | |
|---|---|---|
| $A$ | : | $r_a \in_R \mathbb{Z}_q$, $K_{ah} = P_H^{r_a}$, $alias = E_{K_{ah}}(\mathcal{H}_1(A) \oplus g^{r_a})$ |
| $A \to V$ | : | $H$, $alias$, $g^{r_a}$ |
| $V$ | : | $r_v \in_R \mathbb{Z}_q$ |
| $V \to H$ | : | $alias$, $g^{r_v}$, $g^{r_a}$, $Sig_V(g^{r_v}, g^{r_a}, alias, V)$, $T_1$ |
| $H$ | : | $r_h \in_R \mathbb{Z}_q$, $K_{hv} = \mathcal{H}_2(g^{r_v r_h}, P_V^{r_h})$ |
| $H \to V$ | : | $g^{r_h}$, $E_{K_{hv}}(Sig_H(g^{r_h}, g^{r_v}, \mathcal{H}_1(A) \oplus g^{r_a}, H), \mathcal{H}_1(A) \oplus g^{r_a})$, $T_2$ |
| $V$ | : | $alias' = \mathcal{H}_1(g^{r_v r_a}, \mathcal{H}_1(A))$, $K_{av} = \mathcal{H}_2(g^{r_v r_a}, g^{\hat{S}_V r_a})$ |
| $V \to A$ | : | $g^{r_v}$, $E_{K_{av}}(\mathcal{H}_1(g^{r_v}, g^{r_a}, alias', V), T_2)$, $T_3$ |
| $A \to V$ | : | $E_{K_{av}}(Sig_A(g^{r_a}, g^{r_v}, T_2, V), T_3)$ |

Fig. 8.2. The Go-Kim anonymous roaming protocol.

| | | |
|---|---|---|
| $A$ | : | $r_a \in_R \mathbb{Z}_q$, $K_{ah} = P_H^{r_a}$, $alias = E_{K_{ah}}(\mathcal{H}_1(A) \oplus g^{r_a})$ |
| $A \to M$ | : | $H$, $alias$, $g^{r_a}$ |
| $M$ | : | $r_1 \in_R \mathbb{Z}_q$ |
| $\mathbf{M} \to \mathbf{H}$ | : | $alias$, $g^{r_1}$, $g^{r_a}$, $Sig_M(g^{r_1}, g^{r_a}, alias, M)$, $T_0$ |
| $H$ | : | $r_h \in_R \mathbb{Z}_q$, $K_{hm} = \mathcal{H}_2(g^{r_1 r_h}, P_M^{r_h})$ |
| $H \to M$ | : | $g^{r_h}$, $E_{K_{hm}}(Sig_H(g^{r_h}, g^{r_1}, \mathcal{H}_1(A) \oplus g^{r_a}, H), \mathcal{H}_1(A) \oplus g^{r_a})$, $T_2$ |
| $\mathbf{M} \to \mathbf{V}$ | : | $M$, $alias$, $g^{r_a}$ |
| $V$ | : | $r_v \in_R \mathbb{Z}_q$ |
| $V \to M$ | : | $alias$, $g^{r_v}$, $g^{r_a}$, $Sig_V(g^{r_v}, g^{r_a}, alias, V)$, $T_1$ |
| $M$ | : | $r_2 \in_R \mathbb{Z}_q$, $K_{mv} = \mathcal{H}_2(g^{r_v r_2}, P_V^{r_2})$ |
| $M \to V$ | : | $g^{r_2}$, $E_{K_{mv}}(Sig_M(g^{r_2}, g^{r_v}, \mathcal{H}_1(A) \oplus g^{r_a}, M), \mathcal{H}_1(A) \oplus g^{r_a})$, $T_2$ |
| $V$ | : | $alias' = \mathcal{H}_1(g^{r_v r_a}, \mathcal{H}_1(A))$, $K_{av} = \mathcal{H}_2(g^{r_v r_a}, g^{\hat{S}_V r_a})$ |
| $V \to A$ | : | $g^{r_v}$, $E_{K_{av}}(\mathcal{H}_1(g^{r_v}, g^{r_a}, alias', V), T_2)$, $T_3$ |
| $A \to V$ | : | $E_{K_{av}}(Sig_A(g^{r_a}, g^{r_v}, T_2, V), T_3)$ |

Fig. 8.3. Deposit-case attack against the Go-Kim protocol.

$V$'s private/public key pair such that $P_V = g^{\hat{s}_V}$. Let $T_1$, $T_2$ and $T_3$ be timestamps. The protocol is illustrated in Figure 8.2.

In the protocol, *alias* is used for hiding the real identity of $A$ against eavesdroppers. However, the Subscription Validation is not properly performed in the protocol which makes the deposit-case attack feasible. In Figure 8.3, we show how this attack works. In the attack, $M$ denotes a malicious server.

In this attack, the malicious server $M$ first intercepts the message from $A$ to $V$, it then contacts $A$'s home server $H$, and claims that $A$ is communicating with $M$. $H$ then innocently sends $A$'s real identity to $M$. After that, $M$ launches the deposit-case attack by impersonating $A$ and sending a modified message to $V$ (illustrated as the first message from $M$ to $V$ in Figure 8.3). In the rest of the communications, $M$ can successfully fool $V$ to believe that $M$ is the home server of $A$, while $A$ believes that he has informed $V$ that $H$ is its home server.

Notice that $A$ and $V$ will still agree on the same key $K_{av}$ when the attack completes. Hence the attack is carried out successfully and will not be discovered by any of the three honest parties.

| | | | | | |
|---|---|---|---|---|---|
| $P_i \rightarrow P_j$ | : | $m$ | $P_i \rightarrow P_j$ | : | $m$ |
| $P_i \leftarrow P_j$ | : | $m,\ N_j$ | $P_i \leftarrow P_j$ | : | $m,\ PKE_{P_i}(N_j)$ |
| $P_i \rightarrow P_j$ | : | $m,\ SIG_{P_i}(m, N_j, P_j)$ | $P_i \rightarrow P_j$ | : | $m,\ MAC_{N_j}(m, P_j)$ |

Fig. 8.4. A Signature-based authenticator and A Public-key-encryption-based authenticator.

### 8.3.2. *A Secure AKE Protocol for Roaming Networks*

We now describe an efficient AKE protocol for secure roaming. This protocol was proposed by Yang, Wong and Deng [10]. It is efficient and requires only four rounds of message flows among the three communicating parties, namely the roaming user $A$, the foreign server $V$ and the home server $H$. The protocol has also been proven secure under a formal security model, which is based on the Canetti-Krawczyk model [5]. In the following, before reviewing their protocol, we first describe an authentication tool which is used in their construction.

#### 8.3.2.1. *A one-pass counter-based authenticator*

An authenticator (or "MT-Authentication" in [5,11]) is an authenticated message transfer protocol, it can be built from various cryptographic primitives. Figure 8.4 illustrates two authenticators constructed by Bellare et al. in [11] using public key techniques, where $N_j \in_R \{0,1\}^k$ denotes a random challenge (or nonce), $SIG_{P_i}$ denotes the digital signature function of $P_i$, $PKE_{P_i}$ denotes the public key encryption function of $P_i$ and $MAC_{N_j}$ denotes a Message Authentication Code (MAC) function under key $N_j$.

In [10], Yang, Wong and Deng proposed a new authenticator which consists of only one-pass. This authenticator is important in their construction of a secure and efficient roaming protocol. Below is the details of this one-pass authenticator.

Suppose a party $P_i$ shares a random key $\kappa$ with another party $P_j$. Each of $P_i$ and $P_j$ initiates a counter starting with 0.

- Whenever $P_i$ wants to send a message $m$ to $P_j$, $P_i$ increases its local counter $COUNT_{P_i}$ by one, and sends $m, COUNT_{P_i}, MAC_\kappa(m, COUNT_{P_i}, P_j)$ to $P_j$.
- Upon receiving $m, COUNT_{P_i}, MAC_\kappa(m, COUNT_{P_i}, P_j)$, $P_j$ verifies that the MAC is correct and $COUNT_{P_i} > COUNT_{P_j}$ where $COUNT_{P_j}$ is the local counter of $P_j$. If all the verifications succeed, $P_j$ accept the message and sets $COUNT_{P_j} = COUNT_{P_i}$, otherwise, $P_j$ rejects the message.

The authors proved the security of the above authenticator under the Canetti-Krawczyk model. We refer readers to [10] for the proof.

There is an issue of counter re-synchronization if the database of either party collapses. Therefore, a counter re-synchronization protocol should be provided for practical applications, for example, by using the existing protocol for 3GPP [7].

### 8.3.2.2. *The Yang-Wong-Deng secure roaming protocol*

This protocol consists of two phases: the *user registration phase* and the *roaming phase*. In the user registration phase, a long-term *user authentication key* denoted $authK_A$ will be established between the user and his home network. Usually, this key will be established when the user subscribes to his home server, such as embedding it in the roaming device of the user. In the roaming phase, the user is in a foreign domain and communicating with a foreign server. The AKE protocol for roaming will be carried out by the roaming user, the foreign server and the home server. The purpose of the protocol is to let the roaming user and the foreign server establish a fresh session key so that a secure channel can be built. Below are the details of the protocol.

Let $COUNT_A$ denote the local counter of a roaming user $A$, $MAC_K$ a secure MAC function under key $K$, $SIG_P$ the digital signature function of party $P$, $N_P$ a nonce generated by party $P$, and $s$ the session ID. The Yang-Wong-Deng Secure Roaming Protocol is illustrated in Figure 8.5. The session key established is $g^{xy}$.

In the protocol, foreign server authentication is performed using the signature-based authenticator. However, subscription validation is more complicated. First, $A$ sends an authentication token, which is generated using the counter-based authenticator, to $V$, and $V$ simply forwards the authentication token to $H$. $H$ then verifies the authentication token, if the verification succeeds, $H$ sends an acknowledgement to $V$ for certifying the validity of $A$, here the signature-based authenticator is used to ensure the authenticity of the acknowledgement. Up to this point, readers may think that subscription validation is completed, however, this is not true. After receiving the last message from $V$, $A$ needs to verify that the home server identity he received is correct, the purpose of this step is to prevent the deposit-case attack described in Sec. 8.3.1.

In many roaming applications, the mobile user $A$ is usually a battery-powered mobile device, which is limited in power. Therefore, it is desirable if the computational complexity of a protocol on $A$ is low. In the protocol above, we

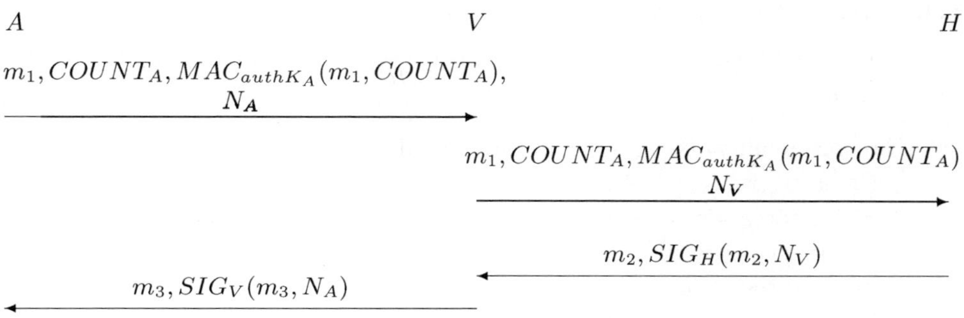


$$m_1 = (A, H, V, s, \alpha = g^x)\ m_2 = (A, H, V, s, \alpha)\ m_3 = (A, H, V, s, \beta = g^y)$$

Fig. 8.5. The Yang-Wong-Deng secure roaming protocol.

can see that all the operations carried out on $A$ are lightweight by assuming that the signature verification for $SIG_V(m_3, N_A)$ is efficient. In addition, we suggest that some appropriate elliptic curve based additive group may be used for efficient computation of $\alpha$, $\beta$ and operations related to the part corresponding to Diffie-Hellman key exchange.

## 8.4. Enhancing User Privacy in AKE Protocols

We now move to the last topic of this chapter. In this topic, we will discuss how to build a secure AKE protocol for secure roaming while maintaining the anonymity of the user. User privacy is a notable security issue, especially on a roaming network. It concerns about exposing the user identities and whereabouts unwillingly without the awareness or consent of the users. For example, in cellular networks, GSM and 3GPP roaming protocols provide a certain degree of user anonymity by using a temporary identity called TMSI (Temporary Mobile Subscriber Identity) rather than the real identity IMSI (International Mobile Subscriber Identity) for each roaming user. However, when TMSI is not available, for example, when the mobile device is turned on, IMSI is sent to the serving network in clear through the air interface.

There are many other applications where user privacy is desirable, for example, the inter-bank ATM networks and the credit card payment systems. Ideally, a user should not reveal anything to a foreign serving network other than the confirmation of the user's good standing with respect to the user's ATM card or credit card issued by the user's home bank. However, current systems are having users give out their personal information inevitably. In this section, we will discuss the security requirements regarding user privacy in AKE protocols, and review some existing techniques and constructions. We separate the existing works into two categories:

(1) user privacy is preserved against eavesdroppers only; and
(2) user privacy is preserved against both eavesdroppers and foreign networks.

### 8.4.1. *User Privacy Against Eavesdroppers*

In general, user privacy against eavesdroppers includes the following two security requirements:

(1) (User Anonymity) Besides the user, the intended communicating party, and any user trusted parties, no one can tell the identity of the user.
(2) (User Untraceability) Besides the user, the intended communicating party, and any user trusted parties, no one is able to identify any previous protocol runs which have the same user involved.

In some situations, the location of the user should be known to a user trusted third party. For example, in the roaming scenario discussed in Sec. 8.3, the home server must trace the locations of its subscribers so that incoming calls can be forwarded to the corresponding serving networks. In the following, we review two protocols which aim to provide user privacy against eavesdroppers.

8.4.1.1. *The Go-Kim anonymous roaming protocol*

In [9], Go and Kim proposed an anonymous roaming protocol, which we have already reviewed in Sec. 8.3.1. Their protocol aims to preserve the anonymity of mobile users against eavesdroppers in roaming networks.

However, it was found by Wong [12] that the Go-Kim anonymous roaming protocol is insecure against malicious insider attack. A malicious foreign server who eavesdrops the communication between a roaming user and an honest foreign server can recover the identity of the user, hence breaking the user anonymity. Before going into the attack, readers may first review the Go-Kim protocol illustrated in Figure 8.2 in Sec. 8.3.1.

**Wong's Attack against the Go-Kim Protocol.** The protocol was originally designed to allow only the home server and the visiting foreign server to know the real identity of the roaming user. No other entity in the system including any other foreign servers which are not engaged in this protocol run should be able to obtain the identity of the user. However, from Figure 8.2 in Sec. 8.3.1, we can see that the *alias* computed by $A$ does not contain $V$. In Step 4, when $H$ receives the message from $V$, there is no proof that $A$ intends to communicate with $V$. In other words, $H$ has no idea if $A$ is actually in the serving network operated by $V$ or some other network operated by another operator. Based on this observation, in [12], Wong presented an attack that breaks the user anonymity of the protocol.

Suppose there is a malicious foreign server $\mathcal{E}$ which is eavesdropping in the radio coverage of $V$. After $A$ sends the first message flow to $V$, $\mathcal{E}$ later connects to $H$ in another session and claims that a user of $H$ is visiting the network operated by $\mathcal{E}$. This is illustrated in step $2'$ in Figure 8.6.

In Step 3', $\mathcal{H}_1(A)$ is obtained by $\mathcal{E}$, using this information, $\mathcal{E}$ can easily identify if the same user is involved in two protocol runs. In other words, the protocol fails to provide user untraceability against eavesdroppers. In addition, the identity of $A$ can be found by an offline exhaustive search. Note that the attacking session between

$$
\begin{array}{lll}
1.\ A \to V & : & H,\ alias,\ g^{r_a} \\
2.\ V \to H & : & alias,\ g^{r_v},\ g^{r_a},\ Sig_V(g^{r_v}, g^{r_a}, alias, V),\ T_1 \\
2'.\ \mathcal{E} \to H & : & alias,\ g^{r_1},\ g^{r_a},\ Sig_{\mathcal{E}}(g^{r_1}, g^{r_a}, alias, \mathcal{E}),\ T_1' \\
3.\ H \to V & : & g^{r_h},\ E_{K_{hv}}(Sig_H(g^{r_h}, g^{r_v}, \mathcal{H}_1(A) \oplus g^{r_a}, H), \mathcal{H}_1(A) \oplus g^{r_a}),\ T_2 \\
3'.\ H \to \mathcal{E} & : & g^{r_2},\ E_{K_{h\mathcal{E}}}(Sig_H(g^{r_2}, g^{r_1}, \mathcal{H}_1(A) \oplus g^{r_a}, H), \mathcal{H}_1(A) \oplus g^{r_a}),\ T_2' \\
4.\ V \to A & : & g^{r_v},\ E_{K_{av}}(\mathcal{H}_1(g^{r_v}, g^{r_a}, alias', V), T_2),\ T_3 \\
5.\ A \to V & : & E_{K_{av}}(Sig_A(g^{r_a}, g^{r_v}, T_2, V), T_3)
\end{array}
$$

Fig. 8.6. Wong's attack against the user anonymity of Go-Kim anonymous roaming protocol.

| | | | | | |
|---|---|---|---|---|---|
| $A \to B$ | : | $PKE_B(A, K_{AB}, count)$ | $A \to B$ | : | $PKE_B(A, r_A, count)$ |
| $A \leftarrow B$ | : | $E_{K_{AB}}(count, r_B)$ | $A \leftarrow B$ | : | $r_B, E_{K_{AB}}(count, r_A)$ |
| $A \to B$ | : | $Sig_A(B, h(count, K_{AB}, r_B))$ | $A \to B$ | : | $Sig_A(B, h(count, r_B, K_{AB}))$ |

Fig. 8.7. The Boyd-Park anonymous key transport and key agreement protocols.

$\mathcal{E}$ and $H$ does not need to be launched in parallel with the original session between $A$ and $V$. It can be launched after an arbitrary period of time.

#### 8.4.1.2. *The Boyd-Park anonymous AKE protocol*

In [13], Boyd and Park proposed an AKE protocol which provides user anonymity against eavesdroppers. They provided two versions, one of which provides key transport and the other key agreement (i.e., both parties contribute to the final session key). Their protocol is illustrated in Figure 8.7, where $r_A$ and $r_B$ denote nonces generated by $A$ and $B$, respectively. $PKE_B$ denotes the public key encryption function of party $B$, $Sig_A$ denotes the digital signature function of party $A$, $E_K$ denotes a symmetric encryption function under key $K$, and *count* denotes a counter maintained by $A$ and $B$. In the key agreement protocol, the session key $K_{AB}$ is computed as $h(r_A, r_B)$ for a suitable hash function $h$.

In the Boyd-Park protocol, it is assumed that $A$ and $B$ have access to the public keys of each other. For example, in the case that $A$ is a mobile user and $B$ is the serving network, $A$ may get the public key of $B$ from the broadcast channel of the network, while $B$ can get the public key of $A$ from $A$'s certificate which can be included inside the encrypted information in the first message.

However, it should be noted that certain signature schemes may leak information on the signer's identity. Therefore, in order to provide user anonymity and untraceability, $A$ must use an "Anonymous Signature" [14] which requires that without the knowledge of the corresponding message, given a signature, it is infeasible to determine who the actual signer is.

### 8.4.2. *User Privacy Against both Eavesdroppers and Foreign Networks*

In some situations, such as those discussed at the beginning of Sec. 8.4, there is no need for the foreign server to know the real identity of the user. The foreign server only needs a proof of the validity and solvency of the user accessing the service and enough information to bill the user's home server. In this case, the security requirements are revised as follows.

(1) (User Anonymity) Besides the user and its home network, no one including the foreign network can tell the identity of the user.
(2) (User Untraceability) Besides the user and its home network, no one including the foreign network is able to identify any previous protocol runs which have the same user involved.

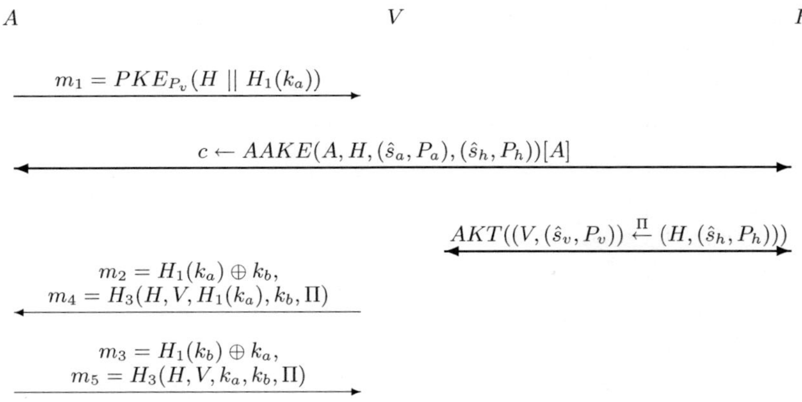


Fig. 8.8. A generic anonymous roaming protocol.

8.4.2.1. *A generic anonymous roaming protocol*

In [15], Yang, Wong and Deng proposed a generic roaming protocol which provides user anonymity and untraceability against eavesdroppers and foreign networks. Their protocol is illustrated in Figure 8.8.

In the protocol, $(\hat{s}_v, P_v)$ denotes the public key pair of $V$. Assume $A$ obtains $P_v$ through the broadcasting channel of $V$, and checks its validity using the associated certificate before running the protocol. Let $(\hat{s}_a, P_a)$ and $(\hat{s}_h, P_h)$ be the public key pairs of $A$ and $H$, respectively. Let $H_1$, $H_2$ and $H_3$ be cryptographic hash functions. Below is the protocol description.

(1) $A$ randomly generates $k_a \in_R \{0,1\}^k$ and sends $m_1 = ENC_{P_v}(H\|H_1(k_a))$ to $V$ where '$\|$' denotes string concatenation.
(2) $V$ decrypts $m_1$ using the private key $\hat{s}_v$ and obtains $H$ and $\alpha$. It then 'informs' (by sending a prespecified message) $H$ that there is a user who claims to be its subscriber.
(3) $A$ and $H$ run an Anonymous AKE (denoted AAKE) protocol via $V$ ($V$ is treated as a router) and obtain

$$c \leftarrow AAKE(A, H, (\hat{s}_a, P_a), (\hat{s}_h, P_h))[A].$$

Here $c$ denotes the agreed key between $A$ and $H$, and "[A]" denotes that $A$'s privacy is preserved during the protocol run. Readers can refer to Figure 8.7 for a concrete AAKE protocol.
(4) $H$ computes $\Pi = H_2(A, H, V, c)$.
(5) $H$ and $V$ run an authenticated key transport protocol

$$AKT((H, (\hat{s}_h, P_h)) \overset{\Pi}{\rightarrow} (V, (\hat{s}_v, P_v))).$$

(6) $V$ randomly generates $k_b \in_R \{0,1\}^k$ and sends $m_2 = \alpha \oplus k_b$ to $A$.
(7) $A$ obtains $k_b$ as $m_2 \oplus H_1(k_a)$ and sends $m_3 = H_1(k_b) \oplus k_a$ to $V$.

(8) $V$ obtains $k_a$ from $m_3$ and checks if $H_1(k_a) = \alpha$. If it is true, continue. Otherwise, $V$ rejects the connection.
(9) Each of $A$ and $V$ computes the session key $\sigma$ as $H_2(H, V, k_a, k_b, \Pi)$ and jointly conduct the following key confirmation steps.
   (a) $V$ sends $m_4 = H_3(H, V, H_1(k_a), k_b, \Pi)$ to $A$.
   (b) $A$ checks if $m_4 = H_3(H, V, H_1(k_a), k_b, \Pi)$. If it is true, $A$ sends $m_5 = H_3(H, V, k_a, k_b, \Pi)$ back to $V$ and accepts the connection. Otherwise, $A$ rejects the connection.
   (c) $V$ checks if $m_5 = H_3(H, V, k_a, k_b, \Pi)$. If it is correct, $V$ accepts the connection. Otherwise, $V$ rejects the connection.

   The messages can be piggybacked in the last two message flows.
(10) Both $A$ and $V$ destroy their copies of $k_a$ and $k_b$ after accepting the connection.

In the protocol, we can see that besides AAKE and $\Pi$, there is no information related to the identity of $A$. Since $H_2$ is assumed to be a cryptographic hash function (e.g., SHA-256), and $c$ is unknown to eavesdroppers and the foreign server, $\Pi$ does not help them obtain any additional information about the identity of $A$. Note that exhaustive search will not work here because of the secrecy of $c$. Therefore, user privacy of the protocol reduces to that of the AAKE scheme.

### 8.4.2.2. *An efficient anonymous roaming protocol*

In the previous section, we have seen a generic anonymous roaming protocol constructed by Yang, Wong and Deng in [15]. Later, in [10], the authors proposed a concrete anonymous roaming protocol which requires only four moves among a roaming user, a foreign server and the home server of the roaming user. The new protocol also achieves user privacy against eavesdroppers and foreign servers. In [10], the authors also proposed a formal security model which captures user anonymity and user untraceability simultaneously, and proved the security of their protocol under this model. Readers who have a background on computational complexity based security models can refer to [10] for the details of the security model. In the following, we only review the protocol (Figure 8.9).

The protocol is a modified version of the roaming protocol discussed in Figure 8.5 in Sec. 8.3.2.2. Several modifications are made in order to preserve user

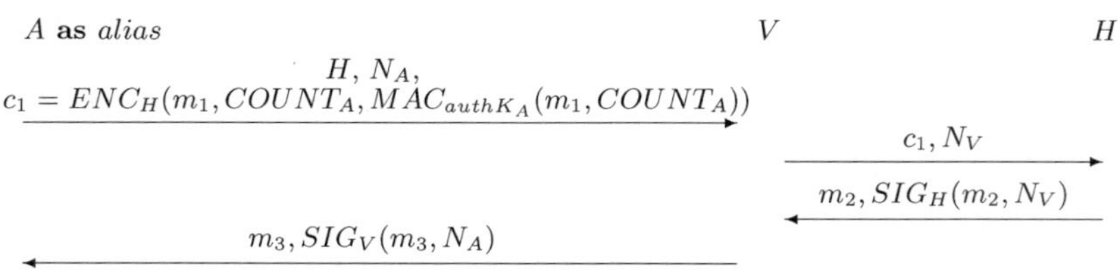


$m_1 = (alias, A, H, V, s, g^x)$ $m_2 = (alias, H, V, s, g^x)$ $m_3 = (alias, H, V, s, g^y)$

Fig. 8.9. An efficient anonymous roaming protocol.

privacy. First of all, the identity of the user should not be sent in clear, an *alias* acting as a *temporary ID* for the roaming user is used. However, the home server needs to know the real identity of the roaming user before certifying him, so the real identity of $A$ is included in $m_1$, and in order to achieve anonymity, all the messages for $H$ are encrypted under $H$'s public key. Similarly, the protocol above could also be implemented efficiently by choosing some appropriate encryption and digital signature schemes. One may choose the schemes so that the encryption and signature verification algorithms are lightweight. In addition, elliptic curve based additive group may be used for efficient computation of the components corresponding to Diffie-Hellman key exchange. All of these are suggested for the purpose of reducing the computational complexity of the user $A$.

## 8.5. Remarks

In this chapter, we discussed three advanced topics on AKE. They are two-factor smart-card-based password AKE protocols; AKE for secure roaming; and user privacy protection in AKE protocols. Furthermore, as we have seen that most of the protocols have been designed so that the mobile user does not need to carry out any expensive operation. This makes the protocols very suitable for implementation on lightweight mobile devices.

## References


[1] W. Diffie and M. E. Hellman, New directions in cryptography, *IEEE Trans. Inform. Theory*, **IT-22**, 644–654 (Nov, 1976).

[2] L. Lamport, Password authentication with insecure communication, *Communications of the ACM*, **24**(11), 770–771 (Nov. 1981).

[3] G. Yang, D. S. Wong, H. Wang, and X. Deng, Two-factor mutual authentication based on smart cards and passwords, *J. Comput. Syst. Sci.*, **74**(7), 1160–1172, (2008).

[4] I. E. Liao, C. C. Lee, and M. S. Hwang, A password authentication scheme over insecure networks, *J. Comput. Syst. Sci.*, **72**(4), 727–740, (2006).

[5] R. Canetti and H. Krawczyk, Analysis of key-exchange protocols and their use for building secure channels. In *Proc. of Eurocrypt'01*, pp. 453–474. Springer-Verlag, (2001). Full paper available at `http://eprint.iacr.org/2001/040/`.

[6] M. Mouly and M.-B. Pautet, *The GSM System for Mobile Communications.* 1992.

[7] *3GPP TS 33.102: 3rd Generation Partnership Project 3GPP, 3G Security, Security Architecture.* Technical Specification Group (TSG) SA, (2003).

[8] G. Yang, D. S. Wong, and X. Deng, Deposit-case attack against secure roaming. In *Information Security and Privacy, 10th Australasian Conference, ACISP 2005*, pp. 417–428. Springer-Verlag, (2005).

[9] J. Go and K. Kim, Wireless authentication protocol preserving user anonymity. In *Proc. of the 2001 Symposium on Cryptography and Information Security (SCIS 2001)*, pp. 159–164 (Jan. 2001).

[10] G. Yang, D. S. Wong, and X. Deng, Formal security definition and efficient construction for roaming with a privacy-preserving extension, *Journal of Universal

*Computer Science, Special Issue on Cryptography in Computer System Security*, **14**(3), 441–462, (2008).
[11] M. Bellare, R. Canetti, and H. Krawczyk, A modular approach to the design and analysis of authentication and key exchange protocols. In *Proc. of STOC'98*, pp. 419–428. ACM, (1998).
[12] D. S. Wong, Security analysis of two anonymous authentication protocols for distributed wireless networks. In *Proc. of the 3rd IEEE Intl. Conf. on Pervasive Computing and Communications Workshops (PerCom 2005 Workshops)*, pp. 284–288. IEEE Computer Society (Mar. 2005).
[13] C. Boyd and D. Park, Public key protocols for wireless communications, *The 1st International Conference on Information Secuirty and Cryptology (ICISC'98)*. pp. 47–57, (1998).
[14] G. Yang, D. S. Wong, X. Deng, and H. Wang, Anonymous signature schemes. In *Proc. of the 9th International Workshop on Practice and Theory in Public Key Cryptography (PKC'06)*, pp. 347–363, (2006).
[15] G. Yang, D. S. Wong, and X. Deng, Anonymous and authenticated key exchange for roaming networks, *IEEE Transactions on Wireless Communications*, **6**(9), 3461–3472, (2007).

# Chapter 9

## DETECTING MISUSED KEYS IN WIRELESS SENSOR NETWORKS

Donggang Liu* and Qi Dong†
*Department of Computer Science and Engineering*
*The University of Texas at Arlington*
*416 Yates Street, Arlington, TX 76001*
* *dliu@uta.edu*
† *qi.dong@uta.edu*

Key management is the cornerstone for secure communication in sensor networks. Researchers have recently developed many techniques to setup pairwise keys between sensor nodes. However, these techniques allow an attacker to compromise a few sensor nodes and learn many pairwise keys used between non-compromised nodes. The attacker can then use these keys to impersonate non-compromised nodes and mislead the sensing application. To deal with this problem, this chapter discusses how to detect misused keys in sensor networks. We introduce a *hidden* layer of protection, which is designed for the security of pairwise keys rather than the messages in the network. It cannot be seen and will not be used by sensor nodes during normal communication. However, it can be checked by some special nodes to identify suspicious keys. With this idea, we develop a serial of techniques to detect misused keys. These techniques make it particularly difficult for an attacker to actively mislead the application using the compromised keys shared between non-compromised nodes. We also show the effectiveness and efficiency of these techniques through analysis and experiments.

### 9.1. Introduction

Recent technological advances have made it possible to deploy wireless sensor networks consisting of a large number of low-cost, low-power, and multi-functional sensor nodes that communicate in short distances through wireless links [1]. Such sensor networks are ideal candidates for a wide range of applications in military and civilian operations such as health monitoring, data acquisition in hazardous environments, and target tracking. The desirable features of wireless sensor networks have attracted many researchers to develop protocols and algorithms to support these various applications.

Sensor networks may be deployed in hostile environments where enemies may be present. It is critical to ensure the integrity, availability, and at times confidentiality of the data collected by sensor nodes in hostile environments. However, providing security for sensor networks is particularly challenging due to the resource constraints on sensor nodes [1] and the threat of node compromises [2].

Key management is the cornerstone of many security services such as authentication and encryption. Since the sensor nodes in the network usually communicate with other sensor nodes or base stations through their neighbors, a critical security service is a way to establish a pairwise key between two neighbors in the network. Research seeking low-cost pairwise key establishment techniques that can survive node compromises in sensor networks becomes quite active in the past three, four years, yielding several novel key pre-distribution schemes [3–10].

To name a few, Eschenauer and Gligor proposed to distribute a random subset of keys from a key pool to every sensor node before deployment such that every pair of sensor nodes will have a certain probability of sharing at least one key after deployment [3]. Chan *et al.* extended this scheme by requiring two sensor nodes share at least $q$ pre-loaded keys to establish a pairwise key [6]. Chan *et al.* also developed a random pairwise keys scheme [6]. This scheme pre-distributes random pairwise keys between a sensor node and a random subset of other sensor nodes, and has the property that the compromise of sensor nodes does not lead to the compromise of any key shared *directly* between two non-compromised sensor nodes. To further enhance the security of key pre-distribution, Liu and Ning and Du *et al.* independently developed two similar threshold-based schemes [4,5]. Chan and Perrig also developed a protocol named PIKE for key establishment by using peer sensor nodes as trusted intermediaries [9].

### 9.1.1. *Motivation*

Despite the recent advances in pairwise key establishment, there are still many open problems. In particular, none of these existing schemes can guarantee source authentication between non-compromised nodes. An attacker can compromise a small number of sensor nodes and learn a quite large number of keys established *directly* or *indirectly* between non-compromised nodes. For example, in the basic probabilistic scheme [3], an attacker can learn a large number of keys in the key pool by compromising a small number of sensor nodes. As a result, it can quickly determine a large fraction of keys used between non-compromised sensor nodes. As another example, in the random pairwise keys scheme [6], a large fraction of pairwise keys are actually established indirectly with the help of intermediate nodes. When an intermediate node is compromised, it is very likely that the keys established through this sensor node have been disclosed to the attacker. Hence, although this scheme provides perfect security guarantee for the keys established directly between sensor nodes, the compromise of sensor nodes will still reveal many keys established indirectly between non-compromised sensor nodes.

*Generally, an attacker can always learn many pairwise keys shared between non-compromised sensor nodes unless a trust server generates and assigns a unique and random key for every two sensor nodes.* For example, we can either use the trusted base station as a KDC to help the sensor nodes establish pairwise keys or pre-load each sensor node a unique key with every other sensor node. However, these ideas will introduce huge communication overhead or huge storage overhead and is not practical for resource-constrained sensor networks [3]. It is thus reasonable to assume that one of those recently developed key pre-distribution techniques is employed in the network. In this case, a few compromised sensor nodes will allow an attacker to know a quite large number of pairwise keys shared between non-compromised sensor nodes.

Once an attacker knows the pairwise key between two non-compromised nodes, it can forge and modify messages between these two nodes and actively mislead the sensing application. Clearly, the detection of these misused keys is of particular importance. This is a unique key management problem for sensor networks due to the resource constraints and the trade-offs we have to make between the storage, communication, computation and the security. However, this problem hasn't been studied by the researchers in sensor network security. The objective here is *to detect misused pairwise keys in sensor networks.*

### 9.1.2. *Contributions*

In this chapter, we present a serial of techniques to detect the misused keys in the network. To the best of our knowledge, this is the first work in this research direction. The main idea is to add a *hidden* layer of protection for the security of the keys rather than the messages in the network. It cannot be seen and will not be used by any sensor node during the normal communication. However, it can be checked by some special nodes (e.g., dedicated sensor nodes or base station) to identify misused keys.

The proposed methods have a number of advantages. First, even if an attacker has learned the keys shared between non-compromised sensor nodes, it is still difficult for him to impersonate non-compromised nodes using these keys and actively mislead the sensing application without being detected. Second, the proposed methods are independent from the detection of compromised nodes. Therefore, they can be used as stand-alone techniques to evaluate whether a given network is under attack. Third, the results generated by our detection approaches can actually help detect compromised nodes. For example, many existing pairwise key establishment techniques such as the grid-based scheme [5] and PIKE [9] are deterministic. In these schemes, we can often figure out which sensor node is involved in the establishment of a given pairwise key. Thus, if a given pairwise key is detected to be misused, we can immediately narrow down the set of suspicious nodes.

### 9.1.3. *Organization*

This chapter is organized as follows. The next section gives the system model and the design goals. Section 9.3 presents the technical detail as well as the analysis for the proposed approaches. Section 9.4 discusses the implementation issues. Section 9.5 reviews related work on sensor network security. Section 9.6 concludes this chapter and discusses some future research directions.

## 9.2. System Models and Design Goals

In this chapter, we consider wireless sensor networks consisting of a large number of resource-constrained sensor nodes and a powerful and resourceful base station. The sensor nodes are randomly scattered to sense and report the conditions and events in the field. The base station is used to collect or process the sensed results or act as a gateway to the traditional networks.

An attacker can launch a wide range of attacks against the network. For example, he can simply perform a denial-of-service (DoS) attack to jam the wireless channel and disable the network operation. Such DoS attack is simple but common to the protocols in every sensor network. There are no effective ways to stop the attacker from mounting such attack. However, in this chapter, we are more interested in the attacks whose goal is to actively mislead the sensing application by inserting forged or modified messages into the network since generating a wrong result or making a wrong decision often causes more damage to the application.

In this chapter, we assume that an attacker can eavesdrop, modify, forge, replay or block any network traffic. We assume that it is computationally infeasible to break the cryptographic primitives such as encryption and decryption. We assume the attacker can compromise a few sensor nodes and learn the keys between non-compromised sensor nodes. For example, in Figure 9.1, the compromise of nodes 6 and 7 will allow the attacker to learn the two keys $K_{2,3}$ and $K_{4,5}$. By checking the messages in the network, the attacker can easily determine the pairs of non-compromised nodes that share these two keys. Based on our previous discussion, we know that this strategy is true for all the existing pairwise key establishment schemes.

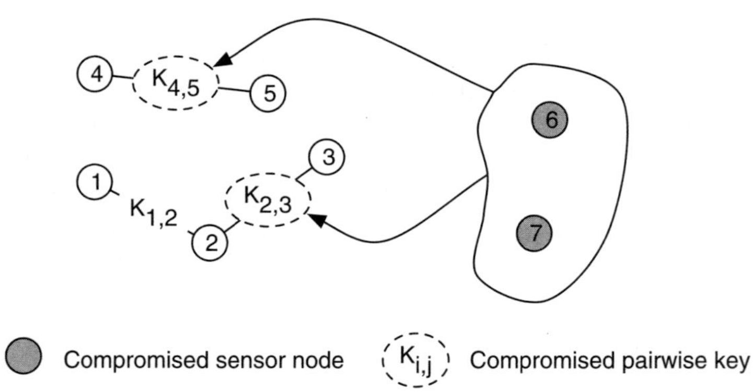


Fig. 9.1. Example of compromised keys.

A problem that is related to what we studied in this chapter is the detection of compromised sensor nodes. Examples of such detection methods include the "Watchdog" and "Pathrater" [11]. Clearly, once a sensor node is detected to be compromised, it is often possible to figure out the pairwise keys that are affected. However, detecting compromised sensor nodes is still a non-trivial problem in sensor networks. To date, there are no effective ways to guarantee such detection. Therefore, we do not assume the detection of compromised sensor nodes in this chapter.

**Design Goals:** As we mentioned, by compromising a few sensor nodes, an attacker can easily obtain many keys established between non-compromised nodes. For all existing pairwise key establishment protocols, there is no further protection for these keys. An attacker can use these compromised keys to impersonate non-compromised nodes and mislead the sensing application. Our overall goal is to provide additional protection for non-compromised nodes even if their shared keys have been disclosed. Specifically, we want to make sure that *the attacker cannot misuse the keys shared between non-compromised nodes.*

## 9.3. The Detection of Misused Keys

This section provides the technical detail on how to detect misused keys in the network. We will start with a simple and naive approach, where the base station makes the detection decisions in a centralized manner. We will then develop a serial of techniques to deal with the limitations of this naive approach and finally generate an efficient distributed detection approach.

The proposed detection schemes are independent from the pairwise key establishment protocol. They can be used for improving the resilience of any pairwise key establishment protocol. Hence, we skip the detail of pairwise key establishment and assume that the pairwise key between any two communicating sensor nodes has already been established. We assume that every message between two sensor nodes are protected by their shared pairwise key. For the sake of presentation, let $K_{u,v}$ be the key established between two nodes $u$ and $v$.

### 9.3.1. *Scheme I: The Naive Approach*

In the naive approach, every sensor node adds a secret value, called the *committing value*, to every outgoing message in addition to the protection achieved by the pairwise key. This committing value will not be used by sensor nodes during the normal communication in sensor networks. However, it can be verified by the base station to detect if the key is misused. Simply speaking, the pairwise keys in the network are used for providing secure communication between sensor nodes, while the committing values are used for providing protection for the usage of keys.

To detect misused pairwise keys, we have the base station check the communication in the network and see if the messages transmitted in the network include incorrect committing values. A message including an incorrect committing value clearly indicates a misused key. Thus, every sensor node samples the messages received from other sensor nodes and generates a *report* to the base station for every sampled message. When the base station receives such report, it can then check if the committing value matches the sampled message. If not, the pairwise key is used improperly. In this way, we can easily detect those misused keys if the attacker forges or modifies the messages between non-compromised sensor nodes to actively mislead the sensing application. The detail of this approach is given below.

- *Committing Messages*: Before deployment, each sensor node $u$ is pre-loaded with a unique random key $K_u$. This key is only known by the base station and node $u$. In the naive approach, a sensor node simply adds a committing value to every outgoing message *other than the report message*. Let $M$ be the message needs to be transmitted by node $u$. The committing value $V$ is computed by $V = H(H(M)||K_u)$, where $H$ is a one-way hash function and "||" denotes the concatenation operation. The final message $\{M, V\}$ will be protected by a proper pairwise key and transmitted over the wireless channel. For convenience, we call this message $\{M, V\}$ the *committed message*. Figure 9.2 shows an example of the packet format after applying our detection approach. For simplicity, we only provide integrity for the messages in this chapter. However, confidentiality can be easily achieved in our method whenever it is required by the sensing application.
- *Sampling and Detection*: When a sensor node $v$ receives a committed message $\{M, V\}$ from another sensor node $u$, it will first authenticate this message using the pairwise key shared with $u$. If the authentication fails, this message will be dropped; otherwise, it will construct a report message $M' = \{u, H(M), V\}$ at a probability of $p$. This report message $M'$ will be protected by the key $K_v$ and delivered to the base station for the detection of misused keys.

  When the base station receives a report $\{u, H(M), V\}$ from node $v$, it checks if $V$ equals $H(H(M)||K_u)$. If not, the key shared between $u$ and $v$ is not trustworthy. The base station will then notify $v$ that its shared key with $u$ is not secure

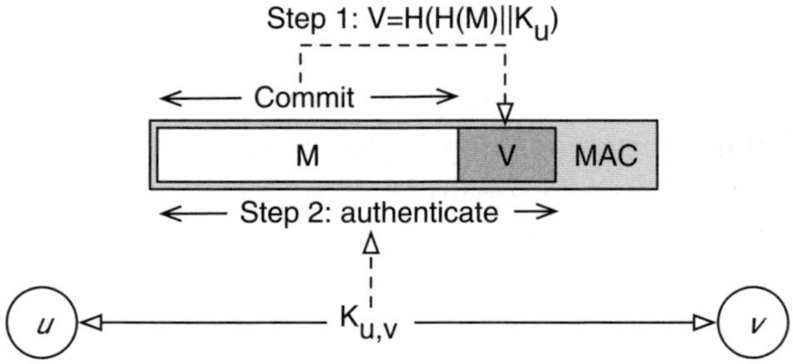


Fig. 9.2. Example packet format in Scheme I.

anymore. The notification message may also include a new pairwise key for the secure communication between $u$ and $v$.

In Scheme I, we can clearly see that an attacker cannot generate correct committing values for those forged or modified messages between two non-compromised sensor nodes $u$ and $v$ even if it has compromised their shared key $K_{u,v}$. The reason is that the attacker has to know $K_u$ in order to generate a correct committing value for any message from $u$ to $v$. While this key is only known by the base station and the non-compromised sensor node $u$. Hence, as long as the report message for one forged or modified message between two non-compromised sensor nodes is successfully delivered to the base station, we can detect that the pairwise key has been misused.

A critical parameter in the proposed approach is the probability $p$ of sending a report to the base station. Assume the attacker has forged or modified $x$ messages between two non-compromised nodes, the probability of this misused key being detected can be estimated by $1-(1-p)^x$ when every report message can successfully reach the base station. Clearly, the more often the attacker misuses a pairwise key, the higher the probability of being detected. For example, if $p = 0.05$, when the attacker forges 10 messages, the misused key will be detected at a probability of 0.4; when the attacker forges 100 messages, the misused key will be detected at a probability of 0.994.

Since every message between two sensor nodes will lead to a report to the base station at a probability of $p$, the percentage of additional messages introduced by our detection approach can be roughly estimated by $p \times d_{avr}$, where $d_{avr}$ is the average hop distance to the base station. For example, if $p = 0.05$, when the average distance to the base station is 10 hops, the number of messages transmitted in the network will be increased by 50 percent. Therefore, we usually prefer a small $p$ for a reasonable communication overhead.

From the above discussion, we can clearly see the limitations of the naive approach. For security purpose, we prefer a large $p$ so that we can detect misused keys with a high probability even if the attacker only forges or modifies a few messages between non-compromised nodes. However, a large $p$ will lead to substantial communication overhead. In the next subsection, we will present an improved method which guarantees the detection of misused keys as long as one report can reach the base station.

### 9.3.2. *Scheme II: Cumulative Commitment*

In the previous approach, a committing value can only be used for the verification of one message. In the improved approach, we propose to *cumulatively commit* the communication between two nodes $u$ and $v$ so that a committing value can be used to verify all the previously transmitted messages. More specifically, a committing value is always generated based on the hash image of all the previous messages to the destination node. In this way, as long as one report can reach the base station, we can tell whether the pairwise key has been misused so far.

For simplicity, we assume that the communication between two *neighbor* sensor nodes is always reliable. This can be easily achieved by using standard fault tolerance techniques such as re-transmission. The details will be skipped in this chapter for simplicity. We also assume that a sequence number is included in every message to deal with the replay attacks. This sequence number is increased by one for every outgoing message. The main improvement we made in Scheme II is the way we generate the committing value. The sampling and detection part will be similar to the naive approach.

- *Committing Messages*: Consider two communicating sensor nodes $u$ and $v$. Both of them maintain a variable $c_{u,v}$ to track the history of the communication from $u$ to $v$. (Another variable $c_{v,u}$ will be needed for the communication from $v$ to $u$.) Initially, we have $c_{u,v} = 0$. For every message $M$ from $u$ to $v$, node $u$ simply updates $c_{u,v} = H(c_{u,v}||M)$ and computes the committing value $V$ as $V = H(c_{u,v}||K_u)$. The final message from $u$ to $v$ is $\{M, V\}$, which will be protected by the key $K_{u,v}$ and delivered to node $v$.
- *Sampling and Detection*: This step is similar to the naive approach in the previous subsection. The only difference is: when a sensor node $v$ receives a committed message $\{M, V\}$ from another sensor node $u$, it updates $c_{u,v}$, which will be the same as the value $c_{u,v}$ at node $u$ under the reliable communication, and then sends the report message $\{u, c_{u,v}, V\}$ to the base station at a probability of $p$.

Scheme II significantly improves the performance of the naive approach. As we mentioned, every report message can be used to tell whether the pairwise key has been misused in any previous communication from the source node to the destination node due to the cumulative commitment. In contrast, the report message in the naive approach can only provide evidences for a single communication. It is very likely that the base station will miss those forged or modified messages even if every report message can be successfully delivered.

Assume every report from a regular sensor node can reach the base station. Consider two non-compromised nodes $u$ and $v$. If an attacker has compromised their shared key $K_{u,v}$ and forged a message from $u$ to $v$, the probability that it will be detected during the transmission of the next $x$ messages from $u$ to $v$ can be estimated by $1 - (1 - p)^{x+1}$. Different from the naive approach, these $x$ messages do not have to be forged or modified messages due to the cumulative commitment. Hence, even if the attacker only forged or modified a single message, the misused key will be detected as long as one report prepared by the destination node reaches the base station.

Certainly, an attacker may choose to forge a few messages and then block the communication from the source node to the destination node. It is very likely that the destination node has not sent any report to the base station yet. In this case, the misuse of this key will not be detected. A simple way to fix this is to have every sensor node buffer the last message received from any neighbor node and always generate a report to the base station if it has been a long time since the receipt of the last message. With this fix, the detection of misused keys between non-compromised sensor nodes is almost guaranteed as long as the destination nodes do not run out of battery.

However, the cumulative commitment approach also has limitations that may affect its application in real-world scenarios. First, it still introduces considerable communication overhead to the base station due to the centralized detection. Second, although it guarantees to detect a misused key when at least one report for the usage of such key can reach the base station, the delay introduced in the detection may still cause problems, especially when we need a small $p$ to reduce the communication to the base station. In the next subsection, we will present a scheme to address these two issues by making the detection part distributed.

### 9.3.3. *Scheme III: Distributed Detection*

A simple solution for distributed detection is to duplicate the base station's keying materials at a number of tamper-resistant nodes and deploy these tamper-resistant nodes in the target field to monitor the network. These tamper-resistant nodes can thus perform the detection of misused keys in the same way as the base station. As long as a sensor node can find a tamper-resistant node in its local area, it can use this node for the detection. However, tamper-resistant packaging is still expensive and can not provide a high level of security. In this chapter, we do not assume the tamper-resistant nodes. We are more interested in the algorithmic solutions.

The main idea in this subsection is to make the detection part of the previous scheme *distributed*. The communication cost to the base station only happens when a misused key is detected. This will greatly reduce the communication overhead and the detection delay. Indeed, we can have a large $p$ to reduce the detection delay without increasing the communication overhead to the base station. Specifically, in the proposed approach, we use a number of dedicated sensor nodes, called the *detecting sensor nodes*, to sample the communication in the network. These detecting sensor nodes have the keying materials that allow them to check the committing values included in the messages and detect the misused keys. Once a key is detected to be compromised, the detecting node will notify the base station to revoke this key.

We assume that the attacker may compromise a few detecting sensor nodes. Once a detecting node is compromised, the attacker can discover all its keying materials. Thus, the keying materials in the detecting sensor nodes are different from that in the base station; but they should still allow the detecting sensor nodes to check the committing values. We assume that the base station is well protected and will not be compromised. The detailed protocol is described below.

- *Initialization*: Let $m$ be the total number of detecting sensor nodes and $n$ be the total number of regular sensor nodes in the network. Every regular sensor node $u$ is pre-loaded with a unique and random key $K_u$. This key is only known by the base station and node $u$. Every detecting sensor node $i$ stores a hash value $H(K_u||i)$ for every regular sensor node $u$. Therefore, every detecting sensor node will be pre-loaded with $n$ hash images, one for each regular sensor node. Figure 9.3(a) shows an example of pre-loaded keys for the regular and detecting sensor nodes when $n = 4$ and $m = 2$.

  Clearly, the above key assignment will introduce substantial storage overhead for the detecting sensor nodes in case of a large sensor network. However, we believe that this is often feasible since the main function of the detecting sensor nodes is to monitor the usage of keys in the network. They can thus use all their memory, including the flash memory, to store these keys. For example, the TelosB motes have 1024Kbytes flash memory [12], which allows a detecting

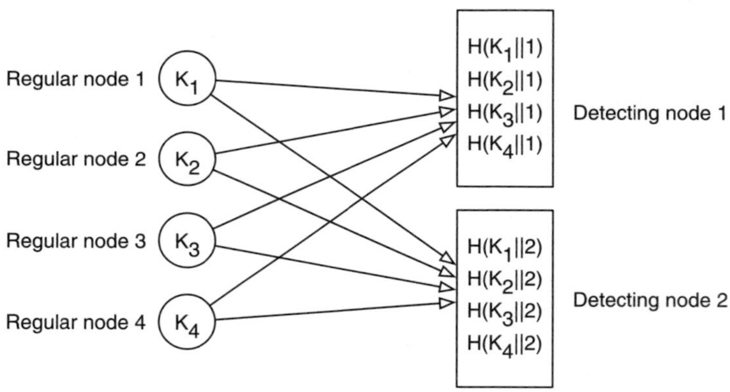


(a) Initialization

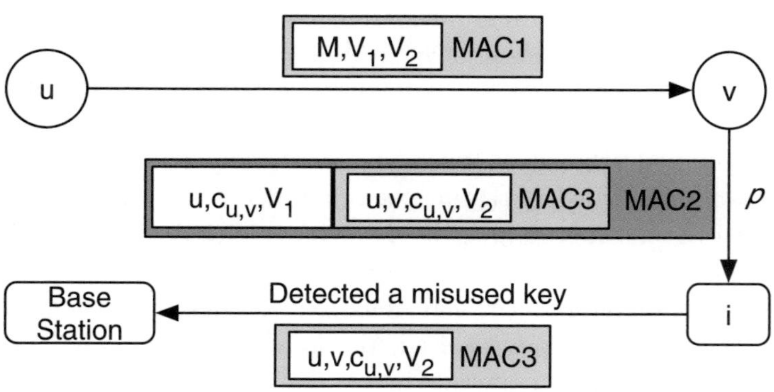


(b) Committing, sampling and detection

Fig. 9.3. Illustration of the steps in Scheme III

sensor node to store keys for a network of 128,000 sensor nodes if every key is 8-byte long.

- *Committing Messages*: After deployment, every sensor node $u$ discovers the set $\mathcal{M}(u)$ of detecting sensor nodes in its neighborhood. The IDs in this list are ranked in an ascend order. For any two communicating neighbor sensor nodes $u$ and $v$, they both need to get the other node's list of neighbor detecting sensor nodes through the secure channel established with the key $K_{u,v}$. Hence, as long as the pairwise key $K_{u,v}$ is still secure, $u$ will know the correct version of $\mathcal{M}(v)$, and $v$ will also know the correct version of $\mathcal{M}(u)$.

  Similar to the previous scheme, both $u$ and $v$ maintain a variable $c_{u,v}$ to track the history of the communication from $u$ to $v$. (Another variable $c_{v,u}$ will be needed for the communication from $v$ to $u$.) Initially, we have $c_{u,v} = 0$. For every new message $M$ from $u$ to $v$, we update $c_{u,v} = H(c_{u,v}||M)$. Let $S$ be the size of $\mathcal{M}(v)$ and $s$ be the sequence number included in $M$. Node $u$ will use the detecting node $i$ at the position $1 + (s \bmod S)$ in $\mathcal{M}(v)$ for detection. The purpose of choosing the detecting sensor node $i$ in this way is to make sure that an attacker cannot always pick a compromised detecting node for its messages.

  Node $u$ then computes two committing values: $V_1 = H(c_{u,v}||H(K_u||i))$ and $V_2 = H(c_{u,v}||K_u)$. $V_1$ will be used by the detecting node $i$ to check the committing value, while $V_2$ will be used only when the detecting node $i$ notices the misuse of the key and needs to notify the base station to revoke the key. The final message from $u$ to $v$ is thus $\{M, V_1, V_2\}$, which will be further protected by the key $K_{u,v}$ and delivered to node $v$.

- *Sampling and Detection*: When $v$ receives a committed message $\{M, V_1, V_2\}$ from $u$, it first gets the ID $i$ of the detecting node at position $1 + (s \bmod S)$ in $\mathcal{M}(v)$ once this message is authenticated, where $s$ is the sequence number included in $M$. Node $v$ then updates the variable $c_{u,v} = H(c_{u,v}||M)$ and send a report to the detecting node $i$ at a probability of $p$. This report includes two protected pieces of information, $\{u, c_{u,v}, V_1\}$ and $\{u, v, c_{u,v}, V_2\}$. The first one is for the detecting node $i$, while the second one is for the base station. The second piece of information will be first protected by $K_v$, and then the whole report will be protected by $H(K_v||i)$. Figure 9.3(b) shows an example of the final scheme, where MAC1 is a message authentication code generated using the key $K_{u,v}$, MAC2 is generated using $H(K_v||i)$, and MAC3 is generated using $K_v$.

  When the detecting node $i$ receives the report from node $v$, it checks if $V_1$ equals $H(c_{u,v}||H(K_u||i))$ after authenticating the report. If not, the key $K_{u,v}$ is misused. In this case, if the misuse of $K_{u,v}$ hasn't been reported to the base station before, the detecting node $i$ will send the second piece of information $\{u, v, c_{u,v}, V_2\}$ to the base station to revoke the key $K_{u,v}$; otherwise, it will ignore the report. When the base station receives this message, it will further check if $V_2$ equals $H(c_{u,v}||K_u)$ after the message is authenticated using the key $K_v$. If not, it will notify $v$ that its shared key with $u$ is not secure anymore. The notification message may include a new pairwise key for the secure communication between $u$ and $v$.

#### 9.3.3.1. *Security analysis*

In the security analysis, we will focus on our final scheme, the distributed detection approach. Clearly, if a sensor node cannot find any detecting node in its local area, it is not possible to perform the detection of misused keys. As a result, we want to make sure that a regular sensor node can find at least one detecting node in its local area with a high probability. A critical parameter for this requirement is the number $m$ of detecting sensor nodes in the network. For simplicity, we assume that the sensor nodes are evenly deployed in the field. Let $b$ be the average number of neighbor nodes for every regular sensor node before the deployment of detecting sensor nodes. After the detecting sensor nodes are evenly deployed in the network, the probability that a regular sensor node cannot find any detecting node in its neighborhood can be estimated by $(1-\frac{b}{n})^m$. The probability of finding at least one detecting sensor node in any given regular sensor node's neighborhood can be estimated by

$$p_{cover}(m,n) = 1 - \left(1-\frac{b}{n}\right)^m \approx 1 - \left(\frac{1}{e}\right)^{\frac{bm}{n}}.$$

Clearly, for densely deployed sensor networks, we can usually deploy a small fraction of additional sensor nodes for detection so that most regular sensor nodes are covered by at least one detecting node. For example, when $b = 50$, we only need to deploy 10% additional sensor nodes ($m = \frac{n}{10}$) to make sure that a regular sensor node can find a detecting sensor node with a probability of 0.99. Additionally, deploying a reasonable fraction of additional sensor nodes are usually acceptable for security sensitive operations. We thus assume that the number $m$ of detecting sensor nodes is large enough so that every sensor node has at least one neighbor detecting sensor node in its neighborhood.

Consider two particular non-compromised sensor nodes $u$ and $v$. There are two cases in terms of the pairwise key $K_{u,v}$. It is either compromised or not compromised. When the key $K_{u,v}$ is still secure, we can clearly see that neither of $u$ and $v$ is compromised. In addition, a non-compromised detecting sensor node will never report a false alarm against this key as shown in the following theorem.

**Theorem 9.1.** *A non-compromised detecting sensor node will never report a false alarm against any non-compromised pairwise key.*

**Proof.** Assume the detecting node $i$ receives an authenticated report from $v$. Let $\{u, c_{u,v}, V_1\}$ be the first piece of information in this report. Since the key between $u$ and $v$ is still secure, and the communication between them is always reliable, we know that both of $u$ and $v$ will have the same copy of $c_{u,v}$. It is therefore guaranteed that $V_1$ equals $H(c_{u,v}||H(K_u||i))$. This means that a non-compromised detecting sensor node will never report false alarms against non-compromised pairwise keys. □

The above theorem indicates that a non-compromised detecting sensor node will never introduce communication overhead to the base station unless it detects a misused key. However, when a detecting node is compromised, it can certainly report a false alarm. *Fortunately, this compromised detecting sensor node is still unable to affect the communication between non-compromised nodes $u$ and $v$.* This can be explained in the following theorem.

**Theorem 9.2.** *A non-compromised pairwise key will never be revoked.*

**Proof.** According to the protocol description, we know that only the base station can revoke the pairwise keys in the network. Let $R = \{u, v, c_{u,v}, V_2\}$ denote the report from a compromised detecting sensor node to the base station. Since $R$ is protected by $K_v$, which is only known by the base station and node $v$, the attacker cannot forge or modify any report. As a result, when the report is authenticated, it is always guaranteed that $V_2$ equals $H(c_{u,v}||K_u)$ as long as the key $K_{u,v}$ is still secure. This means that a non-compromised pairwise key will never be revoked. □

When the pairwise key $K_{u,v}$ is compromised, we will study the *detection rate*, which is the probability of a misused key being detected. Let $f_c$ be the fraction of those detecting sensor nodes that have been compromised. We assume that a report message can always reach the intended detecting node. We note that the keys stored on different detecting nodes are different from each other due to the one-way hash function $H$. We can clearly see that no matter how many detecting nodes are compromised, the secrets on those non-compromised detecting nodes are still safe.

**Theorem 9.3.** *Let $u$ and $v$ be two non-compromised sensor nodes and $x$ be the number of authenticated messages $v$ received since the first misuse of the key $K_{u,v}$. The probability of this misuse being detected is at least $(1-(1-(1-f_c)\times p)^{x+1}) \times p_{cover}(m \times (1-f_c), n)$.*

**Proof.** Clearly, when all the detecting nodes $v$ can reach are compromised, we are unable to protect the usage of the keys for the communication to this sensor node. Based on our previous analysis, the probability that $v$ finds at least one benign detecting node is $p_{cover}(m \times (1-f_c), n)$. In addition, we note that $v$ will generate a report to a detecting node at a probability of $p$ for every authenticated message from $u$. When this detecting node is compromised, the misuse of $K_{u,v}$ will not be detected; otherwise, this misuse of $K_{u,v}$ will be detected at a probability of $p$. Since every detecting node in $\mathcal{M}(v)$ will be used by $u$ at the same probability, the probability of detecting the misuse of $K_{u,v}$ after transmitting a single message can be estimated by $(1-f_c) \times p$. Thus, after the transmission of $x$ messages, the probability of detecting the misuse of this pairwise key is at least $1-(1-(1-f_c) \times p)^{x+1}$. Hence, the overall probability of detecting a misused key is at least $(1-(1-(1-f_c) \times p)^{x+1}) \times p_{cover}(m \times (1-f_c), n)$. □

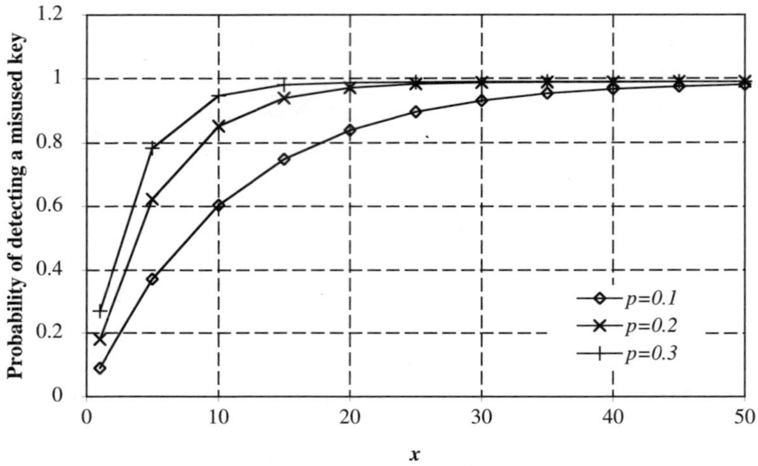


(a) $f_c = 0.1$

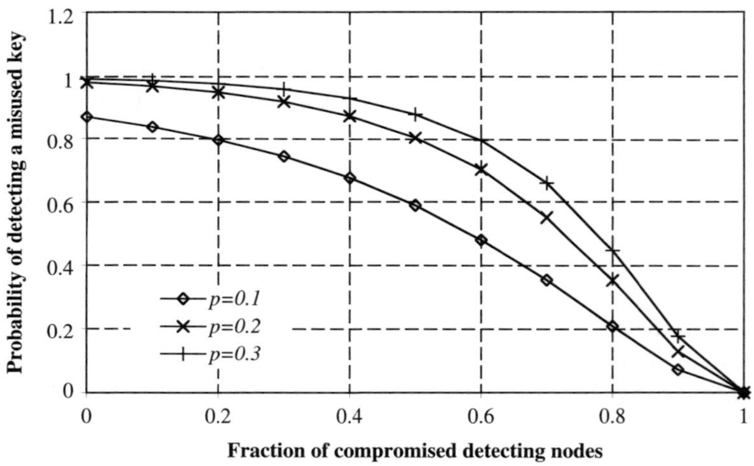


(b) $x = 20$

Fig. 9.4. Probability of detecting a misused key. Assume average number of neighbors $b = 50$ and the total number of detecting nodes $m = \frac{n}{10}$.

Figure 9.4 shows the probability of detecting a misused key under different situations. From Figure 9.4(a), we can clearly see that the detection rate increases quickly with $x$, the number of messages transmitted from the source node to the destination node. It means that any misused pairwise key will be detected with a very high probability as long as the source node is still communicating with the destination node. We also note that increasing the probability $p$ of sending a report will improve the probability of detecting a misused key given only a small number of messages. In other words, increasing $p$ has a positive impact on reducing the detection delay. Since a large $p$ implies more communication overhead, we thus have to make a trade-off between the detection delay and the communication overhead.

Figure 9.4(b) shows that when there are more compromised detecting sensor nodes, we will have less chance of detecting misused keys. In particular, when all the detecting nodes are compromised, we are not able to detect any misused key. Nevertheless, we can clearly see that the performance of our detection approach degrades slowly with the number of compromised detecting sensor nodes.

We would like to mention that the proposed scheme can only detect the misuse of the keys shared between non-compromised sensor nodes. A compromised sensor node can certainly misuse its own keys to mislead the sensing application without being detected. Nevertheless, our detection method prevents the attacker from impersonating those non-compromised sensor nodes or non-existing sensor nodes. As a result, the attacker can only cause damage to the network using the compromised sensor nodes. For example, a compromised sensor node can only communicate with a non-compromised sensor node as "itself". This greatly mitigates the impact of node compromises on the security of network operations.

#### 9.3.3.2. *Overheads*

For every regular sensor node, the additional storage overhead introduced by our detection approach is a shared key with the base station and the space for the lists of nearby detecting sensor nodes and the variables to track the communication history with its neighbor nodes. Note that in most applications, a sensor node only needs to communicate with a few other nodes and only needs to save a few list of neighbor detecting nodes. Thus, the storage overhead at sensor nodes will not be a big problem in our approach. For every detecting node, it needs to store $n$ keys for a network of $n$ sensor nodes. As discussed before, this is often feasible for a reasonable size sensor network since all the sensor memory can be used to store these keys.

As for the computation overhead, our detection approach only involves a few efficient symmetric key operations for the regular sensor nodes. For the detecting sensor nodes, they need to access the flash memory for the keys needed to verify the messages. Certainly, accessing flash memory will be much slower than accessing RAM, and will likely cost more energy. However, because of the limited number of neighbors for every sensor node, a detecting sensor node only needs to retrieve a few keys from its flash memory during the entire lifetime. A detecting sensor node also needs to check every report message. However, this only involve a few number of efficient symmetric key operations.

As for the communication overhead, our detection approach needs two additional fields for the committing values in every outgoing message. A typical size of a committing value is 8-byte long. Hence, this is usually not a problem for the current generation of sensor networks. In addition to this, every sensor node will generate a report message at a probability of $p$ for every message other than the report from its neighbor nodes. Thus, the total number of messages transmitted in the network will be approximately increased by a fraction of $p$. However, these report messages are only transmitted between neighbor nodes and will unlikely generate big impact on the performance of the sensing application. Note that a detecting sensor node also needs to notify the base station for revoking a misused key. However, this only happens when a misused key is detected. We therefore believe that our detection approach is practical for the current generation of sensor networks in terms of the storage, communication and computation overheads.

#### 9.3.3.3. *Advantages*

The main advantage of our approach is the ability of determining whether a particular pairwise key has been misused before. This is particularly meaningful for us in many cases. In the following, we will show the benefits of our detection approach in improving the resilience of a pairwise key establishment technique. We will consider the basic probabilistic key pre-distribution scheme [3], the random subset assignment scheme [5], the matrix-based scheme [4], the random pairwise keys scheme [6], the grid-based scheme [5] and PIKE [9].

For the basic probabilistic key pre-distribution scheme [3], the random subset assignment [5] and the matrix-based scheme [4], a small number of compromised sensor nodes reveal a large fraction of keys in the network. As a result, the attacker will learn a large number of pairwise keys shared between non-compromised sensor nodes. Additionally, the attacker can easily create new sensor nodes using the secrets learned from compromised sensor nodes, leading to a Sybil attack [13]. These newly created sensor nodes can establish keys with legitimate sensor nodes and generate negative impact on the network at a large scale. By applying our detection method, both problems can be mitigated significantly. The misused keys between those non-compromised or newly created sensor nodes can be detected with a high probability.

For the random pairwise keys scheme [6], the grid-based scheme [5] and PIKE [9], an attacker learns nothing about or only a very small fraction of the keys shared directly between non-compromised sensor nodes. However, a large fraction of keys will be established indirectly with the help of one or a few intermediate sensor nodes. In this case, a few compromised nodes will leak many indirect keys. By applying our detection method, we can achieve additional security property. In particular, those indirect pairwise keys between non-compromised sensor nodes can be monitored for security purpose. Once they are misused by the attacker to mislead the sensing application, we are able to detect the misuse at a very high probability as shown in Theorem 9.3.

Our last approach also provides an interesting way to setup pairwise keys for sensor nodes. Specifically, every sensor node can ask one of its neighbor detection sensor node to help it establish a pairwise key with any other regular sensor node. Hence, as long as the detecting sensor node is still secure, its pairwise key will also be secure. To improve security, we can have every sensor node establish multiple keys with the same sensor node using multiple detecting sensor nodes and combine these keys into a single key. In this way, as long as one detecting sensor node is secure, the key is safe. The detection part of our approach then offers an addition security property. When a new detecting sensor node is deployed in a sensor node's local area, it can help detect if there is any key misused in the communication to this node.

## 9.4. Implementation Issues

The security and overheads of our proposed detection approach has been thoroughly discussed in Section 9.3. The result shows that our scheme can *effectively* detect misused keys with a high probability. In this section, we will study the implementation issues. The purpose is to show that our detection approach can be efficiently implemented on resource-constrained sensor nodes.

We have implemented the distributed detection approach using TinyOS [14]. Since the base station is much more resourceful than sensor nodes, adding an additional piece of revocation mechanism is usually not a problem. Hence, we focus on the implementation for the detecting sensor nodes and for the regular sensor nodes. We use RC5 [15] to implement the security primitives such as hash and MAC operations. All the keys and hash values are 8-byte long.

For a detecting sensor node $i$, it needs to listen to the channel for the report message from regular sensor nodes. The detecting node may need to access the flash memory to get the key to check the committing value. If a misused key is detected, it will notify the base station to revoke the key. For a regular sensor node, our detection method is implemented in the communication module. Specifically, whenever a new message other than the report needs to be delivered to other sensor nodes, we add two committing values to the message. Whenever a new message is received from other sensor nodes, we will generate and send a report message to a detecting sensor node at a certain probability after authenticating the message.

From the above discussion, we can see that the proposed scheme can be easily implemented on resource-constrained sensor nodes. The following table summarizes some important characteristics for our implementation on TelosB [12] motes. The RAM size for the regular nodes also include the space for 10 neighbor regular nodes, and each of them has 5 neighbor detecting nodes.

| | | |
|---|---|---|
| Detecting node | Code size with OS | ROM: 13086 bytes<br>RAM: 1205 bytes |
| | # of hash operations | Detect: 2<br>Report: 1 |
| Regular node | Additional code size | ROM: 1668 bytes<br>RAM: 494 bytes |
| | # of hash operations | Commit: 5<br>Report: 6 |

## 9.5. Related Work

The closest related work to the techniques studied in this chapter is pairwise key establishment. Many techniques have been proposed along this research direction, including the basic probabilistic scheme [3], the $q$-composite scheme [6], the random pairwise keys scheme [6], the two threshold-based schemes [4,5] and PIKE [9]. Additionally, the prior deployment and post deployment knowledge were also used to improve the performance of key pre-distribution in various situations [7,8,16]. Our techniques in this chapter address an important issue that hasn't been studied yet. The proposed techniques can improve the resilient of sensor network by detecting misused keys.

There are many other studies on sensor network security, including key management [17–19], tamper-resistant hardware [20], efficient broadcast authentication [21], secure data aggregation and in-networking processing [22–24], and vulnerabilities, attacks, and countermeasures [25,26]. We consider them complementary to our techniques in this chapter.

## 9.6. Conclusion and Future Work

This chapter identifies an important security problem for key management in sensor networks, the detection of misused keys. In this chapter, we present a serial of solutions to detect the misuse of pairwise keys in the network. The analysis indicates that our proposed approaches are efficient and effective for the current generation of sensor networks.

There are still a number of open issues. First, the proposed schemes cannot detect the misused key when one of the sensor nodes related to this key is compromised. It is interesting to see what else we can do to deal with this situation. In addition, we are also interested in the detection of compromised nodes that behave maliciously.

## References


[1] I. Akyildiz, W. Su, Y. Sankarasubramaniam, and E. Cayirci, Wireless sensor networks: A survey, *Computer Networks*, **38**(4), 393–422, (2002).

[2] C. Hartung, J. Balasalle, and R. Han, Node compromise in sensor networks: The need for secure systems. Technical Report CU-CS-990-05, U. Colorado at Boulder (Jan. 2005).

[3] L. Eschenauer and V. D. Gligor, A key-management scheme for distributed sensor networks. In *Proceedings of the 9th ACM Conference on Computer and Communications Security (CCS)*, pp. 41–47 (November, 2002).

[4] W. Du, J. Deng, Y. S. Han, and P. Varshney, A pairwise key pre-distribution scheme for wireless sensor networks. In *Proceedings of 10th ACM Conference on Computer and Communications Security (CCS)*, pp. 42–51 (October, 2003).

[5] D. Liu and P. Ning, Establishing pairwise keys in distributed sensor networks. In *Proceedings of 10th ACM Conference on Computer and Communications Security (CCS)*, pp. 52–61 (October, 2003).

[6] H. Chan, A. Perrig, and D. Song, Random key predistribution schemes for sensor networks. In *IEEE Symposium on Security and Privacy (S&P)*, pp. 197–213 (May, 2003).
[7] W. Du, J. Deng, Y. S. Han, S. Chen, and P. Varshney, A key management scheme for wireless sensor networks using deployment knowledge. In *Proceedings of IEEE INFOCOM* (March, 2004).
[8] D. Liu and P. Ning, Location-based pairwise key establishments for static sensor networks. In *2003 ACM Workshop on Security in Ad Hoc and Sensor Networks (SASN)*, pp. 72–82 (October, 2003).
[9] H. Chan and A. Perrig, PIKE: Peer intermediaries for key establishment in sensor networks. In *Proceedings of IEEE Infocom* (Mar., 2005).
[10] P. Traynor, R. Kumar, H. B. Saad, G. Cao, and T. L. Porta, Liger: Implementing efficient hybrid security mechanisms for heterogeneous sensor networks. In *ACM/USENIX Fourth International Conference on Mobile Systems Applications and Services (MobiSys)*, (2006).
[11] S. Marti, T. J. Giuli, K. Lai, and M. Baker, Mitigating routing misbehavior in mobile ad hoc networks. In *Proceedings of the Sixth annual ACM/IEEE International Conference on Mobile Computing and Networking*, pp. 255–265, (2000).
[12] Crossbow Technology Inc. Wireless sensor networks. http://www.xbow.com/Home/HomePage.aspx. Accessed in February 2006.
[13] J. Newsome, R. Shi, D. Song, and A. Perrig, The sybil attack in sensor networks: Analysis and defenses. In *Proceedings of IEEE International Conference on Information Processing in Sensor Networks (IPSN 2004)* (Apr, 2004).
[14] J. Hill, R. Szewczyk, A. Woo, S. Hollar, D. Culler, and K. S. J. Pister, System architecture directions for networked sensors. In *Architectural Support for Programming Languages and Operating Systems*, pp. 93–104, (2000).
[15] R. Rivest, The RC5 encryption algorithm. In *Proceedings of the 1st International Workshop on Fast Software Encryption*, vol. 809, pp. 86–96, (1994).
[16] D. Huang, M. Mehta, D. Medhi, and L. Harn, Location-aware key management scheme for wireless sensor networks. In *Proceedings of the 2nd ACM workshop on Security of ad hoc and sensor networks (SASN)*, pp. 29–42 (October, 2004).
[17] D. Carman, P. Kruus, and B.J. Matt, Constrains and approaches for distributed sensor network security. Technical report, NAI Labs, (2000).
[18] S. Zhu, S. Setia, and S. Jajodia, LEAP: Efficient security mechanisms for large-scale distributed sensor networks. In *Proceedings of 10th ACM Conference on Computer and Communications Security (CCS)*, pp. 62–72 (October, 2003).
[19] R. Anderson, H. Chan, and A. Perrig, Key infection: Smart trust for smart dust. In *Proceedings of IEEE International Conference on Network Protocols (ICNP 2004)* (Oct., 2004).
[20] S. Basagni, K. Herrin, D. Bruschi, and E. Rosti, Secure pebblenets. In *Proceedings of ACM International Symposium on Mobile ad hoc networking and computing*, pp. 156–163, (2001).
[21] A. Perrig, R. Szewczyk, V. Wen, D. Culler, and D. Tygar, SPINS: Security protocols for sensor networks. In *Proceedings of Seventh Annual International Conference on Mobile Computing and Networks (MobiCom)* (July, 2001).
[22] B. Przydatek, D. Song, and A. Perrig, SIA: Secure information aggregation in sensor networks. In *Proceedings of the 1st ACM Conference on Embedded Networked Sensor Systems (SenSys)* (Nov. 2003).
[23] J. Deng, R. Han, and S. Mishra, Security support for in-network processing in wireless sensor networks. In *2003 ACM Workshop on Security in Ad Hoc and Sensor Networks (SASN)* (October, 2003).

[24] L. Hu and D. Evans, Secure aggregation for wireless networks. In *Workshop on Security and Assurance in Ad Hoc Networks* (January, 2003).
[25] A. D. Wood and J. A. Stankovic, Denial of service in sensor networks, *IEEE Computer*, **35**(10), 54–62, (2002).
[26] C. Karlof and D. Wagner. Secure routing in wireless sensor networks: Attacks and countermeasures. In *Proceedings of 1st IEEE International Workshop on Sensor Network Protocols and Applications* (May, 2003).

# Chapter 10

## A SURVEY OF KEY REVOCATION SCHEMES IN MOBILE AD HOC NETWORKS

Xinxin Fan* and Guang Gong†
*Department of Electrical and Computer Engineering*
*University of Waterloo, Waterloo, Ontario, N2L 3G1, Canada*
**x5fan@engmail.uwaterloo.ca*
*†ggong@calliope.uwaterloo.ca*

Mobile ad hoc networks (MANETs) have been attracting much interest in both academia and industry communities due to their potential applications in a wide range of areas. However, the salient characteristics of MANETs, in particular the absence of infrastructure, mobility and the constrained resources of mobile devices, present enormous challenges when designing the security mechanism in this environment. As an important component of a key management mechanism, an efficient key revocation scheme, which revokes cryptographic keys of malicious nodes and isolate them from the network, is crucial for the security and robustness of MANETs. In this chapter, we provide a survey of key revocation schemes in pure general-purpose MANETs and vehicular ad hoc networks (VANETs), highly successful specializations of (pure) MANETs. We notice that revocation is closely related to the kind of trust among the users as well as between the users and the authorities, which can vary from one application to another. Therefore, there is not a universal solution for key revocation which is applicable to all the scenarios where MANETs are used. Different approaches should be employed based on the requirements and the characteristics of target applications.

### 10.1. Introduction

With the rapid development in network technology, in particular wireless communication, traditional centralized, fixed networks cannot satisfy enormous demands on network connectivity, data storage and information exchange any longer. New types of communication networks based on wireless and multi-hop communication have emerged to provide efficient solutions for the growing number of mobile wireless applications and services. A large family of the new types of wireless communication networks can be best represented by *mobile ad hoc networks (MANETs)*. MANETs provide a relative new paradigm of wireless networking, in which all networking functions (e.g., control, routing, monitoring, mobility management, etc.) are performed by nodes themselves in a decentralized manner and no authority is in charge of controlling and managing the network. While the above pure general-purpose MANETs attract much attention in academia community, they have not yet achieved the envisaged impact in the light of real world implementation and industry deployment. At the same time, with the increasing problems related to traffic and roads, another important and promising application of MANETs, *vehicular ad hoc networks (VANETs)*, will be expected to rapidly penetrate the market and impact the commercial world. VANETs use ad hoc communication techniques for performing efficient driver assistance and car safety. Vehicular network nodes, that is, vehicles and Road-side infrastructure Units (RSUs), will be equipped with sensing, processing, and wireless communication modules, which allow communication between vehicles (V2V) as well as between vehicles and the infrastructures (V2I) to improve traffic safety.

Although a VANET can be regarded as a special form of a MANET, they have significant differences in the following aspects: [28]

- *Network Dynamics*: The speeds of vehicles moving in VANETs are much higher than those of nodes in general-purpose MANETs. Therefore, the vehicles have very short connection time for exchanging information with neighbors. Furthermore, the trajectories of the vehicles are also restricted by factors like road course, encompassing traffic and traffic regulations, whereas nodes in general-purpose MANETs can move to any place and in any direction at their own will.
- *Network Size*: VANETs usually consist of hundreds of millions of vehicles and the size of the network is huge. However, the communication in VANETs is mainly local due to the geographical location of the members, whereas nodes are assumed to be able to communicate with any peer under the general network models of MANETs.
- *Resource Constrains*: Resource constrains such as power, memory, and computation are general assumptions for mobile devices used in MANETs. However, vehicles do not have limitations related to the capacities of the devices and therefore the use of complex cryptographic algorithms and protocols (such as public key cryptography) are feasible in VANETs.
- *Infrastructure*: MANETs do not depend on any established infrastructure or centralized administration, whereas VANETs are assumed to be supported by some fixed infrastructure units that are deployed in some critical sections of the road (such as traffic lights, intersections and stop signs). Furthermore, these infrastructure units can assist vehicles with various services and provide access to stationary networks.

Security support is indispensable in order for these networks and related services to be implemented in real world applications. However, due to the absence of (omnipresent) infrastructure, insecure nature of the wireless communication medium and dynamic changes of the network topology, MANETs and VANETs are vulnerable to a range of attacks and are thus difficult to secure [1,4]. Furthermore, the design of security mechanism should also consider the different features between MANETs and VANETs as described above. In recent years, a number of research contributions have been made to design efficient key management mechanisms for MANETs [5,11,19,20,34,37–39] and VANETs [14,32].

As a component of any key management scheme, key revocation plays a very important role for the security and robustness of MANETs and VANETs. In the context of MANETs and VANETs, key revocation is a kind of mechanism that determines whether a certificate and the corresponding cryptographic key of a network node need to be revoked. When a certificate is issued, its validity is limited by an expiration date. However, due to the potential threats that nodes are compromised by attackers and launch various attacks to the network under the control of the adversaries, there are some circumstances that a certificate and the corresponding cryptographic key of a network node must be revoked prior to its expiration date. Without the valid certificates and cryptographic keys, malicious nodes cannot communicate with other nodes and participate in the network operation. Furthermore, all messages from those nodes will also be ignored by peers. Therefore, if cryptographic certificates and keys are issued by an authority, it must possible, whenever necessary (e.g., key exposure or compromise), for the authority to revoke them, and essentially evict malicious nodes from the network.

In this chapter we will present a survey of typical key revocation schemes in MANETs and VANETs. The rest of this chapter is organized as follows: In section 10.2 we present the motivation for designing new key revocation schemes for MANETs and VANETs. Section 10.3 gives a review of two main categories of solutions and some other new ideas for key revocation in MANETs. In section 10.4, we survey existing solutions for the eviction of misbehaving and faulty vehicles in VANETs. Finally, we conclude this chapter in Section 10.5.

## 10.2. Motivation

In the context of wired networks, implementations of key revocation schemes are usually based on Public Key Infrastructures (PKIs) [13]. When the certificate of some user is to be revoked, a certificate authority (CA) adds user's certificate information into a Certificate Revocation List (CRL) and puts it on an on-line trusted public repository or distributes it to other relevant users in some secure way. Based on such centralized structure, various solutions for the revocation have been proposed such as *Certificate Revocation System* (CRS) [22,26], *Certificate Revocation Tree* (CRT) [16], and *Online Certificate Status Protocol* (OCSP) [21]. One common characteristic of all these methods is the need of good synchronization with the revocation source either by online status checks or by frequently refreshed certificates. Unfortunately, these conventional techniques are difficult to be applied to MANETs because of a number of unique features of MANETs such as the absence of an on-line CA and a centralized repository. In VANETs, although the CA can use the road-side infrastructure as the gateway to distribute the CRLs, the RSUs are not omnipresent (especially in the early deployment stages) and therefore it is hard for vehicles to obtain timely revocation information. Change of network models requires designing new key revocation schemes tailored towards MANETs and VANETs based on the unique features of these networks.

## 10.3. Key Revocation Schemes in MANETs

Two main classes of solutions have been proposed for key revocation in MANETs. The schemes in the first category employ threshold cryptography and network nodes collaborate to revoke keys of malicious nodes. Those in the second category are fully self-organized and each node has its own opinion about the network and other nodes' behavior. These solutions can be implemented with either the certificate-based cryptography (CBC) or identity-based cryptography (IBC). Furthermore, some novel ideas have also been proposed in the literature, which can be used to fast remove malicious nodes from MANETs in particular application scenarios. In this section we will review existing key revocation schemes for MANETs in detail.

### 10.3.1. *System Models of General-Purpose MANETs*

In this subsection, we describe the network model and adversary model for the general-purpose MANETs. These models determine the requirements that a sound key revocation scheme for MANETs should satisfy.

#### 10.3.1.1. *Network model*

A general-purpose MANET consists of an unconstrained number of networking nodes with a random mobility pattern, i.e., nodes moving independently within a given field or keeping stationary in a location for a period of time. In addition, the network topology also changes dynamically when a particular network event, such as node join, leave or failure, occurs. Each node has limited transmission and reception capabilities. Mobile nodes that are within each other's radio range communicate directly via bandwidth-constrained, error-prone insecure wireless links, while those that are far apart rely on other nodes to relay their messages in a multi-hop fashion. As requirements of many network tasks and protocols, each node must be unambiguously identified by a unique identity. It can be a MAC address or an IP address. In order for nodes monitoring various behavior of their direct neighbors within the communication range, the communication links are bidirectional in the network and nodes are in promiscuous mode. Both assumptions are common in many low-layer MANETs protocols such as DSR [15] and AODV [29] routing protocols. Furthermore, identifiers of neighbor nodes can be obtained by running some neighborhood discovery protocols, which are part of many existing routing protocols and therefore can be reused. Moreover, processors of mobile nodes are assumed to be able to perform public-key algorithms. All the above assumptions are quite common and reasonable for most application scenarios of the general-purpose MANETs.

#### 10.3.1.2. *Adversary model*

We term as an *adversary* or *attacker* any node whose behavior deviates from the legitimate MANET protocols. A malicious node can attack a wireless link by eavesdropping, injecting, deleting, and altering packets. It may also mount denial-of-service attacks, such as physical-layer jamming, MAC-layer misbehavior, or routing disruption. Moreover, a malicious node might occasionally compromise and control one or a few well-behaving nodes through software bugs or reverse engineering. We assume that each node in MANETs is installed an Intrusion Detection System [23] which can detect most misbehavior above. The procedure of key revocation involves observations and interactions among well-behaving nodes, which also makes false accusation a very effective attack. The false accusation attack can be independently or collaboratively initiated by some adversaries. These attackers intend to revoke keys of well-behaving nodes by accusing them at their own will.

### 10.3.2. *Key Revocation Schemes Based on Threshold Cryptography*

Key revocation schemes that depend on the use of a centralized trusted third party (TTP) are not well suited to the ad hoc network scenario due to several reasons. Firstly, a CA will be a vulnerable point in the network, especially if it is not distributed. If the CA is compromised, the security of the entire network is breached. More importantly, the CA should be available all the time in order to manage keys of network nodes. A typical approach to solve these problems is to distribute the services of a centralized CA to a set of network nodes using threshold cryptography [36]. And then these network nodes can collaboratively carry out the key revocation. Although this kind of key revocation schemes do not require the establishment of any infrastructure, the use of threshold cryptography may cause tremendous computation and communication overhead on the network. We next describe several key revocation schemes based on threshold cryptography for MANETs. In the following discussion, $N$ denotes the overall number of network nodes and $t$ and $n$ are two positive integers satisfying $t \leq n < N$.

#### 10.3.2.1. *Partially distributed authority*

In the seminal paper by Zhou and Hass [39], the authors use CBC and a $(t, n)$ threshold scheme to distribute the services of the CA to a set of specialized server nodes in MANETs. The system contains three types of nodes, namely, client, server and combiner nodes. The client nodes are the normal users of the network, whereas the server and combiner nodes are part of the CA. The system can tolerate $t - 1$

compromised servers due to the use of threshold cryptography. Although the authors mentioned that the servers can collaborate to revoke the certificates of the malicious nodes, no algorithms about the certificate revocation are provided.

In Ref. 38, Zhang *et al.* designed a key management mechanism called IKM for MANETs by combining IBC and threshold cryptography. The authors described a novel construction method of ID-based public/private keys. In IKM, an external TTP distributes its functionality to $n$ Distributed Private Key Generators (D-PKGs) and bootstraps the network with identity-based cryptography. More specifically, the TTP generates two master keys and only introduces the information of one of master keys into the network using a $(t, n)$ threshold scheme. Therefore, each node has two pairs of keys, a static one issued by the TTP and one that depends on the current time interval issued by the on-line D-PKGs. By this means, IKM guarantees high-level resilience to node compromise attacks. Keys are updated periodically through the broadcasts of the D-PKGs. In their key revocation protocol, each node observing malicious behavior of other nodes securely reports its signed accusations to the preassigned D-PKGs with ID-based signature and encryption schemes. When the number of accusations against a malicious node reaches the revocation threshold in a predetermined time window, the $t$ D-PKGs will collaborate to revoke the key of the malicious node with an ID-based $(t, n)$-threshold signature scheme. Although the design of IKM minimizes the damage from node compromise attacks, the procedure of key revocation involves a lot of expensive pairing computations, which means that the network nodes in MANETs should have sufficient computational and power resources.

#### 10.3.2.2. *Fully distributed authority*

In Refs. 17 and 20, a localized key management scheme was proposed for MANETs. The authors use a $(t, N)$ threshold scheme to distribute the capabilities of the CA to all nodes in MANETs. In addition, the authors also briefly described a localized certificate revocation scheme in a single paragraph. In their scheme, each node monitors the behavior of its one-hop neighboring nodes. The key revocation will happen in two cases. One is when node $A$ observes that one of its neighbors is misbehaving. Node $A$ will directly mark its neighbor as "convicted". Furthermore, node $A$ also disseminates its signed accusations to its $m$-hop neighborhoods with a RSA signature scheme, where $m$ is a design parameter denoting the range of the accusation propagation. The other case is when node $A$ receives an accusation against node $B$ from node $C$. Node A first verifies whether the accuser $C$ can be trusted by checking its own certificate revocation lists. If it is, it verifies the signature of the accuser $C$ and updates its CRLs accordingly. Otherwise node $A$ ignores the accusation received from $C$. When the number of accusations for one node reaches a predefined network-wide revocation threshold, the certificate of that node will be revoked. Furthermore, each node only holds each entry in a CRL for some time $T_{cert}$ (which is defined as the valid period of a certificate) so that it will not provide the certificate update service for a convicted node that still have a valid certificate. Therefore, the convicted node will be evicted from the network after a period of $T_{cert}$. Although the proposed key revocation scheme meets some requirements of MANETs, it is vulnerable to the Sybil attack [8] where an malicious node can create a large number of identities to collect enough shares and reconstruct the CA's private key [5].

In Refs. 34, Saxena *et al.* proposed ID-GAC, an elegant identity-based access control scheme for ad hoc groups such as MANETs. ID-GAC uses a $(t, N)$ threshold scheme to share the master key among all network nodes before the deployment. In particular, the authors presented a membership revocation mechanism based on Membership Revocation Lists (MRLs), which are the analogues of the CRLs used in the traditional PKI. Their scheme is basically similar to those in Refs. 17 and 20 except that the signed accusations are broadcasted to the entire network and a identity-based threshold signature scheme is used to update key shares. The disadvantages of ID-GAC include: (i) Broadcasting accusations to the entire network introduces a lot of communication load; (ii) The procedure of key revocation needs many expensive pairing computations which impose a large computational overhead for mobile devices in MANETs; and (iii) ID-GAC suffers from the same undesirable security drawback as the schemes in Refs. 17 and 20.

### 10.3.3. *Self-Organized Key Revocation Schemes*

The above key revocation schemes use threshold cryptography and therefore some nodes need to collaborate to revoke keys of malicious nodes, whereas several fully self-organized schemes are also proposed in the literature. In self-organized key revocation schemes, each node has its own view about the network and decides whether cryptographic keys of other network nodes should be revoked based on its own observations and the information collected from peers in MANETs. These self-organized key revocation schemes do not require any infrastructure and on-line access to trusted authorities.

In Ref. 5, Capkun *et al.* presented a self-organized key management scheme for MANETs. This scheme uses a PGP-like trust model [40] and allows nodes to certify each other. When a user want to revoke a certificate that he issued, the user sends an explicit revocation statement to the nodes that regularly update that certificate. The disadvantage of this scheme is that the assumption of a transitive trust might be too strong for MANETs.

The scheme proposed in Ref. 7 by Crépeau and Davis is the first self-organized certificate revocation scheme for MANETs. Their protocol uses a weighted accusation scheme and provides the protection against the potentially false accusation attacks from malicious nodes. The scheme is further improved and extended in Ref. 2. Here, the value of a node's trustworthiness determines the weight of its accusation. The weight of node $A$'s accusations depends on the number of accusations against node $A$, as well as the number of additional accusations made by node $A$. The authors presented a method for actually quantifying the trustworthiness of the nodes in MANETs satisfying that accusations from the trustworthy nodes will have higher weight than those from less trustworthy nodes. The underline principle of their scheme is that the weight of a node's accusation is zero if the trustworthiness of the node is the minimum possible value (i.e., the node receives the maximum number of accusations from peers) and the node made the maximum number of accusations that is allowed at the same time. All accusations are frequently broadcasted throughout the entire network. Moreover, the newly joining nodes will receive the signed profile tables of the existing members of the MANET from peers in order to obtain the up-to-date information about the behavior profile of other nodes. The certificate of a node is revoked when the sum of the weighted accusations against the node is equal to or greater than a configurable threshold (revocation quotient). Their scheme does not need the time synchronization and any access to on-line CAs after each node gets the certificate from an off-line CA during network initialization. Furthermore, one-way hash chain is employed to provide the authentication of the data origins and the integrity check of massages. Crépeau *et al.*'s key revocation scheme uses the idea from game theory very tactfully and provides a strong protection against certificates being wrongfully revoked through false accusations attacks from malicious nodes. However their scheme also has the following disadvantages: (i) Broadcasting accusations to the entire network introduces tremendous communication overhead; (ii) Using $\mu$TESLA-based techniques [30] to authenticate accusations is vulnerable to denial-of-service attacks [27]; (iii) The newly joining nodes need to verify a large amount of profile tables received from peers, which means that these nodes should have sufficient computational and power resources.

In Ref. 12, Hoeper and Gong presented self-organized key revocation and key renew schemes for MANETs. These schemes are further analyzed in Ref. 11. The authors introduced a new format involving node's identity, key expiry date, and key version number for ID-based public keys such that new keys can be issued for the same identity after the previous key has been revoked. In their revocation scheme, each node uses a neighborhood watch mechanism to monitor nodes within its communication range. Upon detection of malicious behavior, these observations are then securely propagated to an $m$-hop neighborhood ($m$ denotes the range of the accusation propagation) using the pre-shared secret key obtained from a non-interactive ID-based key agreement protocol. Furthermore, when a node realizes that its private key has been compromised, the node will generate a harakiri message and propagate this message to all its $m$-hop neighbors. Node $A$ will consider node $B$'s public key as revoked if at least one of the following three conditions is true: (i) $A$ observes the malicious behavior of $B$ through the neighborhood watch; (ii) $A$ receives a harakiri message from $B$ declaring that its private key has been compromised; (iii) $A$ receives at least $\delta$ accusations against $B$ from trustworthy nodes within node $A$'s $m$-hop neighborhood, where $\delta$ is a predetermined revocation threshold. The authors also used the majority vote with parameter $\varepsilon$ to mitigate the influence of false accusation attacks from colluding $l$-hop neighbors ($2 \leq l \leq m$). In addition, newly joining nodes can simply join the network and start the key revocation scheme without first verifying a large number of past accusations.

In Ref. 9, Fan and Gong noted that key revocation involves observations and interactions among nodes, and therefore is closely related to reputation and trust of nodes in the network. Moreover, the authors also noticed that some nodes may misbehave accidently (for example, a node cannot forward packages due to temporary network congestion) and last only for a short time. When a node shows this kind of accidental misbehavior, it might not mean that the node has been compromised by an attacker and it is more reasonable to keep collecting information about the behavior of this node instead of immediately characterizing it as malicious and excluding it from the network in this case. Inspired by these observations, the authors designed a self-organized key revocation scheme based on the combination of Dirichlet multinomial model [10] and IBC. Their scheme is within the framework of Bayesian data analysis. After an external trusted third party (TTP) bootstraps the MANET with IBC and classifies nodes' behavior into three categories (i.e., good behavior set, suspicious behavior set, and malicious behavior set), the Dirichlet multinomial model is employed to explicitly quantify the uncertainty about nodes' behavior with probability. Each node updates its global knowledge about key status of peers by observing neighbors' behavior and analyzing other nodes' reports. Moreover, IBC is used to secure the information transmission during interactions of nodes. Two defence lines are set to mitigate potential false statement attacks from malicious nodes. A deviation test based on the statistical pattern of reports is first used to filter out false statements to some extent. If the sender's report passes the deviation test of the receiver, Dempster-Shafer belief theory [35] is used to update the receiver's current knowledge about the behavior of the subject in question with this report. Based on the analysis of collected information, each node finally makes multilevel response. Their scheme consists of five parts: network initialization, neighborhood watch, authenticated information dissemination, filter of false statements, and multilevel response for malicious nodes. A high level description of their key revocation scheme is shown in the following Algorithm 1.

### 10.3.4. *Other Key Revocation Schemes*

In Ref. 19, Luo *et al.* proposed a certificate management scheme called **DICTATE** (**DI**stributed **C**er**T**ification **A**uthority with probabilis**T**ic fr**E**shness) for special MANETs that have intermittent connections to a mother certificate authority (mCA), which is a trusted authority connected to the backbone and known to all network nodes. Their scheme is based on the combination of an offline mCA that issues initial certificates for nodes and a number of online distributed servers

**Algorithm 1** Self-Organized Key Revocation for MANETs

**Step 1.** Network Initialization
- ▷ Generation of system parameters
- ▷ Registration of network nodes
- ▷ Classification of node behavior

**Step 2.** Neighborhood Watch
- ▷ Monitor neighbors' behavior and generate observation matrix
- ▷ Update key status of nodes with direct observations

**Step 3.** Authenticated Information Dissemination
- ▷ Disseminate nodes' direct observations to all $m$-hop neighbors in an authenticated way by using a keyed-hash function

**Step 4.** Filter of False Statements
- ▷ Filter out potentially false statements statistically
- ▷ Update key status of nodes based on Dempster-Shafer theory

**Step 5.** Multilevel Response for Malicious Nodes
- ▷ Revoke keys of nodes showing malicious behavior
- ▷ Cease communication with nodes showing suspicious behavior and keep observing their behavior for further decision

(dCAs) that process certificate update and query requests. To prevent the key compromises, the scheme requires nodes' certificates to be updated periodically. Otherwise the certificates will become invalid. Periodically, there is a check time, at which the dCAs (physically) go back to the mCA for purgation (only distributed CA servers should go through this procedure and clients can still perform their remote operations). During the check time, the mCA, through out-of-band mechanisms, detects compromised servers and has them reinitiated or substituted by new ones. It also refreshes the secret shared among the dCAs.

In Ref. 6, Clulow and Moore introduced the concept of the suicide for solving the problem of the credential revocation in self-organizing systems for the first time. Their work is further extended and analyzed in Ref. 24. The basic idea of the suicide attack is extremely simple: a node who observes another node's malicious behavior simply broadcasts a signed message to the entire network and claims both of them to be dead. Therefore, a good node that unilaterally removes a malicious node from MANETs sacrifices its own participation in the future network operations as well. This radical strategy can fast isolate the malicious nodes from the network and is ideally suited to highly mobile networks or special-purpose MANETs, for example those deployed in a military battlefield, in which all entities belong to a group and have the common benefits and goals. The suicide protocol is fully self-organized and incurs the low communication and storage overhead. The authors also described possible implementations and proposed various countermeasures to mitigate the abuse of this mechanism. More specifically, when a centralized trusted authority is available, it will broadcast the suicide note received from an accuser to the entire network. If there is no trusted authority in MANETs but nodes are capable of performing asymmetric primitives, an accuser will broadcast its signed suicide node accompanied with its public key certificate. To mitigate the abuse of the suicide mechanism, the authors also suggested that accusers attach a timestamp for their suicide nodes in order to resolve potential conflicts. Furthermore, each node should wait a long enough period for duplicate suicide notes and only accept the one with the earliest timestamp.

Besides the suicide attacks, Moore *et al.* also proposed reelection-based key revocation schemes for relatively static MANETs. Reelection is in fact a kind of access control mechanism in which good nodes collaborate to periodically renew their own membership. If a malicious node cannot update its network access token, it will be evicted from the network automatically. The authors describe two implementation options of the reelection protocol. The first one is based on the combination of threshold secret sharing and one-way hash chain techniques. Prior to the deployment, an external authority uses an one-way use to demonstrate their membership in each time period. For each node, the authority then distributes the shares of its network tokens, and the anchor of the hash chain to all its neighbors. Hash tree based authentication mechanism is employed by each node to verify the received shares from its neighbors. The network access token of a malicious node will be automatically revoked when a number of its neighbors delete the stored shares of that token. Another way to implement the reelection is to use the buddy list. The basic idea is that each node periodically and locally broadcasts a buddy list of its approved neighbors, and the receivers cross-reference these lists to determine whether to trust a node or not. A $\mu$TESLA-like broadcast authentication mechanism is used for nodes to authenticate received buddy lists.

## 10.4. Key Revocation Schemes in VANETs

Vehicular ad hoc network is a quite new paradigm of ad hoc networking as well as a highly successful specialization of pure general-purpose MANETs. Most existing works on vehicular network security have proposed the use of a PKI and digital signatures to provide various security services [28,31,32]. The security issues are mainly covered in the second part of the IEEE 1609 WAVE (*Wireless Access in Vehicular Environments*) communication standards that employ the *Dedicated Short Range Communications* (DSRC) protocols and IEEE 802.11p for wireless communication in vehicular environments [14]. The IEEE 1069.2 Draft Standard mainly describes a PKI based approach employing elliptic curve cryptography (ECC) for securing VANETs. It has also mentioned to use the distribution of CRLs and short-lived certificates for the purpose of certificate revocation without elaborating the details and providing a complete solution. Only a few key revocation schemes have been proposed in the literature and we will give a detailed review of these schemes in this section.

### 10.4.1. *System Models of VANETs*

In this subsection, we describe the system model and adversary model for VANETs. These models determine the design rationale for key revocation in VANETs.

#### 10.4.1.1. *System model*

In VANETs, CAs (e.g., automotive authorities in cities) are responsible for the registration and management of identities and credentials for all vehicles. Each vehicle has a unique identity and a public/private key pair. Furthermore, CAs will also equip a public key certificate to each vehicle. According to DSRC, each vehicle on the road broadcasts a traffic safety message every 300 ms, which include the current status of the vehicle such as position, speed, direction, acceleration/deceleration, and traffic events, etc. Routine traffic safety messages are only broadcasted to all neighboring vehicles or to limited regions of the network. Moreover, vehicles also send emergent messages when any abnormal situation or accident happens, such as traffic jam, emergent braking and car collision. These emergent messages will be transmitted to other vehicles in a multi-hop fashion. Vehicles have sufficient computation and power resources and therefore can perform asymmetric primitives. All messages are singed and accompanied by the senders' certificates. When messages are transmitted through a multi-hop path, the position information and timestamp of the last relying node will also be included in the messages. The vehicles will determine whether the received messages should be discard based on the following factors: (i) The time that the messages are received; (ii) The positions of the senders; and (iii) The authenticity and integrity of the messages. Besides vehicles, VANETs also include RSUs which work as the gateway to deliver data between CAs and vehicles. The RSUs are connected to CAs through secure wireline links and deployed in some critical sections of the road. The lack of an omnipresent RSU implies that CAs are not available at all times.

At the date link layer, the DSRC protocol defines typical data transmission ranges (300 to 1000 m) and rates (6 to 27 Mps) in VANETs. Furthermore, VANETs can also take advantage of alternative networks such as cellular and WiMAX to carry traffic information. Another common assumption in VANETs is that each vehicle is equipped with a Tamper Proof Device (TPD) or a Trusted Platform Module (TPM) which stores all cryptographic keys and performs all cryptographic algorithms.

#### 10.4.1.2. *Adversary model*

In VANETs, a large amount of safety-related information is transmitted almost all the time. These life-critical information is therefore the main target of adversaries.

In VANETs, attackers can disseminate false information to affect the behavior of other drivers. Adversaries can also try to control the sensory inputs and incoming safety-related information. Furthermore, it is also possible that attackers launch denial-of-service attacks, such as channel jamming, or injection of dummy messages. Similar to the case of MANETs, in the context of key revocation, adversaries intend to revoke keys of well-behaving vehicles by mounting false accusation attacks independently or collaboratively.

### 10.4.2. *Certificate Revocation Based on Weighted Voting*

In Ref. 33, Raya *et al.* introduced the following two certification revocation protocols for VANETs:

- *Revocation of the Trusted Component (RTC)*: in this protocol, the CA revokes all cryptographic keys of a vehicle by sending a signed revocation message. Other VANET users do not participate in this procedure. After receiving the revocation message, the trusted component in a vehicle will erase all keys, sends an acknowledgement to the CA, and stops signing messages. As a result, this vehicle cannot generate any valid message.
- *Revocation using Compressed Certificate Revocation List ($RC^2RL$)*: this protocol is used if the CA does not receive an acknowledgement from the trusted component or if a subset of keys need to be revoked. In this scheme, the CA generates compressed CRLs based on the Bloom Filter techniques [3], and then distributes the compressed CRLs into the VANETs through one of available channels. After receiving a message, the receiver will use the compressed CRLs to check if the sender's certificate is still valid. Using the compressed CRLs efficiently reduces the size of traditional CRLs as well as keeps false revocations within acceptable error margins.

Furthermore, when the updated revocation information is not available temporarily, the authors also described how to use a localized **MDS** (**M**isbehavior **D**etection **S**ystem) and the **LEAVE** (**L**ocal **E**viction of **A**ttackers by **V**oting **E**valuators) protocol to detect misbehaving and faulty nodes and finally evict them from VANETs. Vehicles use MDS to detect various malicious behavior of their neighbors. If a vehicle observes misbehavior it will broadcast a warning message to all its neighbors. Any vehicle receiving the warning message adds the suspect device to an accusation list. Once enough accusations against a vehicle is collected, it will be locally revoked by LEAVE and a disregard message will also be broadcasted to inform all the neighbors of the adversary to ignore its message. Finally, each vehicle reports its opinion about other nodes' behavior to the CA when in reach of RSUs. Based on the analysis of all the reports, the CA will determine the status of certificate of each vehicle. The design of LEAVE also borrows the idea of the weighted accusation scheme proposed in Refs. 2 and 7 (see Subsection 1.3.3). Furthermore, LEAVE also requires an honest majority in the attacker's neighborhood to thwart false accusation attacks and guarantee the security of the weighted accusation scheme.

### 10.4.3. *Certificate Revocation Based on Suicide Attack*

In Ref. 25, Moore *et al.* showed how to adapt the suicide attack, originally proposed for key revocation in MANETs [24] (see subsection 1.3.4), to VANETs. The authors presented a new protocol, called **Stinger**, to fast isolate the misbehaving and faulty nodes from VANETs. In Stinger, a vehicle can unilaterally remove a suspect neighbor by limiting its own participation. More specifically, if a vehicle $A$ observed that its neighbor $B$ is misbehaving, $A$ will broadcast a singed sting (i.e., suicide node) to all its neighbors for a few times and inform them to ignore messages from both $A$ and $B$. Different from the suicide protocol in MANETs, although messages from $A$ and $B$ will be ignored by other vehicles, Stinger still allows both vehicle to continue receiving and relaying messages, which minimizes the influence that the suicide attack has on a well-behaving vehicle. Given the extremely large scale and numerous network entities of VANETs, Stinger only allows that the singed stings are locally broadcasted for a few times. Therefore, multiple well-behaving vehicles might sacrifice themselves in order to exclude a single adversary. However, this impact is limited and localized, and no single vehicle will ignore two well-behaving ones for the same errant device by checking a local blacklist. Furthermore, in order to thwart the mobile adversaries, Stinger also permits well-behaving vehicles to continue accusing malicious ones even after they have issue one sting. By extensive simulations, the authors compare the security and performance of Stinger and LEAVE (see subsection 1.4.2) in great detail. Their simulations show the following complementary properties of Stinger and LEAVE in both security and performance: (i) Stinger is significantly faster than LEAVE at excluding misbehaving vehicles, but using LEAVE can provide more precise analysis about vehicles' behavior than using Stinger when an adversary abuses the exclusion mechanism; and (ii) Stinger scales better than LEAVE with the increase of the vehicle density, whereas LEAVE is more resilient to false positive rates than Stinger. Based on their simulation results, the authors proposed a hybrid mechanism by balancing the security and performance properties of Stinger and LEAVE.

### 10.4.4. *RSU-Aided Certificate Revocation*

In Ref. 18, Lin *et al.* introduced a RSU-aided certification revocation scheme for VANETs. The authors noted that it is infeasible for each vehicle to obtain the timely certificate revocation information due to the extremely large amount of vehicles in VANETs. Therefore, the authors proposed to use RSUs to assist the dissemination of the revocation information. More specifically, once RSUs obtain the updated certification revocation information from the CA, they will verify validity of certificates of all passing vehicles. If an invalid certificate is found,

RSUs will broadcast a singed warning message to all the approaching vehicles. Hence, these vehicles can update their CRLs and cease the communication with the compromised vehicle. Furthermore, the vehicles receiving updated revocation information also forward this message to others. To thwart the silent attack from a compromised vehicle, the authors also suggested that passing vehicles ask RSUs to sign their certificates. This certificate revocation scheme efficiently uses the existing infrastructure in VANETs and provides an effective way to disseminate the revocation information. However, since the distribution of the RSUs is sparse, there might be a window of vulnerability before the passing vehicles receive the warning messages from the RSUs.

## 10.5. Conclusions

Key revocation is a critical issue for the security and robustness of MANETs, which has been addressed through various mechanisms proposed in the literature. This chapter provides an overview of these techniques, each of which has advantages and disadvantages and suited to specific applications. The salient characteristics of MANETs and VANETs determine the requirements that a well-designed key revocation scheme should satisfy. For general-purpose MANETs, a flexible, efficient and self-organized key revocation scheme is desirable. However, in life-critical VANETs, false safety messages and forged emergent messages should be fast identified and malicious vehicles should be isolated from the network immediately. The efficiency of key revocation is more important than its accuracy in VANET applications. The study of key revocation in general-purpose and specialized MANETs still provides a lot of research opportunities in the future and more schemes should be designed by making efficient use of available network resources as well as keeping in mind the requirements of different network models and application scenarios. Furthermore, how to efficiently detect and identify compromised nodes is another important issue need to be further studied because of its significant influence on the accuracy of existing key revocation schemes.

## References

[1] F. Anjum and P. Mouchtaris, *Security for Wireless Ad Hoc Networks*, John Wiley & Sons, Inc., Hoboken, New Jersey, 2007.

[2] G. Arboit, C. Crépeau, C. R. Davis, and M. Maheswaran, A Localized Certificate Revocation Scheme for Mobile Ad Hoc Networks, *Ad Hoc Network*, **6**(1), 17–31, 2008.

[3] B. Bloom. Space/Time Trade-Offs in Hash Coding with Allowable Errors, *Communications of the ACM*, **13**(7), 422–426, 1970.

[4] L. Buttyán and J.-P. Hubaux, *Security and Cooperation in Wireless Networks*, Cambridge University Press, 2007.

[5] S. Capkun, L. Buttyán, and J.-P. Hubaux, Self-Organized Public-Key Management for Mobile Ad Hoc Networks. *IEEE Transactions on Mobile Computing*, **2**(1), 52–64, 2003.

[6] J. Clulow and T. Moore, Suicide for the Common Good: A New Strategy for Credential Revocation in Self-Organizing Systems, *SIGOPS Operating System Reviews*, **40**(3), 18–21, 2006.
[7] C. Crépeau and C. R. Davis, A Certificate Revocation Scheme for Wireless Ad Hoc Networks, *Proceedings of the 1st ACM Workshop on Security of Ad Hoc and Sensor Networks (SASN'03)*, pp. 54–61, 2003.
[8] J. Douceur, The Sybil Attack, *Proceedings of the 1st International Workshop on Peer-to-Peer Systems (IPTPS'02)*, pp. 251–260, 2002.
[9] X. Fan and G. Gong, Key Revocation Based on Dirichlet Multinomial Model for Mobile Ad Hoc Networks, *Centre for Applied Cryptographic Research (CACR) Technical Reports*, CACR 2008-05, available at `http://www.cacr.math.uwaterloo.ca/techreports/2008/cacr2008-05.pdf`.
[10] A. Gelman, J.B. Carlin, H.S. Stern, and D.B. Rubin, *Bayesian Data Analysis, Second Edition*, Boca Raton, Florida, USA: Chapman & Hall/CRC, 2004.
[11] K. Hoeper, *Authentication and Key Exchange in Mobile Ad Hoc Networks*, Ph.D. thesis, Department of Electrical and Computer Engineering, University of Waterloo, Waterloo, Canada, 2007.
[12] K. Hoeper and G. Gong, Key Revocation for Identity-Based Schemes in Mobile Ad Hoc Networks, *Proceedings of the 5th International Conference on Ad-Hoc, Mobile, and Wireless Networks (ADHOC-NOW 2006)*, ser. LNCS 4104, pp. 224–237, 2006.
[13] R. Housley, W. Polk, W. Ford, and D. Solo, Internet X.509 Public Key Infrastructure Certificate and Certificate Revocation List (CRL) Profile. RFC 3280, 2002.
[14] IEEE P1609.2 Version 1. Standard for Wireless Access in Vehicular Environments — Security Services for Applications and Management Messages, 2006.
[15] D.B. Johnson and D. A. Maltz, Dynamic Source Routing in Ad Hoc Wireless Networks, *Mobile Computing*, Vol. 353, chapter 5, pp. 153–181, Kluwer Academic Publishers, 1996.
[16] P.C. Kocher, On Certificate Revocation and Validation, *Proceedings of the 2nd International Conference on Financial Cryptography (FC'98)*, pp. 172–177, 1998.
[17] J. Kong, P. Zerfos, H. Luo, S. Lu, and L. Zhang, Providing Robust and Ubiquitous Security Support for Mobile Ad Hoc Networks, *Proceedings of the 9th International Conference on Network Protocols (ICNP'01)*, pp. 251–260, 2001.
[18] X. Lin, R. Lu, C. Zhang, H. Zhu, P.-H. Ho, and X. Shen, Security in Vehicular Ad Hoc Networks. *IEEE Communications Magazine*, **46**(4), 88–95, 2008.
[19] J. Luo, J.-P. Hubaux, and P.T. Eugster. DICTATE: Distributed CerTification Authority with probabilisTic frEshness for Ad Hoc Networks. *IEEE Transactions on Dependable and Secure Computing*, **2**(4), 311–323, 2005.
[20] H. Luo, J. Kong, P. Zerfos, S. Lu, and L. Zhang, URSA: Ubiquitous and Roubust Access Control for Mobile Ad Hoc Networks. *IEEE/ACM Transactions on Networking*, **12**(6), 1049–1063, 2004.
[21] A. Malpani, S. Galperin, M. Myers, R. Ankney, and C. Adams, X.509 Internet Public Key Infrastructure Online Certificate Status Protocol — OCSP. RFC 2560, 1999.
[22] S. Micali, Efficient Certificate Revocation. Technical Memo MIT/LCS/TM-542b, Massachusetts Institute of Technology, Laboratory for Computer Science, March 1996.
[23] A. Mishra, K. Nadkarni, and A. Patcha, Intrusion Detection in Wireless Ad Hoc Networks, *IEEE Wireless Communication*, **11**(1), 48–60, Feb. 2004.
[24] T. Moore, J. Clulow, R. Anderson, and S. Nagaraja, New Strategies for Revocation in Ad Hoc Networks, *Proceedings of the Fourth European Workshop on Security and Privacy in Ad Hoc and Sensor Networks (ESAS 2007)*, ser. LNCS 4572, pp. 232–246, 2007.

[25] T. Moore, M. Raya, J. Clulow, P. Papadimitratos, R. Anderson, and J.-P. Hubaux, Fast Exclusion of Errant Devices From Vehicular Networks, to appear in *Proceedings Fifth Annual IEEE Communications Society Conference on Sensor, Mesh and Ad Hoc Communications and Networks (SECON 2008)*, 2008.

[26] M. Naor and K. Nissim, Certificate Revocation and Certificate Update, *Proceedings of the 7th USENIX Security Symposium*, San Antonio, Texas, Jan 1998.

[27] P. Ning, A. Liu, and W. Du, Mitigating DoS Attacks against Broadcast Authentication in Wireless Sensor Networks, *ACM Transactions on Sensor Networks*, **4**(1), 1–35, January 2008.

[28] B. Parno and A. Perrig, Challenges in Securing Vehicular Networks, *Proceedings of the Fourth Workshop on Hot Topics in Networks (HotNets-IV)*, 2005.

[29] C. E. Perkins, E. M. Royer, and S.R. Das, Ad Hoc On Demand Vector (AODV) Routing, *IETF Internet Draft*, Internet Draft (draft-ietf-manet-aodv-09.txt), November 2001, Work in Progress.

[30] A. Perrig, The BiBa One-time Signature and Broadcast Authentication, *Proceedings of the ACM Conference on Computer and Communications Security*, pp. 28–37, 2001.

[31] M. Raya and J.-P. Hubaux, The Security of Vehicular Ad Hoc Networks, *Proceedings of the 3rd ACM Workshop on Security of Ad Hoc and Sensor Networks (SASN 2005)*, pp. 11–21, 2005.

[32] M. Raya and J.-P. Hubaux, Securing Vehicular Ad Hoc Networks, *Journal of Computer Security, Special Issue on Security of Ad Hoc and Sensor Networks*, **15**(1), 39–68, 2007.

[33] M. Raya, P. Papadimitratos, I. Aad, D. Jungels, and J.-P. Hubaux, Eviction of Misbehaving and Faulty Nodes in Vehicular Networks, *IEEE Journal on Selected Areas in Communication*, **25**(8), 1557–1568, 2007.

[34] N. Saxena, G. Tsudik, and J.H. Yi. Identity-Based Access Control for Ad Hoc Groups, *Proceedings of the 7th International Conference on Information Security and Cryptology (ICISC 2004)*, ser. LNCS 3506, pp. 362–379, 2004.

[35] G. Shafer, *A Mathematical Theory of Evidence*, Princeton University, 1976.

[36] A. Shamir, How to Share a Secret, *Communications of the ACM*, **22**(11), 612–613, 1979.

[37] S. Yi and R. Kravets, MOCA: Mobile Certificate Authority for Wireless Ad Hoc Networks, *Proceedings of the 2nd Annual PKI Research Workshop (PKI'03)*, pp. 65–79, 2003.

[38] Y. Zhang, W. Liu, W. Lou, and Y. Fang, Securing Mobile Ad Hoc Networks with Certificateless Public Keys, *IEEE Transactions on Dependable and Secure Computing*, **3**(4), 386–399, 2006.

[39] L. Zhou and Z.J. Hass, Securing Ad Hoc Networks, *IEEE Networks Special Issue on Network Security*, **13**(6), 24–30, 1999.

[40] P. Zimmermann, *The Official PGP User's Guide*, MIT Press, 1995.

# Part IV: Malware

# Chapter 11

## HARDWARE CONTROLLED SYSTEMATIC APPROACH TO DETECT AND PREVENT VIRUS

Meikang Qiu* and Jiande Wu†
*Department of Electrical Engineering,*
*University of New Orleans, New Orleans, LA 70148*
**mqiu@uno.edu*
*†jwu3@uno.edu*

Hung-Chung Huang
*Dept. of Sys. Bio. and Trans. Med.,*
*Texas A&M Health Science Center, Temple, TX 76504, USA*
*hc.jhuang@tamu.edu*

Wenyuan Li
*Dept. of Molec. and Compu. Bio.,*
*University of Southern California*
*wel@usc.edu*

The advent of Internet and mobile devices imposes great challenges for anti-virus and security of computer system. The main problem of the current signature-based anti-virus approaches is that they are based on a passive strategy. This paper reports a active detection and prevention systematic approach in anti-virus. We let user-end computer systems play more active role in protecting themselves and use independent signature-based scanner to heuristically check the signature of system to detect virus. Combined with Digital Immune System, this systematic approach shows great advantages. A controlled experiment has been carried out to identify the pros and cons of our method. The results show that based on our strategy, our method can be a practical solution for computer system against virus.

### 11.1. Introduction

Virus attacks escalated dramatically in these years. In this paper, virus is used to denote any malicious software such as virus, worm, Trojan, etc. According to the statistics by the Computer Emergency Response Team Coordination Center (CERT/CC), 114,855 security incidents were reported in the first three quarters of 2003 while the total number of incidents is \$182,463 from 1988 to 2002. Despite the best efforts of the anti-virus industry, viruses (include worms) infect millions of computers and cost businesses billions of dollars in lost productivity, wasted hours, computer repair, and data recovery. For example, the damages from the MS Blaster and Sobig.F worms in August 2003 alone, were estimated to be at least $500 million and from $500 million to more than one billion dollars, respectively [1].

While it takes more time to find solutions for viruses using the current signature-based anti-virus approaches, viruses are spreading faster. For example, after 24 hours, the MS Blaster worm infected 336,000 computers [2] and the Sobig.F worm produced over 1 million copies [3]. These facts show that using the signature-based anti-virus techniques only can not effectively protect computers from virus attacks any more.

A computer virus is a computer program that can copy itself and infect a computer without permission or knowledge of the user. The term "virus" is also commonly used, albeit erroneously, to refer to many different types of malware and adware programs. The original virus may modify the copies, or the copies may modify themselves, as occurs in a metamorphic virus. A virus can only spread from one computer to another when its host is taken to the uninfected computer, for instance by a user sending it over a network or the Internet, or by carrying it on a removable medium such as a floppy disk, CD, or USB drive. Meanwhile viruses can spread to other computers by infecting files on a network file system or a file system that is accessed by another computer [4].

There are several anti-virus approaches [5]: The ideal solution to the threat of viruses is prevention: Do not allow a virus to get into the system in the first place. But this is impossible to achieve. The next best approach is Detection-Identification-Removal method. When identification or removal is not possible, then discard the infected program and reload a clean backup version.

People usually install anti-virus software that can detect and eliminate known viruses after the computer downloads or runs the executable. There are two common methods that an anti-virus software application uses to detect viruses [4].

- By far the most common method of virus detection is using a list of virus signature definitions. This works by examining the content of the computer's memory (its RAM, and boot sectors) and the files stored on fixed or removable drives (hard drives, floppy drives), and comparing those files against a database of known virus "signatures". The disadvantage of this detection method is that users are only protected from viruses that pre-date their last virus definition update.
- The second method is to use a heuristic algorithm to find viruses based on common behaviors. This method has the ability to detect viruses that anti-virus security firms have yet to create a signature for.

Some anti-virus programs are able to scan opened files in addition to sent and received e-mails 'on the fly' in a similar manner. This practice is known as "on-access scanning." Anti-virus software does not change the underlying capability of host software to transmit viruses. Users must update their software regularly to patch security holes. Anti-virus software also needs to be regularly updated in order to prevent the latest threats [4].

Intrusion detection has been studied for at least two decades since the Anderson's report [6]. Intrusion-detection systems (IDSs) have been deployed more and more widely along with intrusion-prevention techniques such as password authentication and firewalls.

Intrusion-detection techniques can be classified into two categories: *misuse detection* and *anomaly detection.*

- *Misuse detection*: looks for known attacks' signatures, that is, the explicit patterns, and any matched activity is considered an attack. Misuse detection can detect known attacks effectively, though it usually cannot accommodate unknown attacks.
- *Anomaly detection*: models the subject's behaviors, and any significant deviation from the normal behaviors is considered the result of an attack. Anomaly detection has the potential to detect unknown attacks; however, it is not as effective as misuse detection for known attacks. In practice, misuse detection and anomaly detection are often used as complementary components in IDSs.

Each anti-virus approach solves the real problem in different angles and has its pros and cons. Our approach is based on the following two observations:

**Observation 1:** *In spite of numerous intrusion detection techniques, it is impossible to completely prevent viruses from entering a computer system.*

There are four generations of anti-virus software [5]:

- *Simple scanners:* use virus signature to identify a virus.
- *Heuristic scanners:* search for probable virus infection or integrity checking.
- *Activity traps:* only to identify the small set of actions rather than its structure in an infected program.
- *Full-featured protection:* combine all three above.

From this observation, it is impractical to find and patch every security hole in a large computer system. A virus is always possible to enter a system and cause damages during the time period between the initial detection and the download of a signature. The main problem of the current signature-based anti-virus approaches is that they are based on a passive strategy [7]. A signature specifies a generic pattern of a certain type of attack, which is usually independent of any specific system.

In traditional anti-malicious executable detection methods, the suspicious program needs to be examined and a signature extracted from it and included in the anti-malicious executable software database. Typically, using these approaches, we wait for the occurrence of a virus, and then identify the pattern of the virus and produce a signature and solution of the virus. Then users can download the signature and solution to scan and clean the virus. And this signature is used to prevent the further entering of the virus. Taking advantage of the time period between initial detection and the production of a signature, a virus has a lot of time to propagate and can cause a huge damage before a user downloads the signature. To make things worse, viruses start to deploy schemes to counteract these anti-virus approaches. For example, polymorphic virus has been created in such a way that each copy of a polymorphic virus has different bit patterns.

Therefore, it is more difficult and need more time to identify and produce a signature for this kind of viruses. Viruses can also cut off the channel to make an update fail as the MS Blaster worm does: it uses Denial of Services (DoS) to shutdown Microsoft Update Web site and causes a lot of troubles for users to download the update patches.

To solve these problems, our technique focuses on the protection in this time period between the initial detection and the download of a signature. we need to let user-end computer systems play more active role in protecting themselves. In this paper, we address this issue from hardware and software co-design and propose a signature-based system model to protect the internal of a computer and prevent the infection of a virus in the first place. Our basic idea is to protect the files in a computer from system level by secured hardware component and dynamic checking, hence a system is able to detect the infection in the first place and protect themselves from attacks. Combined this active user-end detection and prevention with Digital Immune System, then the damages caused by a virus during this time period can be effectively reduced.

**Observation 2:** *While the current signature-based anti-virus approaches have a lot of limitations, in order to completely kill a virus, we still need them to produce a systematic solution.*

The Digital Immune System [8,9] is an advanced anti-virus approach. The objective of this system is to provide rapid response time so that viruses can be stamped out almost as soon as they are introduced. When any program thought to be infected, the administrative machine encrypts the sample and sends it to a central virus analysis machine to produces a prescription for identifying and removing the virus.

Thus, the need for a more comprehensive approach to security is increasing [10]. Any single protection mechanism is likely vulnerable to some class of intrusions. For example, relying on a protection mechanism that is designed for known types of intrusion implies vulnerability to novel intrusion methods. It is our belief that a multi-faceted approach is most appropriate, in which, similar to natural immune systems, both specific and non-specific protection mechanisms play a role.

We combined the hardware controlled anti-virus user-end approach with traditional Digital Immune System [8,9] together. We use a secure channel to connect with secure company to get prescription and share information. Like human immune system, the local end users have certain ability to solve their problem locally by themselves. When they meet a big problem and can not solve themselves, they will alter the secure company, ask help and if necessary to notify the whole network.

The following section describes the design and rationale of our approach in more detail. Section 11.2 describes the active detection and prevention approach. Section 11.3 explains the systematic anti-virus solution. With a controlled experiment, Section 11.4 tested aforementioned approach and compare it with previous work. Related work is described in Section 11.5. Finally, Section 11.6 draws conclusions and outlines future work.

## 11.2. Active Detection and Prevention Approach

### 11.2.1. *Signature-Based Anti-Virus Technique*

Current virus scanner technology has two parts: a signature-based detector and a heuristic classifier that detects new viruses [11]. The classic signature-based detection algorithm relies on signatures, that is, unique telltale strings, of known malicious executables to generate detection models. Signature-based methods create a unique tag for each malicious program so that future examples of it can be correctly classified with a small error rate.

These methods do not generalize well to detect new malicious binaries because they are created to give a false positive rate as close to zero as possible. Whenever a detection method generalizes to new instances, the trade off is for a higher false positive rate. Heuristic classifiers are generated by a group of virus experts to detect new malicious programs. This kind of analysis can be time-consuming and oftentimes still fail to detect new malicious executables.

In Signature-based detection methods, these signatures are picked to differentiate one malicious executable from another, and from benign programs. These signatures are generated by an expert in the field or an automatic method. Typically, a signature is picked to illustrate the distinct properties of a specific malicious executable. A signature-based scanner was implemented with this method which follows a simple algorithm for signature generation.

First, scanner calculated the byte sequences that were only found in the malicious executable class. These byte sequences were then concatenated together to make a unique signature for each malicious executable example. Thus, each malicious executable signature contained only byte sequences found in the malicious executable class. To make the signature unique, the byte sequences found in each example were concatenated together to form one signature. This was done because a byte sequence that is only found in one class during training could possibly be found in the other class during testing, and lead to false positives in testing. This method was never intended to detect unknown malicious binaries.

This method has some limitations. For example, during the time required for a malicious program to be identified, analyzed and signatures to be distributed, systems are at risk from that program. Our approach provides a defense during that time. With a low false positive rate, the inconvenience to the end user would be minimal while providing ample defense during the time before an update of models is available.

### 11.2.2. *Hardware Controlled Scanner Anti-Virus Method*

Our approach overcomes the limitation of the signature-based anti-virus technique. In traditional heuristic scanner method, heuristic rule was used to search for probable virus infection, such as looking for fragments of code that are often associated with virus or using integrity checking. If the virus is sophisticated enough to change the checksum when it infects a program, one way to counter it is using encrypted hash function. The encryption key is stored separately from the program so that the virus cannot generate a new hash code and encrypt that. But it is impossible to completely prevent virus from entering a computer system. If a virus takes control of the root, it can decrypt the hash function or find the hash key, even more, it can delete the scanner. Then this method will not work. In our approach, the basic idea is as followings:

We have an independent signature scanner and a tool which can connect with the scanner. When the tool (dedicated program) connected with the scanner, write system signature to scanner hardware. Otherwise, the tool will detached with the scanner, hence system can not write signature to scanner hardware. We can think of the tool as an open/close gate. When put it in close state, the memory of scanner can be written. And the scanner will scan the system and store the signature to its memory. When put the gate in open state, the memory can not be written. Figure 11.1 shows the system architecture.

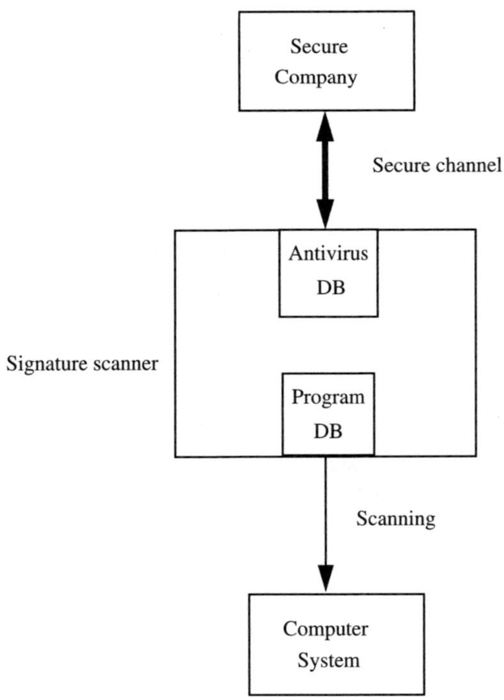


Fig. 11.1. Anti-virus system architecture.

There are two modes in this system: open mode and close mode. The virus can not control the scanner. Only the scanner can get information, that is, to scan the system while the system can not write scanner. The scanner likes a hardware which plug into the system. The tool like two kinds of mode, it can exchange from one to another. Yet in traditional scanner, the system controls the root and the scanner, which is just a kind of software. Virus can break in and control the root, such as the MS Blaster virus.

Our approach is to improve the anti-virus ability of user-end. It is a hardware controlled anti-virus approach, which greatly improved the security of system. When the scanner can not determines whether a suspicious program is a virus, the scanner use secure channel to connect the security company.

This systematic approach does automatic update as followings: First, the scanner will update its signature database as soon as it receives the information from the security company. Second, it will report abnormal behavior to whole system. User-end can detect signature of virus constantly. If user-end can determine a virus, it need not send it to secure company for help and save a lot of time. If it can not determine whether a suspicious program is malicious, then it can ask help from the security company and the company will alarm whole system.

## 11.3. Systematic Anti-Virus Solution

### 11.3.1. *Structure of Active Detection and Prevention Systematic Approach*

Digital Immune System (DIS) developed by IBM [8,9]. The motivation of the development of DIS has been the rising threat of Internet-based virus propagation. This system provides a general-purpose emulation and virus- detection system. The objective of this system is to provide rapid response time so that viruses can be stamped out almost as soon as they are introduced. When a new virus enters an organization, the immune system automatically captures it, analyzes it, adds detection and shielding for it, removes it, and pass information about that virus to systems running IBM anti-virus so that it can be detected before it is allowed to run elsewhere.

Our approach based on the Digital Immune System with an improvement of use-end anti-virus ability. Our contribution is to detect signature change before send the suspicious sample to Administrative machine to analyze.

Like the immune system of living things, we can have a way to detect damage to our body and quickly to react to it. We can quickly repair the damage and order our body to avoid intrusion again. From this nature mechanism, we design our anti-virus method. We create a signature scanner (or detector) which can keep detecting system changes. This scanner likes a co-processor whose job is to check system and guarantee security of system. The signatures stored in scanner and can not be changed. We use the signatures stored in scanner to compare with the signatures in system. If there is a difference, then the files in system have been changed and give a virus warn to system. Some hackers may try to change the signatures in scanner through cyber attack. But this cannot be done since signature can be changed only when the tool connected with the scanner, yet through cyber attack, hackers can not move the tool locally.

We use systematic approach to prescript a solution to infected system. If the user-end can not determine whether a suspicious program is viral, it can send the sample to central analyze machine and ask help from center. Combined the idea of Digital Immune System, this sample can be analyzed completely there. The analyze machine creates an environment in which the infected program can be safely run for analysis. Techniques used for this purpose include emulation, or the creation of a protected environment within which the suspect program can be executed and monitored. The virus analysis machine then produces a prescription for identifying and removing the virus.

Figure 11.2 illustrates the system structure of our approach. The flow chart of our approach is illustrated in Figure 11.3:

We summarize our approach into Algorithm 11.1.

### 11.3.2. *Implementation Issues*

One important issue in implementation is false positive. In signature-based detection, if the signatures are too narrowly defined, some attacks might not be detected, resulting in false negatives; if signatures are too broadly defined, some benign behavior might cause false positives.

In our approach, the false positive will be greatly reduced. Since the detect ability of user-end has been greatly improved, If a virus which has a signature stored in scanner database intrude, the scanner can quickly detects it and provide solution to it. Hence in this situation, the false positive will be avoided. If the scanner can not determine whether the suspicious program is virus, it will send the sample to central analyzer and wait for the conclusion of center. In this situation, the false positive probability is low, same as that of original Digital Immune System.

A critical limitation of signature-based intrusion detection is the inability to detect new viruses that do not match a known signature and might attack an unknown or unannounced vulnerability. Hence how to update the signature database quickly enough is another important issue. If a suspicious program is proved to be a virus, then the center analyzer will extract the signatures of new virus and provide solution to infected client. The database of scanner will then be updated. This update will improve the anti-virus ability of scanner in user-end.

## 11.4. Experiments

In this section, we conduct experiments with different anti-virus methods on a set of test suits. We build a simulation framework to evaluate the effectiveness of our approach. We conducted experiments on three methods: Method 1: Passive

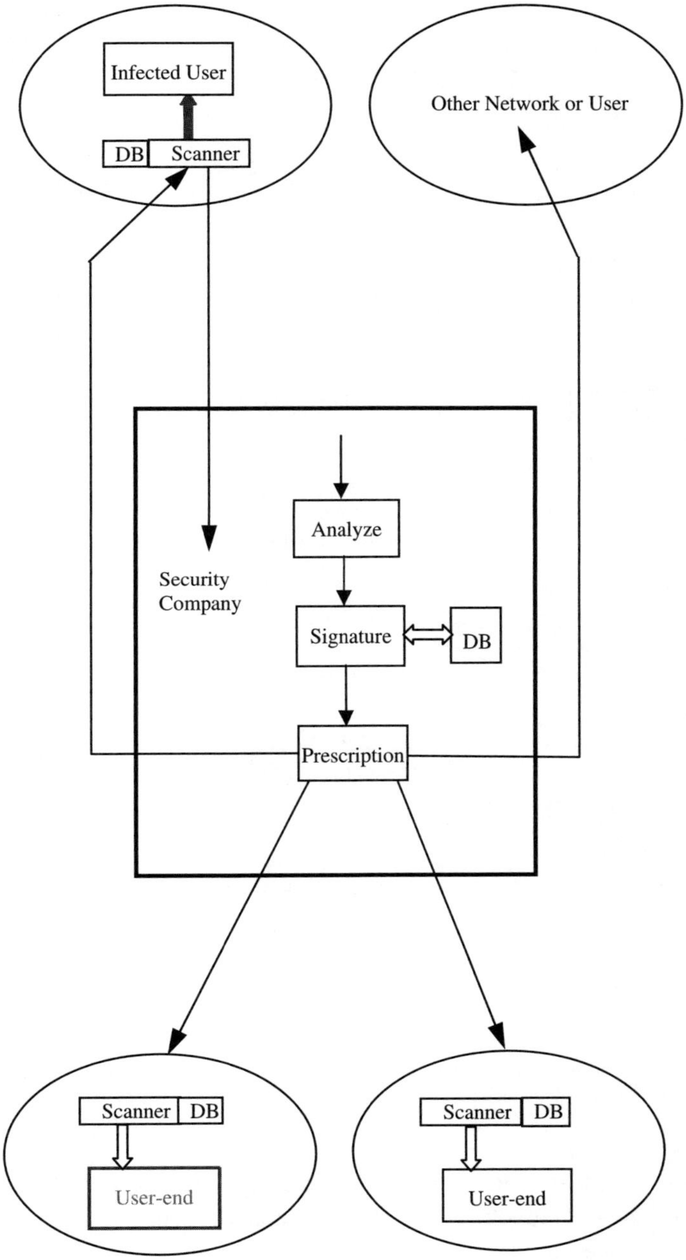


Fig. 11.2. Systematic structure of our approach.

detection and prevention method; Method 2: Hardware controlled active detection and prevention method; Method 3: Our systematic method; The experiments are performed on a Dell Optiplex GX375 with a Pentium 3.4 GHz CPU and 3.0 GB RAM running Red Hat Linux 9.0.

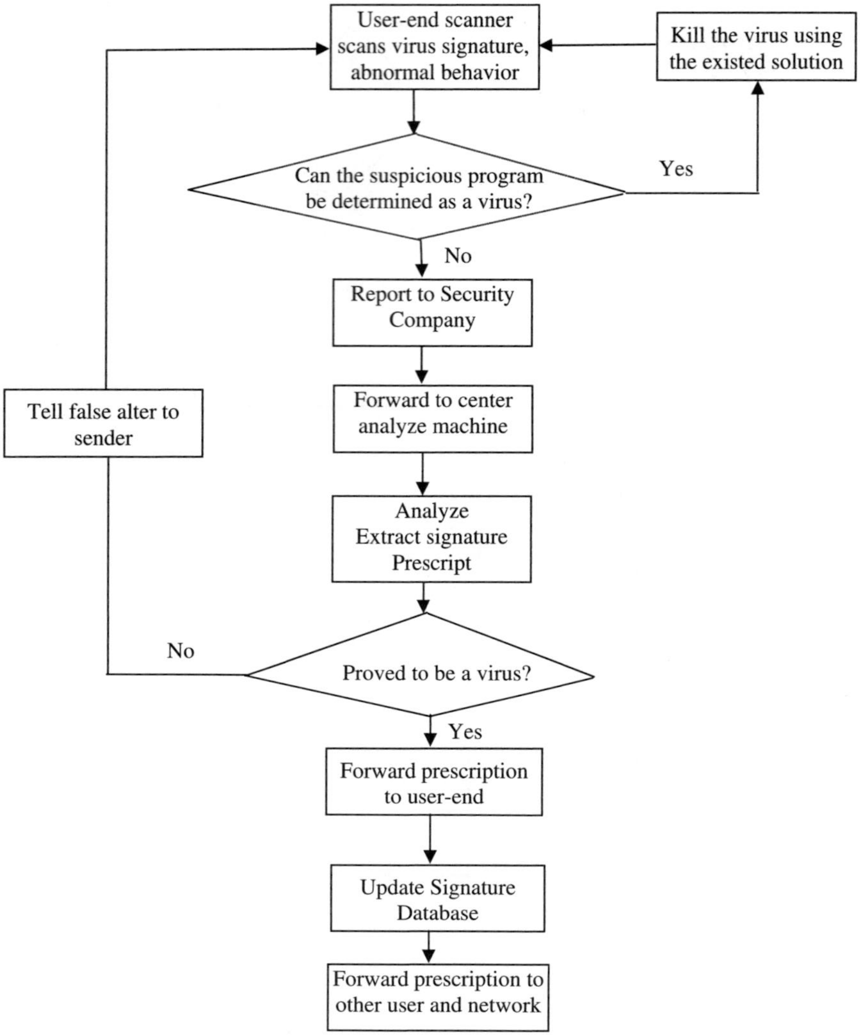


Fig. 11.3. Flow chart of active detection and prevention systematic approach.

There are four test suits used in our experiments. Each test suit represents one type of virus. We classified virus into four types according to self-description and reproductive mechanism [12]. If a virus is not afforded its self-description and reproductive mechanism by an external entity, then we classify it as "Type I" virus. A virus which is afforded either its reproductive mechanism or its self-description is either "Type II" or "Type III", respectively. A virus which is afforded both the self-description and reproductive mechanism by an external entity is "Type IV". There are four test suits, i.e., "Test 1" to "Test 4". corresponding to virus "Type I" to "Type IV".

**Algorithm 11.1** ***Systematic Anti-Virus*** **Algorithm**

**Input:** Computer system, secure company, and scanner.
**Output:** Detect and prevent viruses.

(1) A scanner on each PC uses a variety of heuristics based on system behavior, suspicious changes to programs, or family signature to infer that a virus may be present.

(2) If a scanner matches the signature of a virus with the suspicious program, the scanner will alarm the system and use prescription in its database to kill the virus.

(3) Otherwise, if a scanner can not determine whether a suspicious program is a virus, implement the following:

   (a) The scanner forwards a copy of any program thought to be infected to a security company through secure channel. This channel is encrypted by RSA and can be thought to be secure enough. The scanner encrypts the sample and sends it to the secure company.
   (b) The secure company use their virus analyze machine to analyze the sample. This machine creates an environment in which the infected program can be safely run for analysis. Techniques used for this purpose include emulation, or the creation of a protected environment within which the suspect program can be executed and monitored. The virus analysis machine then produces a prescription for identifying and removing the virus.
   (c) If the sample proved to be virus, implement the following:

      i. The resulting prescription and signature are sent back to the scanner of infected user-end machine.
      ii. The user-end will update its signature database and use the prescription kill the virus.
      iii. The prescription is also forwarded to other user-end in the system.
      iv. Subscribers around the world receive regular anti-virus updates that protect them from the new virus.

   (d) Otherwise, tell false alter to the sender. The sender will release the holder.

---

The experimental results of all our four experiments are shown in Table 11.1. "Exp." is the name of experiments. There are four test suits, from "Test 1" to "Test 4". Column "M1" to "M3" represent the three different methods that we used in these controlled experiments, i.e, "Method 1" to "Method 3". Under "Index" column, there are four different indexes: "Detect accurate", "False positive", "Detect time", and "Convenience". Column "% M1", "% M2" represents the percentage of improvement of detection accurate rate, and reduction in false positive rate and detection time of Method 3 compared to that of Method 1 and Method 2, respectively. The average percentage is shown in the last row of the table.

Table 11.1 shows that our algorithms can greatly improve detection rate and reduce the false positive rate. On average, our approach gives a detection accurate rate improvement of 24.31% comparing with Method 1, and improvement of 8.35% comparing with Method 2.

From the experimental results, we can conclude that Type I viruses are harder to detect at run-time while Type IV viruses are easier to detect. Types II and III

Table 11.1. Experimental results of 3 Methods on various test suits.

| Exp. | Index | M 1 | M 2 | M 3 | M1% | M2% |
|---|---|---|---|---|---|---|
| | Detect accurate | 76.7% | 84.5% | 90.4% | 17.86 | 6.98 |
| Test 4 | False positive | 20.5% | 17.3% | 15.7% | 23.41 | 9.25 |
| | Detect time | 9.7 S | 8.6 S | 8.2 S | 15.46 | 4.65 |
| | Convenience | normal | good | very good | | |
| | Detect accurate | 72.6% | 81.9% | 87.3% | 20.25 | 6.59 |
| Test 3 | False positive | 21.6% | 18.5% | 16.8% | 22.22 | 9.19 |
| | Detect time | 9.8 S | 8.7 S | 8.2 S | 16.33 | 5.75 |
| | Convenience | normal | good | very good | | |
| | Detect accurate | 68.5% | 78.2% | 85.1% | 24.23 | 8.82 |
| Test 2 | False positive | 23.4% | 20.5% | 18.8% | 19.66 | 8.29 |
| | Detect time | 10.1 S | 8.8 S | 8.3 S | 17.82 | 5.68 |
| | Convenience | normal | good | very good | | |
| | Detect accurate | 61.3% | 74.5% | 82.7% | 34.91 | 11.01 |
| Test 1 | False positive | 25.2% | 22.6% | 20.7% | 17.86 | 8.41 |
| | Detect time | 10.2 S | 8.9 S | 8.3 S | 18.63 | 6.74 |
| | Convenience | normal | good | very good | | |
| Average | Detect accurate | | | | 24.31 | 8.35 |
| Saving | False positive | | | | 20.79 | 8.78 |
| | Detect time | | | | 17.06 | 5.71 |

viruses are somewhere in the middle. For example, the accurate rate of our approach on test suit 1 (Type I) is 82.7%, while on test suit 4 (Type IV), it is 90.4%.

The advantages of our algorithms over the passive detection (Method 1) are summarized as follows. First, our algorithm is efficient and provides higher detection accurate rate. Second, our approach has low false positive rate compared to previous approach. Third, our detection speed is faster than previous methods. Finally, our algorithm is very convenient and practical.

## 11.5. Related Work

Several different techniques have been proposed to let systems actively protect themselves against virus attacks. In [13–17], the infection detection and automated response techniques have been developed based on ideas from immunology. In these techniques, the abnormal behaviors of a process are identified from the sequences of sys-calls. While these techniques put more focus on the dynamic status of a program (after a program runs), our technique does more on the static status (before a program runs).

The weakness of aforementioned techniques is that no matter what kind of abnormally behavior, even the user-end can determine the virus, the monitoring program will send the sample to central analyze machine, hence the precious time is lost. Yet we know in most situations, attack come from known virus. Hence the efficiency of the anti-virus system is low. Using our approach, an infected program will be detected when loading and have no chance to run. In recent work, two techniques, virus throttle [18,19] and Angel [20], have been proposed to prevent a computer from participating in network attacks based on the behavior and signature-based algorithm, respectively. The approach we take differs in that we focus on the protection of the internal of a computer.

There has been a lot of research work to use hardware to secure a system [21–31]. The concept of a secure microprocessor with bus-encryption is first introduced in [21], in which the data and addresses are encrypted /decrypted in the internal of a CPU and only encrypted values are stored in external memory. The ABYSS [22] and Ciadel [24] systems further improve the security of this architecture by introducing advanced packaging technology.

In [25], a more general architecture is introduced to support multitask operating system. In [26–28], the XOM architecture is proposed that can provide a higher level of security by implementing the secret keys and tags in the main processor. Since these techniques focuses on defend against hardware tamper and software tamper, where an attacker can physically access a system, the complicated hardware and software models need to be used. To deal with virus attacks, we can assume that an attacker can not physically access a computer. So we only need a simple hardware component that can store keys and generate the signature quickly.

Arbaugh et al. [32] proposed a secure bootstrap architecture that guarantees a secure kernel to be booted up using a "chain" inductively integrity checking with simple hardware component. Based on this secure kernel, we extend the integrity checking to the files and develop a data-block-level signature-based file system model. In our work, each data block has an encrypted signature using a key obtained from a safe hardware component. Two new system calls: signature file() and secure load(), are used to do signature assignment and integrity check for a file, respectively. Signature file() assigns the signatures to a file. And secure load() will check the integrity of a file when it is loaded.

As to virus classification, we use the method in paper [12]. Von Neumann split his automaton into two separate parts: a self-description stored on a tape (analogous to a Turing machine tape), and a reproductive mechanism. The classification of virues involves identifying the parts of the reproductive process which correspond to the self-description and reproductive mechanism. If the reproducer is not assisted in its reproductive process, i.e., if a virus does not use the disk, it will be a Type I reproducer. If a virus uses the disk for its self-description and reproductive mechanism, then this virus will be a Type IV reproducer.

## 11.6. Conclusion and Future Work

### 11.6.1. *Conclusion*

The advent of Internet and mobile devices imposes great challenges for anti-virus and security of computer system. The main problem of the current signature-based anti-virus approaches is that they are based on a passive strategy. This paper reports a new active systematic approach in anti-virus. We let user-end computer systems play more active role in protecting themselves and use hardware controlled scanner to heuristically check the signature of system to detect virus. Combined with Digital Immune System, this active approach shows great advantages. A controlled experiment has been carried out to identify the pros and cons of our method. The results show that based on our strategy, our method can be a practical solution for defending system against malicious software.

### 11.6.2. *Future Work*

We plan to conduct further studies our anti-virus approach:

- First, we will extend the application of our anti-virus approach. For example, in a secure loader system, we use DSA (Digital Signature Algorithm) method to encrypt the entry point of the executable file. Combined with our anti-virus method, the security of the computer system will be greatly improved.
- Second, we will study how to prescript using automated tools and procedures. Third, using statistical method to data mining the signature is an interested problem. We will research on the efficient way of extract signature from new virus and match them quickly and accurately.

## References

[1] A. Salkever, The ever-growing virus crisis. In *Business Week Online, http://www.businessweek.com/technology/content/aug2003/ tc20030826 4386 tc047.htm.*

[2] R. Pethia, Attacks on the internet in 2003. In *Congressional Testimony, http://usinfo.state.gov/journals/itgic/1103/ijge/gj11a.htm.*

[3] G. Law, Sobig.f breaks speed records. In *PC World, http://www.pcworld.com/news/article/0,aid,112108,00.asp.*

[4] Computer virus, *http://en.wikipedia.org/wiki/.*

[5] W. Stallings, Cryptography and network security, principles and practice, *PRENTICE HALL, 2 edition.* pp. 510–514.

[6] P. Ning, S. Jajodia, and X. Y. Wang, Abstraction-based intrusion detection in distributed environments, *ACM Transactions on Information and System Security,* **4**(4), (Nov. 2001).

[7] F. Cohen, A short course in computer viruses. In *John Wiley and Sons*, (1994).

[8] J. Kephart, G. Sorkin, D. Chess, and S. White, Fighting computer viruses, *Scientific American*, (Nov. 1997).

[9] J. Kephart, G. Sorkin, B. Swimmer, and S. White, Blueprint for a computer immune system. In *Proceedings of Virus Bulletin International Conference*, (Oct. 1997).

[10] P. D'haeseleer, S. Forrest, and P. Helman, An immunological approach to change detection: algorithms, analysis and implications, In *IEEE Symposium on Security and Privacy*, pp. 110–119, (May, 1996).

[11] M. Schultz, E. Eskin, F. Zadok, and S. J. Stolfo, Data mining methods for detection of new malicious executables. In *IEEE Symposium on Security and Privacy*, pp. 38–49, (May, 2001).

[12] M. Webster and G. Malcolm, Reproducer classification using the theory of affordances, In *Proceedings of the 2007 IEEE Symposium on Artificial Life*, pp. 115–122, (2007).

[13] S. Forrest, A. S. Perelson, L. Allen, and R. Cherukuri, Self-nonself discrimination in a computer. In *1994 IEEE Symposium on Research in Security and Privacy*, (1994).
[14] S. Forrest, S. A. Hofmeyr, A. Somayaji, and T. A. Longstaff, A sense of self for unix processes. In *1996 IEEE Symposium on Computer Security and Privac*, pp. 120–128, (1996).
[15] S. Forrest, S. Hofmeyr, and A. Somayaji, Computer immunology, *Communications of the ACM*, **40**(10), 88–96, (1997).
[16] S. A. Hofmeyr, A. Somayaji, and S. Forrest, Intrusion detection using sequences of system calls, *Journal of Computer Security*, **6**, 151–180, (1998).
[17] A. Somayaji and S. Forrest, Automated response using system-call delays, In *the 9th USENIX Security Symposium*, (2000).
[18] M. M. Williamson, Throttling viruses: Restricting propagation to defeat malicious mobile code, In *the 18th Annual Computer Security Applications Conference*, pp. 61–68, (Dec. 2002).
[19] J. Twycross and M. M. Williamson, Implementing and testing a virus throttle. In *the 12th USENIX Security Symposium*, pp. 285–294, (Aug. 2003).
[20] D. Bruschi and E. Rosti, Angel: a tool to disarm computer systems. In *New Security Paradigms Workshop*, pp. 63–69, (Sep. 2001).
[21] R. M. Best, Preventing software piracy with crypto-microprocessors. In *IEEE Spring COMPCON 80*, pp. 466–469, (Feb. 1980).
[22] S. H. Weingart, Physical security for the abyss system. In *the IEEE Computer Society Conference on Security and Privacy*, pp. 52–58, (1987).
[23] J. D. Tygar and B. Yee, Dyad: A system for using physically secure coprocessors. In *IP Workshop Proceedings*, (1994).
[24] E. R. Palmer, An introduction to citadel — a secure crypto coprocessor for workstations. In *the IFIP SEC94 Conference*, (1994).
[25] T. Gilmont, J. D. Legat, and J. J. Quisquater, An architecture of security management unit for safe hosting of multiple agents. In *the International Workshop on Intelligent Communications and Multimedia Terminals*, pp. 79–82, (Nov. 1998).
[26] D. Lie, C. Thekkath, M. Mitchell, P. Lincoln, D. Boneh, J. Mitchell, and M. Horowitz, Architectural support for copy and tamper resistant software. In *the 9th InternationalConference on Architectural Support for Programming Languages and Operating Systems*, pp. 168–177, (Nov. 2000).
[27] D. Lie, J. Mitchell, C. Thekkath, and M. Horowitz, Specifying and verifying hardware for tamper-resistant software. In *the 2003 IEEE Symposium on Security and Privacy*, (May 2003).
[28] D. Lie, C. Thekkath, and M. Horowitz, Implementing an untrusted operating system on trusted hardware. In *the 19th ACM Symposium on Operating Systems Principles*, (Oct. 2003).
[29] Z. Shao, C. Xue, Q. Zhuge, M. Qiu, B. Xiao, and E. H.-M. Sha, Security protection and checking for embedded system integration against buffer overflow attacks via hardware/software, *IEEE Trans. on Computers*, **55**(4), 443–453, (Apr., 2006).
[30] D. Serpanos and J. Henkel, Dependability and security will change embedded computing, *IEEE Computer*, **41** (1), 103–105, (Jan. 2008).
[31] S. Gueron, G. Stronqin, J. Seifert, D. Chiou, R. Sendag, and J. Yi, Where does security stand? new vulnerabilities vs. trusted computing, *IEEE Micro.*, **27**(6), 25–35, (Dec. 2007).
[32] W. Arbaugh, D. Farber, and J. Smith, A secure and reliable bootstrap architecture. In *1997 IEEE Symposium on Security and Privacy*, pp. 65–71, (May 1997).

# Chapter 12

## A MATHEMATICAL VIEW OF SELF-REPLICATING MALWARE

Thomas M. Chen
*School of Engineering*
*Swansea University, Singleton Park*
*Swansea SA2 8PP, UK*
*t.m.chen@swansea.ac.uk*

Nasir Jamil
*Dept. of Electrical Engineering*
*Southern Methodist University*
*Dallas, Texas 75275, USA*
*nasir@mail.smu.edu*

Mathematical epidemiology developed from a long history of infectious biological diseases has been applied to model the spread of self-replicating malicious software (namely viruses and worms) in computer networks. The goal of epidemiology is to understand the dynamics of outbreaks and ultimately help design effective defenses. In this chapter, we first review the simple and general homogeneous epidemic models for random scanning worms. A more sophisticated community-of-households model takes into account the effect of the network on the epidemic rate. We use the community of households model to investigate the effectiveness of rate throttling and quarantine as active defenses.

### 12.1. Introduction

An abundant variety of malicious software (malware) pervades the Internet today [1]. A personal encounter with spyware, viruses, worms, Trojan horses, bots, or other type of malware has become a common experience for most PC users. Malware is unwanted and possibly dangerous software that gets installed on an innocent computer often through stealth or deception. Malware can damage the victim computer but might operate covertly without causing any observable changes. Common uses of malware are theft of personal information (e.g., accounts, passwords, Social Security numbers) and remote control of a victim computer to send spam or denial of service attack.

Malware can be broadly classified into self-replicating or not self-replicating. Some common examples of nonself-replicating malware include: spyware designed to covertly steal personal information; Trojan horses that seem to be useful but have a hidden malicious function in their programming; bots carrying out instructions from a remote "bot herder"; and rootkits that modify a computer's operating system in order to be undetectable by usual methods.

Self-replicating malware consists mainly of viruses and worms [2]. Viruses are pieces of code attached parasitically to a normal host program or file. When the host program is executed, the virus code takes over and copies itself to more programs or files. In contrast, worms are standalone programs that seek out target computers across a network. When a vulnerable target is found, the worm copies itself to the target. Worms have become more commonplace as computer networks (namely the Internet) have become ubiquitous.

### 12.1.1. *Methods of Self Replication*

Viruses and worms have the distinct characteristic of self-replication meaning that their code contains specific functions to reproduce copies of themselves. For self-replication, their code must contain three functions to: identify new targets to infect; compromise the new target; and transfer a copy of the virus or worm code. We will discuss only worms here but the self-replication functions of viruses are similar conceptually.

Worms must first locate a new target host across the network. Since hosts have unique 32-bit IP (Internet protocol) addresses, a common method is to generate random (or actually pseudorandom) 32-bit numbers. Random IP addresses are easy to program but do not work very efficiently for three reasons. First, random probing results in targets being probed multiple times. This wasted effort might be avoided by arranging some type of coordination between the worm copies to make each worm cover a different IP address block, but the coordination effort could be complicated and a potential weakness exploitable by security experts.

Second, probed targets may not be vulnerable to the worm. For example, a worm programmed to exploit Windows95 computers may probe thousands of other hosts before finding a Windows95 host. This inefficiency might be avoided by a pre-scanning phase, where the worm author scans the IP address space and builds up a "hit list" of vulnerable hosts before the worm is released. When released, the worm attacks only the addresses on the hit list.

Third, random scanning is inefficient because a worm will be probing across the wide area network most of the time, involving delays and packet losses. Some past examples of worms have favored the same class B or C address space, meaning that the worm attempts to find hosts within the same local network most of the time because closer targets can be reached more quickly.

Another common method to identify new targets is to harvest e-mail addresses from the infected host. PCs usually have an address book and files containing e-mail addresses. The reason for harvesting e-mail addresses is because a possible trust relationship exists with these e-mail addresses. If the worm sends itself to one of these e-mail addresses, it is more likely to be accepted by the recipient.

Other common methods to find new targets include looking at the Windows network neighborhood and querying addresses from DNS (domain name system).

After a new target is identified, the target's security must be compromised. An identified target will typically have defenses, such as spam filters, access control, antivirus programs, and operating system patches (that keep the computer's software up to date). A worm must find a way through these defenses in order to infect the target with a copy of itself.

Worms are often programmed with one or more attacks for compromising a target. A common attack is an exploit of a vulnerability. A vulnerability is a security weakness in a computer's operating system or applications that allows a remote intruder to gain a level of control. Vulnerabilities are categorized according to their seriousness. The most serious vulnerabilities are critical, meaning that an intruder may possibly gain complete control. A common vulnerability is a buffer overflow, which are often critical because they allow an intruder to execute arbitrary code. An exploit is a piece of code written to take advantage of a specific vulnerability.

Another common type of attack is password cracking. Although most systems today have strong password policies, passwords may be possible to guess. Also, many systems are shipped with default administrative accounts and passwords. If the default account is left unchanged, an intruder could easily gain access.

Instead of exploits, other worms attempt social engineering attacks, essentially taking advantage of human deception. For instance, a worm could e-mail itself in a message pretending to be a Windows update or JPG image. The recipient is tricked into opening the attachment, although the most sophisticated attacks only require a message to be previewed.

Some worms have looked for backdoors left by other worms. Backdoors allow covert remote access bypassing the usual access controls.

After a target has been compromised, a worm needs to copy itself to the target. The transfer might be combined with the compromise, or it might be a separate step after the compromise. For example, a worm could e-mail a copy of itself; this single step is an attack and transfers a copy of the worm. On the other hand, a buffer overflow attack could open a remote shell on the target; then a copy of the worm could be transferred by FTP.

### 12.1.2. *Historical Examples*

The Brain virus in 1986 was the first notable virus in the wild, although the computer virus concept had been documented and demonstrated by Fred Cohen earlier in 1983 [3]. The DOS-based Brain virus was interesting for its ability to hide itself in memory by hooking the DOS system calls that could normally detect viruses.

The famous 1988 Robert Morris Jr. worm brought the problem of viruses and worms to widespread attention [4]. The term "worm" had been coined by John Shoch and Jon Hupp earlier in 1979 during their experiments on mobile software at Xerox PARC. The Morris worm was the first to use a combination of attacks to spread quickly to 6,000 Unix computers in a few hours (10 percent of the ARPANET at that time). First, it ran a dictionary attack on password files captured from target systems. Second, it exploited the debug option in the Unix sendmail program which allowed it to transfer a copy of itself. Lastly, it attempted a buffer overflow attack through a vulnerability in the Unix fingerd program.

In March 1999, the Melissa macro virus showed that viruses could spread quickly through e-mail. Melissa spread quickly to 100,000 hosts in three days, setting a new record and forcing many organizations to shut down their e-mail systems. It began as a newsgroup posting promising passwords for erotic web sites. However, the downloaded Word document actually contained a macro that took advantage of functions in Microsoft Word and Microsoft Outlook to propagate. On infected hosts, the macro was executed in Word and launched Outlook to send itself to 50 recipients found in the address book. In addition, it infected the Word NORMAL.DOT template using the VBA macro auto-execute feature; any Word document subsequently saved from the template carried the virus.

Two versions of the Code Red worm appeared in 2001 [5]. On July 12, the first version Code Red I targeted a buffer overflow vulnerability in Microsoft IIS web servers. However, it spread slowly due to a programming error in its pseudorandom address generator causing each worm copy to probe the same set of IP addresses. A week later, Code Red I was apparently revised with the programming error fixed. It was able to infect more than 359,000 servers within 14 hours. A more complex and dangerous version Code Red II was targeted to the same IIS vulnerability on August 4. To spread faster, the worm ran 300 parallel threads on each computer (enabling up to 300 simultaneous TCP connections).

In September 2001, the Nimda worm used five different ways to spread to 450,000 hosts within the first 12 hours: e-mailing a copy of itself; exploiting a buffer overflow vulnerability in Microsoft IIS web servers; infecting network shares; adding Javascript to web pages to infect surfers; and looked for backdoors left by Code Red and Sadmind worms.

The SQL Sapphire/Slammer worm appeared on January 25, 2003, targeted to Microsoft SQL servers [6]. It reportedly infected 90 percent of vulnerable hosts within 10 minutes (about 120,000 servers). The fast spreading rate was achieved by its simple design apparently intended for efficient replication. The entire worm consisted of a single 404-byte UDP packet (including 376 bytes for the worm code). The use of UDP instead of TCP meant that infected hosts could generate new worm copies as quickly as possible without having to wait for responses from targeted machines. The short packet length meant that many worm copies could be sent generated quickly; in contrast, Code Red was about 4,000 bytes and Nimda was 60,000 bytes. The Slammer worm was so efficient that it was limited only by the available bandwidth.

Many other worms have appeared since 2003, which can be perused on the WildList (www.wildlist.org) or lists maintained by major anti-virus companies.

Relatively speaking, worms have become less urgent among security researchers since 2003 because concern has increased for bots and Web-hosted malware.

## 12.2. Related Literature

The first major work in computer epidemiology was performed by Kephart, White, and Chess at IBM Research in the early 1990s [7]. They pointed out a connection between large-scale (macroscopic) behavior of computer viruses and biological viruses, and the lack of epidemiology studies of computer viruses. Mathematical models such as the SIS (susceptible-infective-susceptible) model were borrowed from biological epidemiology [8] to try to gain insights into computer virus spreading. In addition, they simulated viruses to investigate the impact of different network topologies (random, hierarchical, lattice) and response time. Eventually, their research turned to the problem of digital immunity and their work was implemented into commercial antivirus software products.

Code Red incidence data has been the subject of a recent studies because of its global impact (2 billion damages), interesting history, and availability of incidence data. Staniford, Paxson, and Weaver presented additional Code Red I incidence data that exhibited a similar trajectory as the other Code Red I data [9]. They proposed a "random constant spread" model based on mass action (homogeneous) mixing, identical to the traditional simple epidemic or SI (susceptible-infective) model. Although the model was not novel, the study was an interesting exercise to fit a standard epidemic model to actual virus data. Moore, Shannon, and Claffy also presented a good fit of the SI model to Code Red I data [10].

Zou, Gong, and Towsley noted that the SI model did fit the Code Red I incidence data well during its initial rapid spread [11]. However, the SI model did not explain a slight decrease in the spreading rate after the initial rapid spread had reached a peak (shortly before Code Red I shut itself down). First, to explain the slowdown of the infection rate in the later time interval, the SIR (susceptible-infective-removed) model due to Kermack and McKendrick [12] was argued to be more realistic because it could take into account that infected machines can be removed by human countermeasures. Second, it was observed that countermeasures could move both susceptibles and infectives into the removed state, e.g., patching a susceptible machine would make it immune to infection. This implied that the standard SIR model needed to be modified, because the SIR model does not account for any hosts moving from the susceptible state directly to the removed state (without being first infected). Hence, two ad hoc modifications to the standard SIR model were proposed. The infection rate $\beta$ usually assumed to be constant was changed to a time-varying function $\beta(t)$ that is dependent on $I(t)$; specifically, it is inversely proportional so that the infection rate decreases as more machines are infected. Also, a fourth variable $Q(t)$ was introduced to account for the number of susceptibles changed to removed, and the total population becomes $N = S(t)+I(t)+R(t)+Q(t)$ where $S(t)$ is the number of susceptibles, $I(t)$ is the number of infectives, and

$R(t)$ is the number of removed. It was proposed that susceptibles are removed according to

$$\frac{d}{dt}Q(t) = \mu S(t)[I(t) + R(t)] \tag{12.1}$$

The final modified model is therefore Eq. (12.1) and

$$\frac{d}{dt}S(t) = -\beta(t)S(t)I(t) - \frac{d}{dt}Q(t) \tag{12.2}$$

$$\frac{d}{dt}I(t) = \beta(t)S(t)I(t) - \gamma I(t) \tag{12.3}$$

$$\frac{d}{dt}R(t) = \gamma I(t). \tag{12.4}$$

Moore *et al.* attempted to fit the SI model to Slammer incidence data and found a good fit in the initial phase of the outbreak [6]. However, Slammer's probe rate leveled off at some point, attributed to saturation of network links. Slammer had spread so quickly that network links became congested and prevented the worm from spreading faster. Hence, Slammer has been called an example of "bandwidth limited" worms.

## 12.3. Homogeneous Epidemic Models

The simplest epidemic model assumes an infinite population. Each host in the population is in either a susceptible or infective state; hence, this model is often referred to as the SI (susceptible-infective) model. A susceptible host can change its state to infective if it comes into contact with an infective. Once changed, a host remains indefinitely in the infective state.

A single infective will contact other hosts at rate $\beta$, called the probe rate or pairwise contact rate (although some literature refers to $\beta N$ as the pairwise contact rate). The assumption of homogeneity means that other hosts are chosen completely at random and the pairwise contact rate is the same for all pairs of hosts. At time $t$, the number of infective hosts is $I(t)$ and the number of susceptibles is $S(t) = \infty$. By implication, an infective always contacts a host who is susceptible because there are an infinite number of susceptibles.

Suppose that $\Delta t$ is a very small interval of time, then the total number of new contacts in this time interval will be $\beta I(t)\Delta t$. Since every contact results in a new infective, the number of new infectives produced in this time interval will be

$$\Delta I = \beta I(t)\Delta t. \tag{12.5}$$

The rate of change over a small time interval will be

$$\frac{\Delta I}{\Delta t} = \beta I(t). \tag{12.6}$$

Taking $\Delta t \to 0$, the rate of change in infectives is governed by

$$\frac{d}{dt}I(t) = \beta I(t). \tag{12.7}$$

The derivative $dI(t)/dt$ is called the epidemic rate. Eq. (12.7) implies exponential growth from an initial condition $I(0) = I_0$:

$$I(t) = I_0 e^{\beta t}. \tag{12.8}$$

### 12.3.1. *The Simple Homogeneous Epidemic*

Unlimited exponential growth is clearly unrealistic because there can not be an infinite population of susceptibles. The fixed size of a real population imposes a natural slowdown in the epidemic rate as the population becomes more saturated. While each infective is still contacting other hosts at a rate $\beta$, not every contacted host will be in the susceptible state; some contacts will reach an already infected host and therefore be ineffective. In a finite population of $N = S(t) + I(t)$, the probability that a contacted host will be susceptible is

$$P_s = \frac{S(t)}{N} = 1 - \frac{I(t)}{N}. \tag{12.9}$$

The probability $P_s$ might be called the probability of effective contact. In other words, the finite population has the effect of reducing the pairwise contact rate $\beta$ to an "effective" pairwise contact rate of

$$\beta_e = \beta P_s = \beta\left(1 - \frac{I(t)}{N}\right). \tag{12.10}$$

Figure 12.1 shows that the effective pairwise contact rate is lower for the finite population compared to the infinite population.

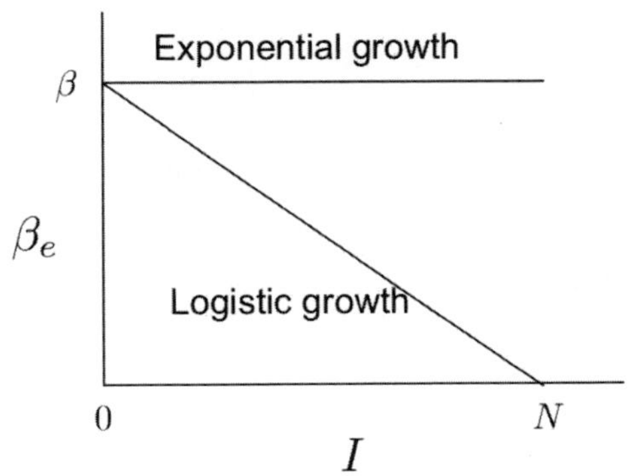


Fig. 12.1. Effective pairwise contact rate for finite and infinite populations.

The total number of new contacts in a small time interval is still $\beta I(t)\Delta t$, but the number of new infectives will be

$$\Delta I = \beta I(t)\left(1 - \frac{I(t)}{N}\right)\Delta t. \tag{12.11}$$

The epidemic rate can be found again by taking $\Delta t \to 0$, leading to

$$\frac{d}{dt}I(t) = \beta I(t)\left(1 - \frac{I(t)}{N}\right). \tag{12.12}$$

Given the initial condition $I(0) = I_0$, the solution is the well known logistic growth

$$I(t) = \frac{I_0 N}{I_0 + (N - I_0)e^{-\beta t}} \tag{12.13}$$

which has been attributed originally to Pierre Verhulst in 1838.

It can be seen that the epidemic rate (12.12) is always positive, implying that the epidemic will always grow until the entire population is eventually saturated. Figure 12.2 shows the familiar "S" shape of the logistic curve.

In addition, Figure 12.3 shows the epidemic rate is initially slow (when $I(t) \approx 0$), reaches a maximum at $I(t) = N/2$, and then slows down (when $I(t)$ approaches $N$).

### 12.3.2. *The General Homogeneous Epidemic*

The simple epidemic model does not take into account the possibility that infected hosts can be disinfected (for example, by antivirus software). The general epidemic model adds a third removed or recovered state and is often referred to as the SIR (susceptible-infective-removed) model attributed to Kermack and McKendrick in 1927. An infective can change to the removed state at some rate, and then stays in the removed state immune from re-infection.

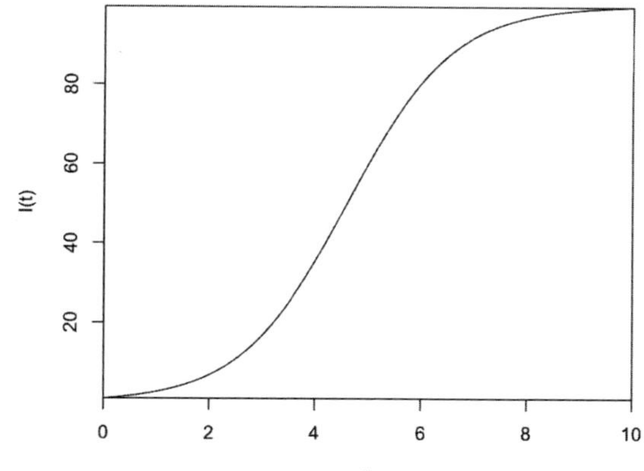


Fig. 12.2. Logistic growth of simple epidemic assuming $N = 100$, $\beta = 1$, $I_0 = 1$.

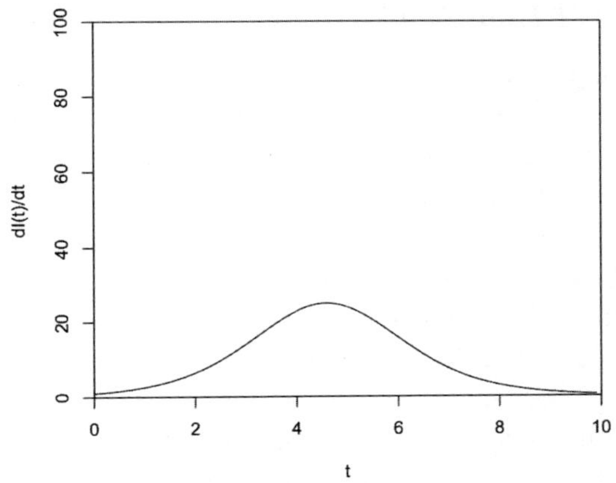


Fig. 12.3. Epidemic rate for simple epidemic assuming $N = 100$, $\beta = 1$, $I_0 = 1$.

The number of removed hosts is $R(t)$, and the population is a fixed size $N = S(t) + I(t) + R(t)$. The modification to the simple epidemic is the additional assumption that infectives change to the removed state at a removal rate $\gamma$. The epidemic rate is now governed by the system of equations:

$$\frac{d}{dt}S(t) = -\beta I(t)S(t)/N \tag{12.14}$$

$$\frac{d}{dt}I(t) = \beta I(t)S(t)/N - \gamma I(t) \tag{12.15}$$

$$\frac{d}{dt}R(t) = \gamma I(t). \tag{12.16}$$

The dynamics of the epidemic depends on the initial number of susceptibles. In Eq. (12.15), note that the epidemic rate will be positive only if $\beta S(t)/N > \gamma$ or $S(t) > N\gamma/\beta$. Thus, if the initial number of susceptibles is more than the threshold $S(0) > N\gamma/\beta$, the epidemic will grow and then later diminish as shown in Figure 12.4. Otherwise, if the initial number of susceptibles is below the threshold $S(0) < N\gamma/\beta$, the epidemic will only diminish without growing.

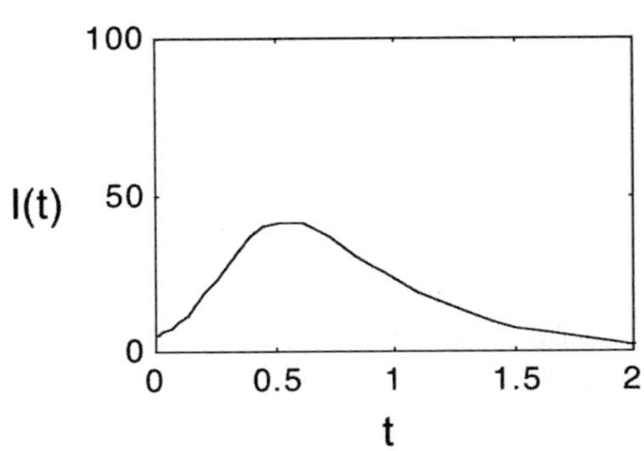


Fig. 12.4. SIR epidemic assuming $N = 100$, $\beta = 0.1$, $I_0 = 5$, $\gamma = 2.5$.

## 12.4. Community of Households Model

Epidemiologists recognized long ago that the assumption of uniform mixing in the homogeneous epidemic models is unrealistic and unnecessarily restrictive. In reality, each individual is not equally likely to make contact with all other individuals. For example, individuals are more likely to mix with others within the same locality. There are many possible ways to model a heterogeneous population. One approach is to assume that the heterogeneous population consists of different subpopulations [13]. The community of households (COH) model, first presented by Rushton and Mautner in 1955, refers to subpopulations as households, where the "inter-household" contact rates between separate households can be different from the "intra-household" contact rates between individuals within the same household [14].

In the context of worms, worm simulations have followed the COH model where the households represent autonomous systems in the Internet [15]. The Internet is known to consist of separately administered but interconnected autonomous systems or routing domains. In the simulations, the infection parameters were estimated to fit historical worm traffic data. Other worm simulations have similarly chosen to model worm propagation through an Internet structured as an interconnection of multiple subnetworks [16].

In the COH model, the population of $N$ is organized into $M$ separate households. The $i$-th household has population $N_i$ and infectives $I_i(t)$. The total population is $N = N_1 + \cdots + N_M$, and the total infection is $I(t) = I_1(t) + \cdots + I_M(t)$. It is assumed that an infective in household $i$ has an intra-household contact rate $\beta_i$ with others in the same household but an inter-household contact rate $\beta_{ij}$ to household $j$. In $\Delta t$ time, infectives in household $i$ contact a total $\beta_i I_i(t)\Delta t$ hosts within the same household, and $\beta_{ji} I_j(t)\Delta t$ hosts in household $i$ are contacted from household $j$ (for all $j \neq i$). For the discussion here, we only address the simple (SI) epidemic and ignore the possibility of removals; an extension to the general SIR epidemic would be straightforward.

The probability that a contact to household $i$ will contact a susceptible (and not an infective) is

$$P_s = 1 - \frac{I_i(t)}{N_i}. \tag{12.17}$$

By implication, the number of new infectives in household $i$ caused by intra-household spreading will be

$$\beta_i I_i(t) \left(1 - \frac{I_i(t)}{N_i}\right) \Delta t. \tag{12.18}$$

In addition, the number of new infectives in household $i$ caused by inter-household spreading from household $j$ will be

$$\beta_{ji} I_j(t) \left(1 - \frac{I_i(t)}{N_i}\right) \Delta t. \tag{12.19}$$

Summing all new infectives in household $i$ and taking $\Delta t \to 0$, the rate of change of infectives in household $i$ is

$$\frac{d}{dt}I_i(t) = \beta_i I_i(t)\left(1 - \frac{I_i(t)}{N_i}\right) + \sum_{j \neq i} \beta_{ji} I_j(t)\left(1 - \frac{I_i(t)}{N_i}\right). \tag{12.20}$$

The COH model is governed by the system of differential equations (12.20) for $i = 1, \ldots, M$.

### 12.4.1. *Symmetric Case of COH Model*

For simplicity, we consider a special symmetric case of the COH model where all households are equal size $N_i = N/M$; all households have the same initial conditions $I_i(0) = I_0/M$; all intra-household contact rates are equal $\beta_i = \beta/M$; and all inter-household contact rates are equal $\beta_{ji} = \alpha\beta/M$. The $\alpha$ coefficient accounts for a possible difference between the intra-household and inter-household contact rates when $\alpha \neq 1$. Normally, we would expect that $\alpha < 1$ in real situations.

The reason for examining the special symmetric case is simplification of the system of differential equations into a single differential equation. It is clear that all households are symmetric under the simplifying assumptions, in the sense that they start with the same initial conditions and then continue to have the same number of infectives per household: $I_1(t) = \cdots = I_M(t) = I(t)/M$. Thus, the system of differential equations simplifies to

$$\frac{d}{dt}I_i(t) = \frac{\beta}{M}\frac{I(t)}{M}\left(1 - \frac{I(t)}{M}\frac{M}{N}\right) + \sum_{j \neq i} \alpha \frac{\beta}{M}\frac{I(t)}{M}\left(1 - \frac{I(t)}{M}\frac{M}{N}\right) \tag{12.21}$$

$$= \beta I(t)\left(1 - \frac{I(t)}{N}\right)\frac{1}{M^2} + \sum_{j \neq i} \alpha\beta I(t)\left(1 - \frac{I(t)}{N}\right)\frac{1}{M^2} \tag{12.22}$$

$$= \beta I(t)\left(1 - \frac{I(t)}{N}\right)\frac{1 + (M-1)\alpha}{M^2} \tag{12.23}$$

for $i = 1, \ldots, M$. Note that every equation in the system is identical and has no dependence on $i$. Since

$$\frac{d}{dt}I_i(t) = \frac{1}{M}\frac{d}{dt}I(t), \tag{12.24}$$

the system of differential equations (12.21) becomes equivalent to the single differential equation

$$\frac{d}{dt}I(t) = \beta I(t)\left(1 - \frac{I(t)}{N}\right)\frac{1 + (M-1)\alpha}{M}. \tag{12.25}$$

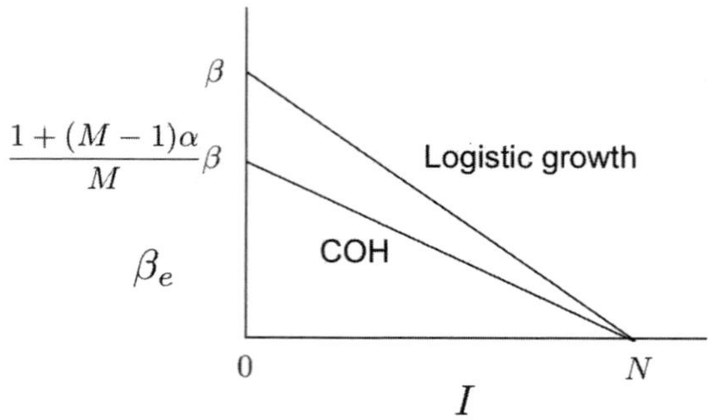


Fig. 12.5. Effective contact rate for COH model and simple homogeneous model.

The effective pairwise contact rate in this case is

$$\beta_e = \beta\left(1 - \frac{I(t)}{N}\right)\frac{1+(M-1)\alpha}{M}. \tag{12.26}$$

Figure 12.5 compares the effective contact rate for the symmetric COH model and the simple homogeneous model (with logistic growth). By comparison with the logistic growth curve, it can be seen that the symmetric COH case with $\alpha < 1$ will exhibit a slower epidemic rate because of slower infections across households. In the worst case $\alpha = 0$, the rate of the SI model is reduced by a factor of $M$. In other words, if all households are isolated from each other, the epidemic rate is reduced by the number of households.

Fortunately, the symmetric COH model (12.25) is straightforward to solve by the method of separation of variables:

$$I(t) = \frac{I_0 N}{I_0 + (N - I_0)e^{-\frac{1+(M-1)\alpha}{M}\beta t}}. \tag{12.27}$$

## 12.5. Epidemic Slowed by Bandwidth Limits

A worm such as SQL Slammer has been called "bandwidth limited" because hosts compromised by Slammer can scan as fast as they can transmit packets [6]. In the case of Slammer, hosts were put into a simple execution loop to send out 404-byte UDP packets containing a copy of the worm to random IP addresses. Slammer was observed to saturate the bandwidth on many links and would probably have taken advantage of more bandwidth had it been available. Limited network resources acted as a natural dampener on the epidemic rate, even in the absence of active defenses (such as quarantine).

The traditional homogeneous models and even the COH model do not take network limitations into consideration. However, the COH model can be modified slightly to account for bandwidth limitations, which we call the community of households with limited inter-household bandwidths (COH-LIHB) model. For the COH model, we now envision logical connection links between each pair of households. The logical link between households $i$ and $j$ has a limited bandwidth $L_{ij}$ measured in maximum rate of contacts per unit time, that imposes an upper bound of $L_{ij}\Delta t$ on the number of contacts made in household $j$ coming from household $i$ in a small time $\Delta t$. In general, the bandwidths in opposite directions may not be the same, i.e., $L_{ij}$ may be different from $L_{ji}$. Intra-household contacts are not affected by the limited bandwidth of the logical links.

Recall that in the COH model, household $i$ received $\beta_{ji} I_j(t)\Delta t$ contacts from household $j$. If $I_j(t)$ is small (i.e., in the early phase of an outbreak), then the rate of contacts will not be affected by the limited bandwidth. However, when $I_j(t)$ is sufficiently large, the rate of contacts will be bounded by the bandwidth to $L_{ji}\Delta t$. That is, the rate of inter-household contacts from household $j$ to household $i$ will be

$$\min(L_{ji}, \beta_{ji} I_j(t)). \tag{12.28}$$

Eq. (12.28) is the basis for the COH-LIHB model.

With substitution of Eq. (12.28) into the COH model, the COH-LIHB model is represented by the modified system of differential equations

$$\frac{d}{dt} I_i(t) = \beta_i I_i(t)\left(1 - \frac{I_i(t)}{N_i}\right) + \sum_{j\neq i} \min(L_{ji}, \beta_{ji} I_j(t))\left(1 - \frac{I_i(t)}{N_i}\right) \tag{12.29}$$

for $i = 1, \ldots, M$.

We would expect the epidemic to progress as usual in the early stages until the size of the epidemic is large enough to reach the bandwidth limits. This will happen when

$$L_{ij} = \beta_{ij} I_i(t) \tag{12.30}$$

for any pair of households $i$ and $j$. At this point in the epidemic, the rate of inter-household contacts will begin to be limited, causing the COH-LIHB epidemic to progress slower compared to the community of households with unlimited bandwidths. As might be expected, the bandwidth limits will have the effect of dampening the epidemic rate in its later stages.

### 12.5.1. *Special Symmetric Case of COH-LIHB Model*

As before, the special symmetric case assumes equal size households $N_i = N/M$; all households have the same initial conditions $I_i(0) = I_0/M$; all intra-household contact rates are equal $\beta_i = \beta/M$; and all inter-household contact rates are equal $\beta_{ji} = \alpha\beta/M$. Furthermore, if the inter-household links have limited bandwidths, we make an assumption that all link bandwidths are equal, $L_{ij} = L$ for all $i$, $j$.

Now the system of differential equations (12.29) for the COH-LIHB model simplifies for this special symmetric case to

$$\frac{d}{dt}I_i(t) = \frac{\beta}{M}\frac{I(t)}{M}\left(1-\frac{I(t)}{M}\frac{M}{N}\right) + \sum_{j\neq i}\min\left(L, \frac{\alpha\beta}{M}\frac{I(t)}{M}\right)\left(1-\frac{I(t)}{M}\frac{M}{N}\right) \tag{12.31}$$

$$= \beta I(t)\left(1-\frac{I(t)}{N}\right)\frac{1}{M^2} + \sum_{j\neq i}\min(LM^2, \alpha\beta I(t))\left(1-\frac{I(t)}{N}\right)\frac{1}{M^2} \tag{12.32}$$

$$= \left(\beta I(t) + (M-1)\min(LM^2, \alpha\beta I(t))\right)\left(1-\frac{I(t)}{N}\right)\frac{1}{M^2} \tag{12.33}$$

for $i = 1, \ldots, M$. Note that every equation in the system is identical and has no dependence on $i$. Since

$$\frac{d}{dt}I_i(t) = \frac{1}{M}\frac{d}{dt}I(t), \tag{12.34}$$

the system of differential equations (12.31) becomes equivalent to the single differential equation

$$\frac{d}{dt}I(t) = \left(\beta I(t) + (M-1)\min(LM^2, \alpha\beta I(t))\right)\left(1-\frac{I(t)}{N}\right)\frac{1}{M}. \tag{12.35}$$

When will the epidemic become affected by bandwidth limitations? Examining the differential equation (12.35), there is change when the epidemic $I(t)$ reaches a level $I_{\text{thresh}}$ such that

$$LM^2 = \alpha\beta I_{\text{thresh}} \tag{12.36}$$

or

$$I_{\text{thresh}} = \frac{LM^2}{\alpha\beta}. \tag{12.37}$$

A consequence of this threshold is that bandwidth limitations will affect the epidemic only if $I_{\text{thresh}} < N$, or in other words, if the link bandwidth

$$L < \frac{\alpha\beta N}{M^2}. \tag{12.38}$$

If Eq. (12.38) is true, the link bandwidth will have a dampening effect on the epidemic before it saturates the susceptible population. On the other hand, if the link bandwidth is sufficiently large,

$$L \geq \frac{\alpha\beta N}{M^2} \tag{12.39}$$

then the epidemic will saturate the population before the worm traffic reaches the bandwidth limits, and the network will have no dampening effect on the progress of the epidemic.

Eq. (12.38) is the interesting case, so we assume here the special symmetric case of the COH-LIHB model where Eq. (12.38) holds and ask how the effect of bandwidth limits can be seen in terms of the effective contact rate. The epidemic will progress in two phases: an early undampened phase without bandwidth limitations, and a later dampened phase where the worm traffic has completely taken the available inter-household bandwidths.

In the initial stages of the epidemic, the limitations on bandwidth have no effect. The initial stages of the epidemic are governed by the partial differential equation

$$\frac{d}{dt}I(t) = \frac{1+(M-1)\alpha}{M}\beta I(t)\left(1-\frac{I(t)}{N}\right). \tag{12.40}$$

When the epidemic exceeds the threshold $I_{\text{thresh}}$, then it becomes limited by the bandwidth of inter-household links and is governed by

$$\frac{d}{dt}I(t) = \frac{\beta I(t)+(M-1)LM^2}{M}\left(1-\frac{I(t)}{N}\right). \tag{12.41}$$

Taking account both phases, the effective contact rate for the special symmetric case of the COH-LIHB model is

$$\beta_e = \begin{cases} \dfrac{1+(M-1)\alpha}{M}\beta\left(1-\dfrac{I(t)}{N}\right) & \text{if } I(t) < I_{\text{thresh}} \\[2ex] \dfrac{\beta I(t)+(M-1)LM^2}{MI(t)}\left(1-\dfrac{I(t)}{N}\right) & \text{if } I(t) \geq I_{\text{thresh}} \end{cases} \tag{12.42}$$

Figure 12.6 shows how the bandwidth limit causes the effective contract rate to "dip" compared to the COH model with unlimited bandwidth. The dip is deeper when $I_{\text{thresh}}$ is smaller (i.e., when the epidemic reaches the bandwidth limits sooner).

The symmetric COH-LIHB model (12.35) can be solved by the method of separation of variables. In the initial phase of the epidemic, the epidemic proceeds as Eq. (12.27) until the epidemic $I(t)$ reaches the threshold $I_{\text{thresh}}$. Let $t_0$ denote

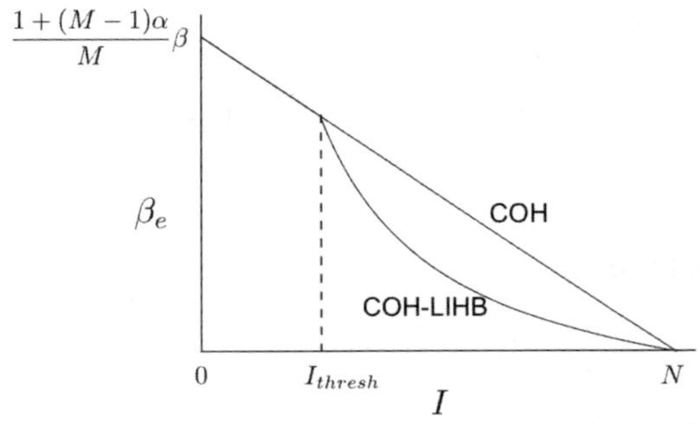


Fig. 12.6. Effective contact rate for COH-LIHB and COH models.

the time when the epidemic reaches the threshold. For $t > t_0$, then the solution of Eq. (12.41) is

$$I(t) = \frac{\beta N I_{\text{thresh}} + (M-1)LM^2 N - (M-1)LM^2 e^{-C(t-t_0)}}{\beta I_{\text{thresh}} + (M-1)LM^2 + (N - I_{\text{thresh}})\beta e^{-C(t-t_0)}} \tag{12.43}$$

where $C = (\beta N + (M-1)LM^2)/MN$.

## 12.6. Active Defenses

Figure 12.6 showed that limited bandwidth in the network acts as a natural dampener on an epidemic. The observation suggests that active defenses may dampen an epidemic even more effectively by imposing artificial bandwidth limits. One obvious approach is dynamic quarantine, an extreme method where the effective contact rate is restricted to zero. Another approach is rate throttling, a less drastic method where the effective contact rate is reduced to a small (non-zero) level.

### 12.6.1. *Dynamic Quarantine*

The COH model can be used to study dynamic quarantine. The idea of dynamic quarantine for worms is the same as quarantine for infectious diseases — to slow down the epidemic to buy more time for disinfection [17]. Current automated worm defenses consist of antivirus software, firewalls, and intrusion detection systems [18]. These defenses attempt to detect worms through misuse detection (signatures) or anomaly detection (based on suspicious behavior) and then block the worm traffic in the network.

In practice, it may time some time $t_0$ to detect a new worm epidemic and activate quarantine. In the initial phase, the epidemic may progress unrestricted according to Eq. (12.27). At time $t_0$, the epidemic will have reached a level

$$I(t_0) = \frac{I_0 N}{I_0 + (N - I_0)e^{-\frac{1+(M-1)\alpha}{M}\beta t_0}}. \tag{12.44}$$

For $t > t_0$, the effect of dynamic quarantine is represented by Eq. (12.25) with $\alpha = 0$. The reduction in the effective contact rate is shown in Figure 12.7. For $t > t_0$, the solution is

$$I(t) = \frac{I(t_0)N}{I(t_0) + (N - I(t_0))e^{-\frac{\beta}{M}(t-t_0)}}. \tag{12.45}$$

### 12.6.2. *Rate Limiting*

While dynamic quarantine can undoubtedly be effective, quarantine works by detecting and blocking worm traffic. Current detection methods are not completely accurate. Signature-based detection depends on known signatures. A new worm without an existing signature will not be detected until a new signature is developed,

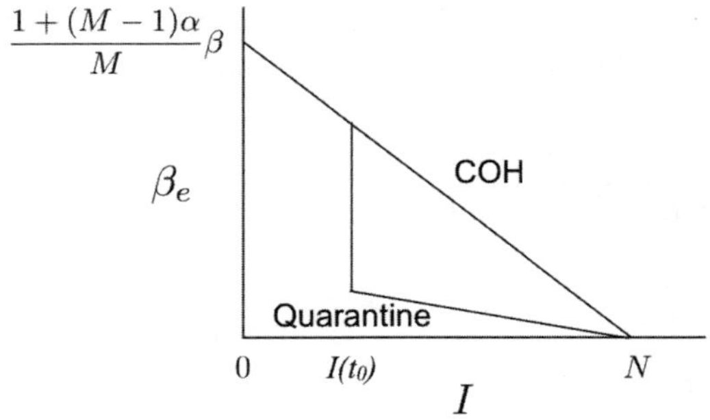


Fig. 12.7. Effective contact rate for dynamic quarantine.

which can take hours to days. On the other hand, behavior-based anomaly detection can potentially detect new worms without an existing signature, but currently suffer from high rates of false positives. A high rate of false positives is problematic when legitimate traffic may be blocked.

As an alternative, rate limiting has been advocated as a "benign" action [19]. The idea is essentially to slow down hosts that are trying to quickly connect to many different other hosts. Suspicious "worm-like" traffic is only delayed, not destroyed. In false positive cases, legitimate traffic may be delayed at worst. Hence detection accuracy is not as critical with rate limiting as with quarantine.

Unlike dynamic quarantine, rate limiting can be applied quickly after the start of a new worm epidemic because detection does not have to be highly accurate. For modeling, we assume a short delay $t_0$. Again before $t_0$, the epidemic may progress unrestricted according to Eq. (12.27). At time $t_0$, the epidemic will have reached a level given by Eq. (12.44).

When rate limiting is activated at time $t_0$, the change in the effective contact rate is similar to bandwidth limits. Indeed, the basic idea of rate limiting is to reduce $L$ close to zero (but not actually zero). The effective contact rate may be visualized as in Figure 12.8. It has the same "dip" as the COH-LIHB model, but the intention of rate limiting is to deepen the dip as much as possible without interfering unduly with legitimate traffic.

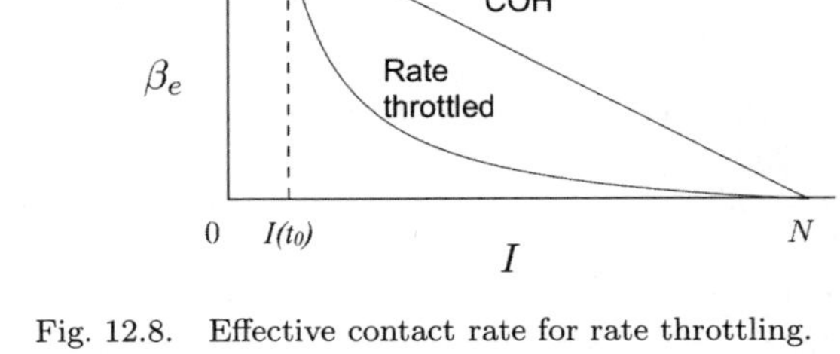


Fig. 12.8. Effective contact rate for rate throttling.

For $t > t_0$, the effect of dynamic quarantine is represented by Eq. (12.41) with some very small $L \neq 0$. Similar to Eq. (12.43), the solution for $t > t_0$ is

$$I(t) = \frac{\beta N I(t_0) + (M-1)LM^2N - (M-1)LM^2e^{-C(t-t_0)}}{\beta I(t_0) + (M-1)LM^2 + (N - I(t_0))\beta e^{-C(t-t_0)}} \tag{12.46}$$

## 12.7. Conclusions

Epidemiology is based on analogies that can be drawn between the macroscopic behavior of malware and human infectious diseases. Traditional deterministic epidemic models have been found to have a reasonably adequate fit to some historic worm incidence data. However, epidemiology is much more than an exercise in data fitting. The ultimate goal of mathematical epidemiology is to bring insights into the design of networks and active defenses against fast-spreading malware.

In particular, we believe that the community of households model is promising for capturing the Internet structure at a high level. We have shown that the modified COH-LIHB model can explain how bandwidth limits in the network can help to dampen a worm outbreak by restricting its ability to make contacts across the network.

The COH model can also be used to examine the effectiveness of active defenses, such as dynamic quarantine and rate limiting that are based on restraining an epidemic by controlling the available bandwidth in the network. We have only studied a special symmetric case of the COH model for simplicity. This has led to some results limited to the specific case where all households are equal. Future research should examine the more general and realistic case where households are not equal.

## References


[1] E. Skoudis, *Malware: Fighting Malicious Code.* (Prentice Hall, Upper Saddle River, 2004).

[2] P. Szor, *The Art of Computer Virus Research and Defense.* (Addison-Wesley, Upper Saddle River, 2005).

[3] F. Cohen, Computer viruses: theory and experiments, *Computers and Sec.*, **6**(4), 22–35, (1987).

[4] E. Spafford, The Internet worm program: an analysis, *ACM Computer Commun. Rev.*, **19**(1), 17–57, (1989).

[5] H. Berghel, The Code Red worm, *Commun. of ACM*, **44**(12), 15–19, (2001).

[6] D. Moore, *et al.*, Inside the Slammer worm, *IEEE Sec. & Privacy*, **1**(4), 33–39, (2003).

[7] J. Kephart, S. White, and D. Chess, Computers and epidemiology, *IEEE Spectrum*, **30**(5), 20–26, (1993).

[8] N. Bailey, *The Mathematical Theory of Infectious Diseases and its Applications*, 2nd ed. (Hafner Press, New York, 1975).

[9] S. Staniford, V. Paxson, and N. Weaver, How to own the Internet in your spare time. In *proc. 11th Usenix Sec. Symp.*, San Francisco (Aug. 2002).

[10] D. Moore, C. Shannon, and K. Claffy, Code-Red: a case study on the spread and victims of an Internet worm. In *proc. 2nd ACM SIGCOMM Workshop on Internet Measurement (IMW)*, Marseille, 273–284, (Nov. 6–8, 2002).

[11] C. Zou, W. Gong, and D. Towsley, Code Red worm propagation modeling and analysis. In *proc. 9th ACM Conf. on Computer and Commun. Sec. (CCS'02)*, Wash. DC, 138–147, (Nov. 2002).

[12] W. Kermack and A. McKendrick, A contribution to the mathematical theory of epidemics, *Proc. Roy. Soc. Lond. A.* **115**, 700–721, (1927).

[13] D. Daley and J. Gani, *Epidemic Modeling: An Introduction.* (Cambridge U. Press, Cambridge, 1999).

[14] N. Becker and J. Hopper, The infectiousness of a disease in a community of households, *Biometrika.* **70**, 29–39, (1983).

[15] M. Liljenstam, *et al.*, A mixed abstraction level simulation model of large-scale Internet worm infestations. In *proc. 10th IEEE/ACM Symp. on Modeling, Analysis, and Simulation of Comp. Telecom. Sys. (MASCOTS 2002)*, Fort Worth, 109–116, (Oct. 2002).

[16] A. Wagner, *et al.*, Experiences with worm propagation simulations. In *proc. ACM Workshop on Rapid Malcode (WORM 2003)*, Wash. DC, 34–41, (Oct. 2003).

[17] T. Chen and N. Jamil, Effectiveness of quarantine in worm epidemics. In *proc. IEEE ICC 2006*, 2142–2147, (June 2006).

[18] D. Moore, *et al.*, Internet quarantine: requirements for containing self-propagating code. In *proc. IEEE Infocom 2003*, San Francisco, 1901–1910, (May 2003).

[19] M. Williamson, Throttling viruses: restricting propagation to defeat malicious mobile code. In *proc. 18th Annual Comp. Sec. Appl. Conf.*, Las Vegas, (Dec. 2002).

# Chapter 13

## WORM PROPAGATION AND INTERACTION IN MOBILE NETWORKS

Sapon Tanachaiwiwat
*Innovative Scheduling, Inc.*
*stanachai@gmail.com*

Ahmed Helmy
*Computer and Information Science and Engineering*
*University of Florida*
*helmy@cise.ufl.edu*

Many worms are shifting their attack targets to the wireless mobile phone. The characteristics of worms in mobile networks are different from random-scan network worms which randomly scan susceptible hosts whose IP addresses are within the worms' targeted IP address ranges. Worms in mobile networks are limited by encounter patterns influenced by human mobility patterns. This spreading pattern is very similar to spread of packet replications in encounter-based networks (frequently-disconnected wireless ad-hoc networks requiring immediate neighbors to store and forward aggregated data for information dissemination). An earlier study in encounter-based networks actually used the term "epidemic routing" to describe the similarity of this routing protocol to disease spreading. Because this type of network is highly dynamic and has no specific boundary, we need a fully distributed security response mechanism. We propose the worm interaction approach that relies upon automated beneficial worm generation. This approach uses an automatically generated beneficial worm to terminate malicious worms and patch the vulnerable hosts to prevent re-infection by malicious worms. For encounter-based worms, we validate our proposed model using extensive synthetic and trace-driven simulations. We find that immunization linearly decreases the infection of susceptible nodes while *on-off* behavior only impacts the duration of infection. Immunization and timely deployment seem to be the most effective to counter the worm attacks in such scenarios while cooperation may help in a specific case. These findings provide insights that we hope would aid in developing counter-worm protocols in future encounter-based networks.

### 13.1. Introduction

Since the Morris worm incident in 1988, worms have been a major threat to Internet users. While more vulnerabilities in operating systems are exposed to malicious attackers, new types of worms as well as other malwares are launched at alarming rate. In addition, more and more worms carry destructive payload enabling them to perform distributed denial-of-service attacks (DDoS), steal username/password or hijack victims' files. Internet worms can be categorized as network worms and email worms. Network worms such as Slammer, Witty, and Code Red aggressively scan and infect vulnerable machines. Mass-mailing worms' propagation such as Kamasutra, Love Bugs, and NetSky rely on social engineering techniques.

In recent years, many worms are shifting their attack targets to the wireless mobile phone. In June 2004, Cabir [47], the first wireless worm running in Symbian mobile phone was discovered. Cabir worm can only reach Bluetooth mobile phones in discoverable mode. This worm was created as "proof-of-concept" with no real threat but can deplete the phone battery quickly due to aggressive scan for other vulnerable Bluetooth devices. It still needs users to accept the "worm" before the phone can be infected. Cabir can only infect one device per activation (after being powered off and then on). Lasco worm [51] (discovered in January, 2005) is a variant of Cabir. In addition to Cabir normal vector, it also infects every .sis file in the infected device but those files are not automatically sent to other devices.

Unlike Cabir, Skulls, another Bluetooth worm, once downloaded and installed on the phone, disables all of the phone's built-in programs such as calendar, clock and notepad functions and replaces icons with images of skulls. Skulls was discovered in Nov, 2004.

In March 2005, Commwarrior [47] is another worm replicates on Symbian phones, spreading via Multimedia Messaging Service (MMS) and Bluetooth as a randomly named .sis file. Hence, unlike Cabir, it can infect phones by sending a MMS message with .sis file as an attachment to the phone number from the device's phonebook. It resets the device if it is the first hour of the 14th of any month. Other Symbian-based worms include Locknut, Dampig and Qdial [51].

In addition to the above Symbian-based worms, Duts and Brador [31, 51] which discovered in 2006, are Windows-CE-based viruses targeting PDAs. Duts is the first worm for devices running under Windows CE .NET including following operating systems: Pocket PC 2000, 2002, 2003. The virus infects executable files that are larger than 4KB in size (the virus itself is 1.5 KB). Unlike Duts, Bradir is a full-scale malicious program that once installed from email-attachment or from the Internet; it installs itself as a 5KB program on the device and then open TCP port 2989 to wait for further instruction. More recent updated list of worms on mobile phones and PDAs can be found in [41, 51].

The characteristics of worms in mobile networks are different from random-scan network worms which randomly scan (probe) susceptible hosts (in the Internet) whose IP addresses are within the worms' targeted IP address ranges. Unlike random scan network worms, which are limited by network bandwidth or link delay, worms in mobile networks are limited by encounter (a scenario where a device moves within a radio range of another device) patterns influenced by human mobility patterns. Many of those worms rely on Bluetooth to broadcast their replications to vulnerable phones, e.g., Cabir and ComWar.M [39, 47, 51]. Since Bluetooth radios have very short range e.g., 10–100 meters, the worms need neighbors in close proximity to spread out their replications. Hence, we call this "encounter-based worms". This spreading pattern is very similar to spread of packet replications in encounter-based networks [26, 49, 58], i.e., flooding the copies of messages to all close neighbors. An earlier study in encounter-based networks actually used the term "epidemic routing" [49] to describe the similarity of this routing protocol to disease spreading.

Unlike the Internet, the encounter-based network is a frequently-disconnected wireless ad-hoc network requiring immediate neighbors to store and forward aggregated data for information dissemination. Using traditional approaches such as gateways or firewalls for worm propagation in encounter-based networks is inappropriate. Because this type of network is highly dynamic and has no specific boundary, we need a fully distributed security response mechanism. We propose the worm interaction approach that relies upon automated beneficial worm generation [8]. This approach uses an automatically generated beneficial worm to terminate malicious worms and patch the vulnerable hosts to prevent re-infection by malicious worms. We define this type of worm interaction as aggressive one-sided interaction [40–46]. Before we can use this approach at full potential, we need to understand the worm interaction in this environment. To achieve this goal, we choose to model such worm behavior mathematically.

Our goal in this chapter is to provide a framework to understand the worm propagations and interaction in encounter-based networks. We want to be able to model the worm interactions mathematically and identify the key components that affect the worm interaction the most. We want to define metrics that measure the effectiveness of worm containment caused by worm interactions and being able to enhance such effectiveness based on the understanding of worm interactions. In addition to worm interaction types and node characteristics, this chapter focuses on modeling the interactions of encounter-based worm with different encounter characteristics. We further investigate whether non-malicious worms generated by automatic reverse-engineering techniques [8] or automatic patching [50] can be used to terminate malicious worms effectively.

The chapter is organized as follows: in Section 2, we discuss the related work. We explain the basic definitions including proposed metrics as well as the Worm Interaction Model in Section 3. In Section 4, we analyze worm interactions in both uniform and realistic encounter networks. We conclude our work in Section 5.

## 13.2. Background

In encounter-based networks, the effectiveness depends greatly on initial nodes selection based on their encounter characteristics [44]. There are many important node characteristics to be considered, but we focus only a fundamental subset including cooperation, immunization, *on-off* behavior and delay. We shall show that these are key node characteristics for worm propagation in encounter-based networks. Other characteristics such as energy consumption and buffer capacity are modeled for anti-packet schemes for epidemic routing in [58]. Trust and other social implications between users are subject to further study.

The majority of routing studies in encounter-based networks usually assume ideal node characteristics including full node cooperation and *always-on* behavior. However, in realistic scenarios, nodes do not always cooperate with others and may be *off* most of the time [25]. In worm propagation studies, many works also assume all nodes to be susceptible (i.e., not immune) to worm infection. An *immune* node does not cooperate with infected nodes and is not infected. To investigate more realistic scenarios, we propose to study the mobile node characteristics and analyze the impact of cooperation, immunization and *on-off* behavior on the worm interactions. Cooperation and *on-off* behavior are expected to have impact on the timing of infection. Intuitively, cooperation makes the network more susceptible to worm attacks. Immunization, however, may help reduce overall infection level. This paper examines the validity of these expectations, using the overall infection level and timing of infection as metrics.

We consider several important network characteristics for encounter-based networks such as network sizes, contact rate, group behaviors and batch arrival. Using realistic mobile network measurements, we find that encounters are *"bursty", multi-group and non-uniform.*

Many studies have attempted to foresee how worm may propagate in mobile ad-hoc networks. In [11], the study models worm propagation in mobile ad-hoc networks (MANETs) based on the *SI* model similar to a random-scan network worm in which each node in the network is identified by IP address. Furthermore, the study also incorporates the congestion of networks that was first introduced by [59] to the model. The worm propagation model is validated using ns-2 simulations with the AODV routing protocols and random-way point mobility. The results show that even with the reaction time to counter attack as low as 12 sec, the probability of infection is still as high as 0.3. Later in [12], the study also shows the effects of mitigation on worm propagation on mobility (speed), congestion, and network delay. In [1], MANET TCP worms are also model and simulated based on the *SI* model which the relationships of worm propagation with various payload sizes and transmission rates are studied. The main differences in characteristics between worm in MANETs and in the Internet are that the network size of MANET is smaller and network can become easily congested. However, a slight delay in propagation is due to packet loss caused by congestion, channel condition and mobility. In addition to AODV, we also study worm propagations and interactions in DSDV and DSR. Our results show that worm can propagate fastest in DSR.

Trace-based worm propagation simulations are used in [2] using Dartmouth syslog for more than 6,000 users. The authors focus on the realistic worm propagation and containment effectiveness in the Wi-Fi environments. They propose several access-point-based defense schemes to use when users join the network such as Unpatched User Shunning, (warning to vulnerable users before globally blocking from the networks), Infected/Unpatched User Shunning, (in addition to vulnerable users, infected users are also warned before they are globally blocked from the networks), Active Disinfect/Patch (infected users are disinfected and vulnerable nodes are patched), and Proactive Patching (scheduled patching to users in advance). Only Active Disinfect/Patch combined with Proactive Patching are effective. Deploying active disinfection and patching by beneficial worm, our schemes are expected to be more effective when compared to the location-based access schemes.

Large-scale simulations based on EpiSim are carried out to see the effect of disease spread [17]. The authors estimate mobility pattern based on census and land-use data. They find that the contact graph between people is a strongly connected small-world-like graph. At the same time, the graph between locations shows the hierarchical scale-free properties suggesting the possibility of effectively deploying outbreak detection in the hubs of the location networks. They conclude that early mass vaccination is the key to suppress the disease outbreak. Removing or containing only high degree people is not sufficient due to the strongly connected graph property. These findings are also consistent with our study even with much smaller scale, i.e., 5,000 nodes and 130 buildings in our case to more than 1,500,000 nodes and 1,800 locations in their case (Portland, Oregon). Hence small targeted vaccination will not be efficient in both cases.

In [37], authors investigate the possibility of city-scale Bluetooth worm infection in the city environment (in Toronto city). From their experiments, they find that the populations of Bluetooth devices are rather homogenous (based on manufacturer) and many of them are discoverable, causing high probability of major outbreaks. In addition, small files (<256 KB) can be easily transferred with walking speeds (1–2 m/s). Our experiments also indicate that even with large file (1 MB), most of the file transfers (close to 100%) are also successful with walking speeds. They also simulate worm propagation using Reality-Mining project trace [16] in which 100 students carrying Bluetooth-enable cell phone to discover all nearby Bluetooth devices for 18 months during 2004–2005. From their experiments, it shows that the numbers of initial infected nodes are not as important as the time the initial worms are launched. For example, the worm released in weekday and day time spreads more rapidly when compared with those launched in weekend and night time. Our findings are also consistent with their conclusion by showing the weekly dynamic of clustering coefficient and distance between nodes. We find worms are likely to spread faster only in specific days during a week. In addition, the speeds of worm propagations are significantly influenced by the batch arrival pattern.

In addition to mobility speed effects on worm propagation in realistic traces, the study in [57] focuses on the effect of synthetic mobility models such as random walk, random way point, random direction and random landmarks on Bluetooth worm propagations using ns-2 network simulations with Bluetooth extension. A worm propagates four-time faster with random landmarks mobility than the worm with random walk mobility does. Similar to IMPORTANT [3], authors conclude that such effect causes by node spatial distribution, link duration distribution and burstiness of successive link duration during each encounter and model it into their worm propagation model. Our work focuses on the uniform encounter pattern that is the outcome of a specific synthetic mobility pattern. For realistic encounter patterns, we also show the burstiness of new node arrival to the network and its effects on worm interactions.

Worm-like message propagation or epidemic routing has been studied for delay tolerant network applications [26, 49, 58] As in worm propagation, a sender in this routing protocol spreads messages to all nodes in close proximity, and those nodes repeatedly spread the copies of messages until the messages reach a destination, similar to flooding. This epidemic routing approach is called "store-carry-forward", minimizing the time for distributing the packets from a source to a destination in dynamic sparse networks with no existing complete paths [56] at the expense of increased buffer space, bandwidth, delay and transmission energy.

Performance modeling for epidemic routing in delay tolerant networks [56] based on ordinary differential equations (ODE) is proposed to evaluate the delivery delay, buffer occupancy, number of nodes that has packets buffered, loss probability and power consumption. The epidemic routing is modeled as $SI$ model with $\beta = 2wR(E[V^*])/A^{21}$ for random way point and random direction model where $w$ = constant for each mobility model, $R$ = radio range, $V^*$ = relative speed between two nodes and $A$ = area of node's movement. The average delivery delay from a source to a destination is $\ln N/(\beta(N-1))$. In our case, however, we are more interested in the delay from source(s) to *all* vulnerable nodes and infected nodes.

Also the concept of anti-packet is proposed to stop unnecessary overhead from forwarding extra packets copies after the destination has received the packets. In their IMMUNE scheme, the nodes that carry the buffered packets will remove the packets after they encounter with destinations. For IMMUNE_TX scheme, to stop unnecessary overhead forwarding, this scheme uses direct encounters between nodes and the destination as well as relies on the anti-packets which transferred during those encounters which are spread out to other nodes that carry the buffered packets. Their VACCINE scheme, similar to IMMUNE_TX, but the anti-packets are generated by the encounters between the destination and any node in the network.

These can be considered as a special case of a single group conservative one-sided interaction with fixed predators for their IMMUNE scheme, a single group conservative one-sided interaction for their IMMUNE_TX scheme and a single group aggressive one-sided interaction for their VACCINE scheme which we consider in our model. Note that their ODEs explain the behaviors after the packets reach destination. The extended models for 2-Hop forwarding, Probabilistic forwarding and Limited-Time forwarding are also presented in their study.

The study in [26] focuses on the performance analysis of epidemic routing under contentions including "finite bandwidth" which limits the number of exchanged packets between encountered nodes, "schedule of transmission" between encountered nodes to avoid interferences and also "interference" itself. Their model is based on random walk mobility. The delay of a packet from source to a destination is derived from a Markovian model.

## 13.3. Worm Interaction Model and Metrics

Because encounter-based networks are highly dynamic and have no specific boundary, we need a fully distributed security response mechanism. We propose the worm interaction approach that relies upon automated beneficial worm generation. Examples of worm interactions in the Internet are shown below.

In July 2001, a German programmer launched a worm Code Green [6] which patches vulnerable systems and removed backdoors left by Code Red II. Code Green randomly scans the Internet for NT servers that infected with the Code Red variant. After Code Green infects the machine, it downloads the patch from the Microsoft website. At the same time, CRClean, another anti-worm, reactively spreads itself to the systems attacking machines running CRClean.

Later in September 2003, a network worm Welchia attempted to terminate another network worm Blaster by deleting Blaster's process and downloading patch from Microsoft website. Even with good intention, Welchia created a large amount of traffic causing severe congestion in the Internet and Microsoft website [39].

A similar scenario occurred between Linux-based worms Li0n worm and Cheese worm where Cheese worm patched a vulnerability exploited by the Li0n worm in 2001 [20]. Cheese worm scans for machines with a secure root shell listening on TCP port 10008, as set up by a variant of the Li0n worm (which exploits a BIND vulnerability). If the shell exists, Cheese worm infect the machine and rewrite inetd.conf. It keeps scanning class B networks until its process is terminated. It is the first worm to automatically exploit the compromise and not the existing vulnerability. We also define this as a conservative one-sided worm interaction and we also model this scenario in Chapter 3.

In 2004, majority of worm outbreaks are caused by the "War of the Worms" between mass mailing worms NetSky, Bagle and MyDoom. The Bagle worms caused 15 outbreaks, NetSky 7 and MyDoom is 3 [47]. This war caused the highest outbreaks in one quarter with 12 outbreaks. Between February to April 2004, the authors of the Bagle worms have released nine separate variants (Worm/Bagle.C-K). Over the same period of time, the author(s) of the NetSky worms released three versions of their own (Worm/NetSky.D-F). NetSky's goal is to disable the Bagle and MyDoom worms. The author(s) of MyDoom have responded with the release of MyDoom.G which is immune to NetSky.

To understand worm interaction, we start by examining the concept of the predator-prey relationships in Section 3.1. In Section 3.2, we explain the basic Susceptible-Infected-Recovered (*SIR*) model which we use as the foundation of our worm interaction model. Then, in Section 3.3, we introduce the basic concept of worm interaction model and finally we propose new metrics in Section 3.3. In Section 3.4, we provide basic worm interaction model analysis. Then we introduce concept of node characteristics and node-characteristic-based worm interaction model in Section 3.5. Then, in Section 3.6, we analyze and compare simulation results between uniform and non-uniform (trace-based) worm interactions.

### 13.3.1. *Predator-Prey Relationships*

For every worm interaction type, there are two basic characters: Predator and Prey. The *Predator*, in our case the beneficial worm, is a worm that terminates and patches against another worm. The *Prey*, in our case the malicious worm, is a worm that is terminated or patched by another worm.

A predator can also be a prey at the same time for some other type of worm. Predator can vaccinate a susceptible host, i.e., infect the susceptible host (vaccinated hosts become predator-infected hosts or predator infected hosts) and apply a patch afterwards to prevent the hosts from prey infection. Manual vaccination, however, is performed by a user or an administrator by applying patches to susceptible hosts.

A termination refers to the removal of prey from infected hosts by predator; and such action causes prey infected hosts to become predator infected hosts. The removal by a user or an administrator, however, is referred to as manual removal. For brevity and clarity, manual vaccination and removal are not considered in this paper.

We choose to use two generic types of interacting worms, A and B, as our basis throughout the paper. A and B can assume the role of predator or prey depending on the type of interactions.

### 13.3.2. *Basic SIR Model*

Epidemic models, a set of ordinary differential equations (ODE), were used to describe the contagious disease spread including *SI*, *SIS*, *SIR SIRS*, *SEIR*, *MSIR*, *SEIRS* and carrier models [18, 28, 48] in which $S$, $I$, $E$, $R$, $M$ stand for Susceptible, Infectious, Exposed, Recovered, Maternally-derived Immune states, respectively. Carrier model means that some of the infected patients may never fully cover (as in tuberculosis) and continue to carry the infection. For maternally-derived immune, new born babies have temporary immunization for several months due to the maternal antibodies.

There's an analogy between computer worm infection and disease spread in that both depend on node's state and encounter pattern (as one node is physically close to another node).

*SIR* model is used as a simple model to predict the epidemic of measles, mumps, and rubella (MMR). This model explains the infection dynamic of the populations that are born susceptible, and can become infected as well as infectious simultaneously. For Susceptible-Exposed-Infectious-Recovered (*SEIR*) model, after a susceptible subject becomes infected (exposed), the infected subject (patient) only become infectious after incubation periods.

In the *SIR* model, vulnerable hosts fall in one of the following states in sequence — susceptible, infected and recovered. *Susceptible* hosts have never had the disease and can catch it. *Infected* hosts have the disease and are contagious (infectious). *Recovered* hosts have already had the disease and are immune or cured and cannot catch the disease again. Following are definitions of the basic *SIR* model.

Let $N$ be the size of *vulnerable* population, $I$ be the number of infected hosts at time $t$, $R$ be the recovered hosts at time $t$, $\beta$ be contact rate i.e., the rate of pair-wise contact between hosts, $\gamma$ be the removal or recovered rate and $S$ which equals to $N - I - R$ be the number of susceptible hosts at time $t$. $\beta$ and $\gamma$ are assumed constant.

The fundamental nonlinear ordinary differential equations of *SIR* model are shown below,

$$\frac{dS}{dt} = -\beta SI \tag{1}$$

$$\frac{dI}{dt} = \beta SI - \gamma I, \tag{2}$$

$$\frac{dR}{dt} = \gamma I. \tag{3}$$

The transitions of states are shown in Figure 13.1. An arrow represents a transition from one state to another. This model does not consider the birth/death of population as well as the spatial distribution of susceptible hosts.

From (2), the epidemic is *sustainable* only if $\frac{dI}{dt} > 0$ which requires $\frac{\beta S}{\gamma} > 1$; such important ratio is called the *Epidemiological Threshold*,

$$E_0 \equiv \frac{\beta S}{\gamma}. \tag{4}$$

We would use the basic *SIR* model as the foundation of our proposed Worm Interaction Model which we will show next.

### 13.3.3. *Worm Interaction Model*

Let $S$ be the number of vulnerable hosts that are not yet infected by any worm, i.e., *susceptible* at time $t$. Let $I_A$ and $I_B$ be the number of infected hosts by prey and predator at time $t$, respectively. Assume that each user encounters another random user with constant pair-wise contact rate $\beta$ (probability per unit of time of encounter between any pair) and uniform encounter (every node has equal chance

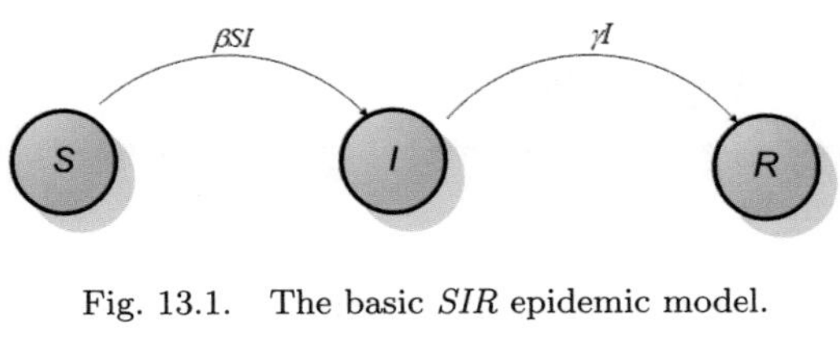


Fig. 13.1. The basic *SIR* epidemic model.

to encounter any other node). We also assume that node's characteristic including cooperation, immunization and *on-off* behavior does not change after infection from prey or predator. We start with the simple case where every node is cooperative, susceptible and always *on*. The state transition diagram in Figure 13.1 and the susceptible rate and infection rates of prey and predator are given by:

$$\frac{dS}{dt} = -\beta S(I_A + I_B) \tag{5}$$

$$\frac{dI_A}{dt} = \beta I_A(S - I_B) \tag{6}$$

$$\frac{dI_B}{dt} = \beta(SI_B + I_AI_B). \tag{7}$$

We call this set of equations "*aggressive one-sided interaction model*" where a predator is able to terminate its prey and vaccinate susceptible hosts. We shall vary this model later to capture various node characteristics.

### 13.3.4. *Metrics*

To gain insight and better quantify the effectiveness of aggressive one-sided worm interaction, we propose to use the following metrics:

- Total Infected hosts (TI): the number of hosts ever infected by prey.
- Maximum Infected hosts (MI): the peak of instantaneous number of prey-infected hosts where $I_A(0) \leq MI \leq TI$.
- Total Life Span (TL): the sum of time of individual nodes ever infected by prey. It can be interpreted as the total damage by prey.
- Average Individual Life Span (AL): the average life span of individual prey-infected hosts where $AL \leq TL$.
- Time to Infect All (TA): the time required for predator to infect all susceptible and prey hosts. Its inverse can be interpreted as average predator infection rate.
- Time to Remove All (TR): the time required for predator to terminate all preys where $TR \leq TA$. Its inverse can be interpreted as prey termination rate.

Our goal is to find the conditions to minimize these metrics based on node characteristics. We discuss details of node characteristics in Section 3.5.

Next we examine the basic worm interaction model and its relationships with above metrics.

### 13.3.5. *Worm Interaction Model Analysis*

If we want to suppress the initial infection ($\frac{dI_A}{dt} = 0$ at $t = 0$), from $(1 - b)$, then the required condition for this is

$$I_B(0) = S(0) \tag{3}$$

where $I_B(0)$ and $S(0)$ are the number of prey-infected hosts and susceptible hosts at $t = 0$ respectively.

We obtain from this condition that

$$TI = MI = I_A(0), \quad I_A(\infty) = 0 \tag{4}$$

where $I_A(\infty)$ is the number of prey-infected hosts at $t = \infty$.

However, we can see from (3) that the threshold can only be obtained by requiring the initial number of predator to be at least equal to number of susceptible hosts (a trivial condition). If that condition cannot be met, i.e., $I_B(0) < S(0)$, then we can only have certain acceptable level of infection and *TI* can be derived from

$$TI = \int_{t=0}^{\infty} \beta S I_A dt \tag{5}$$

*MI* can be found where $\frac{dI_A}{dt} = 0$ at $t > 0$, in which

$$I_B(t) = S(t) \tag{6}$$

Let $Y$ be the initial infected host ratio which is a ratio of predator initial infected hosts to prey initial infected hosts, i.e., $Y = \frac{I_B(0)}{I_A(0)}$ where $0 < Y < N - S(0)$ and $N$ is the total number of nodes in the network.

In Figures 13.3, 13.4 and 13.5, we show the metrics characteristics based on $Y$ and validate our models through the encounter-level simulations. We simulate and model 1,000 mobile nodes with $\beta = 6 \times 10^{-6}\,\text{sec}^{-1}$, $I_A(0) = 1$, and $1 \leq I_B(0)$, $S \leq 998$. Each simulation runs at least 1,000 rounds and we plot the mean values for each $Y$.

We assume uniform and constant $\beta$ as well as $I_A(0)$. We adjust $Y$ to find the optimal range to minimize our proposed metrics where $Y_{min} = 1$ and $Y_{max} = 998$.

In Figure 13.2, we show the relationships of *TI* and *MI* as the function of $Y$. *TI and MI decrease exponentially as Y increases.* The reason we still keep $I_A(0)$ small is to have wider range of $Y$ with the same size of $N$. *MI* (as a fraction of $N$) is more accurately predicted by the model. The ratio of *TI* to *MI* is constant but it gets

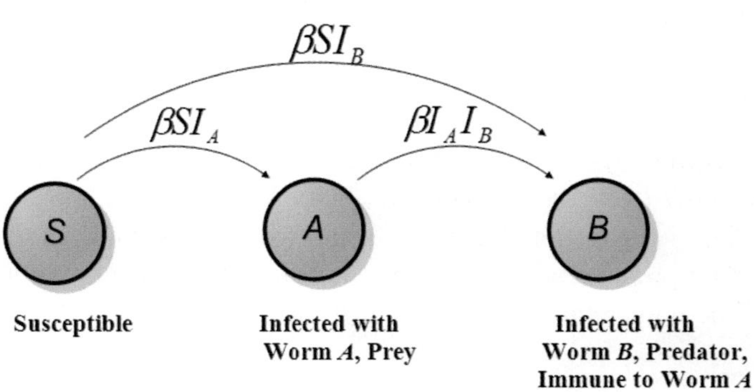


Fig. 13.2. Aggressive one-sided interaction.

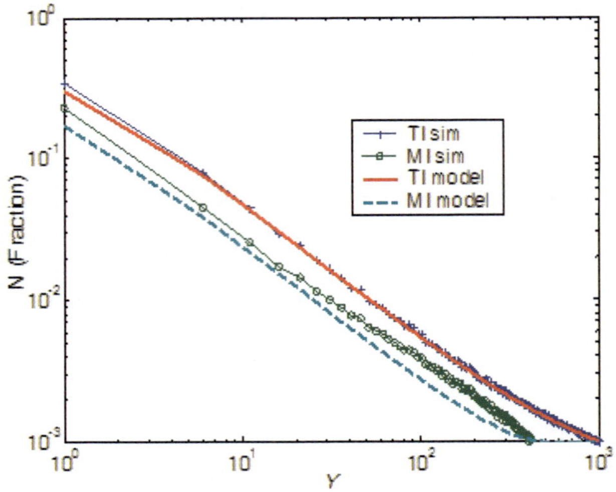


Fig. 13.3. Relationships of $TI$ and $MI$ with $Y$.

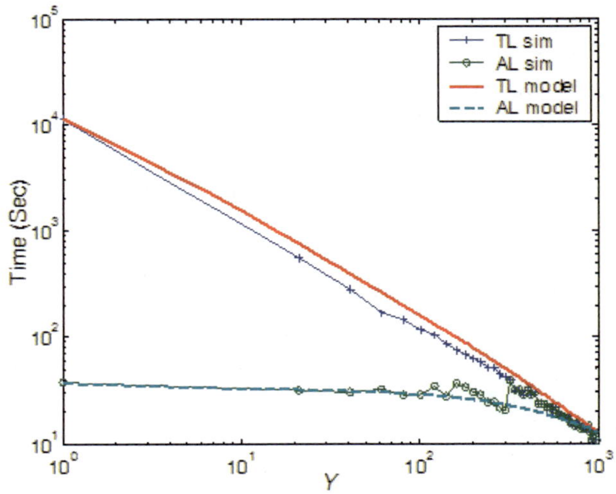


Fig. 13.4. Relationships of $TL$ and $AL$ with $Y$.

smaller towards the largest $Y$. We also find that if $S(0) : I_B(0) : I_A(0)$ is constant then $MI : N$ and $TI : N$ are also constant even $N$ changes.

Because $TL$ is the accumulated life of individual prey until the last prey has been removed by predator whose duration indicated by $TR$. we can simply derive $TL$ based on the numerical solutions from (6) as follows:

$$TL = \sum_{t=o}^{\infty} I_{A_t} \Delta t \tag{6}$$

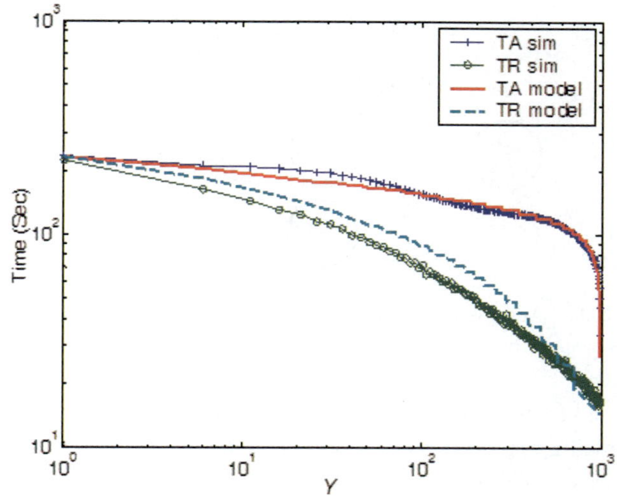


Fig. 13.5. Relationships of *TA* and *TR* with $Y$.

Since $AL$ is the average life span for each node that has been terminated by predator which is equal to the number of nodes that are ever infected, $AL$ can be derived from

$$AL = \frac{TL}{\int_{t=0}^{\infty} \beta I_A I_B dt} = \frac{TL}{\int_{t=0}^{\infty} \beta S I_A dt} = \frac{TL}{TI} \tag{7}$$

*TL* and $AL$ trends are mostly accurately predicted by the model. The $AL$ errors are due to the errors of estimated *TL*.

From Figure 13.4, *TL decreases exponentially as* $Y$ *increases.* $AL$, on the other hand, is almost constant for all $Y$. It is interesting to see that *TL* and $AL$ are merging at their minimum when $Y = Y_{max}$. As we can see that $TL_{min}$ and $AL_{min}$ do not reach zero at $Y_{max}$ because the next encounter time of a prey-infected host with *any* of predator-infected host $(I_B(0))$ requires average of $1/I_B(0)\beta$. Furthermore, from (7), $TL_{min} = TI_{min}AL_{min}$, thus $TL_{min}$ and $AL_{min}$ merge to each other because $TI_{min} = I_A(0) = 1$.

From the observation in Figure 13.4, *TR* reduces much faster than *TA* with the increase of $Y$. *TR* decreases exponentially as $Y$ *increases. TA* starts to be reduced rapidly when $Y \approx Y_{max}$. At $Y_{max}$, we can see that $TA_{min} = TR_{min} = AL_{min}$.

Note that *TA* is also similar to the average time for every node to receive a copy of a message from a random source in an encounter-based network which can be derived as $(2 \ln N + 0.5772)/N\beta$ [13].

### 13.3.6. *Node Characteristics*

Earlier we assume that all nodes are *fully cooperative*, *susceptible* to both prey and predator and "*always-on*", and hence each encounter guarantees a successful message (worm) transfer.

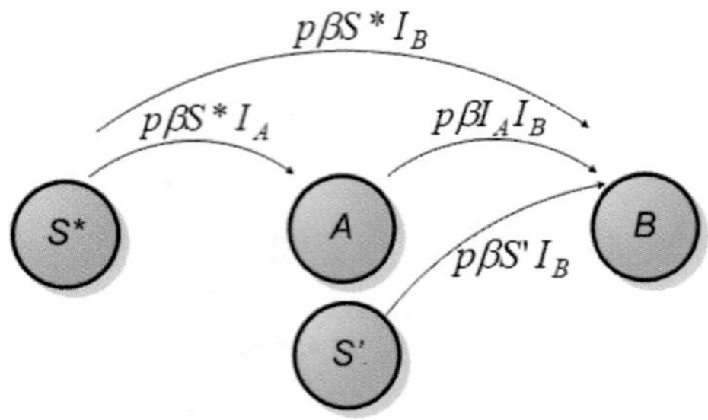


Fig. 13.6. Aggressive one-sided interaction with node characteristics.

In this section, we investigate the scenarios that do not follow above assumptions regarding these three important node characteristics. We assume these characteristics are consistent through out its life time of the networks.

13.3.6.1. *Cooperation*

Cooperation is the willingness of node to forward the message (worm) for other nodes. The opposite characteristic is known as selfishness. Intuitively, cooperation may seem to make the network more vulnerable. However, unlike immunization, cooperation is expected to equally slow down both prey and predator propagations. Hence, the effect of cooperation is hard to anticipate.

13.3.6.2. *Immunization*

Not all nodes are susceptible to the prey either because of their heterogeneous operating systems and their differences of promptness to remove the vulnerability from their machines. Hence partial of nodes can be immune to prey and will slow down the overall prey infection. It is expected to improve the overall targeted metrics that we mention earlier. Because even some nodes are immune to the prey but they still help forwarding the predator to other nodes and it is expected to have no positive impact on $AL$, $TA$ but reduce $TL$ and $TR$ simply because of less number of nodes to be removed.

13.3.6.3. *On-off behavior*

A node is able to accept or forward the packet based on the *on-off* characteristics. In reality, devices are "*on*" or active only a fraction of the time. Activity may be related to mobility. For instance, a mobile phone is usually *on*, while lap top is unlikely to be mobile while *on*. We model the transition from *on* to *off*, and vice versa, probabilistically. The probability is determined at the beginning of each time interval. Hence the contact rate is expected to be proportionally reduced according to the probability that the node cannot forward or accept the packets because of *on-off* status.

Let $c$ be the fraction of $N$ that are willing to be *cooperative* where $0 \leq c \leq 1$ and $N$ is the total number of nodes in the networks. Let $i$ be the fraction of cooperative nodes that are *immune* to prey where $0 \leq i \leq 1$. We assume that initial predator and prey infected hosts are cooperative then the number of susceptible hosts for both prey and predator is $S^*$ where $S^*(0) = c(1-i)N - I_A(0)$ and number of susceptible hosts for predator only is $S'$, where $S'(0) = ciN - I_B(0)$. Note that $N = S^* + S' + I_A + I_B$ and $S = S^* + S'$. We define the probability of "*on*" behavior as $p$ and "*off*" behavior as $1-p$ where $0 \leq p \leq 1$. Hence contact rate for both predator and prey is $p\beta$.

Based on these definitions, the node-characteristic-based aggressive one-sided model can be shown as follows:

$$\frac{dS^*}{dt} = -p\beta S^*(I_A + I_B) \tag{8}$$

$$\frac{dS'}{dt} = -p\beta S' I_B \tag{9}$$

$$\frac{dI_A}{dt} = p\beta I_A(S^* - I_B) \tag{10}$$

$$\frac{dI_B}{dt} = p\beta((S^* + S')I_B + I_A I_B) \tag{11}$$

Similarly to Section 3.4, we use this model to derive metrics that we are interested. The differences between the conditions of this model and that of basic model to minimize the metrics are investigated here.

If we want to suppress the prey initial infection, then we need

$$I_B(0) = S^*(0) \tag{12}$$

Assume small $I_A(0)$ and $I_B(0)$ when compared with $N$, hence $S^*(0) \approx c(1-i)$ $S(0)$; required $I_B(0)$ to stop prey initial infection is therefore also reduced approximately by the factor of $c(1-i)$ when compared with (3). *TI*, similarly derived to (5), is

$$TI = p\int_{t=0}^{\infty} \beta S^* I_A dt \tag{13}$$

As contact rate is changed due to *on-off* behavior, *TA* which $Y = 1$, can be derived as follows:

$$TA = (2\ln N + 0.5772)/pN\beta \tag{14}$$

Our model can also be used to model node-characteristic-based one-worm-type propagation which equivalent to epidemic routing by assigning either $I_B(0) = 0$ or $I_A(0) = 0$ in (8) to (11).

## 13.4. Simulation Results

In this section, we start by validating our models with uniform-encounter simulation. Then, we compare the relationships of node characteristic with our proposed metrics in uniform and non-uniform (trace-based) encounter networks.

### 13.4.1. *Uniform Encounters*

We use encounter-level simulations to simulate uniform encounter of 1,000 mobile nodes with $\beta = 6 \times 10^{-6}\,\text{sec}^{-1}$, and $I_A(0) = I_B(0) = 1$. Each simulation runs 10,000 rounds and we plot the median values for each $i$. The lag time between predator and prey initial infection is 0 sec. We vary cooperation ($c$) from 20% to 100%, immunization ($i$) from 0% to 90% with 100% "*on*" time for the first part of experiments (Figure 13.7(a)–(f)) and we vary "*on*" time from 10% to 90% with 90% cooperation and 10% immunization, for the second part (Figure 13.7(g)–(h)). The first part aims to analyze the impact of cooperation and immunization on worm interaction whereas the second part aims to analyze the *on-off* behavior.

From Figure 13.7(a)–(f) we find that increase of cooperation, surprisingly, reduces malicious worm infection for all the metrics. (Note that increase of cooperation actually increases absolute *TI* and absolute *MI*, but relative *TI* (or $TI/N^*$) and relative *MI* (or $MI/N^*$) are reduced where number of cooperative-susceptible nodes $N^* = c(1 - i)N$).

Similarly, for immunization Figure 13.7(a)–(f) shows that immunization reduces all categories of metrics except $AL$. With the increase of immunization, *TI* is reduced much faster than $TL$, thus increase of immunization increases $AL$. Furthermore, increase of immunization, as expected, reduces *TR* because of less number of possible prey-infected hosts.

*Cooperation reduces AL and TR significantly* than it does to other metrics. *Immunization, however, reduces relative TI, relative MI and TL more significantly* than it does other metrics. With equal increase (20% to 80%), immunization at cooperation = 100% reduces relative *TI*, relative *MI* and *TL* approximately 8.8 times, 2.7 times, and 10.6 times, respectively, more than cooperation does at immunization = 0%. On the other hand, cooperation reduces *TR* approximately 3.3 times more than immunization does. As shown in Figure 13.7(e), unlike immunization, only cooperation can reduce *TA*.

The impact of *on-off* behavior ($p$) is clear in Figure 13.7(g) and (h). As expected, with variant of "*on*" *time*, there is no difference in relative *TI* and relative *MI*. The ratio of contact rate between predator and prey is an indicator of the fraction of infected hosts irrespective of the contact rate. In this case, the ratio of contact rate is always 1.0, and hence the constant of relative *TI* and relative *MI* [11].

*TL*, *AL TA* and *TR exponentially decrease* with the increase of "*on*" *time* causing reduction of inter-encounter time. Our model shows a good agreement with simulation results for most of the scenarios based on node characteristics.

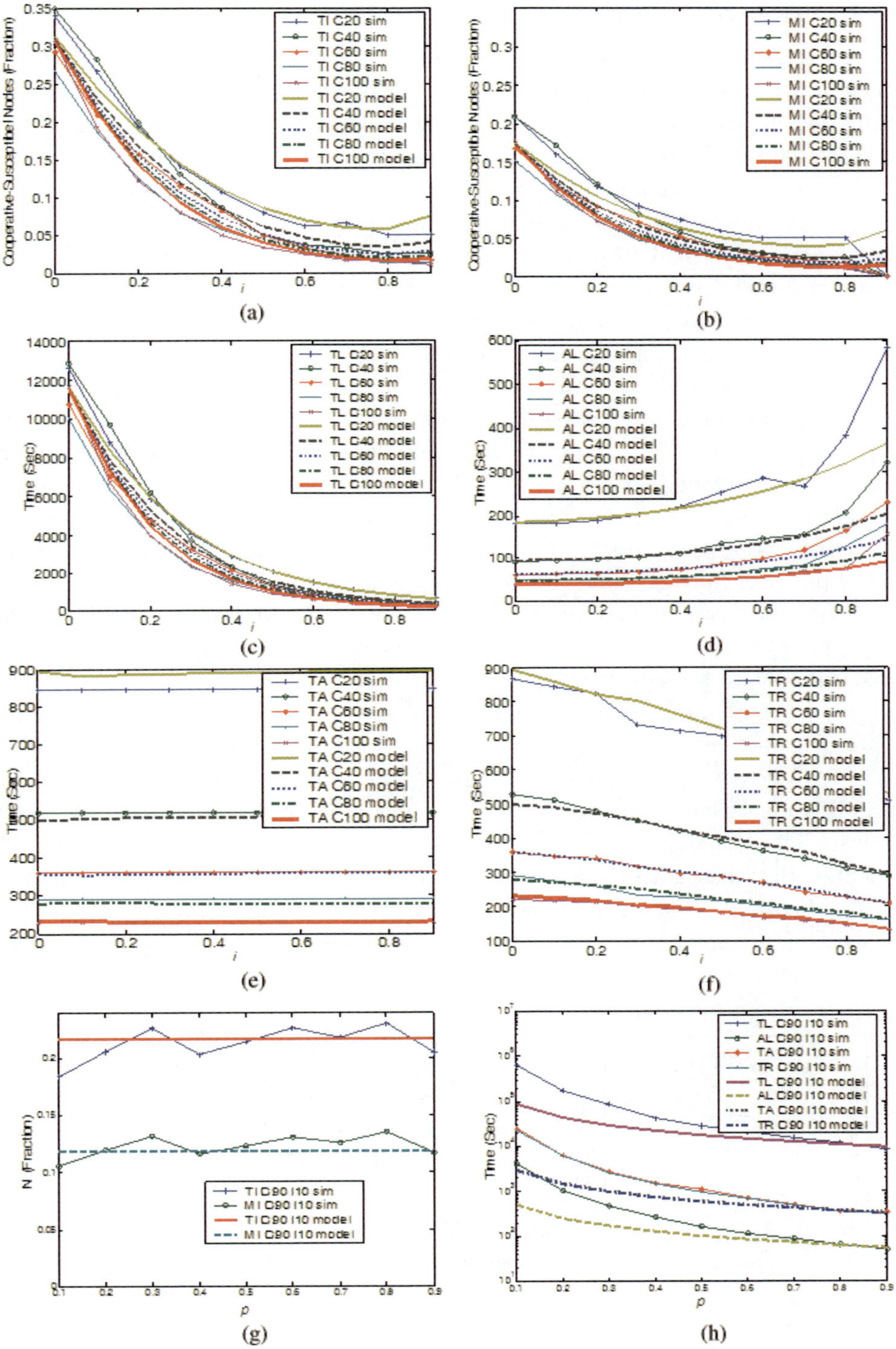


Fig. 13.7. Effects of cooperation ($c$), immunization ($i$) and *on-off* behavior ($p$) on uniform-encounter worm interactions.

### 13.4.2. *Non-uniform Encounters*

We investigate the consistency of the model-based results with those generated by using measurement-based real encounters. We drive our encounter-level simulations using the wireless network traces of the University of Southern California of 62 days in spring 2006 semester [25]. We define an encounter as two nodes sharing the same access point at the same time. We randomly choose 1,000 random nodes from 5,000 most active nodes based on their online time from the trace. Their median $\beta$ is $1.27 \times 10^{-6}\,\text{sec}^{-1}$ and median number of unique encounter node is 94. We use $I_A(0) = 1$ and $I_B(d) = 1$ where $d$ is the delay between initial predator-infected node and initial prey-infected node in the simulation. This delay was introduced as the traced delay between the first arrival of two groups in which the initial predator-infected node and the initial prey-infected node are assumed to be in different groups (and different batch arrivals). First group and second group account approximately for 90% and 10% of total population, respectively. The first group has average contact rate $\beta_{11} = 3.6 \times 10^{-6}\,\text{sec}^{-1}$, the second group has average contact rate $\beta_{22} = 3.3 \times 10^{-6}\,\text{sec}^{-1}$, and the approximated contact rate between groups $\beta_{12} = 4 \times 10^{-7}\,\text{sec}^{-1}$. From the trace, the median arrival delay between initial predator-infected node and initial prey-infected node is 8.7 days (introduced by the gap between the first and the second batch arrivals). Because the first group is in the first batch, hence "*Fast predator*" is also the *early* predator and "Slow predator" is also the *late* predator.

We can see the consistent batch arrival pattern in Figure 13.8(c), each line represents different start new-node arrival time into the networks, i.e., day 0, 10, 20 and 30 where day 0 is January 25, 2006. Because at the beginning of the semester, not all students had returned to campus; hence, the large gap between the batch arrivals. The smaller gaps (1 day) in other start days were caused by the university's schedule that has classes either on Tuesday-Thursday or Monday-Wednesday-Friday. *Hence, the batch arrival patterns are likely to occur in any encounter-based networks due to the users' schedules.* In addition, in Figure 13.8(a)–(b), we find that user's encounter in the trace is highly skewed (non-uniform), i.e., top 20% of user's

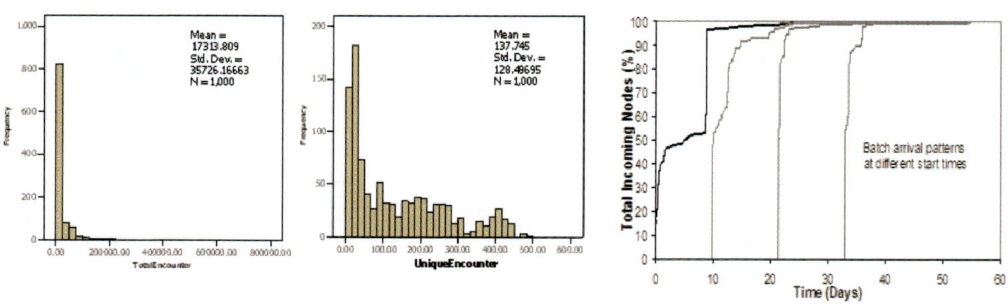


(a) (b) (c)

Fig. 13.8. Trace-based encounter characteristics (a) Total encounters (b) Unique encounters and (c) Batch arrival pattern.

total encounter account for 72% of all users' encounters and 70% of users encounter less than 20% of total unique users which are caused by non-uniform *on-off behavior and location preferences* [25, 26].

We choose to run our trace-driven simulations at day 0 to see the significance of batch arrival patterns on worm interactions. To validate our model accuracy, we compare the trace-driven simulation results with our aggressive one-sided model with node characteristics and group behavior. We also apply the batch arrival and delay to our model and compare the trace-driven simulation results with our model plot.

In our model, we use $\beta_{11} = 3.6 \times 10^{-6}$, $\beta_{22} = 3.3 \times 10^{-6}$, $\beta_{12} = 4 \times 10^{-7}$ with $t_1$ = day 8.7 (second batch arrival, 395 nodes join group 1, 50 nodes join group 2), $t_2$ = day 8.71 (all predator-infected nodes leaving the networks), $t_3$ = day 11.57 (predator-infected nodes rejoin the networks), $t_4$ = day 17.4 (third batch arrival, 50 nodes join group 2), $t_4$ = day 40.5 (fourth batch arrival, 5 nodes join group 2). These batch arrival patterns are approximated from the observed trace and simulations.

In Figure 13.9(c)–(f), this batch arrival patterns and the delay cause significant additions on our proposed metrics especially *TL*, *AL*, *TA*, and *TR* (*TA* is subject to the time of the last-node arrival). In addition, we find that immunization ($i$) is still a very important factor to reduce relative *TI*, relative *MI*, *TL*, and *TR* and *cooperation helps reduce relative TI, relative MI, TL, AL, and TR.*

## 13.5. Summary and Future Works

In this chapter, we discuss the worm propagations in mobile networks. We explain the basic definitions including proposed metrics required for understanding the Worm Interaction Model. Then we propose a node-characteristics-based model and metrics as a performance evaluation framework for worm interactions in encounter-based networks, with focus on cooperation, immunization, and "on-off" behavior. We find that in uniform encounter networks, immunization is the most influential characteristics for total infected hosts, maximum infected hosts and total life span. Cooperation and on-off behaviors greatly affect average individual life span, time-to-infect-all and time-to-remove-all. Our model also shows a very good agreement with uniform-encounter simulation results.

Based on realistic mobile networks measurements, we find that the contact rate and the number of unique encounters of users are not uniform. This causes worm infection behavior to deviate significantly from that of uniform encounter networks, even though the general trends remain similar to the model.

In addition, the level of infection is now determined by the contact rate of the initial predator and prey-infected hosts. A higher contact rate of initial predator (than prey) infected hosts significantly reduces the total infected hosts and maximum infected hosts when compared to those of the opposite scenario. In such networks, immunization seems to be more important factor than

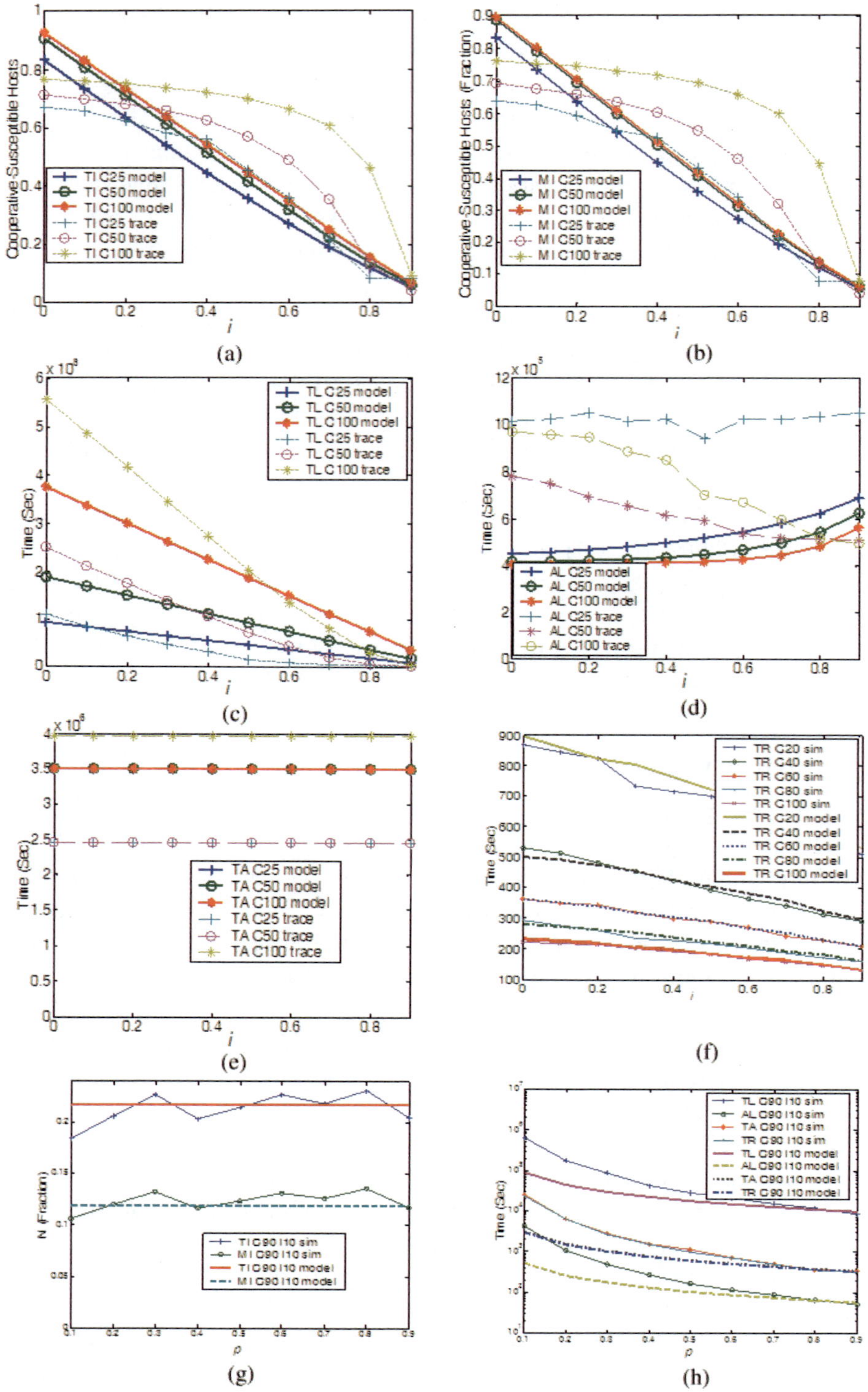


Fig. 13.9. Effects of cooperation ($c$), immunization ($i$) and *on-off* behavior ($p$) on uniform-encounter worm interactions.

cooperation. Hence, enforcing early immunization and having mechanism to find a high-contact-rate node to use as an initial predator-infected host is critical to contain worm propagation in encounter-based networks. We believe that node-characteristics model for uniform encounter networks can be extended with delay and cluster behavior to explain effect of node characteristics on worm interaction in non-uniform encounter networks of the future.

## Acknowledgements

Much of this work was performed at the University of Southern California with support from NSF awards: CAREER 0134650, ACQUIRE 0435505 and Intel.

## References

[1] A. Avritzer, R. G. Cole, and E. J. Weyuker, "Using performance signatures and software rejuvenation for worm mitigation in tactical MANETs", Proceedings of the 6th international Workshop on Software and Performance (Buenes Aires, Argentina, February 05–08, 2007). WOSP'07. ACM Press, New York, NY, 172–180.

[2] E. Anderson, K. Eustice, S. Markstrum, M. Hansen, and P. Reiher, "Mobile contagion: Simulation of infection and defense", Proceedings of the 19th Workshop on Principles of Advanced and Distributed Simulation, pp. 80–87, 2005.

[3] F. Bai, N. Sadagopan, and A. Helmy, "The IMPORTANT Framework for Analyzing the Impact of Mobility on Performance of Routing for Ad Hoc Networks", *AdHoc Networks Journal Elsevier Science*, Vol. 1, Issue 4, pp. 383–403, November 2003.

[4] M. Bishop, "Computer Security: Art and Science",

[5] BRITE: Boston Representative Internet Topology Generator.

[6] R. Buckley, "'Anti-worms' released to clean up Code Red", Information Age http://www.information-age.com/article/2001/september/anti-worms_released_to_clean_up_code_red

[7] CAIDA, ICSI, Silicon Defense, UC Berkeley EECS and UC San Diego CSE, "Analysis of the Sapphire Worm", http://www.caida.org/analysis/security/sapphire

[8] F. Castaneda, E. C. Sezer, and J. Xu, "WORM vs. WORM: preliminary study of an active counter-attack mechanism", ACM workshop on Rapid malcode, 2004.

[9] A. Chaintreau, P. Hui, J. Crowcroft, C. Diot, R. Gass, and J. Scott, "Impact of Human Mobility on the Design of Opportunistic Forwarding Algorithms", IEEE INFOCOM 2006, April 2006.

[10] Z. Chen, L. Gao, and K. Kwiat, "Modeling the Spread of Active Worms", IEEE INFOCOM 2003.

[11] R. G. Cole, "Initial Studies on Worm Propagation in MANETS for Future Army Combat Systems", ASC 2004.

[12] R. G. Cole, N. Phamdo, M. A. Rajab, and A. Terzis, "Requirements of Worm Mitigation Technologies in MANETS", Principles of Advanced and Distribution Simulation, 2005.

[13] D. E. Cooper, P. Ezhilchelvan, and I. Mitrani, "A Family of Encounter-Based Broadcast Protocols for Mobile Ad-hoc Networks", In Proceedings of the Wireless Systems and Mobility in Next Generation Internet. 1st International Workshop of the EURO-NGI Network of Excellence, Dagstuhl Castle, Germany, June 7–9 2004.

[14] R. Dantu, J. Cangussu, and A. Yelimeli, "Dynamic Control of Worm Propagation", Proceedings of the International Conference on Information Technology: Coding and Computing (ITCC'04) Volume 2 — Volume 2 2004.

[15] C. Douligeris and A. Mitrokotsa, "DDoS attacks and defense mechanisms: classification and state-of-the-art", Computer Networks: The International Journal of Computer and Telecommunications Networking 2004.

[16] N. Eagle and A. Pentland, "Reality Mining: Sensing Complex Social Systems", Journal of Personal and Ubiquitous Computing, June 2005.

[17] S. Eubank, H. Guclu, V. S. A. Kumar, M. V. Marathe, A. Srinivasan, Z. Toroczkai, and N. Wang, "Modelling disease outbreaks in realistic urban social networks", *Nature* 429, 180–184 (13 May 2004).

[18] J. C. Frauenthal, "Mathematical Modeling in Epidemiology", Springer-Verlag, New York, 1988.

[19] A. Ganesh, L. Massoulie, and D. Towsley, "The Effect of Network Topology on the Spread of Epidemics", IEEE INFOCOM 2005.

[20] T. C. Green, "'Friendly' Cheese worm reveals many compromised boxes", The Register http://www.theregister.co.uk/2001/05/17/friendly_cheese_worm_reveals_many/

[21] R. Groenevelt, P. Nain, and G. Koole, "The Message Delay in Mobile Ad Hoc Networks", Performance, October 2005.

[22] A. Helmy, "Small Worlds in Wireless Networks", IEEE Communications Letters, pp. 490–492, Vol. 7, No. 10, October 2003.

[23] R. V. Hogg and E. A. Tanis, Probability and Statistical Inference, Prentice Hall, 2001.

[24] W. Hsu and A. Helmy, "On Nodal Encounter Patterns in Wireless LAN Traces", The 2nd IEEE Int.l Workshop on Wireless Network Measurement (WiNMee), April 2006.

[25] W. Hsu and A. Helmy, "On Modeling User Associations in Wireless LAN Traces on University Campuses", The 2nd IEEE Int.l Workshop on Wireless Network Measurement (WiNMee), April 2006.

[26] A. Jindal and K. Psounis, "Performance analysis of epidemic routing under contention", Proceeding of the 2006 international Conference on Communications and Mobile Computing (Vancouver, British Columbia, Canada, July 03–06, 2006). IWCMC'06. ACM Press, New York, NY, 539–544.

[27] J. Kephart, G. Sorkin, D. Chess, and S. White, "Fighting Computer Viruses", Scientific American, November 1997.

[28] W. O. Kermack and A. G. McKendrick, "A Contribution to the Mathematical Theory of Epidemics", Proceedings of the Royal Society 1997; A115: 700–721.

[29] W. Mendenhall and T. Sincich, Statistics for Engineering and the Sciences, Prentice Hall.

[30] D. Moore, C. Shannon, G. M. Voelker, and S. Savage, "Internet Quarantine: Requirements for Containing Self Propagating Code", IEEE INFOCOM 2003.

[31] J. Morales, P. J. Clarke, B. M. G. Kibria, and Y. Deng, "Testing and evaluating virus detectors for handheld devices", *Journal of Computer Virology*, Springer, Vol. 2, 135–147, 2006.

[32] NS-2: the network simulator (http://www.isi.edu/nsnam/ns/).

[33] D. M. Nicol, M. Lijenstam, and J. Liu, "Multiscale Modeling and Simulation of Worm Effects on the Internet Routing Infrastructure", Proceedings of the Performance Tools 2003 Conference Urbana, IL, September 2003.

[34] D. M. Nicol, "Models and Analysis of Active Worm Defense", Proceeding of Mathematical Methods, Models and Architecture for Computer Networks Security Workshop 2005.

[35] Z. Nicoloski, N. Deo, and L. Kucera, "Correlation Model of Worm Propagation on Scale-Free Networks", *Complexus* 2006 Vol. 3, No.1–3, 2006 pp. 169–182.

[36] R. Pastor-Satorras and A. Vespignani, "Epidemic dynamics in finite size scale-free networks", *Physcal Review E*, 65, 2002.

[37] J. Su, K. K. W. Chan, A. G. Miklas, K. Po, A. Akhavan, S. Saroiu, E. Lara, and A. Goel, "A preliminary investigation of worm infections in a bluetooth environment", ACM Workshop on Rapid Malcode (WORM), Alexandria, VA, Oct. 2006.

[38] S. Staniford, V. Paxson, and N. Weaver, "How to own the Internet in your spare time", Proceeding of the USENIX Security Symposium, Monterey, 2002, pp. 149–167.

[39] P. Szor, "The Art of Computer Virus Research and Defense", (Symantec Press) 2005.

[40] S. Tanachaiwiwat and A. Helmy, "VACCINE: War of the Worms in Wired and Wireless Networks", IEEE INFOCOM 2006, Barcelona, Spain Poster and Demo Session (Technical Report CS 05-859, Computer Science Department, USC).

[41] S. Tanachaiwiwat and A. Helmy, "Analyzing the Interactions of Self-Propagating Codes in Multi-hop Networks", Eighth International Symposium on Stabilization, Safety, and Security of Distributed Systems (SSS) accepted as Brief Announcement, November 2006, Dallas, Texas.

[42] S. Tanachaiwiwat and A. Helmy, "Modeling and Analysis of Worm Interactions (War of the Worms)", IEEE Broadnets 2007 Fourth International Conference on Broadband Communications, Networks, and Systems, September 10–14, 2007, Raleigh, North Carolina, 2007.

[43] S. Tanachaiwiwat and A. Helmy, "Worm Ecology in Encounter-based Networks (Invited Paper)", IEEE Broadnets 2007 Fourth International Conference on Broadband Communications, Networks, and Systems, September 10–14, 2007, Raleigh, North Carolina, 2007.

[44] S. Tanachaiwiwat and A. Helmy, "On the Performance Evaluation of Encounter-based Worm Interactions Based on Node Characteristics", ACM Mobicom 2007 Workshop on Challenged Networks, September 14, 2007, Montreal, Quebec, Canada.

[45] S. Tanachaiwiwat and A. Helmy, "Encounter-based Worms: Analysis and Defense", IEEE Conference on Sensor and Ad Hoc Communications and Networks (SECON) 2006 Poster/Demo Session, VA, September 2006.

[46] S. Tanachaiwiwat and A. Helmy, "Encounter-based worms: Analysis and defense, Ad Hoc Networks". Elsevier Journal (2009), doi:10.1016/j.adhoc.2009.02.004.

[47] Trend Micro Annual Virus Report 2004, http://www.trendmicro.com.

[48] H. Trottier and P. Phillippe, "Deterministic Modeling Of Infectious Diseases: Theory And Methods", The Internet Journal of Infectious Diseases ISSN: 1528-8366.

[49] A. Vahdat and D. Becker, "Epidemic routing for partially connected ad hoc networks", Technical Report CS-2000.

[50] M. Vojnovic and A. J. Ganesh, "On the Effectiveness of Automatic Patching", ACM WORM 2005, The 3rd Workshop on Rapid Malcode, George Mason University, Fairfax, VA, USA, Nov 11, 2005.

[51] Viruslist.com, "Information about Viruses, Hackers and Spams", www.viruslist.com.

[52] A. Wagner, T. Dubendorfer, B. Plattner, and R. Hiestand, "Experiences with worm propagation simulations", Proceedings of the ACM Workshop on Rapid Malcode (WORM), Washington 2003.

[53] Y. Wang and C. Wang, "Modelling the effects of timing parameters on virus propagation", Proceedings of the ACM Workshop on Rapid Malcode (WORM), Washington 2003.
[54] N. Weaver, V. Paxson, and S. Staniford, "A taxonomy of computer worms", Proceedings of the ACM Workshop on Rapid Malcode (WORM), Washington, D.C., 2003.
[55] N. Weaver, S. Staniford, and V. Paxson, "Very Fast Containment of Scanning Worms", 13th USENIX Security Symposium, Aug. 2004.
[56] N. Weaver, I. Hamadeh, G. Kesidis, and V. Paxson, "Preliminary Results Using Scale-Down to Explore Worm Dynamics", Proceedings of the ACM Workshop on Rapid Malcode (WORM), Fairfax, VA, Oct. 2004.
[57] G. Yan, L. Cuellar, S. Eidenbenz, H. D. Flores, N. Hengartner, and V. Vu, "Bluetooth Worm Propagation: Mobility Pattern Matters!", ASIACCS, March 2007, Singapore.
[58] X. Zhang, G. Neglia, J. Kurose, and D. Towsley, "Performance Modeling of Epidemic Routing", to appear Elsevier Computer Networks journal, 2007.
[59] C. C. Zou, W. Gong, and D. Towsley, "Code red worm propagation modeling and analysis", Proceedings of the 9th ACM CCS 2002.
[60] C. C. Zou, W. Gong, D. Towsley, and L. Gao, "Monitoring and early detection for Internet worms", Proceedings of the 9th ACM CCS 2003.

# Chapter 14

## WINDOWS ROOTKITS A GAME OF "HIDE AND SEEK"

Sherri Sparks*, Shawn Embleton† and Cliff C. Zou‡
*Clear Hat Consulting, Inc., http://www.clearhatconsulting.com/*
*School of Electrical Engineering and Computer Science,*
*University of Central Florida, Orlando, FL 32816, USA*
**sparks@clearhatconsulting.com*
*†embleton@clearhatconsulting.com*
*‡czou@cs.ucf.edu*

Rootkits are a type of malware that attempt to hide their presence on a system, typically by compromising the communication conduit between an Operating System and its users. In this chapter, we track the evolution of rootkits and the techniques used to defend against them from the earliest rootkits to highly advanced, present day rootkits capable of exploiting processor virtualization extensions and infecting the BIOS.

### 14.1. Introduction

Despite all of the popular press surrounding malicious code like viruses and worms, until the past few years rootkits had remained a relatively hidden threat. If one were asked to classify viruses and worms by a single defining characteristic, the first word to come to mind would probably be *replication*. In contrast, the single defining characteristic of a rootkit is *stealth*. Viruses reproduce, but rootkits hide. They hide by compromising the communication conduit between an Operating System and its users. A rootkit can be defined as "a set of programs which patch and trojan existing execution paths within the system" [1].

Before delving into the low-level technical details, it is helpful to view the problem at a higher level of abstraction. Most modern Operating Systems are based upon the concept of a layered architecture. A layered architecture attempts to divide a computer system into hierarchal groups of related components that communicate according to predefined sets of rules, or interfaces [2]. At the highest level of abstraction, we can divide a system into three layers: users, Operating System (OS), and hardware. In this hierarchy, system users reside at the highest layer while hardware resides at the lowest. The Operating System sits in the middle managing the system's hardware resources. The function of the OS is two-fold. First, it shelters users from the gory details of hardware communication by encapsulating them into convenient services that they can call upon to perform useful work (e.g., creating a file, or opening a network connection). These services, also known as the API (Application Programmer Interface), form the communication conduit between users and the Operating System. Secondarily, the Operating System provides a trusted computing base (TCB) with security mechanisms for user authentication and the means of protecting itself and applications from damaging each other [3]. This layer is further divided into sub-components corresponding to the management of the system's primary resources. They have their own interfaces and commonly include file management, process management, memory management, device management, network communications, and protection/security. Figure 14.1 provides a simplified view of Operating System components and interfaces arranged according to a layered architecture.

The advantage of a layered architecture lies in its extensibility. Because each layer communicates with the layer beneath it according to a defined interface, components in the lower layer can be modified or replaced without affecting the upper layer. The benefits to large commercial Operating Systems, like Windows, are obvious. Unfortunately, the interfaces are also a weak link in such a design because they provide a malicious user with a single point of attack. Since a user's view of the computer system and its resources is strictly mediated by the information the Operating System provides to it via the API interface, a malicious program that modifies the interface controls the entire system. The exploitation of this idea forms the basis of rootkit technology.

A rootkit hides its presence by controlling the interfaces between various Operating System components. It does so by intercepting and then altering the interface communications to suit its purposes (e.g., to hide its presence). Consider an application attempting to determine whether or not the executable file for rootkit

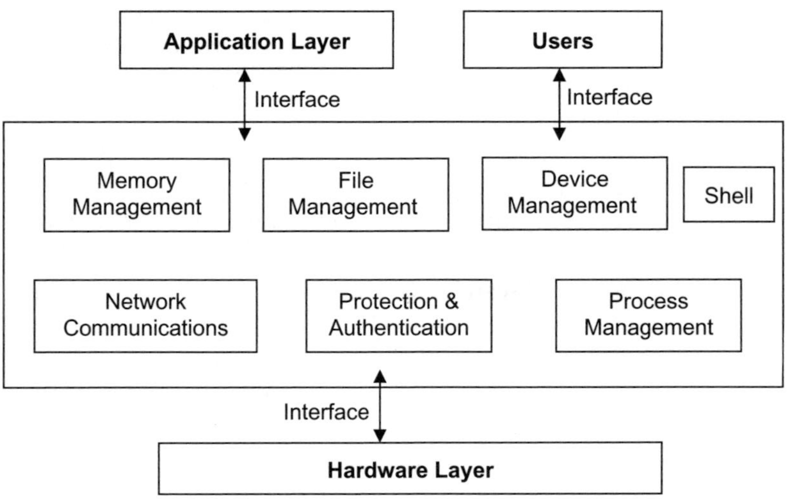


Fig. 14.1. Layered design of Operating System components and interfaces.

X exists on a system. The application does not search for the file by directly going out and reading sectors from the hard disk. Instead, it calls a convenient FindFile API provided by the Operating System. Invisible to the application, rootkit X has compromised the API interface to the file manager. Covertly, the rootkit intercepts the application's call to FindFile and returns an erroneous message indicating that the file does not exist. Thus, the rootkit file is effectively hidden from the application and its users despite the fact that it clearly still exists. As such, we can view rootkits as a form of "man in the middle attack".

In order to obscure its presence, a rootkit may compromise one or more of the primary Operating System components. File management, process management, and network communication components have all been compromised by various rootkits to hide files, processes, and network connections on the computers they are installed upon.

Secondary to hiding itself, a rootkit is generally capable of gathering and manipulating information on a target machine. It may, for example, log a victim user's keystrokes to obtain passwords and other sensitive information, or manipulate the system state to allow a remote attacker to gain control by altering security descriptors and access tokens. Once again, it does this by eavesdropping on communications between the user and the Operating System.

The most common usage of a rootkit is to secure access to a "hacked" system thereby allowing an attacker to return and obtain control of the compromised system at some later date. This clearly poses a concern for system administrators. Nevertheless, an even greater concern arises when we consider the trend toward malicious code hybridization that is the blurring of boundaries between malware species like viruses, worms, spyware, and rootkits. Rootkits bring two powerful cards to the table: extreme stealth and remote control. Viruses have incorporated stealth techniques into their code for a number of years, but modern rootkits take information camouflage to the level of art. It is not difficult to imagine a distributed informational warfare scenario based upon a hybrid species of malicious code that combines the advanced propagation techniques of viruses and worms with the capabilities for stealth and remote control of modern rootkits. It should be noted, however, that in spite of its potential for malicious misuse, rootkit technology has also been used for legitimate purposes. It has, for example, been used by law enforcement to capture evidence in computer crime cases involving child exploitation.

The relative obscurity and scarcity of comprehensive information on non-UNIX rootkits coupled with the popularity of the Microsoft Windows Operating System has led us to focus this chapter on Windows rootkits. In the next section we examine the evolution of rootkit technology. Section III attempts to provide some insights into how various Operating System components have been attacked by rootkits. Section IV and V briefly discuss their technical implementation. This allows us to speculate how the structural organization and design of the Windows Operating System and its underlying hardware architecture may facilitate malicious code injection and render detection more difficult. In section VI, we conclude with a survey of current research in Windows rootkit detection.

## 14.2. Rootkit Evolution

We have already noted that a rootkit hides by compromising the interfaces between the components and layers in a computer system; however, the exact mechanisms of that compromise have evolved significantly since the discovery of the first rootkits. The actual compromise of an interface may be achieved either directly or indirectly using code modifications, data modifications, or a combination of both. Furthermore the location of these modifications may be either to the program file on disk or to its loaded image in memory. Using these divisions we can roughly breakdown rootkit evolution into first, second, and third, and fourth generation techniques with the inter-generational transitions mediated by co-evolutionary adaptation responses to rootkit detection technology.

First generation rootkits relied upon system file masquerade. It is the simplest technique; however, it is also outdated except from a historical perspective. In the early days of Unix rootkits, an attacker would replace a system file with a subversive file that "masqueraded" as the original [4]. The login program was a common target for this type of attack as it could be replaced by a malicious version which captured the passwords of users as they attempted to log into a system. Because this type of attack usually involved physically modifying and replacing system files on disk, it motivated the development of integrity checkers like Tripwire [5]. Integrity checkers function by calculating a check value known as a CRC (Cyclic Redundancy Check) for each file stored on a hard disk and then comparing it to a set of known values. It is based on the premise that a mismatch will indicate weather a system file has been maliciously altered. While successful against file masquerade attacks, rootkit authors quickly developed execution path redirection techniques to counter this form of detection.

Execution path redirection, also referred to in programming parlance as *hooking*, was the primary weapon in the second generation rootkit's arsenal of techniques. Hooking encompasses a class of techniques whereby a program's normal control flow is altered to execute a block of foreign code. Consider the previous example of the application trying to determine if the executable file for rootkit X exists on the system. The rootkit attacks the FindFile API function used by the application to determine if the rootkit file exists. Under the hood, the rootkit has patched the code of the Operating System's FindFile function so that it jumps to the rootki's file hiding function first. This file hiding function checks the name of the file the user is searching for. If it is the rootkit file, it returns "not found". Otherwise, it returns control to the original FindFile function which continues operation as usual. This example illustrates the basic principle of execution path redirection, which is the normal execution path is redirected to execute the rootkit code before the

Operating System's function. It is important to note that execution path redirection is impervious to traditional integrity checkers like Tripwire which typically only check files stored on the hard disk for modifications. These second generation modifications escape the scrutiny of these integrity checkers because they make their changes to the loaded images in memory rather than to the disk images. If masquerade is viewed as the first rung on the rootkit evolutionary ladder, execution path redirection can be viewed as the next step.

Though more difficult to detect than masquerade, execution path redirection remains detectable by memory-based integrity checkers and other heuristic approaches. The details of these approaches are discussed later. The third generation rootkit avoids this problem because it modifies only data, specifically OS kernel data. This technique is referred to as DKOM or Direct Kernel Object Manipulation [6]. Rather than redirecting the code path, DKOM alters the kernel data structures the Operating System code relies upon to function and produce trusted output. The idea is that by controlling the data used in a function, a rootkit can indirectly control the execution path. DKOM attacks are among the most difficult to detect. First, there is no support on the underlying hardware architecture for memory monitoring such as would be required to validate accesses to kernel memory. Secondly, kernel data structures change rapidly making it difficult to differentiate between normal and abnormal contents. We also include filter drivers in the third generation rootkit category. Like DKOM, they are an inherently kernel mode technique. However, rather than modifying kernel data structures, filter drivers exploit the layered nature of the Windows device driver architecture [7]. They insinuate themselves between and upper and lower layer device driver where they are capable of transparently and bidirectionally intercepting and censoring the communications to and from the installed filter.

Fourth generation and beyond rootkits include virtual memory subverting rootkits, virtualization rootkits, System Management Mode rootkits, and other hardware specific rootkits that infect the BIOS or PCI expansion cards. Unlike earlier rootkits which focused upon compromising the Operating System, most of these newer rootkits are Operating System Independent. Being independent from the OS gives them greater stealth because it is not necessary for them to make any detectable changes to the OS.

In summary, a rootkit may be generally characterized by the type and location of its modifications to the Operating System. Figure 14.2 illustrates the evolution of rootkit techniques based upon these characteristics. First generation techniques make direct modifications to program files stored on the hard disk. In contrast, second generation rootkits move the alterations to memory where they are more difficult to detect. These alterations, however, are still usually of a direct nature, and involve the injection of rootkit code to control the execution path. Third generation techniques, likewise, make their changes in memory, however, they seem to universally exploit kernel mode privileges by running as device drivers and

| Generation | Type | Location | Detectability |
|---|---|---|---|
| 1st | Code (direct) | Disk | Easy |
| 2nd | Code & Data (direct) | Memory | Moderate |
| 3rd | Code & Data (indirect) | Memory | Moderate / Difficult |
| 4th + | No changes | Memory | Very Difficult |

Fig. 14.2. A characterization of rootkit modifications to Operating System interfaces by type, location of the modification, and difficulty level of detection.

making more indirect modifications. They control an upper level interface indirectly by modifying the data structures used by the code in a lower layer interface for communicating information to an upper layer. Finally, fourth and beyond generation rootkits operate at the lowest possible level whereby they are able to avoid making any changes to the host Operating System. They tend to run outside the OS and interact directly with the hardware.

## 14.3. Anatomy of the Rootkit Compromise

In addition to classifying rootkits according to their technical implementation methods, it may also be useful to classify them from a functional perspective. Such a classification may be desirable for a system administrator who wishes to determine the extent of the compromise for an infected machine. As we mentioned previously, a rootkit may compromise the interfaces between one or more Operating System components. We therefore begin our functional classification with a brief overview of the kernel components of the Windows architecture and discussion of how they have been targeted by rootkits.

### 14.3.1. *I/O Manager*

The I/O manager is responsible for providing device independent I/O services and managing device driver communication [8]. Communication is based upon a packet driven mechanism where requests are represented by I/O request packets (IRPs) that travel between components. Additionally, the I/O system provides a library of device independent services common to most drivers. These include standard functions like open, close, read, and write as well as more advanced functions for asynchronous and buffered I/O. A kernel rootkit that provides functions for logging keystrokes or network connections often compromises I/O management. It accomplishes this either at a high level by attacking the API interface exposed by the I/O manager or at a low level by intercepting and modifying the I/O request packets of the hardware device. This idea forms the basis for the application of rootkit filter drivers.

### 14.3.2. *Device & File System Drivers*

Device drivers are loadable kernel modules that interface between the I/O manager and the hardware [8]. File system drivers are the basis of Windows 2000 file system management. They receive the high level file I/O requests of applications, drivers, and other OS components and translate them into low level I/O requests destined for a specific hardware device. Rootkits often attack the file management interface in order to hide files or directories. Because rootkits are themselves often implemented as device drivers, there is also a motivation for providing driver hiding functionality.

### 14.3.3. *Object Manager*

The object manager oversees the creation and deletion of the objects Windows uses to represent Operating System resources like process, threads, semaphores, queues, timers, and access tokens [8]. User processes access objects by specifying an identifier known as a handle. A rootkit may compromise the object manager with the intention of modifying security related objects like access tokens. Hiding object handles is another common motivation. (i.e., for example, the handle of a hidden process).

### 14.3.4. *Security Reference Monitor*

The security reference monitor (SRM) enforces security policies. It is responsible for performing run-time access checking on objects and manipulating user privileges [8]. Clearly, a compromise in the SRM undermines the entire trusted computing base. As such, it is not surprising that the SRM has been targeted by rootkit authors. In [1], Greg Hoglund describes the application of a 4 byte patch capable of disabling all security in the NT kernel. Hoglund discovered that an NT function, SeAccessCheck, is solely responsible for controlling object access. What's more, the access check distills down to a simple true/false return value. By patching the function to always return true, access is always granted. This provides yet another illustration of the single point of failure attacks inherent to modular and layered designs.

### 14.3.5. *Process & Thread Manager*

The process and thread manager is responsible for creating, scheduling, and terminating processes and threads [8]. A rootkit attacks this component in order to hide processes or threads from the view of a user or system administrator.

### 14.3.6. *Configuration Manager*

The configuration manager's primary task is to manage the system registry. The registry forms a system-wide database that maintains both global and local settings [8]. Global settings affect the behavior of the entire OS as opposed to local settings which maintain configuration information for individual applications. The registry is arranged in a hierarchal scheme according to keys, subkeys, and values which can be analogized to directories, subdirectories, and files, respectively. One global registry setting that rootkits like to modify contains a list of applications the Operating System needs to load at startup. Modifying this list to include a rootkit exposes it to trivial detection and provides the motivation for the implementation of registry key hiding functions.

### 14.3.7. *Memory Manager*

The Windows Memory manager has two primary tasks. First, it is responsible for translating a process's virtual address space into physical memory so that when a thread running in the context of that process reads or writes the virtual address space, the correct physical address is referenced. Secondarily, it is responsible for paging some of the contents of memory to disk when physical memory resources run low and then bringing that data back into memory when it is needed. Ideally, a rootkit would like to subvert memory management such that it is able to hide the detectable changes its code and any detectable changes its made to the Operating System in memory (i.e., the placement of an inline patch, for example). Such a rootkit is able to alter a detector's view of an arbitrary region of memory. When the detector attempts to read any region of memory modified by the rootkit, it sees a 'normal', unaltered view of memory. Only the rootkit sees the true, altered view of memory.

## 14.4. Technical Survey of Basic Windows Rootkit Techniques

We begin our survey of Windows rootkit techniques with a discussion of execution path redirection, or hooking. Hooking is a technique that can be applied to either user or kernel mode with several variations. These include import/export table hooking, system service dispatch table hooking, interrupt descriptor table hooking, and inline function hooking. The first three variations gain control of the execution path by patching function pointers in a table through which a set of calls or events are routed. The later method gains control by modifying the binary code of a target function. We conclude our survey with an overview of two advanced, strictly kernel mode techniques; filter drivers and DKOM.

### 14.4.1. *Hooking*

The first type of hooking we will discuss is import hooking. Import hooking involves the interception of Win32 library function calls. Many firewalls, antivirus products, and host based intrusion detection systems use these techniques to intercept Operating System APIs in order to monitor a system for suspicious activity. Nevertheless, they are also used by rootkits and other malicious software to alter the behavior of important Operating System functions to hide files, processes, and network ports. API hooking is one of the most common user mode rootkit techniques. This method takes advantage of the dynamic linking mechanism in Windows [9]. Unlike static linking where the code for a linked function is copied into the program executable at compile/link time, code for dynamically linked functions resides outside the program in external libraries called DLLs. As a result, only the information necessary to locate the DLL function is compiled into the program and references to it are resolved at runtime by the Operating System loader. In Windows, this information is contained in the import address table (IAT).

Before an application is loaded, the IAT contains file-relative offsets to the names of the DLL functions referenced by the program. These name pointers are replaced by the real memory addresses of the functions when the Operating System maps the program into memory [10]. The functions contained in the IAT are referred to as "imports". Because code references to the imports are compiled into the executable as indirect jump or call instructions to their corresponding IAT entries, all calls to a given DLL function are routed through a single entry point. This scheme is efficient from the perspective of the Operating System loader; however, it provides a convenient point of attack for the rootkit author wishing to divert the execution path.

Figure 14.3 illustrates this process by showing an application call to the OpenFile API. In this example, the normal execution path (Figure 14.3A) makes an indirect call to contents of address 0x00402000. The address 0x00402000, which is contained within the application Import Address Table, directs the call to the actual memory address of the OpenFile function (0x78000000) located in KERNEL32.DLL. The hooked execution path (3B) differs in only one respect. Here,

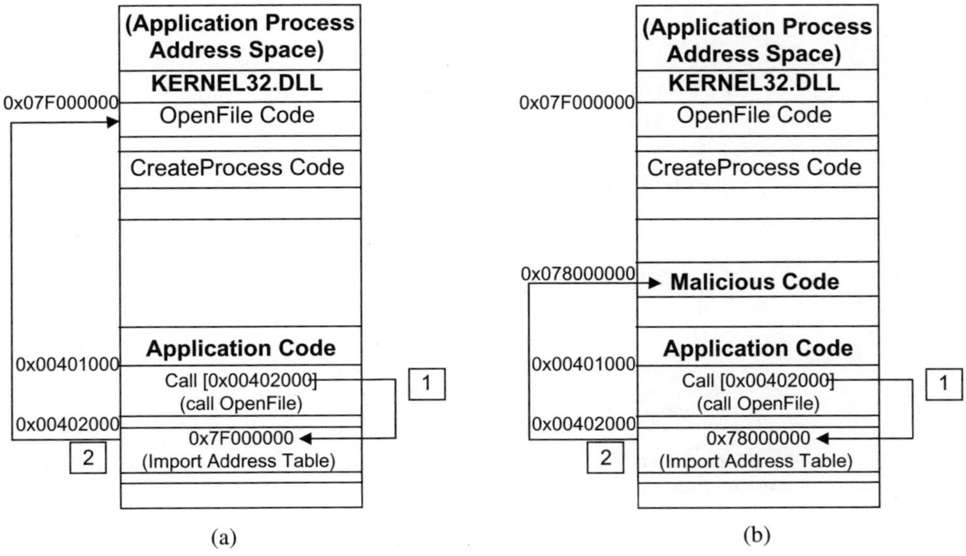


Fig. 14.3. Comparison of a normal (A) and a redirected (B) execution path for an IAT hook.

the IAT entry for OpenFile has been replaced by a pointer to a block of injected code. It is clear that whenever the hooked application now makes a call to OpenFile, execution will be routed to the injected code rather than to the OpenFile API. The injected routine may or may not choose to call the original function. However, if it does, the API call will be completely under its control since it will be able inspect and modify both the parameters and return values for the function. The utility of the technique becomes clear when you consider a rootkit intercepting the OpenFile call of an intrusion detection system. Perhaps the IDS is attempting to determine if the rootkit file exists on the system. The rootkit first intercepts the call and inspects its parameters. If it sees its own name as the target file, it returns an error indicating the file does not exist. Otherwise, it calls the original function and returns the result back to application. A rootkit can apply this concept to virtually any user level Windows API function.

While import table hooking is primarily used to subvert the OS at the application level, the same effect may be accomplished in the kernel by hooking the System Service Dispatch Table (SSDT). Windows system services are implemented in a layered architecture and the Win32 API interface targeted by import and export table hooking affects only the topmost layer. This is the layer exposed to user applications when, for example, they need to call a KERNEL32.DLL function like OpenFile. It is, however, oftentimes just a wrapper for a lower level call into NTDLL.DLL. NTDLL provides the actual interface between user and kernel mode [8]. OpenFile, calls down to NtOpenFile which generates the interrupt that switches

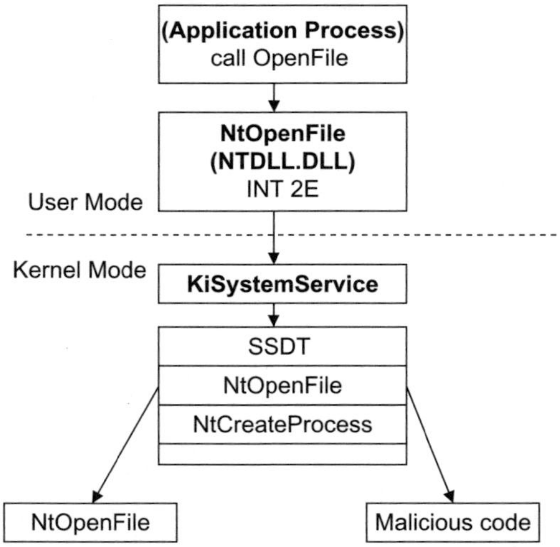


Fig. 14.4. System Service Dispatch Table. Upon invocation of the OpenFile API, execution flows from the user mode function in located in KERNEL32.DLL to the interface in NTDLL.DLL. NTDLL generates the system call interrupt that causes a transition to kernel mode. The interrupt handler, KisystemService, looks up the requested function address in the System Service Descriptor Table (SSDT) and calls it. A rootkit may replace the address in the SSDT to globally intercept Operating System services.

from user to kernel mode. The kernel mode interrupt handler, KiSystemSerivce, looks up the ID of the requested service in the System Service Dispatch Table (SSDT) and calls it on behalf of the user application [11]. Just as application level API calls are funneled to a single entry point in the import table, the kernel API's themselves are funneled to a single entry point in the system service dispatch table. The default service table, KeServiceDescriptorTable, defines the primary kernel services implemented in ntoskrnl.exe. This is the set of services that rootkits are primarily interested in intercepting. Since it exists in kernel memory, SSDT hooking is a purely kernel rootkit technique. Similarly to IAT hooking, it only involves overwriting a single function pointer. Its benefit over user-land IAT hooking lies in the fact that it is a global hook. Whereas an IAT hook must be instantiated in each application process, a hook on the default KeServiceDescriptorTable can intercept user and kernel API calls occurring in any process. This makes it an attractive solution for a rootkit.

In addition to hooking the IAT and SSDT, the possibilities for rootkit call table hooking extend to the hardware level. As previously alluded to, the Operating System provides services to applications and drivers via the software interrupt mechanism. The handlers for these interrupts are located in a structure known as the interrupt descriptor table (IDT). There is one IDT per processor and each IDT contains an array of 8 byte segment descriptors that hold the code segment selectors and offsets for their corresponding interrupt handlers [12]. By replacing an IDT entry, a rootkit is able to control the execution path for both Rootkit with a keylogger that directly hooks the keyboard interrupt Operating System services (implemented via the INT 2E interface under Windows 2000/NT) and other hardware devices. Greg Hoglund illustrates this in NT. In contrast to IAT, SSDT, or IDT hooking which modify a single address in a call table, inline hooking involves the modification of actual program instructions so that they force a jump to a foreign block of executable code.

Hunt and Brubacher discuss this approach in their implementation of the Detours library [13]. The Detours library is designed to dynamically intercept arbitrary Win32 binary functions by patching them in memory at runtime. Detours works by replacing the first few bytes of the target function with a direct jump to the *detour* (hook) function. The overwritten instructions are subsequently saved and inserted into a *trampoline* function which is appended with an unconditional jump pointing to the remainder of the target function. When invoked, the detour function has the choice of calling or not calling the target function as a subroutine via the trampoline. Figure 14.5 illustrates how a rootkit might intercept a function using a detours style inline hook.

An alternate approach to inline hooking involves patching the addresses of every call opcode in the program to point to a given hook procedure [13]. While, in theory, it seems more straightforward than the detours approach, in practice, it is seldom used due to the difficulty and performance cost involved with disassembling a binary image.

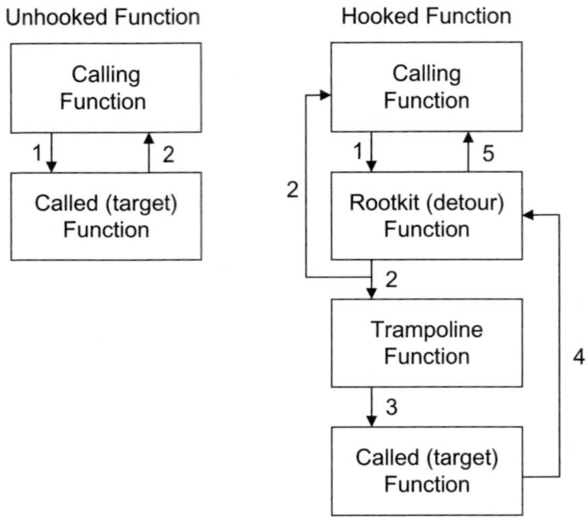


Fig. 14.5. For the case of the unhooked function, the calling function invokes the target function (1). After it has finished execution, the target directly returns control to its caller (2). In the case of the hooked function, when the calling function attempts to invoke the target function, control is immediately passed to the rootkit (or detour) function instead of to the target (1). This is accomplished by patching first few bytes of the target with a direct jump to the rootkit's detour. During execution, the rootkit function determines if it will pass control on to target function via the trampoline or simply return control to the caller without executing the target (2). If it chooses to invoke the trampoline, the trampoline will execute the instructions that were overwritten in the target function when the detour was inserted and then call target (3). Note, here, that the rootkit function has the opportunity to modify the arguments of the target function before calling it. Eventually, the target function returns to the rootkit's detour (4). Finally, the detour returns to the original caller. Note that this step ensures that the rootkit has an opportunity to modify the results of the target function before returning them.

Although the end result of inline hooking is similar to function table hooking in the sense that the execution of a victim function is redirected to a foreign block of code, inline hooking confers a few advantages. First, it allows for generic, non API function hooking. Whereas import hooking can only be used to intercept Operating System API functions, inline hooking can be used to intercept any arbitrary programmer defined function in a binary. Secondarily, and perhaps most importantly for a rootkit, inline hooking is more difficult to detect than the aforementioned call table hooking techniques.

### 14.4.2. *Filter Drivers*

Whereas rootkit hooking techniques often focus on passively concealing data (i.e., hiding processes or files), filter drivers are usually engaged in actively intercepting user data. Common uses for filter drivers include logging key strokes or network activity to capture user passwords or other sensitive information.

Filter drivers provide an interesting subversion of Windows naturally layered architecture. The drivers for Windows devices are arranged into a hierarchal stack.

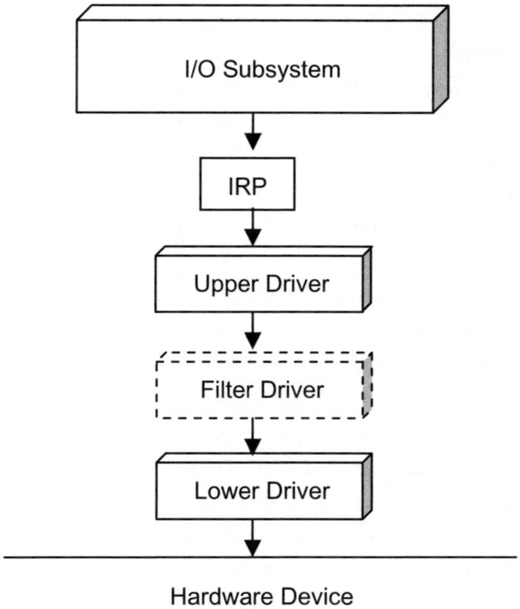


Fig. 14.6. Windows device stack.

Figure 14.6 illustrates this layout. Lower level drivers communicate directly with the hardware and provide an abstraction to upper level drivers. The I/O Manager facilitates driver to driver communication by means of I/O Request Packets (IRPs) that are defined according to operation (read, write, etc). A filter driver differs from a normal driver in that it is capable of being placed transparently between any existing upper and lower drivers in the device stack [7]. While filters are often legitimately used to modify or enhance the functionality of lower level drivers (e.g., by adding encryption support to a low level disk driver), rootkits may also use them to intercept and modify the IRP packets of a hardware device. Like a kernel SSDT hook, the filter is global in scope in the sense that all user mode applications and kernel drivers above the malicious filter will receive the censored data.

### 14.4.3. *Direct Kernel Object Manipulation (DKOM)*

Direct Kernel Object Manipulation (DKOM) compromises the integrity of sensitive Operating System data by manipulating the contents of kernel objects in memory. Under the Windows (NT, 2000, XP) Operating System, objects represent the physical and logical resources of a system and are collectively created and managed by the object manager, an executive kernel component [11]. Kernel objects may include low-level resources like processes, threads, events, semaphores, queues, and timers in addition to higher level structures like device drivers and the file system. Regardless of type, all objects are composed of a standard header and a body which specifies their individual attributes and procedures. The common structure shared by Windows objects enables diverse system resources to be supervised by a single object manager. The responsibilities of the manager subsystem include creating and deleting objects, maintaining object state information, organizing and tracking object handles, and imposing resource quotas. In addition, the object manager works with the Security Reference Monitor to enforce access rights [8]. Every object is associated with an Access Control List (ACL) specifying the actions that can be performed on it.

By requiring processes to access and manipulate objects via handles as opposed to direct pointers, the system is able to check an object's ACL and verify that the process has the proper permissions to perform the requested action. This strategy provides effective security for user mode processes, but is easily bypassed by code running in kernel mode. User mode processes are unable to directly access the kernel memory where objects reside and are therefore forced to rely upon the object handles provided to them by the API interface. Unfortunately, no such memory access restrictions exist for kernel mode code. The result is that kernel objects may be accessed directly by pointers effectively bypassing the access control mechanisms of the Windows object manager.

A DKOM attack exploits this lack of separation between the Operating System and other kernel code by directly accessing and writing to kernel objects stored in memory. Unlike traditional execution path redirection techniques, DKOM attacks avoid code injection and alteration rendering them highly stealthy and difficult to detect. They do, however, make a tradeoff in portability, based as they are, upon the modification of fixed offsets and undocumented Operating System structures. In a system as heavily object based as Windows, the scope of this type of attack is limited only by the attacker's imagination. Nevertheless, some objects present themselves as more profitable targets than others.

Butler *et al.* [14] present a unique class of intrusion: the hidden process, which is based upon the application of DKOM technology to process and thread objects. They observed that Windows maintains a doubly linked list of active processes independent from the process lists used by the scheduler. Furthermore, they discovered that the active process list appears to be the only list queried by user and kernel API functions responsible for enumerating existing processes. By modifying forward and backward pointers in this doubly linked list of active process objects, they were able to unlink a process object from the list and effectively hide it from view. The apparent independence of this list from the scheduler meant that execution of the hidden process continued unimpeded.

This technology has been subsequently implemented in the FU rootkit [15]. FU performs three primary functions via DKOM: process hiding, driver hiding, and access token modification. It should also be noted that it is not uncommon for rootkits and other malware species to contain self-defense code. One can therefore speculate that the reverse of the previous scenario would also be possible: that is disconnecting a process from the scheduler while leaving it in the active process list. In this manner, a malicious piece of code could potentially disconnect an antivirus utility or an intrusion detection system from the processor while leaving it superficially visible. Consequently, the user would falsely believe that all is well with their system. The implications for host based intrusion detection systems (IDS) are clearly that they can no longer trust the Operating System to provide them with uncensored data.

## 14.5. Survey of Advanced Windows Rootkit Techniques

In the following sections we give an overview of some more advanced rootkit techniques. These include Virtual Memory Subversion, Hardware Virtualization Rootkits, System Management Mode Rootkits and hardware based rootkits capable of infecting the BIOS or a peripheral PCI card.

### 14.5.1. *Virtual Memory Subversion*

Once a rootkit is publicly known, Anti-Virus software can develop a signature for it. Furthermore, rootkit changes to the Operating System may be detectable using memory scans that look for changes to critical Operating System components in memory. It is, therefore, advantageous for a rootkit to be able to hide its memory footprint and any changes it makes to the OS.

Memory subversion was first implemented in the Shadow Walker rootkit [16]. The Shadow Walker rootkit demonstrated that it was possible to control the view of memory regions seen by the Operating System and other processes by hooking the paging mechanism and exploiting the Intel split TLB architecture. Using these techniques, it was capable of hiding both its own code and changes to other Operating System components. This enabled it to fool signature, integrity, and heuristic based scans.

The x86 virtual memory architecture is based upon a 2-level paging scheme used to used to translate virtual to physical addresses. The general memory access can be summarized as follows:

1. Lookup in the page directory to determine if the page table for the address is present in main memory.
2. If not, an I/O request is issued to bring in the page table from disk.
3. Lookup in the page table to determine if the requested page is present in main memory.
4. If not, an I/O request is issued to bring in the page from disk.
5. Lookup the requested byte (offset) in the page.

Therefore every memory access, in the best case, actually requires three memory accesses: one to access the page directory, one to access the page table, and one to get the data at the correct offset. In the worst case, it may require an additional two disk I/Os (if the pages are swapped out to disk). Thus, virtual memory incurs a steep performance hit. To help reduce this penalty, modern CPU's use a Translation

Lookaside Buffer (TLB). The TLB is essentially a hardware cache used to hold frequently used virtual to physical mappings. It is able to be searched much faster than the time it would require to look up a translation in the page tables. Thus, the TLB is actually the first component on the memory access path. On a memory access, the TLB is searched first for a valid translation. If it is found, the page table lookup is bypassed. If it is not found, however, the slower page table lookup occurs.

On the x86, there are actually 2 TLBs, a data TLB (DTLB) and an instruction TLB (ITLB). Under normal operation, the DTLB and ITLB contain identical virtual to physical mappings. It is, however, possible to desynchronize them such that they point to 2 different physical frames. The ability to separate read/write and execute accesses by selectivly loading the TLBs is highly advantageous from a rootkit point of view. Consider the case of an inline hook. The modified code is translated through the ITLB to a physical page containing the malicious changes. Therefore, it runs normally. However, any attempts to read (i.e., detect) the changes are translated via the DTLB to a different "virgin" physical page that contains the original unaltered code. Using such a technique, a rootkit is capable of fooling most types of memory based scans.

### 14.5.2. *VMM Rootkits*

Within the past couple of years, Intel and AMD have added hardware virtualization support to their processors. Rootkit authors have figured out how to exploit these new features to develop a new class of rootkits, capable of existing independently of any Operating System. Such rootkits are able to insert an alarming degree of control without modifying a single byte in the OS [18]. Joanna Rutkowska developed the first proof of concept virtual machine based rootkit, named Blue Pill [17]. The Blue Pill rootkit exploits AMD hardware virtualization extensions to migrate a running Windows Operating System into a virtual machine and exerts its control from an external Virtual Machine Monitor (VMM). This process is invisible to the OS. Once installed, the rootkit VMM is capable of transparently intercepting and modifying states and events occuring in the virtualized OS. It can observe and modify keystrokes, network packets, memory, and disk I/O. If the rootkit has virtualized memory, its code footprint will also be invisible. These things make this type of rootkit extremely difficult to detect.

### 14.5.3. *System Management Mode (SMM) Rootkits*

System Management Mode rootkits represent another form of OS independent malware with capabilities similar to the Virtualization based rootkits. System Management Mode (SMM) is a relatively obscure mode on Intel processors used for low-level hardware control like power management and thermal regulation. One of the primary features that makes SMM attractive to rootkits is the fact that it has its own private memory space and execution environment which is invisible to code running outside of SMM (e.g., inside the Operating System). Furthermore, SMM code is completely non-preemptible, lacks any concept of privilege level, and is immune to memory protection mechanisms.

System management mode is entered by means of a System Management Interrupt (SMI) and the System Management Memory Space (SMRAM) is used to hold the processor state information that is saved upon an entry to SMM, including the SMI handler. Normally, the contents of SMRAM are only visible to code executing in SMM. This isolation is ensured by the chipset's rerouting of any non SMM memory accesses to the VGA frame buffer when a special lock bit in an internal chipset register is set. Once set, it is difficult, if not impossible, for security software to read the SMRAM memory space to verify the integrity of the SMM handler. Figure 14.7 illustrates this idea.

An SMM rootkit additionally offers a high degree of control over peripheral hardware. It can transparently interact with the network card, keyboard, mouse, hard disk, video card, and other peripheral devices in a manner that is virtually undetectable to the host Operating System. Paper [19] discusses the implementation of a proof of concept SMM keylogger and network backdoor that interacts with the keyboard and network peripheral components at the chipset level.

### 14.5.4. *BIOS and PCI Rootkits*

In addition to Virtualization and System Management Mode rootkits, researchers have proposed the feasibility of BIOS and PCI expansion card based rootkits. The BIOS is the first code that runs when a system is powered on. It performs diagnostics and initializes the chipset, memory, and peripheral devices. A rootkit that infects the BIOS is capable of controlling hardware at a level similar to an SMM or VMM rootkit with the additional benefit of being able to survive reboots and reinstallations of a new OS. John Heasman developed a proof of concept BIOS rootkit that acts as a simple Windows NT backdoor [20]. He used the Advanced Configuration and Power Interface (ACPI) to patch a kernel API in system memory. Heasman has also discussed the viability of rootkits that would

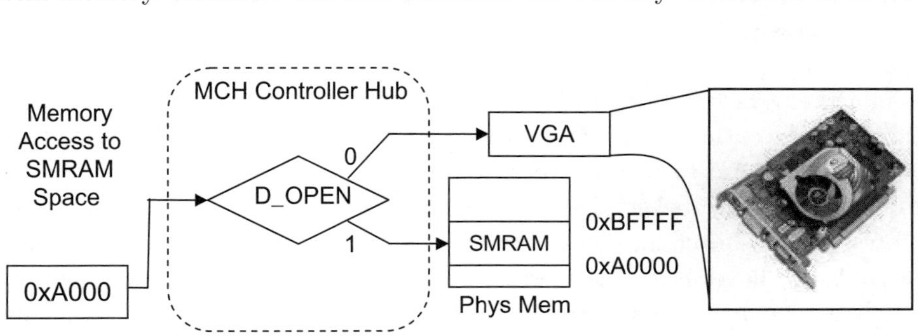


Fig. 14.7. SMRAM memory accesses are filtered by the chipset based upon their origin and the state of the 'open' bit in the SMRAM control register. SMM accesses are normally directed to SMRAM while non-SMM accesses are directed to VGA memory.

exist in the expansion ROM memory available on many peripherals like network cards. Details of this advanced attack can be found in [21]. To the authors knowledge BIOS and PCI based rootkits have not appeared in malware in the wild.

### 14.5.5. *The Big Picture: Rootkit Attack Patterns*

In surveying rootkit attack patterns, it becomes apparent that they exploit common themes related to the design of the Operating System and its abstraction of the underlying hardware. First, the layered, modular design of the Windows Operating System leads to singular points of attack in the trusted computing base. This is most apparent in the exploitation of filter drivers and call table hooking. By modifying a single function pointer, a rootkit is capable of intercepting Operating System API calls and system-wide interrupts. While such abstractions are both necessary and convenient for efficiency and extensibility of the Operating System, we must remember that they afford the same luxuries to rootkits seeking to maliciously "extend" the functionalities of trusted OS components.

Next, we consider the Win32 API. At the risk of being facetious, we might say that Windows provides a sort of "Rootkit API". With user mode functions like CreateRemoteThread and WriteProcessMemory, malicious code injection becomes a trivial task for even lowly user applications. These functions perform exactly as their names imply. They allow a user space process to transcend the normal barriers which protect processes from modifying or damaging each other by switching to the memory context of another running process and injecting code there. While such functions have legitimate uses in system profiling and debugging tools, they are a double edged sword. The clever use of these API's forms the basis of most user mode rootkit techniques.

Lastly, we note that Windows has long fallen short in its usage of the available hardware memory protection mechanisms on the Intel x86 architecture. The x86 protection mechanism recognizes four discrete privilege levels [12]. They are often referred to as "rings" and are numbered 0 through 3. Ring 0, represents the highest privilege level and ring 3 represents the lowest. Code executing at a given privilege can only access modules operating at a level less than or equal to their own.

In practical terms, code executing in the highest ring has full access to the system and enjoys the ability to read or write to any address in memory along with capability of executing all opcodes in the instruction set. While the X86 architecture provides four separate protection rings, the Windows Operating System utilizes only two of them to define its kernel and user modes of operation. Kernel mode, of course, operates at ring 0 and includes core Operating System components and device drivers. As we have seen in the kernel mode rootkit techniques, the implications of running code in ring 0 are truly exhilarating for a rootkit author. With a single memory address pointer, he/she can modify kernel structures in memory, install rogue drivers, change system descriptors, and alter the system page tables at will. In contrast, Windows support subsystems and user applications reside at ring 3.

The difficulty in securing such a system lies in the fact that there is no boundary to separate the Operating System from potentially malicious user code. Designed for compatibility and extensibility, Windows implicitly assumes that kernel mode code is trusted. As such, the Operating System, the intrusion detection system, and the kernel rootkit driver all operate upon an even playing field with equivalent access and system privileges.

Consider the fact that a kernel rootkit by definition has access to the entire memory address apace, including the address space of the intrusion detection system. What is to prevent such a rootkit from compromising the integrity of the detection system's internal procedures or data using a DKOM attack? Conversely, what is to prevent the IDS from disabling the rootkit in a similar fashion?

While kernel rootkits are clearly more dangerous than usermode rootkits, we can see that this lack of separation vulnerability also exists at the user level in the Windows architecture due to the fact that the Operating System's support subsystems reside at the same level of privilege as user applications. Conversely, this trend even extends to more advanced hardware virtualization, SMM, and BIOS rootkits. In general the closer one gets to the hardware, the more power and stealth potential one obtains. Ultimately, however, it remains a cat and mouse game largely about who got to that level of the system (rootkit vs security software) first. In the next section, we outline some of the current research in rootkit detection.

## 14.6. Rootkit Detection

We have surveyed the evolution of rootkit technology as it has progressed from the simple masquerade of system files to advanced kernel object manipulation, hardware virtualization, and BIOS rootkits. It has been, and continues to be, a challenge for host-based intrusion detection systems (HIDS) to keep pace with these developments.

Historically, there have been two approaches to intrusion detection: *misuse* and *anomaly* detection [22]. Misuse detection is based upon the idea of searching a system for known attack signatures. When applied to the detection of malicious code, the attack signature is usually a sequence of bytes found in the malicious executable. Typically, memory and files are both searched for occurrences of this pattern and a positive identification implies the presence of the malicious program. Provided that care is taken in choosing a sufficiently unique signature, misuse detection is a highly accurate method of detection. Because it relies upon a known attack signature, its primary drawback lies in its inability to identify new malicious code variants.

In contrast, anomaly detection does not rely upon known attack patterns. Instead, it attempts to define "normal" system characteristics and behaviors. Deviations from this norm are interpreted as attacks. When applied to malicious code, "normal" may be defined either statically based upon the structural characteristics of the code/file format or dynamically as a sequence of system calls/file accesses or control flow patterns. The benefit of the anomaly based approach lies in its ability to detect both old and new attacks. Unlike misuse detection, however, it is incapable of identifying attacks by name and tends to suffer from a high rate of false positives due to the difficulty in defining "normal" in a dynamically changing system.

A third approach, termed, "host integrity monitoring" observes trusted system components for changes [23]. These components may include system files and portions of kernel memory. Changes in these trusted components are interpreted as a system compromise. Like anomaly detection, host integrity monitoring may be able to identify both old and new attacks by the changes observed in a system. The changes themselves, however, may or may not provide a "signature" for a known attack. The aforementioned three methodologies supply the underpinnings of most current research in rootkit detection. In the following sections, we describe how they have been applied at both the hardware and software levels.

### 14.6.1. *Software Solutions*

Host integrity monitoring seems a natural approach to rootkit detection. Weather rootkits modify system files on disk or engage in more elaborate modifications to loaded components in memory, one fact remains. Kernel code is a static entity and it should not change except in the rare instance where the user has applied an Operating System update. That is, in general, changes to Operating System code are suspicious.

The Tripwire tool represents one of the first efforts to apply this observation towards intrusion detection. Tripwire detects changes in system files by creating an initial baseline database containing their unique CRC values and then periodically recalculating and comparing the CRC's of these files against the trusted baseline [5]. A mismatch during the comparison process indicates a system compromise.

As we mentioned previously, few modern rootkits modify system files, preferring instead to make their changes to memory. Nevertheless, the concept is equally applicable to memory and may be used to detect inline hooks that have modified the code of kernel API functions. Osiris is a free integrity assurance solution for both Windows NT and Unix [24]. It is capable of tracking and reporting changes to the file system, user and group lists, and kernel modules. Despite its utility, the application of host integrity monitoring is limited in scope. This is because it relies upon the static, unchanging nature of kernel code. It falls short, for example, in the detection of a DKOM attack. The rapidly changing nature of kernel data structures makes it impossible to define the baseline upon which the host integrity monitoring approach depends.

Anomaly detection has also been applied to rootkit detection in various forms. Here, we attempt to define normal system characteristics or behavior. Anomaly detection may be used to examine the structural characteristics of functions to detect hooking. For example, the first few instructions of any function are typically related to setting up its stack frame. Statistically, the probability of the first instruction in an unhooked function being a direct jump is quite small and its presence may be an indicator that the function is hooked. Table based hooking methods (IAT, SSDT, IDT) can also be detected heuristically. It is, for example, highly suspicious for the pointer to a system service to be located outside of the address range of the loaded kernel. Such metrics are a valuable part of a rootkit detection application, but are hardly sufficient to indicate the presence of a rootkit by themselves. Used alone, they tend to generate a high false positive rate due to the fact that other applications, including intrusion detection systems and firewalls, hook functions.

VICE is a freeware tool designed to detect Windows hooks [25]. It is capable of detecting inline hooks, IAT and SSDT hooks using the aforementioned heuristic approaches. While it is a valuable analysis tool, it does require a knowledgeable operator to screen out false positives. Execution path analysis has also been used to heuristically detect hooked kernel functions [26]. It uses the x86 single step mechanism to interrupt execution after each instruction so that is able to count the number of executed instructions and look for statistical deviations between hooked and unhooked versions of kernel API functions.

The Patchfinder tool provides a proof of concept implementation of this idea [26]. Finally, where normal integrity checking fails, anomaly detection has been applied to DKOM attacks. It is based upon the cross validation of kernel data structures. This technique is sometimes referred to as *cross view detection.* As noted in the discussion of DKOM, a process which is hidden by unlinking its process object from the Operating System's active process list must still remain in the dispatcher list if it is to continue receiving CPU quantums from the scheduler. Joanna Rutkowska [27] uses this discrepancy as a detection metric for processes hidden using DKOM.

The aforementioned approaches are primarily useful against Operating System dependent rootkit techniques (hooking, DKOM, filter drivers). OS independent rootkits present new challenges to detection. Virtualization rootkits, System Management Mode rootkits, and BIOS rootkits are considerably more difficult to detect and defend against than OS dependent malware. Because it is generally not necessary for these type of rootkits to make visible changes to the Operating System, heuristics are not particularly useful. Furthermore, since both virtualization and SMM rootkits are capable of concealing their memory footprints, signature detection is also of little value. As a result, indirect detection measures like timing or cache discrepancies have been suggested as potential modes of detection [28]. Nevertheless, the considerably more difficult problem remains to decide weather or not a detected discrepancy is malicious or benign.

### 14.6.2. *Hardware Solutions*

On systems that lack support for hardware virtualization, separation between kernel drivers and the Operating System at ring 0 renders virtually all software approaches vulnerable. Rootkit detectors must rely upon some portion of kernel trustworthiness in order to ensure their own correctness. At a bare minimum, they must rely upon the integrity of the Operating System's memory manager. In other words, the scanner implicitly assumes an unaltered view of memory as a basis for the validity of its integrity checks. As we have seen, this is not always a valid assumption. Beyond this, rootkit detectors may rely upon the results of compromised Operating System APIs and that is saying nothing of the more overt attacks. Clearly, a kernel rootkit is capable of compromising a scanner using the same techniques it uses to corrupt the integrity of the Operating System kernel.

The new hardware virtualization extensions on Intel and AMD processors may increase the usefulness of software based approaches because they do have the potential to provide an isolated environment for security software to run in. In short, software approaches are not without value, but a hardware approach may be more powerful and trustworthy since it intrinsically overcomes some of the problems associated with purely software solutions.

The CoPilot project is one such example. CoPilot is a runtime kernel monitor implemented onboard an external PCI card [29]. Its advantages lie in the fact that it does not rely upon the kernel for memory access and does not require any software modifications to the host Operating System. Its trustworthiness, therefore, is independent of kernel correctness. CoPilot works by detecting changes to hashes of critical regions of kernel memory. It can be viewed as sort of hardware based Tripwire tool. The authors report promising results with CoPilot. They report that it has identified over 12 rootkits with less than a 1% degradation in system performance.

## 14.7. Conclusion

What began as a UNIX problem has spread to most of the major Operating System platforms. Unfortunately, the technical details and underlying issues surrounding rootkit implementation on the non-UNIX system have remained somewhat shrouded in obscurity. With a large percentage of the world wide computing base using Microsoft Operating Systems, we have focused our discussion on the Windows rootkit.

The defining characteristic of a rootkit is stealth. Rootkits hide processes, files, and registry keys by intercepting and modifying communications at the interfaces between one or more Operating System components. We have shown how nearly all of the primary Operating System components have been attacked directly or indirectly by rootkits. As rootkit technology advances, however, it appears to be moving away from the Operating System. This is evidenced by emerging research into hardware Virtualization, System Management Mode, BIOS, and PCI based rootkits. These technologies also bring new challenges to the detection and defense against malicious code.

## Acknowledgments

This work was supported by NSF Grant CNS-0627318 and Intel research funds.

## References

[1] Greg Hoglund, "A *REAL* NT Rootkit, patching the NT Kernel," in Phrack Magazine, **9**(55), 1999.
[2] Harvy M. Deitel, Paul J. Deitel, and David R. Choffnes, Operating Systems, Third Edition, Prentice-Hall, 2004.
[3] Charles Pfleeger and Shari Pfleeger, Security In Computing, Third Edition, Prentice-Hall, 2003.
[4] Thimbleby, S. Anderson, and P. Cairns, "A Framework for Modeling Trojans and Computer Virus Infections", *Computer Journal*, **41**(7), 444–458, 1998.
[5] Gene H. Kim and Eugene H. Spafford, "The design and implementation of tripwire: A file system integrity checker", ACM Conference on Computer and Communications Security, pp. 18–29, 1994.
[6] Jamie Butler and Greg Hoglund, "VICE: Catch The Hookers: Plus New Rootkit Techniques", http://www.blackhat.com/presentations/win-usa-04/bh-win-04-butler.pdf, Feb. 2005.
[7] Art Baker and Jerry Lozano, The Windows 2000 Device Driver Book, Second Edition, Prentice-Hall, 2001.
[8] David A. Solomon and Mark E. Russinovich, Inside Windows 2000, Third Edition, Microsoft Press, 2000.
[9] API Spying Techniques For Windows 9x, NT, and 2000, http://www.internals.com/articles/apispy/apispy.htm, Feb. 2005.
[10] Matt Pietrek, "An In-Depth Look into the Win32 Portable Executable File Format", MSDN Magazine, Feb. 2002.
[11] Sven B. Schreiber, Undocumented Windows 2000 Secrets, Addison-Wesley, pp. 281–294, 2001.
[12] Intel Architecture Software Developer's Manual Volume 3: System Programming Manual, Intel, 1997.
[13] Galen Hunt and Doug Brubacher, "Detours: Binary interception of win32 fucntions", in Proceedings of the Third USENIX Windows NT Symposium, 1999.
[14] James Butler, Jeoffery Undercoffer, and John Pinkston, "Hidden Processes: The Implication For Intrusion Detection", in Proceedings of the IEEE Workshop on Information Assurance, pp. 116–120, 2003.
[15] http://www.rootkit.com, Feb. 2005.
[16] Sherri Sparks and James Butler. Shadow Walker: Raising the Bar for Windows Rootkit Detection. In Phrack Volume 0x0B, Issue 0x3D, Phile #0x08 of 0x14. 2005.
[17] J. Rutkowska, Subverting Vista Kernel for Fun and Profit. Presented at Black Hat USA, Aug. 2006.
[18] D. A. Zovi, Hardware Virtualization Rootkits. Presented at Black Hat USA, Aug. 2006.
[19] Shawn Embleton, Sherri Sparks, and Cliff Zou, SMM Rootkits: A New Breed of OS Independent Malware", 2007.
[20] J. Heasman, Implementing and Detecting an ACPI BIOS Rootkit. Presented at Black Hat Federal, 2006.

[21] J. Heasman, Implementing and Detecting a PCI Rootkit. An NGSSoftware Insight Security Research Publication, 2006.
[22] A. Jones and R. Sielken, "Computer System Intrusion Detection", Technical Report, Computer Science Dept., University of Virginia, 1999.
[23] Host Integrity Monitoring: Best Practice For Deployment, http://www.securityfocus.com/infocus/1771, Feb. 2005.
[24] http://osiris.shmoo.com/, Feb. 2005.
[25] James Butler, "VICE", http://www.rootkit.com/vault/fuzen_op/vice.zip, Feb. 2005.
[26] Jan K. Rutkowska, "Execution path analysis: finding kernel based rootkits." in Phrack Magazine Vol. 0x0b, No. 0x3b, Phile #0x0A, 2003.
[27] Joanna Rutkowska and Klister, http://www.rootkit.com/vault/joanna/klister-0.4.zip.
[28] T. Garfinkel, K. Adams, A. Warfield, and J. Franklin, Compatibility is Not Transparency: VMM Detection Mythis and Realities. In HotOS XI: 11th Workshop on Hot Topics in Operating Systems, 2007. USENIX.
[29] Nick L. Petroni, Timothy Fraser, Jesus Molina, and William A. Arbaugh, "Copilot — a Coprocessor-based Kernel Runtime Integrity Monitor", Proceedings of the 13th USENIX Security Symposium, pp. 179–194, 2004.

# Chapter 15

## AN OVERVIEW OF BOT ARMY TECHNOLOGY AND PROSPECTS

Martin R. Stytz
*The Institute for Defense Analyses*
*Calculated Insight, Washington, DC*
*mstytz@att.net*

Sheila B. Banks
*Calculated Insight, Orlando, Fl 32828*
*sbanks@calculated-insight.com*

This chapter discusses bot armies, which are more powerful and dangerous than any other type of malware. Their power and threat derive from the controllability and flexibility of the bots in a bot army. Bot armies, unlike other forms of malware, are controlled and directed throughout all phases of an attack using a command and control structure that is increasingly sophisticated. The bots' flexibility arises from the ability of the bot's software to be updated at any time by the owner of the bot (who is commonly called a bot master or bot herder). A bot army is composed of tens of thousands, possibly millions, of compromised computers that can surreptitiously communicate with each other and their command and control centers; allowing them to execute massive, coordinated attacks upon Internet resources. Defeating bot armies requires more knowledge about them and the people who build and use them. Research into the evolution, construction, control, and uses of bot armies is required, as is analysis of current bot activities for patterns that indicate objectives and operations that have been or are being conducted by bot armies.

### 15.1. Introduction

A botnet is a network of suborned computers running a common set of remotely controlled, malicious software [96]. Botnets use malware called botware and pose one of the most serious security threats to all networks; whether they are civilian or government owned, or carry classified or unclassified message traffic. The attack upon Estonia via cyberspace is a sample of the damage that can be inflicted upon a nation's information infrastructure using relatively primitive botnets [42]. Botnets, remotely controlled and operated by bot masters,[a] can launch massive denial of service attacks, multiple penetration attacks, or any other malicious network activity

[a]The terms bot master and bot herder are typically used interchangeably.

on a massive scale [8, 9, 46, 70, 73, 74, 80, 81, 87, 96]. While bot army activity has, in the past, been limited to fraud, blackmail, and other forms of criminal activity, their potential for causing large-scale damage to the entire Internet, for launching large-scale, coordinated attacks on government computers and networks, and for large-scale, coordinated data gathering from thousands of users and computers on any network is only beginning to be fully appreciated. This chapter will examine the challenges posed by the bot army problem by examining their means for infiltration, operation, control, and cleansing.[b] While it may seem obvious, the reason that bot technology is dangerous is due to the worldwide nature of the Internet coupled with the lack of laws against bot activity, poor enforcement of the few laws that apply to bot activity, and the challenges of international law enforcement and evidence collection (especially on the Internet). The use, creation, or distribution of bots is an illegal activity along with the use, creation, or distribution of any of the technologies that bots employ[c] except for Internet chat, also called Internet relay chat (IRC).

A botnet and its malware allows an unauthorized, remote user to operate the bots using one or more of a variety of covert command and control strategies via the Internet, as illustrated in Figure 15.1.

The bot army computers can be used to spread spam, launch denial-of-service attacks against Web sites, conduct fraudulent activities that are highly sophisticated and organized [29], and prevent authorized network traffic from traversing the network. On the Internet in 2004, it was estimated that over 70% of all spam messages are coming from bot armies; the number today is estimated to be higher. Running a bot army can be highly profitable; for example, in today's civilian "bot army" economy, a bot master[d] can have 100,000 machines under his control and will contract to send a million e-mail. Because of the number of machines under his control, the bot master will have each machine send out only 10 messages. It is very hard for the owner of a machine that is compromised to know that 10 [e-mail] messages went out on any given day. As a result, it's virtually impossible for an average person to know whether or not their machine has been drafted into a bot army. To date, the presence of botnets and the threat they pose have received relatively little attention, but the threat posed by botnets to civilian and government capabilities is growing and the attention that this threat is receiving is also increasing. Botnets are not only used for attacks (such as data theft, phishing, and click fraud), they can also be used to provide subverted computer hosts for illegal services, such as pornography, malware, and warez hosting.

---

[b]A short introduction to the topic of bots and bot armies can be found at http://zine.dal.net/previousissues/issue22/botnet.php, "Knowing Your Enemy: Tracking Botnets".

[c]One exception is the use of rootkit technology to protect copyrights, a controversial use of this powerful technology; see http://www.sysinternals.com/blog/2005/10/sony-rootkits-and-digital-rights.html by Mark Russonovich at "Mark's Blog" for more information.

[d]A bot master or bot herder is the person (or group) who developed and/or controls the bot army.

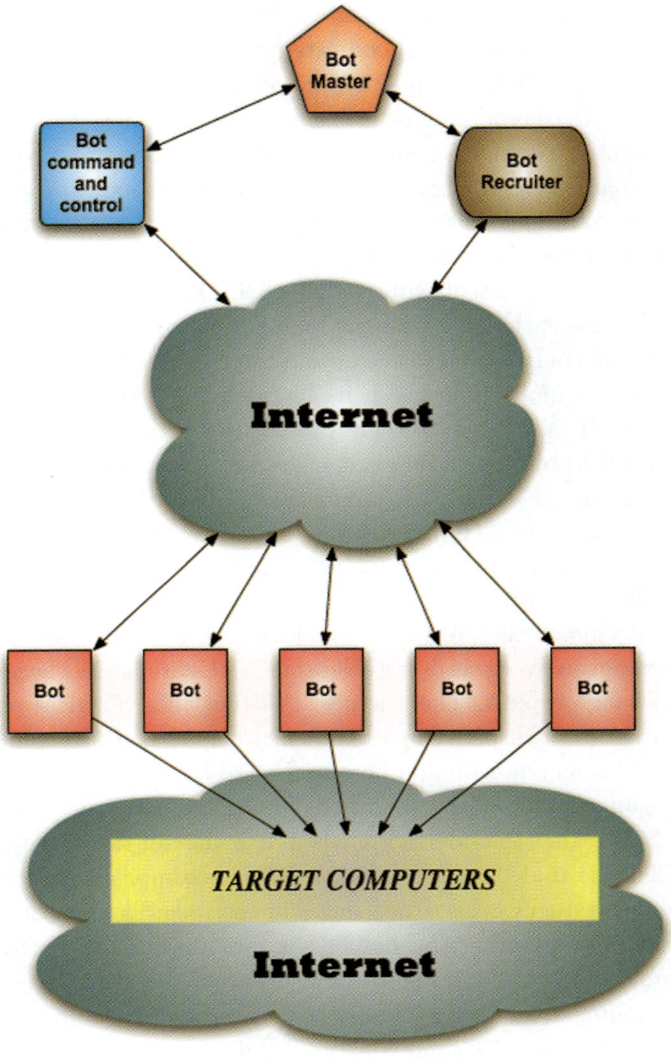


Fig. 15.1. Illustration of a botnet and its environment.

At this time, one of the most powerful bots in the world is the STORM bot, an examination of its capabilities, which are documented in the freely available literature, will provide a useful insight into the potential threat posed by this technology. As a note, STORM, while the leading bot today, could easily lose this position because of the rapid advancements in all aspects of bot technology. STORM generally targets PCs running Windows 200, Windows XP, and Windows server. The STORM bot army is partitioned into subnets that operate and can be "rented" separately. Essentially, the STORM army is composed of several independent divisions. STORM relies upon social engineering to make the first code load, either via an e-mail attachment or via a web site. The bots selectively forward STORM-only spam. Encrypted messages and code are used for command and control and to update bot code. A Trojan horse and a rootkit are among the first capabilities loaded by STORM, then the kernel is changed almost immediately. When the kernel is changed, the changes: (1) hide STORM, (2) disable any software capable of locating STORM, (3) reload STORM whenever the computer reboots, (4) prevent STORM-related processes from appearing in a listing of running processes, and (5) prevent all STORM-related files from appearing in any file listing. The bot modifies any running anti-malware to that it will not detect STORM. STORM is comprised of multiple software loads that are brought together over time to form the complete bot. Command and control is performed using Internet relay chat (IRC). Command and control also has multiple levels in its hierarchy, and the servers at each level frequently change IP addresses. To help protect the bots from defensive measures and to make STORM bot detection via changes in network traffic patterns difficult, the STORM software is designed to set individual bots to "sleep" (or hibernate) for long periods. The core STORM software (whether initially load from a website or via an e-mail attachment) changes 10 or more times per hour, thereby also rendering traditional virus or worm identification techniques useless. The actual websites that download the infection are hidden behind a set of false-front proxies as well, so warnings to avoid certain websites or URLs are useless because the false-front proxies change rapidly. There is also evidence that STORM can hide itself within unused RAM for display chipsets or other chipsets on a Windows computer. Because STORM is so powerful and because bot technology is changing so rapidly, we will provide an overview of the operation of bot army activities and the operation of individual bots rather than delve into the particulars of the operation of specific bots or provide code that demonstrates how a bot accomplishes specific tasks.

To have a bot army, the army must be created by suborning individual computers and by implanting the botcode within them. The general pattern of botnet creation, as illustrated in Figure 15.2, requires a few basic steps: (1) malware creation, (2) command and control software creation, (3) malware propagation, (4) malware infestation, (5) command and control setup, (6) further malware download, and (7) malware check-in for further instructions via the command and control setup. To distribute and control a botnet, a malware author needs to gain access to the Internet in a manner that hides identity and provides as much bandwidth as possible. To facilitate initial contact with the bot after it has infected a computer, the malware author typically encodes an initial contact domain name into the malware binary. In preparation for contact by the bots as they become active after infection, the bot master prepares a command and control computer, or set of computers operating off of a variety of Internet Protocol (IP) addresses. Once infestation of a computer is complete, the bot uses the IP information to acquire additional malware and obtain its operational instructions. Obviously, the bot can acquire additional malware and instructions at any other time in the future as well. The command and control computer(s) are one of two types: a high-bandwidth compromised machine, or a high-capacity co-located computer. The command and control computer or computer suite is set up to run an IRC service to provide command and control of the bots by the bot master (their creator and manager). There are numerous intermediate steps and processes that a bot herder, and the army, must continually perform in order to expand the army, insure its survival, and secure its communications, as shown in Figure 15.2. Establishing and managing a bot army is a complex undertaking, requiring considerable time and resources. As malware defenses improve, the investment required to establish and maintain

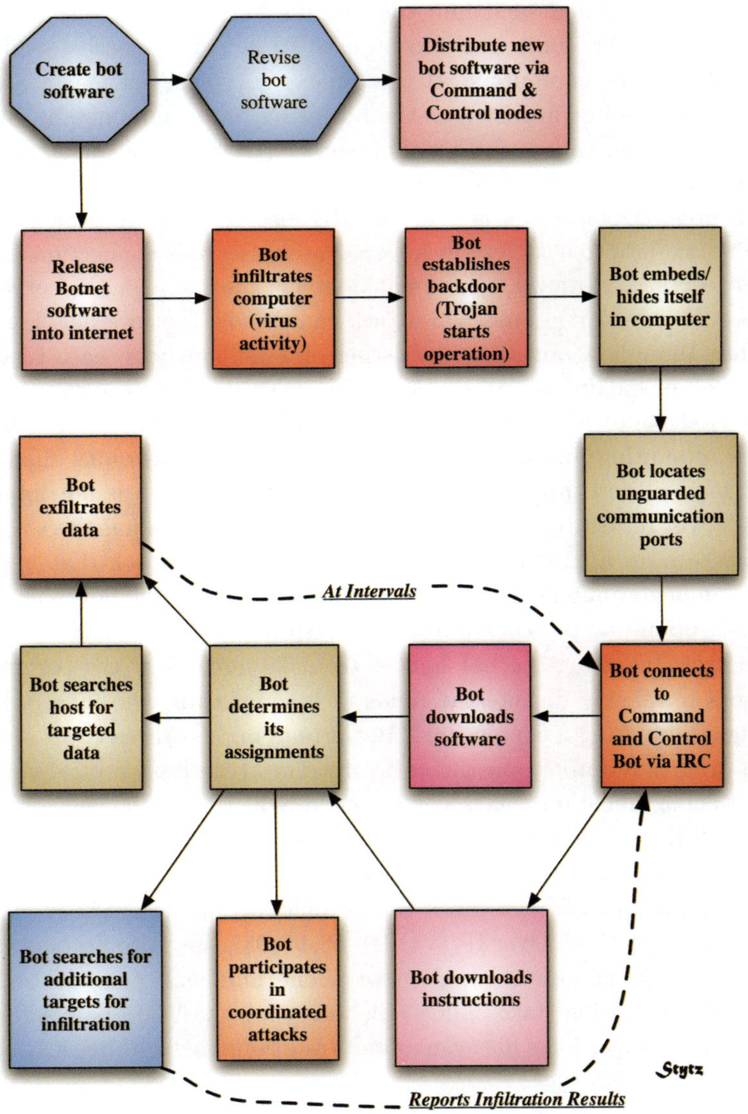


Fig. 15.2. Overview of bot development and expansion process.

a bot army will commensurately increase, indicating that bot armies will soon require substantial funding and resource commitments and that the day of the individual bot master is passing; to be replaced by bot masters working for criminal or state enterprises that have the resources required to establish the bot army and maintain it.

Bot armies have several criminal uses; all of which are under the control of the bot master. The botherder who developed the botware can use IRC channel commands to make the bots spam websites or to make even more bots. The bot herder can also launch attacks against channels he wants to attack, or get the bots to message him and send him the information about anyone who uses the infected computer. The bots can also be used to launch a massive exfiltration of data from all infected computers. At this time, the typical bot master operates to make money, so the bot master uses the bot army to make money by threatening to launch or launching a launch Denial of Service (DOS)[e] attack against servers [6] or by employing one of the other attacks mentioned previously. Due to the scale of a bot army, a DOS attack is very effective because hundreds or thousands of bots all sending data to a server quickly saturates a server's connections and causes the server to crash. However, the threat does not stop at just the server level, it is quite conceivable that a bot DOS attack can disable the Internet. For example, assume that there is a bot army consisting of 1 million bots, each of which can consume 128k of bandwidth at any time. If all of the bots transmit at the same time, the total bandwidth consumed is 128 Billion bytes/second. Ten bot armies of this size, operating in concert, would consume more bandwidth than the main Internet backbone can provide. A bot army of 1 million bots is not impossible to achieve. We will return to this type of threat, and other coming threats of a more serious nature later in this paper. Another effective bot attack that is gaining in popularity among criminals is the click-fraud attack, where the bot master uses the bots to click upon pay-per-click advertising residing upon web pages that the bot master controls (allowing the bot master to make money) or the bot master can use the bots to quickly deplete the funds of a competitor who uses pay-per-click advertising (eliminating a competitor). Bot armies impose three types of costs; one being the drag they impose on the entire Internet (the loss of bandwidth due to normal bot communication), the second being a reduction in the pace of technology adoption, and the third being the economic costs they impose when they attack.

In addition to the current illegal uses of botnets, there are many potential nefarious applications of bot armies that should be of concern. For example, as organizations adopt Voice Over IP (VOIP) [65, 97, 98], they also become vulnerable to attacks directed at determining active phone numbers, de-activating phones, sending false information (fake phone calls), or using the VOIP connection to gain access into an organization's file system and traditional networking services via the

[e] "Distributed Denial of Service", http://www.packetstormsecurity.org/distributed/ddos.txt

telephonic IP connection [92]. There is also the threat of eavesdropping via VOIP, re-direction of VOIP calls, and flooding of VOIP calls [99]. A bot army can effectively conduct these attacks en masse. A further threat is to the national infrastructure that controls water, power, other utilities, as well as other critical systems that provide important services; the so-called SCADA systems.[f] And, of course, data exfiltration from infected hosts to the bot master is always a possibility and a grave concern. Given the potential for bot armies to disrupt or prevent Internet communication, it is rational to assume that criminal elements are interested in developing and exploiting this technology. However, the legal risk faced by civilian bot researchers has served to severely restrict the amount and quality of research on bots and bot armies [63];[g] which gives bot masters an even greater advantage when they attack.

Bot masters can, if they have access to contemporary malware tools, infect any computer with minimal risk of detection [9, 12, 44, 70, 73, 74, 81, 96] as shown in Figure 15.3. The bot master's exposure to detection is limited to the contact that the bot master must maintain with two classes of computers, the bot controllers and the exploit machines. The risk of maintaining these contacts [43] can be reduced using

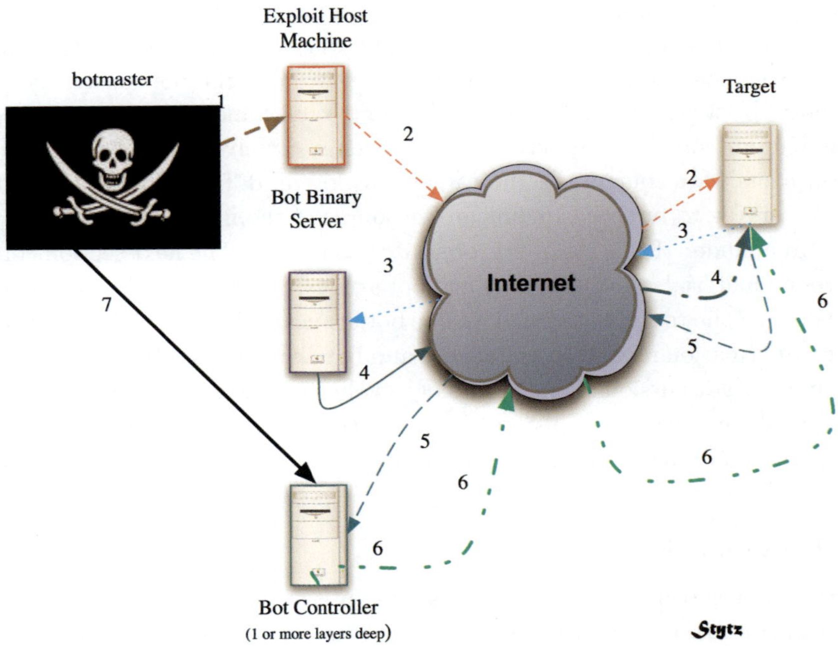


Fig. 15.3. Illustration of Typical bot infestation process.

[f]Supervisory Control and Data Acquisition (SCADA) systems are used to control large-scale chemical, power, and utility systems.
[g]Such as that imposed by the Digital Millenium Copyright Act of 1998, which has been used to prosecute malware researchers [McL03].

a variety of technologies to hide the origination point and the bot army command and control centers for the contact, as we will discuss next.

In general, a computer is infested as follows. Once the bot master has implanted the basic bot code in the exploit machine (step 1) the exploit machine starts to automatically search the Internet for targets. Once a vulnerable machine is located (step 2), the basic bot code is downloaded to the target. The basic bot code then contacts the bot code server host (step 3) to acquire its full complement of malware software (step 4). Once the full complement of software is acquired, the target contacts the controller (step 5) for instructions, which are provided upon demand (step 6) in accordance with the instructions provided by the bot master (step 7). A recent development in botnet technology is their acquisition of the capability to insure sole infestation of the computer by the bot, which is accomplished by instructing the bot to download and execute a hacked version of a commercially available anti-virus program; thereby, insuring that the bot is the only infection on the computer [37, 38]. The bot can scan for viruses as often as desired by the bot master, thereby reducing the risk that the bot or the computer can be hijacked.

Clearly, the bot master is not very vulnerable to detection (due to the number of command and control (C2) nodes between the bot and the bot master) and it is trivial for a bot master to control a large number of bots with minimal risk. Therefore, both closing down a bot army and tracking a bot master remain very difficult tasks [49]. Note that the Internet serves to hide the bot master as well as the contact between the exploit hosts, the control machines, and the bots because all contacts are via the Internet; therefore, even successive packets of information between a malware source and the target may travel different paths through the Internet; serving to further camouflage the source of the malware.

The remainder of this chapter is organized as follows. The next section contains background material relevant to bots and bot armies, concentrating on the operation of botnets and the technologies that enable bot armies to function. The third section presents information related to bot armies and bot army defense techniques. Section Four contains a discussion of bot technology evolution, likely future capabilities, and developments in defenses against bot armies. The Fifth section contains a summary of the paper and a few conclusions concerning bot army technology.

## 15.2. Background

Bots were developed almost as soon as the Internet was capable of supporting them; which is essentially when Internet chat was developed. No one technology is responsible for the rise of bot armies as a threat; instead, it is the development of several technologies that permits bots to pose the threat they do. At its most basic, a bot requires a C2 channel, malware, and a distribution technology. The simplest, and earliest, bots used simple IRC for C2, malware in the form of a packet generator (to conduct a denial of service attack), no host for distribution of additional software for the bot, and a C2 node at a fixed IP address for C2. Technology development has been rapid. In this section we discuss two major topics. The first subsection presents an introduction to botnets and their technology. The second subsection is dedicated to a discussion of the major facilitating technology for botnets, malware.

### 15.2.1. *Botnet and Botnet Operation*

All bots in a bot army use, to a greater or lesser degree, malicious software, which is often called malware [12, 48, 69, 70, 73, 74, 81]. Malware is a term used to describe the software used to build worms, viruses, rootkits, backdoors, Trojan horses, virtual machines [77, 94], and other forms of unauthorized code. The major difference between a bot and a virus or worm is that the botnet uses a worm or virus as a means to gain entry into a computer system and embed itself and use it to perform nefarious activity; whereas, the common worm or virus has as its goal simple propagation. A bot operates without the permission of the computer's owner and, almost always, operates without the knowledge of the computer's owner.

A bot, once implanted, nominally operates as shown in Figure 15.4. For a bot, there are two key connections that must be made as soon as possible after it successfully infiltrates the computer's defenses: a connection to some user application that allows the bot to become active and a connection to the Internet that allows the bot to communicate and to perform attack functions. Furthermore, there is one piece of software that is critical, the rootkit [47, 71, 101], which allows the bot to embed itself in the system, operate, remain undetected, and hide within the file system for the computer. As shown in Figure 15.4, once a bot gains entry, its first task is to be able to insure its ability to execute. To do so, it hooks into an application or the operating system so that it interposes itself between the operating system and application(s). For example, if the normal communication pathway between the operating system and an application is along the execution path labeled A and uses the application's dynamic link library (DLL) along the execution path labeled D; the bot changes the path so that the communication goes through the hook along the path labeled B through C to get to the DLL. Once in the DLL, its alteration allows for the activation of the bot via the path labeled F and for the performance of the function desired by the application along the D execution path. To insure that the bot's activity remains unnoticed and indetectable, execution path A is replaced by execution path labeled A', which insures that the application software appears to be functioning normally from the point of view of the operating system and the user.

The other threat faced by a bot is communication with its command and control system and gaining access to the network [43]. Here again, hooking is critical as it changes the execution path between the operating system and the network. The hooking code is used to change the network interface along the path labeled 1, from that point on the interface will accept requests for communication along the path labeled 1 or the path labeled 3, but the bot controls the destination for incoming information so that its messages are routed only to itself. Normal communication

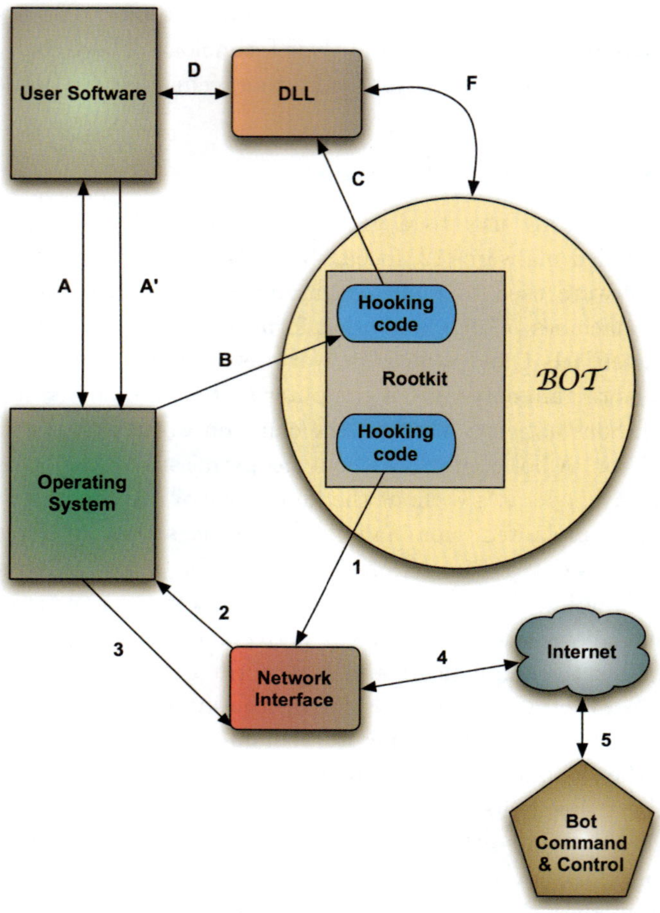


Fig. 15.4. Nominal bot operation within a host.

follows the paths labeled 3 and 4 to access the Internet, and then paths 4 and 2 return any response to the communication to the operating system (and user), as would happen normally. However, when the bot needs to communicate, it sends its message along path 1 to the network interface and from there, along the paths labeled 4 and 5, the bot can communicate with its command and control center. In actuality, the amount of code needed to make all of these changes is relatively small; however, the software changes to the execution paths are more complicated and subtle than illustrated here.

Widespread bot infestations are achieved using a variety of techniques; for example, the bot may infiltrate the computer by being wrapped in a file or e-mail attachment that looks innocent. The bot software may infest the computer using hidden code on a website that the user visited, which automatically downloaded from the website to the computer when the website connection was made. Nevertheless, however the bot software (botware) got there, the bot is now embedded in the computer and, unless the user runs an exceptionally powerful and sensitive anti-virus/anti-malware program, the user will not know the bot is implanted. The result of the infection is that it allows the infected computer to join the bot army that the bot master is building. When the bot master next checks the C2 computer or when sufficient bots have checked in (in the case of autonomous bot net operation) the "army" is ready for operation. A more detailed, but yet nominal, configuration for a bot army is depicted in Figure 15.5.

Current bot armies are very sophisticated, with the capability for different computers (and bots) in the army to perform different and specialized functions while remaining hidden. Typically, within a bot army there are a multitude of computers that have been subverted and that are solely dedicated to the task of recruiting new bots. There are also a number of bots that operate as command and control centers for the bot army; from the bot master point of view, these computers

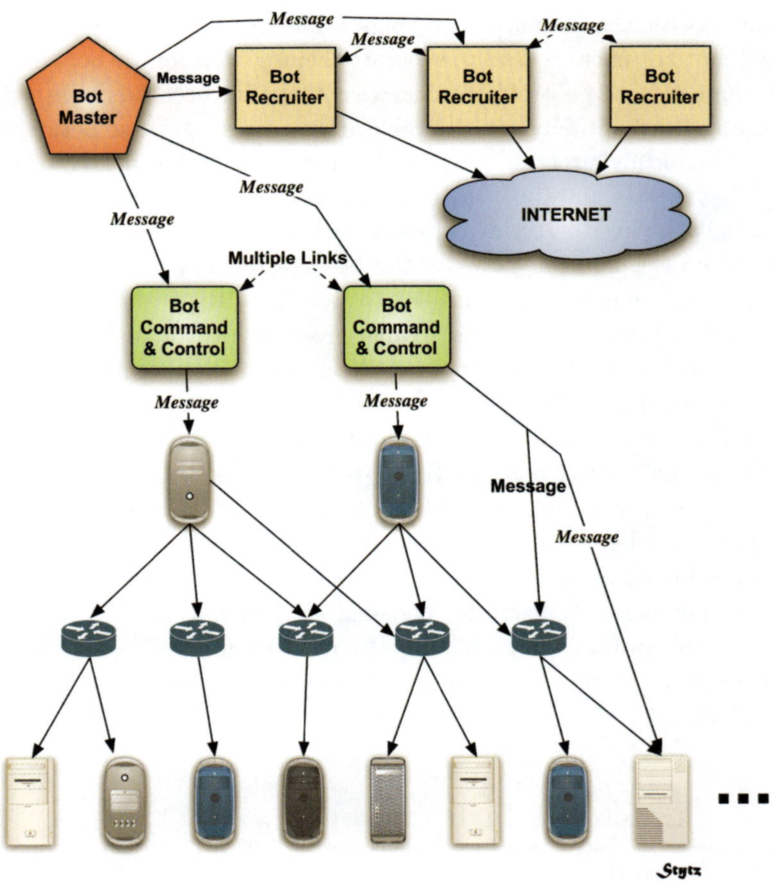


Fig. 15.5. Nominal bot army configuration.

provide an additional benefit to the bot master because they hide the bot master by insulating the bot master from the bots. The insulation both de-couples the main army bots from the bot master and the bot master commands and increases the difficulties that must be overcome in order to locate the bot master because the bot master can control the bots via the command and control centers (or C2 bots). A minimally competent bot master never needs to have direct contact between the bot master and any element of the bot army. A bot master can have multiple levels of C2 bots, allowing them to arbitrarily increase their degree of isolation from the bots they command.

Typically, the bot army that is under the control of a bot master at any time is smaller than the number of bots that have been implanted with the bot master's code. This difference arises generally because of administrative problems in the army; for example, some bots may not have registered, some computers may be off-line (meaning that their bots are inactive), some bots may not be reachable (because their command and control centers have been detected), or the bots are hibernating so that they are harder to detect. The desired or optimum degree of separation between the bot master and bots is not known and has not been publicly researched, but bot masters tend to separate themselves from the bots using several levels of command and control bots. Likewise, there has been no published research that addresses the optimum or desirable degree of separation between the bot master and the army's recruiter bots. The desire for a high degree of separation between a bot master and the army is tempered by the fact that other bot masters are continually trying to recruit compromised bots into their army. As a result, a high degree of separation between the bot master and the bots increases the opportunities for competitor bot masters to steal bots. Experience to date indicates that bot theft by competitors is a serious problem for bot masters. Based upon observations of bot master activity and the types of bot armies that have been defeated and analyzed, there is a tradeoff between the safety/security provided by large degrees of separation and the positive control and secure communication provided by a small degree of separation. Given that the theft of bots or portions of bot armies by competitors is a real threat to bot masters and that the security of communication between the bot master and bots determines the number of effective bots in the army at any given time, there will continue to be a tension between the bot master's desire for personal security and the bot master's desire to effectively control as large an army as possible [8, 36, 43, 46, 51, 55, 75]. This tension has led to the adoption of encryption techniques for communication within bot armies[h] [23, 55].

---

[h] http://www.news.com/Bots-may-get-cloak-of-encryption/2100-7349_3-5952102.html, http://www.news.com/AOL-IM-bot-cloaked-in-encryption/2100-7349_3-6066961.html?part=rss&tag=6066961&subj=news, http://www.securityfocus.com/news/11390, http://www.usenix.org/event/hotbots07/tech/full_papers/chiang/chiang_html/

Since victim computers are recruited for a bot army using viruses, worms, and other techniques that implant bot software in random hosts, a common set of problems faced by botnet authors[i] exists in discovering, organizing, and controlling their bots. The command and control problem is enough of a challenge that it is usually the Achilles heel of any bot army [43]. The command and control (C2) problem is most easily addressed by programming the bots to connect to named machines, commonly called a rallying box' to acquire their operational instructions. For example, to establish a C2 connection between a C2 node and a simple trojan bot, the simple trojan bot will include in its code the name of a C2 machine hard coded as a string in the binary executable for the bot. Upon infection, the victim computer unpacks the string and contacts the C2 server. The bot malware author can then observe the connections and communicate back to the bot in the infected computer. Obviously, there are two problems with this naive approach. The first problem with this approach is that if the C2 rallying box is cleansed, then the bot software has no way to join the army. The second problem with this approach is that the network traffic going into and out of the rallying box is an unmistakable indicator of a bot army and serves to point out to authorities the location and operation of the bots in the army. As a result, bot authors have explored ways to create robust networks to exercise command and control over the bots embedded in their victims. A common technique is to use Internet Relay Chat (IRC) [54] to communicate with bots in a bot army because IRC networks are very resilient, and designed to resist network faults. However, botnet defense can benefit from this choice because watching for unusual Internet relay chat traffic can be and is the common method for detecting the presence of bots and botnets. Cooke [28] describes a variety of other available command and control techniques, such as employing pseudo-random IP addresses to host the C2 bots and to serve as rallying boxes. To protect their bot army, bot herders are encrypting their C2 traffic [23, 55], inserting random traffic to hide the real C2 traffic, and creating a stable of alternate C2 nodes that a bot can contact for instructions if its primary C2 host computer is unreachable. Another approach taken by bot authors to preserve their botnet command and control is to keep their botnets mobile using dynamic DNS (DDNS) [95], a service that facilitates frequent updates and changes in C2 and rallying box machine addresses. This technique is particularly difficult to shut down because each time the botnet command and control (C2) box is shut down, the botnet authors merely create a new command and control box and update the appropriate dynamic DNS entry. The bots perform periodic DNS queries, and migrate their communication to the new C2 location.

An example of the capabilities that a bot provides its bot master is illustrated by an examination of one of the more capable and best-known bots in the recent past, the Agobot. According to the anti-virus vendor Sophos [84], there are more

[i]A botnet author, or bot author, develops the bot army software. The bot author and bot master may, or may not, be the same person or team.

than 500 known different variants of the Agobot. The bot is written in C++ and possesses cross-platform capabilities and the source code is put under the General Public License (GPL). The latest available versions of Agobot have a highly abstract software design, allowing it to be highly modular and it is very easy to add commands or scanners for other vulnerabilities. To make a change, the bot master needs to simply extend the correct C++ method(s) to add the desired feature(s). Agobot uses libcap (a packet sniffing library) and Perl Compatible Regular Expressions (PCRE) to sniff and sort traffic, allowing it to target and compromise specific types of network traffic. Agobot can use NTFS Alternate Data Stream (ADS) and its rootkit capabilities allow it to hide its presence on a compromised host. Furthermore, reverse engineering of this malware is difficult because the deployed bot software includes functions designed to detect debuggers and virtual machines [94] and disable the bot if these defensive tools are detected. Agobot can use a control protocol other than IRC, giving it great flexibility in its C2 structure.

### 15.2.2. *Malware*

All bots rely upon malware, so before continuing the discussion of bots, we will briefly examine their underlying technology[j] and associated terminology [10, 11, 13, 17, 19, 24, 30, 35, 41, 48, 53, 56, 57, 59, 72, 78, 82, 99, 101, 106, 107]. The continual advancements in malware technology have both increased the ease of implanting malware and increased the difficulty of preventing its operation. In general, malware's objective is to gather information about target computers or deny access/service by inserting unsolicited software into a computer system. To date, most anti-malware techniques use the traditional anti-virus approach. The approach consists of a third party developing a database of malware signatures and software that removes the malware associated with each signature, which can be used by a security expert or a user to identify and remove the malware. Over time, the malware signature database continually grows as new malware reports are submitted and analyzed and software designed to remove the malware is developed. While the malware signature database is huge, within the database there are four main classes of malware: (1) virus, (2) worm, (3) wabbit, and (4) Trojan horse. We will discuss each class of malware in turn, but focus on the virus and Trojan as they are the two key technologies used for establishing and maintaining a bot army.

Viruses have used many sorts of techniques and hosts to propagate and execute nefarious acts. When computer viruses first originated, common targets for viruses were executable files embedded within application programs and the boot sectors of floppy disks. Viruses were later placed in documents that are designed to contain macro scripts; execution of the script enabled the virus to infect the host. Recently, viruses have been placed into e-mail as attachments and other Internet traffic so

---

[j]See alse: http://www.malware.com/

that they can infect an unsuspecting user's computer (usually assisted by social engineering techniques). In the case of visuses that are executable files, the virus is designed to insure that when the host code is executed, the viral code is executed as well. Normally, the host program keeps functioning after infection by the virus and appears to be uninfected. Viruses spread from computer to computer when the software or document they are embedded within is transferred from one computer to the other.

Computer worms [69] are similar to viruses in action but they are not embedded in host files (or other types of host code) and are built to be self-propagating and infect other computers without assistance or hiding within host documents or code. They do modify their host operating system, however, at least to the extent that they need to insure that they are started as part of the boot process. A third, but uncommon, type of self-replicating malware is the wabbit. Unlike viruses, wabbits do not infect host programs or documents. Unlike worms, wabbits do not use network functionality in order to spread to other computers.

Trojan horse software is malware software disguised within legitimate software. Trojan horses cannot replicate themselves, in contrast to viruses or worms. The fundamental differences between a Trojan horse and a computer virus are that a Trojan horse is combination of a normal computer program and malware and the Trojan does not possess the means to spread itself. A Trojan horse can be transmitted by deliberately attaching it to otherwise useful software or it can spread by using social engineering to trick users into believing that the malicious software is useful. To complicate matters, some Trojans can spread or activate other malware, such as viruses,[k] allowing the combination of malware to inflict more damage than a single type of malware. In a Trojan horse, the useful, or seemingly useful, functions placed into the software (or documents) used to induce a user to use the software serve as camouflage for these undesired functions. In practice, Trojan horses typically contain spying functions or backdoor functions that allow a computer, unbeknownst to the owner, to be remotely controlled across the network by another computer or a human. Because Trojan horses often have harmful functions, there is the misconception that such functions define a Trojan horse, they do not. Originally Trojan horses were not designed to spread themselves. They relied on social engineering techniques to induce people to allow the proffered program to perform actions that they would not have otherwise allowed. Current Trojans contain functions that enable them to spread. Trojan horses can be designed to do various harmful things, the type and degree of damage is generally limited only by the imagination of the hacker. Example Trojan capabilities are erasing or overwriting data on a computer, corrupting files in a subtle way, and enabling the spread of other malware such as viruses.

---

[k]These programs are called 'droppers'.

Since malware, especially bots, are designed to be inherently indetectable, there are few reliable indicators of the presence of malware. First, a malware infection causes unusual behavior on a system, which is usually not noticeable until the infection is severe. The malware may have been designed to propagate, as in the case of viruses, or to inflict havoc or damage on a system, which is what Trojans actually do. Other types of malware such as droppers introduce other malware to systems. In any event, unexpected behavior ensues and central processing unit (CPU) cycles and/or network bandwidth and/or hard drive capacity are consumed by the malware. A second indicator is that malware also tends to use process names that look nearly identical to common process names. For example, WSOCK32.DLL, a common memory process that has the responsibility for managing the library of socket functions in Windows can be spoofed using the name WSOCK33.DLL. Sometimes the names being used to spoof the system are actually valid names for the operating system but the path (hard drive directory address) given for the spoofed process is different from the path to the true function. For example, the KERNEL32.DLL process is supposed to be found in the \Windows\System32 directory but some malware takes advantage of Windows and places the malware in the \Windows\System directory. Finally, there are other indications of malware infection such as a recently executed and supposedly terminated program being found active in memory when it should not be (because it was terminated and its memory should have been freed and given to another process). Another symptom of infection is the appearance of multiple copies of a program in memory even though there is no application with that name installed by the user. One other symptom of a malware infection is that, if upon closing all applications and checking the memory usage there is memory that is still in use then there may be an infection, especially if there is no indication that there is a reason for memory activity, such as supervisory process activity.

However, locating malware is merely the first step; the malware must be removed from the computer and that is not a trivial task. Malware and bot software, like all software, must be stored somewhere on the computer if it is to execute after a shutdown. For bots, persistent storage of the bot software is crucial since it is the only way to insure that the bots persist in operation on the infected computer. Because bot software will be removed if it is found, bot software authors include code in the bot software to allow the bot to hide within the computer and its files. By hiding the bot software, the bot software author insures that the bot can restart after the cleansing completes or the computer reboots. Because bot software is malicious, taking a simple, naïve approach to removing malware is dangerous because the operation can destroy the contents of the computer's storage devices or provide a false sense of security because the malware may be designed to destroy the computer's contents or hide itself among the hard drive's files if it detects any cleansing activity.

Malware and bot software can insure its repeated execution by storing itself anywhere on the system and making an entry into the Windows system registry to insure that it starts execution whenever the system starts or reboots. Another technique used to insure repeated malware execution is to modify the System.ini and Win.ini files by adding links to the malware within these files thereby insuring that the malware is started whenever the computer reboots. A third malware restart technique, that can be used if the malware is a macro, is for the malware to attach itself to a large number of legitimate pieces of software, such as Microsoft Word or Excel, and thereby broadly hide itself and execute whenever any of the infected host applications execute.

## 15.3. Bot Capability Evolution and Bot Defense

In the previous section, we briefly introduced the basics of bot army organization and operation. In this section, we examine bot army capabilities, organization, and operation in more detail. As we indicated, the minimal capabilities required by a bot army are a C2 computer, a C2 communications channel, malware (for insertion and exploitation), and a distribution technology. The simplest, and earliest, bots used simple IRC for C2, malware in the form of a packet generator (to conduct a denial of service attack), no dedicated hosts for distribution of additional bot software to augment bot capabilities, and a C2 node at a fixed IP address for C2 of the bot army by the bot master. This simple configuration and relatively small software load has been replaced by sophisticated software and C2 configurations.

### 15.3.1. *Bot Army Capabilities*

Bot technology has improved dramatically in the last few years, and as a result, bots are increasingly capable and malicious. The modern era of bot army activity dates from February 2000, when a Canadian hacker commanded his bot army to attack CNN.com, Amazon.com, eBay.com, Dell Computer (at dell.com), and other sites with a huge volume of traffic [66]. The traffic volume was sufficient to take the targeted computer systems off-line. Bot technologies and capabilities have made significant progress since this first, relatively naïve modern bot attack.

Bot technological evolution is difficult to describe or depict due to its speed, lack of coordination among bot software developers, the ability of relatively small changes in software to yield dramatic improvements in capabilities, and the many technologies that play a role in advancing bot capabilities. Advances in CPU performance and increases in network bandwidth enable improvements in bot performance and make it easier for bot masters to mask their operation. Conversely, improvements in operating systems generally tend to impede improvements in bot performance and operation, since these improvements tend to improve the security of the system. Improvements in Internet anonymyzing technology, dynamic IP address allocation, encryption, process migration, IRC, inter-process communication, and all malware serve to improve bot technology and capabilities. Simply put, any improvement in Internet usability, security, or performance also improves the capabilities of bot armies much more than the defenses against bot armies. The evolution of bot technology parallels the evolution of Internet technology. The technology that underlies bot armies is not inherently criminal; it is the morality and ethics of the user of the technology and not the technology itself that determines if the technology will be used for criminal purposes.

Bot technology (from the point of view of the employment of their foundational technologies as offensive tools) has developed at a pace that far exceeds the ability of current cyber defense development technologies to prevent bot incursions or to prevent exploitation of compromised resources. New developments in bot army technologies are announced daily. Bot masters exploit technological advances and newly discovered vulnerabilities as rapidly as they are available and long before the flaws they exploit can be fixed or defended. For example, a Microsoft security patch released on 5 August 2006 contained a security flaw that was exploited by a bot army by 12 August 2006 [37, 38]. The developers of bots are agile, increasingly malicious, and technically sophisticated. There is little that technology or appeals to morality can do to dissuade them from attacking; and bot masters feel increasingly secure from detection due to their improvements in C2 infrastructure and secure bot communication. Given the difficulty both of cleansing an infected computer and of finding bot masters, intrusion prevention holds out the best promise for defeating the botnet threat at this time. Indeed, according to the public literature, bot masters are caught only because they make a mistake that allows follow-up forensic investigations to locate them; they are not caught as a result of preemptive action or active search for bot activity. Development of technology for detecting bot controllers, bot hosts, and bot master location should be a top research priority, even though it may be difficult. Unfortunately, little research is underway in any of these areas at this time.

Removing (or busting) a bot army is a far more formidable task than locating a bot master. To remove an army, the deletion activity must locate and remove the bots before the bots or the bot master can determine that a search/deletion effort is underway. As a practical matter, the need to hide bots and to prevent their capture and reverse engineering of their software requires the bot search/deletion activity to be accomplished in a matter of minutes unless the bot controller can be disabled immediately. Obviously, the best way to destroy a bot army is to stealthily acquire a single bot and its bot code and analyze it to locate its self-destruct mechanism(s) and capabilities. Bot code self-mutates so that it is difficult to detect and so that it can adapt to and overcome new defensive techniques autonomously [17]. Most bot masters include a self-destruct command in their bot's code to make forensic analysis difficult and to increase the difficulty of locating the bot master. However, to preserve the bot, the self-destruct command generally must come from either certain specified IP addresses and/or is encrypted; either way the removal process is difficult and must replicate in its entirety the self-destruct command that the bot master would issue. However, if the self-destruct sequence can be obtained, an entire bot army can be removed worldwide in a matter of moments. Given the difficulty of acquiring the self-destruct signal, the typical bot army defensive strategy is to block the infestation, either at each computer or at firewalls (or both) by watching for bot infestation signature traffic on the network. However, if the defensive measures fail, which occurs often, then the infestation must be removed by both removing the bots as well as the C2, botware host, and bot exploitation hosts one by one. This task is formidable because of the number of bots and because the C2, botware host, and bot exploitation hosts are well hidden, capable of migration, and often operate via intermediaries in order to coordinate their activities and to warn each other of possible attempts to remove the bot army or to capture it by another bot master.

Botware is well hidden, capable of migration, and often operates via intermediaries because bot masters are highly motivated to continue to infest computers with bots and to improve the sophistication of the bots they employ. Providing the required degree of sophistication for the software used by the bot army and thereby staying ahead of defensive efforts requires considerable ongoing effort. Hence, we can assume that a bot master will always attempt to maximize the sophistication of their bots when they are deployed, especially as regards their robustness, mobility, and stealth because of the effort required to develop the bot and the ease with which some critical malware elements can be obtained. Robustness allows the bots and bot army to continue to operate effectively even when some of the C2 and software distribution hosts are compromised or if some of the bot's code is compromised on its host. Mobility allows bots to migrate among hosts, thereby expediting infestation and helping to maintain a bot army's membership. Stealth permits the bot to operate and communicate without detection and also serves to help to hide the bot software from discovery in any host that it infects. So, unless the bot master makes a mistake, it will remain difficult to detect a bot or bot army. Fortunately, it is well known that as code increases in complexity, the chances of an error being inserted into the software also increases. Therefore, by increasing the degree of sophistication of the defense against botnets, we increase the chances that the bot masters will make a mistake in their software that will, in turn, enable the defenders to more easily detect and defeat the bot armies. However, in order to accomplish this goal, bot defense should cooperate internationally, since the bot masters also operate and coordinate their actions internationally.

### 15.3.2. *Bot Army Technology Development*

Bot army technology is advancing very rapidly, with some of its technical components advancing every day and with notable advances in bot army technology occurring every few months. Based upon the literature reviewed, a significant advance occurs at least once per year; which indicates that this technology is far from maturing and that major improvements in bot army technology are yet to come.

A number of technological factors promote and abet the development of even more formidable capabilities for bot armies in the future, all of which bodes ill for bot defense and for computer security in general. These factors include malware technology improvements, innovations in bot army topology,[l] improvements in bot army command and control, malware use, and ever-increasing difficulty of malware and bot detection. For example, random topologies for a bot army communication network renders them difficult to detect, so botnets increasingly employ random topology technologies. As a result, user patching fails to diminish the number of bots in the botnet and searching for and eliminating individual bot nodes can at best remove a few nodes. The result is asymptotically the same for the bot army population as random loss, which is easily counteracted by bot masters. Botnets with random topologies (including structured P2P networks [53]) are extremely resilient to any defensive measures and deserve further study. Due to legal restrictions in the United States, it is difficult to perform the required research on botnets and, therefore it is difficult to point to specific research that points to the future of malware.[m] However, developments in the component technologies for botnets do provide some indications about what the future holds.

If we accept as a working proposition that the rate of progress of a given technology can be estimated by extrapolating the rate of progress of its component technologies, we can estimate the likely future of botnets. All botnets rely upon malware technology, indeed their effectiveness and capacity for harm is closely tied to the state of malware technology. Therefore, anticipated developments in malware can provide a guide to the future capabilities of botnets. Simply, the bot masters have the technological and numbers advantage, they are motivated, the returns are massive for a small investment, and the chances of being caught are small. The chances of successful prosecution are even smaller. Attacker botnet technology is evolving faster than defensive technology, and defenders are cutting research funding that would provide the needed insight into botnet operation and its employment of malware. The botnet situation appears to be headed in a direction wherein matters will get worse before they improve. One example of the current power of botnets will serve to illustrate the potential future power of botnets. It is well known that bot armies are extremely powerful tools for denial of service attacks. At the current time, even simple queries on Google™ can consume inordinate amounts of bandwidth on every network[n] using a technique called "Google hacking".[o] There is no known

---

[l]A topology is an arrangement of the nodes and links in a network, the study of topology is a subset of graph theory, http://physinfo.ulb.ac.be/cit_courseware/networks/pt2_1.htm [91].
[m]Such as that imposed by the Digital Millenium Copyright Act of 1998, which has been used to prosecute malware researchers [McL03].
[n]http://www.informit.com/articles/article.asp?p=170880&seqNum=2&rl=1 has a "Google hacking" mini-guide.
[o]See http://www.acunetix.com/websitesecurity/google-hacking.htm and http://johnny.ihackstuff.com and http://www.gcn.com/online/vol1_no1/45868-1.html

countermeasure for this type of attack; all that can be done is to block requests from IP domain ranges or domain names associated with an attack.

A review of the presentations of the last two years' worth of BlackHat conferences [15] leads to several conclusions relevant to advancement in botnet technologies. Probably the most distressing fact is that botnet attacks are now being executed for money, profit, or other gain; not to demonstrate technical prowess. Botnet activity is a criminal activity on an international scale, with any bot-related tool or skill available at a price [44]. Attacks will only stop when the hackers' risk/reward calculus changes dramatically; and the prospect of such a change is slight in the near term. No commercial software, such as the Windows$^{TM}$ operating system software, is secure against botnets because virtually all outsourced software is being made with backdoors in it, which allows for unauthorized, illegal access to computer systems. In addition to the backdoors that are present, the number of botnet exploits and their sophistication is increasing. The indicators are that there are hundreds of non-publicly available exploits currently in use, exploits that we are currently unable to be defended against. There are no commonly accepted estimates of the total number of exploits in use. The botnet defense challenge is further highlighted by the fact that bot and malware attacks continue to increase in sophistication; they are harder to detect, faster in their propagation from host to host, and that the most effective tools and techniques are close-held.

Deterrence and prosecution of cyber attacks will continue to be difficult, because attacks from overseas predominate the set of botnet attacks and because of the increasing sophistication of botnet attacks. Another factor that increases the difficulty of attack attribution is the recent appearance of fire and forget bot armies. The fire and forget bot army innovation allows a bot master to obtain further distance from the activity of a bot army because the bot master need only set up a command and control center and recruitment center for bots, manage these centers remotely, and allow the command centers to manage the attacks. The bot army operates completely autonomously in this new incarnation of the concept. If the bot army is intended to make money for the bot master, the trail from the attacked financial accounts to the destination financial accounts may lead to the bot master, but this is the only usable trail to the bot master as the trail from the bot master to the bots is too difficult to follow and from which to gather evidence. As noted above, bot attack sophistication is increasing and one of the more troublesome areas is that the bot master's attack toolkit armor for the bot software is improving. This development, of course, increases the resilience of the bots and makes each successful penetration more valuable and long lasting. An additional recent element of sophistication is the use of photographic files, such as JPG and GIF files, to hold attack code for transport to a target computer. As the image is loaded into a browser or e-mail reader, the image file causes photographic parser software to be activated, which parses the image and converts it from the transport format (JPG for example) to a display format.[p] During the image unpacking process the malware embedded in the image is activated and installs itself on the targeted machine. Because the photograph is the attack vector and malware transport medium, users have almost no opportunity to prevent the attack from succeeding and the malware almost always enters the targeted computer. The efficacy of this attack is limited by the amount of malware that can be embedded in the picture, not by any defense that can currently be mounted.

Coupled with the advancements in malware technology, another component of future challenges posed by bot armies is the improvements in rootkit technologies coupled with their wider use. Rootkits[q] are becoming easier to create due to the availability of free and commercial tools for creating rootkits, books that assist in the development of rootkits, and the availability of rootkit development services via the web. In addition, complete exploit development toolsets have appeared that provide great assistance to rootkit and malware development authors. Malware and botware development technology is so advanced that a hacker can literally "point-and-click" their way to the development of a powerful botnet and exploits. In short, the sophistication of botnet attacks can be expected to increase while at the same time the knowledge and skill required to assemble sophisticated attacks is decreasing. For example, it is now possible for an attacker to assemble a bot army whose bots are able to run within a virtual machine outside of the host computer's operating system, the so-called "Blue Pill." Rutkowska has demonstrated the "Blue Pill" capability [77] and at this time, Vista$^{\text{TM}}$ is vulnerable to this attack [67, 68, 83]. Using the "Blue Pill", a bot can insure that no other malware is executing on the machine, and this capability has already been observed in the wild. Using the "Blue Pill", a bot master would, indeed, "own" the computer in every sense of the word. Furthermore, consider that software productivity and quality has a great degree of variability among software developers [76]; therefore, sophisticated bot armies are undoubtedly being developed by some of the best programmers in the world, programmers who must possess a deep understanding of the operating systems and applications they are targeting so that the bot can accomplish its task. In the bot army domain, as for any other software development effort, it seems that the quality of the hackers (software developers) is much more important than the number of hackers available for a task; a general rule of thumb is that a few good hackers will always outperform a large number of average hackers. All of these factors, when considered in aggregate, indicate that the bot army threat will become worse, that bots and bot armies will become more sophisticated and difficult to find, and that bot armies will be able to do more damage than ever before.

---

[p]http://blog.trendmicro.com/digital-photo-frames-frameup/
http://www.enterpriseitplanet.com/security/features/article.php/3409471

[q]Rootkits can also be an effective defensive/forensics tool [14] and can be detected using some tools under specific circumstances [105].

One area of great future concern is the continuing search for and development of economic, easy, and effective means for hiding communications between the bot master, the main control computers and the bots. The current technology of choice is Onion routing [34, 64]. Onion routing is the name for a set of projects dedicated to researching, designing, building, and analyzing techniques for assembling anonymous communications systems. In Onion routing, the focus is on practical systems for low-latency Internet-based connections that impede traffic analysis, eavesdropping, and other attacks both by outsiders (e.g., Internet routers) and insiders (the Onion routing servers). Onion Routing operates by preventing the transport medium from knowing who is communicating with whom — the network knows only that communication is occurring. The content of the communication is hidden from eavesdroppers up to the point where the traffic leaves the onion routing network. The protection provided by Onion routing is independent of which end of the communication wishes to hide their identity. For example, the sender and receiver may wish to identify and even authenticate to each other, but do not wish others to know that they are communicating. Onion routing protects against a form of Internet surveillance known as "traffic analysis." Traffic analysis can be used to infer who is talking to whom over a public network. Knowing the source and destination of Internet traffic allows others to track behavior, interests, and duties. Within the Internet, traffic analysis operates by taking advantage of the content of packet headers. Internet data packets have two parts: a data payload and a header used for routing. The data payload is what is being sent from sender to recipient, whether it is an email message, a web page, or an audio file. Even if the data is encrypted, traffic analysis still reveals a great deal about what is being done and, possibly, what data is being transferred because it focuses on the header, which discloses source, destination, size, timing, and other information. For example, the most powerful current type of traffic analysis uses sophisticated statistical techniques to track communications patterns of many different organizations and individuals. Encryption does not help against these statistical analysis based attacks because encryption only hides the content of Internet traffic, not the headers. To defeat traffic analysis and preserve anonymity, Onion routed data travels between source and recipient using different intermediate packet relay servers for each packet. The sender and recipient accomplish Onion routing by building an overlay network that consists of a private network that employs encrypted connections between servers. The connections are built one hop at a time, each connection only knows the preceding hop in the private network from whom it receives data and the next hop on the private network to whom it sends data, and each hop on each pathway has a separate encryption key. Pathways in the virtual private network change frequently, further complicating the traffic analysis problem. The utility of this technology for bot armies is obvious, Onion routing enables protected, nearly anonymous communication between bot masters and their bots, and allows bots to securely communicate with each other because our current tools for detecting bot communication are ineffective against onion routing.

One prominent trend among botnets is the use of multiple IP sources to launch attacks and spread bots, thereby allowing botnets to rapidly increase in size. The use of web pages for spreading bots in addition to their use for command and control is also a very promising tool for spreading bots. Web pages are difficult to secure because the multitude of technologies and overlapping responsibilities combine to make vulnerabilities that are readily exploited in a manner that is difficult to detect. The technological barriers that must be overcome to launch a web-based attack are very low. The low technological barriers to attacks are complemented by the high complexity of web-based applications in OSI layer 7,[r] thereby yielding tempting and easily penetrated pathways into computer systems. Increasing computer power will only make the use of web pages to propagate hidden commands and infection vectors easier (such as by using steganography[s] to hide bot commands and malware). There are now web-based attacks comprised of software that is self-replicating and that automatically finds and exploits its targeted vulnerabilities; hence, the bot master can just release the bot software into the net and wait for bots to register as the software moves from site to site.

### 15.3.3. *Defending Against Bot Armies*

For the bot army defender of the future, prospects are bleak.[t] As of this time, most defensive security products, though effective, are far from perfect or seamless; require continual updates; and are not sufficiently effective to be able to insure that bots cannot penetrate the computer. Unfortunately, most bot security incidents are detected because of poor computer performance, higher than normal network activity, persistent crashing of the system, failure of software to load/run, inability to install new applications, inability to save new files, or other software failure. The presence of a bot on a computer is generally not indicated via defensive warnings or detection systems. The bot defenses do not detect the bot software as it tries to infiltrate the computer or during operation, rather it is only the secondary indicators that reveal the presence of a bot after the infection has occurred and corrupted the computer. Bot armies are usually only detected when the bot master makes a significant mistake, which allows the defenses to identify a bot or bot army and attempt to remove it. Botnet defense has one bright spot, however, most attacks rely upon user interaction to initiate the infection. If the user fails to open an attachment containing the attack payload, does not go to the website containing the attack

[r] Such as e-mail and web browsers, the protocols in this layer are easily understood, mandate few security operations, but are very powerful.

[s] *Steganography* means *covered writing* as derived from Greek. It includes a vast array of methods of secret communications that conceal the very existence of the message. Among these methods are invisible inks, microdots, character arrangement (other than the cryptographic methods of permutation and substitution), digital signatures, covert channels and spread-spectrum communications. http://www.jjtc.com/stegdoc/steg1995.html

[t] http://www.smh.com.au/news/security/now-is-the-winter-of-our-malware-discontent/2008/04/08/1207420317465.html

payload, or fails to perform some other affirmative action, most bots cannot enter and infest the user's computer. Therefore, training to build a defensive and cautious attitude toward all Internet communications is the best current defense against bot armies. But, as will be discussed, much more research into botnet defense is required.

An advancement that has been made in bot defense is the modeling of bot army growth and propagation. These models are drawn from the medical literature. In the medical literature [2, 3, 5, 7, 17, 18, 21, 22, 31, 32, 39, 45, 50, 61, 63] infection transmission is usually portrayed using the general disease transmission and outcome diagram presented in Figure 15.6. The transfer diagram portrays, in an abstract format, the potential sources, infestation pathways, and outcomes for fatal disease transmission. There is a large body of work that has been developed to describe and model disease transmission and disease infestation vectors for various diseases, a much larger body of work than we can discuss here in reasonable detail. (The actual model used for a given disease is modified from this general model based upon the type of infection, transfer modality, and potential for re-infection.)

To exploit existing epidemiology research, we suggest using the same symbology shown in Figure 15.6 for each stage of bot infestation, but that the meaning of the symbols should be changed to suit the botnet modeling challenge. In medicine, typically, M is the class (or portion) of the population born with passive immunity (due to the mother). In our formulation **M** is the class of computers (hardware or software) that are not infected with malware during manufacture or development that can, nevertheless, be exploited to enable bot infestation. In medicine, S is employed to represent the class of the population that has lost its maternally acquired passive immunity plus the portion of the population that never had immunity, with the transfer from the class M to class S determined by the rate at which passive immunity disappears. In medicine, S represents the susceptible population. In our formulation, the class **S** is used to represent the class of computers

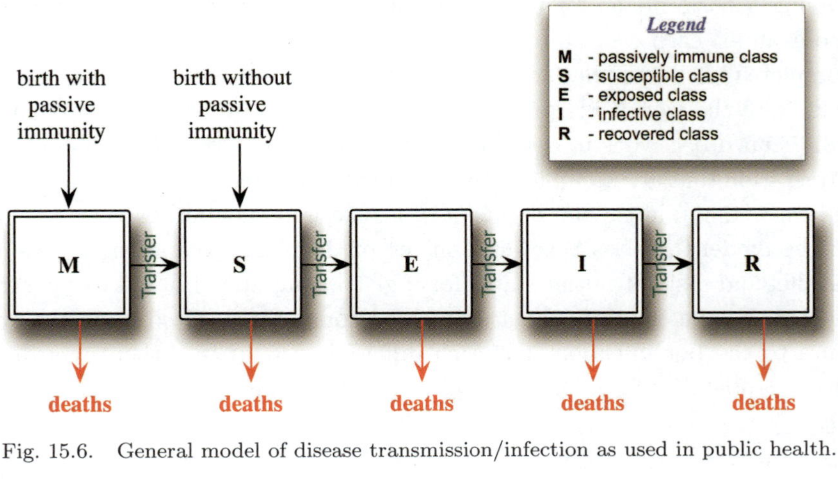


Fig. 15.6. General model of disease transmission/infection as used in public health.

(hardware or software) that are infected during manufacture with malware that can be exploited to enable bot infestation (hence these computers are more susceptible than expected).

In medicine, the class E is the set of individuals who have been exposed to the infection but do not show signs of infection. In our formulation, the class **E** is the set of computers that have been attacked, that have been infected, and in whom the infection has not been detected. Note the size of the set (**M** + **S**) is not equal to the entire set of computers that have been constructed, and the probability of a computer changing state from class **M** to **E** is not the same as the probability of a computer changing state from class **S** to **E**. In medicine, the class I is typically comprised of the set of individuals in whom the latency (or dormancy) period for the infection has passed, who can transmit the infection, and who exhibit signs of infection. In our formulation, the class **I** is the set of computers that have been infected, are transmitting the infection, are performing the task(s) that the bot was intended to perform, that show (or contain) signs of bot infection, and in whom the infection has not been detected. The members of the set **I** are the most active bots in the bot army and the most likely to be detected; for a given bot army the number of computers in the class **I** is less than or equal to the number of computers in the class **E**, with part of the difference being the number of bots that are lying dormant. In medicine, the class R is the set of individuals for whom the infection period has ended and who have acquired permanent infection-acquired immunity; they are sometimes referred to as the infection's reservoir. In our formulation, the class **R** is the set of computers that have been infected, whose infection has been detected, and whose bot software has been removed. However, these bots can, potentially become susceptible to the bot and become re-infected; to account for this possibility cleansed computers that have lost their immunity are placed back into the set **S** and are treated the same as any computer that lacks passive immunity from the bot infection. Figure 15.7 presents our model and the relationships between the classes of bot infection that we have defined.

Having a basic model for the classes of susceptibility for botnet infection, we need to examine each class in more detail to present the basis for the development of a complete model, one that accounts for all of the significant steps in a bot army's lifecycle since the worldwide penetration of computers by bots is estimated to be 90% [87]. Our objective is to develop comprehensive but closed-form models of bot army operation that are useful for smaller sets of computers, and the model outlined above is a first step in the development of the desired capability.

In the model the class **S** is not a subset of the class **M**, and these two classes are parallel and disjoint initial states for a given computer. Both states contribute to the class **E** (the class of currently infected computers), based upon the type of exposure to the bot infection. For each different type of bot, there is a different transition probability from the class **M** to the class **E** and from the class **S** to the class **E**.

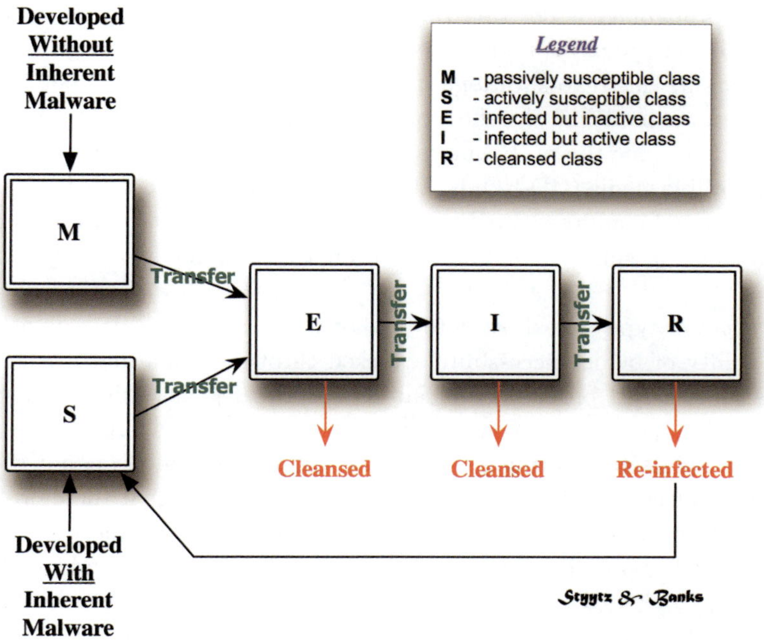


Fig. 15.7. General model of bot infection.

The class $\underline{\mathbf{E}}$, the class of infected but inactive computers, is comprised of two subclasses: (1) the subclass of infected computers that provide command and control for the botnet, called $\underline{\mathbf{E}}_{\mathrm{C}}$ and (2) the subclass of infected computers that are designed to be merely the bots, called $\underline{\mathbf{E}}_{\mathrm{B}}$, but have not yet been activated. The class $\underline{\mathbf{I}}$ is drawn from the class of computers in the class $\underline{\mathbf{E}}_{\mathrm{B}}$. The members of the class $\underline{\mathbf{I}}$ perform botnet tasks and/or actively attempt to infect additional computers and place them into the botnet either as a command and control member or a plain bot. Because there are two subclasses in class $\underline{\mathbf{E}}$, there are four transfer probabilities that affect the transition from class $\underline{\mathbf{E}}$ to $\underline{\mathbf{I}}$ that must be considered; $\underline{\mathbf{E}}_{\mathrm{C}} \Rightarrow$ command and control, $\underline{\mathbf{E}}_{\mathrm{C}} \Rightarrow$ bot, $\underline{\mathbf{E}}_{\mathrm{B}} \Rightarrow$ command and control, and $\underline{\mathbf{E}}_{\mathrm{B}} \Rightarrow$ bot. Historically, the class $\underline{\mathbf{E}}$ is a more difficult to detect class of bots than the bots in class $\underline{\mathbf{I}}$ (bots in class $\underline{\mathbf{E}}$ have a lower probability of detection than those in class $\underline{\mathbf{I}}$), and the transition $\underline{\mathbf{E}}_{\mathrm{B}} \Rightarrow$ bot is the transition most likely to be detected. As regards detection, each subclass in classes $\underline{\mathbf{E}}$ and $\underline{\mathbf{I}}$ have their own detection probabilities, and those probabilities are used to determine the transition rate from each of the subclasses to class $\underline{\mathbf{R}}$. The probabilities of detection for each subclass in $\underline{\mathbf{E}}$ and $\underline{\mathbf{I}}$ are related to the volume of data transmitted by the members of the subclass, frequency of transmission, the activity of each subclass of bot within its host computer, and the bot's defenses. Note that since there is no "natural" immunity conferred on a computer after having been cleansed of a bot infection, it is possible for a previously infected computer to be re-infected by the same bot again. This probability is portrayed by a transition probability from state **R** back to one of the state **S** and is represented by $P_R$.

There are at least two additional factors that affect a model of bot infestation. The first factor is modeling the effect of types of exposure to bot software (botware) in order to determine the probability of being attacked through the network, USB drives, removable media (CD-ROMs, DVD-ROMs, etc,), or other media. The second factor that must be addressed is how to model the probability of an infection by a particular bot, $P_I$, since this number determines the number of computers in the class **I**.

The effect of types of exposure to bot software, called $P_{BotWare}$, is modeled by the probability of being successfully attacked through media and is a component of the variable called probability of an attack, $P_P$. $P_P$ has other components in addition to $P_{BotWare}$, other components of $P_P$ include the probability that the hardware was infected during manufacture, $P_{PH}$, and the probability that the software was infected during manufacture, $P_{PS}$. It is known that these probabilities are independent; that is, $P_{BotWare}$ is not related to $P_{PH}$, which is not related to or dependent upon $P_{PS}$. Rather, all probabilities operate independently, so $P_P = P_{BotWare} + P_{PS} + P_{PH}$. The computer security literature indicates that several infections due to manufacturing can be in place simultaneously in both the hardware and software. However, since we are not trying to determine the probability of a particular computer being infected, but instead the probability that a set of computers is infected by a specific bot, the mean infection rate of hardware and software due to manufacturing will be sufficient for our purposes. The infection rate for hardware is, currently, classified but is known to be non-zero, small, and less than entirely pervasive. For our purposes here, $P_{PH}$ is assigned a reasonable number. The infection rate for software is quite high and is due to two factors. The first factor is deliberate insertion of malware for later use, and its value is classified. The second factor is the persistent problem of software errors, and is generally related to both the complexity of the software and the number of lines of code. Schneider [79] empirically determined that the expected number of software errors (B) in a software development project to is related to: (1) the overall reported months of programmer effort for the project (E), (2) the number of subprograms (n), and (3) the count of thousands of coded source statements (S). These estimators, developed by Schneider [79], are given in the following two equations:

$$B \approx 7.6E^{0,667*}S^{0.333} \tag{15.1}$$

and

$$B \approx n^{*}((S/n)/.045)^{1.667} \tag{15.2}$$

In general, the error count in software is a relatively accurate estimate of the number of errors that can be exploited by malware [100]. Therefore, we use Schneider's model to allow us to approximate B, as described in equations 1 and 2, and employ a reasonable estimate for the number of deliberately inserted pieces of malware (in hardware or software); the sum of these figures divided by the count of thousands of coded source statements (S) gives us our approximate value for $P_{PS}$; $P_{PS} = B + (P_{SH} + P)/n$.

The model can be used for modeling multiple bot army attacks, each type of botnet is modeled individually. $P_I$ for a particular botnet is computed for the complete set of computers in the simulation, not for a single computer; thereby allowing us to estimate the size of the infected set for a particular bot. As indicated by the preceding discussion, there are many factors that determine the probability of infection for a particular bot. A baseline model for bot infection can be built based upon the known progression and effect of a bot attack. The baseline model is the probability of an attack, $P_A$, times the probability of a successful penetration, $P_P$, times the probability of a successful exploitation, $P_E$. Therefore,

$$P_I = P_A * P_P * P_E \tag{15.3}$$

$\mathbf{P_I}$ will, for a given computer population, determine the number of computers in the set **E̲** and **I̲**. However, there are multiple factors that affect this basic formula and that must be considered. One factor that affects the formula is that $\mathbf{P_A}$ and $\mathbf{P_P}$, which are applied to the size of the sets **M̲** and **S̲** for a given bot and gives rise to the set **E̲** for all computers for a particular bot, are dependant upon separate probabilities for attack and penetration for hardware, $P_{AH}$, $P_{PH}$, and software $P_{AS}$ and $P_{PS}$ for a given bot. The size of the sets **M̲** and **S̲** are related to both $P_{AH}$ and $P_{AS}$ because a computer must both be vulnerable to attack and in a position on the network to be attacked (an isolated, powered-down computer cannot be attacked in a meaningful manner) in order for it to be exposed to the bot infection. The different values for **M̲** and **S̲** are due to the presence of defenses against the bot attack that were inserted into the computer during construction or after deployment; therefore, for specific values of $P_{AH}$ and $P_{AS}$ we should expect the number of computers that transition from state **M̲** to **E̲** to be greater than the number of computers that transition from the state **S̲** to **E̲**. The number of computers in the set **E̲** for a particular bot is dependant upon the values for $P_{AH}$ and $P_{AS}$ and the values for $P_{PH}$ and $P_{PS}$. If the hardware and software for a particular computer were developed to insure that the hardware and software have no malware that enables a particular bot infection and the defenses against bot infection are strong, then the values for $P_{PH}$ and $P_{PS}$ are small because the computer can be considered to have "passive" immunity to the bot infection and must be infected via transmission of malware that can not exploit inside assistance and bot defenses must be overcome. The equation expresses this intuition concerning bot infestation. However, it is difficult to assemble a computer that is immune to all bot infections; therefore, the probability of attack upon a computer's hardware and software by a bot must be considered in relation to all bots and in relation to the possibility that a bot infestation can be designed both to exploit covert malware[u] and to conduct an un-aided penetration. Because of the reported volume of attacks against any computer connected to the Internet, we assume that $P_{AS}$ has a value of 1.0. The value for $P_{AH}$ is very small and can be set to any reasonable value. We assume that $P_E$ has a value very close to 1.0 because any competent bot developer will insure that the bot software executes within the target environment if the bot software successfully penetrates the defenses erected against bot infestation (such as firewalls, passwords, virus scanners, worm scanners, two-factor authentication, and other malware defenses.)

Within the bot army research and development community, another crucial research and development thrust should be aimed at gaining insight into effective techniques for impeding the spread of the bot software, either by forcing single navigation threads for bot attack vectors or by forcing a noticeable increase in computational overhead so that a user would know that an attempt at infection is underway. Botnet propagation modeling will be useful in this research as it is one of the few tools that can be employed to determine the relative effectiveness of different defensive techniques. Embedded defensive intelligence systems that would assist the user in detecting malware infections, detecting attempts at infection, and detecting bots are also needed, but can not be deployed without further research in order to make them effective.

One promising, but rarely used due to cost, technology available today for detecting and defending against botnets is the honeypot [33, 49, 71, 85] as illustrated in Figure 15.8. A honeypot derives its botnet defensive value from its ability to be

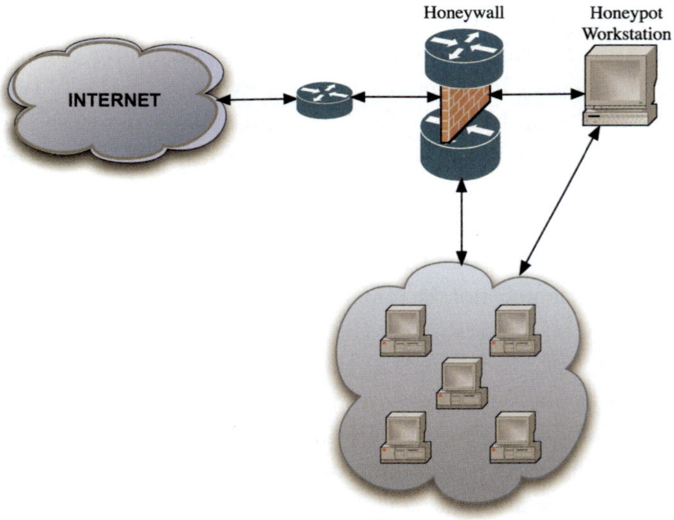


Fig. 15.8. Honeypot (Honeynet) Diagram.

[u]That is, malware inserted into the software or hardware during their development or manufacture.

probed, attacked, and compromised so that the defender can capture and analyze the attackers every action. Honeypots (aka honeynets) are a technique for discovering the tools and tactics of attackers, whether the attacker is a worm, virus, or bot. A honeypot is a computer trap designed to detect, deflect, confine, and record attempts at unauthorized penetration of information systems and is based upon a firewall [110]. The entire honeypot has no purpose other than to try to attract and dissect malware. A firewall is a key component of the honeypot because it is the computer or network router that controls network access and traffic and controls access to network resources behind the firewall. Firewalls employ proxy server, packet filtering, application gating, and circuit gating techniques to route access to resources behind the firewall and to hide the true Internet addresses of computers behind the firewall. Essentially, a firewall routes network traffic to the target computer in the honeypot and uses it as a sacrificial computer. If the target computer is properly configured (i.e., very vulnerable) it normally takes only a couple of minutes before the target is compromised. The hidden monitor computers watch the target's behavior by being connected to each other and to the target by a network, as illustrated in Figure 15.8. In general, the firewall hides the resources of the honeynet so that an attacker can only find the target computer and not the monitoring computers. When an attacker penetrates the honeypot's firewall and invades the target computer, the monitoring computers log and analyze the actions of the attacking software. By using honeynets, defenders can safely observe a bot army in action at the individual bot level — a task that is difficult using other techniques.

Honeynets allow a defender to determine the IP addresses and servers used by attackers, to trap the software used by the bot, and to observe communication patterns and commands issued by bot masters. A honeynet allows defenders to acquire sensitive information from a botnet that, in turn, enables the defender to place a fake bot into a botnet, and begin the process of disarming/disabling the botnet. The information required to disarm a botnet includes the DNS/IP-address of IRC server(s) used by the bot army and the port number(s) and password(s) used to connect to IRC-server(s). Other critical information that can be obtained is the name of the bot and ident structure and the channel to join and the channel-password. A honeynet also allows bot defensive researchers to determine the DNS/IP-address(es) that the captured bot wants to connect to and the corresponding port number(s). As data is acquired about the bot army, the defenders can acquire enough information to prevent the bot from receiving valid commands from the master channel. While learning how to disable a bot is important, a more important achievement is learning how to mimic a bot or bot controller so that the components of the bot army can be disabled. However, turning off a bot is difficult because bot herders use unique commands to control their bots and change commands often. Disabling and turning off bots is made even more difficult because the operation of each bot army is different and small changes in bot C2 can result in significant changes in the way that bots operate and respond to commands. However, due to the amount of data that can be acquired by a honeynet, it is possible to reconstruct the actions of attackers, the tools they use, and observe them in detail and determine how to mimic a bot or turn a bot so that a bot army can be disarmed.

Honeypots are important because they provide important insight into the command and control of botnets, and for now and the foreseeable future, command and control will be the Achilles heel of botnets. The tension between the need to keep a small degree of separation between the bot master and the bots in order to keep them under control and prevent their theft and between the need to stay as far away from the bots as possible in order to minimize the ability to attribute the activity of the bot army to the bot master will not go away. The development of fire and forget bot armies eliminates this problem; however, this approach is an expensive solution to the problem of maintaining bot master anonymity and the results obtained by this approach are uncertain from the point of view of the bot master. Another approach to resolving the bot master anonymity problem that has appeared is the use of small botnets that can be combined in an ad hoc manner to form large attack swarms as desired by the bot master [96]. Therefore, because the C2 nodes are so critical to the operation of a bot army one of the better approaches that the defense can pursue is to turn bots off is to hunt down and eliminate bot C2 computers instead of trying to eliminate individual bots.

A promising defensive technique for the prevention of bot activity is the use of "sandboxing" of applications so that an infection in one application on a computer cannot spread to other applications, the operating system, or the file system. The most promising of these techniques for sandboxing is the use of virtual machines, as illustrated in Figure 15.9, to implement the sandboxes [1, 4, 20, 40, 62, 94]. A virtual machine operating system provides two important capabilities. The first capability is the ability to host and manage a number of applications running directly within the host operating system. The second capability is the ability to host and manage a number of guest operating systems within a virtual machine. In general, the guest operating systems are not modified to operate within the virtual machine's operating system host and, theoretically, are not aware and cannot determine if they are running within their intended computer hardware and operating system or a virtual representation of it. Note that the same operating system can be used in multiple virtual machines on the same computer simultaneously. As a result, theoretically any bot within a virtual machine is not able to determine if it can access the actual computer hardware or not and is, in effect, trapped within a single-computer honeynet.

Because of the resources required to develop and deploy a significant bot army, bot army theft [8, 51, 55, 75] and bot army security will increase in importance for bot masters. While it is possible to build a complete bot using simple "point and click" technology, the most sophisticated bot armies will not be built this way. Instead, sophisticated bot armies will employ a mixture of readily available bot software and customized bot software components that are used to increase the

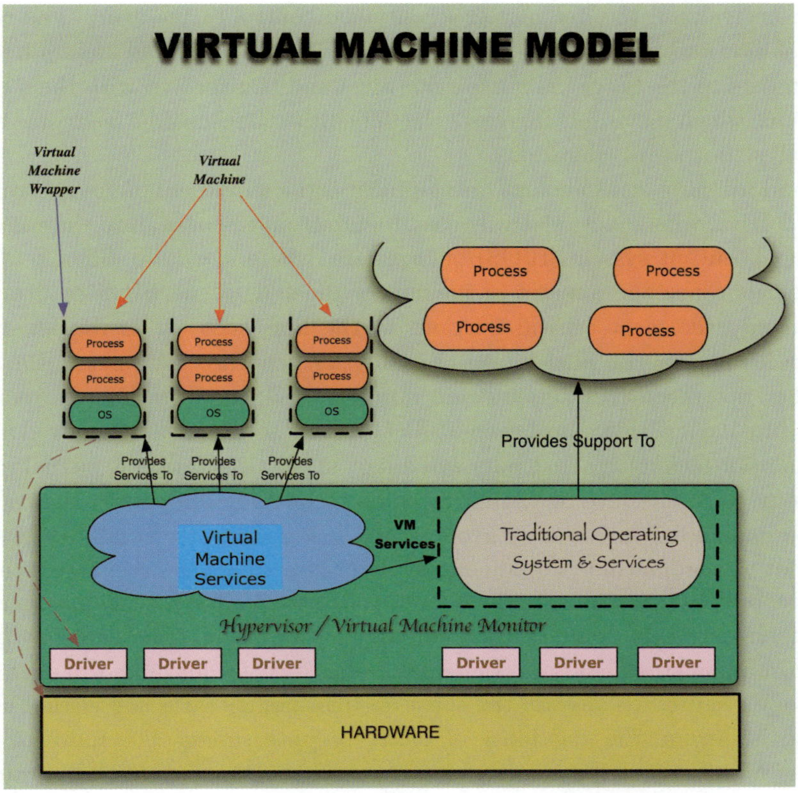


Fig. 15.9. Exemplar virtual machine model.

effectiveness and security of the army. Sophisticated bot armies are valuable but challenging to build and implant. Stealing primitive bots and then augmenting their security properties is easier and almost as good a building from scratch. Therefore, improving internal bot army security is required in order to preserve the size of a botmaster's army and to preserve the safety/anonymity of the bot master. In addition, to preserve the security of their bot armies and the performance of the armies, there will be a gradual move from the current C2 structure for bot armies to a more de-centralized, hierarchical, amorphous, secure, and mobile C2 structure. The C2 structures on the horizon will incorporate both peer-to-peer and random communication between bots and C2 nodes in order to maximize their survivability and minimize their detectability and communication latency. Therefore, as indicated previously, bot defense should concentrate on eliminating bot army C2 nodes because this process effectively renders the bots harmless. Developing the technologies needed to eliminate future C2 nodes will, however, require a significant international legal and research effort because the C2 nodes for an army can be distributed worldwide and it is likely that any given bot army in the future will have multiple, parallel, redundant C2 systems in place so as to insure the army's survival and the bot master's continued control of the army. The required degree of international cooperation will be difficult to achieve and maintain because key countries in the botnet arena are not open and transparent with their Internet operations, which inevitably increases the difficulties that must be overcome to track and analyze bot army operations.

An additional bot technology development is the movement of bot software from the hard drive, where it is relatively easy to detect and remove, into the computer's basic input/output system (BIOS) or firmware, where it will be difficult to detect and remove. Since the amount of memory dedicated to the BIOS or firmware is limited, only the most critical portions of the bot, such as its rootkit and bot software loader, will be placed into the BIOS or firmware. By placing the rootkit and other bot reconstitution software into the BIOS or firmware, the bot could reconstitute itself within a host even if all of its other software were removed from the host. Another technology that bots will adopt in the near future is virtual machine technology [77]. The lure of virtual machine technology for bots is that a virtual machine implanted/operated by a bot would make the bot virtually indetectable, as the bot virtual machine would completely encase all of the other software on the host. The best way, and maybe the only way, to detect a bot virtual machine would be to determine that some of the computer's computing cycles are not be used for known applications and are, therefore, being used for an unknown reason. The technology required to operate the software that can detect a bot virtual machine infection is beyond the capability of most computer users. The move to virtual machines for offense by bots and defense (to prevent malware infection) promises to raise the bot defense and offense challenges to a new level of technical difficulty, and indicates the importance of defeating bot armies by attacking their weakest points, their C2 structure, rather than attempting to defeat them solely by defending and cleansing individual computers.

## 15.4. Summary

Bot armies are a new, powerful, and dangerous type of malware. Their menace arises from the bot armies' ability to be controlled and directed throughout all phases of an attack and exploit by using an increasingly complex command and control structure that takes maximum advantage of the security vulnerabilities that exist in contemporary software. A bot army is composed of tens of thousands, if not millions, of compromised computers that can surreptitiously communicate with each other, allowing them to execute massive, coordinated attacks.

Bot armies are used for two reasons: (1) they can execute multiple overt actions against targets and (2) they can provide multiple coordinated and covert listening/recording points within targeted networks and computer systems. As with most covert data gathering efforts, the greatest value for a bot army is attained when the listening device achieves unnoticed longevity within the target systems. The movement of information and the characteristics of information within the target environment are all useful data that can be exfiltrated from the target via the bot army's connections.

Future bot army technologies will benefit from improvements in cyber attack technologies at a rate that far outstrips foreseen improvements in cyber defensive technologies. Bots will become increasingly stealthy, mobile, controllable, specialized, amorphous, and sophisticated and bot armies will increase in their capabilities. Bot armies will be able to be readily infused with specialized technologies for a special-purpose attack and just as readily drop those technologies and adopt new ones in order to execute their next assignment. The current typical bot master (for a average-sized botnet) is not highly proficient in computer technologies and does not need sophisticated software development skills. This bot master skill profile will change and in a few years typical bot masters will be more skilled and their bot armies will be correspondingly more effective, powerful, and difficult to detect. Defenses will also improve to a degree, but bot offensive techniques will retain their advantage over the defense over the near-term. Clearly, relying on detecting bot communication is not a viable long-term strategy for defeating botnets. Instead, all characteristics of bots, botnets, command and control, and their communication patterns should be used in the hunt for and elimination of bot armies; hence, host performance assessment tools and network traffic monitors are needed in order to determine if a bot army has infested a network. Removal of C2 nodes for the bot army will remain the best approach for defeating and disarming bot armies. Nevertheless, more research to characterize bot army performance and operation is crucial.

Unfortunately, the technology for bot detection or bot army infestation detection has not significantly advanced in the last decade. There is a great need to develop means to identify, analyze, diagnose, and predict the activities of bot armies as well as to develop new means for detecting the presence of bots and bot armies. The bot detection challenge has been seriously compounded by the failure to develop the tools needed to perform the analysis that would provide insight into the intent and objectives of an invading bot army. Research in bot army intent and objectives analysis has not even begun. However, some progress has been made in the development of bot army propagation modeling [26, 86, 88 – 90, 93, 103–105, 108, 109]. Bot army propagation models are based upon the research performed to develop infectious disease propagation models [2, 3, 5, 7, 17, 18, 21, 39, 45, 50, 61, 63, 88–90] and, like them, are used to make probabilistic statements about a computer population and its susceptibility to a specific infection.

Bot armies do not spell the end of the Internet or of the ability to freely explore the web. However, they do pose a significant threat to commercial infrastructure and to government operations; especially if they continue to improve in their capabilities at a significantly faster rate than defensive bot technologies. While the days of the individual bot master seem to be ending, there is no reason to expect that hackers and their ethic will pass away or that hackers will not remain at the forefront of malware and bot technology development [27]. The major software developers are working to eliminate the vulnerabilities that allow bots to infest a computer; however, merely eliminating vulnerabilities will not end the bot threat because new software and software upgrades introduce vulnerabilities faster than they are eliminated. At the present time, the best apparent approach to ending the bot threat is research and development to build tools that enable the rapid detection and elimination of bot army C2 nodes. Additionally, a wide-ranging, broadly scoped research effort is needed.

Research aimed at determining the likely configurations of bot armies and their topology is also needed, as insight into likely topologies of bot armies as they become larger will assist in the take down of bot armies. Research is also required to develop technologies to determine which C2 nodes are crucial and must be disabled and which C2 nodes are most likely to have redundant links that must also be located and disabled if a portion of a bot army is to be truly isolated and shutdown. Research to develop new technologies that can defeat new approaches developed by botmasters to accomplish bot infestation and bot hiding is also needed; the bot herders are already conducting the research they will need. Bot defenders need to replicate bot master research so that defenders will know how to defeat bots and detect the bots and bot armies that employ the newest malware technologies. Failure to conduct the necessary defensive research and to pursue the development of technologies that can be used to defeat bots and bot armies leaves the Internet vulnerable to a large-scale bot army attack that could disable or destroy crucial portions of the national information infrastructure. The threat is clear and pressing, it is time to devote resources that can develop mitigations to current and coming bot army threats.

A key question that must be answered is what are the likely and, as of this writing, the most effective means for defeating bot armies. Developing technologically effective solutions will not be inexpensive but is attainable. Bots can be eliminated by a three-pronged research and development effort: one prong would devise better software development technologies, one prong would develop better understanding of bot armies, bot C2, and bot software propagation, and one prong would develop an improved Internet infrastructure. The required changes in software development are obvious. We require software design and implementation technologies that guarantee that security is designed into the software and insures that there are no techniques that bots or other malware employ can use to infiltrate and subvert systems, which means that the software error rate must be dramatically reduced. The second research thrust would target the bots, their characteristics, their C2 structures, their operations, and their defenses so that they can be isolated and eliminated. The third research and development effort needs to target the design and development of Internet technologies that place security as a top priority and that insure that current and future communication techniques employed by bots and malware for anonymous or source-free communication are not possible. Additionally, tools and infrastructure that prevent an attacker from transmitting software to a target computer anonymously must be developed. Simultaneously, legitimate communications must be guaranteed to be both secure and private. These three major research thrusts for improved software development, bot operational understanding, and Internet infrastructure should be augmented by the research directed toward the development of software and network security tools that can rapidly and autonomously test for all known bot attack vectors and rapidly incorporate information concerning new bot attack vectors; thereby preventing bots from gaining a foothold within their computer hosts. Like all other pathogens, bots require a host in order to thrive and survive; defensive bot research should be aimed at depriving bots of the computer hosts that they require. However, achieving this objective will not be easy. Botmasters are skilled, motivated, and willing to take technical risks to achieve their objectives.

Bot armies are a new and formidable threat to all networks and the computers attached to them. A bot army's combination of breadth of Internet coverage, speed of attack, detached operation, repurposing after deployment and insertion, broad spectrum of uses, and scale of attack make bot armies both a powerful and unique class of threat. If, as appears likely, bots acquire a limited artificial intelligence capability they could readily exhibit swarm behaviors that would be sophisticated, coordinated, and, in the aggregate, much more powerful than the best bot armies deployed today. Defending against this new class of bot armies will be extremely difficult for three reasons: the bots' will be able to change their behaviors without a command from a bot master, different portions of the same army could exhibit different behaviors (making it difficult to determine the extent of an infestation), and the bots will be able to operate in tight coordination to accomplish their objective(s). A large and vigorous research effort that addresses current and future bot army capabilities and that develops potent defensive techniques is needed.

## References


[1] R.J. Adair, R.U. Bayles, L.W. Comeau, and R.J. Creasy, "A Virtual Machine System for the 360/40", Cambridge, MA: *IBM Scientific Center Report 320-2007*, May 1966.

[2] L.J.S. Allen, "Some Discrete Time SI, SIR, and SIS Epidemic Models", *Mathematical Biosciences*, Vol. 124, pp. 83–105, 1994.

[3] E.J. Allen, "Jump Diffusion Model for the Global Spread of an Amphibian Disease", *International Journal of Numerical Analysis and Modeling*, Vol. 1, No. 2, pp. 173–187, 2004.

[4] G.M. Amdahl, G.A. Blaauw, and F.P. Brooks, "Architecture of the IBM System/360", *IBM Journal of Research and Development*, Vol. 8, No. 2, pp. 87–101, 1964.

[5] R.M. Anderson and R.M. May, eds., *Infectious Diseases of Humans: Dynamics and Control*, Oxford University Press, Oxford, UK, 1991.

[6] J. Aquilina, "Ancheta", Department of Justice, 3 November, http://www.usdoj.gov/criminal/cybercrime/anchetaArrest.htm, 2005.

[7] N.T.J. Bailey, *The Mathematical Theory of Infectious Diseases*, 2nd ed, Haufner, NY, 1975.

[8] P. Barford and V. Yegneswaran, "An Inside Look at Botnets", *Special Workshop on Malware Detection, Advances in Information Security*, Springer Verlag, 2006.
[9] A.P. Barros, A. Fucs, and V. Pereira, "New Botnet Trends and Threats", *BlackHat Europe 2007*, Amsterdam, Netherlands, 2007.
[10] H. Berghel, "Digital Village: Malware Month", *Communications of the ACM*, Vol. 46, Issue 12, December 2003.
[11] H. Berghel, "Digital Village: The Code Red Worm", *Communications of the ACM*, Vol. 44, Issue 12, December 2001.
[12] J. Bethencourt, D. Song, and B. Waters, "Analysis Resistent Malware", *Proceedings of Network and Distributed Systems Security (NDSS)*, San Diego, CA, 2008.
[13] S. Bhatkar, R. Sekar, and D. DuVarney, "Efficient Techniques for Comprehensive Protection from Memory Error Exploits", *Proceedings of the 14th USENIX Security Symposium*, August 2005.
[14] B. Bilby, "Low-Down and Dirty: Anti-Forensics Rootkits, *RuxCon 2006*, Sydney, AU, 2006.
[15] BlackHat Briefings, *Blackhat Conference Proceedings 2006 and 2007*, http://www.blackhat.com/html/bh-link/briefings.html, 2006, 2007.
[16] F. Brauer, "Models for the Spread of Universally Fatal Diseases", *Journal of Mathematical Biology*, Vol. 28, pp. 451–462, 1990.
[17] D. Bruschi, L. Martignoni, and M. Monga, "Code Normalization for Self-Mutating Malware", *IEEE Security & Privacy*, Vol. 5, No. 2, pp. 46–54, 2007.
[18] S.N. Busenberg, and K.P. Hadeler, "Demography and Epidemics", *Mathematics of Biosciences*, Vol. 101, pp. 41–62, 1990.
[19] L. Carettoni, C. Merloni, and S. Zanero, "Studying Bluetooth Malware Propagation: The Bluebag Project," *IEEE Security and Privacy*, Vol. 5, No. 2, pp. 17–25, 2007.
[20] R.P. Case and A. Padegs, "Architecture of the IBM System/370", *Communications of the ACM*, Vol. 21, No. 1, pp. 73–96, January 1978.
[21] A.D. Cliff, "Incorporating Spatial Components into Models of of Epidemic Spread", *Epidemic Models: Their Structure and Relation to Data*, Mollison, (ed.), Cambridge University, UK, 1996.
[22] L.N. de Castro and J. Timmis, *Artificial Immune Systems: A New Computational Intelligence Approach*, Springer, London, 2002.
[23] K. Chiang and L. Lloyd, "A Case Study of the Rustock Rootkit and Spam Bot", *HotBots'07: First Workshop in Hot Topics in Understanding Botnets*, April 10, Cambridge, MA, 2007.
[24] M. Curphey and R. Araujo, "Web Application Security Assessment Tools", *IEEE Security and Privacy*, Vol. 4, No. 4, pp. 32–41, 2006.
[25] CNN, "Botnets No. 1 emerging Internet threat", http://www.gtisc.gatech.edu/pdf/cnn_botnets_013106.pdf, 2006.
[26] V. Colizza, S. Hu, S. Myers, S. Stamm, A. Tsow, and A. Vespignani, "Crimeware in Firmware", in *Crimeware: Understanding New Attacks and Defenses*, M. Jakobsson, and Z. Ramzan, eds., Addison-Wesley, pp. 103–272, 2008.
[27] G. Conti, "Hacking and Innovation", *Communications of the ACM*', Vol. 49, No. 6, pp. 33–36, June 2006.
[28] E. Cooke and F. Jahanian, "The Zombie Roundup: Understanding, Detecting, And Disrupting Botnets", *Steps to Reducing Unwanted Traffic on the Internet Workshop (SRUTI '05)*, Cambridge, MA, 2005.

[29] CSO, CSO Online, 7 August, http://www2.csoonline.com/blog_view.html/?CID=23687&source=csonewswatch, 2006.

[30] M. Dalla Preda, M. Christodorescu, S. Jha, and S. Debray, "A Semantics-Based Approach to Malware Detection", *Proceedings of the 34*th *Annual Symposium on Principles of Programming Languages (POPL 2007)*, 2007 .

[31] D. Dasgupta, Ed., *Artificial Immune Systems and Their Applications*, Springer, Berlin, 1999.

[32] D. Dasgupta and F. Gonzalez, "Artificial Immune Systems In Intrusion Detection", *Enhancing Computer Security with Smart Technology*, V. Rao Vemuri, ed., Auerbach Publications, pp. 165–208, 2005.

[33] C.K. Dimitriadis, "Improving Core Network Security with Honeypots", *IEEE Security & Privacy*, Vol. 5, No. 4, pp. 40–47, July/August 2007.

[34] R. Dingledine, N. Mathewson, and P. Syverson, "TOR: The Second Generation Onion Router", *Proceedings of the 13*th *USENIX Security Symposium*, August 2004.

[35] J. Erickson, *Hacking: The Art of Exploitation*. No Starch Press, San Francisco, 2003.

[36] Evron, Gadi, "Battling Botnets and Online Mobs", *Georgetown Journal of International Affairs*, Winter/Spring, pp. 121–126, 2008.

[37] EWeek, "Spam Trojan Installs Own Anti-Virus Scanner", http://www.eweek.com/article2/0,1895,2034680,00.asp, 2006.

[38] EWeek, "Botnet Herders Attack MS06-040 Worm Hole", http://www.eweek.com/article2/0,1895,2002966,00.asp, 2006.

[39] E. Filiol, M. Helenius, and S. Zanero, "Open Problems in Computer Virology", *Journal of Computer Virology*, Vol. 1, pp. 55–66, 2006.

[40] K. Fraser, S. Hand, I. Pratt, and A. Warfield, "Safe Hardware Access with the Xen Virtual Machine Monitor", *Proceedings of the 1st Workshop on Operating System and Architectural Support for the on-demand IT Infrastructure*, Boston, MA, October 2004.

[41] V. Gratzer and D. Naccache, "Alien vs Quine", *IEEE Security and Privacy*, Vol. 5, No. 2, pp. 26–31, 2007.

[42] Greenemeier, Larry, "Estonian Attacks Raise Concern Over Cyber 'Nuclear Winter", *Information Week*, May 24, at [http://www.informationweek.com/news/showArticle.jhtml?articleID=199701774], 2007.

[43] G. Gu, J. Zhang, and W. Lee, "BotSniffer: Detecting Botnet Command and Control Channels in Network Traffic", *Proceedings of Network and Distributed Systems Security (NDSS)*, San Diego, CA, 2008.

[44] Hack Report, "Honeynet Founder Lance Spitzner: Hackers not afraid of being caught", http://hackreport.net/2006/11/28/honeynet-founder-lance-spitzner-hackers-not-afraid-of-being-caught/, 2006.

[45] H.W. Hethcote, "The Mathematics of Infectious Diseases", *SIAM Review*, Vol. 42, No. 4, pp. 599–653, 2000.

[46] J. Hoagland, Z. Ramzan, and S. Satish, "Bot Networks", in *Crimeware: Understanding New Attacks and Defenses*, M. Jakobsson, and Z. Ramzan, eds., Addison-Wesley, pp. 183–224, 2008.

[47] G. Hoglund and J. Butler, *Rootkits: Subverting the Windows Kernel*, Addison-Wesley, Boston, 2005.

[48] G. Hoglund and G. McGraw, *Exploiting Software: How to Break Code*. Addison-Wesley, Boston, 2004.

[49] Honeynet Project "Know your Enemy: Tracking Botnets", http://www.honeynet.org/papers/bots/, 2006.
[50] J.M. Hyman and J. Li, "Differential Susceptibility and Infectivity Epidemic Models", *Mathematical Biosciences and Engineering*, Vol. 3, No. 1, pp. 89–100, January 2006.
[51] N. Ianelli and A. Hackworth, *Botnets as a Vehicle for Online Crime*, Cert Coordination Center, http://www.cert.org/archive/pdf/Botnets.pdf, 2005.
[52] D. Illett, "Interview with Steve Linford", ZDNet UK, 2004.
[53] M. Jakobsson and Z. Ramzan, *Crimeware: Understanding New Attacks and Defenses*. Addison-Wesley, Upper Saddle River New Jersey, 2008.
[54] C. Kalt, "Internet relay chat: Architecture". http://www.faqs.org/rfcs/rfc2810.html, 2000.
[55] A. Karasaridis, B. Rexroad, and D. Hoeflin, "Wide-scale Botnet Detection and Characterization", *HotBots'07: First Workshop in Hot Topics in Understanding Botnets*, April 10, Cambridge, MA, 2007.
[56] D.M. Kienzle and M.C. Elder, "Internet WORMS: Past, Present, And Future: Recent Worms: A Survey And Trends", *Proceedings of the 2003 ACM Workshop on Rapid Malcode*, October 2003.
[57] D. Loguinov, A. Kumar, V. Rai, and S. Ganesh, "Graph-Theoretic Analysis of Structured Peer-to-Peer Systems: Routing Distances and Fault Resistance", *SIGCOMM '03: Special Interest Group on Data Communication*, Karlsruhe, Germany, August 25–29, pp. 395–406, 2003.
[58] R. Lyda and J. Hamrock, "Using Entropy Analysis to Find Encrypted and Packed Malware, *IEEE Security and Privacy*, Vol. 5, No. 2, pp. 40–45, 2007.
[59] G. McGraw and G. Morrisett, "Attacking Malicious Code: Report to the Infosec Research Council", *IEEE Software*, Vol. 17, No. 5, pp. 33–41, September 2000.
[60] L. McLaughlin, "After ElComSoft DMCA Still Worries Developers, Rsearchers", *IEEE Software*, Vol. 20, No. 2, pp. 86–91, 2003.
[61] J.A.J. Metz and F. vanden Bosch, "Velocities of Epidemic Spread", in *Epidemic Models: Their Structure and Relation to Data*, D. Mollison (ed.), Cambridge University Press, UK, pp. 150–186, 1996.
[62] R.A. Meyer and L.H. Seawright, "A Virtual Machine Time-Sharing System", *IBM Systems Journal*, Vol. 9, No. 3, pp. 199–218, 1970.
[63] D. Mollison, *Epidemic Models: Their Structure and Relation to Data*, D. Mollison (ed.), Cambridge University Press, UK, 1996.
[64] Navy Research Laboratory, "Onion Routing", http://www.onion-router.net/, 2006.
[65] M. Nassar, S. Niccolini, R. State, and T. Ewald, "Holistic Voip Intrusion Detection And Prevention System", *Proceedings Of The 1st International Conference On Principles, Systems And Applications Of IP Telecommunications*, New York, NY, pp. 1–9, 2007.
[66] Netcraft, "Akamai attack highlights threat from bot networks", http://news.netcraft.com/archives/2004/06/16/akamai_attack_highlights_threat_from_bot_networks.html, 2004.
[67] *PCWorld*, "Indetectable Vista Malware", http://blogs.pcworld.com/staffblog/archives/002525.html, 2006.
[68] PCAdvisor, "Undetactable Vista Malware?", http://www.pcadvisor.co.uk/blogs/index.cfm?entryid=311&blogid=4, 2006.
[69] V. Paxson, S. Staniford, and R. Cunningham, "Internet WORMS: Past, Present, And Future: A Taxonomy Of Computer Worms", *Proceedings of the 2003 ACM Workshop on Rapid Malcode*, October 2003.

[70] T. Peng, C. Leckie, and K. Ramamohanarao, "Survey Of Network-Based Defense Mechanisms Countering The Dos And Ddos Problems", *ACM Computing Surveys*, Vol. 39, No. 1, 2007.

[71] C.P. Pfleeger and S.L. Pfleeger, *Security in Computing*, 4th ed., Prentice-Hall, Upper Saddle River: NJ, 2006.

[72] J.C. Rabek, R.I. Khazan, S.M. Lewandowski, and R.K. Cunningham, "Defensive Technology: Detection Of Injected, Dynamically Generated, And Obfuscated Malicious Code", *Proceedings of the 2003 ACM Workshop on Rapid Malcode*, October 2003.

[73] M.A. Rajab, J. Zarfoss, F. Monrose, and A. Terzis, "A Multifaceted Approach To Understanding The Botnet Phenomenon", *Proceedings Of The 6th ACM SIGCOMM Conference On Internet Measurement*, Rio de Janiero, Brazil, pp. 41–52, 2006.

[74] M. Rajab, J. Zarfoss, F. Monrose, and A. Terzis, "My Botnet is Bigger Than Yours (Maybe Better Than Yours): Why Size Estimates Remain Challenging", *First Workshop on Hot Topics in Understanding Botnets (HotBots)*, April 10, Cambridge, MA, 2007.

[75] Realtime Community, "Botnet Threats", http://www.realtime-websecurity.com/061205_sullivan.asp.

[76] D.J. Reifer, "Industry Software Cost, Quality, and Productivity Benchmarks", *Software Tech News*, Vol. 7, No. 2, July; also at: http://www.softwaretechnews.com/stn7-2/reifer.html, 2004.

[77] J. Rutkowska, "Bots Using Virtual Machines: The Blue Pill", http://www.eweek.com/article2/0,1895,1983037,00.asp, http://searchservervirtualization.tech-target.com/tip/0,289483,sid94_gci1220291,00.html?bucket=ETA&topic=303465, or http://theinvisiblethings.blogspot.com/2006/06/introducing-blue-pill.html, 2006.

[78] S. Savage, "Large-Scale Worm Detection", *ARO-DHS Special Workshop on Malware Detection*, August 2005.

[79] V. Schneider, "Approximations for the Halstead Software Science Software Error Rate and Project Effort Estimators", *ACM SIGMETRICS Performance Evaluation Review*, Vol. 16, No. 2–4, pp. 22–29, February 1989.

[80] G.P. Schaffer, "Worms and Viruses and Botnets, Oh My!: Rational Responses to Emerging Internet Threats, *IEEE Security and Privacy*, Vol. 4, No. 3, pp. 52–58, 2006.

[81] T. Schluessler, S. Goglin, and E. Johnson, "Is A Bot At The Controls?: Detecting Input Data Attacks", *Proceedings Of The 6th ACM SIGCOMM Workshop On Network And System Support For Games*, Melbourne, Australia, pp. 1–6, 2007.

[82] E. Skoudis and L. Zeltser, *Malware: Fighting Malicious Code*, Prentice Hall.; Weaver, N.Y, 2003.

[83] Slashdot, "Vista Designed to make malware easy", http://it.slashdot.org/article.pl?sid=06/12/03/1453244&from=rss, 2006

[84] Sophos, "Stopping Zombies, Botnets, And Other E-Mail Borne Threats", http://www.sophos.com/security/whitepapers/sophos-zombies-wpus; also http://www.us-cert.gov/current/archive/2004/05/03/archive.html, 2004.

[85] L. Spitzer, *Honeypots: Tracking Hackers*, Addison-Wesley: Boston: MA, 2003.

[86] J. Su, A.G. Miklas, K.K.W. Chan, K. Po, A. Akhavan, S. Saroiu, d. E. Lara, and A. Goel, "A Preliminary Investigation of Worm Infections In A Bluetooth Environment", *Proceedings of WORM'06*, 2006.

[87] Swatit, "Bots, Drones, Zombies, Worms and Other Things That Go Bump In The Night", http://swatit.org/bots/, 2006.

[88] A.O. Tarakanov, V.A. Skormin, and S.P. Sokolova, *Immunocomputing: Principles and Applications*. Springer, New York, 2003.

[89] A.O. Tarakanov and G. Nicosia, "Foundations of Immunocomputing", *Proc. 1st IEEE Symposium on Foundations of Computational Intelligence (FOCI'07)*, Honolulu, Hawaii, pp. 503–508, 2007.

[90] A.O. Tarakanov, "Immunocomputing for Intelligent Intrusion Detection", *IEEE Computational Intelligence Magazine*, pp. 22–30, May 2008.

[91] A.S. Tanenbaum, *Computer Networks*, 4th ed. Prentice Hall: Boston, 2002.

[92] TechNewsWorld, Report: Cell Phones, VOIP Fraud to Grow in '07, http://www.technewsworld.com/story/53398.html.

[93] R.W. Thommes and M.J. Coates, "Epidemiological Modeling of Peer-to-Peer Viruses and Pollution", *Proceedings of IEEE Infocom'06*, 2006.

[94] R. Uhlig, G. Neiger, D. Rodgers, A.L. Santoni, F.C.M. Martins, A.V. Anderson, S.M. Bennett, A. Kagi, F.H. Leung, and L. Smith, "Intel Virtualization Technology", *IEEE Computer*, Vol. 38, No. 5, pp. 48–56, 2005.

[95] P. Vixie, S. Thomson, Y. Rekhter, and J. Bound, "Dynamic Updates In The Domain Name System (DNS Update)". http://www.faqs.org/rfcs/rfc2136.html, 1997.

[96] R. Vogt, J. Aycock, and M.J. Jacobson, "Army of Botnets", *Proceedings of Network and Distributed Systems Security (NDSS)*, San Diego, CA, 2007.

[97] T. Wallingford, *Switching to VOIP*, O'Reilly: Sebastopol, CA, 2005.

[98] T. Wallingford, *VoIP Hacks: Tips & Tools for Internet Telephony (Hacks)*, O'Reilly: Sebastopol, CA, 2005.

[99] N. Weaver, V. Paxson, S. Staniford, and R. Cunningham, "A Taxonomy Of Computer Worms", *2003 ACM Workshop on Rapid Malcode (WORM'03)*, ACM SIGSAC, October, 2003.

[100] Websense Security Labs, "New Skype Worm", http://www.websense.com/securitylabs/alerts/alert.php?AlertID=716, 19 December, 2006.

[101] J. Whitaker, Personal communication, 2002–2006.

[102] C. Willems, T. Holz, and F. Freiling, "Toward Automated Dynamic Malware Analysis Using CWSandbox", *IEEE Security and Privacy*, Vol. 5, No. 2, pp. 32–39, 2007.

[103] G. Yan and S. Eidenbenz, "Bluetooth Worms: Models, Dynamics, and Defense Implications", *Proceedings of ACSAC'06*, December 2006.

[104] G. Yan, L. Cuellar, S. Eidenbenz, H.D. Flores, N. Hengartner, and V. Vu, "Bluetooth Worm Propagation: Mobility Pattern Matters!", *Proceedings of ACM ASIACCS'07*, March 2007.

[105] G. Yan and S. Eidenbenz, "Modeling Propagation Dynamics of Bluetooth Worms", *Proceedings of ICDCS'07*, Toronto, Canada, June 2007.

[106] H. Yin, X. Liang, and D. Song, "Hookfinder: Identifying and Understanding Malware Hooking Behaviors", *Proceedings of Network and Distributed Systems Security (NDSS)*, San Diego, CA, 2008.

[107] S. Zanero, "Issues in Modeling User Behavior in Computer Virus Propagation", *Proceedings of the 1st International Workshop on the Theory of Computer Viruses*, 2006.

[108] C.C. Zou, W. Gong, and D. Towsley, "Code Red Worm Propagation Modeling and Analysis", *Proceedings ACM CCS'02*, October 2002.

[109] C.C. Zou, D. Towsley, and W. Gong, "Email Worm Modeling And Defense", *Proceedings of the 13th International Conference on Computer Communications and Networks*, 2003

[110] E.D. Zwicky, S. Cooper, and D.B. Chapman, *Building Internet Firewalls (2nd ed.)*. O'Reilly: Sebastopol, CA, 2000.

# Part V: Latest Security-Related Topics on Computer Networking

# Chapter 16

## PERFORMANCE OF BRIDGING ALGORITHMS IN IEEE 802.15.3 MULTI-PICONET NETWORKS

Jelena Mišić*, Muhi Ahmed Ibne Khair† and Vojislav B. Mišić*
*Ryerson University, Toronto, Ontario, Canada
† University of Manitoba, Winnipeg, Manitoba, Canada

In this chapter, we introduce the bridging problem from the viewpoint of the recent IEEE 802.15.3 high data rate WPAN, and present alternative solutions that are possible in 802.15.3 networks. Then, we investigate the performance of a network with two piconets interconnected in a parent-child manner and linked through a bridge device which operates in a master-slave fashion. We have designed an adaptive bandwidth allocation algorithm for bridge down link CTA allocation, and examined the impact of the value of the smoothing constant and threshold hysteresis on the throughput, blocking probability, and average queue size for the downlink queue at the bridge.

### 16.1. Introduction

The IEEE 802.15.3 standard for high data rate Wireless Personal Area Networks (HR-WPANs) is designed to fulfill the requirements of high data rate suitable for multimedia applications whilst ensuring low end-to-end delay [1]. Devices in 802.15.3 networks are organized in small networks called piconets, each of which is formed, controlled, and maintained by a single dedicated device referred to as the piconet coordinator (PNC). However, there are many applications in which a multi-piconet network must be used: for example, small scale mesh networks [2] could be implemented using 802.15.3 standard. 802.15.3 networks can also be used in multimedia sensor networks, where their high data rate ensures reliable transmission of still images or video feeds from the sensors, e.g., in surveillance or military applications.

The 802.15.3 standard provides the basic piconet interconnection capability in the form of parent-child piconet topology, in which the time on the working channel is shared among the two piconets. However, the standards does not give much guidance as to the actual algorithm for topology construction, not does it provide the algorithms for bandwidth allocation which is needed to achieve the desired performance levels of a multi-piconet network.

In this chapter, we investigate the performance of a two-piconet network in a parent-child topology where the child piconet coordinator acts as the master-slave bridge to allow communication between the two piconets. We describe two adaptive algorithms for bandwidth allocation and examine their performance through extensive simulation. We show that the second algorithm provides much better performance despite its relative computational simplicity.

The chapter is organized as follows. In Section 16.2 we describe the major characteristics of the 802.15.3 standard, and highlight the way in which multi-piconet operation may be achieved in Section 16.3. Section 16.4 presents the bridging algorithms, while Section 16.5 discusses some related work. In Section 16.6, we examine the performance of fixed bandwidth allocation and describe an adaptive algorithm with symmetrical thresholds, which is then modified to include hysteresis in Section 16.7. Finally, Section 16.8 concludes the chapter and provides some directions for future research.

## 16.2. Operation of 802.15.3 Networks

The IEEE 802.15.3 standard describes the requirements for physical (PHY) and medium access control (MAC) layer protocols for a high data rate wireless personal area network. Its high data rate and low latency make it suitable for multimedia applications, but also ensure easy reconfigurability and high resilience to interference, since it operates in the unlicensed Industrial, Scientific, and Medical (ISM) band at 2.4GHz. (Note that this band is shared with a number of other communication technologies such as 802.11b/g WLANs, 802.15.1 Bluetooth piconets, 802.15.4 low data rate WPANs, and others.)

An 802.15.3 network is formed in an ad hoc fashion: upon discovering a free channel, the PNC capable device starts the piconet by simply transmitting period beacon frames; other devices that detect those frames then request admission, or association (as it is referred to in the 802.15.3 standard). The coordinator duties include transmission of periodic beacon frames for synchronization, admission of new devices to the piconet, as well as allocation of dedicated time periods to allow unhindered packet transmission by the requesting device.

Time in an 802.15.3 piconet is structured in superframes delimited by successive beacon frame transmissions from the piconet coordinator. Each superframe contains three distinct parts: the beacon frame, the contention access period (CAP), and the channel time allocation period (CTAP), as shown in Figure 16.1. During the Contention Access Period, devices compete with each other for access; a form of CSMA-CA algorithm is used. This period is used to send requests for CTAs (defined below) and other administrative information, but it can also be used for transmission of smaller amounts of asynchronous data.

The Channel Time Allocation Period contains a number of individual sub-periods (referred to as Channel Time Allocation, or CTA) which are allocated by the piconet coordinator upon explicit requests by the devices that have data to transmit. Requests for CTAs are sent during the Contention Access Period; as

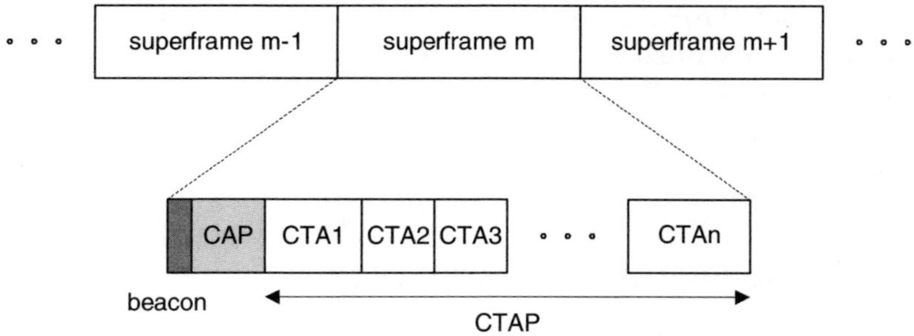


Fig. 16.1. Superframe structure in an 802.15.3 network.

such, they are subject to collision with similar requests from other devices. The decision to grant the allocation request or not rests exclusively with the piconet coordinator, which announces its decision in the next beacon frame; CTA allocation may be temporary or may last until explicit deallocation by the piconet coordinator. Once a device is allocated a CTA, other devices may not use it, and contention-free access is guaranteed. Special CTAs known as Management Channel Time Allocation (MCTA) are used for communication and dissemination of administrative information between the piconet coordinator and its devices.

Unlike other WPANs such as Bluetooth and 802.15.4, direct device-to-device communication is possible in an 802.15.3 piconet. In case the communicating devices are not within the transmission range of each other, the piconet coordinator (which, by default, must be able to communicate with both) may be involved as an intermediary, leading in effect to multi-hop intra-piconet communication. It is worth noting that problems of this nature may be alleviated by adjusting the transmission power, but also by making use of the adaptive data rate facility provided by the 802.15.3 standard. Namely, if transmission at the full data rate of 55 Mbps suffers from too may errors because the signal-to-noise-plus-interference ratio (SINR) is too low, different modulation schemes with lower data rate may be used to give additional resilience. This problem and its solutions, however, are beyond the scope of the present chapter.

Reliable data transfer in 802.15.3 networks is achieved by utilizing acknowledgements and retransmission of non-acknowledged packets. The standard defines three acknowledgment modes:

- no acknowledgement (No-ACK) is typically used for delay sensitive but loss tolerant traffic such as multimedia (typically transferred through UDP or some similar protocol);
- immediate acknowledgement (Imm-ACK) means that each packet is immediately acknowledged with a small packet sent back to the sender of the original packet; and
- delayed acknowledgement (Dly-ACK), where an acknowledgment packet is sent after successfully receiving a batch of successive data packets; obviously, this

allows for higher throughput due to reduced acknowledgment overhead — but the application requirements must tolerate the delay incurred in this case, and some means of selective retransmission must be employed to maintain efficiency.

## 16.3. Interconnecting IEEE 802.15.3 Piconets

The 802.15.3 standard contains provisions for the coexistence of multiple piconets in the same (or partially overlapping) physical space. Since the data rate is high, up to 55 Mbps, the channel width is large and there are, in fact, only five channels available in the ISM band for use of 802.15.3 networks. If 802.11-compatible WLAN (or, perhaps, several of them) is/are present in the vicinity, the number of available channels is reduced to only three in order to prevent excessive interference between the networks adhering to two standards. As a result, the formation of multiple piconets must utilize time division multiplexing, rather than the frequency division one, as is the case with Bluetooth. Namely, a piconet can allocate a special CTA during which another piconet can operate. There are two types of such piconets: a child piconet and a neighbor piconet.

A child piconet is the one in which the piconet coordinator is a member of the parent piconet, as shown in Figure 16.2(a). It is formed when a PNC-capable device which is a member of the parent piconet sends a request to the parent piconet coordinator, asking for a special CTA known as a private CTA. Regular CTA requests include the device addresses of both the sender and the receiver; a request for a private CTA is distinguished by virtue of containing the same device address as both the sending and the receiving node. When the parent piconet coordinator allocates the required CTA, the child piconet coordinator may begin sending beacon frames of its own within that CTA, and thus may form another piconet which operates on the same channel as the parent piconet, but is independent from it. The private CTA is, effectively, the active portion of the superframe of the child piconet. The child superframe consists, then, of this private CTA which can be used for communication between child piconet coordinator (PNC) and its devices (DEVs); the remainder of the parent superframe is reserved time — it can't be used for communication in the child piconet. Figure 16.2(b) shows the communication patterns in this topology.

The timing relationship of superframes in parent and child piconets is shown in Figure 16.2(a), where the top part corresponds to the parent piconet and the bottom part to the child piconet. Note that the distinction is logical rather than physical, since the piconets share the same RF channel.

A given piconet can have multiple child piconets, and a child piconet may have another child of its own. Obviously, the available channel time is shared between those piconets, at the expense of decreased throughput and increased delay; but the effective transmission range may be increased.

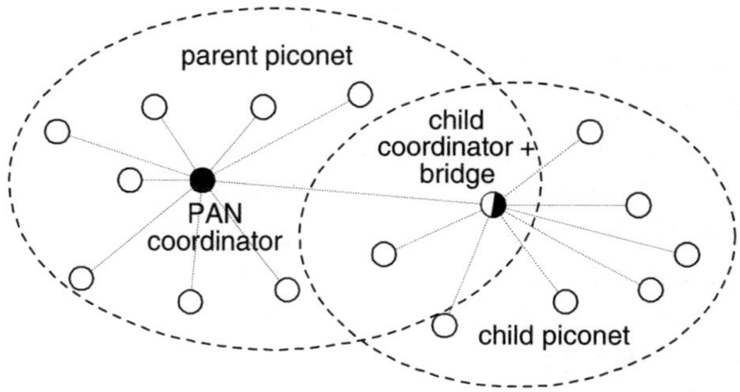


(a) Topology.

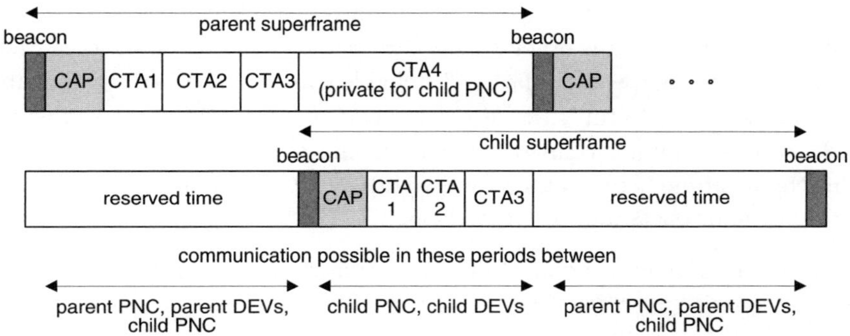


(b) Communication patterns.

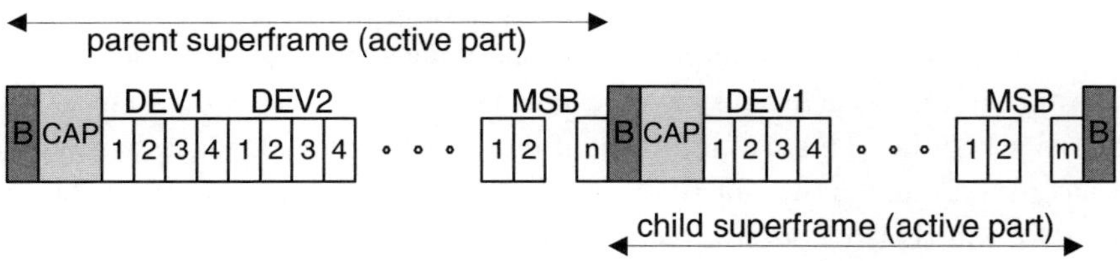


(c) Superframe structure. MSB denotes the CTA allocated to the MS bridge.

Fig. 16.2. Parent-child interconnection.

**Challenges.** As can be seen from the discussion above, the main challenge in forming a multi-piconet network that uses the same RF channel — i.e., a complex network in which *all* piconets are related through parent-child relationships — is to develop a network-wide distributed scheduling algorithm that will allocate channel time to all devices in an efficient and fair manner. Since time division multiplexing among each parent-child piconet pair is used, we need not worry about collisions between transmissions originating from different piconets in the network which plague MAC protocols based on CSMA-CA such as 802.15.4 [3]: transmissions during allocated CTAs are guaranteed to be conflict-free. However, transmission scheduling and bandwidth allocation pose significant difficulties, in particular when multiple piconets are connected. It is worth noting that the problem of optimal scheduling in a multi-piconet Bluetooth environment (which also uses TDMA) has been shown to be NP-complete [4].

The need to wait until the appropriate active portion of the superframe incurs some additional delays besides the usual transmission delay and access delay in the outbound queue of the source device; furthermore, the bridge device operates its own queues (one for each direction of the traffic) and these can also add delay to the total packet transmission time. Further problems arise from the finite size of various device buffers which packets have to pass on their route from the source node in one piconet, to the destination node in another one. Once these buffers are full, newly arrived packets will be rejected, which leads to packet losses or, if acknowledgments are used, more frequent retransmissions. In the latter case, efficiency is reduced, and the probability of overflowing other buffers earlier in the packet route increases, thus causing rapid performance degradation. If reliable transfer is needed, the possibility of packet blocking necessitates the use of Imm-ACK or Dly-ACK acknowledgment policy. In addition, we must devise an efficient and fair algorithm to partition the available channel time between the piconets, taking into account the traffic intensity both within the piconets and between them.

**Using different RF channels.** Multi-piconet networks can also be created using a different scenario, in which several multi-piconet networks operate in the same physical space but on different RF channels. While *physical* conflicts between transmissions originating from different multi-piconet networks are still absent by virtue of frequency division multiplexing, *scheduling* conflicts between the piconets will be the main source of complexity, as the device that wants to act as a bridge must alternatively synchronize with piconets that operate according to entirely unrelated schedules. This precludes the use of Master-Slave bridges to interconnect such piconets. Namely, the Master-Slave bridges must not abstain from their duties as the PNCs in their respective piconets for prolonged periods of time. As a result, piconets operating on different RF channels favor interconnection through Slave-Slave bridges, i.e., devices that act as ordinary nodes in each of the piconets they belong to. As such devices have no coordinator duties, their absence from a given piconet will not cause any problems there. In fact, their absence might even go unnoticed if there happens to be no traffic directed to such devices during that time interval.

**Neighbor piconets.** The 802.15.3 standard also provides the concept of the neighbor piconet, which is intended to enable an 802.15.3 piconet to coexist with another network that may or may not use the 802.15.3 communication protocols; for example, an 802.11 WLAN in which one of the devices is 802.15.3-capable. A PNC-capable device that wants to form a neighbor piconet will first associate with the parent piconet, but not as an ordinary piconet member; the parent piconet coordinator may reject the association request if it does not support neighbor piconets. If the request is granted, the device then requests a private CTA from the coordinator of the parent piconet. once a private CTA is allocated, the neighbor piconet can begin to operate. The neighbor piconet coordinator may exchange commands with the parent piconet coordinator, but no data exchange is allowed. In other words, the neighbor piconet is simply a means to share the channel time between the two networks. Since, unlike the child piconet, data communications between the two piconets are not possible, this mechanism is unsuitable for the creation of multi-piconet networks.

## 16.4. Implementing Multi-Piconet Networks with 802.15.3

In this Section we will first explain the interconnection (bridging) mechanism, followed by our proposed scheduling algorithm for channel time allocation in a multi-piconet network. The superframe structure of our MAC protocol follows the IEEE 802.15.3 MAC superframe and the channel time allocation is based on TDMA, during the guaranteed access period, and CSMA/CA, during the contention period.

Two common approaches, namely the Master-Slave bridge and the Slave-Slave bridge are used for piconet interconnection in different networks. In the case of a Master-Slave bridge, Figure 16.3(a), the bridge device is the PNC for Piconet 2 and a normal member of Piconet 1. In the case of a Slave-Slave bridge, Figure 16.3(b), the bridge device is an ordinary member (DEV) in both piconets. We can combine both types of bridges in a multi-piconet environment in order to cover larger areas.

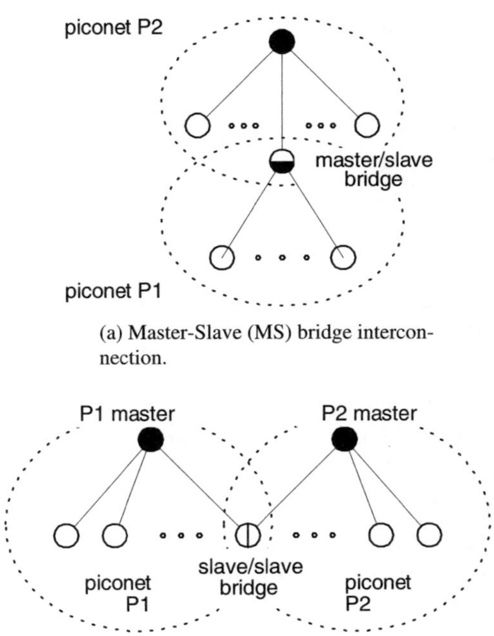


(a) Master-Slave (MS) bridge interconnection.

(b) Slave-Slave (SS) bridge interconnection.

Fig. 16.3. Bridge topologies for multi-piconet networks.

The choice of the type of interconnection depends on location of the bridge device within the network. The interconnection will be established through a Master-Slave bridge if a PNC-capable device is located in such a way that it can easily control one piconet and participate in the other one. On the other hand, the Slave-Slave bridge can be used if no suitable PNC-capable device can be found, or if the two piconets operate on different RF channels, possibly because the traffic volume is too high to be serviced with half the available bandwidth.

**Operation of the Master-Slave bridge.** The bridge establishes a connection between a parent and a child piconet where the bridge device acts as the PNC of the child piconet. The bridge device maintains two queues to temporarily store, and subsequently deliver, the traffic in both directions. As can be seen from Figure 16.2(a), the superframe duration is the same for both parent and child piconets; in fact, the child superframe is simply a private CTA from the parent superframe. The only setup operation needed in this case is for the child piconet PNC to request a private CTA as explained above. Once such a CTA is allocated by the parent piconet PNC, the child piconet PNC simply begins to send beacons at the beginning of the CTA, which is also the beginning of its own superframe. Devices that need to send data to the other piconet can simply request their own CTAs from their respective PNCs.

**Operation of the Slave-Slave bridge.** A device that is already associated with a piconet can detect the presence of a new piconet by receiving a beacon sent by its PNC, or a control packet with a piconet identification number (PNCID) that is different from the existing one. Whenever a prospective bridge device detects the presence of two piconets within its transmission range, it initiates the connection establishment algorithm (Algorithm 16.1). First, the device waits for the MCTA period or CAP period to send a request command for bridging. Then it will use the four-way handshake (RTS-CTS-DATA-ACK) to send the request command, piggybacking its current scheduling information to the neighbour PNC. The neighbour PNC adjusts its scheduling information based on the received scheduling information from its neighbour piconet. If the PNC is a Master-Slave bridge in its own right, it will request a private CTA from its parent PNC, trying to accommodate the demands of the bridge device. The bridge requirements are, simply, that the neighbouring child piconets obtain channel time for transmission (i.e., private CTAs) without interfering with each other. A positive response from the parent PNC establishes the connection between the child piconets. After the connection establishment, the bridge device needs to maintain a table that keeps track of the scheduled times of activity in each piconet. The PNCID uniquely identifies each record in the table and helps the bridge device switch in a timely fashion between different piconets.

**Channel Scheduling.** The channel time scheduling of the network under consideration will be based on average queue size of the devices. The queue size of an ordinary device (i.e., not a PNC or a bridge device) primarily depends on

**Algorithm 16.1** The Slave-Slave bridge connection.

scan presence of overlapped coverage
**if** scan == positive **then**
  send join-request to neighbour PNC using four way handshaking protocol
  receive feedback from neighbour PNC
  update scheduling table with PNCID and received scheduling information
**end if**

packet arrival rate of that device. The queue size for a bridge device is based on the incoming packet queue sizes from neighbour piconets and outgoing packet queue sizes to the neighbour piconets. The bridge device will use the average of these two queues size to determine its channel time requirement. The devices send requests for channel time based on the average queue size to their respective PNCs. The PNC uses Algorithm 16.2 based on the request from the bridge in question. In case of a request from a bridge device, the PNC schedules channel time and a private CTA (for the child piconet) in such a way that there will be no overlap of channel time between the two adjacent piconets.

A representative topology that employs both types of bridge interconnection is shown in Figure 16.4. In this network, the parent piconets P1 and P2 are located

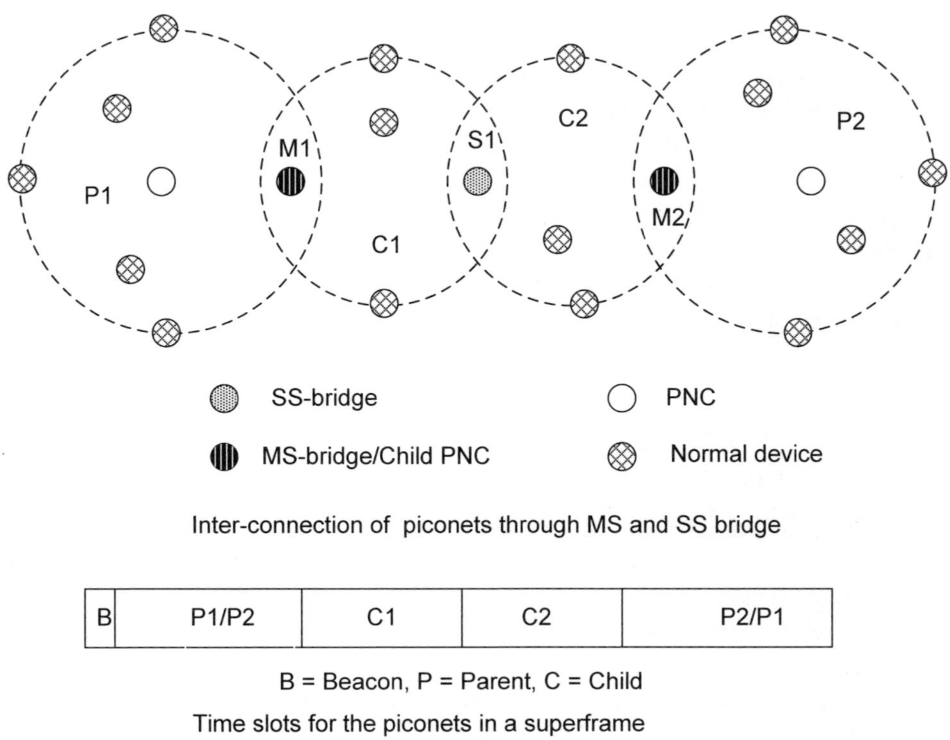


Fig. 16.4. A multi-piconet structure that employs both types of bridge interconnection.

beyond each other's transmission ranges and, thus, can operate on the same RF channel. However, the presence of two child piconets that can hear each other — they are, in fact, interconnected — presents a challenge for scheduling. In order to resolve this, the two parent piconets P1 and P2 will assign channel time for their children in different time slots, based on the scheduling information they exchanged during connection establishment. Let us consider time slots in the superframe in Figure 16.4. The time slots represented by P1/P2 (or P2/P1) imply that P1 and P2 can communicate at the same time. On the other hand, when a child piconet is operating, no other piconet in its range can talk. In this case we can assume that a single superframe (actually two superframes from two different parent piconets) are divided into four time slots. Within each time slot, the devices will have guaranteed channel time and contention period. There are also MCTAs in each time slot during which a new node can join or a bridge can establish a connection. There is a chance of conflict during the MCTA period as the new devices do not have any knowledge of the current scheduling information resulting in the hidden terminal problem. We will use the four way handshaking protocol to resolve this problem.

**Algorithm 16.2** Scheduling of channel time.

```
if request command from Master-Slave bridge then
   assign private CTA anywhere in the superframe
end if
if request command from Slave-Slave bridge then
   check piggyback data for neighbour scheduling information
   if no scheduling information then
      request for scheduling information
   end if
end if
scheduling information received
calculate required channel time based on average queue size
determine private CTA position
assign private CTA and channel time
```

## 16.5. Related Work

The MAC protocols for wireless multi-piconet networks are different from the traditional wireless MACs in terms of self organization, distributed nature, multi-hop, and mobility. Multi-piconet networks can be designed with a single RF channel or multiple RF channels. For simplicity, we will focus on a single channel network with a parent-child interconnection.

Multi-piconet networks have often been developed using the IEEE 802.11 DCF MAC protocol, and most of the research work in this area was based on using the features of 802.11 MAC protocol, possibly slightly modified to improve network performance. Bicket *et al.* [5] have evaluated the performance of 802.11b networks; their experiments have shown that an ad hoc network implemented using 802.11b technology can achieve sustained throughput of around 630 Kbps, significantly below the supported data rate of 11 Mbps. Similarly, Yamada *et al.* [6] have identified two problems of 802.11b based networks: limited throughput and degradation of fairness. To solve these problems they have introduced two new control packets, namely Invite-to-Send (ITS) and Copied CTS (CCTS). The use of ITS and CCTS packets has brought some improvements in throughput, but at the cost of increased control overhead and delay. Also, the overhead due to ITS and CCTS packets and end-to-end packet delay will increase with the network load. However, in an 802.15.3 network, data communications are accomplished using dedicated time periods, hence there is no need to introduce additional control packets such as ITS and CCTS.

MACA was developed to solve the hidden and exposed terminal problems of traditional CSMA [7] protocols. In MACA, the sender and receiver exchange RTS and CTS control packets before sending a data packet to avoid collisions. Fullmer and Garcia-Luna-Aceves [8] describe the scenario where MACA fails to avoid collisions due to hidden terminals. MACA may also make a device wait for a long period to access the medium because its use of the BEB [a] algorithm [7].

To overcome the problems of MACA, a new solution was proposed by Bharghavan et al. called Media Access Protocol for Wireless LANs (MACAW) [9]. Basically MACAW is a modification of the BEB algorithm in MACA. It introduces acknowledgement and data-sending (DS) control packets producing the RTS-CTS-DS-DATA-ACK sequence for data transfer. The IEEE 802.11 standard [10] has been developed by adopting the CSMA and MACAW with further modifications to support wireless LANs.

However, neither IEEE 802.11 MAC nor MACAW provide support for real time data transfers because of the absence of guaranteed time slots. Therefore, Lin and Gerla [11] proposed an enhanced version of MACA called MACA with Piggybacked Reservation (MACA/PR) to support real-time traffic. The MACA/PR protocol is a contention based protocol with a reservation mechanism. It has been designed to support multimedia data in multihop mobile wireless network providing guaranteed bandwidth through reservation. Every node keeps the reservation information of sending and receiving windows of all the neighbour nodes in a table, which is refreshed after every successful RTS-CTS-DATA-ACK (known as four way handshaking protocol) cycle. The RTS and CTS packets are exchanged for the first packet in the transfer of a series of real-time data packets. The reservation information for the next data packet is piggybacked with the prior data packet and the receiver confirms this reservation in the acknowledgement control packet.

[a] In Binary Exponential Backoff (BEB), a device doubles the size of its backoff window if a collision is detected.

The limitation of MACA/PR is that it requires help from the network layer routing protocol. However, MACA/PR has better performance in terms of latency, packet loss, mobility, and bandwidth share than both asynchronous packet radio network (PRNET [b]) and synchronous TDMA based MACs. The use of fixed reserved time slots in MACA/PR can result in wastage of bandwidth. Manoj and Ram Murthy [12] have proposed a modification to the reservation mechanism of MACA/PR to prevent bandwidth wastage. In the modified scheme, the reserved slots can be placed at any position in the superframe and unused resources (channel time) are released after a successful transmission.

We note that the 802.15.3 MAC uses TDMA based channel allocation to provide guaranteed time slots for data transfer. However, the piggybacked reservation information of MACA/PR can be employed together with the TDMA based MAC to support real-time data transfer along with best-effort traffic in 802.15.3 based multi-piconet networks.

Xiao [13] has performed a detailed performance evaluation of the IEEE 802.15.3 [1] and IEEE 802.15.3a [14] standards through simulation and mathematical analysis. He has also done a throughput analysis of the 802.11 [10] protocol, which uses backoff with counter freezing during inactive portions of the superframe. The freezing and backoff techniques are essentially the same in the 802.11 and 802.15.3 MACs, except that different ways of calculating the backoff time are utilized. The backoff and freezing have an impact on the performance of the network; especially the backoff has a direct impact on the delay parameter. Large backoff windows can result in longer delays. On the other hand, small backoff windows may increase the probability of collisions. Xiao used the backoff procedures defined in the 802.11 and 802.15.3 MAC specifications; this work gives us performance of the protocol in terms of throughput over various payload sizes, but the performance of reliable transmission in error-prone wireless network during contention period needs more study.

## 16.6. Fixed vs. Adaptive CTA Allocation

To investigate the performance of an 802.15.3 network formed by two piconets interconnected with a MS bridge, we have built a simulator using the object oriented Petri Net engine Artifex by RSoftDesign, Inc. [15]. In the topology considered, the parent piconet consisted of nine devices, while the child piconet consisted of five devices (not counting either coordinator). The child piconet coordinator is also the bridge toward the parent piconet. Each of the ordinary nodes in either piconet has Poisson traffic with a specified packet arrival rate, with packets of 1200 bytes each (chosen to correspond to an average IP packet size). Packet destinations are randomly selected within the same piconet with the total probability of $P_l$, and in the other piconet with the probability of $1 - P_l$. For convenience, we refer to the traffic from the parent to child piconet as downlink traffic, and the traffic in the

[b]In a PRNET, the devices use the same channel and share it dynamically.

opposite direction as uplink traffic. The structure of the superframe is shown in Figure 16.2(c). Each of the ordinary devices is allocated a CTA sufficient for four packets, while the bridge device is allocated an additional CTA with $b$ packet slots for inter-piconet traffic; this holds for both parent and child piconet superframes. In this manner, the total superframe duration is close to the maximum value of $65.535\,ms$ prescribed by the standard [1].

The total run length of our simulation is 100 seconds, after the initial warm up period of 6 seconds. We have varied the packet arrival rate from 10 to 50 packets/s, while the locality probability was varied from 0.65 to 0.9. The size of the downlink queue at the bridge was fixed at 100 packets. Measured bridge throughput is shown in Figure 16.5 as a function of packet arrival rate (in packets per second per node) and locality probability $P_l$. The number of packet slots in the CTA allocated to bridge downlink traffic (which, in Figure 16.2(c), corresponds to the MSB period in child piconet superframe) has been varied from $b = 3$ to 7. As can be seen, higher bandwidth allocation results in higher throughput and reduced blocking probability at the bridge; but at the same time, it takes some time away either at the expense of CTAs allocated to other devices. Higher bandwidth may also be wasted if there is no traffic.

A much better solution would be to allocate the bandwidth to the bridge in an adaptive manner. This, however, is complicated by the essentially random character of inter-piconet traffic due to Poisson packet arrivals. To smooth those fluctuations, we apply a simple transformation known as exponentially weighted moving average, or EWMA [16]. In this approach, the bandwidth allocated by the bridge is determined on the basis of exponentially smoothed value of bridge downlink queue size, which is recalculated at each new packet arrival as

$$\overline{Q}_{i+1} = \alpha Q_{i+1} + (1 - \alpha)\overline{Q}_i \tag{16.1}$$

where $Q$ and $\overline{Q}$ denote the instantaneous and smoothed bridge downlink queue size, while the index refers to the time instant of packet arrival. The level of smoothing depends primarily on the smoothing constant $\alpha$: the higher its value, the more weight is assigned to most recent reading. The actual bandwidth allocation follows Algorithm 16.3. Changes may be explicitly requested by the bridge and granted by the coordinator of the child piconet; alternatively, the bridge can just report the instantaneous queue size in each superframe, and the coordinator can use the algorithm to calculate the required bandwidth allocation itself.

**Algorithm 16.3** Adaptive CTA allocation for down link.

1: $Q_{i+1}$ measured and/or reported by the bridge
2: $\overline{Q}_{i+1} = \alpha Q_{i+1} + (1 - \alpha)\overline{Q}_i$
3: $\text{CTAforDLqueue} = (\overline{Q}_{i+1} - q_0) \bmod \Delta q + b_0$

Measured results for bridge throughput are shown in the diagrams in the left hand column of Figure 16.6, for different values of the smoothing constant $\alpha$; we

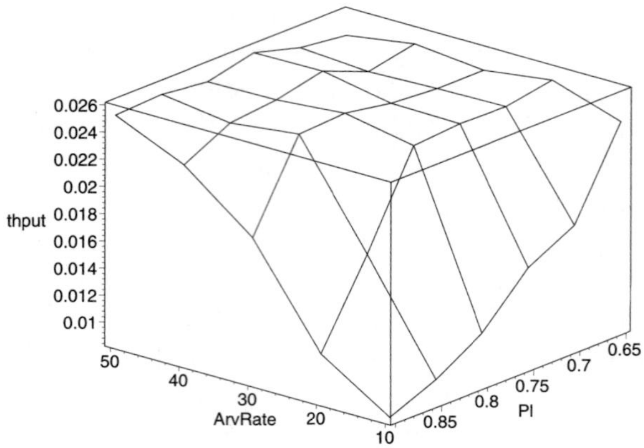


(a) Throughput at $b = 3$.

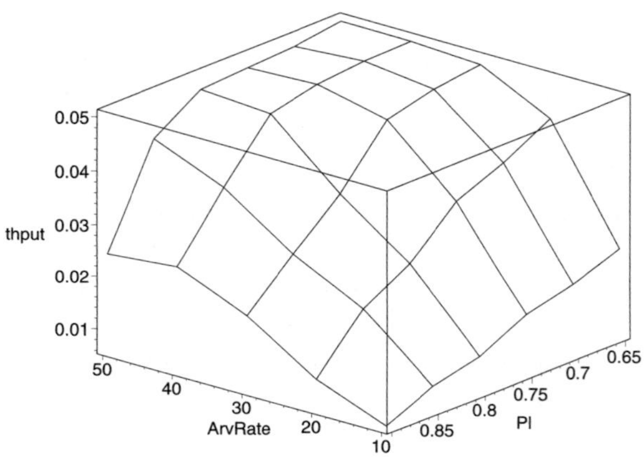


(b) Throughput at $b = 5$.

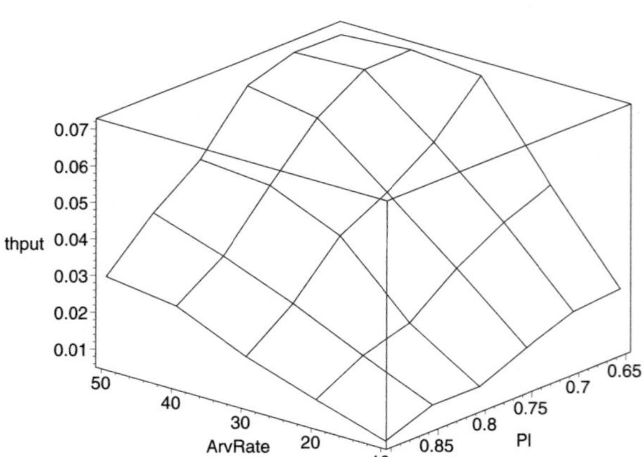


(c) Throughput at $b = 7$.

Fig. 16.5. Bridge throughput under fixed bandwidth allocation.

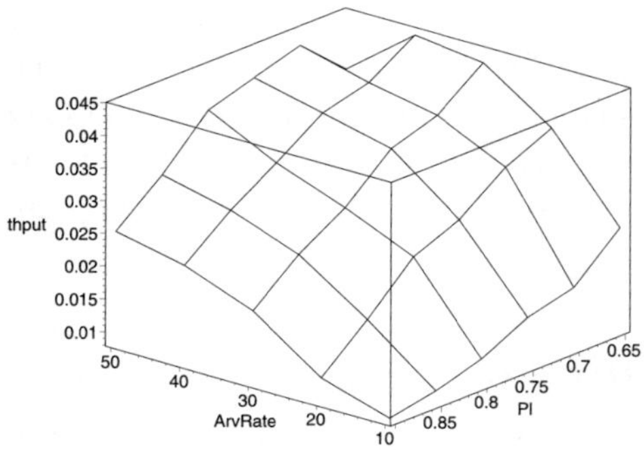


(a) Throughput, α = 0 .3.

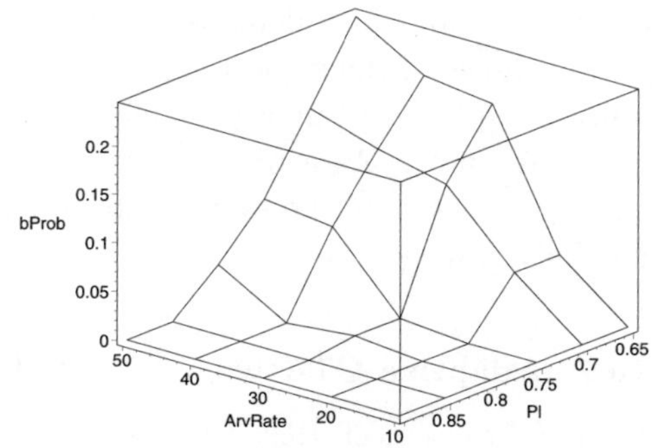


(b) Blocking probability, α = 0 .3.

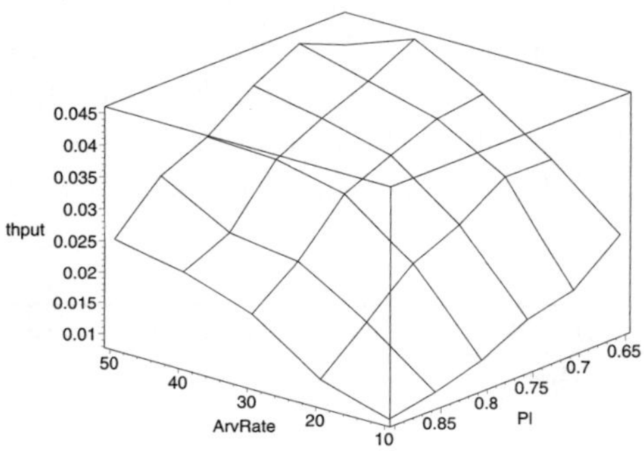


(c) Throughput, α = 0 .5.

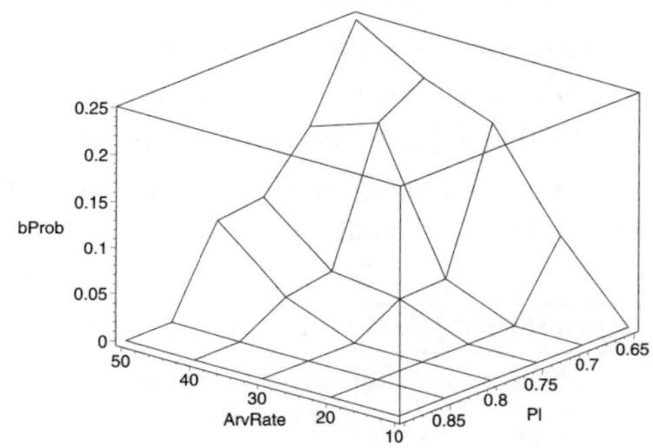


(d) Blocking probability, α = 0 .5.

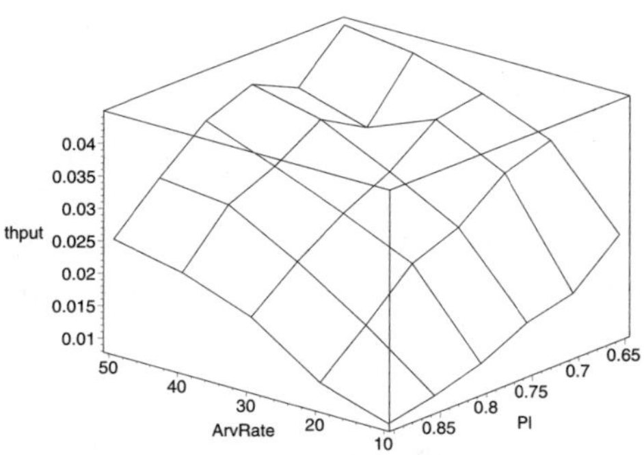


(e) Throughput, α = 0 .7.

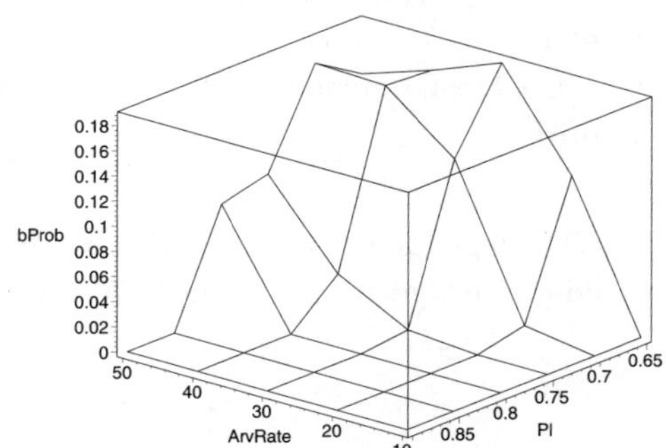


(f) Blocking probability, α = 0 .7.

Fig. 16.6. Bridge throughput and blocking probability under adaptive bandwidth allocation.

have set $b_0 = 3$, $q_0 = \Delta q = 20$. As can be seen, the adaptive algorithm manages to maintain the throughput at values close to the one obtained under fixed bandwidth allocation with $b = 5$. On the basis of these measurements, it seems that the value $\alpha = 0.5$ would be the best choice for the smoothing constant, although the differences are rather small.

Unfortunately, exponential smoothing does not solve all problems, as can be seen from the diagrams of blocking probability, shown in the right hand column of Figure 16.6, which demonstrate that this parameter is not significantly affected by the choice of the smoothing constant $\alpha$. Namely, as soon as a packet leaves the downlink queue, the allocation will be adjusted downward, and the queue will take longer to empty. As a result, the amount of bandwidth allocated to the bridge is still too sensitive to the average downlink queue size, and benefits of adaptivity are not fully realized.

## 16.7. Adaptive CTA with Threshold Hysteresis

In order to correct this, we have introduced a small amount of hysteresis into the adaptive bandwidth allocation algorithm. Namely, the thresholds for allocation adjustment will differ, depending on the direction of the adjustment, and upward adjustments will have higher thresholds than their downward counterparts. In this manner, when a sufficient number of packets arrive to the downlink queue, the bandwidth allocation will remain high until the bulk of the increase is processed, i.e., delivered to their respective destinations. The modified algorithm is shown as Algorithm 16.4 below.

**Algorithm 16.4** Adaptive CTA allocation with hysteresis threshold for downlink.

```
Q_{i+1} measured and/or reported by the bridge
Q̄_{i+1} = αQ_{i+1} + (1 − α)Q̄_i
if Q̄_{i+1} > Q̄_i then
    CTAforDLqueue = (Q̄_{i+1} − q_0) mod Δq + b_0
else
    CTAforDLqueue = (Q̄_{i+1} − (q_0 − χ)) mod Δq + b_0
end if
```

The dependency between the bandwidth allocation and average queue size in the adaptive algorithm with hysteresis can be graphically depicted as in Figure 16.7.

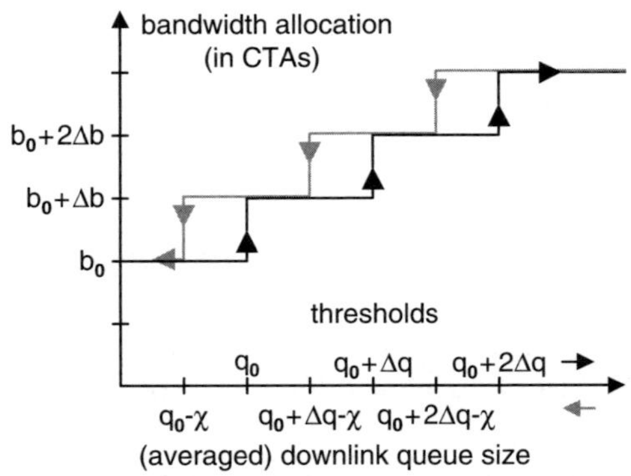


Fig. 16.7. Adaptive CTA allocation with hysteresis.

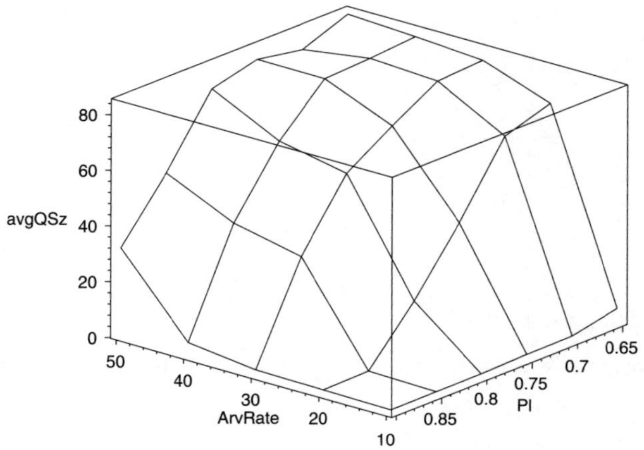


(a) Average queue size at α = 0.3.

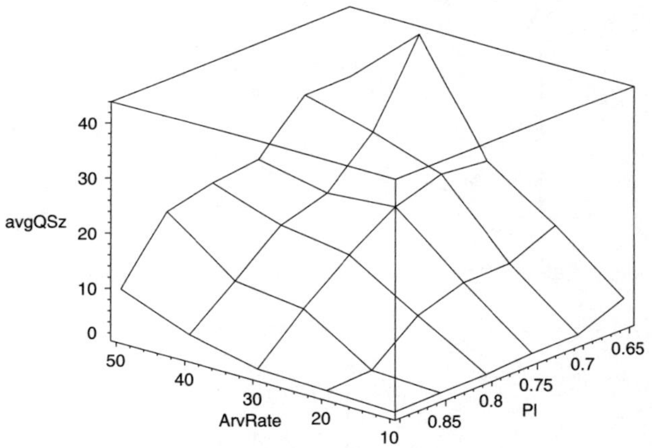


(b) Average queue size at α = 0.5.

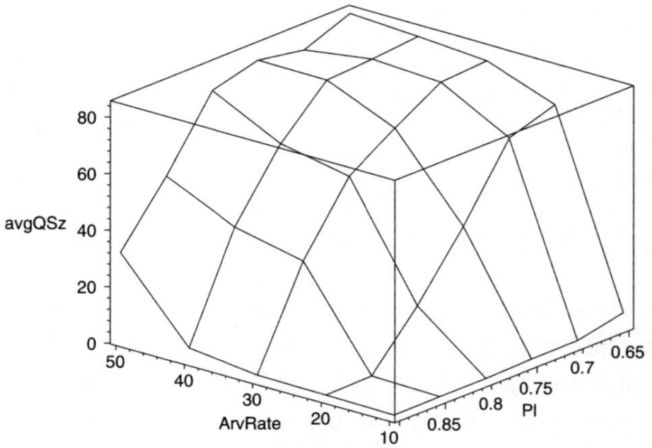


(c) Average queue size at α = 0.7.

Fig. 16.8. Average queue size under adaptive algorithm with hysteresis.

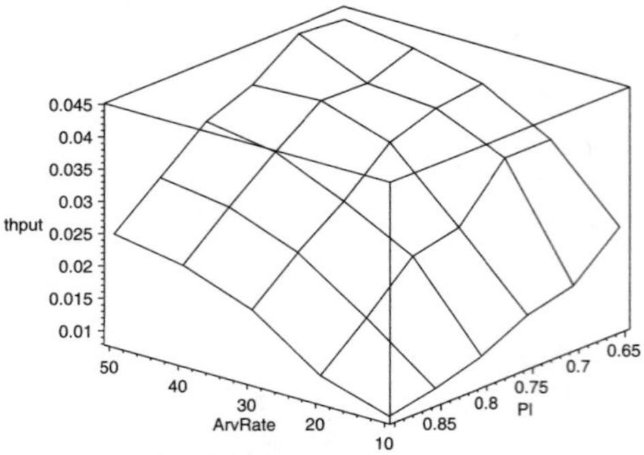


(a) Throughput at $\alpha = 0.7$.

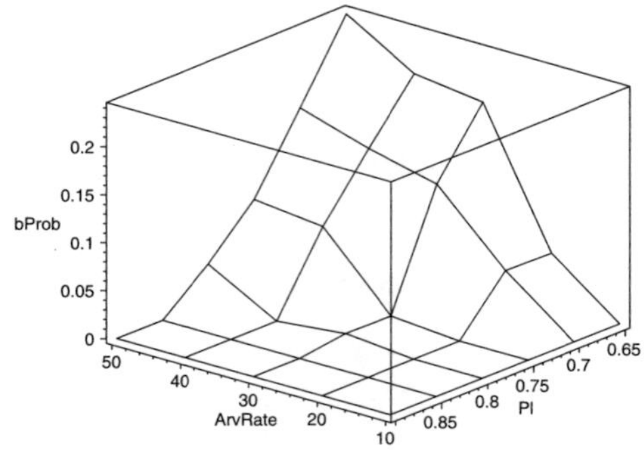


(b) Blocking probablility at $\alpha = 0.7$.

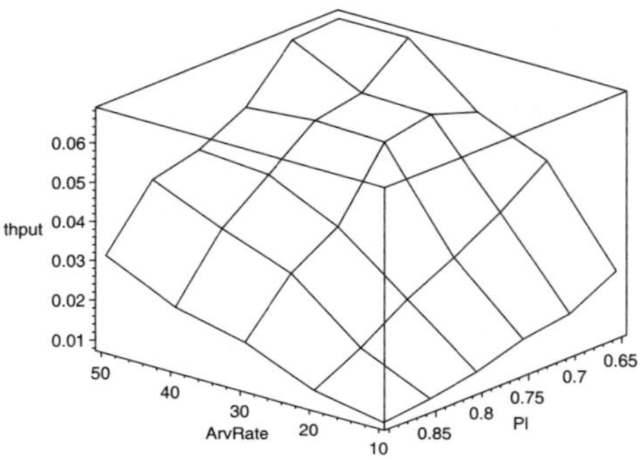


(c) Throughput at $\alpha = 0.5$.

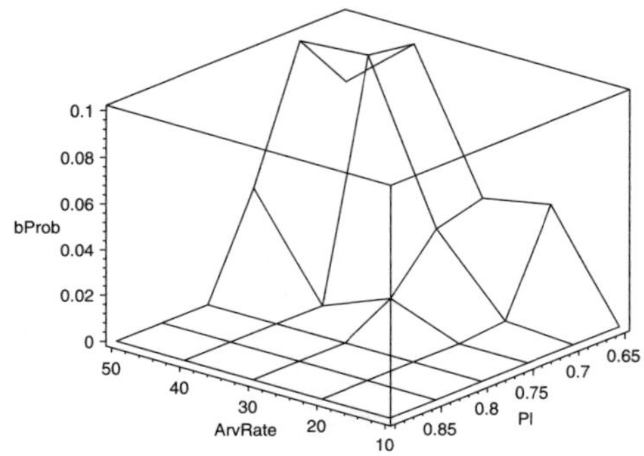


(d) Blocking probablility at $\alpha = 0.5$.

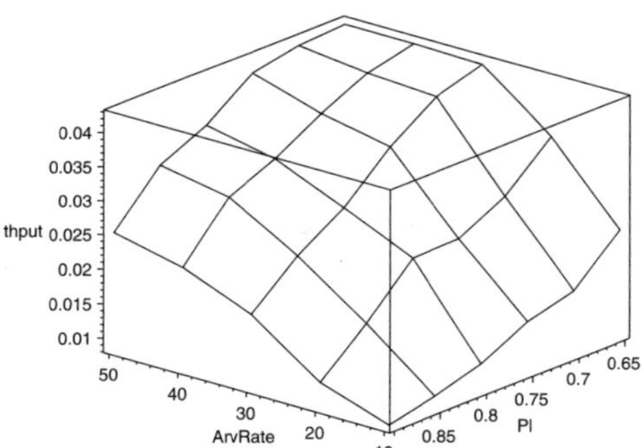


(e) Throughput at $\alpha = 0.3$.

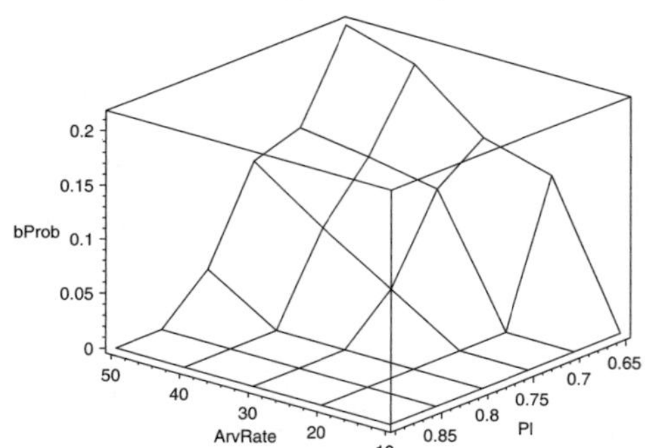


(f) Blocking probablility at $\alpha = 0.3$.

Fig. 16.9. Performance of adaptive algorithm with hysteresis.

The measured results, including throughput, blocking probability at the bridge, and average downlink queue size, are shown in Figure 16.8. For illustration, we have shown these results for three values of the smoothing constant $\alpha$.

Finally, Figure 16.9 shows the corresponding throughput and blocking probability. As can be seen, throughput shows a marked improvement in the case $\alpha = 0.5$, being close to the value achieved under fixed bandwidth allocation with $b = 7$, Figure 16.5(c). Furthermore, blocking probability is much lower than for other values of $\alpha$, and it remains lower in a wider range of values of packet arrival rate and locality probability. Similar observation can be made for the average downlink queue size at the bridge, which in the most part of the observed range stays well below the maximum size of 100 packets. This confirms the validity of the adaptive bandwidth allocation approach.

## 16.8. Conclusion

In this chapter, we have considered the performance of a two-piconet network built upon the recent IEEE 802.15.3 high data rate WPAN standard. The parent and child piconets are interconnected through a Master-Slave bridge which also acts as the coordinator of the child piconet. We have shown that an adaptive algorithm for allocating downlink bandwidth to the bridge, utilizing threshold hysteresis, can easily outperform any fixed bandwidth allocation algorithm. Further work will focus on extensions to control the bandwidth allocation for uplink traffic, as well as that of ordinary nodes in the network.

## References


[1] Standard for part 15.3: Wireless medium access control (MAC) and physical layer (PHY) specifications for high rate wireless personal area networks (WPAN). IEEE standard 802.15.3, IEEE, New York, NY, (2003).

[2] I.F. Akyildiz, X. Wang, and W. Wang, Wireless mesh networks: a survey, *Computer Networks*. **47**, 445–487 (March, 2005).

[3] J. Mišić and V.B. Mišić, *Wireless Personal Area Networks: Performance, Interconnections and Security with IEEE 802.15.4*. (John Wiley and Sons, New York, NY, Jan. 2008).

[4] N. Johansson, U. Körner, and L. Tassiulas, A distributed scheduling algorithm for a Bluetooth scatternet. In *Proceedings of the International Teletraffic Congress — ITC-17*, pp. 61–72, Salvador de Bahia, Brazil (Sept., 2001).

[5] J. Bicket, D. Aguayo, S. Biswas, and R. Morris, Architecture and evaluation of an unplanned 802.11b mesh network. In *11th ACM International Conference on Mobile Computing and Networking*, vol. 1, pp. 31–42, Cologne, Germany (September, 2005).

[6] A. Yamada, A. Fujiwara, and Y. Matsumoto, Enhancement of mesh network oriented IEEE 802.11 MAC protocol. In *10th Asia-Pacific Conference on Communications and 5th International Symposium on Multi-Dimensional Mobile Communications*, vol. 1, pp. 142–146, Kanagawa, Japan (September, 2004).

[7] C. Ram Murthy and B. Manoj, *Ad Hoc Wireless Networks, Architecture and Protocols*. (Prentice Hall, Upper Saddle River, NJ, 2004).

[8] C.L. Fullmer and J.J. Garcia-Luna-Aceves, Floor acquisition multiple access (FAMA) for packet-radioi networks. In *ACM SIGCOMM '95*, pp. 262–273, Cambridge, MA (September, 1995).

[9] V. Bharghavan, A. Demers, S. Shenker, and L. Zhang, MACAW: a media access protocol for wireless LAN's. In *ACM SIGCOMM '94*, pp. 212–225, London, UK (August, 1994).

[10] Standard for wireless LAN medium access control (MAC) and physical layer (PHY) specifications. IEEE standard 802.11, IEEE, New York, NY (May, 1997).

[11] C.R. Lin and M. Gerla, MACA/PR: an asynchronous multimedia multihop wireless network. In *IEEE INFOCOM '97*, pp. 118–125, Kobe, Japan (March, 1997).

[12] B.S. Manoj and C.S. Ram Murthy, Real-time support for ad hoc wireless networks. In *IEEE ICON '02*, pp. 335–340, Grand Copthorne Waterfront, Singapore (August, 2002).
[13] Y. Xiao, MAC layer issues and throughput analysis for the IEEE 802.15.3a UWB, *Dynamics of Continuous, Discrete and Impulsive Systems, Series B: Applications & Algorithms.* **12**, 443–462 (June, 2005).
[14] *IEEE 802.15 WPAN high rate alternative PHY Task Group 3a (TG3a).* (Available online at `http://www.ieee802.org/15/pub/TG3a.html`, August 2006).
[15] *Artifex v.4.4.2.* (RSoft Design, Inc., San Jose, CA, 2003).
[16] S. Delurgio, *Forecasting — Principles, and Application.* (McGraw-Hill/Irwin, New York, 1998).

# Chapter 17

## AUTHENTICATION AND BILLING FOR WLAN/CELLULAR NETWORK INTERWORKING

Minghui Shi*, Yixin Jiang†, Xuemin Shen‡ and Jon W. Mark§
*Department of Electrical and Computer Engineering,*
*University of Waterloo, 200 University Ave. W.,*
*Waterloo, Ontario, Canada*
**mshi@bbcr.uwaterloo.ca*
*†yixin@bbcr.uwaterloo.ca*
*‡xshen@bbcr.uwaterloo.ca*
*§jwmark@bbcr.uwaterloo.ca*

Dongmei Zhao
*Department of Electrical and Computer Engineering,*
*McMaster University, Hamilton, Canada*
*dzhao@ece.mcmaster.ca*

Humphrey Rutagenwa
*Radio Communications Technologies,*
*Communications Research Centre, Ottawa, Canada*
*humphrey.rutagemwa@crc.ca*

In this chapter, an agent based integrated service model for WLAN/cellular networks and relevant authentication and event-tracking for billing support schemes are proposed. The service model does not require cumbersome peer-to-peer roaming agreements to provide seamless user roaming between WLAN hotspots and cellular networks, which are operated by independent wireless network service providers. The proposed authentication and event-tracking schemes take the anonymity and intraceability of mobile users into consideration and operate independently so that the integrated billing service can be applied to cellular network even if it still uses a traditional authentication scheme. In addition, the proposed modified dual directional hash chain (MDDHC) based billing support mechanism features mutual non-repudiation. Security analysis and overhead evaluation are given to demonstrate that the proposed service model and the supporting schemes are secure and efficient.

### 17.1. Introduction

WLAN (Wireless Local Area Network) functionality has become the de facto standard component in mobile devices. More and more WLAN hotspots serviced by Wireless Internet Service Providers (WISPs) have been deployed in airports, cafes,

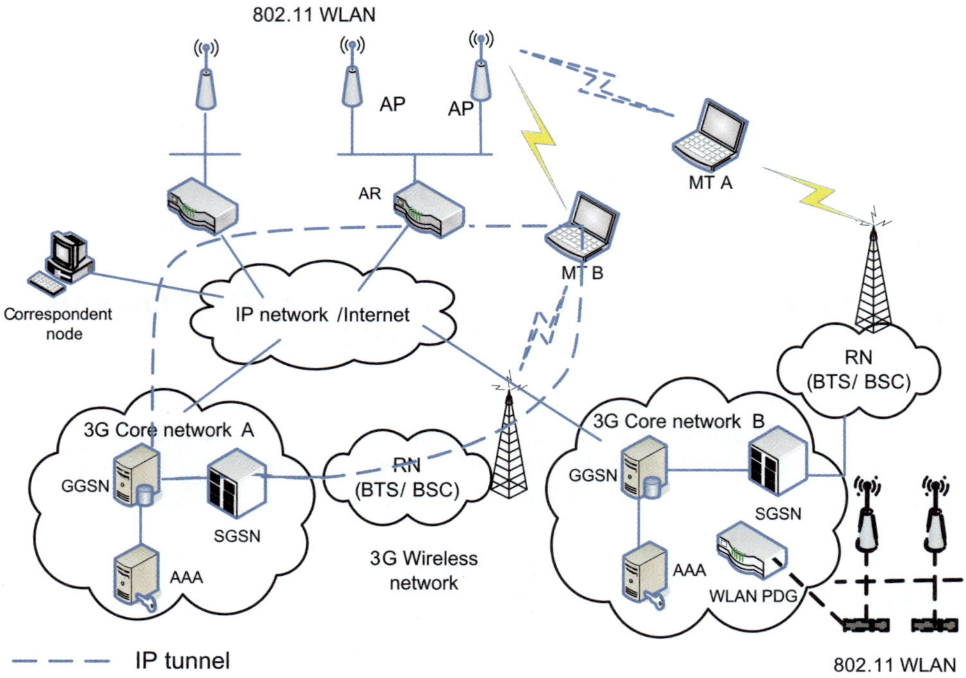


Fig. 17.1. Integrated 802.11 WLAN and 3G cellular networks.

book stores, etc. Mobile devices having both cellular phone and WLAN capability are available [1]. The mobile users naturally demand integrating multiple mobile computing services into a single entity.

In Figure 17.1, the interworking between WLAN and 3G cellular networks through an IP network. Mobile IP (MIP) protocol [2,3] is applied to support IP mobility for mobile clients. Data can be transported along two different paths, as shown in dashed lines in the figure, depending on which access interface that the mobile terminal is associated with. The Home Agent (*HA*) and the Foreign Agent (*FA*) are added to support Mobile IP. The Gateway GPRS Serving Node (GGSN) is modified to act as a *FA* for the cellular network. The WLAN hotspot may have its gateway as a *FA*. The Mobile Terminals (*MT*s) are provided with MIP clients and can support both IEEE802.11 and 3G access technologies. Depending on the inter-dependence between WLAN and the cellular network, the coupling between them can be tight or loose. In tight-coupling, the 802.11 network injects data directly to the 3G core network and therefore appears to the 3G core network as another 3G access network via WLAN Packet Data Gateway (PDG). Tight-coupling is usually preferred by the cellular network carriers for their own WLAN hotspots. In loose-coupling, the 802.11 gateway connects to the Internet and does not have any direct link to 3G network elements. Depending on the ownership of the WLAN hotspots, a loosely coupled integrated architecture is preferred [4] due to its flexibility by independent hotspots, and a tightly coupled architecture is used by cellular network carrier owned hotspots. However for cellular/WLAN integrated service to be deployed, there are several critical issues in service and security.

*No seamless user authentication for WLAN hotspot*: Although user roaming is well defined in cellular network through AAA, it is still an open issue in WLAN networks operated by multiple service providers. Many WISPs (Wireless Internet Service Providers) provide public WLAN Internet access at the hotspots using Network Access Server (NAS). NAS allows only legitimate customers to use the service and provides intra-domain roaming because the hotspots from one WISP share the same customer base. However, it lacks an architecture to provide inter-domain roaming and Mobile IP support. Currently, multiple accounts for those service providers are required for a user to use the service in corresponding network territories. Due to the manual interaction between the users and a log on webpage, seamless network service offering is not available. On the other hand, since the network structure of the cellular network is quite different (much more complex and expensive) from WLAN hotspot's, it is difficult to import the authentication scheme [5,6] used in cellular network to the WLAN hotspot.

*Inefficient peer-to-peer roaming service agreement*: The number of WISPs is much larger than the cellular counterpart, mainly because of the simplicity and low cost of setting up a WLAN hotspot. For example, each wireless enabled router at home can be considered as a WLAN hotspot. Peer-to-peer service agreement is exercised by cellular network service providers quite well. However, it is not practical in the WLAN case. Assume there are m WISPs, $m(m-1)/2$ agreements in total and $(m-1)$ agreements for each WISP are required to achieve roaming within the network.

*Difficulty to have universal roaming service*: It is difficult for a service provider to have roaming agreement with every network service provider. The issue is fine for using cellular network, since cellular networks overlap each other and a user very likely is able to find a usable one. However, WLAN hotspot does not overlap with each other, and this can result in a user not being able to use the service in some hotspots at all. Therefore, universal roaming service cannot be achieved.

*User identity privacy*: Disclosure of a user identity may also allow unauthorized entities to track his moving history and current location. Any illegal access to information related to the user's location without his attention can be a serious violation of privacy. The anonymity and intraceability of user identity is not considered in the current wireless communication architecture.

*Ubiquitous billing support*: Billing across network carriers could be an issue considering there may not be no direct roaming agreement. When the service provider is metering the usage, it may have problem to determine if the $MT$ has left the service session if it is shut down abnormally due to power, software and/or network glitches.

There are extensive research works related to WLAN/cellular network interworking. Most of them focus on proposing integration architecture [7–9] and modifying network components, such as gateway [10], analyzing switching performance of integrated service [11]. However, most solutions are suitable for the service providers who operate their own WLAN and cellular networks. In [12], an authentication scheme via a secured Web page for login over a hypertext transport protocol secured (HTTPS) connection is proposed. This type of solution requires interactions from the user and cannot be used in seamless roaming service. In [13], a roaming and authentication framework for WLAN/cellular network integration is proposed. However, the anonymity and intraceability of user identity, which was not included in [13], has become an important security property for roaming services. In [14], a single hash chain based undeniable billing support is proposed, where digital signature is applied to the *MT* side to prevent the *FA* falsely claim extended service to the *MT*. Due to the heavy computation of digital signature, it may not be desirable due to the fact that *MT* is a low powered device.

In this chapter, a novel wireless/cellular network integrated service model is proposed. Under the coordination of a service agent, integrated wireless network service can be offered by independent WLANs and cellular networks, which are not affiliated by peer-to-peer roaming agreements. Therefore, many small WLAN service providers are able to join the integrated networks, which could greatly increase the integrated network service coverage. On the other hand, the end users do not have to be a customer of major wireless network operators and they can purchase the service from the service agent instead. The corresponding advantages include reduced support cost, more communication convenience and higher revenue. The proposed authentication scheme for integrated network service can be elastically applied to both WLAN and cellular networks, or WLAN only. It also effectively reduces the extra overhead caused by the service agent. It is self-adaptive to the various authentication scenarios due to different ownership of WLAN hotspots. The supporting processes, such as user authentication for roaming and event-tracking for billing support schemes, are operated in parallel with the authentication process, such that they can be flexibly deployed to those which do not adopt the proposed authentication scheme, such as the cellular network. Based on a Modified Dual Directional Hash Chain (MDDHC), the proposed schemes offer mutually undeniable billing support and, at the same time, resource consuming digital signature is avoided. It is shown that the MDDHC based billing mechanism requires less computation and communication overhead than [14], which makes it more suitable for low power wireless communication devices. In addition, the proposed schemes protect mobile users' privacy by incorporating user anonymity and intraceability feature, so that the user's real identity is not revealed and his/her mobility cannot be traced.

The rest of the chapter is organized as follows. In Section 17.2, an overview of the proposed service model architecture for cellular/WLAN integration is presented. In Section17.3 and Section 17.4, the messaging scheme for the proposed service model and related supplementary operations are described in detail, respectively. Security analysis and overhead evaluation are given in Section 17.5, followed by the

Table 17.1. Description of symbols.

| Symbol | Explanation |
|---|---|
| $ID_X$ | $X$'s ID number or a unique global machine number |
| $PID_j$ | $i$th pseudo identity |
| $k_i$ | $i$th session key |
| $k_{XY}$ | Shared key between $X$ and $Y$ |
| $Pub_X$ | $X$'s public key |
| $E_k\{\}$ | Symmetric encryption using shared key $k$ |
| $E_k <>$ | Asymmetric encryption using public key $k$ |
| $Sig_x$ | Digital signature signed by $X$ |
| $H()$ | Hash function |
| $H^x()$ | x times hash operations recursively |
| $F()$ | One way function with defined bit length output |
| $\|\|$ | Concatenation operation |
| $flag_{operation}$ | A pre-defined fixed number mapped for *operation* |

conclusions in Section 17.6. The common symbols, which will be used in the chapter thereafter, are explained in Table 17.1.

## 17.2. WLAN/cellular Integrated Service Model Architecture

Figure 17.2 shows a typical deployment of cellular networks and WLAN hotspots in a coverage area. There are $m$ cellular networks, $m = 1, 2, 3, \ldots$, and $n$ WLAN hotspots are randomly located around to offer high speed network/Internet access service within the area. Due to the disjoint deployment, WLAN hotspots only offer "stationary" wireless network access. Mobile network access service is offered by WLAN/cellular network integrated infrastructure. The WLAN AP (hotspot) and cellular BS labels are numbered by their network operators, i.e., service providers. According to the current WLAN deployment strategy, which avoids unnecessary multiple hardware setup investment, it is assumed that there is only one service provider operating WLAN service at one spot area. Therefore there is no direct WLAN network level handover anytime. A cellular network service provider usually operates WLAN Internet access service at the same time. Let WLAN AP $x, x \in \{1, \ldots, m\}$, be linked with cellular network $x$. For example, one service provider operates both cellular network 1 and WLAN hotspots numbered as WLAN AP 1. The rest of the WLAN APs are operated by third party WISPs. A multi-mode mobile terminal can either connect to a WLAN hotspot or cellular network at the user's discretion.

We introduce an additional role called service agent ($SA$) to the WLAN/cellular integrated network architecture to improve service flexibility and deal with the roaming agreement issue when the number of WLAN operators is large. Cellular network and WLAN are encouraged to have the one-for-all roaming agreement with the $SA$ directly so that cumbersome peer-to-peer roaming agreements are no longer needed. In the ideal case, one agreement per service provider can achieve universal user roaming. On the other hand, the one-for-all roaming agreement can

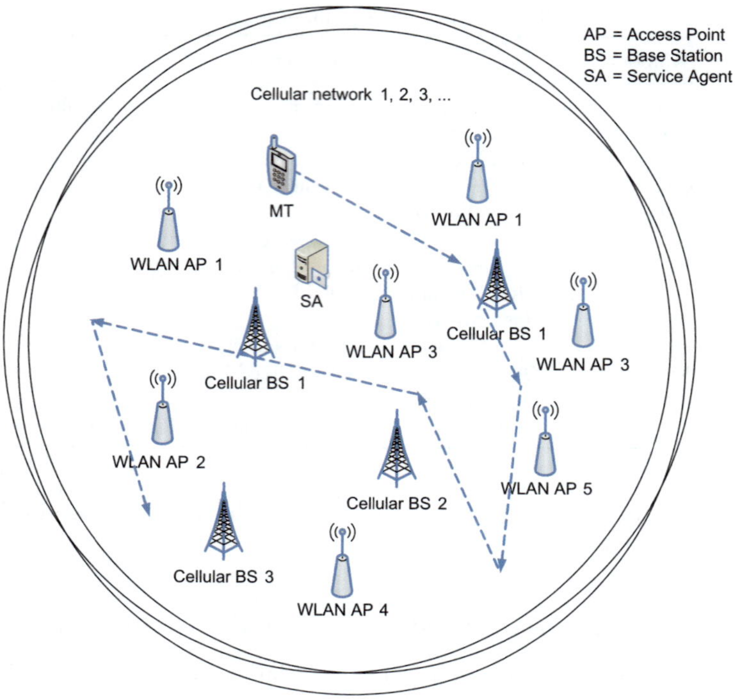


Fig. 17.2. Typical cellular network and WLAN hotspots deployment. The numbers in the cellular network BS and the WLAN AP labels are coded based on their network operators. *SA* is the proposed additional network component.

co-exist with peer-to-peer roaming agreement. A practical strategy could be that a service provider optionally sets up peer-to-peer agreement with a few major service providers for better performance and a one-for-all roaming agreement with the *SA* for universal roaming completion.

In the proposed service model, the *MT* does not have to be a customer of any physical network operator. The *SA* can provide cellular/WLAN integrated service itself, which is driven by the following business motivation: the *SA* purchases bulk wireless service from physical network operators and sells wireless integrated service to the customers so that the network operators spend less support cost for end users, the customers receive improved network access convenience and the *SA* gets more profit.

In order to make clear network operation layout, we abstract the real network parties in a roaming scenario into parties as shown in Figure 17.3. The network which houses the Foreign agent (*FA*) and the *MT* is visiting could be either a WLAN or a cellular network. *HA* is the *MT*'s home network knowing everything about the *MT*, such as identify, shared secret key, etc. Figure 17.3 also shows that the functions and messaging schemes of the proposed service model, which are composed by three layers: 1) authentication and registration plane; 2) pseudo-identifier (*PID*)

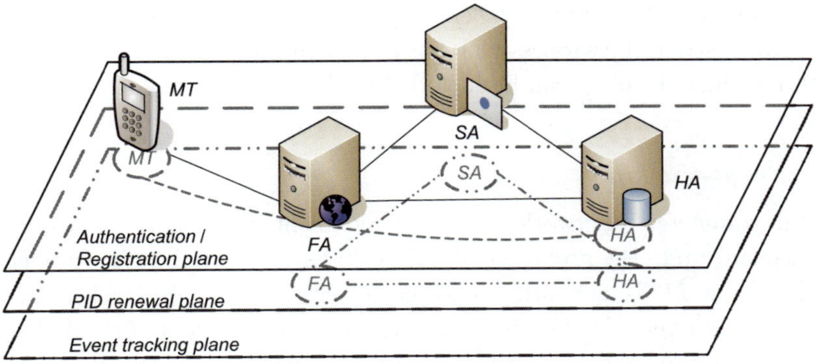


Fig. 17.3. Overview of service model function and messaging scheme.

renewal for privacy protection of user identity; and 3) event-tracking plane for inter-operator billing. The technical details of these functions are given later in this section. The advantage of independent function layer design is to allow the event-tracking, which is a key component for integrated service billing, to be easily and uniformly adopted by all network operators with few modifications, or information re-mapping of existing authentication process, especially in cellular network.

### 17.2.1. *Authentication and Registration*

Before the *MT* accesses the network service, authentication is performed to verify its legitimacy, and the *MT* is registered in the network if it is authenticated successfully. Meanwhile, the *MT* should avoid rogue service provider via authentication as well. Since the authentication process in the cellular network is mature and has been working well, the proposed authentication scheme is mainly for WLAN hotspots. It can also be adopted by the cellular network operators if a uniform authentication scheme is preferred. In the authentication plane shown in Figure 17.3, the *SA* acts as an authority, which is trusted by all the parties, and assists that mutual verification of the *FA* and the *HA*. Considering the power of the *MT* and wireless transmission environment, the authentication scheme is designed such that most part of authentication process is executed by servers in the wired network. The messaging part, which directly involves with the *MT*, consists of two messages and uses symmetric cryptography only.

### 17.2.2. *PID Renewal*

The anonymity of user identity is achieved by a dynamic user identifier (*PID*). An *MT* does not use its real identity for network authentication and registration all the time, including when it is roaming in foreign networks. The *PID* is refreshed periodically and whenever the *MT* sees the necessity, such as after each authentication session. Independent design of *PID* renewal process allows the *MT* to decide when and how often *PID* should be refreshed according to its preference for anonymity strength, wireless channel condition and battery status. An option for *PID* refreshment policy can be included in the *MT*'s preference menu.

### 17.2.3. *Event-tracking*

Successful commercial network service deployment cannot live without proper billing mechanism. In the proposed WLAN/cellular integrated service model, billing is based on the *MT*'s network accessing activities, which is tracked by a data structure named Event ID. An event ID is defined as an incident of the *MT* accessing the network resource and is distributed to proper network operators by the event-tracking process, which is running independently from the authentication process. The revenue is partitioned later based on the Event ID records.

### 17.2.4. *Service Session Setup*

#### 17.2.4.1. *Overview of dual directional hash chain*

We first introduce the concept of one-way hash function, which is the foundation of the DDHC. A hash function Hash(.) takes a binary string of arbitrary length as input, and outputs a binary string of fixed length. A one-way function $H$ satisfies the following two properties: 1) given $x$, it is easy to compute $y$ such that $y = \text{Hash}(x)$; 2) given $y$, it is computationally infeasible to compute $x$ such that $y = \text{Hash}(x)$. The security features of the proposed group-wise key distribution schemes are based on one-way property of hash function.

A one-way hash chain, as illustrated by forward or backward hash chains in Figure 17.4, is formed by recursively hashing $x$ and lining them up in sequence. Let us take the forward hash chain as an example. Due to the one-way property of the hash function, given any value of node $n$ in the chain, it is computationally infeasible to calculate the forward elements, but is easy to compute backward elements.

A DDHC (Figure 17.4) is composed of two one-way hash chains with equal length, a forward hash chain and a backward hash chain. It can be derived as follows: 1) Generating two random key seed values, seed (fwd) and seed (bwd), for the forward and the backward hash chains, respectively; 2) Repeatedly applying the same one-way function on each seed to generate two hash chains of equal length.

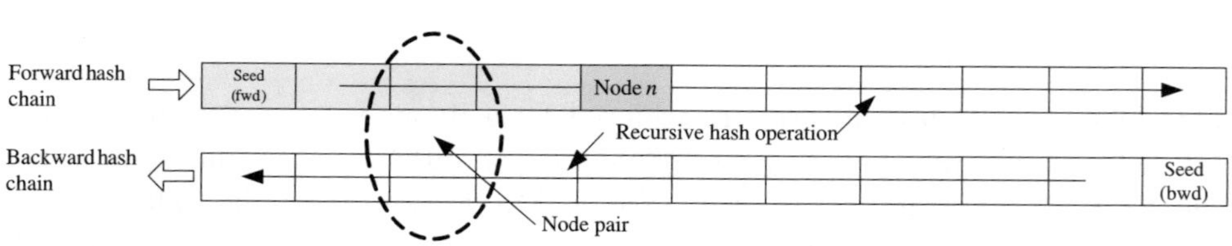


Fig. 17.4. Structure of dual directional hash chain.

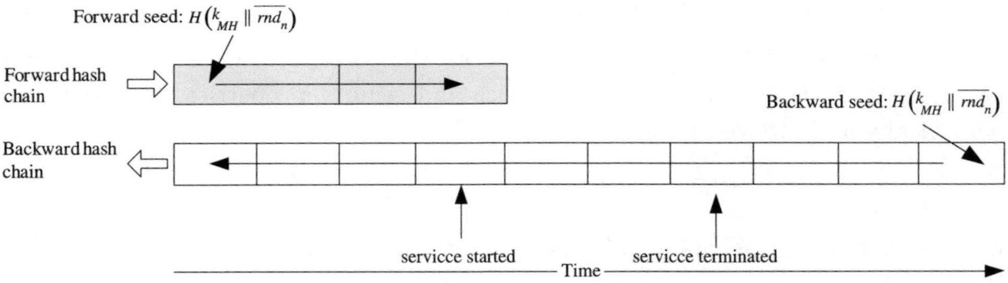


Fig. 17.5. MDDHC setup at *MT*.

The DDHC offers both forward and backward secrecy. Given the end nodes of a window within the chain, the combination the corresponding nodes in the forward and backward chains offers security measure in terms of that a party cannot generate the node pairs outside of the window.

17.2.4.2. *Dual directional hash chain setup at MT*

In the proposed framework, the DDHC is modified to suite the particular use for billing support in mobile communications environment. MDDHC is used to refer DDHC in this chapter thereafter. As shown in Figure 17.5, the *MT* sets $H(k_{MH}||rnd_n)$ as the seed for backward chain, where $k_{MH}$ is the shared secret key between the *MT* and the *HA*, and $rnd_n$ is the random number of $n$th MDDHC. The *MT* sets $H(k_{MH}||\overline{rnd_n})$ as the seed for forward chain, where $\overline{rnd_n} = \mathrm{NOT}(rnd_n)$.

The mask window begins from the time when the service session is started, and ends at the time when the service session is terminated. The concept of node pair only applies to the beginning end of the window. In this particular DDHC application, the forward hash chain ends at the node of "service started" since it is no longer needed for protecting service session beyond that point.

Assume $t_{billing}$ is the metering unit of billing. During its idle time, the *MT* generates multiple MDDHCs with length $l_n = \lceil T/t_{billing} \rceil$, and different *rnds*, where $T$ should be a bit longer than typical maximum service session duration. The *MT* only stores the nodes of the entire backward hash chain, the seed of the forward hash chain, and the corresponding *rnd*.

## 17.3. Messaging Scheme

The messaging scheme for the proposed cellular/WLAN integrated service model includes an authentication scheme with its variations, *PID* renewal scheme and event-tracking scheme. The scheme subsets inherited from the authentication process and the supplementary processes are developed to reduce the authentication latency, enhance the anonymity of user identity and support billing. We will describe those functions in detail in the following subsections.

### 17.3.1. *Anonymity of User Identity*

In the proposed scheme, *PID* is derived from the user's real identity. Additional parameters are added to achieve dynamics and secrecy properties. It is renewed periodically and after each authentication. The series of *PID* is defined as

$$PID_{j+x} = F(PID_{j+x-1}||H^x(k_i)||k_{HM}), \tag{1}$$

where $k_i$ is the $i$th session key negotiated after each successful authentication, $k_{HM}$ is the shared session key between the mobile terminal and the home network, $j = 1, 2, \ldots$, and $x = 0, 1, 2, \ldots F(\,)$ is a one way function which generates the same bit length as *PID*. Function $H^x(\,)$ is a hash chain function which computes the hash value of $k_i$ $x$ times and outputs the variable itself if $x = 0$. The function is used for *PID* renewal, which will be discussed in details in Section 17.4.1. In the implementation, the *MT* keeps the results of the last hash operation; therefore multiple hash operations are not required for each *PID* renewal. The initial value $PID_0$ is defined as the identity of the mobile user $ID_M$. The home network always keeps the mapping relationship of a mobile terminal's *PID* and real identity ($PID_j \leftrightarrow ID_M$). Eq. (1) conceals the real identity $ID_M$ in $PID_j$ and provides anonymity of the user identity for an *MT* without increasing the computational complexity.

### 17.3.2. *Proposed Authentication Process*

We first introduce the full version of the authentication process for the proposed service agent based on WLAN/cellular integrated service model followed by the description of the inherited sub-sets. Assume an *MT* is accessing a WLAN hotspot (*FA*) for the first time. Figure 17.6 shows the message flow of the proposed authentication scheme. The major authentication stages in the figure are described as follows. 1) the *MT* submits the authentication request and encapsulated session key negotiation to the *FA*; 2) the *FA* forwards the message from the *MT* to the *SA* and requests the *HA* for verification; 3) the *SA* returns the identity information of the *HA*, and forwards the authentication message from the *MT* to the *HA*; 4) the *HA* verifies the identities of the *MT* and the *FA*, and returns the session key to the *FA*; 5) the *FA* sends the proof of its knowledge of the session key to the *MT*. The detailed authentication scheme proceeds as follows:
Step 1. ($MT \rightarrow FA$)

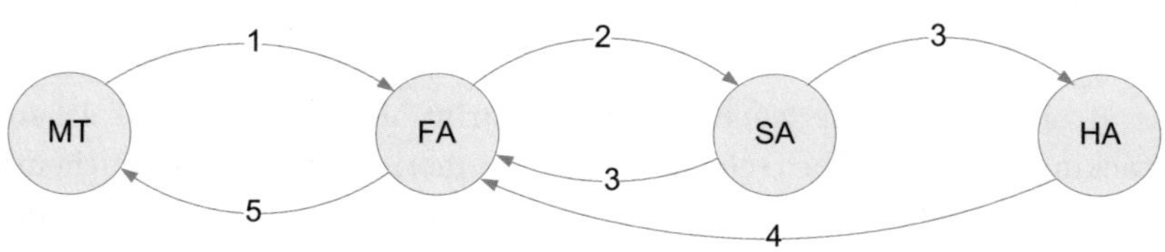


Fig. 17.6. General authentication message flow of the proposed authentication scheme.

The $MT$ sets the other party of the authentication to its home network, and generates a random number as a nonce $N_M$ and a random number as session key $k_i$, which can be used to encrypt the information in the communications session after the authentication is processed successfully. The $MT$ can use its International Mobile Subscriber Identity (IMSI) [15] for $ID_M$, and sends Message (2) to the $FA$ with current time stamp $ts_1$.

$$MT \rightarrow FA : PID_j || ID_H || E_{k_{MH}} \{ID_M || N_M || k_i || ts_1\}. \tag{2}$$

where $PID_j || ID_H$ represents the modified AAA (Authentication, Authorization and Accounting) user name in the form of username@domain. An alternative form of the authentication request for the case in which the $FA$ already has the information of the $MT$ will be discussed in Section 17.3.3.1.

Step 2. ($FA \rightarrow SA$)

On receiving Message (2) from the $MT$, the $FA$ sets $Msg_M$ to $PID_j || ID_H || E_{k_{MH}} \{ID_M || N_M || k_i || ts_1\}$ and generates a serial number $sn_i$, which includes the $FA$'s network operator code, station code and an event sequence code, for the authentication event. Attaching the current timestamp, the $FA$ sends Message (3) to the $SA$:

$$FA \rightarrow SA : ID_F || E_{k_{SF}} \{Msg_M || sn_i || ts_2\} : sig_F. \tag{3}$$

Step 3. ($SA \rightarrow FA, HA$)

The $SA$ checks the integrity of Message (3) by verifying $ID_F$ and the attached digital signature of the $FA$. The $SA$ decrypts Message (3) by $k_{SF}$ and looks into $Msg_M$ to get $ID_H$. Note that the $SA$ cannot read $ID_M || k_i || ts$ in $Msg_M$, since it is encrypted by $k_{MH}$. The $SA$ is aware that the authentication request is intended for the $HA$. The $SA$ searches the database, and fetches $pub_F$ and $pub_H$. The $SA$ set $Msg_F$ to $Msg_M || sn_i || ts_2$. Besides forwarding the necessary information to the $HA$, the $SA$ also acts as PKI authority and sends the certified public key information to both the $FA$ and the $HA$, which will be used by them to verify each other. For publicly available information, such as public key, encryption is not necessary. Digital signature is used to guarantee the integrity. The $SA$ sends Message (4) to the $HA$:

$$SA \rightarrow HA : ID_S || ID_F || pub_F || E_{k_{SH}} \{Msg_F || ts_3\} : sig_S, \tag{4}$$

and Message (5) to the $FA$:

$$SA \rightarrow FA : ID_S || ID_H || pub_H || ts_3 : sig_S. \tag{5}$$

Step 4. ($HA \rightarrow FA$)

The $HA$ checks the integrity of Message (4) by verifying $ID_S$ and the attached digital signature of the $SA$. The $HA$ retrieves $Msg_F$, the identity and the public key of the $FA$, and $PID_j$ by using the shared key $k_{SH}$. The $HA$ searches the $ID_M \leftrightarrow PID_j$ mapping database, and locates the identity of the $MT$ who initiates the authentication process and the corresponding $k_{MH}$. The $HA$ further decrypts $Msg_H$ encapsulated in $Msg_F$ by using $k_{MH}$ and retrieves $ID_M$ of the mobile user, the nonce $N_M$ and the proposed session key $k_i$. The $HA$ checks the validity of timing relationships of all the timestamps $ts_1, \ldots, ts_3$ to prevent replay attack and verify the identity of the $MT$ by comparing the decrypted $ID_M$ and $PID_j$ with the stored copy. Then the $HA$ sends Message (6) to the $FA$:

$$HA \rightarrow FA : ID_H || E_{k_F} < N_M || k_i || PID_j || ts_4 >: sig_H. \quad (6)$$

Step 5. ($FA \rightarrow MT$)

The $FA$ should have received Message (5) from the $SA$ sent in 0 and Message (6) from the $HA$ in the above step. When the $FA$ receives Message (5), it checks the timestamp $ts_3$, and the message integrity by verifying $ID_S$ and the attached digital signature of the $SA$. The $FA$ then stores the identity and the public key of the $HA$ for later use if the verification is positive. When the $FA$ receives Message (6), it checks the message integrity again by verifying $ID_H$ and the attached digital signature of the $HA$. It also checks if the timestamp is reasonable. The $FA$ decrypts the message using the public key of the $HA$ retrieved from Message (5), and gets $PID_j$, the nonce $N_M$ and the session key $k_i$ proposed by the $MT$ in 0, which indicates the $HA$ has acknowledged the $MT$ and approved its roaming privilege. Since the decryption of Message (6) depends on the reception of Message (5), the $FA$ will store Message (6) temporarily if it is received before Message (5). The $FA$ generates a ticket $Tk_i = TkID_i || ref_i || exp_i$, where $TkID_i$ denotes the ticket ID, $ref_i$ denotes the ticket reference code, and $exp_i$ denotes the ticket expiration time. The $FA$ stores the mapping relationship $Tk_i \leftrightarrow k_i \leftrightarrow PID_j$. The purpose of the ticket will be discussed in the next subsection. The $FA$ sends Message to the $HA$:

$$FA \rightarrow MT : ID_F || E_{k_i}\{H(N_M) || N_F || Tk_i || ts_5\} \quad (7)$$

Step 6. ($MT \rightarrow FA$)

After the $MT$ receives Message (7), it checks the identity of the $FA$ and tries to decrypt the message using $k_i$. If the decrypted $H(n_M)$ is correct and $ts_5$ is reasonable, it indicates that both the $FA$ and the $HA$ approves the roaming service request. The $MT$ stores the $Tk_i \leftrightarrow k_i \leftrightarrow ID_F$ mapping for later use. The $MT$ sends Message (8) as the acknowledgement of receiving Message (7) and begins to send communication data to the network operated by the $FA$.

$$MT \rightarrow FA : PID_j || E_{k_i}\{H(N_F) || rnd_n || l_n || x_n || y_{x_n} || ts_6 || comm\_data\}, \quad (8)$$

where $rnd_n, l_n$ and $x_n$ denotes the random component of the seed, length of MDDHC$_n$ and the position of the start endpoint of the window of MDDHC$_n$, and $y_{x_n}$ denotes the node pair at $x_n$ of the MDDHC$_n$.

After receiving Message (8) from the $MT$, the $FA$ retrieves and stores $rnd_n$, $l_n$, $x_n$ and $y_{x_n}$ as part of the metering record of the on-going service session. The recorded parameters are used to form Event ID, which will be introduced in Section 17.4.2. So far, the *MT* and the *FA* have been mutually authenticated. Current WLAN hotspots do not apply data encryption over the wireless link at all, because many WLAN security protocols, such as WEP, WPA, WPA2 (IEEE 802.11i), etc., are more inclined to individual users and centralized corporation environment. $k_i$ can be used to secure the communication between the *MT* and the *FA*.

### 17.3.3. *Variation of the Proposed Authentication Scheme*

One of the key advantages of the proposed authentication scheme is its self-adaptation. We discuss two common alternatives, in the following subsections: 1) the *MT* re-visits the *FA*; and 2) the *MT* purchases integrated service from the *SA*/peer-to-peer roaming agreement exists.

#### 17.3.3.1. *Localized authentication*

Localized authentication is defined as authentication between the *MT* and a network operator who has the *MT*'s certain type of credential. One example of localized authentication is that the *MT* authenticates with the *FA* when the *MT* re-visits the *FA*. The definition of "re-visit *FA*" is that the *MT* visits any hotspot operated by the *FA* for the second time or more by discovering the hotspot from its beacon or SSID, which is constantly broadcasted. The hotspot is not necessary to be the same hotspot that the *MT* visited for the first time. Under this definition, occurrence of this "re-visit" case would be quite common. Recall the ticket $Tk_i = TkID_i||ref_i||exp_i$, which is introduced in 0 in the above subsection. $Tk_i$ is the certificate issued by the *FA* to the *MT* to indicate that the *MT* has been verified by its home network and registered with the *FA* before. Since the storage of tickets requires extra memory space, the $exp_i$ parameter defines the absolute time when the ticket is expired so that both the *MT* and the *FA* do not keep the ticket forever. If the *MT* re-visits the *FA* after $exp_i$ timeout, a full authentication process is required as described in the above subsection. Otherwise, a subset of the proposed authentication scheme, which is composed by 0, 0 and 0, is executed as follows.

$$MT \rightarrow FA : PID_{j+c}||TkID_i||E_{k_i}\{ref_i||N_M||k_{i+1}||ts_1\}; \quad (9)$$

$$FA \rightarrow MT : ID_F||E_{k_{i+1}}\{H(N_M)||N_F||Tk_{i+1}||ts_5\}; \quad (10)$$

$$MT \rightarrow FA : PID_{j+c}||E_{k_{i+1}}\{H(N_F)||rnd_n||l_n||x_n||y_{x_n}||ts_6||comm\_data\} \quad (11)$$

From Message (9), the *FA* locates the corresponding $Tk_i \leftrightarrow k_i \leftrightarrow PID_j$ mapping according to $TkID_{i-1}$ and retrieves $k_{i-1}$. The *FA* then decrypts Message (9) and verifies weather $ref_i$ matches $TkID_i$ and if $ts_1$ is within the tolerant range. If it is true, the *FA* accepts the new session $k_{i+1}$. The *FA* grants the access of the *MT* and sends Message (10) to the *MT* with a new ticket. The parameter $PID_{j+c}$ in

Message (9) is due to the *PID* renewal, which will be discussed in Section 17.4.1. Message (11) serves as an acknowledgement.

Note that in this case, the *FA* assumes the good standing status of the *MT*. The *HA* should notify the *FA* to revoke the ticket once it finds out the *MT* is no longer good. The most recent *FA* list that served the *MT* can be obtained by searching the Event IDs in the *MT*'s service record.

Localized authentication also occurs in the following two cases: 1) the *MT* accesses a network (WLAN hotspot, for example) operated by its home network when it is in the home network; and 2) the *MT* accesses WLAN hotspots operated by the visiting cellular network, which supports ticket and *PID*.

#### 17.3.3.2. *Integrated service offered by SA/existence of peer-to-peer roaming agreement*

Both cases are actually equivalent. So we begin with the former, which is the other operation mode of the proposed network infrastructure. In this case, the *MT* does not belong to any real network operator and it registers with the *SA*, which is denoted as $SA'$ for notational convenience. Therefore $SA'$ is considered as residing in the *MT*'s home network and takes over the work which is designated to the *HA* in Section 17.3.2. Since the *FA* and the *SA* have direct service agreement and share pre-set secret key, the public key exchange in 0 is not necessary and there is no need to do asymmetric encryption. The subset of the proposed authentication scheme, which is composed by all the steps except 0 with minor parameter modifications, is executed as follows.

$$MT \rightarrow FA : PID_j||ID_S||E_{k_{MS}}\{ID_M||N_M||k_i||ts_1\}; \tag{12}$$

$$FA \rightarrow SA : ID_F||E_{k_{SF}}\{Msg_M||sn_i||ts_2\} : sig_F; \tag{13}$$

$$SA \rightarrow FA : ID_S||E_{k_{SF}}\{N_M||k_i||PID_j||ts_4\} : sig_S; \tag{14}$$

$$FA \rightarrow MT : ID_F||E_{k_i}\{H(N_M)||N_F||Tk_i||ts_5\}; \tag{15}$$

$$MT \rightarrow FA : PID_j||E_{k_i}\{H(N_F)||l_n||x_n||y_{x_n}||ts_6||comm\_data\} \tag{16}$$

For the second case, we just need to replace *SA* by *HA* in the above messages. Note that the *HA* and the *FA* have shared secret key $k_{HF}$ in this case.

## 17.4. Supplementary Operations

Two supplementary operations are developed to improve the anonymity of the user identity and commercial deployment: *PID* renewal and event-tracking.

### 17.4.1. *PID Renewal Process*

According to the algorithm for computing the $PID_j$ series described in Section 17.3.1, both the *MT* and the *HA* can compute the next *PID* independently since both of them always hold updated $PID_j$ and $H^x(k_i)$. Therefore the main purposes of the *PID* renewal message exchanges are *PID* synchronization and recovery in case the $PID_j$ and/or $H^x(k_i)$ values that they are holding are out of synchronization for some reason. The following steps show *PID* renewal operation in the normal case.

$$MT \to HA : PID_j||E_{k_{HM}}\{ID_M||flag_{pid.renewal}\}; \tag{17}$$

$$HA \to MT : ID_H||E_{k_{HM}}\{H(k_{HM})||PID_{j+1}\}. \tag{18}$$

In the first step, the *MT* sends Message (17) to the *HA*. $flag_{pid.renewal}$ tells the *HA* that the *MT* is going to renew its *PID*. After the message is received by the *HA*, the *HA* locates $ID_M$ and the corresponding $k_{HM}$ by searching the $PID_j$ in the $PID_j \leftrightarrow ID_M$ mapping database. The *HA* then decrypts Message (17) and verifies if the decrypted $ID_M$ matches the record. If it is true, the *HA* sends Message (18) to the *MT*. The message includes $PID_{j+1}$ computed by the *HA*. After the *MT* computes $PID_{j+1}$ itself, it verifies if both results match each other. If it is true, the *MT* starts to apply the renewed *PID*. Otherwise, the *MT* will continue to use $PID_j$ until proper acknowledgement is received from the *HA*. Meanwhile the proposed renewal process is able to detect the exceptions and the *MT* and the *HA* process the exceptional cases as follows.

Out-of-synchronization $PID_j$: the *HA* is unable to locate information in the $PID_j \leftrightarrow ID_M$ mapping database. The *HA* then sends Message (19) instead of Message (18) to the *MT*.

$$HA \to MT : ID_H||flag_{pid.incorrect} : sig_H. \tag{19}$$

Since the *MT* will not apply a new *PID* until it receives correct acknowledgement from the *HA*, the *PID* at the *HA* must be $PID_{j-1}$.

Out-of- synchronization $H^x(k_i)$ : $PID_{j+1}$ in Message (17) does not match the *MT*'s computational result although $H(k_{HM})$ shows the message is sent by the *HA*. If either case happens, the *MT* sends Message (20) to the *HA* for the *PID* recovery process so that the *HA* is able to reconstruct $PID_{j+1}$.

$$MT \to HA : \begin{cases} PID_{j-1}||E_{k_{HM}\{ID_{MS}||flag_{pid.incorrect}||H^x(k_i)\}}, & \text{case 1} \\ PID_j||E_{k_{HM}\{ID_{MS}||flag_{hash.incorrect}||H^x(k_i)\}}, & \text{case 2} \end{cases}. \tag{20}$$

The *HA* sends Message (18) to the *MT* again for acknowledgement and the *PID* renewal process is completed.

### 17.4.2. *Event-tracking for Billing Support*

Commercial network service deployment cannot be released without a billing mechanism. In the proposed WLAN/cellular integrated service model, billing is based on the *MT*'s network accessing activities. We assume that the WLAN/cellular integrated service is offered by multiple regional networks under different administration. The mobile user will get single bill periodically, such as monthly, from its home network. The charge by the foreign networks for the service to the mobile user will also go through the home network. The billing charge is based on the time of usage, which is measured by the length of MDDHC. Note that proposed billing support can also be applied to network traffic based charge, in which case the length of MDDHC represents the network traffic instead of service time, as shown in this work.

### 17.4.2.1. *Heart beat of MT*

When the *MT* is accessing the service offered by the *FA*, starting from $y_{x_n+1}$, the *MT* periodically release a node one by one, or heart beat, along the time in the backward hash chain of the MDDHC at around metering interval:

$$M \rightarrow F : PID_j || E_{k_i}\{y_{x_{n+r}} || ts\}, \tag{21}$$

where $r$ denotes the metering interval passed. Upon receiving Message (21), the *FA* updates service end value by overwriting $y_{x_{n+r-1}}$ by $y_{x_{n+r}}$. When the *MT* finishes the service session at node $R$ normally, the *FA* should have the node pair $y_{x_n}$ as service session start value and the node $y_{x_{n+R}}$ as service session end value. If the service session is terminated abnormally, the *FA* will not receive the heart beat any more. After pre-determined grace period, the *FA* uses the latest $y_{x_{n+r}}$ as the final service session end value. If the *FA* receives the heart beat within the grace period, the *FA* continues the service session and updates the service session end value using the received $y_{x_{n+r}}$. The affection of missing a few heart beats to proper billing can be neglected. Such measure solves incorrect billing when the *MT* does not disconnect from the service session based on normal procedure.

Sometimes, the service session may be longer than the length of one MDDHC. In such case, the *MT* should be aware of this case since it knows the total length of the MDDHC-in-use. The *MT* will do a ticket ID type authentication with the *FA* to apply another MDDHC in background. Such situation is viewed by the network as two consecutive service sessions from any aspect. Since the *FA* has the information of total length of the MDDHC-in-use, it can predict the upcoming authentication, such as fetch the *MT*'s ticket credential into the cache, etc.

### 17.4.2.2. *Distribution of event ID*

The activity of the *MT* is tracked by a data structure named Event ID as shown in Figure 17.7. An event is defined as an incident of the *MT* accessing the network resource. An Event ID is distributed to proper network operators by event-tracking process, which is running independently from the authentication process. The revenue is partitioned later based on the Event ID records.

Most of the data fields have either appeared before in the literature or self-explanatory, so they do not need to be introduced again. In Event ID data, the

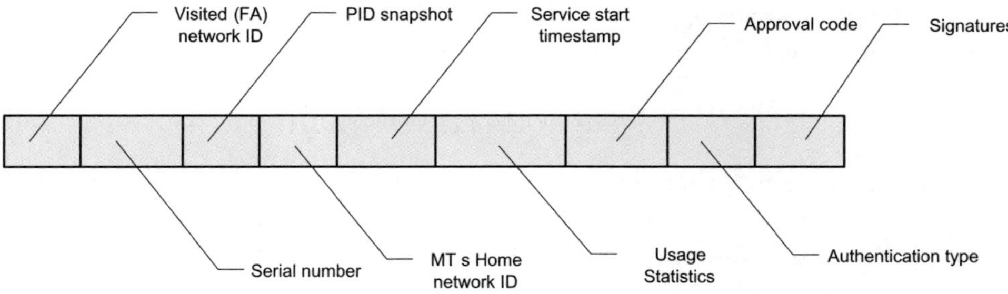


Fig. 17.7. Event ID data structure.

usage statistics field includes the *MT* network activities data, such as connection time, upload/download traffic bandwidth, zone and/or service weight, etc. How to adopt these parameters into billing generation solely depends on the roaming agreements and is beyond the scope of this work. Approval code is a reference number indicating that the event claim is approved by the *MT*'s home network. The attested signatures from the involved network operators show that they agree with those data.

Since different authentication modes have been developed in Sections 17.3.2 and 17.3.3, the distribution of Event ID varies, as shown in Table 17.2. For example, In the "Re-visit" case, the *SA* is not involved and it is unnecessary to send Event ID to the *SA*. However, the *HA* still requires Event ID for billing purpose.

Based on the nature of billing mechanism, we classify network operators into three categories: (roaming) service provider, home network and (roaming) service coordinator. Table 17.2 summaries the roles in the four scenarios. During the authentication process, the network operators keep the received messages at least until Event ID distribution completes. Event-tracking is implemented as follows.

After the *FA* receives Message (8), the service session starts. Meanwhile, the *FA* fills in fields of the event ID data structure and constructs

$$EventID_i^{FA} = ID_F||sn_i||PID_j||ID_H||ts_6||(n||rnd_n||x_n||y_{x_n})||null||1 : sig_F, \tag{22}$$

Table 17.2. Event ID distribution.

| Scenario | Auth. Type | Service provider | *MT*'s home network | Service Coordinator | Event ID distribution |
|---|---|---|---|---|---|
| Normal | 1 | *FA* | *HA* | *SA* | *FA, HA, SA* |
| Re-visit | 2 | *FA* | *HA* | - | *FA, HA* |
| Service purchased from SA | 3 | *FA* | *SA* | - | *FA, SA* |
| Peer-to-peer roaming agreement | 4 | *FA* | *HA* | - | *FA, HA* |

where *null* indicates not applicable. the *FA* sends Message (23) to he *MT*'s home agent, which is the *HA* or, in service type 3, the *SA*[a]

$$FA \rightarrow HA : ID_F||E_{k_H}\{EventID_i^{SA}\}. \tag{23}$$

After the *HA* or the *SA* receives Message (23), it can re-construct the MDDHC that the *MT* uses for the corresponding service session by using $rnd_n$ in the Event ID and $k_{MH}$ that the *HA* already possesses. Then the *HA* checks if $y_{x_n}$ matches the node pair at position $x_n$ of the re-constructed MDDHC, i.e., $y_{x_n} = (H^{x_n}(k_{MH}||\overline{rnd_n}), H^{l_n-x_n}(k_{MH}||rnd_n))$. If it holds, the *HA* returns Message (24) to the *FA* and the *SA*, respectively

$$\begin{aligned} &HA \rightarrow SA : ID_H||E_{k_{SH}}\{EventID_i^{FA}||apv : sig_H\}, \\ &HA \rightarrow FA : ID_H||E_{k_F}\langle EventID_i^{FA}||apv : sig_H\rangle, \end{aligned} \tag{24}$$

where *apv* denotes the approval code. Note that in case of service type 2, 3 and 4, the *HA* only needs to send Message (24) to the *FA*.

After *MT* finishes the network access session in the service area, such as the hotspots or cellular cells operated by the *FA*, the *FA* fills in fields of the event ID data structure and constructs $EventID_i^{FA}$

$$EventID_i^{FA} = \begin{cases} ID_F||sn_i||PID_j||ID_H||ts||(n||y_{x_{n+R}})||1 : sig_F, & \text{type=1} \\ ID_F||TkID_i||PID_{j+c}||ID||ts_5||(n||y_{x_{n+R}})||2 : sig_F, & \text{type=2} \\ ID_F||sn_i||PID_j||ID_s||ts||(n||y_{x_{n+R}})||3 : sig_F, & \text{type=3} \\ ID_F||sn_i||PID_j||ID_H||ts||(n||y_{x_{n+R}})||4 : sig_F, & \text{type=4} \end{cases}, \tag{25}$$

where *ts* denote the latest timestamp that the last Message (21). Similar to the *FA* distributes the Event ID to the *HA* and/or the *SA* described earlier, the *FA* sends the encrypted $EventID_i^{FA}$ in Eq. (25) to the *HA* or, if the *MT*'s integrated service is offered by the *SA*, the *SA*. The $HA^a$ locates the re-constructed MDDHC$_n$ and matches $y_{x_{n+R}}$ along the MDDHC$_n$ and try to find $R$. If the matching process succeeds, i.e., $y_{x_n} = H^{l_n-x_{n+R}}(k_{MH}||rnd_n)$ is located, the total time of the service is computed as $t_{ss} = R \cdot t_{billing}$.

The *FA* sends Message (26) to the *MT*'s home network (*HA*)

$$SA \rightarrow HA : ID_F||E_{k'_{FH}}\{EventID_i^{FA}\}, \tag{26}$$

where the *HA* could be *HA* or the *SA*, and $k'_{FH}$ could be $k_{HF}$ or $k_{SF}$ depending on the authentication type. After it receives Message (26), the *HA* checks the data fields

[a]For simplicity, we use "*HA*" to include both cases.

with the local corresponding information and confirms if the following conditions are satisfied during the claimed service time:

- the *MT* is not being serviced by other networks;
- the *MT* is not in power-off state;
- optionally, the *MT*'s is located within the network service provider's physical location by checking the *MT*'s care-of-address or by location-aware application [16].

If all tests are passed, the *HA* attaches the approval code and its digital signature, and sends Message (27) to the *FA*

$$HA \rightarrow FA : ID_H^{'}||E_{k_{FH}^{'}}\{EventID_i^{FA}||apv : sig_H^{'}\}. \qquad (27)$$

Note that authentication type 2 differs from other types. The *HA* is not notified when the *FA* offers service to the *MT*. The key verification point is to validate $PID_{j+c}$ in conjunction with the three test conditions.

### 17.5. Performance Evaluation

In this section we analyze the security correctness of the proposed protocol and overhead evaluation of the proposed messaging scheme.

#### 17.5.1. *Security Analysis*

A secure protocol design for roaming services requires: 1) prevention of fraud by ensuring that the mobile user and network entity are authentic, that is, there is a mutual authentication mechanism between a network entity and a mobile user; 2) assuring mutual agreement and freshness of the session key; 3) prevention of replaying attack, so that intruders are not able to obtain sensitive data by relaying a previously intercepted message; 4) privacy of mobile user's location information during the communication so that it is requisite to provide the mechanism for user anonymity [17].

To prove the correctness of the authentication provided by the proposed security protocol, we use the logic of authentication developed by Burrows, Abadi and Needham (BAN logic) [18]. Since the conventional notation for security protocols is not convenient for manipulation in the logic of authentication, they introduce the rules to annotate protocols transforming each message into a logic formula. The BAN logic is the most widely used logic for analyzing authentication protocols [19]. We propose a different notation for the specific session key. We assume that from the security viewpoint, the function of the unique session key is the same as for public key. The notation of BAN Logic is listed in Table 17.3.[b]

[b]Table 17.3 is organized from [14].

Table 17.3. Notaions of BAN logic.

| Symbol | Explanation |
|---|---|
| $P\mid\equiv X$ : | $P$ believes $X$, or $P$ would be entitled to believe $X$. In particular, the principal $P$ may act as through $X$ is true. This construct is central to the logic. |
| $P \triangleleft X$ : | $P$ sees $X$. Someone has sent a message containing $X$ to $P$, who can read and repeat $X$ (possibly after doing some decryption) |
| $P\mid\sim X$ : | $P$ once said $X$. The principal $P$ at some time sent a message including the statement $X$. It is not known whether the message was sent long age or during the current run of the protocol, but it is known that $P$ believed $X$ when he sent the message. |
| $P\mid\Rightarrow X$ : | $P$ has jurisdiction over $X$. The principal $P$ is an authority on $X$ and should be trusted on this matter. This construct is used when a principal has delegated authority over some statement. For example, encryption keys need to be generated with some care, and in some protocols certain servers are trusted to do this properly. This may be expressed by the assumption that the principals believe that the server has jurisdiction over statements about the quality of keys. |
| $\#(X)$ : | The formula $X$ is fresh, that is, $X$ has not been sent in a message at any time before the current run of the protocol. This is usually true for nonce, that is, expressions generated for the purpose of being fresh. A nonce commonly includes a timestamp or a number that is used only once such as a sequence number. |
| $P \overset{K}{\leftrightarrow} Q$ : | $P$ and $Q$ may use the shared key $K$ to communicate. The key $K$ is good, in that it will never be discovered by any principal except $P$ or $Q$, or a principal trusted by either $P$ or $Q$. |
| $\overset{K}{\mapsto} P$ : | $P$ has $K$ as a public key. The matching secret key (the inverse of $K$ denoted $K^{-1}$) will never be discovered by any principal except $P$ or a principal trusted by $P$. |
| $P \overset{X}{\rightleftharpoons} Q$ : | The formula $X$ is secret known only to $P$ and $Q$. And possibly to principals trusted by them. Only $P$ and $Q$ may use $X$ to prove their identities to one another. Often, $X$ is fresh as well as secret. An example of a shared secret is a password. |
| $\{X\}_k$ : | This represents the formula $X$ encrypted under the key $K$. Formally, $\{X\}_k$ is an abbreviation for an expression of the form $\{X\}_k$ from $P$. We make the realistic assumption that each message is mentioned for this purpose. In the interests of brevity, we typically omit this in our examples. |
| $\langle X\rangle_Y$ : | This represents $X$ combined with the formula $Y$; it is intended that $Y$ be a secret, and that its presence prove the identity of whoever utters $\langle X\rangle_Y$. In implementations, $X$ is simply concatenated with the password $Y$; our notation highlights that $Y$ plays a special role, as proof or origin for $X$. The notation is intentionally reminiscent of that for encryption, which also guarantees the identity of the source of a message through knowledge of a certain kind of secret. |

17.5.1.1. *Proof of the proposed authentication scheme*[c]

Addition Notation:

*A*: *MT*(*A*': *MT*'s *PID*), $B$ : *FA*, $C$ : *SA*, $D$ : *HA*

Security scheme:

1. $A \rightarrow B : A', H, \{A, N_A, k_i, t_1\}_{k_{AD}}$ from (2)
2. $B \rightarrow C : \{\{A', H, \{A, N_A, k_i, ts_1\}_{k_{AD}}, sn_i, t_2\}_{k_{BC}}\}_{k_B^{-1}}$ from (3)

[c]Because of space limitation, only the full version of the authentication scheme is proved. The subset of authentication schemes for the special cases should comply with this proof.

3. $C \rightarrow D : \{B, k_B, \{A', H, \{A, N_A, k_i, ts_1\}_{k_{AD}}, sn_i, t_2\}_{k_{CD}}, t_3\}_{k_C^{-1}}$ from (4)
4. $C \rightarrow B : \{D, k_D, t_3\}_{k_C^{-1}}$ from (5)
5. $D \rightarrow B : \{\{N_A, k_i, A', t_4\}_{k_B}\}_{k_D^{-1}}$ from (6)
6. $B \rightarrow A : \{H(N_A), N_B, t_5\}_{k_i}$ from (7)
7. $A \rightarrow B : \{H(N_B), t_6, comm\_data\}_{k_i}$

Idealized protocol:

$$i3.\ C \rightarrow D : \left\{ \overset{K_B}{\mapsto} B, \{\{A, k, N_A\}_{k_{AD}}\}_{k_{CD}} \right\}_{k_C^{-1}}$$
$$i4.\ C \rightarrow B : \left\{ \overset{K_D}{\mapsto} D \right\}_{k_C^{-1}}$$
$$i5.\ D \rightarrow B : \left\{ \{k, N_A\}_{k_B} \right\}_{k_D^{-1}}$$
$$i6.\ B \rightarrow A : \left\{ \langle A \overset{N_B}{\rightleftharpoons} B \rangle_{N_A} \right\}_k$$
$$i7.\ A \rightarrow B : \left\{ \langle A \overset{N_A}{\rightleftharpoons} B \rangle_{N_B} \right\}_k$$

Messages 1 and 2 are omitted, since Message 2 simply passes Message 1 to $C$ and the content of Message 1 is included in Message 3.

It is assumed that each principal knows its own secret key, and believes its own nonce and other's timestamp are fresh. The service agent also knows other's public key. The above assumptions are summarized as follows:

A1. $A| \equiv A \overset{k_{AD}}{\leftrightarrow} D$ A2. $A| \equiv \#(N_A)$
A3. $A| \equiv \#(k)$

B1. $B| \equiv \overset{k_B}{\mapsto} B$ B2. $B| \equiv \overset{k_C}{\mapsto} C$
B3. $B| \equiv B \overset{k_{BC}}{\leftrightarrow} C$ B4. $B| \equiv C| \Rightarrow \overset{k_D}{\mapsto} D$
B5. $B| \equiv \#(N_B)$

C1. $C| \equiv C \overset{k_{CD}}{\leftrightarrow} D$ C2. $C| \equiv \overset{k_C}{\mapsto} C$
C3. $C| \equiv \overset{k_B}{\mapsto} B$ C4. $C| \equiv \overset{k_D}{\mapsto} D$
C5. $C| \equiv B \overset{k_{BC}}{\leftrightarrow} C$

D1. $D| \equiv \overset{k_D}{\mapsto} D$ D2. $D| \equiv \overset{k_C}{\mapsto} C$
D3. $D| \equiv C \overset{k_{CD}}{\leftrightarrow} D$ D4. $D| \equiv C| \Rightarrow \overset{k_B}{\mapsto} B$
D5. $D| \equiv A \overset{k_{AD}}{\leftrightarrow} D$

Proof:
From $i3$:

$$D \triangleleft \{\{A, k, N_A\}_{k_{AD}}\}_{k_{CD}}, \tag{28}$$

and

$$D \triangleleft \left\{ \overset{K_B}{\mapsto} B \right\}_{k_C^{-1}}. \tag{29}$$

Applying D3 and D5 to (28), we have

$$D| \equiv A| \sim k, N_A. \tag{30}$$

By checking the timestamp, $D$ believe $N_A$ and $k$ are fresh, we further have

$$D| \equiv A| \equiv k, \tag{31}$$

$$D| \equiv A| \equiv N_A. \tag{32}$$

Applying C2, C3, D2 and D4 to (29), we have

$$D| \equiv C| \equiv \overset{K_B}{\mapsto} B, \tag{33}$$

$$D| \equiv \overset{K_B}{\mapsto} B. \tag{34}$$

Similarly, from $i4$, applying C2, C4, B2 and B4, we have

$$B| \equiv C| \equiv \overset{K_D}{\mapsto} D, \tag{35}$$

$$B| \equiv \overset{K_D}{\mapsto} D. \tag{36}$$

From $i5$:

$$B \triangleleft \{\{N_A, k\}_{k_B}\}_{k_D^{-1}}. \tag{37}$$

Applying (34), (36) and B1, we have

$$B| \equiv D| \sim k, N_A. \tag{38}$$

Applying (31) and (32), we have

$$B| \equiv D| \equiv A| \equiv k, \tag{39}$$

$$B| \equiv D| \equiv A| \equiv N_A, \tag{40}$$

From $i6$:

$$A \triangleleft \{N_A, N_B\}_k. \tag{41}$$

Applying A2 and A3, we have

$$A| \equiv B| \sim N_B, N_A \tag{42}$$

By checking the timestamp, $A$ believes $N_B$ is fresh. We have

$$A| \equiv B| \equiv A \overset{N_B}{\mapsto} B, \tag{43}$$

Applying A1,

$$A| \equiv D| \equiv N_A, \tag{44}$$

$$A| \equiv D| \equiv k, \tag{45}$$

$$A| \equiv B| \equiv D| \equiv N_A, \tag{46}$$

$$A| \equiv B| \equiv D| \equiv k, \tag{47}$$

$$A| \equiv D| \equiv N_A, \tag{48}$$

$$A| \equiv D| \equiv k, \tag{49}$$

Since $B$ does not know $N_A$ and $k$, unless they are told by $D$, and at the same time, $A$ trusts its home network $D$,

$$A| \equiv B| \equiv A \overset{N_A}{\mapsto} B \tag{50}$$

$$A| \equiv B| \equiv A \overset{k}{\leftrightarrow} B \tag{51}$$

From $i7$:

$$B \triangleleft \{N_B\}_k \tag{52}$$

Applying B5 and (50), we have

$$B| \equiv A| \sim N_b \tag{53}$$

$$B| \equiv A| \equiv A \overset{k}{\leftrightarrow} B \tag{54}$$

$$B| \equiv A| \equiv A \overset{N_A}{\mapsto} B \tag{55}$$

Therefore the main conclusions are (50), (51), (54) and (55), which show that $A$ and $B$ are mutually authenticated. At the same time, $k$ and $N_A$ are shared with $A$'s trusted party $D$ as well, which allow the service provider to be able to decrypt the communication when they are requested by law enforcement units.

17.5.1.2. *Robustness of proposed security schemes*

The proposed security schemes are robust to resist certain attacks and sniffing. The intruder cannot impersonate all the parties. In both authentication and event-tracking schemes, the messages between wired parties, such as service providers and service agents, are identified by their digital signature. The proposed authentication scheme can resist replay and middle man attack. The intruder cannot act as the $MT$ since he cannot generate a meaningful Message (2), which can be detected by the $HA$.

User anonymity and intraceability are implemented by dynamic $PID$. The dynamics is achieved by recursive hash operations of the session key and the confidentiality is achieved by the involvement of secret shared key and one way function so that the *FA* cannot generate a valid *PID* series while knowing the session key. Depending on the user's preference and the unit's power condition, *PID* can be regularly refreshed. Since the *PID* refresh is an independent process, the *PID* can be used in cellular networks to replace IMEI when the traditional authentication is used so that user anonymity and intraceability are supported in the entire integrated network. The *PID* recovery processes have the capability of detecting and restoring unsynchronized *PID* in the *HA* due to reasons such as poor wireless channel or software fault.

Replay attack and middle man attack are prevented by implementing an encrypted timestamp mechanism. The intruder cannot update the encrypted timestamp in the replayed message, which can be identified by the legitimate users if its timestamp is out of the pre-defined range.

#### 17.5.1.3. *Dispute resolution*

The proposed MDDHC based billing support mechanism can avoid repudiation from the *FA* and the *MT*. The dispute in this work includes the following cases:

- for the *FA*, over-claim and false claim the service provided;
- for the *MT* and the *HA*, denial of the entire or partial service received;[d]
- for the *SA*, false claim of non-existed service coordination.

The *FA* may claim more service time offered to the *MT*. The *FA* is able to generate the elements on the left hand side of $y_{x_n}$ in the backward hash chain. However, the *FA* cannot compute the corresponding elements in the forward hash chain due to the one way property of the hash chain. Similarly, the *FA* cannot compute the elements on the right hand side of $y_{x_{n+J}}$. Therefore, the knowledge of the MHHDC of *FA* is limited to the window defined by $y_{x_n} y_{x_{n+J}}$, and it cannot over-claim the actual service session duration time.

The MDDHC's seed is the concatenation of the shared secret key between the *MT* and the *HA*, and a random number. While the random number offers the diversity of the MDDHCs, the shared secret key component ensures the MDDHC at the *FA* is generated by the *MT* only. Therefore neither the *FA* nor the *SA* is able to generate a valid MHHDC by themselves to falsely claim the service session that does not exist. For the same reason, if the *FA* holds $y_{x_n}$ and $y_{x_{n+J}}$, it indicates that the *MT* must have received the entire service during the corresponding time that begins at $x_n$ and ends at $x_n + J$. At the same time, the *FA* does not need to hold all the elements in between to prove the service usage by the *MT*. Missing receiving a few $y_{x_{n+j}}$ due to network connectivity problem, etc. is also tolerable to the proposed billing mechanism.

---

[d]We consider the *MT* and the *HA* as one group, and the service offered by the *FA* is received by the *MT-HA* group because of the security and business relationship between the *MT* and the *HA*.

### 17.5.2. *Overhead Analysis*

The overhead is critical since the security protocols are implemented in the mobile devices in the wireless environment. Therefore, heavy computation by the mobile is not feasible [20–22]. Since the bandwidth is lower and the channel error is higher in the wireless networks than those in the wired networks, it is important for the security protocols to minimize the message size and the number of message exchanges.

By applying the dual one way property of MDDHC, digital signature operation for the billing support, which is costly in both computing and communication, at the *MT* is not required. Assume that the data length of parameters in authentication messages related to the *MT* is set as shown in Table 17.4. The total authentication message exchange via the wireless link is less than 1 kb. The cryptographic algorithm and parameter length can be adjusted to balance communication/computation overhead and security strength.

The cryptographic operations at the *MT* are symmetric encryption/decryption and hash, which are efficient in computation, communication and power consumption. In order to further reduce the service access latency, the *MT* pre-computes multiple MDDHCs with different lengths during its idle time so that the MDDHC is immediately available when the *MT* accesses the service. The storage requirement of the MDDHCs is not high. From Table 17.4, if the *MT* would like to generate one MDDHC for 8 hours with metering cycle 2 minutes, the required storage allocation is 8 kB. In practice, the *MT* should generate multiple shorter MDDHCs for several hours' use, which consumes even less simultaneous storage space.

In the following subsections, dynamic overhead characteristics of the proposed service model will be discussed. We first describe our analytical model. Then, we develop general expressions that describe the performance metrics of our interests. Finally, we present and discuss numerical results from various network scenarios and settings.

Table 17.4. Data length of parameters.

| Parameter | Data Length (HEX digits) |
|---|---|
| $ID_M/PID$ | 15 |
| ID network (IP address) | 8 |
| Nonce | 16 |
| Session key | 32 |
| Timestamp | 8 |
| Hash function output | 16 |
| Ticket ID | 8 |
| Ref | 4 |
| Exp | 8 |
| Node in MDDHC | 32 |

17.5.2.1. *Analytical model*

The integrated WLANs and the cellular networks under consideration are shown in Figure 17.2. Cellular networks usually have wide coverage area whereas WLANs hotspots have small coverage area and are only available within distinct hotspots. When a mobile terminal roams to a new area it usually registers in one of the cellular networks and does not switch to other cellular networks. Therefore, it is reasonable to assume that a single large cellular network is overlaid on disjoint WLAN hotspots. Without loss of generality, we consider one cellular network covering $n$WLANs hotspots.

In order to analyze the overhead performance, we consider a simplified but reasonable model where a mobile user roams as shown in Figure 17.8. We assume that the residence times in the in wireless networks are exponentially distributed random variables with parameters $\lambda_i$ (for $i = 0, 1, \ldots, n$). To differentiate accessing rate to WLAN hotspot $i$, we further consider the parameter $\alpha_i$ (for $i = 1, 2, \ldots, n$), which is defined as the probability of a mobile user roaming from the cellular network to WLAN hotspot $i$. Therefore,

$$\sum_{i=1}^{n} \alpha_i = 1. \tag{56}$$

Let $X(t) \in \{\text{Celluar1}, \text{WLAN1}, \ldots, \text{WLAN}n\}$ denote a process that tracks the network which the $MT$ is connected to at time $t$. Therefore, the process $X(t)$ can be modeled as a continuous time Markov process. By sampling the random process $X(t)$ after time instances $t_k = k\tau$, where $\tau \ll (1/\lambda_i)$, for $i = 0, 1, \ldots, n$, the new sampled process $X(t_k)$ is a Markov chain [23], in the state space $\{0, 1, \ldots, n\}$, defined

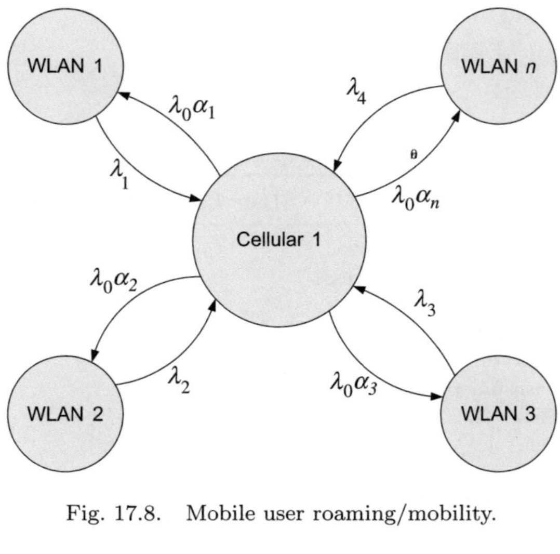


Fig. 17.8. Mobile user roaming/mobility.

by the transition probability matrix

$$\mathbf{P} = \begin{bmatrix} 1-p_0 & \alpha_1 p_0 & \alpha_2 p_0 & \cdot & \cdot & \cdot & \alpha_n p_0 \\ p_1 & 1-p_1 & 0 & & & & \\ p_2 & 0 & 1-p_2 & & & & \\ \cdot & & & \cdot & & & \\ \cdot & & & & \cdot & & \\ \cdot & & & & & \cdot & \\ p_n & 0 & 0 & 0 & 0 & 0 & 1-p_n \end{bmatrix}, \tag{57}$$

where $p_i = 1 - e^{-\lambda_i \tau}$, for $i = 0, 1, \ldots, n$. For a given network setup, the mean residence time(s) $(1/\lambda_i), \forall i$, the roaming probability $\alpha_i$ in WLAN hotspots, and the sampling time interval $\tau$ can be obtained empirically.

17.5.2.2. *Performance analysis*

The metrics of our interest in studying the performance is the overhead cost, which is defined as the average cost per network roaming. The overhead cost $C$can be computed as

$$C = \frac{1}{2} C_0 + \frac{1}{2} \sum_{i=1}^{n} \alpha_i C_i, \tag{58}$$

where $C_i = \Pr_i\{\text{ticket hit}\} C_i^{ticket} + (1 - \Pr_i\{\text{ticket hit}\}) C_i^{no\_ticket} \cdot C_0, C_i^{ticket}$, and $C_i^{no\_ticket}$ are average overhead costs in roaming cellular network, WLAN hotspot $i$ with cached credentials, i.e., ticket $TK_i$, and WLAN hotspot $i$ without cached credentials, respectively. $\Pr_i\{\text{ticket hit}\}$ is the ticket hit probability in WLAN hotspot $i$, defined as the probability of revisiting the WLAN hotspot $i$ before the timeout $t_i^{ticket}$ set for cached credential expires. $\Pr_i\{\text{ticket hit}\}$ is equal to the probability of revisiting the WLAN hotspot $i$ within the time interval $t_i^{ticket}$. Therefore, $\Pr_i\{\text{ticket hit}\}$ can be found as the $i$th element in the first row of the $k$-step transition matrix computed as $\mathbf{Z}^k$, where $k = \left\lfloor \frac{t_i^{ticket}}{\tau} \right\rfloor$. The matrix $\mathbf{Z}$ is obtained by replacing the $i$th row of the matrix $\mathbf{P}$, defined in (57), by the $i$th row of its identity matrix.

17.5.2.3. *Numerical results*

Numerical results are obtained by considering the scenario where a mobile user roams to a region with one cellular network and three types of WLAN hotspots. The cellular network is a foreign network and has roaming agreement with the mobile user's home network. The first type of WLAN hotspot (WLAN1) is affiliated with the cellular network and both networks are tightly-coupled. The second type of WLAN hotspot (WLAN2) is owned by third party service provider. The third type of WLAN hotspot (WLAN3) is owned by the mobile user's home cellular networks.

Table 17.5. Parameters for numerical results.

| Parameter | values |
|---|---|
| Mean residence times $(1/\lambda_0, 1/\lambda_1, 1/\lambda_2, 1/\lambda_3)$ | (100,100,100,100) slots |
| Symmetrical WLAN hotspots roaming probability $(\alpha_1, \alpha_2, \alpha_3)$ | (1/3,1/3,1/3) |
| Asymmetrical WLAN hotspots roaming probability $(\alpha_1, \alpha_2, \alpha_3)$ | (1/4,1/2,1/4) |
| Number of service providers in WLAN1 and 3 | 1 |
| Number of service providers in WLAN2 | 10 |
| Sampling time interval $(\tau)$ | 1 slot |
| Cellular network average roaming overhead cost $(C_0)$ in traditional scheme | 2 hops |
| Cellular network average roaming overhead cost $(C_0)$ in proposed scheme | 2 hops |
| WLAN 1, 2, and 3 hotspots average roaming overhead cost with/without cached credentials $(\{C_i^{ticket}/C_i^{no\_ticket}\})$ in traditional scheme | (2/2,2/4,2/4) hops |
| WLAN 1, 2, and 3 hotspot average roaming overhead cost with/without cached credentials $(\{C_i^{ticket}/C_i^{no\_ticket}\})$ in proposed scheme | (2/2,2/5,2/4) hops |

The second and the third WLAN hotspots have capability to cache mobile terminal credentials and they are loosely-coupled to the cellular network. The overhead cost is computed by using (58) and the parameter values are given in the Table 17.5. The WLAN1 ticket timeout $\left(t_1^{ticket}\right)$ is set to zero. The WLAN2 ticket timeout $\left(t_2^{ticket}\right)$ and WLAN3 ticket timeout $\left(t_3^{ticket}\right)$ take on different values.

In Figure 17.9, the overhead costs for traditional and proposed schemes are compared at various values of WLAN2 ticket timeouts $\left(t_2^{ticket}\right)$ for asymmetrical and symmetrical WLAN hotspots roaming probabilities. In each case, WLAN3 ticket timeout $\left(t_3^{ticket}\right)$ is set to zero (i.e., no user's credentials are cached in WLAN3). From Figure 17.9, it can be seen that, as the WLAN2 ticket timeout increases, the overhead costs of both proposed and traditional schemes decrease and converge to the limiting point. Furthermore, at the low values of the WLAN2 ticket timeout, the traditional scheme has lower overhead cost than proposed scheme; however, as WLAN2 ticket timeout increases the difference in overhead cost decreases to zero. The observations suggest that by choosing an appropriate value of the WLAN2 ticket timeout, the proposed scheme can provide a better and more convenient roaming than the traditional scheme with the same overhead cost.

The overhead cost of the proposed scheme is further studied at various values of WLAN2 ticket timeouts for low WLAN3 ticket timeout $\left(t_3^{ticket} = 0\right)$ and high WLAN3 ticket timeout $\left(t_3^{ticket} = 2000 \text{ slots}\right)$, respectively, for asymmetrical and symmetrical WLAN hotspots roaming probabilities. Figure 17.10 shows that the overhead cost performance of the proposed scheme can be further improved by increasing the WLAN3 ticket timeout. However, the amount of improvement depends on the symmetry of the roaming probabilities $(\alpha_1, \alpha_2, \alpha_3)$.

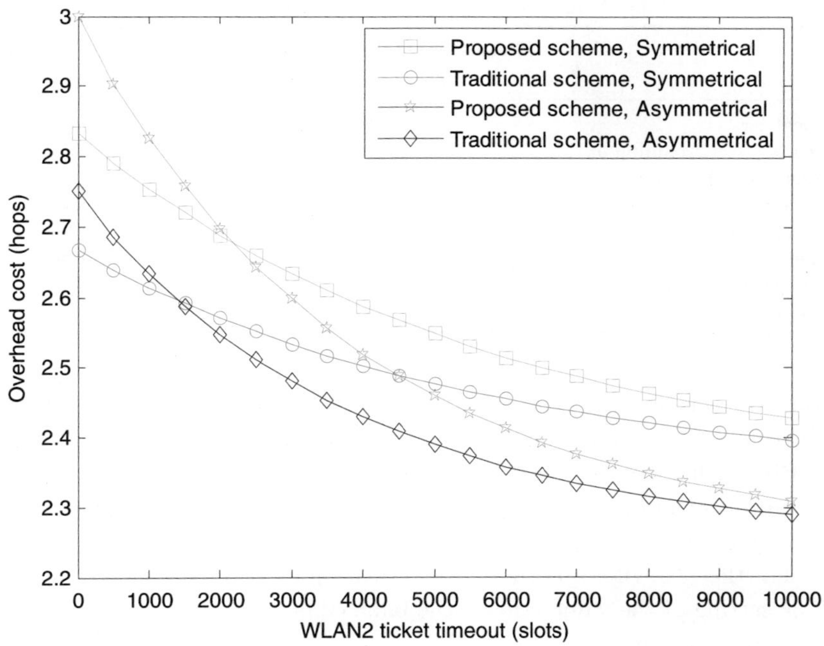


Fig. 17.9. Overhead cost vs. WLAN2 ticket timeout for proposed and traditional schemes.

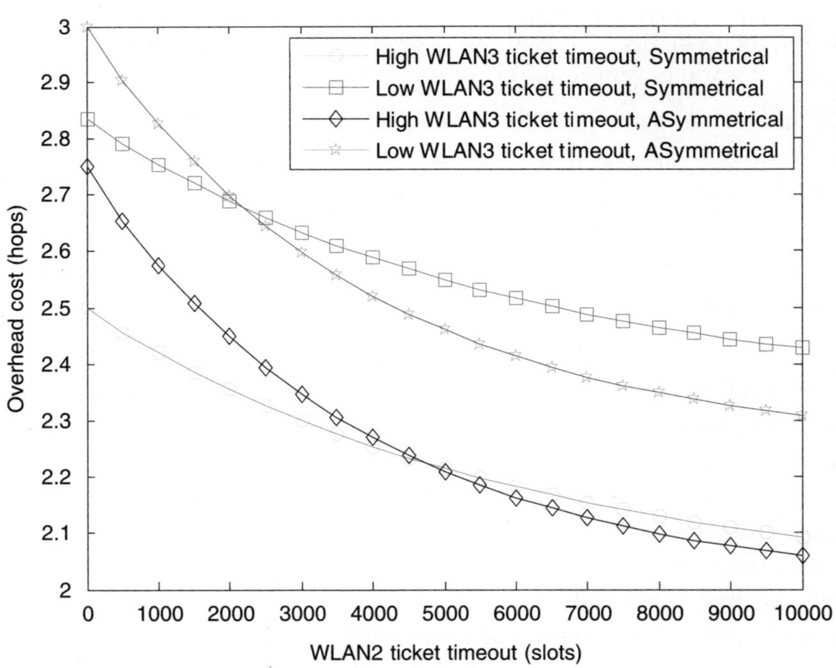


Fig. 17.10. Overhead cost vs. WLAN2 ticket timeout for high and low WLAN3 ticket timeout.

Table 17.6. Comparison of billing support schemes.

| | Event ID billing support | Cellular network billing support | Billing support in [9] |
|---|---|---|---|
| Local service | Yes | Yes | Yes |
| Peer-to-peer. roaming auth. | Yes | Yes | Yes |
| Agent based roaming auth. | Yes | No | No |
| Localized/cached auth. | Yes | No | No |
| Service offered by agent | Yes | No | No |
| Adaptive | Good | Poor | Poor |
| Mutual undeniable | Yes | No | Yes |
| Computation | Low | Low | High |

From the performance analysis, it is observed that the ticket greatly reduces the authentication latency. However the ticket also allows the *FA* to link the *MT*'s current PID with the previous PID stored in its database. On the other hand, the latency improvement becomes smaller and smaller when the ticket timeout increases. Therefore, it is neither suitable nor necessary to choose very large ticket expiration time so that the *MT* will do normal authentication to break the linage from time to time. The setting of the value reflects the balance between the latency performance and the identity intraceability strength.

### 17.5.3. *Characteristics Comparison of Billing Support*

The proposed event ID billing support can accommodate various user authentication scenarios in both local and roaming network access. Table 17.6 shows that the advantages of the proposed billing support scheme over billing support used in cellular network is the capability of adaptively handling special modes, such as re-visiting and agent based network access service, for the integrated network. Since *PID* is used to index the usage record, user anonymity is preserved in billing messages.

## 17.6. Conclusions

In this chapter, a service agent based WLAN/cellular network integrated service model, and relevant authentication and event-tracking for billing support schemes have been proposed. The service model does not require cumbersome peer-to-peer roaming agreements to support seamless user roaming between WLAN hotspots and cellular networks operated by independent wireless network service providers. The proposed authentication and event-tracking schemes take both anonymity and intraceability of the mobile users into consideration, and operate independently so that the integrated billing service can be applied to the cellular networks even if they still use the traditional authentication scheme. Both Security analysis and overhead evaluation have demonstrated the security and the efficiency of the proposed WLAN/cellular network integrated service model.

## Acknowledgements

This work has been partially supported by a grant from the Bell University Laboratories (BUL) and a Natural Sciences and Engineering Research Council (NSERC) of Canada Postdoctoral Fellowship.

## References

[1] Cisco Systems Inc., "Wireless LAN Technologies, Products, & Trends," *Technical report*, Apr. 2004.

[2] C. Perkins, "IP mobility support for IPv4," *IETF RFC 3344*, 2002.

[3] D. Johnson, C. Perkins, and J. Arkko, "Mobility support in IPv6," *IETF RFC 3775*, 2004.

[4] M. Buddhikot, G. Chandranmenon, S. Han, Y.W. Lee, S. Miller, and L. Salgarelli, "Integration of 802.11 and third-generation wireless data networks," *Proc. of IEEE INFOCOM'03*, Vol. 1, pp. 503–512, Apr. 2003.

[5] G. Rose and G.M. Koien, Access security in CDMA2000, including a comparison with UMTS access security, *IEEE Wireless Communications Special Issue on Mobility and Resource Management*, Vol. 11, pp. 19–25, 2004.

[6] G.M. Koien, "An introduction to access security in UMTS," *IEEE Wireless Communications*, Vol. 11, pp. 8–18, 2004.

[7] W. Song, W. Zhuang, and A. Saleh, "Interworking of 3G cellular networks and wireless LANs," *Int. J. Wireless and Mobile Computing*, Vol. 2, pp. 237–247, 2007.

[8] S. Mohanty, "A new architecture for 3G and WLAN integration and inter-system handover management," *Wireless Networks* Vol. 12, pp. 733–745, 2006.

[9] Y. Li, K.-W. Lee, J.-E. Kang, and Y.-Z. Cho, "A novel loose coupling interworking scheme between UMTS and WLAN systems for multihomed mobile stations," *Proc. of the 5th ACM international workshop on Mobility management and wireless access* pp. 155–158, Oct. 2007.

[10] V.W.-S. Feng, L.-Y. Wu, Y.-B. Lin, and W.E. Chen, "WGSN: WLAN-based GPRS environment support node with push mechanism," *The Computer Journal*, Vol. 47, pp. 405–417, 2004.

[11] M. Shi, L. Xu, X. Shen, and J.W. Mark, "Fast vertical handoff for cellular and WLAN interworking," *Wiley's Wireless Communications and Mobile Computing*, Vol. 7, pp. 82–89, 2008.

[12] M. Buddhikot, G. Chandranmenon, S. Han, Y.W. Lee, S. Miller, and L. Salgarelli, "Design and implementation of a WLAN/cdma2000 interworking architecture," *IEEE Communications Magazine*, Vol. 41, pp. 90–100, 2003.

[13] M. Shi, X. Shen, and J.W. Mark, "IEEE802.11 roaming and authentication in wireless LAN/cellular mobile networks," *IEEE Wireless Communications*, Vol. 11, pp. 66–75, Aug. 2004.

[14] J. Zhou and K.-Y. Lam, "Undeniable billing in Mobile Communications," *MOBICOM'98*, pp. 284–290, 1998.

[15] 3GPP, "Universal Mobile Telecommunications System (UMTS); characteristics of the universal subscriber identity module (USIM) application," *3GPP TS 31.102 version 7.4.1 Release 7*, 2006.

[16] M. Hazas, J. Scott, and J. Krumm, "Location-aware computing comes of age," *IEEE Computer*, Vol. 37, pp. 95–97, 2004.

[17] S. Patel, "Weakness of northern American wireless authentication protocol," *IEEE Personal Communications Magazine*, Vol. 4, pp. 40–44, 1997.

[18] M. Burrows, M. Abadi, and R. Needham, "A logic of authentication," *ACM Transactions on Computer Systems*,1990.

[19] B. Schneier, *Applied Cryptography: Protocols, Algorithms, and Source Code in C, 2nd Edition*: Wiley, 1996.

[20] D.S. Wong and A.H. Chan, "Mutual authentication and key exchange for low power wireless communications," *Proc. of IEEE Military Communications Conf., MILCOM 2001*, Vol. 1, pp. 39–43, 2001.

[21] K. Shim, "Cryptanalysis of mutual authentication and key exchange for low power wireless communications," *IEEE Communications Letters*, Vol. 7, pp. 248–250, 2003.

[22] S.L. Ng and C. Mitchell, "Comments on mutual authentication and key exchange protocols for low power wireless communications," *IEEE Communications Letters*, Vol. 8, pp. 262–263, 2004.

[23] R.A. Howard, *Dynamic Probabilistic Systems - Volume I: Markov Models*: Dover Publications, 1971.

# Chapter 18

## CONSTRUCTION OF FAULT-TOLERANT VIRTUAL BACKBONES IN WIRELESS NETWORKS

Donghyun Kim[†], Xiaofeng Gao[‡], Feng Zou[§] and Weili Wu[*,¶]
[†]*Department of Mathematics and Computer Science, North Carolina Central University, 1801 Fayetteville St. Durham, NC27707, USA*
[‡]*School of Science and Technology, Georgia Gwinnett College, 1000 University Center Lane, Lawrenceville, GA 30043, USA*
*Department of Computer Science, University of Texas at Dallas, 800 W. Campbell Road, Richardson, TX 75080, USA*
[†]*donghyun.kim@nccu.edu*
[‡]*xgao@gcc.edu*
[§]*phenix.zou@student.utdallas.edu*
[¶]*weiliwu@utdallas.edu*

Many people have been studying wireless networks due to their usefulness. For many years, people studied virtual backbones for wireless networks to make the network more energy-efficient and practical. Frequently, people design a virtual backbone as a subset of nodes which is 1-connected and adjacent to all other non-backbone nodes. The topology of wireless network can changes frequently due to many reasons. Therefore, a virtual backbone can be broken easily and becomes useless. In this article, we study the problem of computing the minimum $k$-connected $m$-dominating set, which models the question of how to construct fault-tolerant virtual backbones for wireless networks. We summarize recent solutions from many literatures and introduce related theoretical results. At the end, we make a conclusion and discuss future research directions.

### 18.1. Introduction

Wireless networks including ad-hoc and sensor networks are composed of a number of wireless mobile nodes. A wireless node usually has a relatively short data transmission range and therefore a signal generated by one node can only arrive at those nodes within the maximum transmission range of the sender. There is no pre-defined physical backbone infrastructure for message routing and topology control in wireless networks. Thus, any two nodes can communicate with each

*This work is supported in part by National Science Foundation under grant CCF-9208913 and CCF-0728851.

other directly only if they are within the maximum transmission range of each other. Otherwise, messages have to be relayed through some intermediate nodes to reach their destinations. In this way, a set of wireless nodes can construct a network temporarily. Because of such characteristic, wireless networks have a broad range of applications such as disaster rescue, environmental monitoring, battlefield surveillance, conferences, concert, traffic control, health applications, etc. [1,2].

To make a wireless network more cost-effective and practical, some issues have to be resolved. The worse of all, there are many cases in which wireless nodes have a limited source of energy and are not rechargeable. In this reason, it is very important to develop proper management schemes to extend the lifetime of wireless networks. One important management scheme is "routing" because in wireless network, a node consumes most of its energy for communication rather than other activities including computation. Recently, Ni *et al.* have shown in their simulations that flooding scheme which is served as a building block of many existing routing algorithms causes significant amount of collisions and is very energy inefficient [3].

It is generally believed that Ephremides *et al.* made the first attempt to introduce a backbone-like structure of telephone networks to wireless networks [4]. In a wireless network employing the virtual backbone, a node in the network can be either a backbone node or not. Any non-backbone node has to be adjacent to at least one backbone node. In addition, the set of backbone nodes has to be connected. Then, the routing path search space for each message is reduced from the whole network to the set of backbone nodes. Introducing a virtual backbone to a wireless network has several apparent benefits. Most of all, by limiting the number of nodes involved in message routing, less nodes need to maintain routing information. Therefore, any routing protocol over virtual backbone can converge faster. Also, the amount of collisions inside the networks, which is the major contributor of the critical broadcasting storm problem, is reduced. Recently, Shang *et al.* showed that by introducing virtual backbones into a wireless network, the overhead of major routing algorithms can be reduced dramatically [5]. At last, the backbone can be used to support broadcasting and multicasting in wireless networks.

It is obvious that the benefits of a virtual backbone can be magnified if its size is reduced. In this reason, many people focus on constructing smaller virtual backbones [6–31]. Guha and Kuller first used Connected Dominating Set (CDS) to model the problem of generating a smallest virtual backbone [6]. Since computing a minimum CDS is one of well-known early NP-hard problems introduced and proved by Garey and Johnson [32], Guha and Kuller introduced approximation algorithms to compute small size CDSs in general graphs which represent homogeneous wireless networks. So far, there have been extensive researches about designing a good approximation algorithm for this problem.

One remarkable characteristic of wireless networks is that their topology can be altered frequently due to the mobility, energy exhaustion, or temporal communication error of wireless nodes. Therefore, in a wireless network employing a virtual backbone, a non-backbone node may lose every adjacent backbone node or the backbone itself can be disconnected due to the reasons and the lifetime of the virtual backbone can be shortened, which is undesirable. To make virtual backbones more cost-effective and practical, the virtual backbone has to be fault-tolerant. The requirements of the fault-tolerance can be summarized as follows. First, each non-backbone node has to be adjacent to multiple backbone nodes so that when some of neighboring backbone nodes die, the non-backbone node still can send and receive messages. Second, to make the backbone structure resilient from the node failures, it must be multiple-connected.

Dai and Wu first noticed the necessity of fault-tolerance for virtual backbones and proposed the problem of computing $k$-connected $m$-dominating set in which $k$ and $m$ are system parameters which decide the degree of fault-tolerance of the CDS [26]. They also introduced three algorithms to compute $k$-connected $k$-dominating set. The first one is a probabilistic algorithm, namely $k$-Gossip, which is an extension of Gossip algorithm in [33]. In Gossip algorithm, to reduce the amount of message duplications in flooding, a node forwards a message it received with a probability $p$. Similarly, in $k$-Gossip, a node joins current CDS with a probability $p_k$. The second is a deterministic algorithm, which can be recognized as an extension of the coverage condition in [34]. The last one is also a probabilistic algorithm, namely, Color-Based $k$-CDS Construction. This algorithm first partitions the whole graph into several parts and then computes a CDS for each pecie. Later, the union of the CDSs becomes a $k$-connected $k$-dominating set. All of three algorithms are localized ones but none of them guarantees the size bound of resulting CDSs. Wang *et al.* introduced Connecting Dominating Set Augmentation (CDSA), which is a centralized algorithm to compute 2-connected 1-dominating set and showed that its performance ratio is 54.154 [27]. CDSA is based on the observation that two 2-connected subgraph in a graph can be augmented by adding a path from the subgraph to the other part of the graph. The work by Shang *et al.* introduces three centralized approximation algorithms [30]. The first one computes a 1-connected 1-dominating set by using an algorithm in [13] and evolves it to a 1-connected $m$-dominating set by adding $m-1$ MISs. The second algorithm increases the connectivity of a 1-connected $m$-dominating set using an idea similar with Wang *et al.*'s in [27]. The last algorithm assumes the existence of an approximation algorithm to compute $k$-connected $k$-dominating set and develops it to a $k$-connected $m$-dominating set by adding MISs $(m-k)$ times.

My T. Thai *et al.* first introduced a centralized approximation algorithm to compute $k$-connected $m$-dominating set [28]. This work assumes an input graph is $\max(k, m)$ connected and consists of three sub-algorithms [28]. The first one is for computing a 1-connected $m$-dominating set. The second one calculates a $k$-connected $k$-dominating set based on the first algorithm. The last one builds a $k$-connected $m$-dominating set using the second algorithm. Recently, Wu *et al.* proposed a centralized approximation algorithm, CGA, and a distributed algorithm, DDA, to compute $k$-connected $m$-dominating sets for any $k$ and $m$ pair [29]. CGA is a simple algorithm which first computes 1-connected $m$-dominating set and later makes it $k$-connected. The basic strategy of CGA is that it first adds nodes to a subset of nodes until the set becomes $m$-dominating set and later keeps

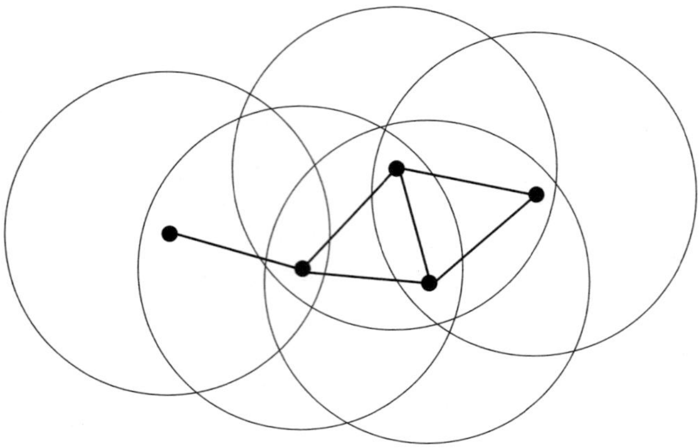

Fig. 18.1. An example of unit disk graph.

inserting nodes to the set until a subgraph induced by this set becomes $k$-connected. DDA is a 3-phase algorithm and the first distributed approximation algorithm to compute $k$-connected $m$-dominating sets. More recently, Wu *et al.* proposed two approximation algorithms, ICGA and LDA, which are the improved versions of CGA and DDA, respectively [31].

In this article, we focus on the construction of fault-tolerant virtual backbones for homogeneous wireless networks, which can be modeled as the $k$-connected $m$-dominating set problem. Existing algorithms for this problem can be categorized into probabilistic and deterministic ones. The deterministic ones can be classified as centralized and distributed ones. In the rest of this article, we summarize the recent literatures related to each category. At the end, we also discuss about future research directions.

## 18.2. Notations and Definitions

In this section, we introduce some notations and definitions which are repeatedly used in the rest of this chapter. $G = (V, E)$ represents a connected graph, which consists of a set of vertices $V = V(G)$ and a set of edges $E = E(G)$. Depending on context, $G$ can be unidirectional or bidirectional.

To embed a physical wireless network to a graph, the following two models which are frequently used.

**Definition 18.1 (Unit Disk Graph).** A graph $G = (V, E)$ is called a Unit Disk Graph (UDG) if for any two nodes $v, u \in V$, which are the centers of same size disks, there is a bidirectional edge between $v$ and $u$ if and only if the distance between the two nodes is no more than the unit distance, 1.

Huson and Sen first used a UDG to model a homogenous wireless networks [36]. In a UDG, each vertex represents a node in the network and a disk whose center is $v$

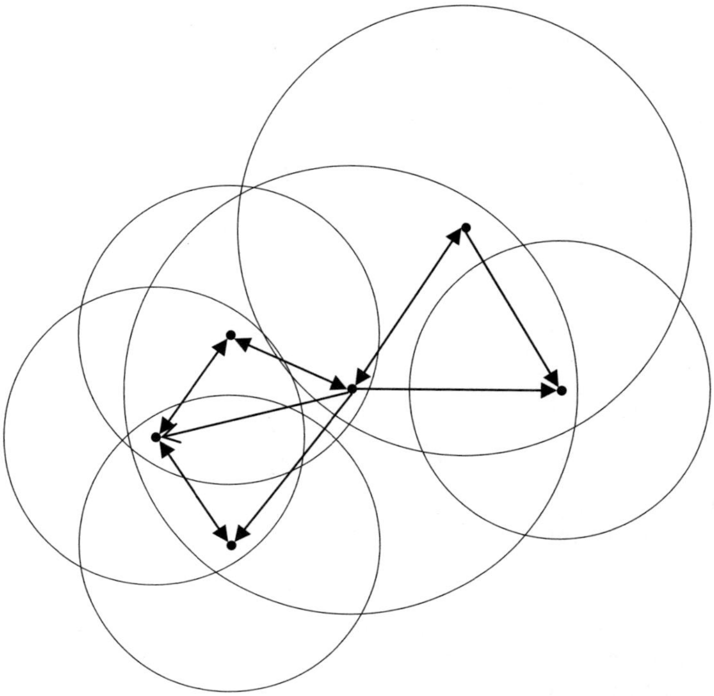

Fig. 18.2. An example of disk graph.

is the communication range of $v$. Since all nodes have the same physical properties, the size of each disk is same. There is an edge between two vertices $u$ and $v$ if $u$ is inside $v$'s disk or vice versa. More detailed information about UDG can be found in [37].

**Definition 18.2 (Disk Graph).** A graph $G = (V, E)$ is called a Disk Graph (DG) if for any two nodes $v, u \in V$ and $r$, which is the radius of a disk whose center is $v$, there is a directional edge from $v$ to $u$ if and only if the distance from $v$ to $u$ is no more than $r$.

Unlike UDG, DG is usually used to model non-homogeneous wireless networks in which nodes may have different transmission ranges and thus there can be a directional link between nodes. Since UDG is a subset of DG, any algorithm working in DGs can work in UDGs.

**Definition 18.3 (Disk Graph with Bidirectional Links).** A DG $G = (V, E)$ is called a DG with Bidirectional links (DGB) if every edge in $E(G)$ is bidirectional.

**Definition 18.4 (Dominating Set).** A Dominating Set (DS) of a graph $G$ is a subset $V'(G) \subseteq V(G)$ such that $\forall(v, w) \in E(G)$, $v \in V'(G)$ or $w \in V'(G)$.

In graph theory, Independent Set (IS) is a set of nodes which are not adjacent to each other. We say an IS $I$ of $G$ is a Maximal Independent Set (MIS) of $G$ if we

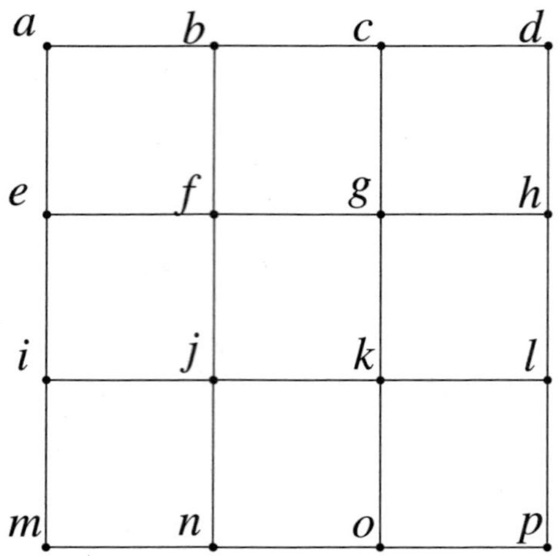


Fig. 18.3. An example 2-connected graph. $A = \{a, c, j, l, m, o\}$ is a DS. $B = A \cup \{b, f, i, k\}$ is a CDS. $C = \{a, c, f, h, i, k, n, p\}$ is a 2-DS. $D = C \cup \{b, d, e, l, m, o\}$ is a 2-CDS.

add any node from $G \setminus I$ to $I$, $I$ is not an IS anymore. Since an MIS of $G$ is a DS of $G$ and generating an MIS is very easy, computing an MIS is one of popular way to generate a DS. Computing a minimum size DS is a very well-known NP-hard problem [35]. Also, finding a minimum size IS is NP-hard.

**Definition 18.5 (Connected Dominating Set).** A Connected Dominating Set (CDS) $C$ of $G$ is a DS of $G$ such that a subgraph of $G$ induced by $C$ is connected.

In many papers, nodes in a CDS are mentioned as the **dominators**, and outside the CDS as the **dominatees**. One easy way to generate a CDS is computing an MIS $I$ first and then connecting $I$ using a Steiner tree or spanning tree algorithm. CDS problem is used to model the problem of computing a minimum-size virtual backbone for wireless networks in [6] for the first time. Recently, this is the most popular approach to build a CDS in this research field.

**Definition 18.6 ($m$-Dominating Set).** $V'(G) \subseteq V(G)$ is a $m$-Dominating Set ($m$-DS) of $G$ if all nodes not in $V'(G)$ has at least $m$ distinct neighbors in $V'(G)$.

**Definition 18.7 ($k$-Vertex Connectivity).** $G$ is $k$-vertex connected if $G \setminus G'$ is still connected for any $G' \subseteq G$ such that $|V(G')| \leq k - 1$.

**Definition 18.8 ($k$-Connected $m$-Dominating Set).** A $k$-DS is a $k$-Connected $m$-Dominating Set of $G$ if a subgraph induced by a $m$-DS of $G$ is $k$-vertex connected.

In this paper, both $(k, m)$-CDS and $C_{k,m}$ represent a $k$-connected $m$-dominating set. Also, $k$-CDS is $(k, k)$-CDS.

**Definition 18.9 (Open and Closed Neighbor Set).** For any $v \in V$, $N(v) = \{u|(v,u) \in E\}$ is called the open neighbor set of $v$ and $N[v] = N(v) \cup \{v\}$ is called the closed neighbor set of $v$.

**Definition 18.10 (Separating Set and Cut-Vertex).** A separating set of a graph $G$ is a subset $S \subseteq V(G)$ such that $G \backslash S$ is a disconnected graph. When $|S| = 1$, the only element of $S$ is called to a cut-vertex.

**Definition 18.11 (Block and $k$-Block).** We call $B \subseteq V(G)$ as a block if $B$ is a maximal connected subgraph with no cut-vertex. Similarly, $k$-block is defined as a maximal $k$-connected subgraph of $G$ with no separating set whose size is less then $k$.

**Definition 18.12 (Leaf Block and $k$-Leaf Block).** A leaf block of $G$ is a block in $G$ having only one cut-vertex. Likewise, a $k$-leaf block is a $k$-block having only one separating set whose size is $k-1$.

## 18.3. Probabilistic Schemes

In this section, we describe two localized algorithms to find a $k$-CDS of a DG $G$. Since both of them are probabilistic algorithms, their final outcomes may not be $k$-CDSs. On the other hand, by adjusting system parameters, the chance of having a $k$-CDS can be improved.

**$k$-Gossip [26]** Originally, Gossip protocol was introduced by Hou and Tipper to alleviate the problem of flooding-based routing algorithm [33]. In this protocol, each node has a probability $p$ and with this probability, it forwards a message received. Based on the Gossip protocol, Dai and Wu proposed $k$-Gossip, which can be recognized as an extension of Gossip, in which each node has a backbone status with a probability $p_k$ [26]. Even though $k$-Gossip is intended to compute $k$-CDSs, by modifying $p_k$ value, it can be used to get $(k,m)$-CDSs with high probability.

$k$-Gossip is a localized algorithm and works on DG. The perfect value of $p_k$ for a wireless network, which leads to the construction of a small $k$-CDS, depends on $k$, the number of nodes $n$ in the network, the size of deploy area, and the maximum transmission range of each node. The upper bound of $p_k$ that makes $k$-gossip algorithms to almost always have $k$ coverage in a network is studied by Kumar, Lai, and Balogh [34]. $k$-Gossip does not require any control message exchange between nodes and incurs very low overhead at each node. The smaller $p_k$ value is, the lower the probability of successfully constructing a $k$-CDS within a trial is. Similarly, with a larger $p_k$ value, the expected size of a $k$-CDS, $n \times p_k$, can be increased greatly.

**Color-Based $k$-CDS Construction [26]** Color-Based $k$-CDS Construction (CBKC) is a probabilistic localized algorithm to compute a $k$-CDS in a DG [26]. This algorithm divides all nodes in a graph into $k$ parts and computes a CDS for each partition such that the union of every CDS is $k$-CDS with high probability. More detailed algorithm is as below.

**Algorithm 18.1** CBKC (G (V,E), k).

Each $v \in V(G)$ picks a random color $c(1 \leq c \leq k)$. Then, $V(G)$ is divided into $k$ disjoint subsets $V_1(G), V_2(G), \ldots, V_k(G)$. Each $V_c(G)$ contains nodes with color $c$.
For each color $c$, a localized 1-CDS algorithm $\mathcal{A}$ is applied to construct a virtual backbone $V_c'(G) \subset V_c(G)$ that covers the original network.
$\cup_{c=1}^{k} V_c'(G)$ is a $k$-CDS.

CBKC does not guarantee that the resulting subgraph is a $k$-CDS. However, the authors showed that if every node in the network is randomly deployed in a finite square area and the node number is more than a constant $n_k$, then CBKC almost always generates a $k$-CDS.

## 18.4. Deterministic Schemes

### 18.4.1. *Centralized Algorithms*

**CDS Augmentation Algorithm for Constructing (2, 1)-CDS [27]** Wang *et al.* noticed that there is no approximation algorithm to construct an approximation algorithm for computing $(k, m)$-CDS and proposed the CDS Augmentation Algorithm (CDSA) to compute $(2, 1)$-CDS of a UDG [27]. Basically, CDSA generates a 1-CDS in a graph firstly by any existing approximation algorithm and then iteratively increases the subgraph of the 1-CDS so that it can be 2-connected. In each augmentation step, CDSA finds a block, which is a 2-connected subgraph, and adds a path between the block and the rest of the 1-CDS so that the block can be augmented. More detailed algorithm description is as follows.

**Algorithm 18.2** CBKC (G (V,E)).

1: If $G$ is not 2-connected, stop the algorithm and returns error. Otherwise, execute any 1-CDS computation algorithm and get $C$, which is a 1-CDS of $G$.
2: Find every block of $C$. We call the list of all blocks in $C$ as $B$.
3: **while** $B$ has more than one block **do**
4: Find one leaf block $L$ in $B$.
5: For all $u \in L$ and all $v \in V \setminus L$, pick $u$ and $v$ such that the shortest path between $u$ and $v$ over $V \setminus \{C \cup L\}$ can be minimized. Let $P$ be the set of nodes in this path. Then, update $C = C \cup P$.
6: **end while**

**Lemma 18.1.** *At each augmentation in Line* 4 *of Algorithm* 18.2*, at most* 8 *nodes are added* [27].

**Theorem 18.1.** *The approximation ratio of CDSA is* 62.154 [27].

**Proof.** We denote $OPT$, $MCDS$, $CDS$, and $2CDS$ as a minimal $(2,1)$-CDS, a minimal 1-CDS, a 1-CDS computed by any 1-CDS algorithm, and $(2,1)$-CDS computed by this algorithm, respectively. To compute a 1-CDS, Min *et al.*'s 8-approximation algorithm can be used and we have $|CDS| \leq 8|MCDS| + 1$ [18]. By Lemma 18.1, $|2CDS| \leq |CDS| + 8(|CDS| - 1) = 9|CDS| - 8$. In summary, $|2CDS| \leq 9|CDS| - 8 \leq 9(8|MCDS| + 1) - 8 \leq 9(8|OPT| + 1) - 8 = 72|OPT| + 1$ for all $|OPT| \geq 2$. Recently, Kim *et al.* proposed a 6.906-approximation algorithm to compute 1-CDS [25] and if this is used, the performance ratio of CDSA can be improved to $6.906 + 8 \times 6.906 = 62.154$. □

**A Centralized Algorithm for Constructing $(1,m)$-CDS and $(2,m)$-CDS [30]** The main contribution of this paper is that it introduced the first approximation algorithm to compute $(1,m)$-CDS and and $(2,m)$-CDS of a UDG. In addition, given the existence of an approximation algorithm to compute $(k,k)$-CDS, it shows how to compute $(k,m)$-CDS.

(1) **Algorithm for Computing $(1,m)$-CDS**: The basic idea of this algorithm is that first compute 1-CDS and repeatedly add an MIS for $k-1$ times. Then, the union of a 1-CDS and $k-1$ MISs is $(1,m)$-CDS. A more formal description of the algorithm is as below.

---

**Algorithm 18.3** for computing $(1,m)$-CDS.

Choose an MIS $I_1$ of $G$ and a set $C$ such that $I_1 \cup C$ is a 1-CDS.
**for** $i = 2$ to $m$ **do**
    Construct an MIS $I_i$ in $G \setminus (I_1 \cup \cdots \cup I_{i-1})$.
**end for**
$D_A = I_1 \cup \cdots \cup I_m \cup C$.
Return $D_A$.

---

Since this algorithm is used as a building block in other algorithms, we present the detailed performance analysis of this algorithm more detail. Lemma 18.2 shows the relationship between an MIS and a $m$-dominating set.

**Lemma 18.2.** *Let $G = (V, E)$ be a UDG and $m$ be a natural number such that $\delta(G) \geq m - 1$, where $\delta(G)$ is the minimum degree of $G$. Let $D^*_m$ be a minimum $m$-dominating set of $G$ and $I$ an MIS of $G$. Then $|I| \leq max\{\frac{5}{m}, 1\}|D^*_m|$* [30].

**Proof.** Denote $I_0 = I \cap D^*_m$, $X = I \setminus I_0$, and $Y = D^*_m \setminus I_0$. Also, for all $u \in X$, let $c_u = |N(u) \cap Y|$ and for all $v \in Y$, let $d_v = |N(v) \cap X|$. Then, the followings are true. First, $X$ and $Y$ are two disjoin set by their definition. Second, $\sum_{u \in X} c_u \geq m|X|$ since $D^*_m$ is a $m$-dominating set of $G$. Third, since in a UDG, a node can have at most five independent neighbors, $d_v \leq 5$ and therefore, $5|Y| \geq \sum_{v \in Y} d_v$. Fourth, $|X| \leq \frac{5}{m}|Y|$ is true since $\sum_{u \in X} c_u = |\{(u,v) \in E : u \in X, v \in Y\}| = \sum_{v \in Y} d_v$. At last, $|I| = |X| + |I_0| \leq \frac{5}{m}|D^*_m \setminus I_0| + |I_0| \leq max\{\frac{5}{m}, 1\}|D^*_m|$. □

**Theorem 18.2.** *Algorithm* 18.3 *generates* $(1, m)$*-CDS correctly and its performance ratio is* $(5 + \frac{5}{m})$ *for* $m \le 5$ *and* 7 *for* $m > 5$ [30].

**Proof.** Assume $D_A = I_1 \cup \cdots \cup I_m \cup C$ is generated by Algorithm 18.3. Let $D_m^*$ be a minimum $m$-dominating set of $G$. Now, suppose $v \in V(G) \setminus D_A$ is not $m$-dominated by $D_A$. Since for $1 \le i \le m$, each $I_i$ is an MIS of nodes in $V(G) \setminus (I_1 \cup \cdots \cup I_i)$, $v$ has to have at least one neighbor in each $I_i$. Therefore, $v$ must have at least $m$ neighbors in $D_A$ and $D_A$ is a $m$-dominating set.

Now, denote $S_i = I_i \cap D_m^*$ for $1 \le i \le m$. Then, in Algorithm 18.3, each $I_i \setminus S_i$ is an independent set and $(I_i \setminus S_i) \cap D_m^* = \emptyset$. Then by Lemma 18.2, $|I_i \setminus S_i| \le \frac{5}{m}|D_m^* \setminus S_i|$ and

$$|I_i \cup \cdots \cup I_m| = \sum_{i=1}^{m} |S_i| + \sum_{i=1}^{m} |I_i \setminus S_i| \le \sum_{i=1}^{m} |S_i| + \sum_{i=1}^{m} \frac{5}{m}|D_m^* \setminus S_i|$$

$$= \left(1 - \frac{5}{m}\right) \sum_{i=1}^{m} |S_i| + 5|D_m^*|.$$

In addition, since $\sum_{i=1}^{m} |S_i| \le |D_m^*|$, $|I_1 \cup \cdots \cup I_m| \le 5|D_m^*|$ for $m \le 5$ and $|I_1 \cup \cdots \cup I_m| \le 6|D_m^*|$ for $m > 5$. In some $C_{1,1}$ construction algorithm like the one in [13] or CDS-BD-C2 in [25], $|C| \le |I_1|$ and by Lemma 18.2, $|C| \le max\{\frac{5}{m}, 1\}|D_m^*|$. In conclusion, the size of $D_A$, which is a $m$-dominating set by Algorithm 18.3 is bounded by $(5 + \frac{5}{m})|D_m^*|$ for $m \le 5$ and $7|D_m^*|$ for $m > 5$ and the theorem holds true. □

(2) **Algorithm for Computing** $(2, m)$**-CDS**: The basic idea of this algorithm is firstly computing $(1, m)$-CDS using Algorithm 18.3, and then increasing its connectivity using the idea of Wang *et al.*'s [27]. More specifically, this algorithm consists of the following four steps.

---

**Algorithm 18.4** for computing $(2, m)$-CDS.

---

1: Use Algorithm 18.3 to construct a $C_{1,m}$ and set $D_B = C_{1,m}$.
2: Computes all blocks in the $C_{1,m}$ using the depth first search. For this purpose, the algorithm proposed by Tarjan *et al.* [39] can be used.
3: Pick a leaf block $L$. Find a shortest path $P$ between $L$ and $V(G) \setminus L$ such that $P$ must be adjacent to a non cut-vertex in $L$ and $P \cup L = \emptyset$. Then, add all nodes in $P$ to $D_B$.
4: Repeat Step 2 and 3 until $D_B$ is 2-connected.

---

To analyze the upper bound of $D_B$, which is a $(2, m)$-CDS, we need to know how many nodes are added to make the $C_{1,m}$ in Line 1 of Algorithm 18.3 to be 2-connected.

**Lemma 18.3.** *In Line* 3 *of Algorithm* 18.4, *P contains at most* 2 *nodes* [30].

One remarkable characteristic of MIS is that the distance between two nearest MIS nodes is at most three hops, and by this property Lemma 18.3 can be proved.

**Lemma 18.4.** *The number of cut-vertices in $C_{1,m}$ by Algorithm 18.3 is bounded by the number of vertices in $D_A$ which is 1-CDS and generated at the first step of Algorithm 18.3 [30].*

It is easy to see that the number of cut-vertices in any $C_{1,1}$ is bounded by its size (i.e. the number of nodes in it). Also, making $C_{1,1}$ to a $m$-dominating set does not increase the number of cut-vertex since if a leaf block $L$ has a cut-vertex $v$, $v$ has to belong to $C_{1,1}$.

**Theorem 18.3.** *The approximation ratio of Algorithm 18.4 is $(5+\frac{25}{m})$ for $2 \le m \le 5$ and 11 for $m > 5$ [30].*

**Proof.** Denote $D^*_m$ be an optimal $(1,m)$-CDS and $D_{opt}$ be an optimal $(2,m)$-CDS. Then, $D^*_m \le D_{opt}$. By Lemmas 18.3 and 18.4, at most $2|C_{1,1}|$ are added to make $|C_{1,m}|$ to $|C_{2,m}|$, where $C_{1,1}$ is a 1-connected 1-dominating set by the first step of Algorithm 18.3 and $C_{1,m}$ is the output of Algorithm 18.3. Since $C_{1,1} = |C| + |I_1|$ in the Algorithm 18.3 and $|C| \le I_1$, $C_{1,1} = 2|I_1| \le 2max\{\frac{5}{m}, 1\}|D^*_m|$ and $C_{2,m} \le C_{1,m} + 2C_{1,1} \le C_{1,m} + 4max\{\frac{5}{m}, 1\}|D^*_m|$. Therefore, by Theorem 18.2, $|D_B| \le (5+\frac{25}{m})|D_{opt}|$ for $2 \le m \le 5$ and $|D_B| \le 11|D_{opt}|$ for $m > 5$, where $D_B$ which is $C_{2,m}$ generated by Algorithm 18.4. □

(3) **Algorithm for Computing $(k,m)$-CDS**: This algorithm assumes that we have an $\alpha$-approximation algorithm $A_{(k,k)}$ to compute a $(k,k)$-CDS. If $k < m$, $(k,m)$-CDS can be computed by choosing MIS $m-k$ times with $A_{(k,k)}$. More formal description is as follows.

---

**Algorithm 18.5** for computing $(k,m)$-CDS.

---

Produce $S$, which is a $(k,k)$-CDS of $G$ using algorithm $A_{(k,k)}$
**for** $i = 1$ to $m-k$ **do**
    Generate an MIS $I_i$ from $G \setminus (S \cup I_1 \cup \cdots \cup I_{i-1})$
**end for**
$D_C = I_1 \cup \cdots \cup I_{m-k} \cup S$
return $D_C$

---

**Theorem 18.4.** *If we have an $\alpha$-approximation algorithm $A_{(k,k)}$ for computing k-CDS, then there is an $(\alpha+6)$-approximation algorithm for computing $(k,m)$-CDSs for the case of $k > m$ [30].*

**Proof.** From the proof of Theorem 18.3, we have $|I_1 \cup \cdots \cup I_m| \leq 6|D_{opt}|$, where $|D_{opt}|$ is an optimal $(k,m)$-CDS. Since $|S| \leq \alpha|D_{opt}|$ is given, the performance ratio of Algorithm 18.5 is $\alpha + 6$ for $m > k$. □

**A Centralized Algorithm for Constructing $(k,m)$-CDS [28]** The main contribution of this paper is that it is the first literature that introduces a centralized $(k,m)$-CDS computation algorithm. It presents an algorithm to compute $(1,m)$-CDS and build another algorithm to compute $(k,k)$-CDS based on the first one. Then, the authors explain how to make an approximation algorithm to compute a $(k,m)$-CDS based on the previous results. Unlike many others, the authors assume the input graph of this algorithm is a DGB, which is a more general graph than UDG.

(1) **CDSMIS: Connected Dominating Set by Maximal Independent Set Algorithm for $(1,m)$-CDS**: this algorithm looks similar as Algorithm 18.3. On the other hand, it computes an MIS first and connects them using the algorithm in [23] so that the union of them can be a $C_{1,1}$. The algorithm makes the $C_{1,1}$ to a $C_{1,m}$ by repeatedly selecting an MIS and adding it to the $C_{1,1}$, which is same to Algorithm 18.3's approach. More formal description is as below.

**Algorithm 18.6** CDSMIS for Computing $(1,m)$-CDS.

Construct a 1-CDS $C = I_1 \cup B$ from a given graph $G$, where $I_1$ is an MIS and $B$ is a set of Steiner nodes.
Remove $I_1$ from $G$
**for** $i = 2$ to $m$ **do**
  Construct an MIS $I_i$ in $G \setminus (I_1 \cup \cdots \cup I_{i-1})$
  $C = C \cup I_i$
**end for**
Return $C$

In a non-homogeneous network, the transmission range of each node is different. Let $r_{max}$ and $r_{min}$ be the maximum and minimum transmission range of all nodes inside the network. Then, we define the **transmission range ratio** to $r = \frac{r_{max}}{r_{min}}$. When $r = 1$ in a graph, DGB is equal to UDG. Therefore, all the analysis in this paper can be applied to UDGs.

**Lemma 18.5.** *In Algorithm* 18.6, $|I_1 \cup \cdots \cup I_m| \leq (K+m)|C^*_m|$, *where* $C^*_m$ *is an optimal* $(1,m)$*-CDS* [28].

**Lemma 18.6.** *The size of $B$ in Algorithm* 18.6 *is at most* $(2 + \ln K)C(T^*)$, *where* $C(T^*)$ *is the number of optimal Steiner node to connect* $I_1$ [28].

**Theorem 18.5.** *The approximation ratio of CDSMIS in a DGB is* $(K + m + \ln K + 2)$ [28].

**Proof.** By Lemmas 18.5 and 18.6 , $|C| = |B| + |I_1| \cup \cdots \cup |I_m| \leq (2 + \ln K)$ $C(T^*) + (K + m)|C^*_m| \leq (2 + \ln K)|C^*_1| + (K + m)|C^*_m| \leq (K + m + \ln K + 2)$ $|C^*_m|$, where $C^*_1$ is an optimal 1-CDS. □

(2) **CDSAN: Connected Dominating Set by Adding Nodes for $k$-CDS**: CDSAN is based on CDSMIS. It iteratively increases the connectivity of a $C_{1,k}$, which is computed by CDSMIS. To do this, the authors use the followings idea: if there is at least two $(i + 1)$-blocks in the current $C_{i,k}$, find the shortest path in the original graph such that the path connects a $(i + 1)$-leaf block in $C_{i,k}$ to another part of $C_{i,k}$ and the path does not have any node in $C_{i,k}$ except the two end points. Initially, $i$ is 2 and this procedure is repeated until $C_{1,k}$ becomes $C_{2,k}$. Then $i$ is increased by 1. We go over the two previous steps until we have a $C_{k,k}$. More detailed description of the CDSAN is as follows.

**Lemma 18.7.** *At most* 2 *new nodes are added into* $C$ *at each augmenting step. That is, the shortest path* $P_{ij}$ *has at most* 2 *nodes not in* $C$ [28].

**Lemma 18.8.** *Denote* $C'_{1,k}$ *as a* $(1, k)$*-CDS generated by CDSMIS. Then, we employ at most* $|C'_{1,k}| - 1$ *augmenting steps in each iteration to increase the connectivity of* $C_{i,k}$ *to* $C_{i+1,k}$ *in Algorithm* 18.7 [28].

**Theorem 18.6.** *The performance ratio of CDSAN which computes* $k$*-CDSs is* $(K + \ln K + k + 2)(2k - 1)$ *in a DGB* [28].

**Proof.** Let $C^*_k$ be an optimal $k$-CDS and $C$ be a solution obtained by executing CDSAN. From Theorem 18.5, we already know that $|C'_{1,k}| \leq (K + m + \ln K + 2)|C^*_m|$, where $C'_{1,k}$ be a $(1, k)$-CDS generated by CDSMIS and $C^*_m$ is an optimal $m$-dominating set. Since $C = C'_{1,k} + B$, where $B$ is a set of nodes added by CDSAN to increase the connectivity of $C'_{1,k}$, we need to know the upper bound of $B$. By Lemmas 18.7 and 18.8 , we add at most $|C'_{1,k} - 1|$ nodes to increase the connectivity by one and we have to repeat this $(k - 1)$ times. Therefore, $|C| \leq |C'_{1,k}| + 2(k-1)(|C'_{1,k}| - 1) \leq (2k-1)|C'_{1,k}| \leq (K - \ln K + k + 2)(2k - 1)$ $|C^*_k|$ and the theorem remains true. □

(3) **Solution for $(k, m)$-CDS**: the idea of building a $(k, m)$-CDS in this paper is that first it computes a $C_{1,m}$ using CDSMIS and then, augments it to $C_{k,m}$ using CDSAN. This approach works only if an input graph is $\max(k, m)$-connected. If $m \geq k$, the performance ratio of this algorithm is $|C'_{k,m}| \leq |C'_{1,m}| + 2(k - 1)$ $(|C'_{1,m}| - 1) \leq (2k - 1)|C'_{1,m}| \leq (K + \ln K + m + 2)(2k - 1)|C^*_{k,m}|$, where $|C^*_{k,m}|$ is an optimal $(k, m)$-CDS. On the other hand, if $m < k$, we must compute a $C_{1,k}$ first, instead of $C_{1,m}$ using CDSMIS and augment it to $C_{k,k}$, which is also $C_{k,m}$. In this case, its approximation ratio is that of $C'_{k,k}$.

**Algorithm 18.7** CDSAN for $k$-CDS.

Construct a $(1, k)$-CDS $C$ in a given graph $G$ using Algorithm 18.6.
Set $k' = 2$
Let $B$ be a list of all $k'$-blocks in $C$
**while** $k' \leq k$ **do**
  **while** $B$ includes more than one $k'$-block **do**
    Let $l$ be the list of all $k'$ leaf-blocks in $B$.
    **for** each node $v \in V(L)$ and $v$ is not a node in separating set **do**
      **for** each node $u \in C \setminus V(L)$ **do**
        Build $G'$ from G by deleting all nodes in $C \setminus \{u, v\}$ and all edges adjacent to those nodes
        **if** there is a path between $u$ and $v$ in $G'$ **then**
          Let $P_{uv}$ is the nodes which are in the shortest path between $u$ and $v$ such that $P_{uv} \cup C = \emptyset$
        **end if**
        $P = P \cup P_{uv}$
      **end for**
    **end for**
    $P_{ij}$ = the path with the shortest length in $P$
    $C = C \cup$ intermediate nodes on $P_{ij}$
    Compute all $k'$-blocks in $C$ and put them in $B$.
  **end while**
  $k' + +$
**end while**
Return $C$, which is a $C_{k,k}$

**CGA: A Centralized Heuristic Algorithm for Constructing $(k, m)$-CDS [29]** The centralized approximation algorithm to compute $(k, m)$-CDS by My T. Thai *et al.* assumes that an input graph to the algorithm is at least $\max(k, m)$ connected [28]. Wu *et al.* pointed out this restriction and proposed the CGA, a centralized algorithm for constructing $(k, m)$-CDS for any $k$ and $m$ pair [29]. Algorithm 18.8 is the description of CGA. It consists of two sub-procedures, FINDKMCDS and OPTIMIZATION. In the first procedure, a $(1, m)$-CDS is computed and it is augmented to a $(k, m)$-CDS. In the second one, the resulting $(k, m)$-CDS is optimized. CGA is a heuristic algorithm to generate $(k, m)$-CDS, and its performance ratio is not given. The time complexity of CGA is $O(|V|^{3.5} \cdot |E|)$.

**ICGA: A Centralized Approximation Algorithm for Constructing $(k, m)$-CDS [31]** Before discussing the algorithm itself, we introduce two important lemmas.

**Algorithm 18.8** $CGA(G(V,E),k,m)$.

```
procedure FINDKMCDS(G(V,E), k, m)
    Sort nodes in non-increasing order in G based on their ID.
    C ← ∅
    for i = 1 to |V| do
        if node i has less than m neighbors in C then
            Add node i into C.
        end if
    end for
    while C is not k connected do
        Select one node in V \ C and add it to C.
    end while
end procedure
procedure OPTIMIZATION(C, k, m)
    Sort nodes in non-increasing order in G based on their ID.
    for i = 1 to |C| do
        if node i has more than m neighbors in C then
            if C is still k-connected without node i then
                Delete node i from C.
            end if
        end if
    end for
end procedure
```

**Lemma 18.9.** *Give a $k$-connected graph $G$ and $S$, which is a set of nodes such that each node $x \in S$ has at least $k$ neighbors in $G$, $G \cup S$ is a $k$-connected graph* [31].

**Lemma 18.10.** *Given a $k$-connected graph $G$ and a connected set $F$ such that each node $x \in F$ has at least $k$ neighbors in $G$, $G \cup F$ is a $(k+1)$-connected graph* [31].

Authors in [31] introduced IGCA, which is an improved version of CGA in [29]. The ICGA consists of following the two steps:

(1) Construct a $(1,m)$-CDS, $C'_{1,m}$.
(2) Augment $C'_{1,m}$ for $k$-connectivity using Lemma 18.10.

To construct a $C_{1,1}$, the authors use CDS-BD-C2 in [25]. Denote $C'_{1,1}$ be a $(1,1)$-CDS generated by CDS-BD-C2. Then, IGCA builds a $C'_{1,m}$ from a $C'_{1,1}$ using the idea in Algorithm 18.3. Then, a connected set $F_{1 \le i \le k}$, which $i$-dominates $C'_{i,m}$, is sequentially added to $C'_{i,m}$ according to Lemma 18.10. Algorithm 18.9 below is more detailed description of ICGA.

**Algorithm 18.9** *ICGA*$(G(V,E),k,m)$.

Build a CDS $C'_{1,1}$ using CDS-BD-C2 in [25].
Set $C'_{1,m} = C'_{1,1}$ and color all nodes in $C'_{1,m}$ black.
**while** There is a white node $x \in V(G) \setminus C$ whose black neighbor is less then $m$ **do**
  Denote $n_i$ be the number of white neighbors of a white node $v_i$.
  Pick a node $v_i$ such that $|n_i|$ is the maximum and set $C'_{1,m} = C'_{1,m} \cup \{v_i\}$.
**end while**
**for** $i = 1$ to $k-1$ **do**
  **if** $C'_{i,m}$ is $(i+1)$-connected **then**
    $C'_{i+1,m} = C'_{i,m}$
  **else**
    Find a connected set $F_i$ which can $i$ dominate $C'_{i,m}$.
    Set $C'_{i+1,m} = C'_{1,m} \cup F_i$
  **end if**
**end for**
Remove any redundant nodes from $C'_{k,m}$ by executing the procedure OPTIMIZATION in Algorithm 18.8.
Return $C'_{k,m}$.

**Theorem 18.7.** *The performance ratio of ICGA is f, where*

$$f = \begin{cases} \begin{cases} 5k + \dfrac{5}{m} + 5H_{k-1} & m \le 5 \\ 7k & m \ge 6 \end{cases} & k \le 6 \\ \begin{cases} 7k-7 & m \le 5 \\ 7k & m \ge 6 \end{cases} & k \ge 7 \end{cases},$$

*where $H_{k-1}$ is the $(k-1)$th harmonic number* [31].

### 18.4.2. *Distributed Algorithms*

**$k$-Coverage Condition [26]** In [38], Wu and Dai proposed the following coverage condition to construct a 1-CDS: Assume two nodes $u$ and $w$ are adjacent to a node $v$. Then, $v$ has a non-backbone status if there is a replacement path that connects $u$ and $w$ via several intermediate nodes (if any) with higher priorities than $v$. This condition can be extended to $k$-coverage condition as follows: $v$ has a non-backbone status if $k$ node disjoint replacement paths exist that connect $u$ and $w$ via several intermediate nodes (if any) with higher ID's than $v$ [26]. By applying this rule to a $k$-connected $k$-dominating graph $G$, we can get a $k$-CDS of $G$. In detail, at the beginning, we set $C_{k,k}$ as an empty set. For each pair of nodes which are adjacent to the same node $v$, the algorithm checks whether there are $k$ disjoint path which consist of nodes in $C_{k,k}$. If not, $v$ must be added to $C_{k,k}$. For this computation, maximum flow algorithm can be used. Thus, to verify if two neighbors are $k$-connected, it takes $O(k\delta^2)$ time and the overall computation cost at each node is $O(k\delta^4)$, where $\delta$ is the maximum degree.

**The First Distributed Approximation Algorithm for Constructing $(k,m)$-CDS [29]** This algorithm, DDA in short, is the first deterministic distributed algorithm to compute $(k,m)$-CDS with performance ratio analysis. DDA consists of three steps. In the first steps, DDA computes $(1,1)$-CDS by using a localized (1,1)-CDS construction algorithm, $r$-CDS in [19]. To build a $(1,m)$-CDS, DDA adds $m-1$ MISs to the (1,1)-CDS by using MIS computation algorithm in $r$-CDS. In the last step, DDA adds more nodes to the $(1,m)$-CDS so that it can be $k$-connected. The last step follows Lemma 18.11 below and it guarantees the resulting CDS is $k$-connected.

**Lemma 18.11.** *If $G$ is a $k$-connected graph, and $G'$ is obtained from $G$ by adding a new node $v$ with at least kneighbors in $G$, then $G'$ is also a $k$-connected graph* [29].

In this algorithm, each node can be a black node or white node. A node can have Initialization, Pending, or Done status and before the third step, every node is in the Initialization status. A node maintains the followings two structures. Requestor List is used to store the IDs of nodes who request this node to join current $k$-connected component. Black Adjacent List is used to remember the black neighbors of this node. The first and second steps come from previous results, and thus this paper concentrates on the third step. The last step begins after computing a $k$-connected subgraph, which will be a part of $(k,m)$-CDS. This can be done by adding some nodes to a subset of current $(1,m)$-CDS. After this, every node in the subgraph broadcasts a KC message, which will be introduced below, to its neighbors. A node $x$ which receives a KC message try to be a member of current $k$-connected subgraph by broadcasting RC message. This message is forwarded to neighbors and once this arrives at one of nodes in the $k$-connected subgraph, a confirmation message is sent back to the node $x$. At the end, the set of black nodes will be a $(k,m)$-CDS. In DDA, wireless nodes are exchanging six types of messages. For more detailed description of each message can be found in [29]. Now, we introduce several lemmas and give the analysis of the performance ratio of this algorithm.

**Lemma 18.12.** *Every subset of an MIS is no more than three hops away from its complement* [29].

Denote $C_0$ as a (1,1)-CDS. Then, by [19], after the first phase, we have $|C_0| \leq 43|S|$, where $S$ be an MIS. In the second phase, since $m-1$ MISs are added, the number of MIS nodes is $|C| = |C_0| + (m-1)|S| \leq (m+4)|S|$. In the phase three, at most $k^2$ nodes can be added for each black node in $C$ by Lemma 18.12. Therefore, $|C| \leq (k^2+1)(m+42)|S|$. Since we have $|S| \leq \frac{5}{m}|D_m^*|$ by Lemma 18.2,

$|C| \leq \frac{5}{m}(k^2+1)(m+42)opt$, where $opt$ is an optimal $(k,m)$-CDS and therefore, the performance ratio of DDA is $\frac{5}{m}(k^2+1)(m+42)$.

**Theorem 18.8.** *The message complexity and time complexity of DDA is $O(|V|\triangle^2)$ and $O(m\triangle + Diam)$, respectively, where $\triangle$ is the maximum node degree and Diam is the diameter of the network* [29].

**LDA: Distributed Local Decision Algorithm for Constructing $(k,m)$-CDS [31]** The message complexity of DDA is $O(|V|\triangle^2)$, where $\triangle$ is the maximum degree [29]. Even though DDA is the first deterministic distributed algorithm to compute $(k,m)$-CDSs for any $k$ and $m$ pair, their high message complexity is quite burdensome in wireless networks.

Wu and Li pointed out the problem of DDA and introduced a new distributed localized algorithm, namely Local Decision Algorithm (LDA). This algorithm computes $(k,m)$-CDSs for any $k$ and $m$ pair similar as [29]. However, rather than exchanging lots of messages among several nodes over multiple hops, each node negotiates only with their neighbors. In this way, the work of constructing $(k,m)$-CDS can be localized. We start our explanation by introducing some notations.

- $GL(v)$ is a graph induced by a node $v$ and all of its neighbors.
- $LVC(v)$, **local vertex connectivity** of node $v$, is the vertex connectivity degree of $GL(v)$.
- $S_{cn}(v,u)$ is a **common node set** of nodes $v$ and $u$, which is equal to $N[v] \cap N[u]$.
- Given $v,u \in V$, a set $X \subseteq V \setminus \{v,u\}$ is called a $v,u$**-separator** or $v,u$**-cut** if there is no path between $v$ and $u$ in $G \setminus X$.
- $\triangle$ is the maximum node degree.
- $Diam$ is the diameter of the network.

Clearly, the minimum size of a $v,u$-separator equals to the maximum number of pairwise internal disjoint $v,u$-paths. Therefore, if the minimum size of any pair separator is larger than $k$, the whole graph $G$ is at least $k$ connected. Algorithm 18.10 is the brief description of LDA.

---

**Algorithm 18.10** LDA $(G(V,E),k,m)$.

1: Build a $(1,m)$-CDS, $C'_{1,m}$ using MDSA.
2: Each black nodes in $C'_{1,1} \subseteq C'_{1,m}$ negotiates with its parents or siblings in $C'_{1,1}$ such that the size of $S_{cbn}$ between them can be at least $k$.
3: Construct a local $k$ vertex-connected subraph.

---

LDA consists of three phases. In the first phase, it computes a $C_{1,m}$ by executing MDSA. In the second phase, a black nodes in $C_{1,1}$, which is a subset of $C_{1,m}$ computed in the previous phase, negotiates a common black node set with its parent or siblings in the $C_{1,1}$ so that $|S_{cbn}| \geq k$ can be true. In the last phase, LDA builds a local $k$ vertex connected subgraph, $G_k$, which contains all the nodes in $C_{1,1}$, $C_{1,m}$, and $S_{cbn}$s and marks all the nodes in $G_k$ in black. The authors presented Lemma 18.13 to prove the correctness of this approach.

**Lemma 18.13.** *Given nodes $u$ and $v$ as neighbors, $N[u]$ and $N[v]$ are their closed neighbor sets, respectively. For a node set $P$, $P \subseteq N[u], v, u \in P, LVC(P) = k$ and a node set $Q, Q \subseteq N[v], v, u \in Q, LVC(Q) = k$. If $|P \cap Q| \geq k$, then $LVC(P \cup Q) = k$. That means the graph superimposed by $P$ and $Q$ is $k$ vertex-connected* [31].

Theorems 18.9 and 18.10 shows the performance ratio and complexity of LDA more detailed proofs can be found in [31].

**Theorem 18.9.** *The approximation ratio of LDA is $max\{\frac{5}{m}, 1\}2\triangle$* [31].

**Theorem 18.10.** *The time and message complexity of LDA is $O(\triangle|V|)$ and $O((m + \triangle) \cdot Diam)$* [31].

Since the message complexity is bounded by $O((\triangle + 1)|V|)$ in the first phase, and $O(\triangle|V|)$ in the negotiation phase, the total message complexity of LDA is bounded by $O(\triangle|V|)$ and therefore LDA has much smaller message complexity than DDA's, which is $O(|V|\triangle^2)$.

## 18.5. Conclusion Remarks

In this article, we introduce recent advances in generating fault-tolerant virtual backbones for wireless networks. In most literatures, UDG is used to model a homogeneous wireless network. Besides, to model the problem of computing a minimum size fault-tolerant virtual backbone, minimum $k$-connected $m$-dominating set problem is used. In the early researches, centralized approximation algorithms are studied and more recently, some distributed solutions are introduced. We show that time complexity of the centralized one is quite high. Likewise, the message and time complexities of distributed one is not low. Therefore, one can effort to reduce those complexities. Recently, Kim *et al.* introduced approximation algorithms to compute 1-CDS with bounded diameters [25] and Zhang *et al.* improved this result and presented a $(2, 1)$-CDS computation algorithm with bounded diameters [40]. However, a generalized version of those algorithm for any $k$ and $m$ pair is not invented yet. Therefore, this can be another good future work.

## References


[1] I.F. Akyildiz, W. Su, Y. Sankarasubramaniam, and E. Cayirci, "A Survey on Sensor Networks," *IEEE Communications Magazine*, Vol. 40, pp. 102–114, August 2002.

[2] C.R. Dow, P.J. Lin, S.C. Chen, J.H. Lin, and S.F. Hwang, "A Study of Recent Research Trends and Experimental Guidelines in Mobile Ad Hoc Networks," in *Proc. of the 19th International Conference on Advanced Information Networking and Applications (AINA'05)*, pp. 72–77, Taiwan, March 2005.

[3] S. Ni, Y. Tseng, Y. Chen, and J. Sheu, "The Broadcast Storm Problem in a Mobile Ad Hoc Network," in *Proc. of the 5th Annual ACM/IEEE International Conference on Mobile Computing and Networking (MOBICOM'99)*, pp. 152–162, Washington, USA, August 1999.

[4] A. Ephremides, J. Wieselthier, and D. Baker, "A Design Concept for Reliable Mobile Radio Networks with Frequency Hopping Signaling," *Proceeding of the IEEE*, Vol. 75, Issue 1, pp. 56–73, 1987.

[5] P. Sinha, R. Sivakumar, and V. Bharghavan, "Enhancing Ad Hoc Routing with Dynamic Virtual Infrastructures," in *Proc. of the 20th Annual Joint Conference of the IEEE Computer and Communications Societies*, Vol. 3, pp. 1763–1772, 2001.

[6] S. Guha and S. Khuller, "Approximation Algorithms for Connected Dominating Sets," *Algorithmica*, Vol. 20, pp. 374–387, April 1998.

[7] B. Das and V. Bharghavan, "Routing in Ad Hoc Networks Using Minimum Connected Dominating Sets," in *Proc. of International Conference on Communications (ICC'97)*, pp. 376–380, Montreal, Canada, June 1997.

[8] B. Das, R. Sivakumar, and V. Bharghavan, "Routing in Ad Hoc Networks Using a Spine", in *Proc. of International Conferfence on Computers and Communication Networks*, 1997.

[9] R. Sivakumar, B. Das, and V. Bharghavan, "An improved spine-based infrastructure for routing in ad hoc networks," in *Proc. of The 3rd IEEE Symposium on Computers and Communications (ISCC'98)*, Athens, Greece, June 1998.

[10] J. Wu and H. Li, "On Calculating Connected Dominating Set for Efficient Routing in Ad Hoc Wireless Networks," in *Proc. of the 3rd ACM Internationl Workshop Discrete Algorithm and Methods for Mobile Computing and Communications*, pp. 7–14, Washington, USA, 1999.

[11] J. Wu, M. Gao, and I. Stojmenovic, "On Calculating Power-Aware Connected Dominating Sets for Efficient Routing in Ad Hoc Wireless Networks," in *Proc. of International Conference on Parallel Processing (ICPP'99)*, pp. 346–356, Fukushima, Japan, Sep. 2001.

[12] M. Cardei, X. Cheng, X. Cheng, and D.-Z. Du, "Connected Domination in Multihop Ad Hoc Wireless Networks," in *Proc. of International Conference on Computer Science and Informatics*, March 2002.

[13] P.-J. Wan, K. M. Alzoubi, and O. Frieder, "Distributed Construction of Connected Dominating Set in Wireless Ad Hoc Networks," in *Proc. of the 21st Annual Joint Conference of the IEEE Computer and Communications Societies (INFOCOM'02)*, New York, USA, June 2002.

[14] K.M. Alzoubi, P.-J. Wan, and O. Frieder, "New Distributed Algorithm for Connected Dominating Set in Wireless Ad Hoc Networks," in *Proc. of the 35th Hawaii International Conference on System Scicences (HICSS'02)*, pp. 297, Hawaii, 2002.

[15] K.M. Alzoubi, P.-J. Wan, and O. Frieder, "Distributed Heuristics for Connected Dominating Sets in Wireless Ad Hoc Networks," *Journal of Communications and Networks*, Vol. 4, No. 1, March 2002.

[16] J. Wu, B. Wu, and I. Stojmenovic, "Power-Aware Broadcasting and Activity Scheduling in Ad Hoc Wireless Networks Using Connected Dominating Sets," *Wireless Communications and Mobile Computing*, Vol. 3, No. 2, pp. 425–438, March 2003.

[17] L. Ruan, H. Du, X. Jia, W. Wu, Y. Li, and K.-I. Ko, "A Greedy Approximation for Minimum Connected Dominating Sets," *Journal of Theoretical Computer Science*, Vol. 329, pp. 325–330, Dec. 2004.

[18] M. Min, F. Wang, D.-Z. Du, and P.M. Pardalos, "A reliable Virtual Backbone Scheme in Mobile Ad Hoc Networks," in *Proc. of IEEE International Conference on Mobile Ad Hoc and Sensor Systems (MASS)*, 2004.

[19] Y. Li, S. Zhu, My T. Thai, and D-Zhu Du, "Localized Construction of Connected Dominating Set in Wireless Networks," *NSF International Workshop on Theoretical Aspects of Wireless Ad Hoc, Sensor and Peer-to-Peer Networks (TAWN04)*, Chicago, June 2004.

[20] K. Mohammed, L. Gewali, and V. Muthukumar, "Generating Quality Dominating Sets for Sensor Network," in *Proc. of the 6th International Conference on Computational Intelligence and Multimedia Applications (ICCIMA'05)*, pp. 204–211, Nevada, USA, August 2005.

[21] Y. Zeng, X. Jia, and Y. He, "Energy Efficient Distributed Connected Dominating Sets Construction in Wireless Sensor Networks," in *Proc. of International Wireless Communications and Mobile Computing Conference (IWCMC'06)*, pp. 797–802, Vancouver, Canada, July 2006.

[22] S. Funke, A. Kesselman, U. Meyer, and M. Segal, "A Simple Improved Distributed Algorithm for Minimum CDS in Unit Disk Graphs," *ACM Transactions on Sensor Network*, **2**(3), pp. 444–453, August 2006.

[23] M.T. Thai, F. Wang, D. Liu, S. Zhu and D.-Z. Du, "Connected Dominating Sets in Wireless Networks with Different Transmission Ranges," *IEEE Transactions on Mobile Computing*, **6**(7), July 2007.

[24] S.C.H. Huang, P.-J. Wan, C.T. Vu, Y. Li, and F. Yao, "Nearly Constant Approximation for Data Aggregation Scheduling in Wireless Sensor Networks," in *Proc. of the 26th Annual Joint Conference of the IEEE Computer and Communications Societies (INFOCOM'07)*, pp. 366–372, Anchorage, AK, May 2007.

[25] D. Kim, Y. Wu, Y. Li, F. Zou, D.-Z. Du, "Constructing Minimum Connected Dominating Sets with Bounded Diameters in Wireless Networks," *IEEE Transactions on Parallel and Distributed Systems*, 07 May 2008. IEEE Computer Society Digital Library. IEEE Computer Society, 23 May 2008 ¡http://doi.ieeecomputersociety.org/10.1109/TPDS.2008.74¿

[26] F. Dai and J. Wu, "On Constructing $k$-Connected $k$-Dominating Set in Wireless Network," in *Proc. of 19th IEEE International Parallel and Distributed Processing Symposium (IPDPS'05)*, 2005.

[27] F. Wang, M.T. Thai, D.-Z. Du, "2-connected Virtual Backbone in Wireless Network," *IEEE Transactions on Wireless Communications*, accepted with revisions, 2007.

[28] M.T. Thai, N. Zhang, R. Tiwari, and X. Xu, "On Approximation Algorithms of $k$-Connected $m$-Dominating Sets in Disk Graphs," *Theoretical Computer Science*, Vol. 358, pp. 49–59, 2007.

[29] Y. Wu, F. Wang, M.T. Thai, and Y. Li, "Constructing $k$-Connected $m$-Dominating Sets in Wireless Sensor Networks", in *Proc. of 2007 Military Communications Conference (MILCOM07)*, Orlando, FL, October 29–31, 2007.

[30] W. Shang, F. Yao, P. Wan, and X. Hu, "On Minimum $m$-Connected $k$-Dominating Set Problem in Unit Disc Graphs," *Journal of Combinatorial Optimization*, Dec. 2007.

[31] Y. Wu and Y. Li, "Construction Algorithms for $k$-Connected $m$-Dominating Sets in Wireless Sensor Networks," *9th ACM International Symposium on Mobile Ad Hoc Networking and Computing (Mobihoc 2008)*, Hong Kong, China, May 26–30, 2008.

[32] M.R. Garey and D.S. Johnson, "Computers and Intractability: A Guide to the Theory of NP-completeness," Freeman, San Francisco, 1978.

[33] X. Hou and D. Tipper, "Gossip-based Sleep Protocol (GSP) for Energy Efficient Routing in Wireless Ad Hoc Networks," in *Proc. of WCNC*, Mar. 2004.

[34] S. Kumar, T.H. Lai, and J. Balogh, "On $k$-Coverage in a Mostly Sleeping Sensor Network," in *Proc. of Mobicom*, pp. 144–158, Sep./Oct. 2004.

[35] D.S. Johnson, "Approximation Algorithms for Combinatorial Problems," *Journal of Computer System Science*, Vol. 9, pp. 256–278, 1974.

[36] M.L. Huson and A. Sen, "Broadcast Scheduling Algorithms for Radio Networks," *IEEE Military Communications Conference (MILCOM '95)*, Vol. 2, pp. 647–651, 1995.

[37] B.N. Clark, C.J. Colbourn, and D.S. Johnson, "Unit Disk Graphs", *Discrete Mathematics*, Vol. 86, pp. 165–177, Dec. 1990.

[38] J. Wu and F. Dai, "A Generic Distributed Broadcast Scheme in Ad Hoc Wireless Network," *IEEE Transactions on Computers*, Vol. 53, pp. 1343–1354, Oct. 2004.

[39] Tarjan R., "Depth First Search and Linear Graph Algorithms," *SIAM Journal on Computing*, Vol. 1, Issue 2, pp. 146–160, 1972.

[40] N. Zhang, I. Shin, F. Zou, W. Wu, and My T. Thai, "Trade-off Scheme for Fault Tolerant Connected Dominating Sets on Size and Diameter," in *Proc. of ACM International Workshop on Foudations of Wireless Ad Hoc and Sensor Networking and Computing (FOWANC)*, in conjunction with MobiHoc, 2008.

# Chapter 19

## SERVICE IOT FOR DIGITAL RIGHTS MANAGEMENT (DRM)

Whai-En Chen
*Institute of Computer Science and Information Engineering,*
*National I-Lan University*
*wechen@niu.edu.tw*

Ting-Kai Huang
*Department of computer Science, National Chiao Tung University*
*1001, Ta Hsueh Road, Hsinchu, Taiwan 310*
*huangtk.iit95g@nctu.edu.tw*

Chun-Chieh Wang
*Information and Communications Research Laboratories,*
*Industrial Technology Research Institute*
*195 Chung Hsing Rd., Sec.4 Chu Tung,*
*Hsin Chu, Taiwan 310*
*wangjj@itri.org.tw*

This chapter describes a conformance and interoperability test tool for Digital Rights Management (DRM) developed on an Open Mobile Alliance (OMA) service interoperability test platform. DRM is a security (protection) mechanism that allows a content issuer to manage the media objects to be delivered to the users with copyright protection. In DRM, the users then access DRM Content (i.e., the protected media objects) according to the Rights Objects. Before a DRM application is launched for a mobile device, it is essential to conduct testing to ensure that the DRM mechanism is correctly implemented. Based on the Testing and Test Control Notation version 3 (TTCN-3) specifications, we show how DRM test cases can be efficiently implemented.

### 19.1. Introduction

*Open Mobile Alliance* (OMA) *Digital Rights Management* (DRM) distributes the media objects (e.g., a movie, an MP3 music file, and so on) with secured business models that can control the usage of the content and manage the content lifecycle [1]. When a user attempts to access the content, he/she may choose a free preview version or a complete version with charge.

### 19.1.1. *OMA DRM*

OMA DRM allows a content issuer to manage DRM Content to be delivered to the users with copyright protection. In the DRM architecture, the user can access DRM Content through a DRM agent (Figure 19.1 ①), where the DRM agent is installed in the mobile device to management the usage of DRM Content. The content issuer (Figure 19.1 ③) is responsible for packaging the media objects into DRM Content and delivering DRM content to the users. A rights issuer (RI; Figure 19.1 ④) is responsible for producing the Rights Objects. Each Rights Object is associated with a piece of DRM Content.

DRM Content is accessed by the DRM agent under the control of the Rights Objects. A Rights Object specifies permissions, constraints and other features, which indicates how DRM Content can be used. Consider an example where DRM Content consists of a movie and two pictures, and DRM Agent 2 (Figure 19.1 ②) attempts to play the movie for two times and display the pictures for unlimited times. DRM Agent 2 may download DRM Content from the content issuer or another DRM agent (e.g., DRM Agent 1 in Figure 19.1 ①) that previously downloaded the same DRM Content through the DRM mechanism. DRM Agent 2 must utilize the *Rights Object Acquisition Protocol* (ROAP) to acquire a Rights Object from the rights issuer, and then accesses DRM Content according to the Rights Object. The format of the Rights Object in this example is illustrated in Figure 19.2. The asset field (Figure 19.2①) specifies the identity, the hash value and the key information of DRM Content. The hash value ensures the integrity of DRM Content. The key information identifies the encryption method used to encrypt the *content encryption key* (CEK) and contains the Base64-encoded value of the

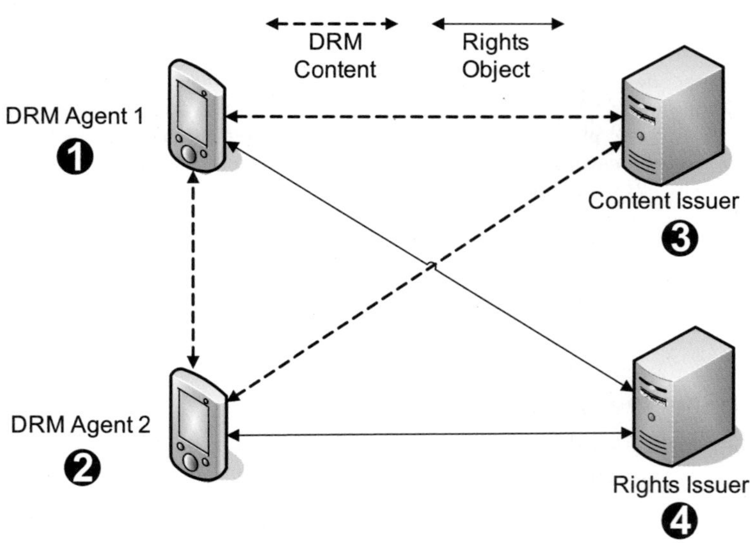


Fig. 19.1. The DRM architecture.

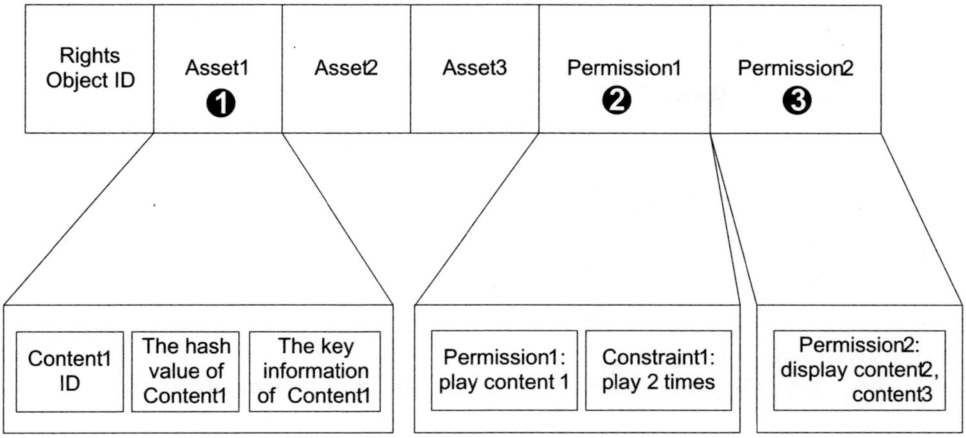


Fig. 19.2. The Rights Object format.

encrypted CEK. The permission field (e.g., Figure 19.2②) specifies the permissions (e.g., to play the movie) and the constraints (e.g., to play the movie two times). The Permission 2 (Figure 19.2③) only specifies the permissions without any constraint, which means that the DRM agent is granted unlimited display rights.

### 19.1.2. *NTP-DRMT*

Before a DRM application can be launched for service, it is essential to conduct testing to ensure that the DRM mechanism is correctly implemented in a mobile device. Although such tests can be done manually, it is more appropriate to automatically validate the DRM mechanism through a test tool. Under Taiwan's *National Telecommunications Program* (NTP), we have developed an OMA service interoperability test platform based on the *Testing and Test Control Notation version 3* (TTCN-3) specifications [9–14]. Several OMA *Push-to-talk over Cellular* (PoC) test cases were deployed on this platform [17]. In this chapter, we implement a *DRM conformance and interoperability test tool* (called NTP–DRMT) on this platform. NTP-DRMT verifies the adherence to normative requirements described in the OMA DRM technical specifications [7, 8]. The conformance test cases verify whether the DRM agent follows the standard regulations described in [7]. The interoperability test cases verify whether the *system under test* (SUT; Figure 19.3②), which is implemented based on the specifications, works satisfactory in various commercial mobile telecommunication networks [8]. Figure 19.3 shows the conformance and interoperability test environment for DRM. In this figure, NTP-DRMT (Figure 19.3 ④) acts as the DRM network entities (including the content issuer and the rights issuer) in all test procedures. It communicates with the SUT through a real cellular network or a cellular network emulator (Figure 19.3 ③) such as Anritsu MD8470A [18]. In the DRM conformance test procedures, NTP-DRMT waits for the SUT to request a Rights Object or DRM

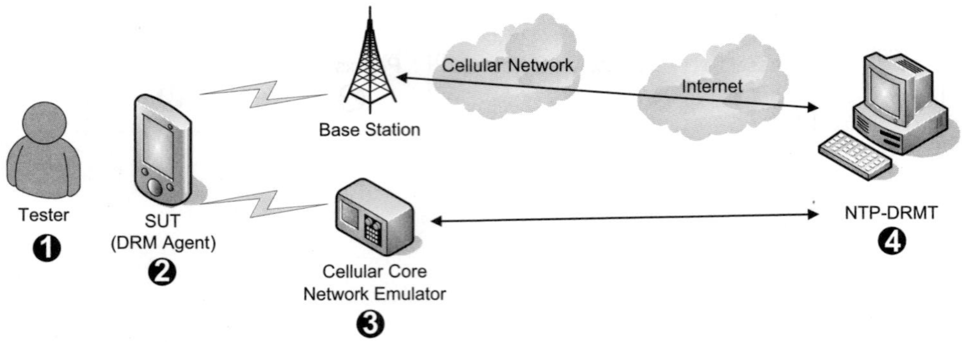


Fig. 19.3. Conformance and interoperability test environment for OMA DRM.

Content. This request is issued by a tester (Figure 19.3 ①). After the SUT receives the response, the tester verifies if the results displayed by the SUT are correct. The tester then reports the verdict (e.g., pass or fail) to NTP-DRMT. In the DRM interoperability test procedures, NTP-DRMT waits for the SUT to request DRM Content and the associated Rights Objects through different commercial mobile networks. The tester then verifies if the SUT is capable of executing the interoperability test cases and reports the verdict to NTP-DRMT.

### 19.1.3. *Test Procedure for the DRM Registration*

In this chapter, we utilize the DRM registration procedure to illustrate how the test cases are implemented in NTP-DRMT. The DRM registration procedure is illustrated in Figure 19.4. When a user attempts to access new DRM Content, the DRM agent first sends an HTTP_GET (Figure 19.4 ①) message to the rights issuer to request the Rights Object. The rights issuer verifies the HTTP_GET message and then the rights issuer replies a ROAP Trigger message (Figure 19.4②). This message is used to trigger the ROAP message exchange. The DRM agent then sends a Device Hello message (Figure 19.4③) to provide device information (such as the Device ID and the ROAP version) and initiate the registration procedure. The rights issuer verifies the Device Hello message and replies a RI Hello message (Figure 19.4 ④). The RI Hello message provides RI preferences and decisions according to the values provided by the DRM agent. The DRM agent then sends a Register Request message (Figure 19.4 ⑤). The rights issuer verifies the Register Request message and checks if the session ID, the device nonce, the request time and the signature in the Register Request message are correct. Then the rights issuer replies a Register Respose message (Figure 19.4⑥). Upon the receipt of this message, the registration procedure is complete, and the DRM agent can acquire the Rights Object.

In the remainder of this chapter, we will describe the design and implementation of NTP-DRMT. Then we use examples to show how the DRM test cases are developed in this test tool.

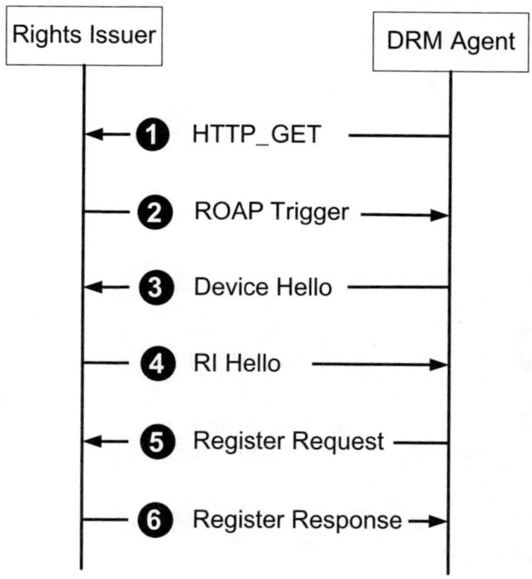


Fig. 19.4. The test case for DRM registration procedure.

## 19.2. TTCN-3 Based Test System

The test system NTP-DRMT is implemented based on TTCN-3. This system manages DRM test execution, interprets/executes compiled TTCN-3 code, and implements proper communications with the SUT. As illustrated in Figure 19.5, NTP-DRMT consists of the following parts.

The *Test Management and Control* (TMC; Figure 19.5 ①) is responsible for the test execution control and the test event logging. The *TTCN-3 Executable* (TE; Figure 19.5 ②) is responsible for the interpretation or the execution of the DRM modules (i.e., abstract test suites). The *SUT Adapter* (SA; Figure 19.5 ③) adapts the TTCN-3 communication between the TE and the SUT (Figure 19.5 ⑤). The *Platform Adapter* (PA; Figure 19.5 ④) adapts the TE to an operating system (e.g., Microsoft Windows XP and 2003) by creating a single notion of time for NTP-DRMT and implementing the external functions as well as timers.

Two interfaces are defined inside NTP-DRMT. The *TTCN-3 Control Interface* (TCI; Figure 19.5 Ⓐ) specifies the interface between the TMC and the TE. The *TTCN-3 Runtime Interface* (TRI; Figure 19.5 Ⓑ) defines the interface between the TE and the SA/PA. A third interface *Test System Interface* (TSI; Figure 19.5 Ⓒ) specifies the interface of the test system towards the SUT.

### 19.2.1. *DRM Test Management and Control (TMC)*

The TMC consists of three entities: the *Test Management* (TM; Figures 19.5⑥), the *Test Logging* (TL; Figure 19.5 ⑦) and the *External CoDecs* (ECDs; Figure 19.5 ⑧).

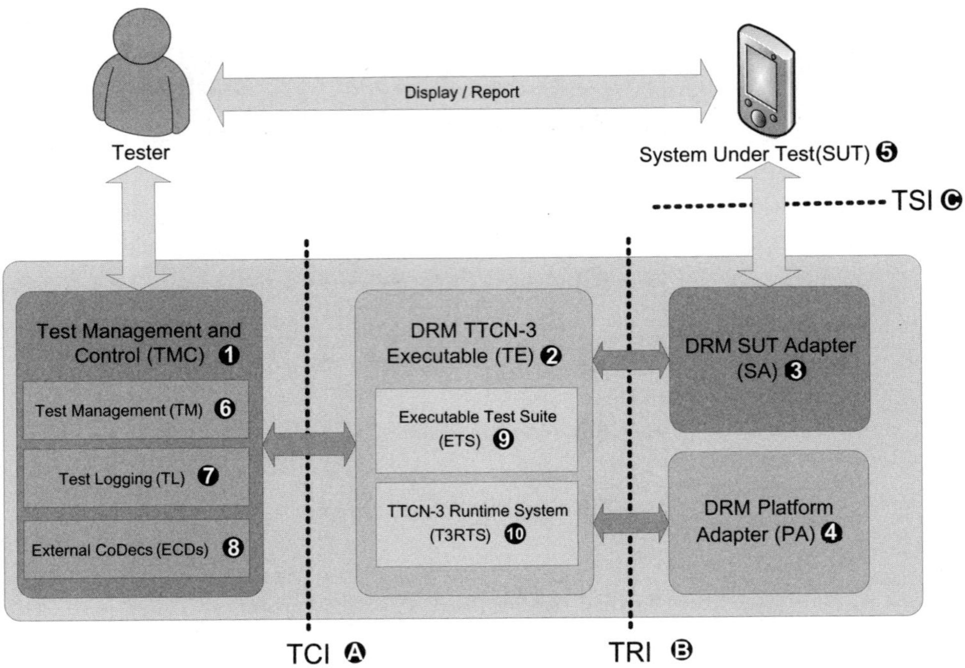


Fig. 19.5. TTCN-3 based NTP-DRMT.

The TM is responsible for controlling the creation and the execution of tests. In DRM test execution, the TM invokes the DRM modules (e.g., tc_ConRoap module which will be described in Figure 19.7) to propagate the module parameters and/or extra testing information to the TE.

The TL is responsible for maintaining the test log, such as the logging information about test component creation, start and termination, and data delivery to/from the SUT. The logging requests to the TL are posted externally from the TE or internally from the TM. Figure 19.6 shows a graphical test log that describes the interactions between MTC (i.e., NTP-DRMT; Figure 19.6 ①) and SYSTEM (i.e., the SUT; Figure 19.6 ②) based on the registration test case. When NTP-DRMT receives an HTTP_GET message (Figure 19.4 ① and Figure 19.6 ③) from the SUT, NTP-DRMT verifies the HTTP_GET message and replies a ROAP Trigger message (Figure 19.4 ② and Figure 19.6 ⑤) to the SUT. Then NTP-DRMT receives the Device Hello message (Figure 16.4 ③ and Figure 19.6 ⑥), verifies this message and replies a RI Hello message (Figure 16.4 ④ and Figure 19.6 ⑧). Upon receipt of the Register Request message (Figure 19.4 ⑤ and Figure 19.6 ⑨), NTP-DRMT verifies this message and replies a Register Response message (Figure 19.4 ⑥ and Figure 19.6 ⑪). Every "match" box (Figure 19.6 ④, ⑦ and ⑩) indicates that the received message matches the pass criteria described in the conformance test

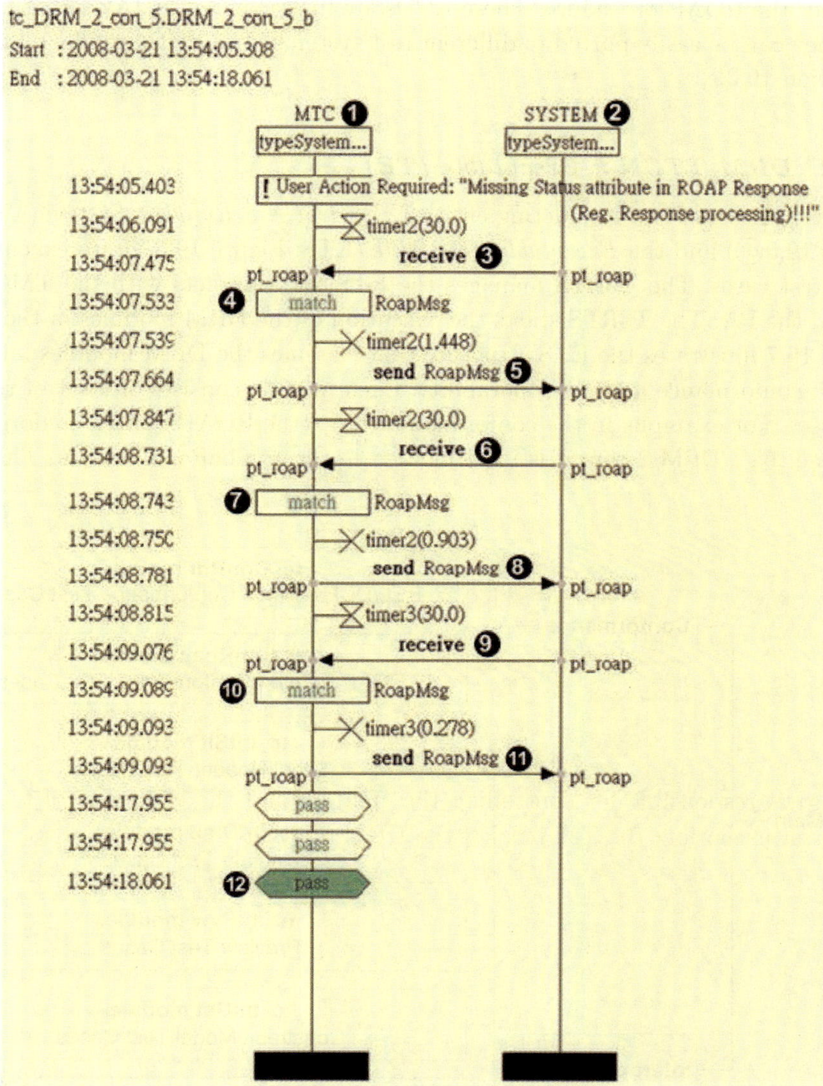


Fig. 19.6. Graphical test log for DRM registration.

specification. The final "pass" box (Figure 19.6 ⑫) indicates that the SUT passes this test case.

The ECDs are invoked by the TE for encoding or decoding the messages. Specifically, the TE passes the TTCN-3 values to an appropriate encoder to produce the encoded messages. The received messages are passed to an appropriate decoder to translate the received messages into the TTCN-3 values. In NTP-DRMT, there are two ECDs in the `DRM_Codec.java` file; one for the HTTP procedure and the other for the ROAP procedure. These ECDs are implemented in JAVA language so that they can be easily ported to different test systems. The ECDs will be described in Section 19.3.

### 19.2.2. *DRM TTCN-3 Executable (TE)*

The TE consists of two interacting entities, the *TTCN-3 Runtime System* (T3RTS; Figure 19.5⑩) and the *Executable Test Suite* (ETS; Figure 19.5 ⑨), to execute the DRM test cases. The T3RTS manages the ETS and interacts with the TMC, the SA and the PA. The T3RTS starts the execution of the DRM modules in the ETS. Figure 19.7 illustrates the ETS structure that classifies the DRM modules into two groups: conformance and interoperability. Each module consists of a set of related test cases. For example, in the conformance group, the ROAP related conformance test case (e.g., DRM_2_con_5) is implemented in the tc_ConRoap module. This test

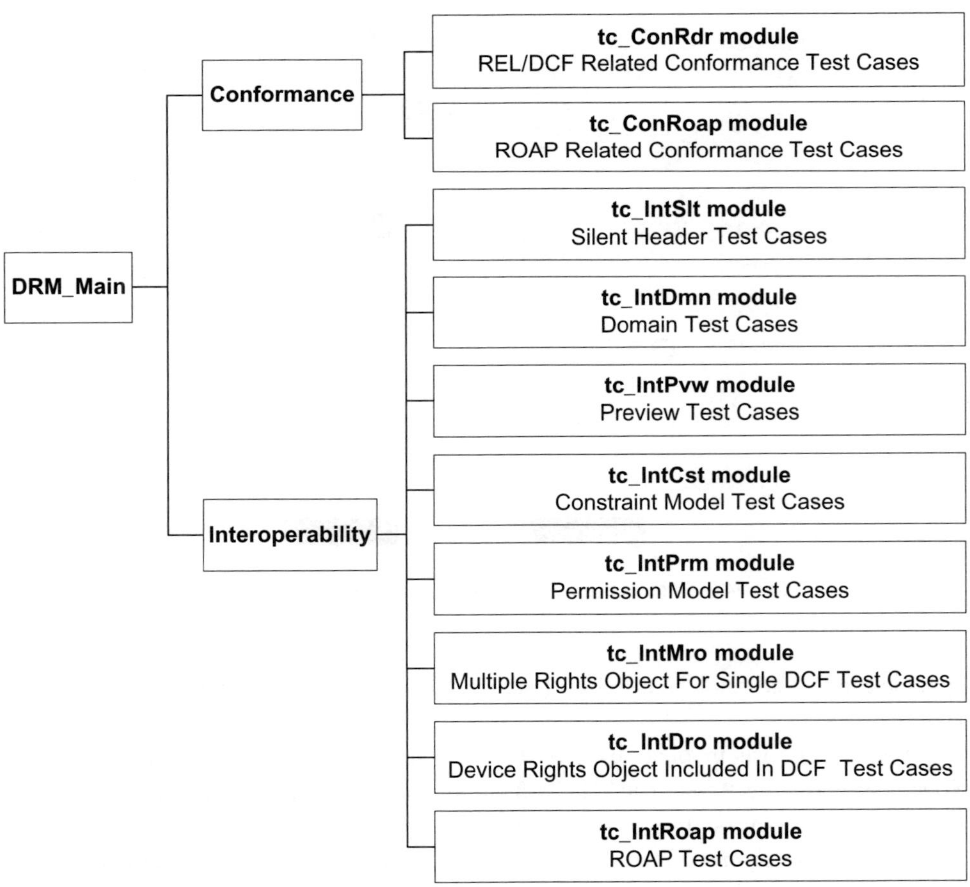


Fig. 19.7. The structure of the DRM ETS.

case is invoked by the T3RTS when NTP-DRMT receives an HTTP_GET message (which is described in Section 1.3) to trigger the registration procedure.

### 19.2.3. *DRM SUT Adapter (SA)*

The SA adapts the communications between the TE and the SUT. The SA interacts with the TE through the TRI. Specifically, to correctly deliver HTTP and ROAP messages to and from the SUT, the TE calls the TRI functions that associate the test component ports to the TSI port and invokes the ECDs (Figure 19.8 ① and ②) for the message encoding/decoding. The test component ports, pt_http (Figure 19.8③) and pt_roap (Figure 19.8 ④), are mapped to the HTTP socket (Figure 19.8 ⑤) in the SA. The SA binds the socket to the TSI port 8080 for the interaction with the SUT.

The SA is responsible for propagating the DRM requests (e.g., sending a ROAP message through the `pt_roap.send` function) from the TE to the SUT and notifying the TE of any received test events form the SUT (e.g., receiving a ROAP message

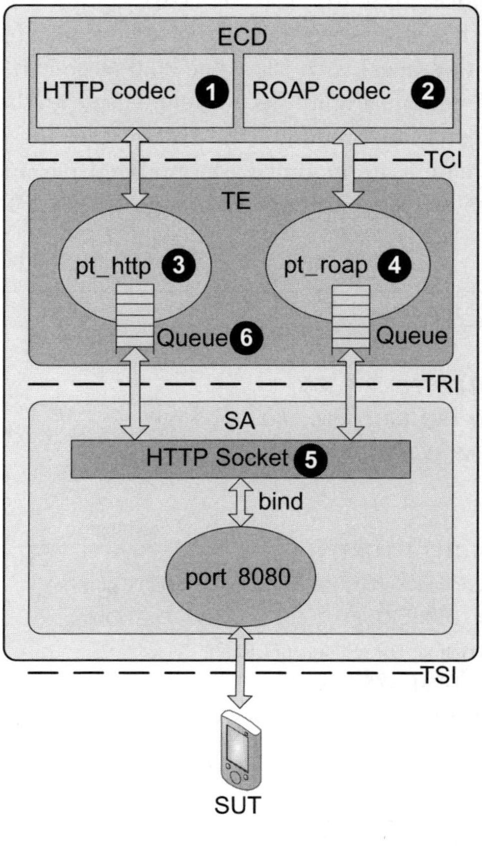


Fig. 19.8. Interaction between the SA and the TE in NTP-DRMT.

through the `pt_roap.receive` function) by buffering them in the TE's port queues (Figure 19.8 ⑥).

## 19.3. TTCN-3 Interfaces for DRM

This section elaborates on the NTP-DRMT control and runtime interfaces. We first describe the *TTCN-3 Control Interface* (TCI), and then the *TTCN-3 Runtime Interface* (TRI).

### 19.3.1. *The TTCN-3 Control Interface (TCI) for DRM*

The TCI between the TE and the TMC has three sub-interfaces: the *Test Management Interface* (TCI-TM), the *Test Logging Interface* (TCI-TL) and the *Coding/Decoding Interface* (TCI-CD). The TCI-TM supports the operations for controlling the test execution and providing the module parameters. The TCI-TM program segment in Figure 19.9 illustrates some DRM module parameters. Line 1 of Figure 19.9 assigns the TSI port HTTP_PORT with the value 8080. Line 2 assigns the test system *Uniform Resource Locator* (URL). Line 3 assigns the maximum waiting time between a sent message and a received message (e.g., the ROAP Trigger and the Device Hello messages) with the value 30.0 (seconds).

The extension function (Figure 19.9 ④–⑥) displays the descriptions of the parameters to the tester and reminds the tester that these parameters can be changed. If the parameters are modified, the updated parameters are provided to the test system as the module parameters through the TCI-TM.

```
group SysParameters {
     modulepar {
①         integer HTTP_PORT := 8080;
②         charstring DRMURL :="http://localhost:8080";
③         float DRM_SYS_WAIT := 30.0;
     }
     with {
④         extension (HTTP _PORT)
              "Description: Specify the port number of HTTP protocol";
⑤         extension (DRMURL)
              "Description: The test system URL.";
⑥         extension (DRM_SYS_WAIT)
              "Description: Maximum time between a sent message and a received message.";
     }
}
```

Fig. 19.9. An example of DRM module parameter.

```
① if(DRM_Verify_Signature(v_recvMsg.roReq.sign)){
(1.1)      f_DRM_2_con_31_a_senRORsp(v_recvMsg);
           return SC_SUCCESS;
   } else {
②          log("Signature verifyfailed");
           returnSC_FAIL;
   }
```

Fig. 19.10. DRM test logging example.

The TCI-TL includes the operations for retrieving the information about the test execution. Figure 19.10 illustrates a TCI-TL program segment that checks whether the signature is correct and logs the error if the signature is incorrect in the received ROAP message. In Figure 19.10 ①, NTP-DRMT checks if the signature in the received message is correct. If yes, NTP-DRMT replies a response message (Figure 19.10 (1.1)). Otherwise, NTP-DRMT logs the error information and shows the error message in the test log.

The TCI-CD provides the operations to access the ECDs. In NTP-DRMT, TCI-CD is implemented in `DRM_Codec.java` described in Section 2.1. Parts of the program are listed in Figure 19.11. In this example, if no encoding rule is matched, then Figure 19.11 ④ is executed for the exception handling. In Figure 19.11 ②, an HTTP message is encoded as follows. Figure 19.11(2.1)–(2.5) construct the HTTP

```
public TriMessage encode(Value value) {
① try{
②    if (value.getType().getName().equals("HttpMsg")){
(2.1)       RecordValue rvMsg = (RecordValue)value;
(2.2)       StringBuffer sb=new StringBuffer();
(2.3)       sb.append("CON"+"");
(2.4)       sb.append(Encode.Charstring(rvMsg,"file")+"");
(2.5)       sb.append(Encode.Charstring(rvMsg,"conType"));
(2.6)       return new TriMessageImpl(sb.toString().getBytes());
      }
③    else if (value.getType().getName().equals("RoapMsg")) {
            ....// ROAP message encoding
        }
④ }catch (IOException e) {
            RB.tciTMProvided.tciError("Encoding error : "+e.getMessage());
      }
}
```

Fig. 19.11. DRM encode operation.

```
public Value decode(TriMessage message, Type decodingHypothesis) {
①     if(decodingHypothesis.getName().equals("HttpMsg")){
(1.1)     RecordValue ret = (RecordValue)decodingHypothesis.newInstance();
(1.2)     Decode.Enumerated(ret, "msgType","HTTP_GET");
(1.3)     Decode.Charstring(ret, "uri", new String(message.getEncodedMessage()));
(1.4)     return ret;
      }
②     else if(decodingHypothesis.getName().equals("RoapMsg")) {
          .... // ROAP message decoding
      }
      return null;
}
```

Fig. 19.12. DRM decode operation.

message structure, append content and set the content type (e.g., image/gif or audio/wav). Figure 19.11 (2.6) generates a byte string from this HTTP message structure. Figure 19.11 ③ encodes a ROAP message, and the details are omitted.

The DRM decode operation invoked by the TE decodes a message according to the decoding rules and returns a TTCN-3 value. Parts of the program are listed as follows. Figure 19.12 ① and ② decode the message as an HTTP or a ROAP message according to the message type. For example, in Figure 19.12 ①, the HTTP message decodes into a structured TTCN-3 value. Figure 19.12 (1.2) sets the "msgType" to HTTP_GET, and Figure 19.12 (1.3) retrieves the *Uniform Resource Identifier* (URI).

### 19.3.2. *The TTCN-3 Runtime Interface (TRI) for DRM*

The TRI supports the communication of the ETS with the SUT [13]. This interface is implemented in the SA to initialize the TSI and establish connections to the SUT. The TRI is implemented in a JAVA program `DRM_TestAdapter.java` consisting of the connection and the communication operations shown in Figure 19.13.

The connection operations include the map and the unmap operations. Through the connection operations, the test component ports are mapped/unmapped to the TSI port. An example is the `triMap` function (Figure 19.13 ①) called by the TE when the TE executes the map operation (Figure 19.15 ①). This operation instructs the SA to establish a dynamic connection to the SUT.

The TRI also supports the communication operations which are used to exchange messages with the SUT. The communication operations include the enqueue and the send operations. An example is the `triEnqueueMsg` function (Figure 19.13 ②) called by the SA after the SA has received a message from the SUT. This operation passes the message to the test component port of the TE.

```
public class DRM_TestAdapter extends TestAdapter {
①   public TriStatus triMap(final TriPortId compPortId, final TriPortId tsiPortId) {
        TriStatus mapStatus = CsaDef.triMap(compPortId, tsiPortId);
        if (tsiPortId.getPortName().equals("pt_http")) {
        .... // bind Socket to port 8080, and wait for packets
②               Cte.triEnqueueMsg(tsiPortId, new TriAddressImpl(new byte[]{}),
                    compPortId.getComponent(), new TriMessageImpl(msg));
    }
.       ... //other map functions
        return mapStatus;
    }

③   public TriStatus triUnmap(TriPortId compPortId, TriPortId tsiPortId) {
        CsaDef.triUnMap(compPortId, tsiPortId);
            ...//unmap functions
        returnsuper.triUnmap(compPortId, tsiPortId);
    }

④   public TriStatus triSend(TriComponentId compId, TriPortId tsiPortId,
        TriAddressaddress, TriMessage message) {
        if (tsiPortId.getPortName().equals("pt_roap")) {
        ...//send aROAPmessage
        }
        else if (tsiPortId.getPortName().equals("pt_http")) {
                FileInputStreamfr=message.getEncodedMessage();
                ByteArrayOutputStream os=new ByteArrayOutputStream();
                byte data[]=new byte[1];
                while(fr.read(data)!=-1)
                        os.write(data);
                out.write(os.toByteArray());
                returnnewTriStatusImpl();
        }
    }
}
```

Fig. 19.13. DRM adapter operation.

Note that the test component port has been mapped to the TSI port beforehand. Another example is the `triSend` function (Figure 19.13 ④) called by the TE when the TE executes the send operation (Figure 19.16 ④). This operation instructs the SA to send a message to the SUT. For DRM testing, two types of the messages are sent by the `triSend` function: RoapMsg for ROAP and HttpMsg for HTTP.

## 19.4. A DRM Conformance Test Scenario

We use a conformance test case "missing State in RI Hello processing" to show how the DRM test suites are implemented. This test case verifies if the SUT correctly handles an incorrect RI Hello message without "Status" in the DRM registration procedure. The "Status" is used to indicate if the preceding request was successfully or not. If the SUT receives this message, it should display an error message and terminate the connection.

The conformance test case is implemented by a *Finite State Machine* (FSM). Figure 19.14 shows the state diagram of the DRM conformance test case "missing State in RI Hello processing".

- At **State 1** (Waiting for HTTP_GET), if the HTTP_GET message is received from the SUT, the TE sends a ROAP Trigger message to the SUT and changes the FSM to **State 2** (Waiting for Device Hello). If any ROAP message is received at this state, the TE sets the verdict to "fail" and stops the FSM at **State 4**

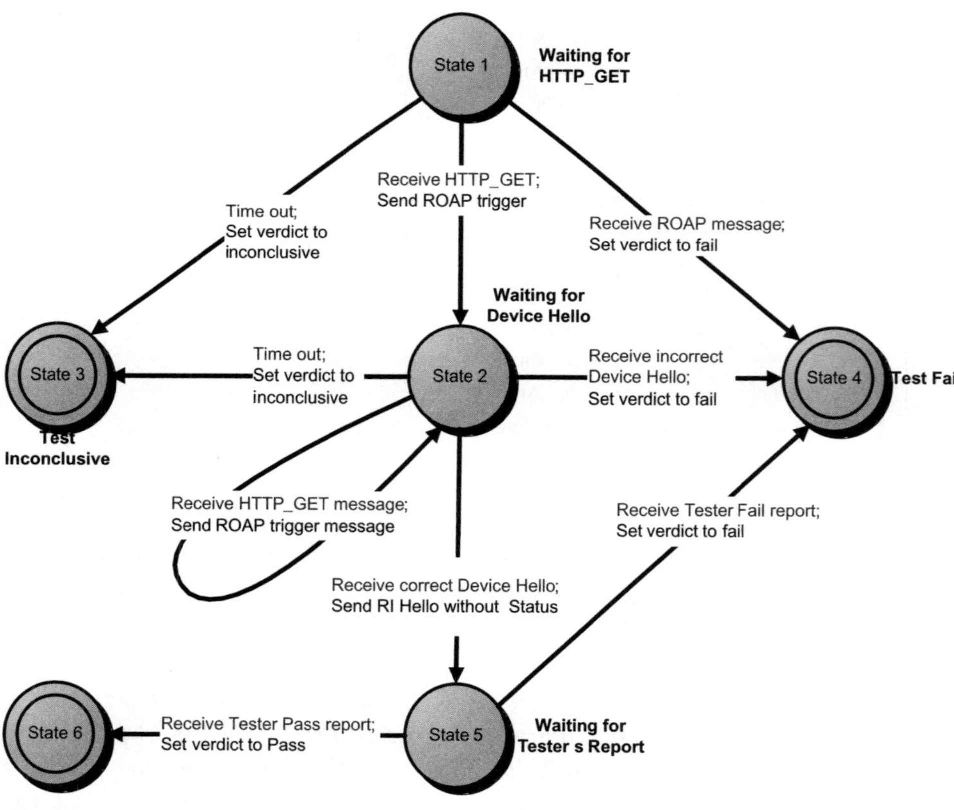


Fig. 19.14. DRM "missing State in RI Hello processing" test case state diagram.

(Test Fail). If the timer expires and the TE does not receive any message, the TE sets the verdict to "inconc" and stops the FSM at **State 3** (Test Inconclusive).

- At **State 2**, if the Device Hello message sent from the SUT is correct, then the TE sends an incorrect RI Hello message to the SUT and changes the FSM to **State 5** (Waiting for Tester Post Result). If an HTTP_GET message is received at this state, the TE resends the ROAP Trigger message and waits for the Device Hello message. If an incorrect Device Hello message is received at this state, the TE sets the verdict to "fail" and stops the FSM at **State 4**. If the timer expires, the TE sets the verdict to "inconc" and stops the FSM at **State 3**.
- **State 3** is the "Test Inconclusive" state.
- **State 4** is the "Test Fail" state.
- At **State 5**, if the tester reports pass, the TE sets the verdict to "pass" and changes the FSM to **State 6** (Test Pass). If the tester reports fail, the TE sets the verdict to "fail" and stops the FSM at **State 4**.
- **State 6** is the "Test Pass" state.

Figure 19.15 illustrates the program segment for the test case. When the test starts, the TE first maps the two test component ports to the TSI port (Figure 19.15 ①; the `triMap` operation at the TRI is invoked). Then it pops up an action window (Figure 19.15 ②) that notifies the tester (Figure 19.3 ①) what the test case is and asks the tester to send an HTTP_GET message from the SUT (Figure 19.3 ②). In Figure 19.15 ③, the TE sets the waiting time. Then the TE invokes the `f_DRM_2_con_5_a_reg` function (Figure 19.15 ④) to check whether the received messages from the SUT are correct.

In the `f_DRM_2_con_5_a_rcvMsg` function, the `t_tMsg` timer starts at the PA (Figure 19.16 ①), and the FSM is initialized to wait at State 1. When an HTTP_GET message from the SUT is received, the `pt_http.receive` function is executed (Figure 19.16 ②), the TE invokes the decode operation in Figure 19.12. After the message is decoded, the TE stops the `t_tMsg` timer at the PA (Figure 19.16 ③) and invokes `f_sndRegTrig` function (Figure 19.16 ④) to send a ROAP Trigger to the SUT. Then the TE goes to execute Figure 19.16 ⑦, and the FSM is moved to State 2. If a ROAP message is received (Figure 19.16⑤), the test result (SC_FAIL) is returned and the FSM is moved to State 4. If the TE does not receive any message from the SUT after the `t_tMsg` timer expires, the PA notifies the TE of this timeout event (Figure 19.16⑥). The `f_DRM_2_con_5_a_rcvMsg` function returns SC_TIME_OUT and the FSM is moved to State 3. The TE sets the verdict to "inconc" (Figure 19.15⑥) to indicate that an inconsistent exception occurs.

If the HTTP_GET message is received (Figure 19.16 ⑧ and Figure 19.14 State 2), then the TE resends the ROAP Trigger to the SUT. If the TE receives a Device Hello message (Figure 19.16 ⑨), then the TE checks whether the header in the Device Hello message contains the DRM feature-tag "devhello version" (Figure 19.16 ⑩). If the check of the message is failed, the `f_DRM_2_con_5_a_rcvMsg` function returns SC_FAIL to indicate the failure and the FSM is moved to State 4.

```
testcase DRM_2_con_5_a() runs on DrmComp system DrmComp{
①   map(mtc:pt_http, system:pt_http);
    map(mtc:pt_roap, system:pt_ http);
②   f_action("Missing Status attribute in ROAP Response (RI Hello processing) !
            Please send a HTTP message ");
③   v_sysWait := DRM_SYS_WAIT;
④   result:= f_DRM_2_con_5_a_ rcvMsg ();

⑤   if (result.rc = SC_FAIL) {
        setverdict(fail);
    }
⑥   else if (result.rc = SC_TIME_OUT) {
        setverdict(inconc);
    }
    else {
⑦       if(DRMConfirmBox("DRM Device receive RI Hello response without status !!!")){
                setverdict(pass);
        }
        else{
                setverdict(fail);
        }
    }
⑧   unmap(mtc:pt_http, system:pt_http);
    unmap(mtc:pt_roap, system:pt_ http);
}
```

Fig. 19.15. DRM conformance test case "missing State in RI Hello processing".

If the received Device Hello message is correct, then the TE sends an incorrect RI Hello message (without "Status") to the SUT and the FSM is moved to State 5. If the `t_tMsg` timer expires, the `f_DRM_2_con_5_a_rcvMsg` function returns SC_TIME_OUT (Figure 19.16 ⑪) and the FSM is moved to State 3.

Finally, if the `f_DRM_2_con_5_a_rcvMsg` function returns SC_FAIL or SC_TIME_OUT, the TE sets the verdict to "fail" or "inconc" (Figure 19.15 ⑤ and ⑥). Otherwise, the TE pops up a confirm box (Figure 19.15 ⑦) to notify the tester to check whether the result displayed by the SUT is correct and waits for the tester's report (Figure 19.14 State 5). Then the TE sets the verdict to "pass" (the FSM is moved to State 6) or "fail" (the FSM is moved to State 4) according to the tester's report. After the verdict is set, the TE removes the bindings between the test component ports and the TSI port (Figure 19.15 ⑧) using the `triUnmap` operation.

```
function f_DRM_2_con_5_a_rcvMsg () runs on DrmComp return RetResult{
①    t_tMsg.start(v_sysWait);
     alt{
②          []pt_http.receive(a_httpget){
③                   t_tMsg.stop;
④                   f_sndRegTrig();
            }
⑤          [] pt_roap.receive(){
                       t_tMsg.stop;
                       ret.c:= SC_FAIL;
                       return ret;
            }
⑥          []t_t Msg.timeout{
                       log("timeout and nothing received");
                       ret.rc:=SC_TIME_OUT;
                       return ret;
            }
     }
⑦    t_tMsg.start(v_sysWait);
     alt{
⑧           []pt_http.receive(a_httpget){
                       t_tMsg.stop;
                       f_sndRegTrig();
                       repeat;
            }
⑨          []pt_roap.receive(v_devhello) -> value v_recvMsg{
               t_tMsg.stop;
⑩ if(not ispresent(v_ devhello.version)){
                       ret.rc:=SC_FAIL;
                       return ret;
             }
             …//check other headers in the received Device Hello message

             f_DRM_2_con_5_a_sndRiHello();
             ret.rc:=SC_SUCCESS;
             return ret;
            }
⑪          []t_tMsg.timeout{
             log("timeout and nothing received");
             ret.rc:=SC_TIME_OUT;
             return ret;
           }
     }
}
```

Fig. 19.16. The f_DRM_2_con_5_a_rcvMsg function.

## 19.5. Conclusions

This chapter described the architecture and the operations of NTP-DRMT which is a DRM test system developed based on the TTCN-3 specifications. This system has been jointly developed by the *National Telecommunications Program* (NTP) and the *Industrial Technology Research Institute* (ITRI) in Taiwan. We used the DRM registration procedure to illustrate how the conformance test can be implemented in NTP-DRMT. The conformance and interoperability test cases are conformed to the OMA Enabler Test Specification (Conformance) for DRM-V2_0 [7] and the OMA Enabler Test Specification for DRM Interoperability [8]. Currently, 493 DRM test cases have been developed in NTP-DRMT.

## 19.6. Acknowledgement

The authors would like to thank professor Yi-Bing Lin for his valuable comments that improve the quality of this article and Pai-Tsan Huang for his help in developing NTP-DRMT. This work was sponsored in part by NSC 96-2219-E-009-019, NSC 96-2218-E-197-004, ITRI/NCTU JRC project, NCHC project, and MoE project.

## References

[1] Open Mobile Alliance, "DRM Specification", OMA-TS-DRM-DRM-V2_0- 2006 0303-A, 2006.

[2] Open Mobile Alliance, "DRM Architecture", OMA-AD-DRM-V2_0-20060303-A, 2006.

[3] Open Mobile Alliance, "DRM Content Format", OMA-TS-DRM-DCF-V2_0-20060303-A, 2006.

[4] Open Mobile Alliance, "DRM Rights Expression Language", OMA-TS-DRM-REL-V2_0-20060303-A, 2006.

[5] Open Mobile Alliance, "OMA DRM Requirements", OMA-RD-DRM-V2_0-20060303-A, 2006.

[6] Open Mobile Alliance, "Enabler Release Definition for DRM V2.0", OMA-ERELD-DRM-V2_0-20060303-A, 2006.

[7] Open Mobile Alliance, "Enabler Test Specification (Conformance) for DRM- V2_0", OMA-ETS-DRM_ CON_Test_Client-V2_0-20060615-C, 2006.

[8] Open Mobile Alliance, "Enabler Test Specification for DRM Interoperability", OMA-ETS-DRM-INT- V2_0-20060704-C, 2006.

[9] ETSI, "Methods for Testing and Specification (MTS); The Testing and Test Control Notation version 3; Part 1: TTCN-3 Core Language", ETSI ES 201 873-1, V3.1.1, 2005.

[10] ETSI, "Methods for Testing and Specification (MTS); The Testing and Test Control Notation version 3; Part 2: TTCN-3 Tabular presentation Format (TFT)", ETSI ES 201 873-2 V3.1.1, 2005.

[11] ETSI, "Methods for Testing and Specification (MTS); The Testing and Test Control Notation version 3; Part 3: TTCN-3 Graphical presentation Format (GFT)", ETSI ES 201 873-3 V3.1.1, 2005.

[12] ETSI, "Methods for Testing and Specification (MTS); The Testing and Test Control Notation version 3; Part 4: TTCN-3 Operational Semantics", ETSI ES 201 873-4 V3.1.1, 2005.
[13] ETSI, "Methods for Testing and Specification (MTS); The Testing and Test Control Notation version 3; Part 5: TTCN-3 Runtime Interface (TRI)", ETSI ES 201 873-5 V3.1.1, 2005.
[14] ETSI, "Methods for Testing and Specification (MTS); The Testing and Test Control Notation version 3; Part 6: TTCN-3 Control Interface (TCI )", ETSI ES 201 873-6, V3.1.1, 2005.
[15] ETSI, "Methods for Testing and Specification (MTS); The Testing and Test Control Notation version 3; Part 7: Using ASN.1 with TTCN-3", ETSI ES 201 873-7 V3.1.1, 2005.
[16] Lin, Y.-B., Liang, C.-F., Chen, K.-H., Liao, H.-Y. "NTP-SIOT: A Test Tool for Advanced Mobile Services", IEEE Network. November/December 2006, pp. 2–7.
[17] Lin, Y.-B., Wang, C.C., Lu, C.H., Hsu, M.R. "NTP-PoCT: A Conformance Test Tool for Push-to-talk over Cellular Network", Wireless Communications and Mobile Computing. John Wiley & Sons, 2007.
[18] Anritsu Corporation, MD8470A Signaling Tester Product Introduction, http://www.us.anritsu.com/products/ ARO/North/Eng/showProd.aspx?ID=659.

## Appendix A: The Conformance and Interoperability Test Cases

**The conformance test cases**

| Test case ID | Test case description |
|---|---|
| DRM-2.0-con-1 | ROAP trigger with expired RI context |
| DRM-2.0-con-3 | Missing Signature in Leave Domain trigger |
| DRM-2.0-con-4 | Invalid Signature in Leave Domain trigger |
| DRM-2.0-con-5 | Missing Status attribute in ROAP Response |
| DRM-2.0-con-6 | Status $\neq$ Success in ROAP Response |
| DRM-2.0-con-7 | Missing Signature in ROAP Response |
| DRM-2.0-con-8 | Invalid Signature in ROAP Response |
| DRM-2.0-con-9 | 1-pass RO Response processing reception while expired RI context |
| DRM-2.0-con-29 | Missing Session ID in Register Response processing |
| DRM-2.0-con-30 | Invalid Session ID in Register Response processing |
| DRM-2.0-con-31 | Missing Device ID in ROAP response; 2 pass RO acquisition and Join Domain. |
| DRM-2.0-con-32 | Invalid Device ID in ROAP response; 2 pass RO acquisition and Join Domain. |
| DRM-2.0-con-33 | Missing Device ID in 1-pass RO Response processing |
| DRM-2.0-con-34 | Invalid Device ID in 1-pass RO Response processing |
| DRM-2.0-con-35 | Missing Device Nonce in ROAP response |
| DRM-2.0-con-35 | Missing Device Nonce in Leave Domain Response processing |
| DRM-2.0-con-36 | Invalid Device Nonce in ROAP response |
| DRM-2.0-con-37 | Missing RI ID in ROAP response |
| DRM-2.0-con-38 | Invalid RI ID in ROAP response |
| DRM-2.0-con-40 | Install Device RO from RO Response processing; Invalid Signature |
| DRM-2.0-con-41 | Install Device RO from RO Response processing; Missing MAC element |

(*Continued*)

(*Continued*)

| Test case ID | Test case description |
|---|---|
| DRM-2.0-con-42 | Install Device RO from RO Response processing; Invalid MAC element |
| DRM-2.0-con-43 | Install Device RO from RO Response processing; Missing RI ID |
| DRM-2.0-con-44 | Install Device RO from RO Response processing; Invalid RI ID |
| DRM-2.0-con-45 | Install Device RO from RO Response processing; Missing Signature |
| DRM-2.0-con-46 | Install Device RO from RO Response processing; Invalid Signature |
| DRM-2.0-con-47 | Install Device RO from RO Response processing; Missing MAC element |
| DRM-2.0-con-48 | Install Device RO from DCF; Invalid MAC element |
| DRM-2.0-con-49 | Install Device RO from DCF; Missing RI ID |
| DRM-2.0-con-50 | Install Device RO from DCF; Invalid RI ID |
| DRM-2.0-con-51 | Install Device RO from DCF; RI Context Expired |
| DRM-2.0-con-52 | Consume rights in Device RO; Invalid Hash value |
| DRM-2.0-con-53 | Install Domain Context; Missing MAC |
| DRM-2.0-con-54 | Install Domain Context; Invalid MAC |
| DRM-2.0-con-55 | Install Domain Context; Missing RI ID in DomainKey |
| DRM-2.0-con-56 | Install Domain Context; Invalid RI ID in DomainKey |
| DRM-2.0-con-57 | Delete Domain Context |
| DRM-2.0-con-58 | Install Domain RO; No valid RI context with corresponding RI ID |
| DRM-2.0-con-59 | Install Domain RO; Missing Signature |
| DRM-2.0-con-60 | Install Domain RO; Invalid Signature |
| DRM-2.0-con-61 | Install Domain RO; Missing Domain ID |
| DRM-2.0-con-62 | Install Domain RO; Invalid Domain Generation |
| DRM-2.0-con-63 | Install Domain RO; Device not in the domain |
| DRM-2.0-con-64 | Install Domain RO; Missing MAC. |
| DRM-2.0-con-65 | Install Domain RO; Invalid MAC. |
| DRM-2.0-con-66 | Install Domain RO; RI Context Expired |
| DRM-2.0-con-67 | Replay protection – Stateful RO with RITS; Future RITS |
| DRM-2.0-con-68 | Replay protection – Stateful RO with RITS; In Replay cache |
| DRM-2.0-con-69 | Replay protection – Stateful RO with RITS; Early RITS |
| DRM-2.0-con-70 | Replay protection – Stateful RO without RITS; In Replay cache |
| DRM-2.0-con-71 | Parent Rights object; Invalid Rights issuer |
| DRM-2.0-con-72 | Nonce generation on Device without system shutdown |
| DRM-2.0-con-73 | Nonce generation on Device with system shutdown |
| DRM-2.0-con-74 | Wrong permissions for an image object |
| DRM-2.0-con-75 | Wrong permissions for a sound object |
| DRM-2.0-con-76 | Wrong permissions for an application object |
| DRM-2.0-con-77 | Unknown permissions |
| DRM-2.0-con-78 | Export permissions ("move") for DCFs with stateless rights object |
| DRM-2.0-con-79 | Export permissions ("copy") for DCFs with stateless rights object |
| DRM-2.0-con-80 | Export permissions ("move") for DCFs with stateful rights object |
| DRM-2.0-con-81 | Export permissions ("copy") for DCFs with stateful rights object |
| DRM-2.0-con-82 | Export permissions not present for DCF |
| DRM-2.0-con-83 | Instant Preview |
| DRM-2.0-con-85 | Erroneous Count constraint |
| DRM-2.0-con-86 | Erroneous Timed-Count constraint |
| DRM-2.0-con-87 | Erroneous Datetime constraint |
| DRM-2.0-con-88 | Erroneous Interval constraint |
| DRM-2.0-con-89 | Erroneous Accumulated constraint |

(*Continued*)

(*Continued*)

| **The Interoperability test cases** | |
|---|---|
| Test case ID | Test case description |
| DRM-2.0-int-1 | To test “Forward Lock” DRM 1.0 functionality. |
| DRM-2.0-int-2 | To test DRM 1.0 “Combined Delivery” functionality |
| DRM-2.0-int-3 | To test DRM 1.0 “Separate Delivery” functionality |
| DRM-2.0-int-4 | To test RO Registration and RO Acquisition |
| DRM-2.0-int-5 | To test RO Registration with existing RI Context |
| DRM-2.0-int-6 | To test RO Acquisition without existing RI Context |
| DRM-2.0-int-7 | To test 1-pass RO Acquisition with existing RI Context |
| DRM-2.0-int-8 | To test 1-pass RO Acquisition without existing RI Context |
| DRM-2.0-int-10 | To test a situation where an RO is included in the DCF |
| DRM-2.0-int-11 | To test behavior in the presence of a group RO for multiple DCFs, using the Group ID mechanism |
| DRM-2.0-int-12 | To test behavior in the presence of an individual RO for a content item which has a Group ID |
| DRM-2.0-int-13 | To test behavior in the presence of several rights objects for one piece of content |
| DRM-2.0-int-14 | To test behavior in the presence of several rights objects for one piece of content |
| DRM-2.0-int-15 | To test DRM Agent’s capability to process Multipart DCFs from the RI |
| DRM-2.0-int-16 | To test behavior in the presence of multiple ROs for a multipart DCF |
| DRM-2.0-int-17 | To test behavior when different content items in a multipart DCF are associated with different groups |
| DRM-2.0-int-18 | To test “Superdistribution” functionality. The protected content is sent from one DRM Agent to another. The rights object is obtained by ROAP session to the rights issuing service. |
| DRM-2.0-int-19 | To test the TransactionID mechanism in connection with Superdistribution |
| DRM-2.0-int-20 | To test <display> and <print> permissions |
| DRM-2.0-int-21 | To test <play> permission |
| DRM-2.0-int-22 | To test <execute> permission for an application object |
| DRM-2.0-int-23 | To test <count> constraint for a DCF |
| DRM-2.0-int-24 | To test <timed-count> constraint for a DCF |
| DRM-2.0-int-25 | To test <datetime> constraint for a DCF |
| DRM-2.0-int-26 | To test <interval> constraint for a DCF |
| DRM-2.0-int-27 | To test <accumulated> constraint for a DCF |
| DRM-2.0-int-28 | To test <individual> constraint for a DCF |
| DRM-2.0-int-29 | To test <system> constraint for a DCF |
| DRM-2.0-int-30 | To test the effect of having multiple constraints |
| DRM-2.0-int-31 | To test the REL Permission Model in the case that the rights include a stateful top level constraint |
| DRM-2.0-int-32 | Initiate ROAP from DCF Preview Header with existing RI Context & domain name NOT in Domain Name Whitelist |
| DRM-2.0-int-33 | Initiate ROAP from DCF Preview Header with existing RI Context & domain name in the Domain Name Whitelist |
| DRM-2.0-int-34 | To test inheritance model when stateful constraints are involved |
| DRM-2.0-int-35 | To test a case where the Parent Rights Object |
| DRM-2.0-int-36 | To test inheritance model when a child RO is a group RO |

(*Continued*)

(*Continued*)

| Test case ID | Test case description |
|---|---|
| DRM-2.0-int-37 | Trigger-initiated domain join without existing RI Context |
| DRM-2.0-int-38 | Trigger-initiated domain join with valid RI Context and no existing Domain<br>Context for this RI |
| DRM-2.0-int-39 | Automatically-initiated domain upgrade with valid RI Context and existing Domain Context for this RI |
| DRM-2.0-int-40 | Trigger-initiated domain join with valid RI Context and existing Domain Context for this RI |
| DRM-2.0-int-41 | Domain RO Acquisition with existing RI Context |
| DRM-2.0-int-42 | To test delivering the DomainRO inside a DCF |
| DRM-2.0-int-43 | To test if different devices related with the same domain are able to share DCFs |
| DRM-2.0-int-44 | Device leaves a domain after receiving a LeaveDomain trigger |
| DRM-2.0-int-45 | Initiate ROAP from DCF Silent Header with existing RI Context and domain name NOT in Domain Name Whitelist |
| DRM-2.0-int-46 | Initiate ROAP from DCF Silent Header with existing RI Context and domain name NOT in Domain Name Whitelist |

# Chapter 20

## PATIENT PRIVACY IN HEALTHCARE WIRELESS SENSOR NETWORKS

Jelena Mišić and Vojislav B. Mišić
*Ryerson University, Toronto, Ontario, Canada*

Patient data privacy is one of the foremost security concerns in healthcare applications. However, the requirements for strong cryptography must often be balanced against the requirements for energy efficiency, esp. in the case when the patients wear a body network using lightweight wireless sensor networks that operate on battery power. In this chapter, we describe two algorithms for key distribution. The first algorithm relies on the central trusted security server to authenticate that the participants indeed belong to the patient's group and to generate the session key. In the second algorithm, participants can authenticate each other using certificates and are largely independent of the central trusted security server. In both cases, the patient's security processor has a lead role in authenticating group membership and the key generation process. In the second algorithm, elliptic curve cryptography is used to reduce energy consumption by cryptographic computations. Using the data from commercial devices compliant with the IEEE 802.15.4 low data rate WPAN technology, we show that this approach can successfully be implemented with low power motes.

### 20.1. Introduction

Wireless Sensor Networks (WSNs) in healthcare applications are the edge component of a fully connected clinical information system. Each patient carries his or her own body sensor network, or piconet, which is built from lightweight, battery-operated sensor devices. The sensor devices monitor different health parameters (such as body temperature, heartbeat rate, blood pressure, or other physiological variables of interest) and send relevant data to the piconet coordinator, a dedicated device within the piconet. The piconet coordinator is connected to the clinical information system network through an access point in a room or ward. In this manner, patient's health data collected by her piconet coordinator may be sent to the central database of the clinical information system in a timely and reliable manner. Figure 20.1 shows the simplified architecture of the clinical information system. Note that access points are shared among several patients, as well as by a number of clinicians and nurses (or, rather, their wireless devices) whenever they may be within the transmission range of the respective access points.

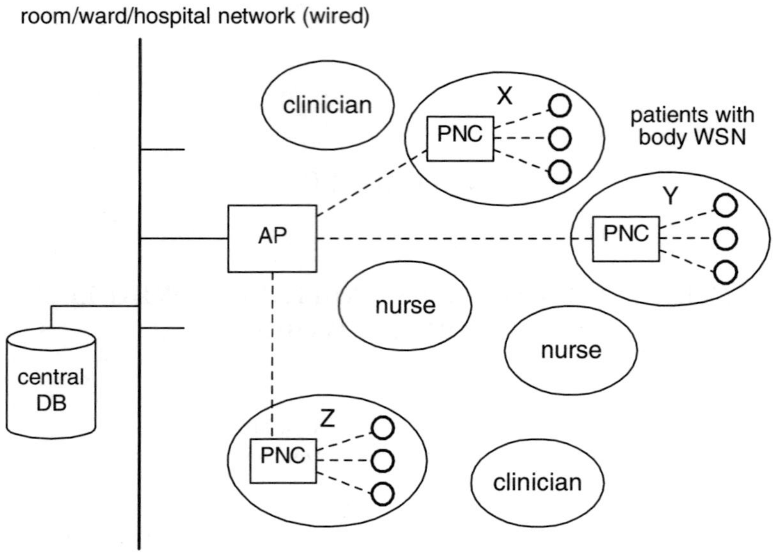


Fig. 20.1. Simplified network architecture of a clinical information system.

One of the major requirements for any healthcare information system, including clinical information systems, is that integrity and privacy of monitored health data must be adequately protected. This requirement must be upheld form the time data is collected, throughout the process by which the data is stored in the patient's medical record, and at all times afterwards [5]. Access to that data should be limited to the patient's attending group of clinicians, which includes the patient's attending clinician and the attending nurse [1,5]. When necessary, other clinicians and/or nurses may be allowed access as well, but their access must be limited only to the subset of data needed to reach qualified decisions regarding patient's treatment. Finally, the patient must give explicit consent to the treatment, and must be informed of any access to her record. As these requirements are far from trivial, discretionary access control such as the one enforced through access control lists is not sufficient. Instead, it becomes necessary to apply mandatory access control, supported through appropriate cryptographic techniques, for both the patient and the members of the attending group of clinicians. As a result, the piconet coordinator of the patient's body piconet must also function as the Patient Security Processor (PSP), whilst the wireless devices of the principal clinician and nurse must possess dedicated security processors that function as the Clinician Security Processor (CSP) and Nurse Security Processor (NSP), respectively. Together with a Central Trusted Security Server (CTSS), the three security processors partake and collaborate to provide the necessary security related functionality; in particular, they need to enforce the chosen access control policy (or policies). The security architecture describing the CTSS and three security processors is schematically shown in Figure 20.2.

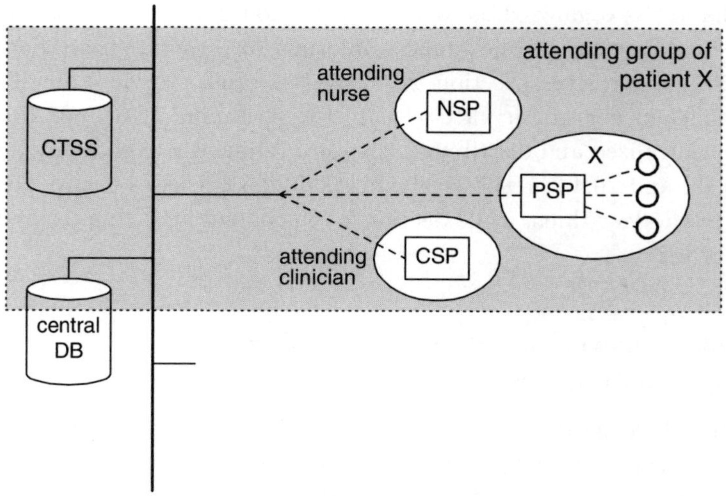


Fig. 20.2. Security architecture: a patient and her attending group of clinicians.

However, the requirements for strong cryptography must often be balanced against the requirements for energy efficiency, esp. in the case when the body network uses lightweight, battery-operated wireless sensors. In other words, all the cryptographic algorithms necessary to support the desired set of security requirements must be carefully evaluated with respect to their computational complexity and energy efficiency. This is particularly important for key generation and distribution algorithms. In this chapter, we discuss two algorithms for key distribution. The first algorithm is a centralized one; it relies on the CTSS to authenticate the participants (i.e., to verify that they indeed belong to the patient's attending group of clinicians) and to generate the session key that will be used for subsequent communications. In the second algorithm, participants (i.e., their respective security processors) authenticate each other using certificates, and are thus largely independent of the central authority of the CTSS (which nevertheless has to be informed of the new key so that is can subsequently use it). In both algorithms, the patient's security processor has a lead role in authenticating group membership and the key generation process. The second algorithm uses elliptic curve cryptography, since it provides good protection at moderate key sizes and thus leads to lower power consumption than the better known RSA [7,10].

Both algorithms presented here are independent of the particular technology used for data communications, but their applicability in practice must be validated using the power consumption data of commercial devices. We have focused on the devices compliant with the recently introduced IEEE 802.15.4 low data rate WPAN technology, which is often used to implement wireless sensor networks, and is thus a suitable candidate for the implementation of the body piconets described above. Our results indicate that the second algorithm can successfully be implemented with low power 802.15.4 motes.

The chapter is organized as follows. In Section 20.2, we present more details about the architecture of the clinical information system, from both network and security perspectives. Section 20.3 gives a brief overview of elliptic curve cryptography and low power CPU architectures running IEEE 802.15.4 protocol stack. The centralized and distributed key establishment protocols are described in Section 20.4.1 and 20.4.2, respectively. Section 20.5 discusses energy consumption of the proposed algorithms, while Section 20.6 concludes the chapter and discusses our future work.

## 20.2. Clinical Information System: Architectural and Security Issues

In the architecture shown in Figure 20.2, the CTSS participates in the process of key generation between the patient and the group of clinicians. The central Medical Database (DB) stores results of sensor measurements from the body sensor network; those measurements are authenticated, timestamped, and encrypted. CTSS and DB should be located at a physically secure location.

As mentioned above, the coordinator of the patient's body sensor network (piconet) also functions as the PSP (Patient Security Processor). The PSP moves with the patient and monitors all data communications. It also participates in the key generation protocol with the members of the attending group of clinicians; this key is used to encrypt all patient's records prior to insertion in the DB. That same key may be used to protect the communications between the PSP (in its capacity as the body piconet coordinator) and the sensor devices in the piconet, as explained in Section 20.4.3 below.

The PSP must be implemented on a trusted hardware, operating system, and application platform, since it controls all major functions of the patient's body piconet, including event detection reliability of the sensing function; location reporting which accompanies sensed data; and finally, power management, which monitors the traffic and determines sleep times for individual nodes in order to maximize the network lifetime. Moreover, all of these functions must provide integrity, availability, and confidentiality.

The star topology, beacon enabled mode of IEEE 802.15.4 networks suits this architecture well since it supports many sensing nodes communicating directly with the piconet (cluster) coordinator [11]. In our case, the coordinator embodies the functions of the data collecting device, bridge towards the access point and the rest of the clinical information system, but also those of the PSP. Individual network nodes contain a sensing subsystem which monitors the physiological parameters on the patient's body and collects the data, and the radio subsystem which sends that data, authenticated and encrypted, to the coordinator/PSP which forwards them (possibly aggregated) to the room access point.

The room access point is, in turn, connected to the central medical record database, to which it forwards encrypted and authenticated patient data through a suitable wired or wireless network. Some data aggregation may take place at the access point as well. From the networking point of view, the access point is simply an interconnection device which interconnects Personal Area Network technology with the hospital network.

The room access point is also used by the wireless devices that function as security processors for the medical personnel, in particular the clinician and nurse who belong to the patient's group of attending clinicians. From the application point of view, clinicians and nurses need to access the patient data and report back what actions have been taken as part of the treatment. From the security standpoint, their security processors (CSP and NSP) are responsible for authentication of other participants, encryption of data traffic, and key generation and distribution, together with their counterpart that belongs to the patient. Each security processor has a dedicated symmetric key which encrypts data communications with CTSS. We will denote these keys as $k_{cc}$, $k_{cn}$ and $k_{cp}$, for clinician, nurse and patient-owned keys, respectively.

Coexistence of several patients' and clinicians' wireless devices (piconets and security processors) within the transmission range of each other is facilitated by the availability of several RF channels in the 802.15.4 standard — 16 channels are available if the 802.15.4 network operates in the ISM band at 2.4GHz [11]. Alternative ways of sharing the RF spectrum are also possible, i.e., by using other WPAN standards such as Bluetooth [13] or 802.11 [16].

## 20.3. ECC and Hardware Platform for Healthcare WSNs

As healthcare WSNs are typically formed by low cost, battery operated devices, it is of utmost importance to deploy energy efficient cryptographic algorithms for protecting the privacy and integrity of relevant data and communications in general.

Recently, Elliptic Key Cryptography (ECC) has been demonstrated as relatively computationally lightweight solution which provides security levels comparable to that of much better known RSA. In particular, for the same level of security, ECC has much smaller key sizes compared to RSA [7,10], as shown in Table 20.1. Use of smaller keys results in faster key exchanges, user authentication, and digital signature generation and verification. Furthermore, smaller key size make them more suitable for storage in limited memory resources of wireless sensor nodes.

Computational (and consequently energy consumption) difference between integer based and elliptic curve algorithm resides in the way in which the public

Table 20.1. Key sizes (in bits) giving equivalent security.

| Algorithm | Integer | ECC | Symmetric key |
|---|---|---|---|
| | 512 | 106 | 64 |
| | 1024 | 163 | 80 |
| | 2048 | 210 | 112 |

key (e.g., for Diffie-Hellman exchange) is computed. In case of RSA, modular exponentiation of the private key is required; in case of ECC, a simpler scalar point multiplication of the secret key with selected base point on the elliptic curve is needed. The inverse operation, i.e., the recovery of the private key in ECC, given that the public key and the base point are known, is known as the elliptic curve discrete logarithm problem. The first measurements from 8-bit Atmel ATmega CPU architecture [3] reported in References 12 and 22 indicate almost 40% reduction of computational time.

Efficiency of implementation of ECC cryptography in WSN depends on the choice of elliptic curve parameters [10] and the computational capabilities of the hardware platform. The general form of elliptic curve equation is $y^2 + a_1xy + a_3y = x^3 + a_2x^2 + a_4x + a_6$, where $a_i \in \mathcal{F}$ [10]. In this case, $\mathcal{F}$ is a Galois field over sets $p$ or $2^p$, where $p$ is a prime. An implementation over $\mathcal{F}_{2^p}$ is reported in Reference 12, while an implementation over $\mathcal{F}_p$ is reported in Reference 9. Hardware platforms which support elliptic curve scalar point multiplications (spm) are also rapidly evolving since general purpose 8-bit architectures are not very suitable for large integer based arithmetic operations. For example, a recent 16-bit microcontroller Tmote_sky [15] uses 8MHz, 16-bit RISC microcontroller with maximal current consumption during computation (radio is off) of 2.4 mA [15]; assuming a supply voltage of 3V, this translates into power consumption of 7.2 mW. Alternatively, a dedicated hardware architecture can be used, as described in Reference 8, which supports elliptic curve operations and consumes 400 $\mu$W at clock frequency of 500 kHz. Also, a recent hardware co-processor for ECC scalar point multiplication was proposed offering energy consumption on 8-bit architecture of 1mJ per multiplication [4]. Nevertheless, the ECC scalar point multiplication is computationally most expensive operation in the ECC based key exchange algorithm.

An ECC key length of 160 bits gives 80 bits of equivalent symmetric key security and is probably sufficient for the whole network lifetime which does not exceed couple of years. However, as indicated in Reference 20 and re-stated for WSN in Reference 2, the longer the key that is used, the greater the chance that it will be compromised, and consequently the greater will be the loss caused by that compromise. Therefore, it is beneficial for the WSN to periodically update the session key; the problem is, then, how to generate a new session key and how to securely distribute it to all the participants — in this case, the CTSS and the security processors of the patient and the members of her attending clinician's group. Depending on the period of key exchange, the length of the ECC key may be reduced to less than 160 bits, which results in faster computation and lower energy consumption.

It is recommended that each entity should have two public/private key pairs: one of these should be used for digital signature, while the other should be used for symmetric key exchange [20]. Keys for the digital signatures must last throughout the entire network lifetime, they should be at least 160 bits long, and they should be stored in digital certificates. The same requirement holds for the key used by the Certifying Authority that signs all the certificates, i.e., the node signature keys. For signature, a suitable algorithm such as the Elliptic Curve Digital Signature Algorithm ECDSA [10] is used.

## 20.4. Key Generation for the Patient Group

We assume that the patient group consists of the responsible (principal) clinician, nurse, and the patient herself; it might contain more clinicians and nurses as well. No person from this group must have the capability to derive the key without the participation of other members. As we mentioned previously, each group member communicates with the CTSS using a dedicated symmetric encryption key shared between its security processor and CTSS. Together, this small group of users must interact with CTSS and generate a dedicated secret session key $L$. If the patient is unable to participate in the decisions regarding her healthcare, then her part of the key generation must be undertaken by an authorized proxy or by the central hospital authority. In an emergency, the central hospital authority, together with the responsible (principal) clinician, should be able to reconstruct the patient key. These details of these procedures are, however, beyond the scope of this chapter.

The key will be used as encryption key of an symmetric encryption system such as AES (Advanced Encryption Standard) [5,20] which is supported by Tmote_sky devices [15]. The rationale behind choosing a symmetric key-based cryptographic protocol is simply performance: encryption using public key cryptography takes a long time and generates high packet payload, which may be a problem for existing wireless technologies and existing low power sensor nodes.

The interaction between the clinician, the nurse, and the patient takes place in a number of sessions. One session corresponds to a limited time period during which the membership of the access list used to control access to the patient medical record remains unchanged. When the contents of the access control list change due to an addition or deletion of an authorized user, or perhaps because of updates for the rights of an existing user, a new session must be created. A new session is also created when the predefined time period expires. Each session uses a new secret session key, which is generated by the CTSS based on the data received from the group members. All measurements taken by the sensors, as well as the observations, prescriptions, and recommendations made or taken by the clinician(s), are encrypted by this key. The audit record for the session is further authenticated by the key derived by the interaction of all group members.

Before the key is generated, mutual authentication of the members of the patient's group needs to be conducted and patient needs to be informed about medical personnel involved in the healthcare session. Therefore, PSP needs to receive and verify identities of CSP and NSP. This can be done in two ways. One way involves CTSS which will actually conduct the authentication on PSP's behalf as presented in subsection 20.4.1. CTSS can also generate the shared session key.

In the second approach involved parties can authenticate each other using certificates and derive the session key without or with the participation of CTSS as discussed in subsection 20.4.2.

### 20.4.1. *Mutual Authentication and Key Generation using CTSS*

First approach to mutual authentication involves the CTSS which will assist in authenticating the parties. This approach is remotely similar to the classical one proposed in Reference 17. Protocol will start with PSP sending its authenticating record

$$A_p = n||PSP_{id}||CSP_{id}||NSP_{id}||\{rand_p||n||PSP_{id}||CSP_{id}||NSP_{id}\}k_{cp}$$

as shown in Figure 20.3(a), which includes the identities of all involved parties ($PSP_{id}$, $CSP_{id}$ and $NSP_{id}$), its challenge $rand_p$, and the sequence number of the transaction $n$. One part of the record is encrypted with the secret symmetric key $k_{cp}$ shared between PSP and CTSS, which will help CTSS to determine that the authenticator is really generated by PSP and that PSP really intends to communicate with NSP and CSP. CSP and NSP will generate similar authenticating records

$$A_c = n||PSP_{id}||CSP_{id}||NSP_{id}||\{rand_c||n||PSP_{id}||CSP_{id}||NSP_{id}\}k_{cc}$$

and

$$A_n = n||PSP_{id}||CSP_{id}||NSP_{id}||\{rand_c||n||PSP_{id}||CSP_{id}||NSP_{id}\}k_{cn}$$

encrypted by secret keys $k_{cc}$ and $k_{cn}$, respectively, as shown in Figure 20.3(b). Note that the arrivals of authentication records from CSP and NSP to PSP need not be synchronized in time and therefore no timestamps are needed.

When PSP collects the authentication records $A_c$ and $A_n$ it knows that all parties are informed about group membership and forthcoming healthcare transaction, as shown in Figure 20.3(c). In order to make sure that group membership will not be changed and that it will not be removed from the list in the next steps, PSP will forward the request for the session key to the CTSS in the following record:

$$R = n||PSP_{id}||CSP_{id}||NSP_{id}||A_p||A_c||A_n$$

If the task of forwarding record $R$ is not given to PSP, it might be possible for CSP and NSP to collude and forward only their authenticators, but without listing the PSP or additional devices, to the CTSS, and thus compromise the key generation process.

CTSS checks whether the contents of authentication records list can be decrypted with the secret keys of the members whose IDs are listed. It further checks whether group membership is the same in all authentication records. If these checks pass, the CTSS generates a symmetric session key $L$ and stores it together

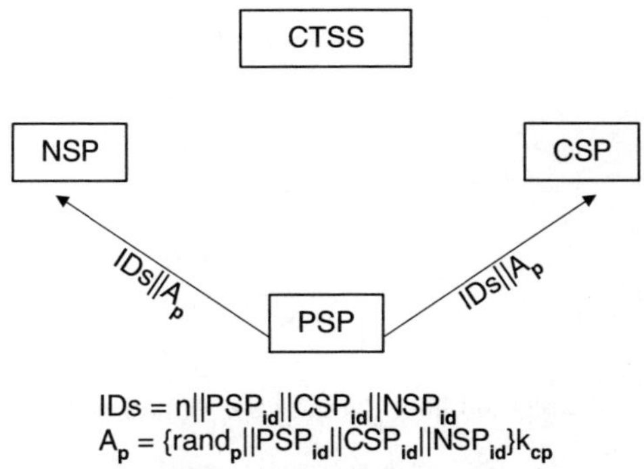


(a) PSP distributes its authenticating record.

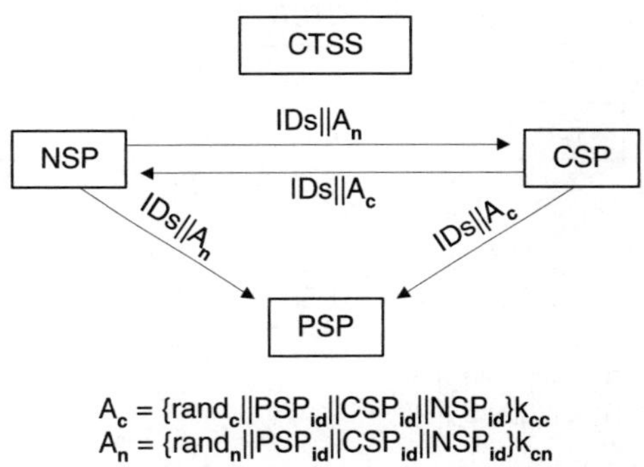


(b) CSP and NSP distribute their authentication records.

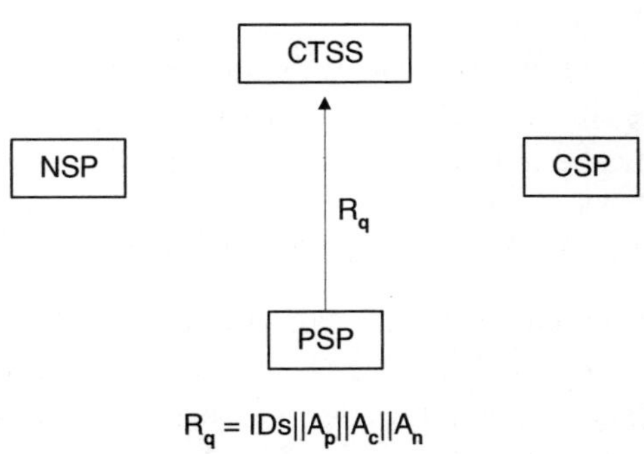


(c) PSP forwards all authentication records to CTSS.

Fig. 20.3. Mutual authentication and session key distribution using keys shared with CTSS.

with the timestamp and IDs of the patient, clinician, and nurse. Then, the CTSS concatenates the session key $L$ with the random challenge from each group member and encrypts it with the secret key shared with that group member. The CTSS will forward the result of this checking to all involved parties, as shown in Figure 20.4(a), be it a positive or negative acknowledgement. Positive acknowledgement contains the session sequence number $n$ and three concatenated key records.

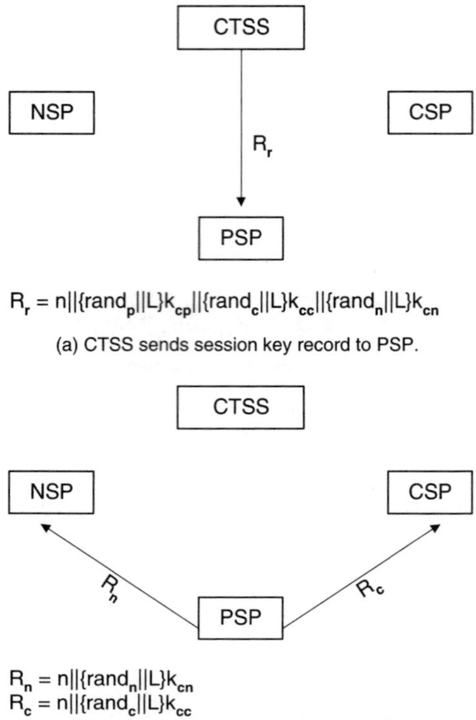


(a) CTSS sends session key record to PSP.

(b) PSP forwards appropriate records to CSP and NSP.

Fig. 20.4. Mutual authentication and session key distribution using keys shared with CTSS.

Each key record contains the corresponding random challenge $rand_p$, $rand_c$, or $rand_n$, and the session key $L$ encrypted with corresponding secret key between CTSS and each involved party ($k_{cp}$, $k_{cc}$ or $k_{cn}$), as follows:

$$R_r = n||\{rand_p||L\}k_{cp}||\{rand_c||L\}k_{cc}||\{rand_n||L\}k_{cn}$$

In the last step, presented in Figure 20.4(b), the PSP distributes appropriate session key records, i.e., $n||\{rand_c||L\}k_{cc}$ and $n||\{rand_n||L\}k_{cn}$ to CSP and NSP, respectively. They decrypt the records with their secret keys $k_{cc}$ and $k_{cn}$, respectively. Upon comparing the received challenge with the original one, they can confirm that the CTSS has generated the record. Note that any phase of this protocol can be interrupted if the received records do not match expected format.

This approach for mutual authentication with ensuring patient's privacy does not require certificates, but relies on the secrecy of the keys $k_{cp}$, $k_{cc}$ and $k_{cn}$ instead. It also relies on the availability of networking channels between the CSP, NSP, and PSP, on one side, and the CTSS, on the other. It also puts computational burden on the CTSS which has to perform the actual authentication. Finally, it makes the CTSS the single most critical point of failure, since it is the only entity authorized to generate the keys, which may or may not be acceptable for a clinical information system. In the latter case, a decentralized approach such as the one discussed in the next Subsection may be more appropriate.

### 20.4.2. *Scaled Multi-Party SSL Protocol with Ephemeral ECC Diffie-Hellman Key Exchange*

Second approach involves exchange of certificates among all parties. We can't use classical X.509 RSA-1024 certificates since they have a length of more than 700 bytes and are thus unsuitable for use in a WSN. However, WSNs allow the digital certificates to contain only identity (ID), public key, and hash of these fields, signed by a Certifying Authority (CA). In the clinical information system application, the role of Certifying Authority may be undertaken by the CTSS. The size of certificate can be further reduced by using ECC, since the size of the ECC signature is equal to approximately two key sizes. For example, with ECC keys of 160 bits, the certificate contains only 86 bytes, as demonstrated in Reference 22. Such certificate can be transmitted in one IEEE 802.15.4 packet which has maximum packet size of 126 bytes [11].

**Step 1** — **Certificate exchange:** In the first step, PSP, CSP, and NSP exchange certificates (with signature keys), as shown in Figure 20.5(a). Certificates with signature keys need to be exchanged whenever new personnel is added to the access list of the patient's record, or when considerably long time has elapsed after the last certificate exchange. Certificates contain public keys for signature verifications. Private signature keys are denoted as $k_{sp}$, $k_{sc}$ and $k_{sn}$ for PSP, CSP, and NSP, respectively.

**Step 2** — **Exchange of challenges:** In the second step, PSP, CSP and NSP exchange acknowledgements for certificates, as shown in Figure 20.5(b). If identity verification was successful, the authenticator node (PSP, CSP or NSP) will send a positive acknowledgement, followed by the new sequence number of the session and a new random challenge. If certificate verification was not successful at this point, any party can interrupt the protocol with a negative acknowledgement. If certificates have been exchanged relatively recently, some sessions may start without exchanging certificates. However, a new sequence number and random challenges need to be exchanged each time when the session key needs to be updated.

**Step 3** — **Request to CTSS:** If all parties have submitted positive acknowledgements, the PSP broadcasts request for session to CTSS, CSP, and NSP, as shown in Figure 20.5(c).

Upon receiving request for a session, the CTSS may take two courses of action, depending on how much autonomy should be given to the PSP, CSP, and NSP. If fully autonomous operation of PSP, CSP and NSP is desirable, then the CTSS should merely note that new session $n$ is to be created between the three of PSP, NSP and CSP. It will leave the key generation process entirely to the PSP, CSP and

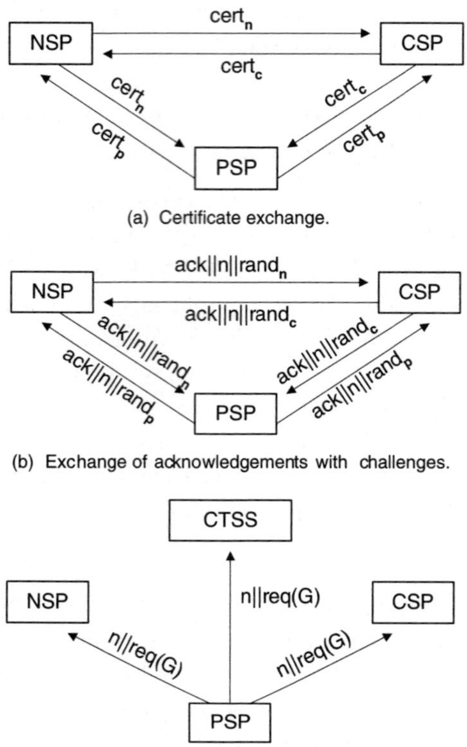


(a) Certificate exchange.

(b) Exchange of acknowledgements with challenges.

(c) Request for the start of key generation process.

Fig. 20.5. Mutual authentication using ECC certificates.

NSP. In this case, PSP, NSP and CSP should have all necessary information for key generation, and they should proceed without the participation of CTSS, except for storing the final key value.

However, in some critical applications the CTSS may undertake a supervisory role in the key generation process. In this work we will discuss this, more general scenario, in which the CTSS coordinates with PSP, CSP and NSP in key distribution process; the case with fully autonomous key generation is just a subset of it.

We will illustrate this approach using multi-party Diffie-Hellman technique with ephemeral key exchange, which is one of the suggested approaches for Secure Socket Layer handshake (SSL) [5]. However, traditional SSL uses the classic Diffie-Hellman key exchange based on Discrete Logarithm Problem [6]. In order to adapt it for use in WSNs, it has to be translated to Elliptic Curve discrete logarithm problem, as discussed in References 7 and 12.

**Step 4 — Base point distribution:** In this step, shown in Figure 20.6(a), the CTSS sends to the PSP, CSP, and NSP the ECC base point $G$ encrypted with dedicated symmetric keys $k_{cp}$, $k_{cc}$, and $k_{cn}$, respectively (these keys protect communications between the CTSS and the PSP, CSP, and NSP,

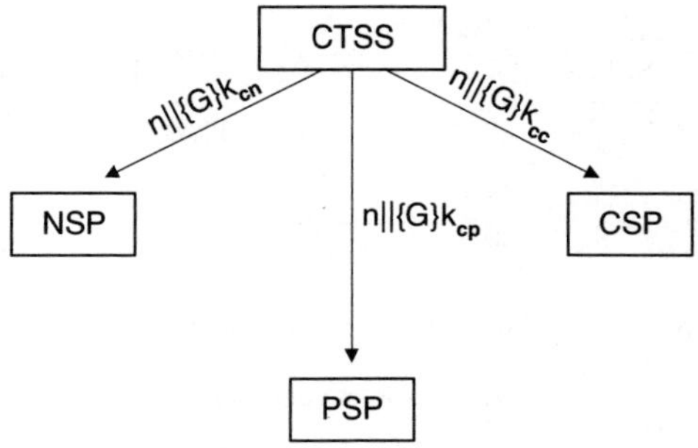


(a) Distribution of base ECC point.

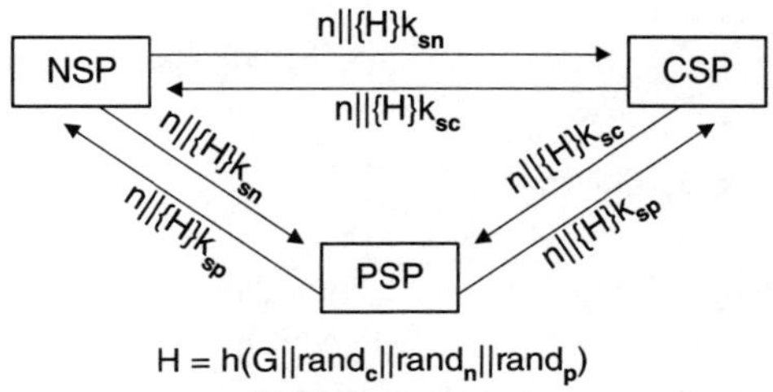


(b) Confirmation.

Fig. 20.6. Distribution of the base ECC point and acknowledgement.

respectively). Note that the ECC base point may be pre-installed in the security processors' certificates, which means that it is constant during the lifetime of the certificate.

**Step 5** — **Confirmation of the reception of base point:** In this step, shown in Figure 20.6(b), the PSP, CSP, and NSP exchange the hash $h(G||rand_c||rand_p||rand_n)$ signed with their private signature keys $k_{sp}$, $k_{sc}$, and $k_{sn}$, respectively.

**Step 6** — **Symmetric key generation:** In this step, the shared symmetric key for the patient group is generated. To reduce complexity, we divide this step in four sub-steps, labeled (6-1) through (6-4).

(6-1) First, the PSP generates a private key $k_p$ and a public key $k_p \cdot G$. It then sends the public key to the NSP, followed by the hash of three challenges concatenated with the base point $G$ and the public key, and encrypted with its private signature key $k_{sp}$, i.e.,

$$sig_p = \{h((k_p \cdot G)||rand_c||rand_n||rand_p||G)\}k_{sp}.$$

Analogous actions are taken by the NSP and CSP, as can be seen from Figure 20.7(a).

(6-2) Then, the PSP computes the scalar point product $k_c \cdot k_p \cdot G$ and sends this value to the CSP, followed by the signature

$$sig_p = \{h((k_p \cdot k_c \cdot G)||rand_c||rand_n||rand_p||G)\}k_{sp}.$$

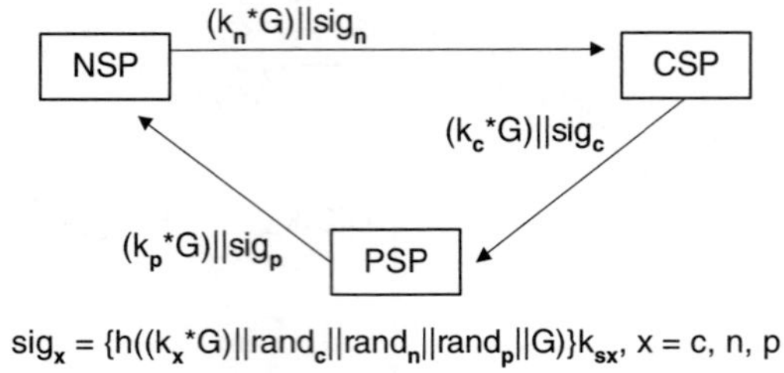


(a) Distribution of public keys.

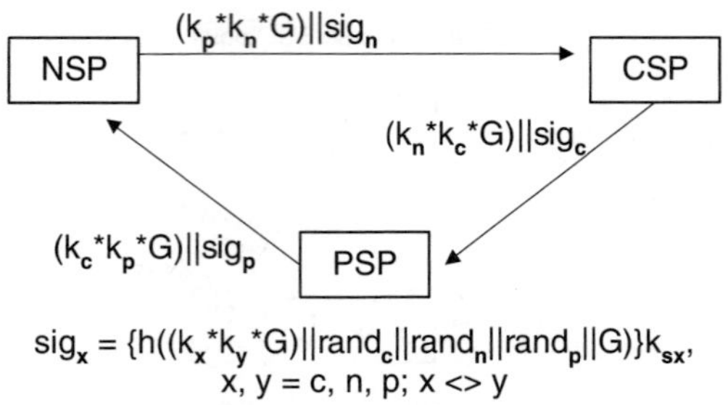


(b) Distribution of products among the members.

Fig. 20.7. Symmetric key generation, first two phases.

Analogous actions are taken by the NSP and CSP, as shown in Figure 20.7(b).

(6-3) Having learned about all three keys, the PSP computes $k_n \cdot k_c \cdot k_p \cdot G$ and sends this value to the CTSS encrypted with the secret symmetric key $k_{cp}$ which is shared between the PSP and the CTSS. That same value is sent by the CSP and NSP, except that their respective secret keys are used for encryption. These actions are presented in Figure 20.8(a).

(6-4) Finally, CTSS generates its own private key $k_s$ and computes the secret key as

$$L = k_s \cdot k_n \cdot k_c \cdot k_p \cdot G.$$

The key $L$ will be sent to the PSP, CSP, and NSP, each time encrypted with their respective secret keys, $k_{cp}$, $k_{cc}$, and $k_{cn}$. These actions are presented in Figure 20.8(b).

### 20.4.3. *Maintenance of the Session Key*

The CTSS stores the session key $L$ together with the timestamp and ID's of the patient, clinician and nurse. Patient data encrypted with this key can be accessed only by the clinician and the nurse who participated in key generation. The session key is also assigned a lifetime by the CTSS, and it has to be re-computed when the lifetime expires. The responsible clinician has the authority to add other clinicians

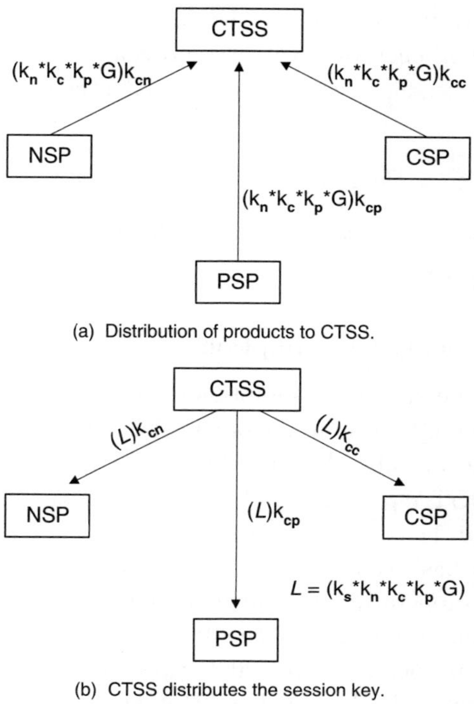


Fig. 20.8. Symmetric key generation, last two phases.

to the access list of the patient record. However, in this case new session key has to be re-computed with the participation of all members of the access list. Therefore, the patient must participate in the key generation process, which will require her consent. When the new session key is computed, the value of the old session key has to be stored in the patient record encrypted with the new session key.

Data packets are authenticated by using keyed-hash message authentication code (HMAC) [5]. For hash function, which will be denoted as $H$, we can adopt the Secure Hash Algorithm (SHA) [18]. Let us denote the $i$-th packet containing measurements of some health variable as $P_i$, the timestamp which records the time of packet generation as $T_{s,i}$, its Medium Access Control header as $A_i$, and its payload as $D_i$. The packet authentication code for packet $i$, PAC$_i$, can then be calculated as

$$PAC_i = H((L \oplus opad)||H(L \oplus ipad||A_i||T_{s,i}||D_i)).$$

### 20.4.4. *Distribution of the Session Key*

When the session key $L$ is calculated, the PSP has to distribute it securely to the wireless sensor nodes in its piconet. When the patient wireless sensor network begins operating, the PSP and each node exchange certificates with signature keys and challenges. Certificates with signature keys need to be exchanged only once during the lifetime of the node. On the other hand, new challenges need to be exchanged each time when the session key needs to be updated. In the next step, PSP sends the new session key $L[n]$ encrypted with the previous session key $L[n-1]$ (here $n$ denotes index of key exchange cycle). This data is authenticated by concatenating it with the signature

$$sig_p = \{h(L[n]||L[n-1]||rand_p||rand_i)\}k_{sp}$$

where $rand_p$ denotes the challenge sent by the PSP, while $rand_i$ denotes the challenge sent by wireless node $n_i$.

## 20.5. Analysis of Energy Consumption

Let us now estimate the energy consumption of the first, centralized algorithm for key generation. For energy consumption of hashing, we have scaled results from [22] derived for 8-bit microcontroller ATMEL ATmega128L using relationships between TelosB and MICA2DOT reported in Reference 19 and further comparison of data sheets for TelosB and Tmote_sky. We have adopted the energy consumption for calculation of SHA-1 hash value to be 0.814 μJ/byte. For energy consumption of encryption/decryption operation we scaled the numbers reported in Reference 22 to 0.25 μJ/byte for encryption and 0.39 μJ/byte for decryption.

For comparison purposes, Table 20.2 gives the energy consumption of a Tmote_sky mote operating in the ISM band [15]. For reference, transmission power of 0 dBm allows the transmission range of about 50 meters indoors and up to 125 meters outdoors, depending on terrain conditions. The impact of collisions, interference, and noise is not taken into account; more details can be found in Reference 14. Values in the Table are calculated for the nominal supply voltage of 2.85 V, which can be supplied by standard 1.5 V batteries. Battery capacity depends on the implementation: typical values for AA batteries are 400 to 900 mAh (milli-Amp-hours) for zinc-carbon batteries, and about 40 to 60% more for zinc-chloride batteries or rechargeable nickel-cadmium ones.

These results show that the energy expenditure of security computations, as seen from the PSP or one of its sensor nodes, is minuscule compared to the energy expenditure of data communication (in particular, reception).

However, our second, decentralized algorithm relies on public key cryptography which is computationally more demanding. Public key computation, shared key computation, and digital signature generation will require one ECC-spm each,

Table 20.2. Current and energy consumption for the Tmote_sky mote.

| operating mode of the radio subsystem | energy consumption at 2.85 V supply voltage (per byte, without collisions) |
|---|---|
| transmitting at 0 dBm | 1.58 μJ |
| transmitting at −3 dBm | 1.38 μJ |
| receiving | 1.79 μJ |
| switched off (idle) | 1.82 nJ |

while digital signature verifications takes two spm [4,12]. Since the analysis from [19] is based on the TelosB [21] mote, which uses the same microcontroller as Tmote_sky but consumes 4 mA, we have used the results for energy consumption from [19] scaled with factor 0.6. Therefore, we assumed that an ECC spm takes 0.5 s and consumes 3.6 mJ. We estimated time and energy for signature generation on Tmote_sky as 0.52 s and 3.75 mJ, while 1.02 s and 7.44 mJ are needed for signature verification [19].

Therefore, the phase which concerns the distribution of base ECC point requires symmetric key decryption by each node; this consumes several dozen of $\mu$J. The phase with confirmation depicted in Figure 20.6(b) requires one digital signature generation and two digital signature verifications, for a total of five ECC-spm. The phase with public key distribution depicted in Figure 20.7(a) will have one public key computation, one digital signature generation, and one digital signature verification per participating node (PSP, CSP and NSP). This results in four spm per node. The phase in which intermediate key products are distributed will require the same number of spm per node as shown in Figure 20.7(b). Distribution of products depicted in Figure 20.8(a) requires one spm and symmetric key encryption per node. Finally, the last phase depicted in Figure 20.8(a) requires only symmetric key decryption by each node. Therefore, one key distribution cycle takes 14 spm or, when using Tmote_sky microcontrollers, around 52.5 mJ. This value is much higher than in the first algorithm, and in fact is much higher than the communication cost. This should come as no surprise, given that the main burden of key generation in the first algorithm rests on the CTSS, which operates from a virtually infinite power source, while the second algorithm relies on computationally demanding actions executed by the security processors themselves.

Obviously, the number of confirmations, intermediate products and cycles to distribute them, and the total energy consumption, will depend on the number of participants — i.e., the number of members on the access list on the patient record.

## 20.6. Conclusion

In this chapter we have presented two algorithms for key distribution in healthcare wireless sensor networks in order to enforce patient's privacy. The first algorithm relies on a central trusted security server to approve membership of the patient's group and to generate the session key. In the second algorithm, participants are less dependent on the central trusted security server, and can authenticate each other using certificates. In both algorithms, the patient's security processor has insight into group membership and leads the key generation process. Both algorithms have their respective strengths and weaknesses. For example, the first, centralized algorithm is more communication intensive, esp. towards the CTSS. Together with the prominent role played by the CTSS, this essentially means that CTSS is a central point of failure. On the other hand, the second algorithm relies on mutual authentication and could, in theory, work even without a CTSS. The price to be paid for this is the computational burden of public key cryptography. In order to ease this burden, we propose to use elliptic curve cryptography which leads to reduced energy consumption required by cryptographic computations. Using the energy consumption data of a commercial 802.5.4 sensor node with a low power microcontroller, we have evaluated the energy consumption of the second, decentralized algorithm. The results show that the use of public key cryptography is feasible, which means that the proposed algorithm can safely be used in practical applications.

## References

[1] R.J. Anderson. A security policy model for clinical information systems. *IEEE Symposium on Security and Privacy*, pp. 34–48, Oakland, CA, May 1996.

[2] B. Arazi, I. Elhanany, O. Arazi, and H. Qi. Revisiting public-key cryptography for wireless sensor networks. *IEEE Computer*, **38**(11):103–105, 2005.

[3] Atmega128(l) — 8-bit AVR microcontroller with 128 k bytes in-system programmable flash. datasheet, ATMEL Corporation, 2006.

[4] G. Bertoni, L. Breveglieri, and M. Venturi. Power aware design of an elliptic curve coprocessor for 8 bit platforms. *PerCom 2006 Workshops*, Mar. 2006.

[5] M. Bishop. *Computer Security — Art and Science*. Pearson Education, Inc., Boston, MA, 2003.

[6] W. Diffie and M.E. Hellman. New directions in cryptography. *it*, **22**(6):644–654, 1976.

[7] A. Fiskiran and R. Lee. Workload characterization of elliptic curve cryptography and other network security for constrained environments. *WWC-5*, pages 127–137, 2002.

[8] G. Gaubatz, J.-P. Kaps, E. Ozturk, and B. Sunar. State of the art in ultra-low power public key cryptography for wireless sensor networks. *PerCom 2005 Workshops*, pages 146–150, 2005.

[9] J. Großschädl. TinySA: A security architecture for wireless sensor networks. In *Proceedings of CoNEXT 2006*, 2006.

[10] D. Hankerson, A. Menezes, and S. Vanstone. *Guide to Elliptic Curve Cryptography.* Springer-Verlag, New York, 2004.

[11] IEEE. Wireless MAC and PHY specifications for low rate WPAN. IEEE Std 802.15.4-2006, IEEE, New York, NY, 2006.

[12] D.J. Malan, M. Welsh, and M.D. Smith. A public-key infrastructure for key distribution in TinyOS based on elliptic curve cryptography. *SECON 2004*, pages 71–80, 2004.

[13] J. Mišić and V.B. Mišić. *Performance Modeling and Analysis of Bluetooth Networks: Network Formation, Polling, Scheduling, and Traffic Control.* CRC Press, Boca Raton, FL, 2005.

[14] J. Mišić and V.B. Mišić. *Wireless Personal Area Networks: Performance, Interconnections, and Security with IEEE 802.15.4*. John Wiley & Sons, New York, NY, 2008.

[15] Moteiv. Tmote_sky low power wireless sensor module, 2006.

[16] B. O'Hara and A. Petrick. *IEEE 802.11 Handbook: a Designers Companion.* IEEE Press, New York, NY, 1999.

[17] D. Otway and O. Rees. Efficient and Timely Mutual Authentication Operating Systems Review, **21**(1), pp. 8–10, 1987.

[18] NIST. *Digital Signature Standard.* US Department of Commerce, Gaithersburg, MD, 1994.
[19] K. Piotrowski and S. Peter. How public key cryptography influences wireless sensor node lifetime. *Fourth ACM workshop on Security of Ad hoc and sensor networks*, pp. 169–176, 2006.
[20] B. Schneier. *Applied Cryptography.* John Wiley & Sons, Inc., New York, N.Y., 2nd edition, 1996.
[21] TelosB mote platform datasheet. mote datasheet, CrossBow Technology, 2006.
[22] A.S. Wander, N. Gura, H. Eberle, V. Gupta, and S.C. Shantz. Energy analysis of public-key cryptography for wireless sensor networks. *PerCom 2005*, pp. 324–328, Mar. 2005.

# Chapter 21

## SECURITY IMPLEMENTATION IN REAL WIRELESS SENSORS: A REVIEW

Fei Hu* and Nidhi Verma
*Department of Computer Engineering*
*College of Engineering, RIT, Rochester, New York*
**fei.hu@rit.edu*

Yang Xiao
*Department of Computer Science*
*University of Alabama, Tuscaloosa, AL 35487–0290*
*yangxiao@ieee.org*

Wireless sensor networks, consisting of micro-sensors for the purpose of monitoring physical environments, have emerged as important new applications for wireless technology. Fusion of networking with wireless sensor technology has led to development of key attributes like severely constrained computation and energy resources, and ad hoc networking environment. This chapter provides a review of security issues of wireless sensor networks, and compares and contrasts various security methods available for these networks today.

### 21.1. Introduction

Wireless sensor networks (WSNs) used for monitoring physical environment have come up as a result of the integration of wireless communications and embedded computing technologies. A WSN consists of hundred or thousands of sensor nodes, low power devices equipped with one or more sensors. Besides sensors, a sensor node typically contains signal processing circuits, microcontrollers, and a wireless transmitter/receiver. By feeding information about the physical world into the existing information infrastructure, these networks are expected to lead to a future where computing is closely coupled with the physical world. Potential applications include monitoring remote or inhospitable locations, target tracking in battlefields, disaster relief networks, early fire detection in forests, and environmental monitoring. While recent research has focused on energy efficiency, network protocols, and distributed databases, there are some attentions given to security [1–22]. In many applications, security aspects are as important as performance and low energy consumption. Besides battlefield applications, security is critical in sensors in critical systems such as airports, hospitals, etc. WSNs have distinctive features, and the most important two are being constrained energy and computational resources.

This chapter will summarize and compare the most famous and implemented security architectures on various platforms including flavors of authentications, bits for key, communication, computation overhead, etc. The chapter begins with Tinysec, followed by ECC (Elliptic Curve Cryptography), LEAP (Localized Encryption and Authentication Protocol), SPINS (security Protocol for sensor networks) (Snep and Tesla), MPA (Multi Path Authentication), LHAP (Light weight hop by hop Authentication Protocol). The chapter ends with a tabular comparison of the above mentioned security architectures.

## 21.2. TinySec: A Link Layer Security Design

TinySec [1] is a link layer architecture designed by a team of 3 dedicated individuals from the University of California, Berkeley. It is said to be the first fully-implemented link layer security architecture for wireless sensor networks.

TinySec is a more recent solution to the sensor link layer security problem. The TinySec protocol provides access control, message integrity, and message confidentiality. TinySec explicitly omits replay protection, recommending it be performed at the application layer. The designers of the protocol emphasized usability and transparency in hopes of increasing TinySec's adoption. To this end, TinySec has been incorporated into the official release of TinyOS, the small, event-driven operating system designed for sensor motes. TinySec has been fully implemented and exhibits promising performance. Encryption and authentication can be performed in software with only 10% energy overhead and 8% increased latency.

### 21.2.1. *Reasons of the Need of Link Layer Security*

Link Layer security is needed, primarily because it is transparent and covers message integrity, authenticity, and confidentiality. Also the end to end security will not be possible since the communication frequency is dense and at times many sensors may not the same change in environment parameters and send similar data to the base station. It will also increase the data length and use more energy.

#### 21.2.1.1. *TinySec design*

TinySec Operates in the following two modes: (1) Authenticated Encryption (TinySec–AE) and Authentication Only (TinySec–Auth). With the authenticated encryption, TinySec encrypts the data packet and authenticates the packet with a Message Authentication Code (MAC). The MAC is computed after the data has been encrypted along with the packet header. In authentication only mode, data is not encrypted but TinySec authenticates the entire packet with a MAC.

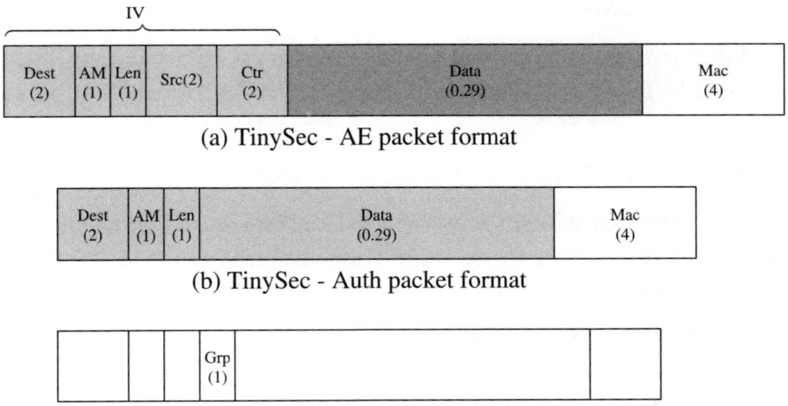


(a) TinySec - AE packet format

(b) TinySec - Auth packet format

(c) TinyOS - Data Packet

Fig. 21.1. TinySec Data Packet (Legends: **Dest:** Destination address; **AM:** Active Message type; it is similar to port numbers in TCP/IP. The AM type specifies the appropriate handler function to decrypt, extract and interpret the message on the receiver side; **Len:** Length).

### 21.2.2. *TinySec Packet Format*

After seeing the different modes of Tinysec, let us see the Tinysec and TinyOS data packets in Figure 21.1. We will later compare these two data packets and observe interesting facts.

As observed, these fields in Figure 21.1 are unencrypted because it can be sent in that fashion and also it may lead to saving some power since a sensor node may go back to sleep mode after determining that the message is not addressed to it.

If the address and AM type are encrypted, early rejection cannot be invoked until these fields are decrypted. This wastes energy. Encrypting the length field adds little to security since the length of message can be inferred regardless.

To detect transmission errors, TinyOS senders compute a 16-bit cycle redundancy check (CRC) over the packet. The receiver re-computes the CRC during reception and verifies it with the received CRC field. If they are equal, the receiver accepts the packet and rejects it otherwise. However, CRCs provide no security against malicious modification or forgery of packets.

To guarantee message integrity and authenticity, TinySec replaces the CRC with a MAC. The MAC protects the entire packet, including the destination address, AM type, length, source address and counter (if present), and the data (whether encrypted or not). This protects the data from tampering. It also prevents attackers from redirecting a packet intended for one node to another node, and prevents packet truncation and other attacks. Since MACs detect malicious changes, they also detect transmission errors, and TinySec does not require a CRC. The TinyOS packet format contains a group field to prevent different sensor networks from interfering with each other. It can be thought of as a kind of weak access control mechanism for non-malicious environments.

### 21.2.3. *Using TinySec in TinyOS Applications*

TinySec is fairly easy to apply to the traditional non-security communication stack. In order to enable TinySec, include to Makefile, "TINYSEC=true", or in command line type:

"make platform_name_pc_mica_mica2 TINYSEC=true"

By default TinySec will only authenticate all messages, without encryption. TinySecMode has two commands to setup transmit and receive mode. For example, enable TinySec default settings by using

```
# add the following line in the Makefile
TINYSEC=true
COMPONENT=Blink
include ../Makerules
```

### 21.2.4. *Different Modes of Operation in TinySec*

There are different modes of operation for transmission and receiving in TinySec.

#### 21.2.4.1. *Enabling TinySec mode*

In order to change the modes of operations, *TinySecMode* interface must be used which can be exported using the *TinySecC* component. Here are the steps to wire and setup.

a. Add "TINYSEC=true" in *Makefile.*
b. In the interface file (*.nc), export from *TinySecC* component the *TinySecMode* interface.
c. Wire the module component to the *TinySecC.*
d. In the module file (*M.nc), add in "uses", the TinySecMode interface.
e. Call the commands to change the transmission/receive mode.

#### 21.2.4.2. *Key management*

TinySec uses symmetric keys to encrypt and authenticate messages. When TinySec is first used a default key is created in a file called: *~/.tinyos_keyfile*, which looks like this:

```
# TinySec Keyfile. By default, the first key will be used.
# You can import other keys by appending them to the file.
default A9FB5D03138166ABD1639B360E4263D4
```

When programming devices from different computers, they must all have the same key-file. When TinySec is enabled, the concept of "groups" no longer exists. The motes will only receive messages from motes that share the same key, which is enforced cryptographically.

Notice that the key stored in the ".tinyos_keyfile" is composed of 32 hex values. TinySec uses key size of 8 bytes or 16 hex values. The first 16 hex values are used as the key for encryption, and the last 16 hex values are used for authentication.

#### 21.2.4.3. *Updating keys*

*TinySecControl* enables the user to update TinySec keys and reset the initialization vector (IV), with these following commands:

```
command result_t updateMACKey(uint8_t * MACKey);
command result_t getMACKey(uint8_t * result);
command result_t updateEncryptionKey(uint8_t * encryptionKey);
command result_t getEncryptionKey(uint8_t * result);
command result_t resetIV();
command result_t getIV(uint8_t * result)
```

### 21.2.5. *Advantages of TinySec*

- It is called lightweight because it doesn't add much overhead unlike 802.11, GSM, Bluetooth etc.
- It is identified as a generic security package because it can be paired with other high level algorithms and be used as an open research platform for evaluating them. Also developers can easily integrate into other sensor network applications.
- TinySec is portable to a variety of hardware and radio platforms. It also has a software cryptographic module and doesn't need any hardware assistance like Bluetooth, GSM etc.
- TinySec can be used for secure pair wise communication in public key cryptography.

## 21.3. Elliptic Curve Cryptography

### 21.3.1. *Introduction*

Elliptic curve systems applied to cryptography were first proposed in 1985 independently by Neal Koblitz from the University of Washington, and Victor Miller, who was then at IBM, Yorktown Heights. Elliptic curve cryptography (ECC) is an approach of public-key cryptography based on the mathematics of elliptic curves. It provides fast decryption and digital signature processing. The main benefit of ECC is that under certain situations it uses smaller keys than other methods — such as RSA — while providing an equivalent or higher level of security. ECC uses points on an elliptic curve to derive a 163-bit public key that is equivalent in strength to a 1024-bit RSA key. Hence smaller number of keys leads to faster key operation and less memory needed. It is said to be ideal for resource-constrained systems because it provides more "security per bit" than other types of asymmetric cryptography. One drawback, however, is that the implementation of encryption and decryption operations may take longer than in other schemes.

### 21.3.2. *Motivation for using Elliptic Curve Cryptography*

As previously mentioned before, RSA and ECC are both public key algorithms. RSA [7] is the most used public key algorithm but ECC [8] can provide the same security at much smaller key size. RSA-1024 is equivalent to ECC-160 bit key [9]. It has also been also calculated that by the year 2010 we have to use RSA-2048 but in case of ECC: ECC-224 will be needed! In this section we will see the comparison between both and learn why ECC is better for the embedded sensor network as a public key algorithm. The energy analysis has been done on the Mica2dots [2], which is one of the popular research platforms for WSN [9]. It has been noted that the power required to transmit 1 bit is equivalent to roughly 2090 clock cycles of execution on the Mica2dot microcontroller. The cost of receiving one byte ($28.6\,\mu$J) is roughly half of that required to transmit a byte ($59.2\,\mu$J). During transmission and reception, the microcontroller is powered on along with the wireless transceiver. The usual packet size is 32 for the payload and 9 bytes for the header. The header, ensuing an 8-byte preamble, consists of source, destination, length, packet ID, CRC, and a control byte. Receiving one 41-byte packet (including 8-byte preamble) costs $49*28.6\,\mu\text{J} = 1.40\,\text{mJ}$ and transmitting one 41-byte packet costs $49*59.2\,\mu\text{J} = 2.90\,\text{mJ}$. To summarize, we have the following table (Table 21.1).

### 21.3.3. *Math for RSA vs. ECC*

Verification of RSA is cheap but what makes it expensive is the signature for authentication. This is due to the fact that RSA-based key exchange protocol relies on party A to encrypt a randomly generated secret key with party B's public key, and party B decrypting the key using its private key. Now for ECC the signature algorithm is called: Elliptic Curve Digital Signature Algorithm (ECDSA) [10]. For ECDSA the signature and verification both are inexpensive. The transition from RSA-1024 to RSA-2048 the energy cost of signing increases by a factor of more than seven, while ECDSA-224 signing is less than three times as expensive as ECDSA-160 signing. With ECC, both parties perform a single Elliptic Curve Diffie-Hellman (ECDH) operation to derive the secret key. From [9], we have Table 21.2.

The above is measured in mille Joules. Hence with the facts, figures and numbers we can clearly say that ECC is a better choice.

Table 21.1. Energy consumption.

| | |
|---|---|
| Effective data rate | 12.4 kbps |
| Energy to transmit | $59.2\,\mu$J/byte |
| Energy to receive | $28.6\,\mu$J/byte |

Table 21.2. Comparison chat for RSA and ECC.

| | Signature | | Key exchange | |
|---|---|---|---|---|
| Algorithm | Sign | Verify | Client | Server |
| RSA–1024 | 304 | 11.9 | 15.4 | 304 |
| ECDSA–160 | 22.82 | 45.09[3] | 22.3 | 22.3 |
| RSA–2048 | 2302.7 | 53.7 | 57.2 | 2302.7 |
| ECDSA–224 | 61.54 | 121.98[3] | 60.4 | 60.4 |

### 21.3.4. *Asymmetric Cryptography as a Fine Balance*

It has been claimed that public key cryptosystems are not feasible to implement in these tiny devices because they are constrained with less resources but this is not true [12]. Asymmetric cryptography is a marvelous technology. Its uses are many and varied.

For many situations in distributed network environments, asymmetric cryptography is a must during communications. For instance, key distribution or any kind of network protocol or application requires secure communications such as buying something on the Internet, when the vendor is using a secure server.

But asymmetric cryptography is demanding and complex, by nature. The hard problems in number theory — the key to the algorithms' functionality — are all intrinsically difficult.

In short, asymmetric cryptography is demanding, but looking at the cryptosystem for more security per bit, ECC is a better choice.

#### 21.3.4.1. *Why asymmetric cryptography?*

Asymmetric cryptographic algorithms do not use a single key as in symmetric cryptographic algorithms such as AES, but a key pair. One of the keys (the public key) is used for encryption, and its corresponding private key must be used for decryption. The critical feature of asymmetric cryptography, which makes it useful, is this key pair — and more specifically, a particular feature of the key pair: the fact that one of the keys cannot be obtained from the other. In all asymmetric cryptosystems, as mentioned above, the key length is the parameter that determines how difficult both the forward and inverse algorithms are.

Hence, the inverse operation rapidly becomes more difficult as key length increases than does the forward operation, as shown in Figure 21.2.

ECC is a set of algorithms for key generation, encryption and decryption and perform asymmetric cryptography.

### 21.3.5. *Authentication with Asymmetric Cryptography*

In the case of asymmetric authentication methods there are two main entities: private key (in the possession of the entity wishing to prove its identity) and the

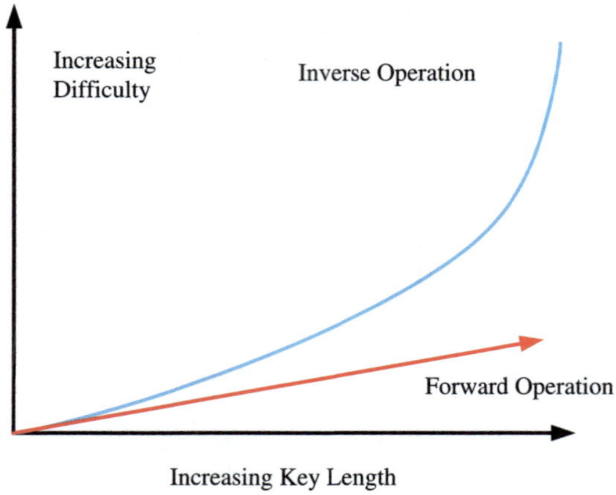


Fig. 21.2. Key length vs. increased security.

public key (in the possession of anyone who wishes to verify the identity of the entity possessing the private key).

The public key can verify the knowledge of the private key but the private key cannot be derived from the public key. This is the critical feature of asymmetric cryptographic schemes that makes them so useful.

This property is useful for a number of reasons: it greatly simplifies key exchange, as one example, and it solves one critical problem symmetric cryptography cannot solve — the problem of guaranteeing unique authentication and non-repudiation. Symmetric hashing/authentication methods — ones for which there is only one key, and both parties in the exchange use it both for authentication and for signature generation — have the distinct disadvantage that they do not, on their own, offer any way to distinguish which party to the exchange signed a given message. If both or all parties must know the key, based on cryptography alone, you cannot distinguish which signed any given message, because any of them could have. In asymmetric authentication schemes, only one party knows the private key, with which the message is signed. Any number may know the public key. Since the private key cannot be derived from the public, the signature serves as a unique identifier. If the message verifies as having been signed by the person with knowledge of the private key, we can narrow down who sent the message to one. But any number of people may have knowledge of the public key, and all of them can therefore verify the identity of the sender.

### 21.3.6. *How are Elliptic Curves Used?*

The crucial property of an elliptic curve is that we can define a rule for "adding" two points which are on the curve, to obtain a 3rd point which is also on the curve. Having defined addition of two points, we can also define multiplication $k * P$ where

$k$ is a positive integer and $P$ is a point as the sum of $k$ copies of $P$, thus we have

$$2 * P = P + P$$
$$3 * P = P + P + P$$

For example, Alice, Bob, Cathy, and David agree on a (non-secret) elliptic curve and a (non-secret) fixed curve point $F$. Alice chooses a secret random integer $Ak$ which is her secret key, and publishes the curve point $AP = Ak * F$ as her public key. Bob, Cathy and David do the same. Now suppose that Alice wishes to send a message to Bob. One method is for Alice to simply compute $Ak * BP$ and use the result as the secret key for a conventional symmetric block cipher (say DES). Bob can compute the same number by calculating: $Bk * AP$, since $Bk * AP = Bk * (Ak * F) = (Bk * Ak) * F = Ak * (Bk * F) = Ak * BP$.

Although the starting point and public key are known, it is extremely difficult to backtrack and derive the private key. An essential property for cryptography is that a group has a finite number of points.

### 21.3.7. *The Diffie Hellman/DSA Cryptosystems and the Discrete Logarithm Problem*

Diffie Hellman along with the Digital Signature Algorithm (DSA) based on it is another of the asymmetric cryptosystems in general use.

ECC, in a sense, is an evolved form of Diffie Hellman. Therefore, to understand how ECC works, it helps to understand how Diffie Hellman works first.

Diffie Hellman uses a problem known as the discrete logarithm problem as its central, asymmetric operation. The discrete log problem concerns finding a logarithm of a number within a finite field arithmetic system.

Prime fields are fields whose sets are prime, and they have a prime number of members. These are of particular interest in asymmetric cryptography because, over a prime field, exponentiation turns out to be a relatively easy operation, while the inverse computing the logarithm is very difficult.

To generate a key pair in the discrete logarithm (DL) system, therefore, the calculation is as follows: $y = (gx) \mod p$, where $p$ is a large prime — the field size, $x$ and $g$ are smaller than $p$, $y$ is the public key, and $x$ is used as the private key. In Diffie Hellman, we wish to make the operations 'easy' or tractable, we harness to the operation in the field which is (relatively) easy — exponentiation. Therefore, encryption using the public key is an exponentiation operation. Decryption using the private key is as well. Decryption using the public key, however, would require performing the difficult inverse operation — solving the discrete logarithm problem. The discrete logarithm problem, using the values in the equation $y = (gx) \mod p$, is simply finding $x$ given only $y$, $g$ and $p$.

If multiplying $g$ by $x$, the result into the field (performed the modulo operation) is as often as necessary to keep the result smaller than $p$. Now, knowing $y$, $g$ and $p$, the problem is to find out what value of $x$ used. It turns out that for large enough values of $p$, where $p$ is prime, this is extraordinarily difficult to do — much more difficult than just finding $y$ from $g$, $x$ and $p$. ECC defines its group differently, and is, in fact, the difference in how the group is defined and particularly how the mathematical operations within the group are defined that give ECC its greater security for a given key size.

### 21.3.8. *The Elliptic Curve Discrete Logarithm Problem*

The elliptic curve discrete logarithm problem [11] is the cornerstone of much of present-day elliptic curve cryptography. It relies on the natural group law on a non-singular elliptic curve which allows one to add points on the curve together. Given an elliptic curve $E$ over a finite field $F$, a point on that curve, $P$, and another point you know to be an integer multiple of that point, $Q$, the problem is to find the integer $n$ such that $nP = Q$.

The problem is computationally difficult unless the curve has a 'bad' number of points over the given field, where the term 'bad' encompasses various collections of numbers of points which make the elliptic curve discrete logarithm problem breakable. For example, if the number of points on $E$ over $F$ is the same as the number of elements of $F$, then the curve is vulnerable to attack. It is because of these issues that point-counting on elliptic curves is such a hot topic in elliptic curve cryptography.

The inverse operation to point multiplication finding a log in a group defined on an elliptic curve over a prime field is defined as follows: given points $Q$ and $P$, to find the integer $k$ such that $Q = kP \mod s$.

This is the elliptic curve discrete logarithm problem and this is the inverse operation in the cryptosystem, the one we effectively have to perform to get the plaintext back from the cipher text, given only the public key.

Now naively, the obvious, certain way of finding $k$ would be to perform repeated addition operations stepping through $P$, $2P$, $3P$, and so on, until we find $kP$. Begin by doubling $P$, then adding $P$ to $2P$ finding $3P$, then $3P$ to $P$ finding $4P$ and so on. This is the brute force method. The difficulty with this approach is by using a large enough prime field, and the number of possible values for $k$ becomes inconveniently large. It is so inconveniently large that it's quite not practical to create a sufficiently large prime field that searching through the possible values of $k$ would take all the processor time currently available on the planet thousands of years.

### 21.3.9. *Elliptic Curve Groups*

Many cryptosystems require the use of algebraic groups [2]. Elliptic curves may be used to form elliptic curve groups. A group is a set of elements with custom-defined arithmetic operations on those elements. For elliptic curve groups, these specific operations are defined geometrically. Introducing more stringent properties to the elements of a group, such as limiting the number of points on an elliptic curve, creates an underlying field for an elliptic curve group. Elliptic curves are first examined over real numbers in order to illustrate the geometrical properties of elliptic curve groups. Thereafter, elliptic curves groups are examined with the underlying fields of $F_p$ (*where p is a prime*) and $F_2$m (*a binary representation with* $2^m$ *elements*).

### 21.3.10. *Advantages of ECC*

ECC offers considerably greater security for a given key size.

The smaller key size also makes possible much more compact implementations for a given level of security. This means faster cryptographic operations, running on smaller chips or more compact software. This also means less heat production and less power consumption — all of which is of particular advantage in constrained devices, but of some advantage anywhere else.

There are extremely efficient, compact hardware implementations available for ECC exponentiation operations, offering potential reductions in implementation footprint even beyond those due to the smaller key length alone.

## 21.4. LEAP: Localized Encryption & Authentication Protocol

LEAP stands for Localized Encryption and Authentication Protocol [5]; it is a protocol for managing the key for the sensor networks. These sensor network are supposed to construe the network security so that even a node gets compromised it doesn't affect the immediate network neighborhood of the compromised node.

With the help of application level information and use of node level density, the nodes can be turned off as per requirement.

The design module is based on the pragmatic observation that different messages may have different security requirement based on the source and destination nodes. Hence LEAP supports the establishment of four types of keys for each sensor node:

- An Individual key shared with the base station,
- A Pair Wise key shared with another sensor node,
- Cluster key shared with multiple neighboring nodes,
- Group key that is shared by all the nodes in the network, depending on the number of nodes in the network.

The key based system is based on symmetric key schemes. The degree of key sharing between nodes in the system is a major deciding factor. The most practical approach for embedding or bootstrapping secret keys in sensor networks is to use pre-deployed keying in which keys are loaded into sensor nodes before they are deployed. There are two extremes for sharing the keys: One is the extreme use of shared key all throughout the network and other extreme is sharing pair wise keys for all pairs of nodes. With the pair wise keys the probability that the nodes will be compromised is rare but under this approach, each node will need a unique key for every other node that it communicates with. Moreover, in many sensor networks, the immediate neighbors of a sensor node cannot be predicted in advance; consequently, these pair wise shared keys will need to be established after the network is deployed.

One mode of communication is passive participation in which in-network processing of s sensor node can take certain actions based on overheard messages. But for this the entire network should share the same key so that intermediate nodes can encrypt/decrypt the messages. On the other hand, if a pair wise shared key is used for encrypting or authenticating a message, it effectively precludes passive participation in the sensor network.

LEAP also includes an efficient protocol for inter-node traffic authentication based on the use of one-way key chains. A salient feature of the authentication protocol is that it supports source authentication. Assumptions made by this protocol to be established include that every node has space for storing up to hundreds of bytes of keying materials; the sensor nodes can be deployed via aerial scattering or by physical installation; also if a node is sabotaged all the information is lost and the adversary can inject/eavesdrop/fake model/network hog or use any other method to compromise the nodes.

Now the four main categories of keys are as follows subsections [5].

### 21.4.1. *Individual Key*

Every node has a unique key that it shares pair wise with the base station. This key is used for secure communication between a node and the base station. This can be used to send individual observation and data collected by nodes. It can be used by the base station too to send individual commands, authentications etc. This key is generated and pre-loaded into each node prior to its deployment. In this scheme the controller might only keep its master key to save the storage for keeping all the individual keys. When it needs to communicate with an individual node $u$, it computes its individual key based on a pseudo random function on the fly. Due to the computational efficiency of pseudo random functions, the computational overhead is negligible.

### 21.4.2. *Group Key*

This is a globally shared key that is used by the base station for encrypting messages that are broadcasted to the whole group. Since the group key is shared among all the nodes in the network, an efficient re keying mechanism is necessary for updating this key after a compromised node is revoked.

### 21.4.3. *Cluster Key*

This category of key is shared by a node and all its neighbors, and it is mainly used for securing locally broadcast messages, specifically in heterogeneous systems, e.g., routing control information, or securing sensor messages.

### 21.4.4. *Pair wise Shared Key*

Every node shares a pair wise key with each of its immediate neighbors. This will be used to communication sensitive information, data commands that require privacy or source authentication. F or example, a node can use its pair wise keys to secure the distribution of its cluster key to its neighbors, or to secure the transmissions of its sensor readings to an aggregation node. For nodes whose neighborhood relationships are predetermined, e.g., via physical installation, pair wise key establishment is simply done by preloading the sensor nodes with the corresponding keys.

### 21.4.5. *Multi-hop Pair wise Shared Keys*

These keys are used to send readings to an aggregation node or the cluster head that is multiple hops away. This can be extend from the (one-hop) pair wise shared key establishment scheme discussed above for the establishment of two-hop pair wise keys. Specifically, once a node discovers its neighbors in the *neighbor discovery* phase, it then broadcasts their ids. As a result, a node discovers all the nodes that can be reached in two hops. It can then establish a pair wise shared key with all the nodes that are two hops away using the same scheme it used for one-hop pair wise key establishment.

### 21.4.6. *Group Keys*

A group key is a key shared by all the nodes in the network, and it is necessary when the controller is distributing a secure message, e.g., a query on some event of interest or a confidential instruction, to all the nodes in the network. One way for the base station to distribute a message $M$ securely to all the nodes is using hop-by-hop translation. Specifically, the base station encrypts $M$ with its cluster key and then broadcasts the message. Each neighbor receiving the message decrypts it to obtain $M$, re-encrypts $M$ with its own cluster key, and then re-broadcasts the message. The process is repeated until all the nodes receive $M$. However, this approach has a major drawback, i.e., each intermediate node needs to encrypt and decrypt the message, thus consuming a non-trivial amount of energy on computation.

Under LEAP [5], $\mu$TESLA is implemented as broadcast authentication protocol. $\mu$TESLA assures the authenticity of a broadcast message by using one-way key chain and delayed key disclosure.

### 21.4.7. *Advantages of LEAP*

The combinational use of LEAP's keys can give rise to a robust key structure:

LEAP uses $\mu$TESLA for inter-node traffic authentication based on the use of one-way key chains.

The mechanism enabled easy flow of net work processing at the same time posing a thick wall to the outer nodes and invaders which may want to compromise the network nodes.

The key establishment and key updating procedures used by LEAP are efficient and the storage requirements per node are small.

LEAP provides a flexible way to provide security, by using combination of its keys it can form a robust network and the same can be relaxed by implementing one kind of key and authentication scheme can prevent/increase the difficulty of launching security attacks on sensor networks.

## 21.5. SPINS: Security Protocols for Sensor Networks

SPINS [6] present a suite of security protocols in the form of two building blocks are follows:

SNEP (data confidentiality and 2 party authentication)
$\mu$TESLA (one way authenticated broadcast)

The network is bootstrapped with shared secret key between nodes and the base station.

SNEP advocates low communication overhead by adding only 8 bytes per message. It provides two flavors of data freshness: weak and strong. Strong data freshness is achieved when the randomly long unpredictable number (called nonce) is used in case of repetitive data to preserve semantic security for e.g., 'yes' and 'no'.

Data sent from point $A$ to point $B$ comprises of requested message $R$ and MAC. The requested message is composed of encrypted $K_{\text{encr}}$ key & counter $C$. It is like beaconing and adds an additional layer of indirection and privacy. MAC is a function of $K_{\text{mac}}$ (derived from Master key), nonce and counter. Data ready to send is stated as follows: $\{R\}_{\langle \text{Kencr},C\rangle}$, MAC $(K_{\text{mac}}, N_a|C|\{R\}_{\langle \text{Kencr},C\rangle})$.

The Counter $C$ is used to save energy instead of sending long randomized data over RF channel. Weak data freshness is achieved by using only the counter as follows: data from node $A$ to node $B$ is encrypted with $K_{\text{encr}}$ and $C$. It is later concatenated with MAC which is a function of $K_{\text{mac}}$ and encrypted data. In notational language, data ready to send is stated as follows: $\{D\}_{\langle \text{Kencr},C\rangle}$, MAC $(K_{\text{mac}}, C|\{D\}_{\langle \text{Kencr},C\rangle})$.

$\mu$TESLA promotes symmetric key communication by loosely time synchronizing the nodes with the base station. It implements modified one way authentication from TESLA as follows. To send an authenticated packet, the base station simply computes a MAC on the packet with a key that is secret at that point in time. When a node gets a packet, it can verify that the corresponding MAC key was not yet disclosed by the base station (based on its loosely synchronized clock, its maximum synchronization error, and the time schedule at which keys are disclosed). Since a receiving node is assured that the MAC key is known only by the base station, the receiving node is assured that no adversary could have altered the packet in transit. The node stores the packet in a buffer. At the time of key disclosure, the base station broadcasts the verification key to all receivers. When a node receives the disclosed key, it can easily verify the correctness of the key. If the key is correct, the node can now use it to authenticate the packet stored in its buffer. Two main points worth mentioning is that this requires additional buffer, processing time and proper time synchronization. Also MAC key is a key of a key chain, generated by a public one-way function $F$. To generate the one-way key chain, the sender chooses the last key Kn of the chain randomly, and repeatedly applies $F$ to compute all other keys: $\text{Ki} = F(\text{Ki} + 1)$.

Energy Costs are as follows: Encryption Computation $<1\%$, Encryption Transmission $<1\%$, Freshness Transmission 7%, Computation $<1\%$, MAC Computation 2%, MAC Transmission 20%, and Data Transmission 71%.

The advantages of SNEP include: achieving semantic security, providing 2 flavors of data freshness, data authentication by using MAC, and low communication overhead per application.

## 21.6. MPA: Multi Path Authentication

Multi-path authentication (MPA) [8] in the sensor nodes is used to verify the claimed identity of an entity. This is done by implementing authentication protocols. It is an entirely different branch from security and data encryption. This methodology considers message authentication protocol in low power sensors. It governs multi path authentication to reduce energy consumption.

### 21.6.1. *Types of Message Passing*

- **Content based** under which data is routed as per the content. If the nodes register for certain contents, they receive the required data. Also this assumes that network has broadcast media and saves the memory as nodes save small routing information if any.
- **Aggregation** for which sensor data is passed around to find higher order events that can't be reliably inferred from other sensor node. It is best practices when the data is aggregated within the network and not at the base station.
- **Base oriented** communication which is governed by base station. It acts as the central authority and governs all communication media.

For all of the above message passing schemes the authentication can be covered under one of the follows:

- **End to end** authentication checks credentials of the source and destination. This can be intervened by the base station or the nodes can be self sufficient and verify other nodes credentials on its own.
- **Hop by hop** authentication fragments the authentication per hop or stops, this puts each node under strict requirement.
- **Multi path** routing does not rely on a single node to forward messages correctly. Instead the data is sent on many alternating paths in parallel. If different

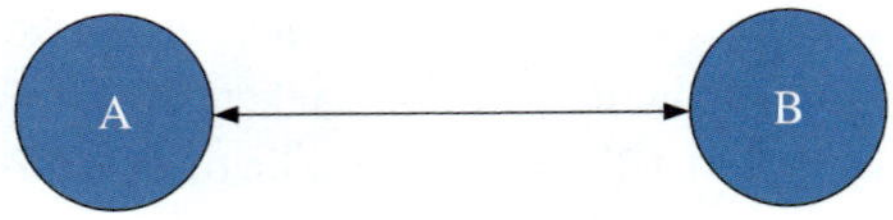


Fig. 21.3. End-to-End authentication.

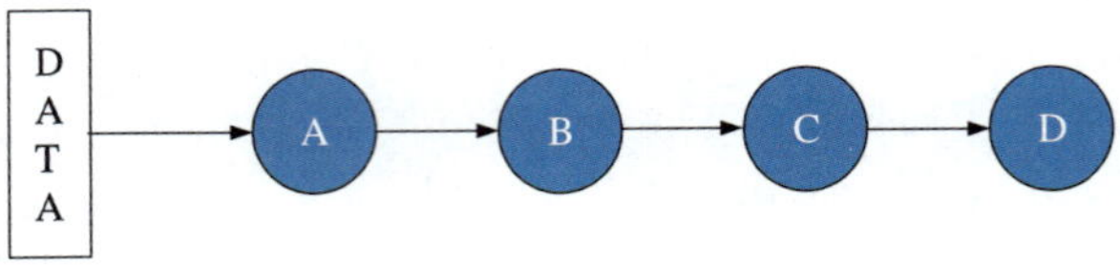


Fig. 21.4. Hop-by-Hop authentication.

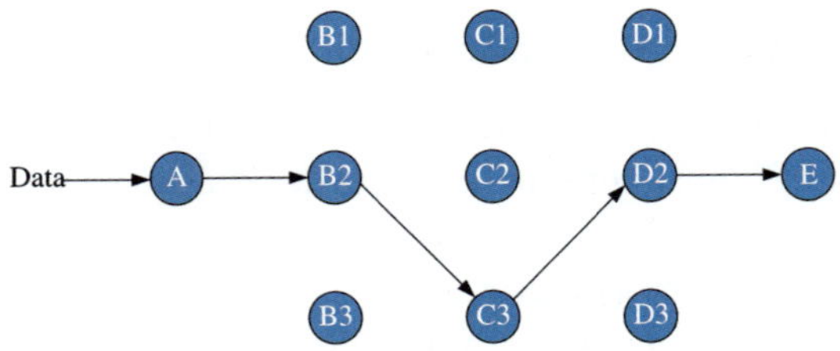


Fig. 21.5. Virtual multipath authentication.

versions of a message are received, the recipient chooses the majority version. All other paths can be marked as untrustworthy, since they delivered a presumably incorrect message.

When combined with hop to hop authentication it forms **multi path authentication**. One step further is the virtual multi path authentication for which data is restricted on one physical media where authentication path is virtual. One necessary condition is that the nodes need to share pair wise keys.

### 21.6.2. *Distribution of Keys*

The distribution of these pair wise shared keys can be random, or can be based on a regular pattern. A regular distribution guarantees that there exists a number of node disjoint authentication paths between any two communicating nodes. When there are two authentication schemes per communication path it is called canvas scheme. Initially, each node shares a secret key with each of its neighbors. Neighbors include all nodes that are reachable either through a direct communication link, or through at most one intermediate node (which has to be a direct neighbor).

### 21.6.3. *Message Passing*

Message forwarding works as follows. A message traveling a path $S0, S1, S2, \ldots, Sn$ is authenticated twice before it is forwarded. S0 creates MACs intended for nodes S1 and S2. S0 can only reach S1 directly and relies on S1 to transmit the MAC intended for S2. Before S1 forwards the message, it creates two new authentication codes itself for S2 and S3. This is continued until the message reaches its final destination.

Before a node forwards a message, it checks the authentication codes from the two preceding nodes. If both codes indicate that the message has not been manipulated, the node forwards the message. An exception arises when a message is created, where only one MAC needs to be checked by the immediate neighbor of the source node.

### 21.6.4. *Key Setup*

The key setup for the Canvas scheme is straightforward. Each node is assigned an identity that uniquely determines a limited set of key values being drawn from a common set. The identity can be made public without helping a potential attacker. Based on their identities, two nodes can determine their common subset of key values. This subset is unique to this pair of nodes with high probability and can be used to exchange a secret key without the use of computationally intensive public key cryptography. A node establishes a unique secret key with each of its neighbors, including the ones that are not directly reachable, based on their identities.

### 21.6.5. *Compromising Situation*

It is obvious that two adjacent nodes can cooperatively compromise the communication path. They are able to manipulate and inject arbitrary messages that are routed through them. This seems to be only a slight improvement over simple hop-to-hop authentication at first. Instead of compromising one node, an attacker now has to gain control over two of them. Since they are co-located, an attack should be easy. Thus it seems nothing much is gained.

### 21.6.6. *Assess Metric*

The network can be assessed by 'live paths'. A path is called live if and only if its both endpoints are not compromised. Hence if an endpoint is compromised, it does not contribute meaningfully to the overall result of a computation. This is true even if end-to-end security measures are available. The set of live paths is thus an indicator of the quality of the network. Additionally, this path is called "functional" if it is both live and the endpoints can communicate securely. With simple hop-to-hop authentication, a path becomes non-functional if at least one node on the path is compromised. With the Canvas scheme, a path remains functional unless two adjacent nodes are compromised. Note that under end-to-end security, a live path is always functional.

### 21.6.7. *Advantages of MPA*

MPA exhibits concept in sensor networks: cooperation of neighboring nodes and authentication of messages eliminates the impact of maliciously behaving nodes.

### 21.6.8. *Disadvantages of MPA*

- More nodes need to spend energy on routing.
- Multiple disjoint paths require a minimum degree of connectivity.
- Some nodes may be only loosely connected to the network and cannot profit from multi path routing.
- It is more demanding to find and maintain sets of disjoint paths between two communication endpoints, compared to a single path.
- In the worst case, multi path routing boils down to (partial) flooding of the network.

## 21.7. LHAP: Light-weight Hop-by-hop Authentication Protocol

LHAP [4] is a light weight authentication protocol which is scalable. It resides in between the data link layer and the network layer.

It implements hop by hop authentication and one way TESLA for packet authentication. In a nut shell all intermediate authenticates packets they receive before forwarding them. The ones received from unauthorized nodes are dropped.

### 21.7.1. *Traffic Authentication*

It uses one way key chain like TESLA for authentication but he key disclosure is not delayed. It adds delay per hop and a major delay when it reaches the destination. Also requires having storage requirement as per delay, network node density and nature of application.

Each node generates a one way key chain. Any new node receiving the data adds to this chain of key traffic. Neighboring nodes receiving this packet can verify the authenticity of this packet by checking the validity of key traffic or key chain. For instance if node $A$ decides to send out message $M$ to other nodes it shall send out the following: $A \rightarrow *$ (broadcast): $M$, $K_A^F(i)$, where $K_A^F$ is is the traffic key chain for $A$ and '$i$' is the $i$-th key element.

The receiving parties shall verify the authenticity of this packet based on the most recent traffic key $K_A^F(j)$ where $j < i$. The advantages are as follows:

- Authentication is enabled and available only from immediate neighbors hence it avoids replay attacks.

- It allows instant verification of traffic.
- The cuts the necessity of disclosing keys periodically hence saving network bandwidth and energy.

### 21.7.2. *Trust Development*

It encompasses bootstrapping, trust maintenance and trust maintenance. New nodes can add to the network by gaining trust, i.e., exchanging authentic traffic keys. This can be done by using public key based method which is not well suited for resource constrained sensory modules. This can be reduced by using TESLA. In TESLA nodes use digital signatures to bootstrap. It pre-computes one way key chain and TESLA key chain. It later signs the commitments of these key chains and broadcasts to the neighbors. To maintain the trust relationship, a node broadcasts its latest released TRAFFIC keys periodically, authenticated by its TESLA keys. Thus its neighbors will drop the replayed packets authenticated by any earlier set of keys. This process is called "Key up date" message. When a node does not receive a valid "Key up date" message from a neighbor within a TESLA interval, it will terminate its trust of this neighbor. The time out can happen due to lack of energy or beyond transmission range. If the two nodes come within transmission range, they will need to run the trust bootstrapping process to reestablish a trust relationship.

### 21.7.3. *Advantages of LHAP*

- It helps prevents resource consumption attacks.
- Also new nodes have to exercise some inexpensive authentication operations to bootstrap to the network.
- It is transparent and independent of network routing protocols.
- It presents light weight trust management and packet authentication.

### 21.7.4. *Disadvantages of LHAP*

- An attacker only needs to compromise one node in order to break the security of the system.
- If the global key is made known, it is difficult to identify the compromised node.
- It is expensive to recover from a compromise because it usually involves a group key update.

## 21.8. Comparisons

Comparison tables (Tables 3 and 4) as follows is listed for the above described protocols on key structure, number of bits in the key, modes of operation, authentication flavors, memory, computation, communication overhead and energy costs associated.

Table 21.3. Comparison.

| | TinySec | ECC | LEAP |
|---|---|---|---|
| **Key structure** | Uses Symmetric key structure. | Asymmetric key cryptography. | Symmetric key system by bootstrapping pre-deployed keys (with assumption that each node can store 100's of keys) |
| **Bits for keys** | 32 hex values | 160 bit keys | |
| **Modes** | Skipjack (CBC) | Public and Private key | Different key groups: individual key, pair wise key, Cluster key, Group key |
| **Authentication flavors** | Auth-Encrypt and Auth | | One-way key chain along with delayed key disclosure |
| **Memory overhead** | | | $d$ neighbors, $L$ number of keys a node stores, the total number of keys a node stores is $3d + 2 + L$. |
| **Computational overhead** | | | Average symmetric operation $= 2(d-1)2/(N-1) + 2$ Where $d =$ connection degree and $N =$ network size |
| **Energy costs communication overhead** | | | Updating a cluster key, Avg (keys sent/received) $= (d-1)2/(N-1)$ group rekeying $= O(\log N)$. |

Table 21.4. Comparison.

| | SPINS | MPA | LHAP |
|---|---|---|---|
| **Key structure** | Network is bootstrapped with shared secret key | Pair wise shared secret key | Instant authentication only from neighbors. Public key scheme used for new nodes. |
| **Bits for keys** | Covered in memory overhead | n/a | n/a |
| **Modes** | Two modules: SNEP: Two flavors (weak and strong) uTESLA | n/a | Traffic authentication and traffic managements |
| **Authentication flavors** | Snep: two party authentication uTESLA: delayed time one way authentication | Multi path | Hop by hop authentication with modified tesla scheme |
| **Memory overhead** | SNEP adds 8 bytes and for uTESLA the security modules require 200 bytes.<br>MAC uses 8 bytes for every 30 bytes<br>Also buffer space for one key disclosure required. | With each message block 3 MAC's have to be computed and sent | 1 traffic key per packet. Public key certificate when nodes join the network.<br>1 ACK packet per new neighbor Keyupdate packet = 2 MAC keys |
| **Computational overhead** | Key Setup requires 686 bytes | | auth: Several hash function<br>Trust mgmt: 1 digital signature, 2 Verify signature per join, Several hash function for key update |
| **Energy costs** | Data Tx: 71% MAC = 20% Encryption computation and transmission = 1% each Data freshness = 7% | Pair wise key set up costs heavily on the energy | |
| **Communication overhead** | Max of 2 set up operations and 2 CTR encryptions to check validity of disclosed Tesla. For check integrity requires 2 key setup, 2 CTR, 4 MAC operations | 1 symmetric key operation (verification and MAC creation) are necessary at each hop. | |

## Acknowledgments

This work is partially supported by the US National Science Foundation (NSF) under grants CNS-0716211 and CNS-0716455.

## References

[1] C. Karlof, N. Sastry, and D. Wagner, "TinySec: a link layer security architecture for wireless sensor networks", Proceedings of the 2nd international conference on Embedded networked sensor systems, November 2004.
[2] M. Rosing, Implementing elliptic curve cryptography, Greenwich: Manning, c1999.
[3] D.J. Malan, M. Welsh, and M.D. Smith, "A public-key infrastructure for key distribution in TinyOS based on elliptic curve cryptography". IEEE SECON 2004.
[4] S. Zhu, S. Xu, Setia, and S. Jajodia, "LHAP: a lightweight hop-by-hop authentication protocol for ad-hoc networks". Distributed Computing Systems Workshops, 2003. Proceedings 23rd International Conference on 19–22, May 2003.
[5] S. Zhu, S. Setia, and S. Jajodia, "LEAP: efficient security mechanisms for large-scale distributed sensor networks", Proceedings of the 10th ACM conference on Computer and communications security, Washington D.C., USA.
[6] A. Perrig, R. Szewczyk, J.D. Tygar, V. Wen, and D.E. Culler, "SPINS: Security Protocols for Sensor Networks", Wireless Network 8, 5 (Sep. 2002).
[7] N. Engelbrecht and W.T. Penzhorn, "Secure Authentication Protocols Used for Low Power Wireless Sensor Networks", ISIE 2005.
[8] H. Vogt, "Exploring Message Authentication in Sensor Networks", 1st European Workshop on Security in Ad Hoc and Sensor Networks (ESAS 2004), Heidelberg, 5–6, Aug. 2004.
[9] Advanced Network technologies division, National Institute of Standards and Technologyb http://w3.antd.nist.gov/wahn_ssn.shtml.
[10] P. Agrawal, T.S. Teck, and A.L. Ananda, "A lightweight protocol for wireless sensor networks", IEEE WCNC 2003.
[11] http://www.certicom.com/index.php?action=ecc,home.
[12] J. Abraham and K.S. Ramanathan, "Security Protocols for Wireless Sensor Networks based on Tiny Diffusion and Elliptic Curves", in Proceedings of Network and Communications Systems, 2006.
[13] X. Du, M. Guizani, Y. Xiao, S. Ci, and H. Chen, "Routing-Driven Elliptic Curve Cryptography based Key Management Scheme for Heterogeneous Sensor Networks", IEEE Transactions on Wireless Communications, accepted and to appear.
[14] X. Du, M. Guizani, Y. Xiao, and H. Chen, "Secure and Efficient Time Synchronization in Heterogeneous Sensor Networks", IEEE Transactions on Vehicular Technology, Vol. 57, No. 3, May 2008.
[15] X. Du, M. Guizani, Y. Xiao, and H. Chen, "Two Tier Secure Routing Protocol for Heterogeneous Sensor Networks", IEEE Transactions on Wireless Communications, Vol. 6, No. 9, pp. 3395–3401, Sep. 2007.
[16] Y. Xiao, H. Chen, B. Sun, R. Wang, and S. Sethi, "MAC Security and Security Overhead Analysis in the IEEE 802.15.4 Wireless Sensor Networks", EURASIP Journal on Wireless Communications and Networking, vol. 2006, Article ID 93830, 12 pages, 2006. doi:10.1155/WCN/2006/93830.
[17] K. Wu, D. Dreef, B. Sun, and Y. Xiao, "Secure Data Aggregation without Persistent Cryptographic Operations in Wireless Sensor Networks", (Elsevier)

Ad Hoc Networks, special issue on Security in Ad Hoc and Sensor Networks, Vol. 5, No. 1, pp. 100–111, Jan. 2007.

[18] X. Du, Y. Xiao, M. Guizani, and H. Chen, "Efficient Key Management Schemes for Heterogeneous Sensor Networks," (Elsevier) Ad Hoc Networks, special issue on Security in Ad Hoc and Sensor Networks, Vol. 5, No. 1, pp. 24–34, Jan. 2007.

[19] Sun, C. Li, K. Wu, and Y. Xiao, "A Lightweight Secure Protocol for Wireless Sensor Networks", Computer Communications Journal, special issue on Wireless Sensor Networks: Performance, Reliability, Security and Beyond, Vol. 29, Nos. 13–14, pp. 2556–2568, Aug. 2006

[20] Y. Xiao, S. Yu, K. Wu, Q. Ni, C. Janecek, and J. Nordstad, "Radio Frequency Identification: Technologies, Applications, and Research Issues", Wireless Communications and Mobile Computing (WCMC) Journal, John Wiley & Sons, Vol. 7, No. 4, pp. 457–472, May 2007.

[21] X. Du, Y. Xiao, H. Chen, and Q. Wu, "Secure Cell Relay Routing Protocol for Sensor Networks", Wireless Communications and Mobile Computing (WCMC) Journal, John Wiley & Sons, Special issue on Wireless Network Security, Vol. 6, No. 3, pp. 375–391, May 2, 2006.

[22] Y. Xiao, X. Shen, B. Sun, and L. Cai, "Security and Privacy in RFID and Applications in Telemedicine", IEEE Communications Magazine, Special issue on Quality Assurance and Devices in Telemedicine, pp. 64–72, Apr. 2006.